BRIAN "BOX" BROWN

CHILD STAR

W9-CBW-430

BRIAN "BOX" BROWN

CHILD STAR

:01

First Second
NEW YORK

PART ONE

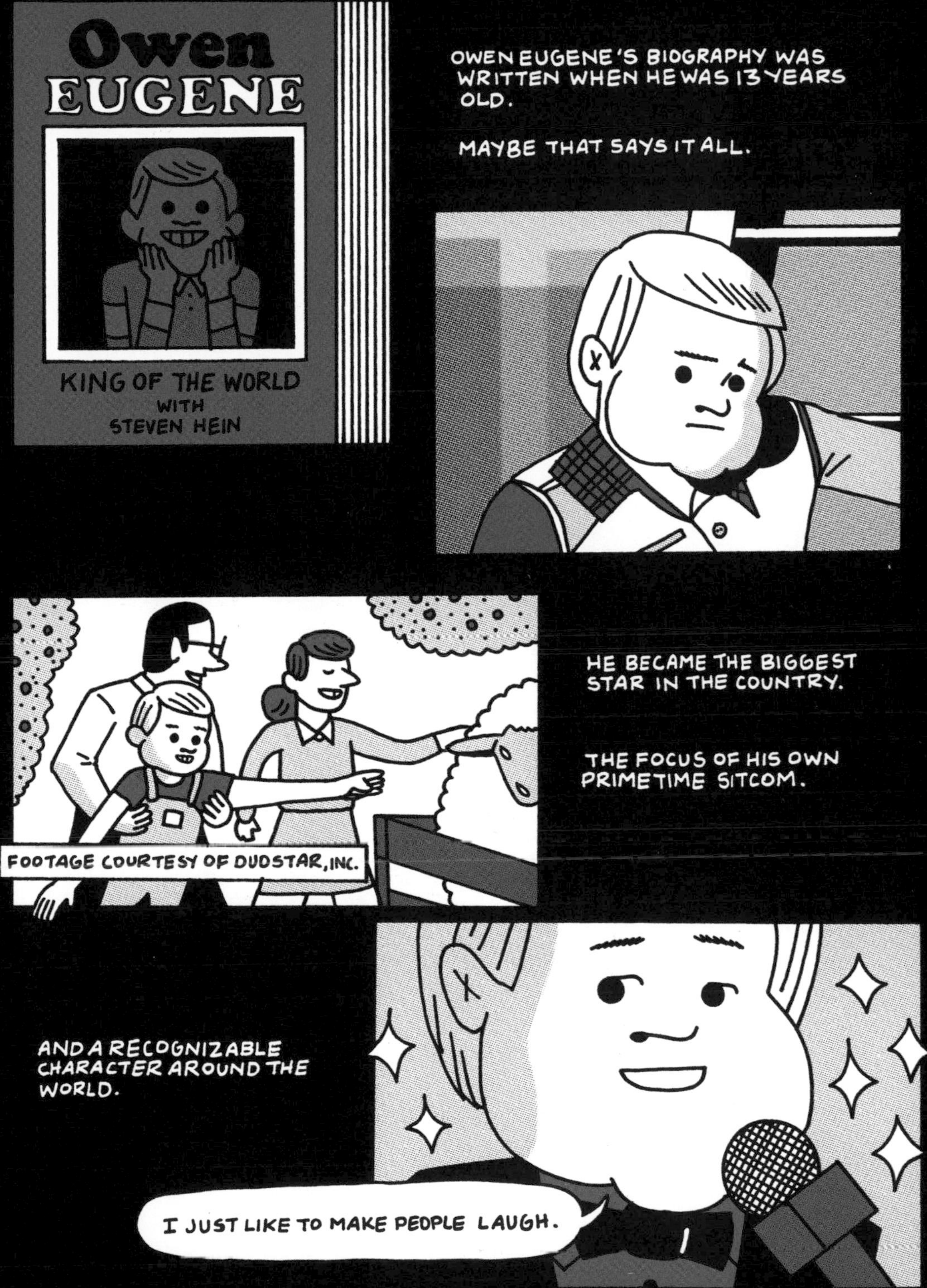
Owen
EUGENE
KING OF THE WORLD
WITH
STEVEN HEIN
OWEN EUGENE'S BIOGRAPHY WAS WRITTEN WHEN HE WAS 13 YEARS OLD.
MAYBE THAT SAYS IT ALL.
HE BECAME THE BIGGEST STAR IN THE COUNTRY.
FOOTAGE COURTESY OF DUDSTAR, INC.
THE FOCUS OF HIS OWN PRIMETIME SITCOM.
AND A RECOGNIZABLE CHARACTER AROUND THE WORLD.
I JUST LIKE TO MAKE PEOPLE LAUGH.

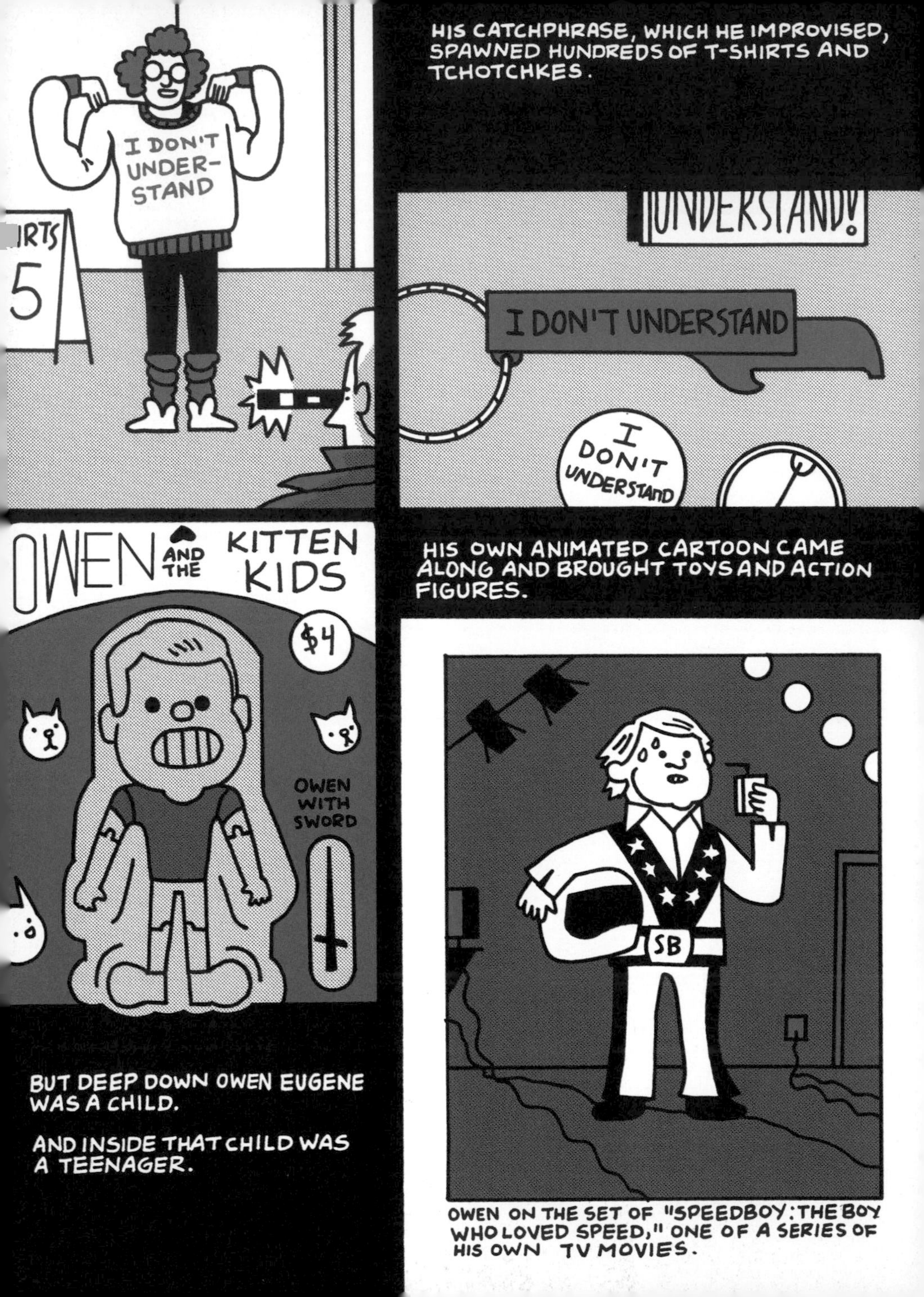
I DON'T UNDER-STAND
IRTS
5
HIS CATCHPHRASE, WHICH HE IMPROVISED, SPAWNED HUNDREDS OF T-SHIRTS AND TCHOTCHKES.
UNDERSTAND!
I DON'T UNDERSTAND
I DON'T UNDERSTAND
OWEN AND THE KITTEN KIDS
$4
OWEN WITH SWORD
BUT DEEP DOWN OWEN EUGENE WAS A CHILD.
AND INSIDE THAT CHILD WAS A TEENAGER.
HIS OWN ANIMATED CARTOON CAME ALONG AND BROUGHT TOYS AND ACTION FIGURES.
SB
OWEN ON THE SET OF "SPEEDBOY: THE BOY WHO LOVED SPEED," ONE OF A SERIES OF HIS OWN TV MOVIES.

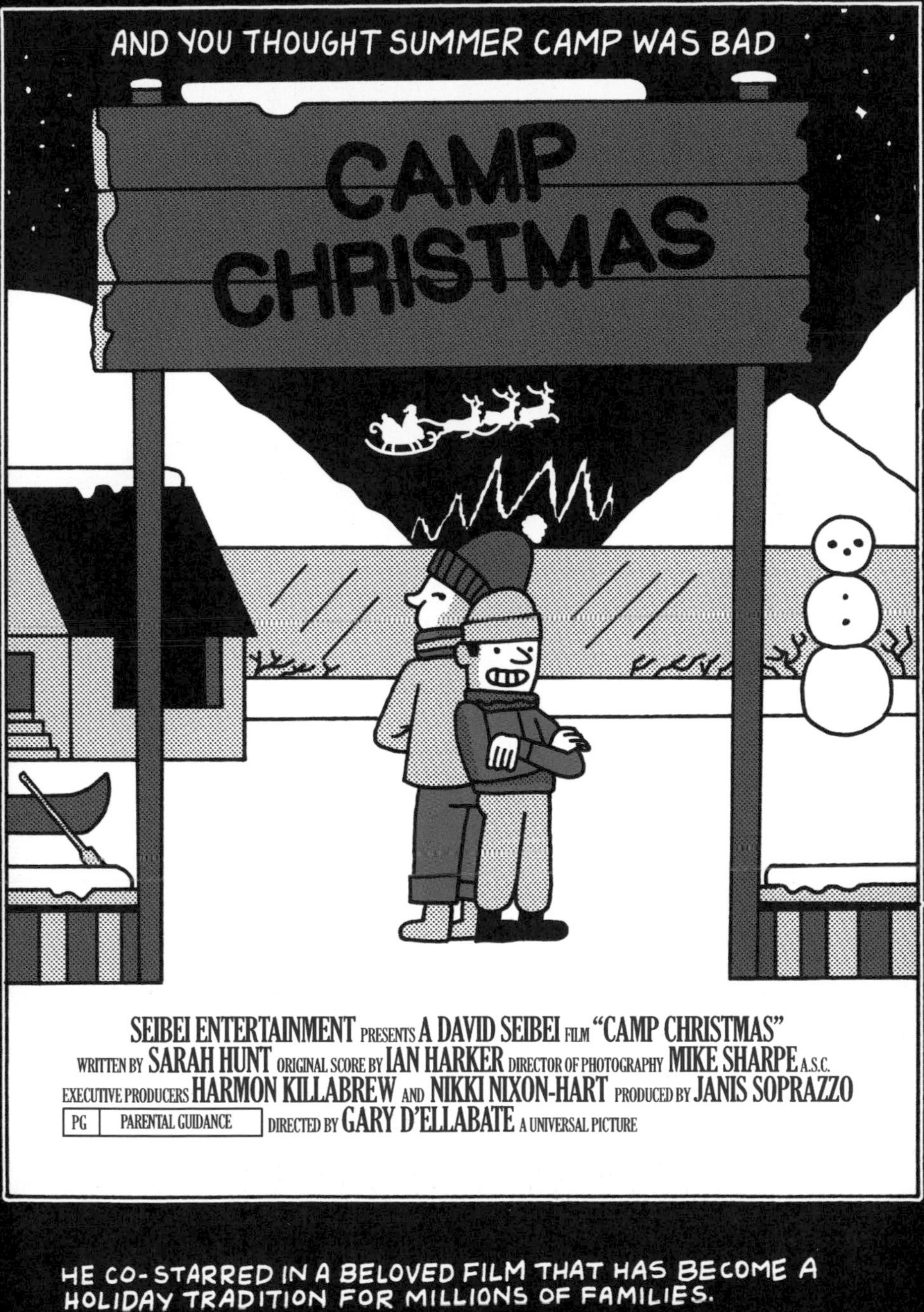
AND YOU THOUGHT SUMMER CAMP WAS BAD
CAMP CHRISTMAS
SEIBEI ENTERTAINMENT PRESENTS A DAVID SEIBEI FILM "CAMP CHRISTMAS"
WRITTEN BY SARAH HUNT ORIGINAL SCORE BY IAN HARKER DIRECTOR OF PHOTOGRAPHY MIKE SHARPE A.S.C.
EXECUTIVE PRODUCERS HARMON KILLABREW AND NIKKI NIXON-HART PRODUCED BY JANIS SOPRAZZO
PG PARENTAL GUIDANCE
DIRECTED BY GARY D'ELLABATE A UNIVERSAL PICTURE
HE CO-STARRED IN A BELOVED FILM THAT HAS BECOME A HOLIDAY TRADITION FOR MILLIONS OF FAMILIES.

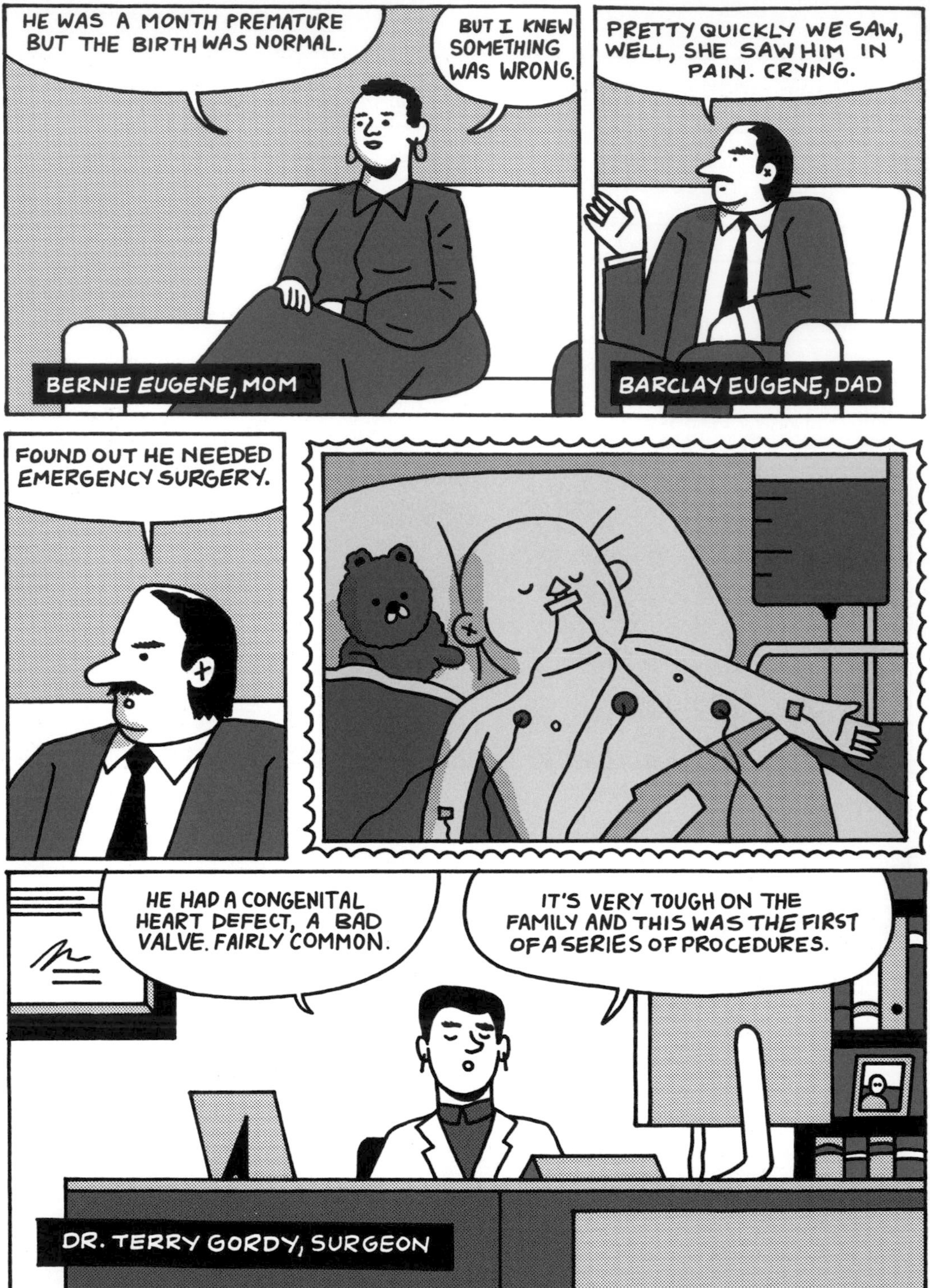
HE WAS A MONTH PREMATURE BUT THE BIRTH WAS NORMAL.
BUT I KNEW SOMETHING WAS WRONG.
BERNIE EUGENE, MOM
PRETTY QUICKLY WE SAW, WELL, SHE SAW HIM IN PAIN. CRYING.
BARCLAY EUGENE, DAD
FOUND OUT HE NEEDED EMERGENCY SURGERY.
HE HAD A CONGENITAL HEART DEFECT, A BAD VALVE. FAIRLY COMMON.
IT'S VERY TOUGH ON THE FAMILY AND THIS WAS THE FIRST OF A SERIES OF PROCEDURES.
DR. TERRY GORDY, SURGEON

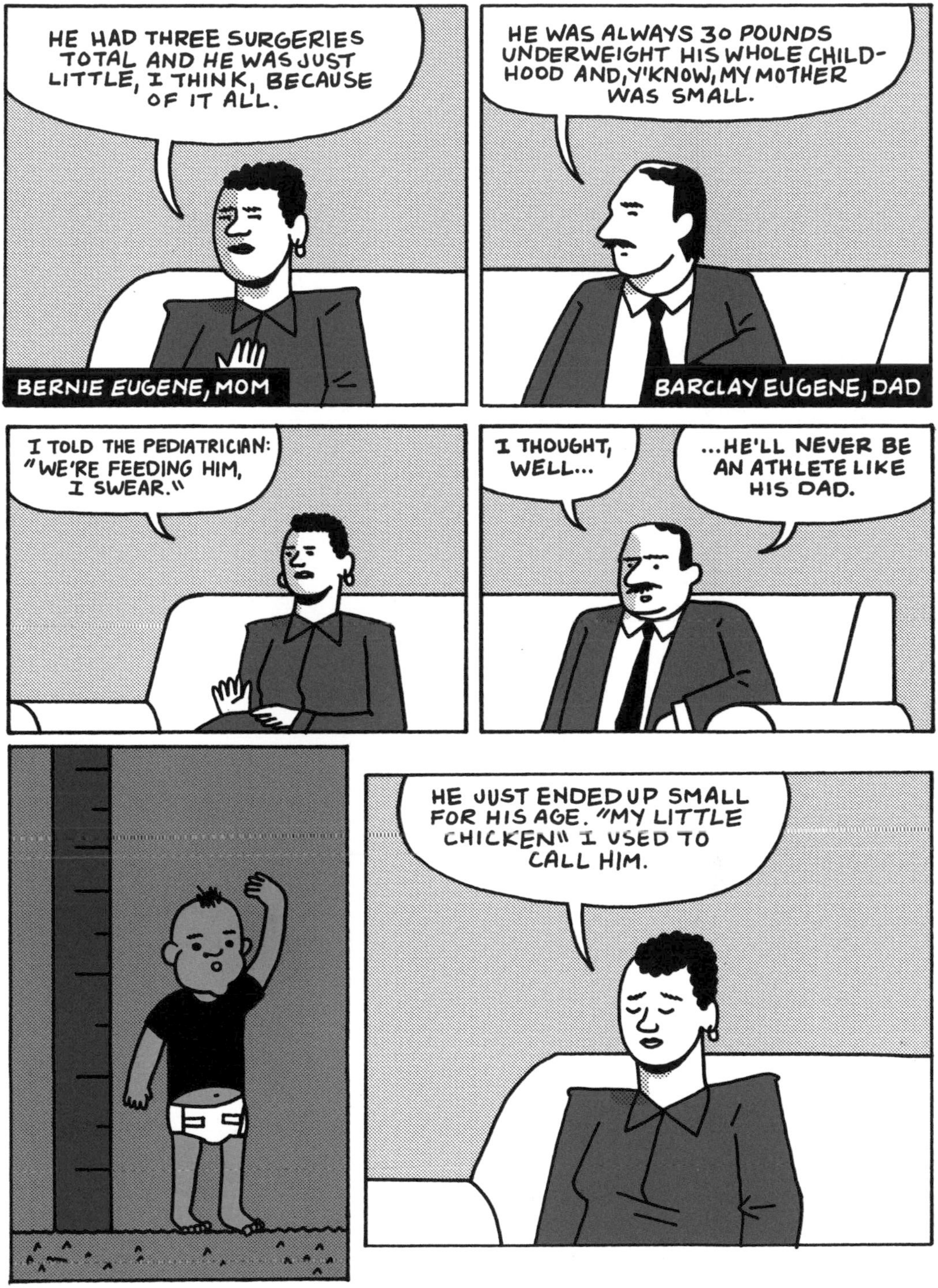
HE HAD THREE SURGERIES TOTAL AND HE WAS JUST LITTLE, I THINK, BECAUSE OF IT ALL.
BERNIE EUGENE, MOM
HE WAS ALWAYS 30 POUNDS UNDERWEIGHT HIS WHOLE CHILDHOOD AND, Y'KNOW, MY MOTHER WAS SMALL.
BARCLAY EUGENE, DAD
I TOLD THE PEDIATRICIAN: "WE'RE FEEDING HIM, I SWEAR."
I THOUGHT, WELL...
...HE'LL NEVER BE AN ATHLETE LIKE HIS DAD.
HE JUST ENDED UP SMALL FOR HIS AGE. "MY LITTLE CHICKEN" I USED TO CALL HIM.

"EVERYONE'S FRIEND" PILOT EPISODE 9/12/79

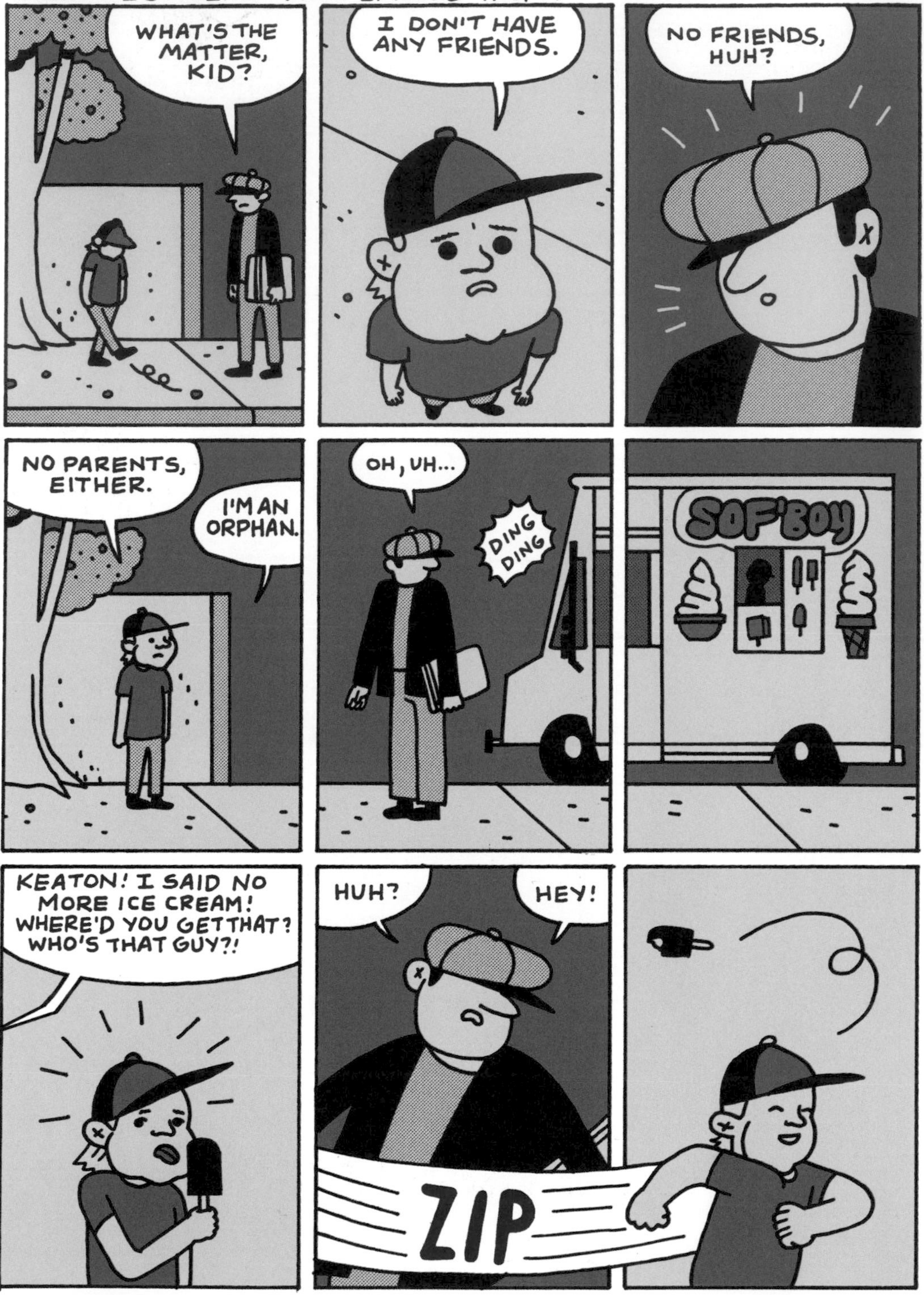
WHAT'S THE MATTER, KID?
I DON'T HAVE ANY FRIENDS.
NO FRIENDS, HUH?
NO PARENTS, EITHER.
I'M AN ORPHAN.
OH, UH...
DING DING
SOF'BOY
KEATON! I SAID NO MORE ICE CREAM! WHERE'D YOU GET THAT? WHO'S THAT GUY?!
HUH?
HEY!
ZIP

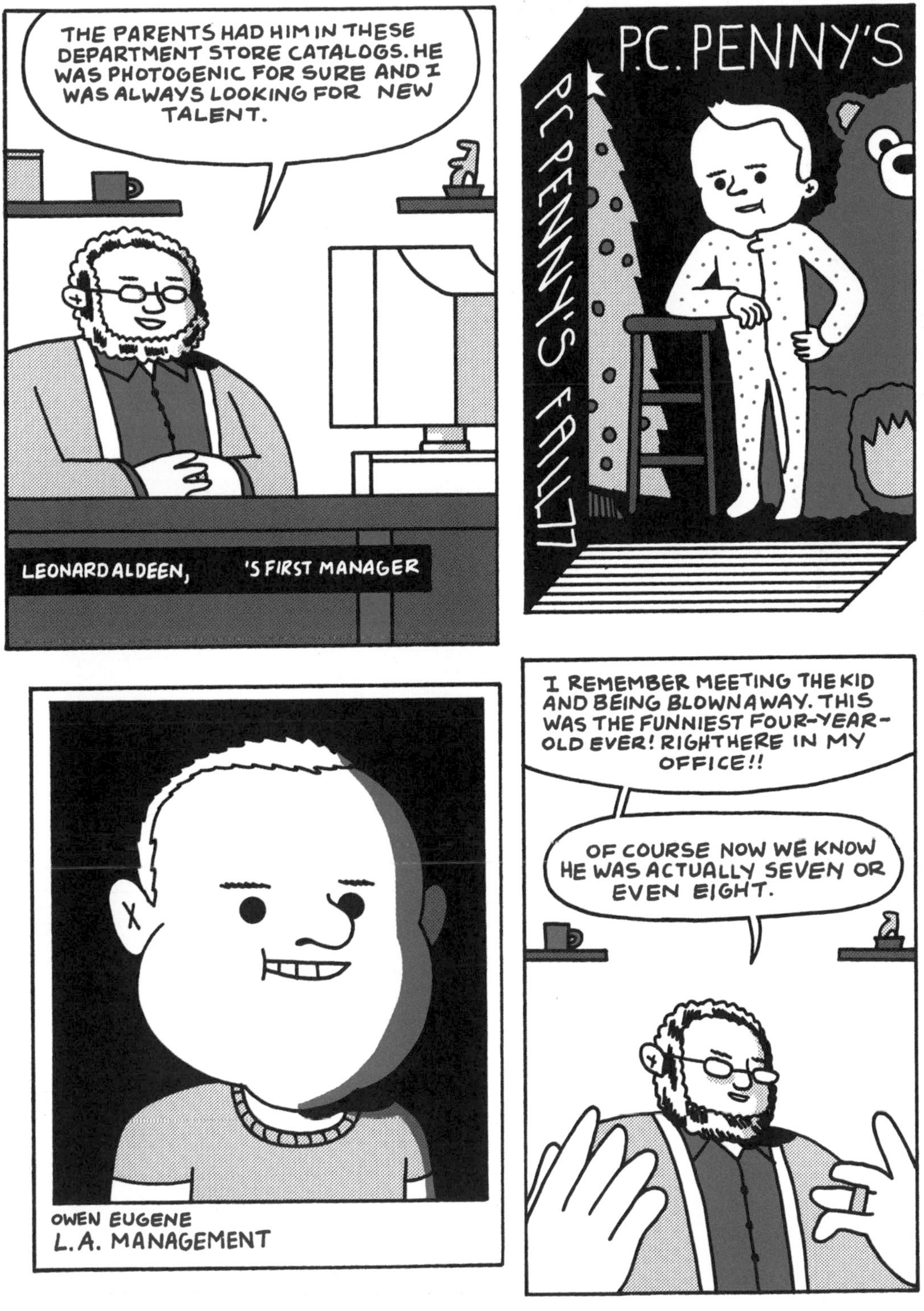
THE PARENTS HAD HIM IN THESE DEPARTMENT STORE CATALOGS. HE WAS PHOTOGENIC FOR SURE AND I WAS ALWAYS LOOKING FOR NEW TALENT.
LEONARD ALDEEN, 'S FIRST MANAGER
P.C. PENNY'S
P.C. PENNY'S FALL 77
OWEN EUGENE
L.A. MANAGEMENT
I REMEMBER MEETING THE KID AND BEING BLOWN AWAY. THIS WAS THE FUNNIEST FOUR-YEAR-OLD EVER! RIGHT HERE IN MY OFFICE!!
OF COURSE NOW WE KNOW HE WAS ACTUALLY SEVEN OR EVEN EIGHT.

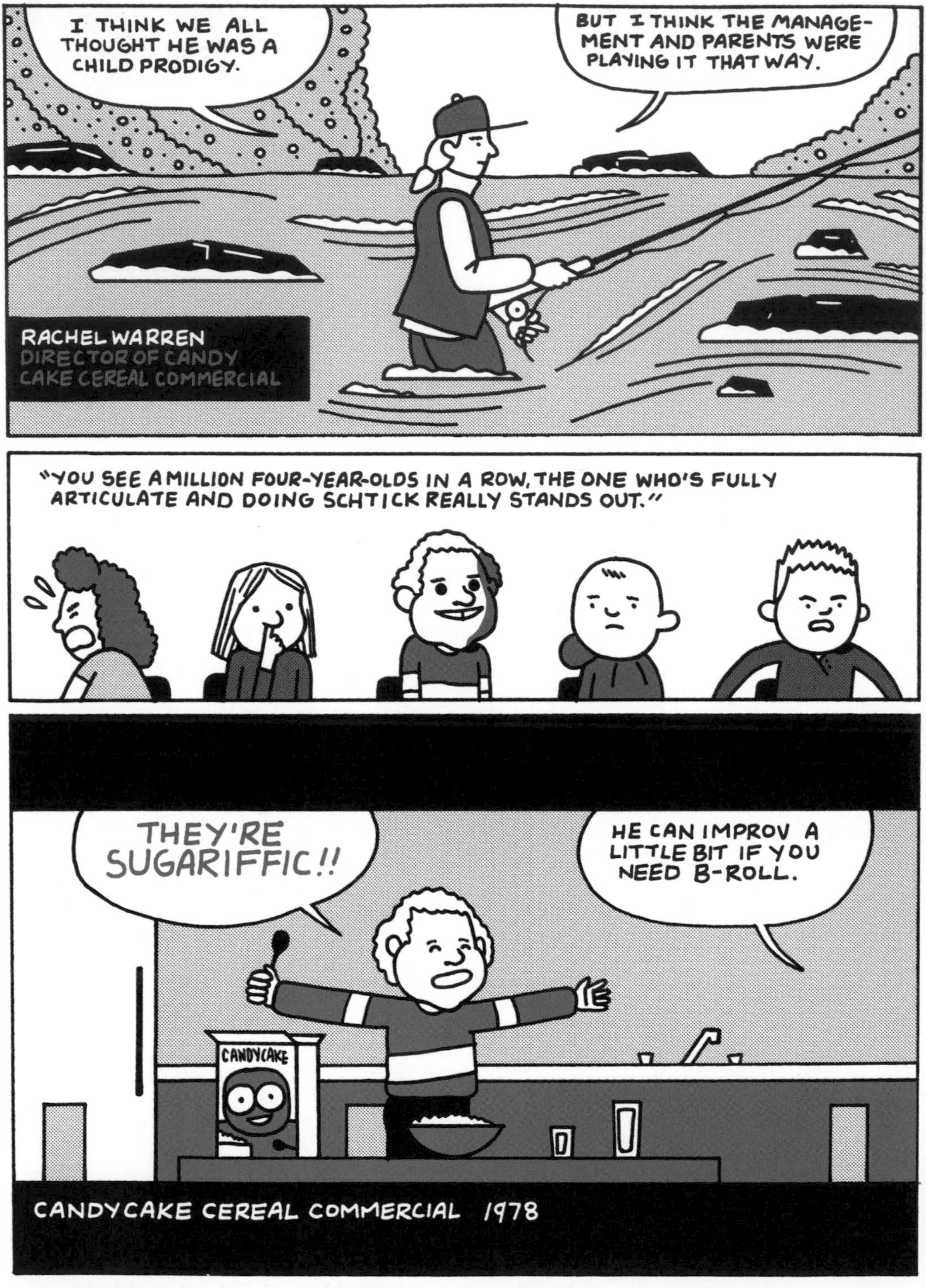

I THINK WE ALL THOUGHT HE WAS A CHILD PRODIGY.
BUT I THINK THE MANAGEMENT AND PARENTS WERE PLAYING IT THAT WAY.
RACHEL WARREN
DIRECTOR OF CANDY CAKE CEREAL COMMERCIAL
"YOU SEE A MILLION FOUR-YEAR-OLDS IN A ROW, THE ONE WHO'S FULLY ARTICULATE AND DOING SCHTICK REALLY STANDS OUT."
THEY'RE SUGARIFFIC!!
HE CAN IMPROV A LITTLE BIT IF YOU NEED B-ROLL.
CANDYCAKE
CANDYCAKE CEREAL COMMERCIAL 1978

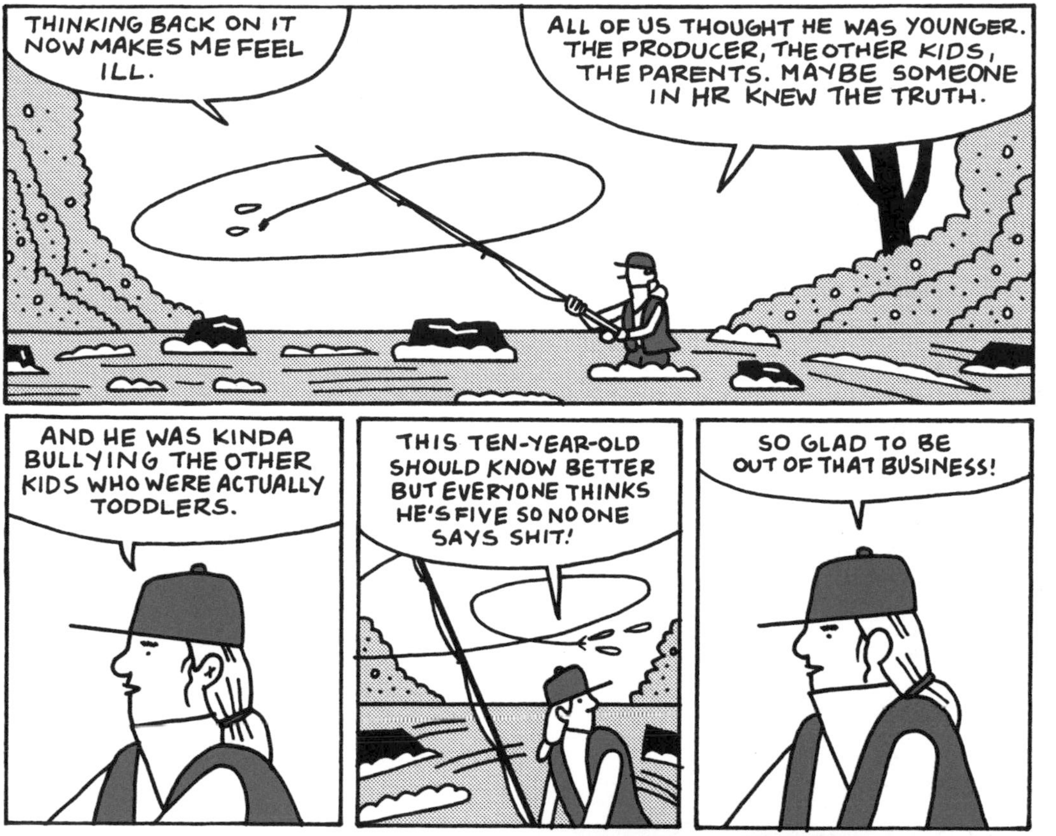
THINKING BACK ON IT NOW MAKES ME FEEL ILL.
ALL OF US THOUGHT HE WAS YOUNGER. THE PRODUCER, THE OTHER KIDS, THE PARENTS. MAYBE SOMEONE IN HR KNEW THE TRUTH.
AND HE WAS KINDA BULLYING THE OTHER KIDS WHO WERE ACTUALLY TODDLERS.
THIS TEN-YEAR-OLD SHOULD KNOW BETTER BUT EVERYONE THINKS HE'S FIVE SO NO ONE SAYS SHIT!
SO GLAD TO BE OUT OF THAT BUSINESS!

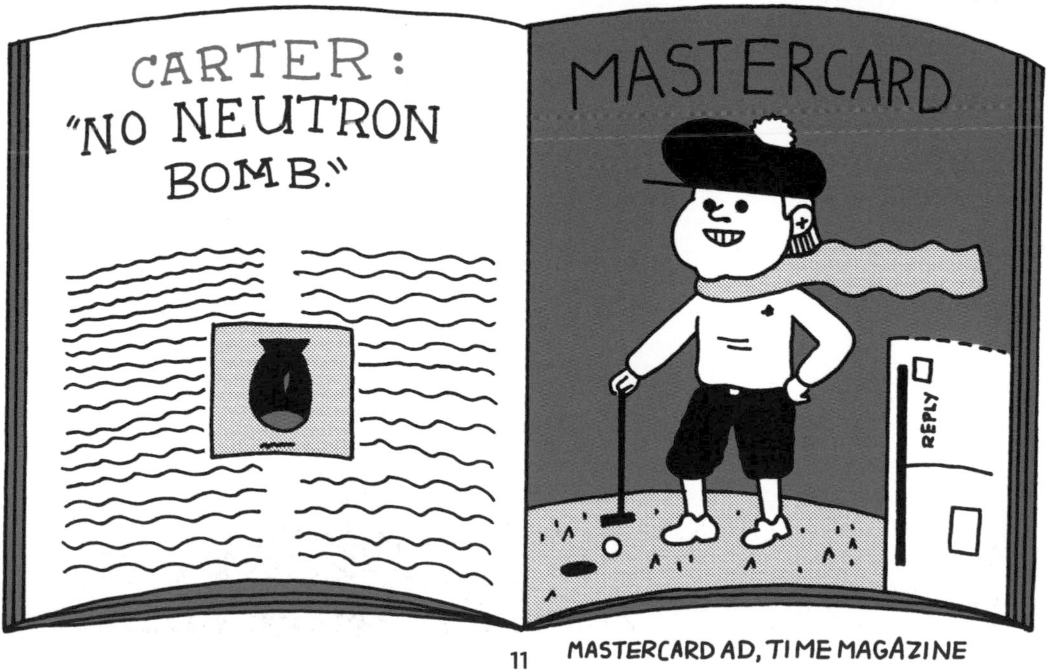
CARTER: "NO NEUTRON BOMB."
MASTERCARD
REPLY

MASTERCARD AD, TIME MAGAZINE

DUMBO POPS COMMERCIAL (MOSTLY IMPROVISED) 5/7/79

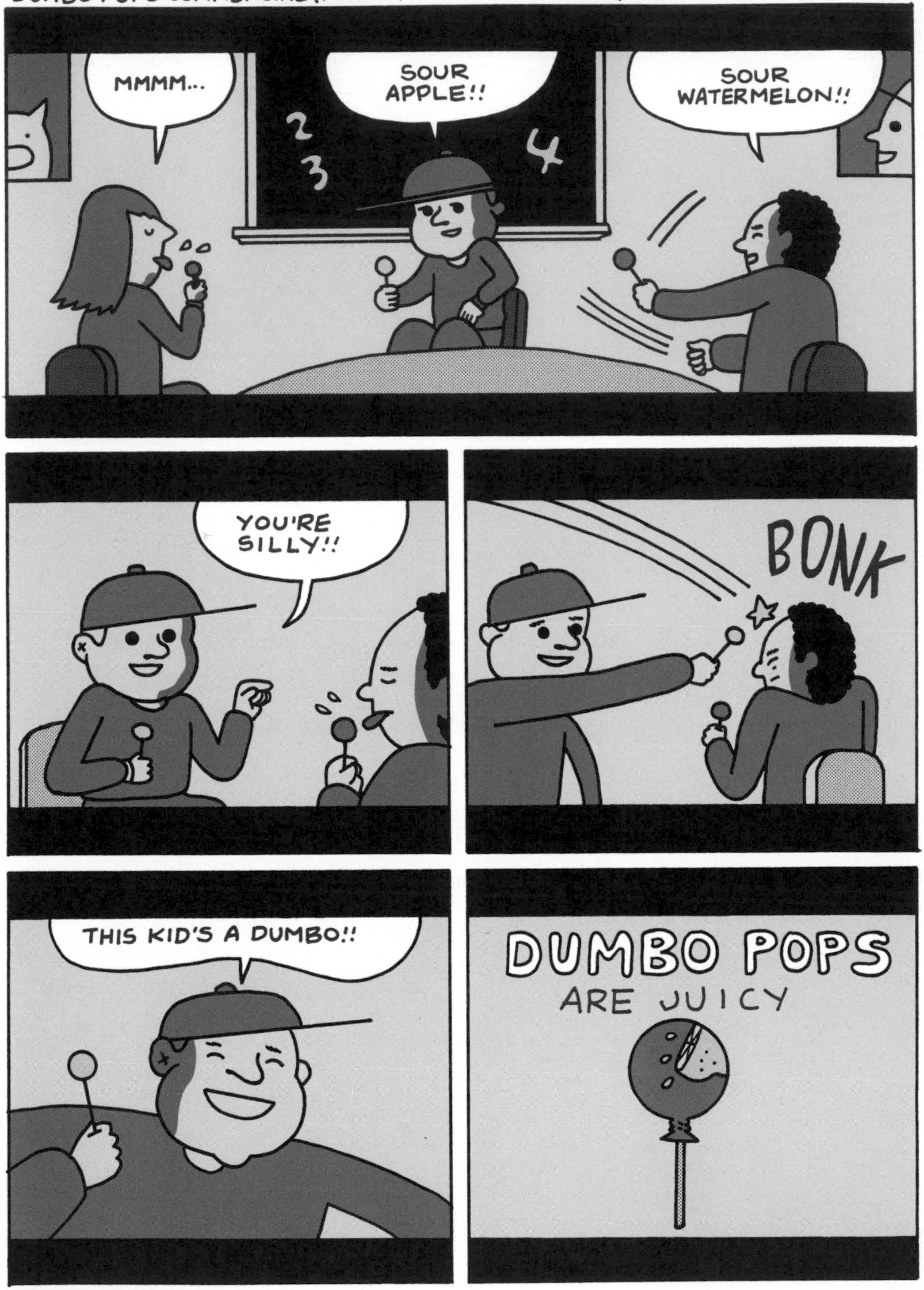
MMMM...
SOUR APPLE!!
SOUR WATERMELON!!
YOU'RE SILLY!!
BONK
THIS KID'S A DUMBO!!
DUMBO POPS
ARE JUICY

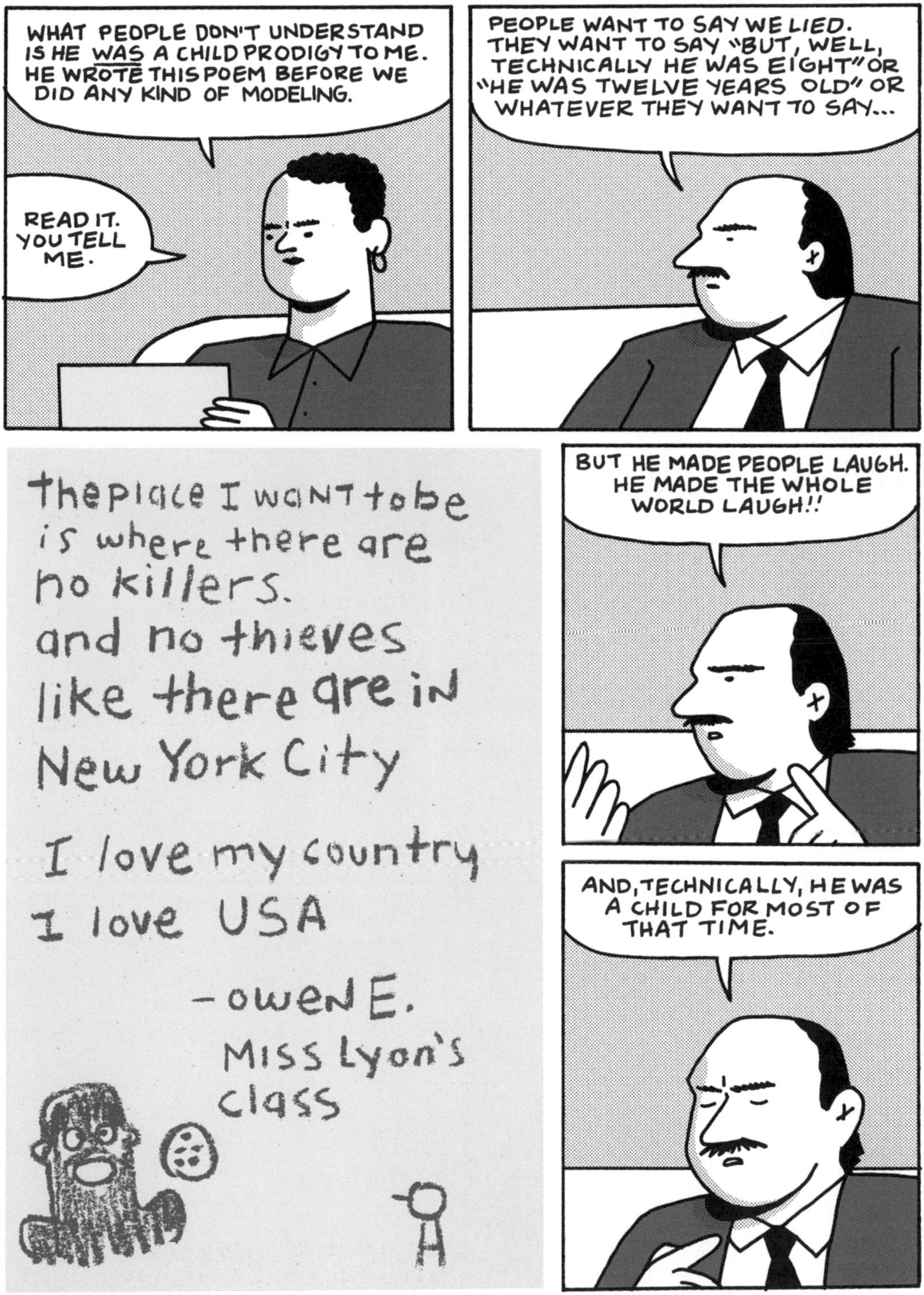
WHAT PEOPLE DON'T UNDERSTAND IS HE WAS A CHILD PRODIGY TO ME. HE WROTE THIS POEM BEFORE WE DID ANY KIND OF MODELING.
READ IT. YOU TELL ME.
PEOPLE WANT TO SAY WE LIED. THEY WANT TO SAY "BUT, WELL, TECHNICALLY HE WAS EIGHT" OR "HE WAS TWELVE YEARS OLD" OR WHATEVER THEY WANT TO SAY...
the place I want to be
is where there are
no killers.
and no thieves
like there are in
New York City
I love my country
I love USA
-owen E.
Miss Lyon's
class
BUT HE MADE PEOPLE LAUGH. HE MADE THE WHOLE WORLD LAUGH!!
AND, TECHNICALLY, HE WAS A CHILD FOR MOST OF THAT TIME.

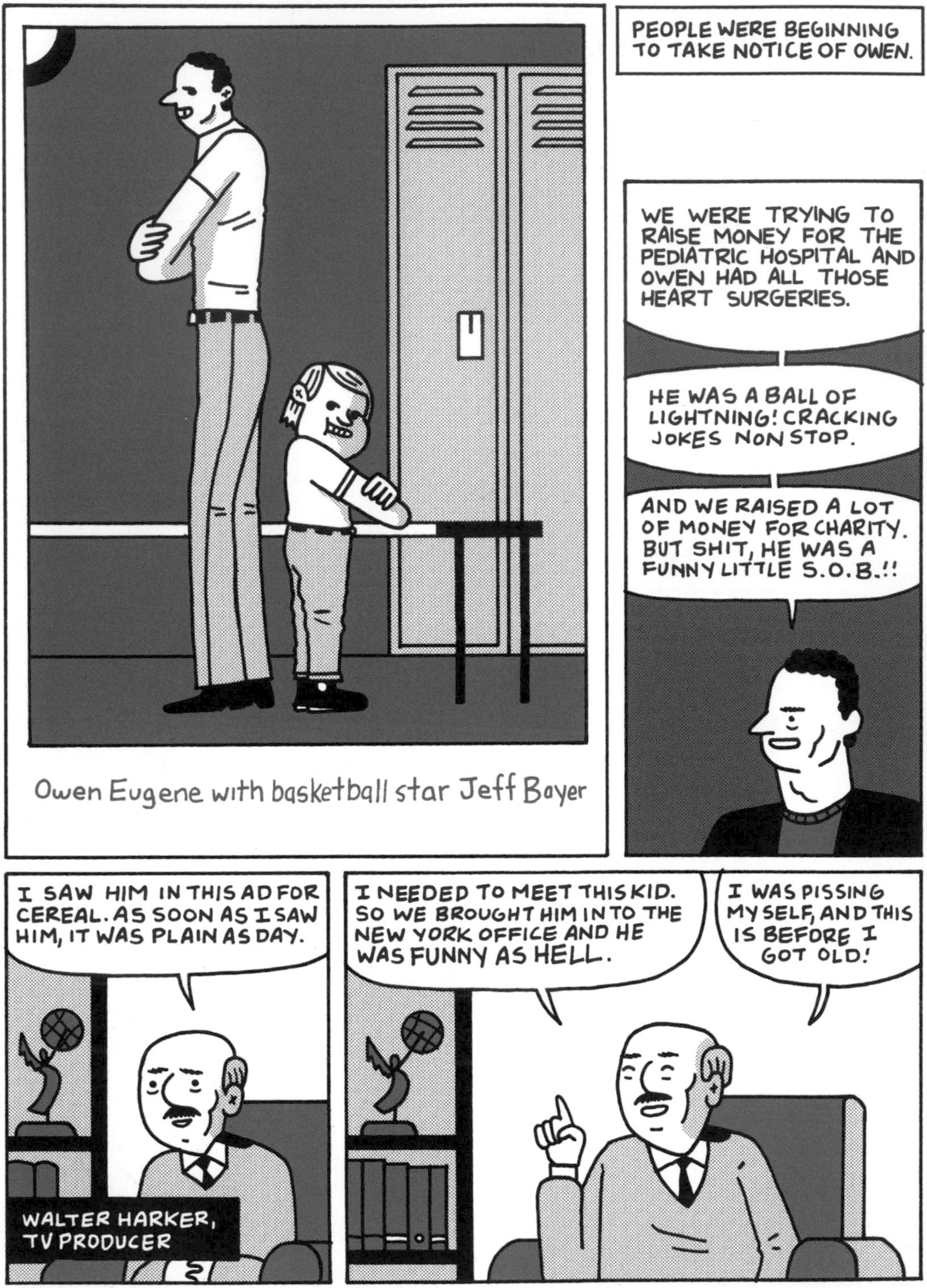
PEOPLE WERE BEGINNING TO TAKE NOTICE OF OWEN.
WE WERE TRYING TO RAISE MONEY FOR THE PEDIATRIC HOSPITAL AND OWEN HAD ALL THOSE HEART SURGERIES.
HE WAS A BALL OF LIGHTNING! CRACKING JOKES NON STOP.
AND WE RAISED A LOT OF MONEY FOR CHARITY. BUT SHIT, HE WAS A FUNNY LITTLE S.O.B.!!
I SAW HIM IN THIS AD FOR CEREAL. AS SOON AS I SAW HIM, IT WAS PLAIN AS DAY.
WALTER HARKER, TV PRODUCER
I NEEDED TO MEET THIS KID. SO WE BROUGHT HIM IN TO THE NEW YORK OFFICE AND HE WAS FUNNY AS HELL.
I WAS PISSING MYSELF, AND THIS IS BEFORE I GOT OLD!
Owen Eugene with basketball star Jeff Bayer

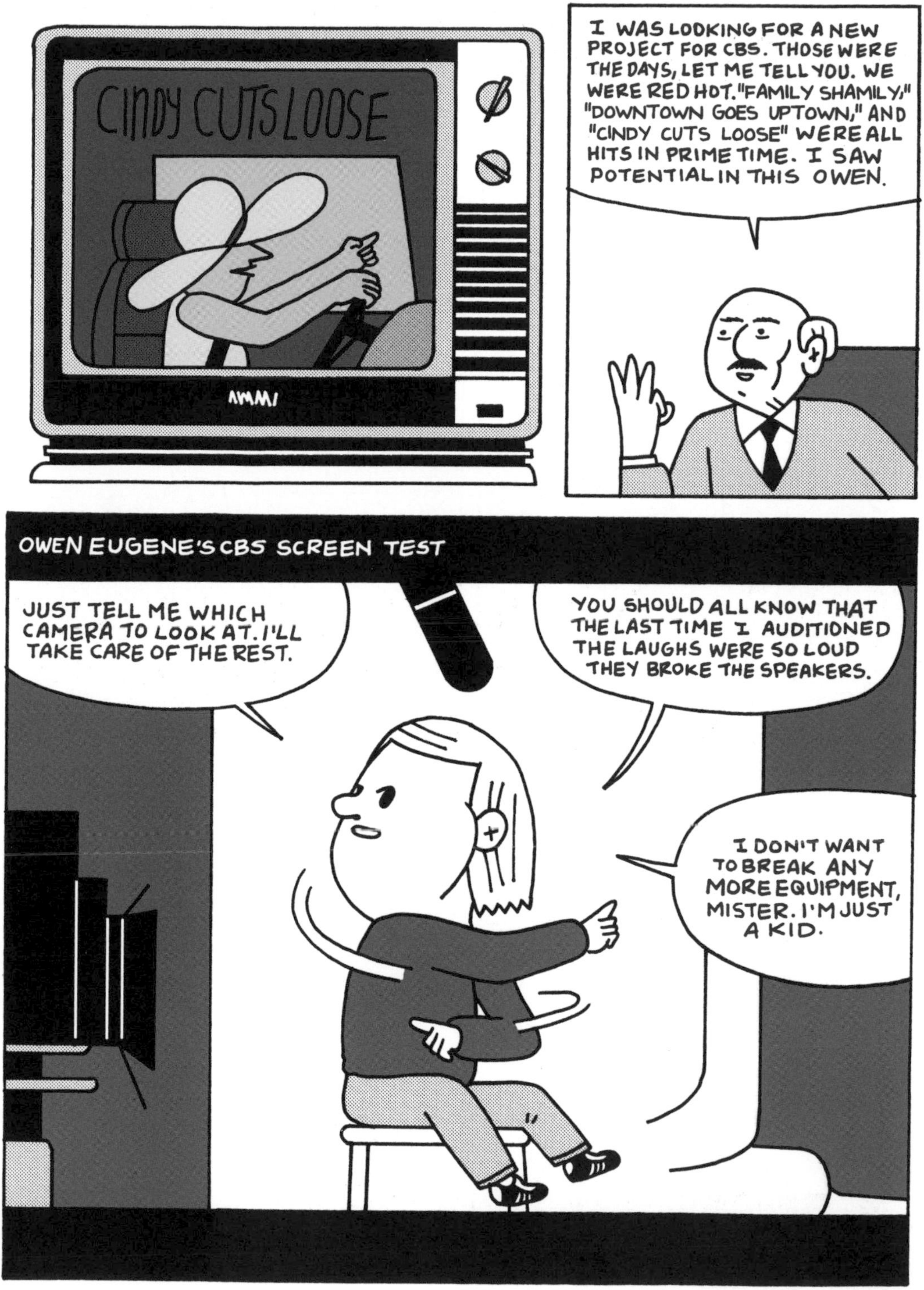
CINDY CUTS LOOSE
I WAS LOOKING FOR A NEW PROJECT FOR CBS. THOSE WERE THE DAYS, LET ME TELL YOU. WE WERE RED HOT. "FAMILY SHAMILY," "DOWNTOWN GOES UPTOWN," AND "CINDY CUTS LOOSE" WERE ALL HITS IN PRIME TIME. I SAW POTENTIAL IN THIS OWEN.
OWEN EUGENE'S CBS SCREEN TEST
JUST TELL ME WHICH CAMERA TO LOOK AT. I'LL TAKE CARE OF THE REST.
YOU SHOULD ALL KNOW THAT THE LAST TIME I AUDITIONED THE LAUGHS WERE SO LOUD THEY BROKE THE SPEAKERS.
I DON'T WANT TO BREAK ANY MORE EQUIPMENT, MISTER. I'M JUST A KID.

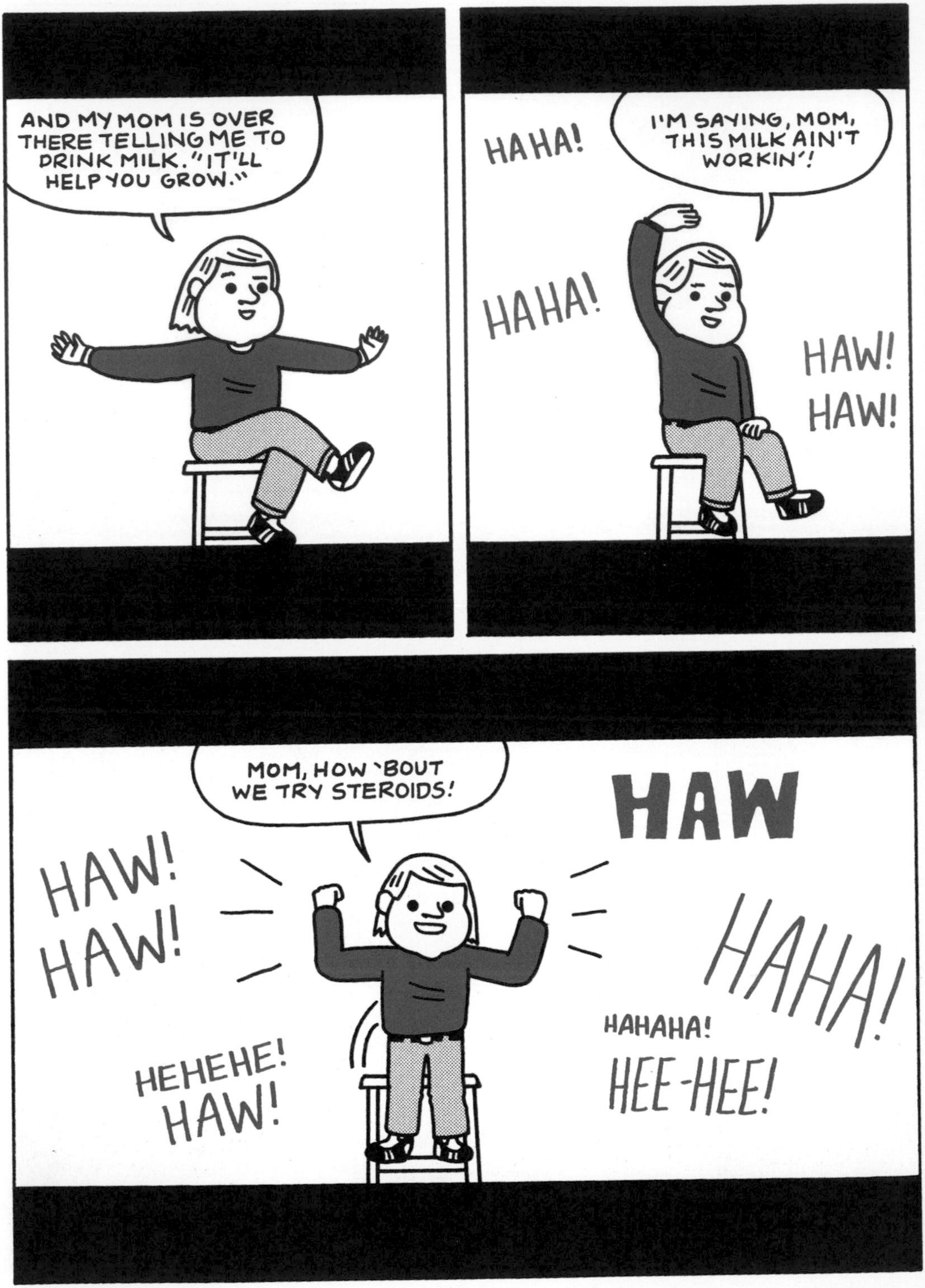
AND MY MOM IS OVER THERE TELLING ME TO DRINK MILK. "IT'LL HELP YOU GROW."
HAHA!
I'M SAYING, MOM, THIS MILK AIN'T WORKIN'!
HAHA!
HAW! HAW!
MOM, HOW 'BOUT WE TRY STEROIDS!
HAW
HAW! HAW!
HAHA!
HAHAHA!
HEHEHE! HAW!
HEE-HEE!

THEY SAID THEY WERE DOING A TV PILOT AND AND A TV MOVIE.

WE HAD TO GO TO L.A.

WHEN I SAW THAT CONTRACT... WE WERE... HAPPY.

THOSE WERE HAPPY DAYS.

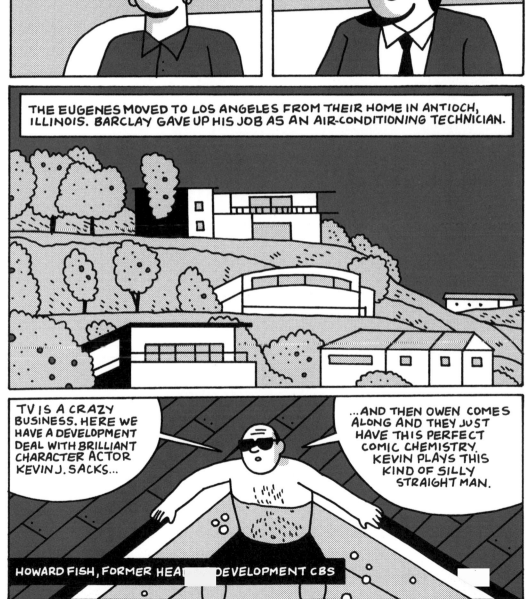

THE EUGENES MOVED TO LOS ANGELES FROM THEIR HOME IN ANTIOCH, ILLINOIS. BARCLAY GAVE UP HIS JOB AS AN AIR-CONDITIONING TECHNICIAN.

TV IS A CRAZY BUSINESS. HERE WE HAVE A DEVELOPMENT DEAL WITH BRILLIANT CHARACTER ACTOR KEVIN J. SACKS...

...AND THEN OWEN COMES ALONG AND THEY JUST HAVE THIS PERFECT COMIC CHEMISTRY. KEVIN PLAYS THIS KIND OF SILLY STRAIGHT MAN.

HOWARD FISH, FORMER HEAD OF DEVELOPMENT CBS

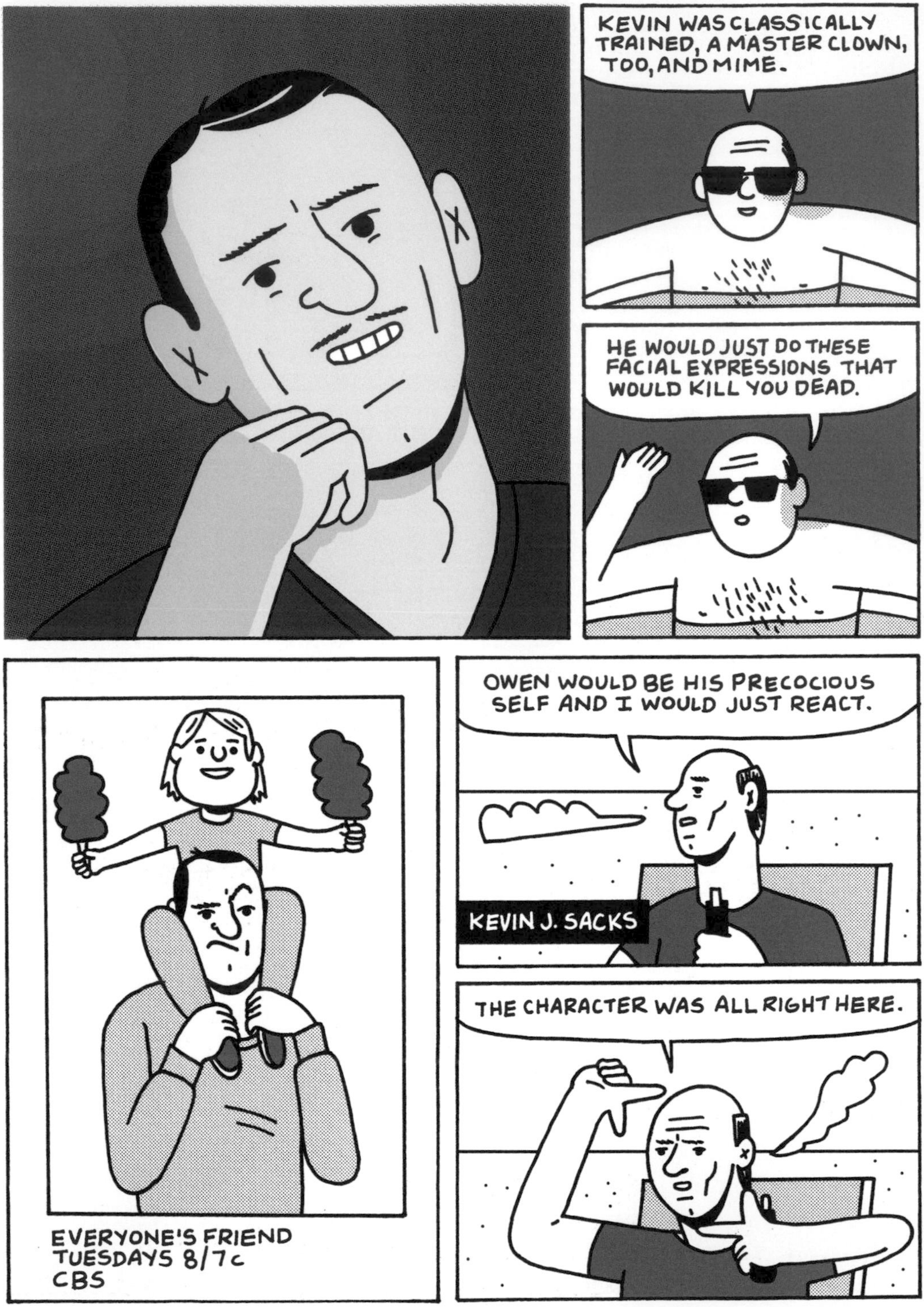

KEVIN WAS CLASSICALLY TRAINED, A MASTER CLOWN, TOO, AND MIME.
HE WOULD JUST DO THESE FACIAL EXPRESSIONS THAT WOULD KILL YOU DEAD.
EVERYONE'S FRIEND
TUESDAYS 8/7c
CBS
OWEN WOULD BE HIS PRECOCIOUS SELF AND I WOULD JUST REACT.
KEVIN J. SACKS
THE CHARACTER WAS ALL RIGHT HERE.

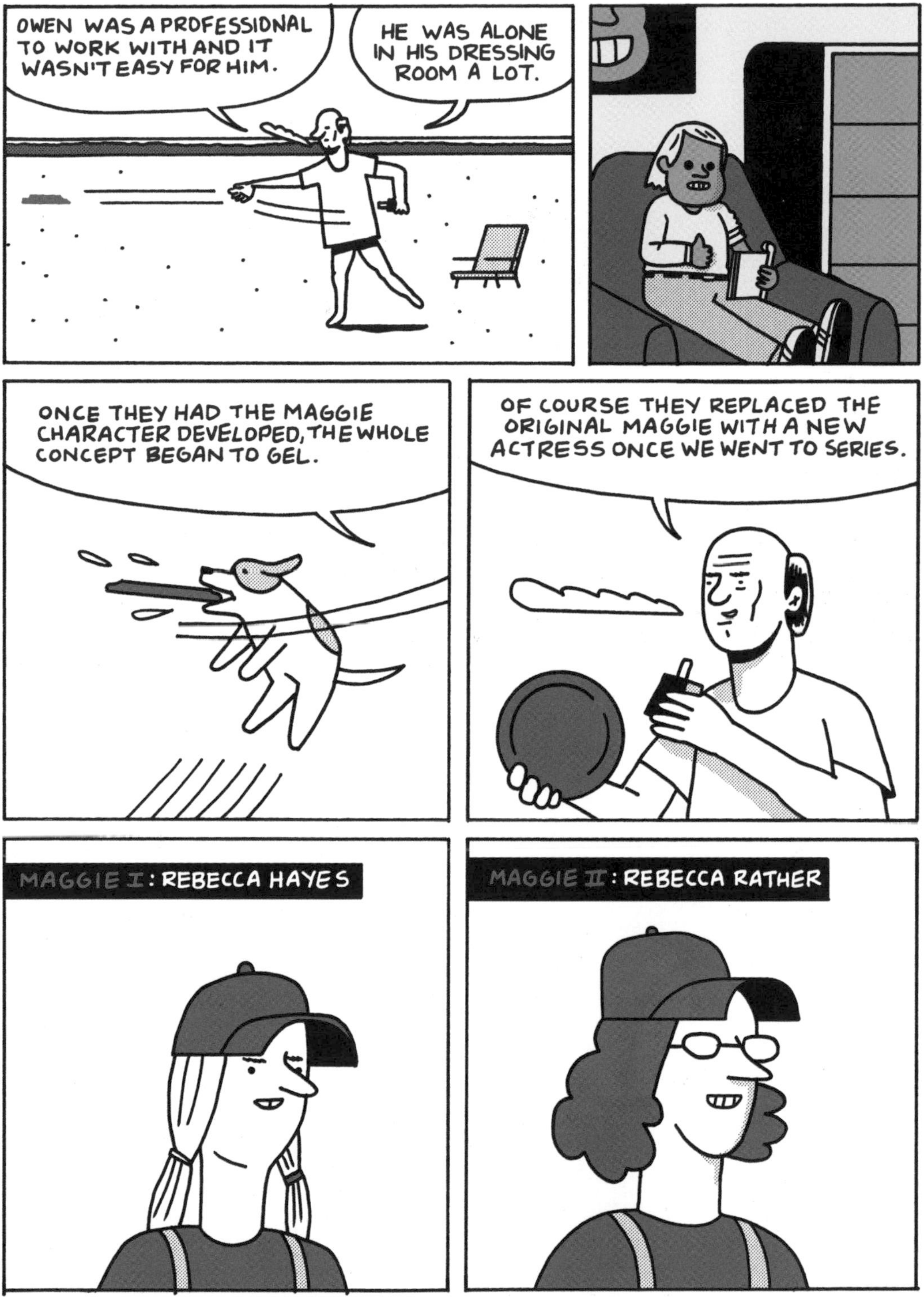
OWEN WAS A PROFESSIONAL TO WORK WITH AND IT WASN'T EASY FOR HIM.
HE WAS ALONE IN HIS DRESSING ROOM A LOT.
ONCE THEY HAD THE MAGGIE CHARACTER DEVELOPED, THE WHOLE CONCEPT BEGAN TO GEL.
OF COURSE THEY REPLACED THE ORIGINAL MAGGIE WITH A NEW ACTRESS ONCE WE WENT TO SERIES.
MAGGIE I: REBECCA HAYES
MAGGIE II: REBECCA RATHER

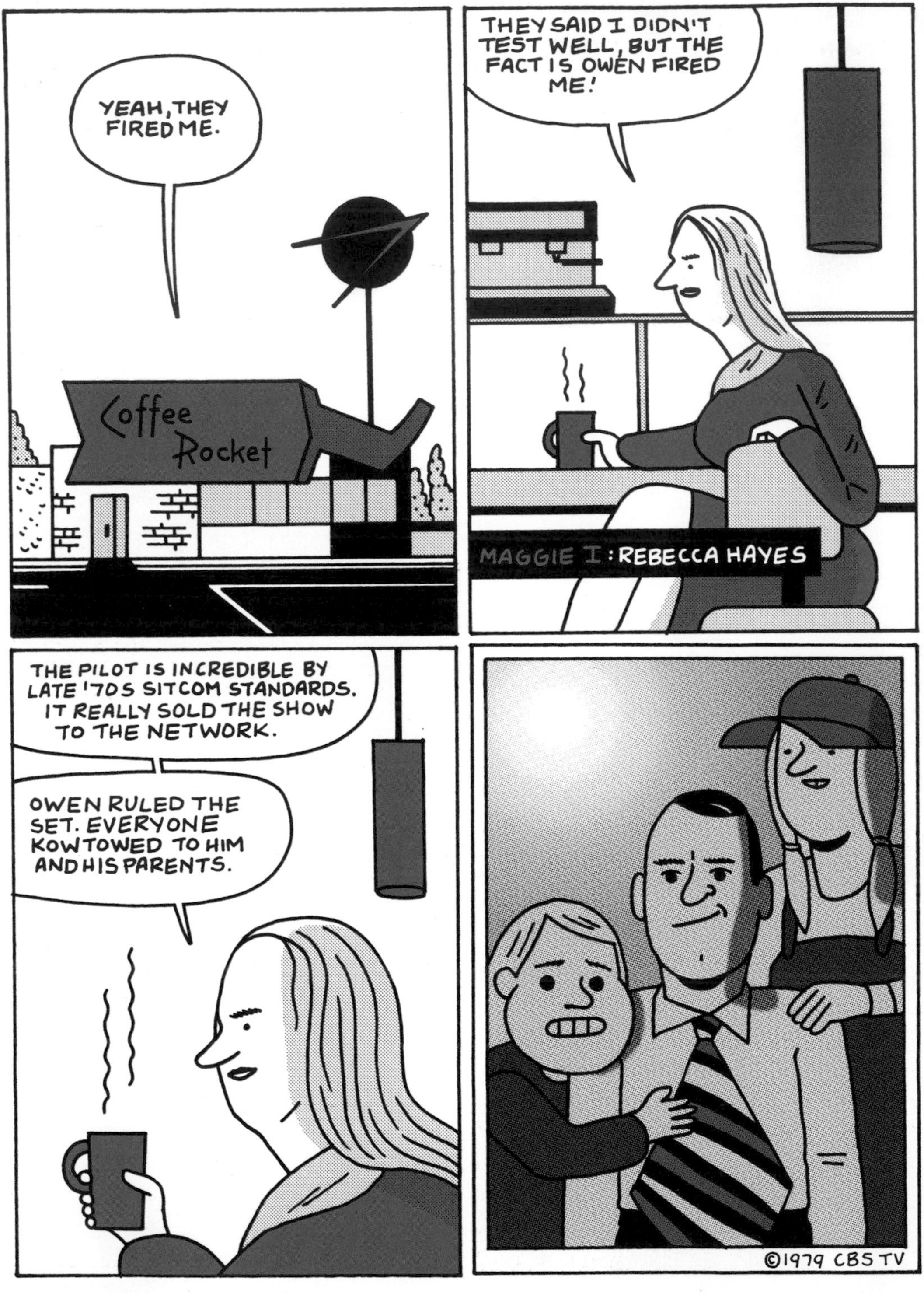
YEAH, THEY FIRED ME.
Coffee Rocket
THEY SAID I DIDN'T TEST WELL, BUT THE FACT IS OWEN FIRED ME!
MAGGIE I : REBECCA HAYES
THE PILOT IS INCREDIBLE BY LATE '70S SITCOM STANDARDS. IT REALLY SOLD THE SHOW TO THE NETWORK.
OWEN RULED THE SET. EVERYONE KOWTOWED TO HIM AND HIS PARENTS.
©1979 CBS TV

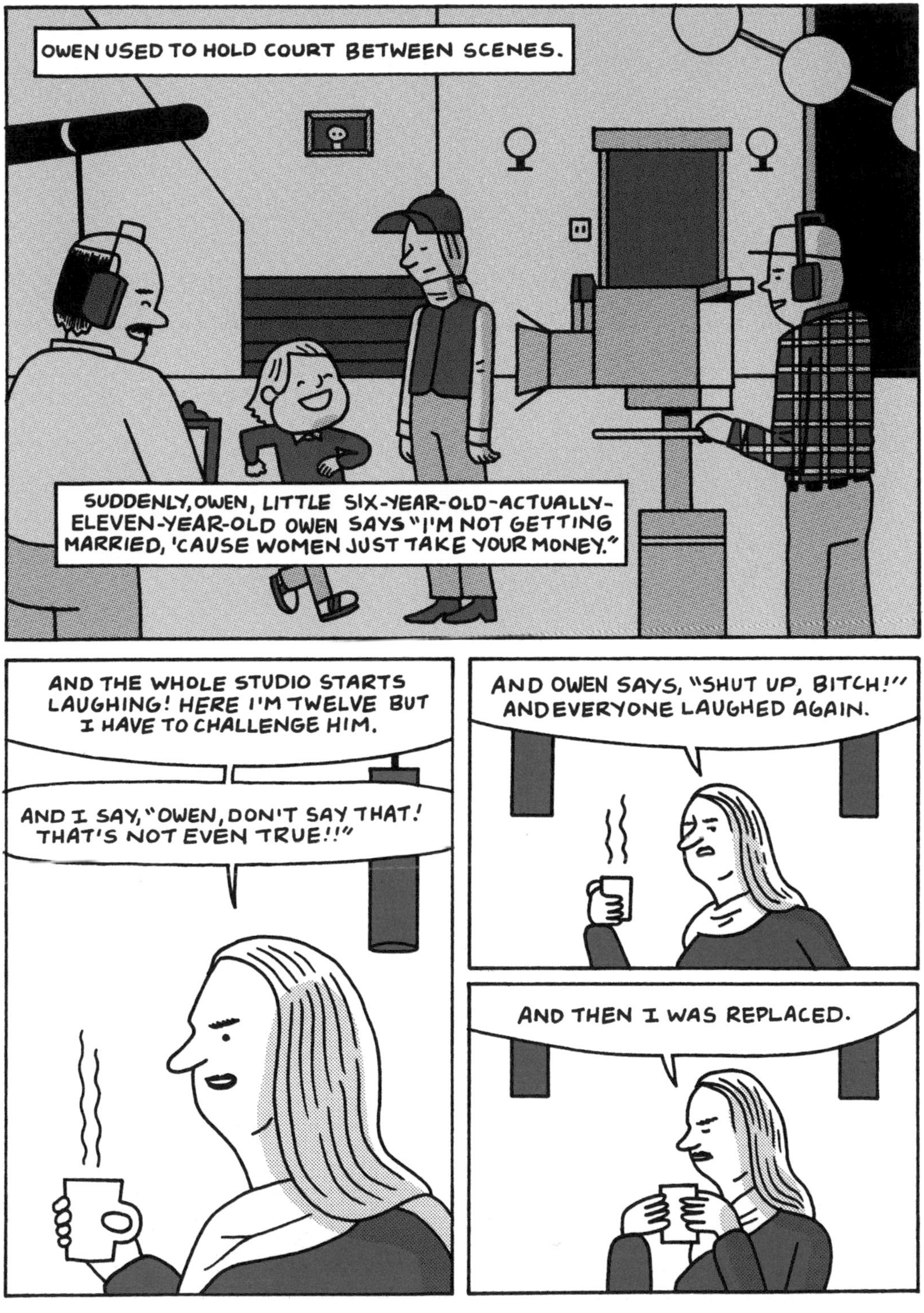
OWEN USED TO HOLD COURT BETWEEN SCENES.
SUDDENLY, OWEN, LITTLE SIX-YEAR-OLD-ACTUALLY-ELEVEN-YEAR-OLD OWEN SAYS "I'M NOT GETTING MARRIED, 'CAUSE WOMEN JUST TAKE YOUR MONEY."
AND THE WHOLE STUDIO STARTS LAUGHING! HERE I'M TWELVE BUT I HAVE TO CHALLENGE HIM.
AND I SAY, "OWEN, DON'T SAY THAT! THAT'S NOT EVEN TRUE!!"
AND OWEN SAYS, "SHUT UP, BITCH!" AND EVERYONE LAUGHED AGAIN.
AND THEN I WAS REPLACED.

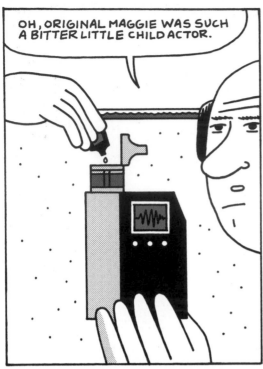

OH, ORIGINAL MAGGIE WAS SUCH A BITTER LITTLE CHILD ACTOR.

IT WAS OBVIOUS TO EVERYONE.

I'M SURE IT WAS A GOOD LESSON FOR HER ABOUT THE PECKING ORDER.

DON'T FUCK WITH NUMBER ONE ON THE CALL SHEET.

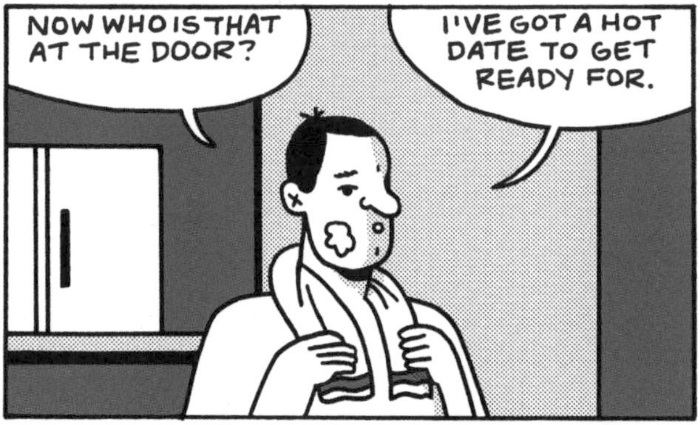
NOW WHO IS THAT AT THE DOOR?
I'VE GOT A HOT DATE TO GET READY FOR.

THE PILOT SET UP THE PREMISE:

Everyone's Friend

Tuesday

8:00PM

Single dad Connie Hammond gets an unexpected message from his estranged ex-girlfriend.

Connie's old flame, who had joined a commune years before, has died and she's left him as the next of kin for her two children!
Look out, Connie! Keaton and Maggie are gonna turn your world upside down! Say goodbye to your swinging bachelor lifestyle!

KEVIN J. SACKS
of "Highway Girl"
OWEN EUGENE
REBECCA HAYES

CLOSED CAPTIONED

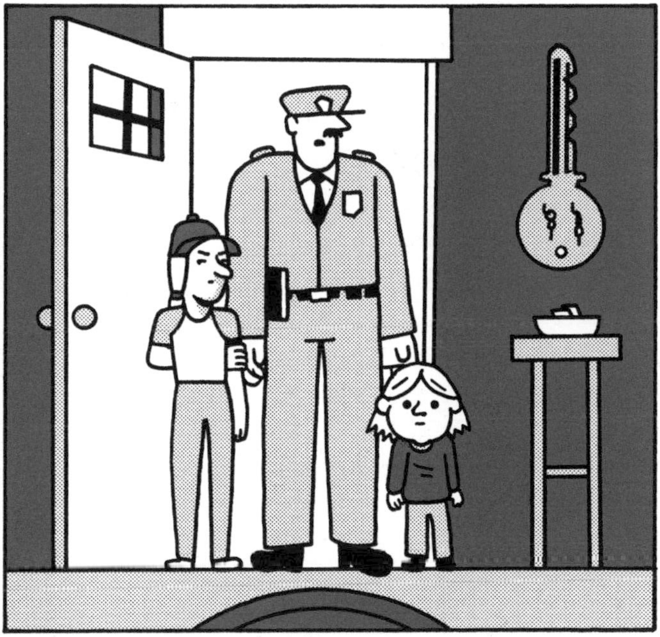

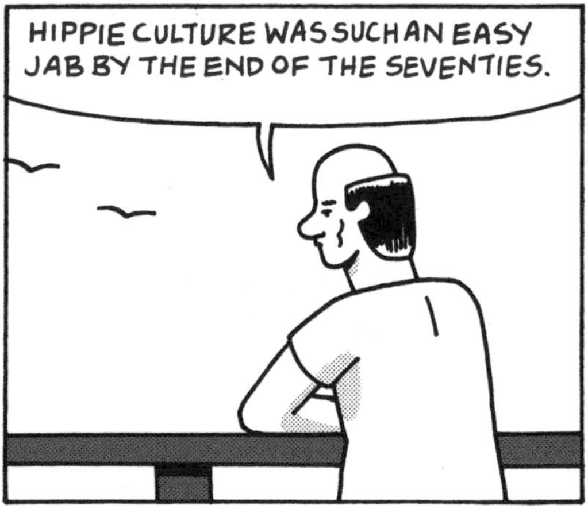
HIPPIE CULTURE WAS SUCH AN EASY JAB BY THE END OF THE SEVENTIES.

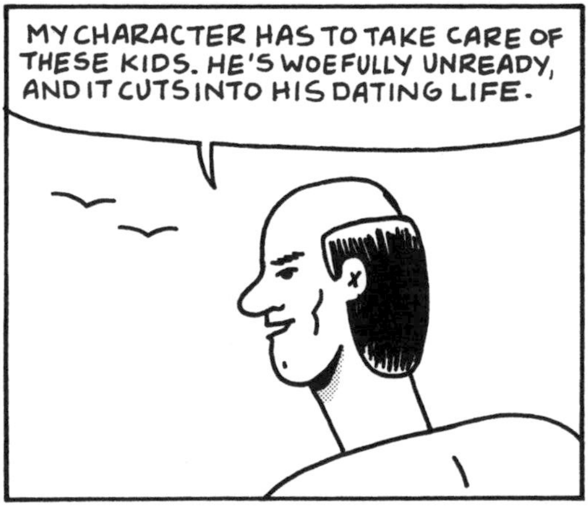
MY CHARACTER HAS TO TAKE CARE OF THESE KIDS. HE'S WOEFULLY UNREADY, AND IT CUTS INTO HIS DATING LIFE.

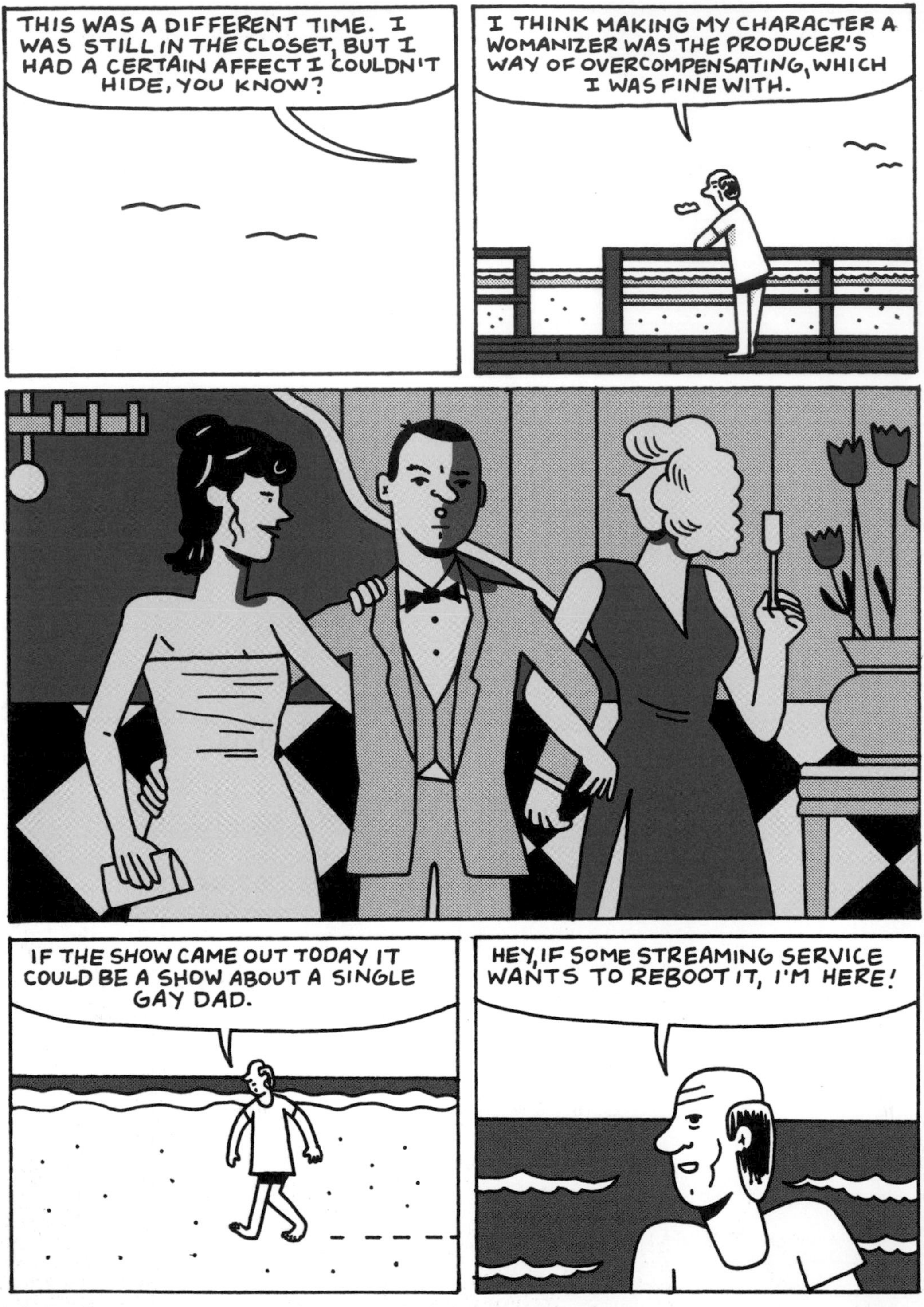
THIS WAS A DIFFERENT TIME. I WAS STILL IN THE CLOSET, BUT I HAD A CERTAIN AFFECT I COULDN'T HIDE, YOU KNOW?
I THINK MAKING MY CHARACTER A WOMANIZER WAS THE PRODUCER'S WAY OF OVERCOMPENSATING, WHICH I WAS FINE WITH.
IF THE SHOW CAME OUT TODAY IT COULD BE A SHOW ABOUT A SINGLE GAY DAD.
HEY, IF SOME STREAMING SERVICE WANTS TO REBOOT IT, I'M HERE!

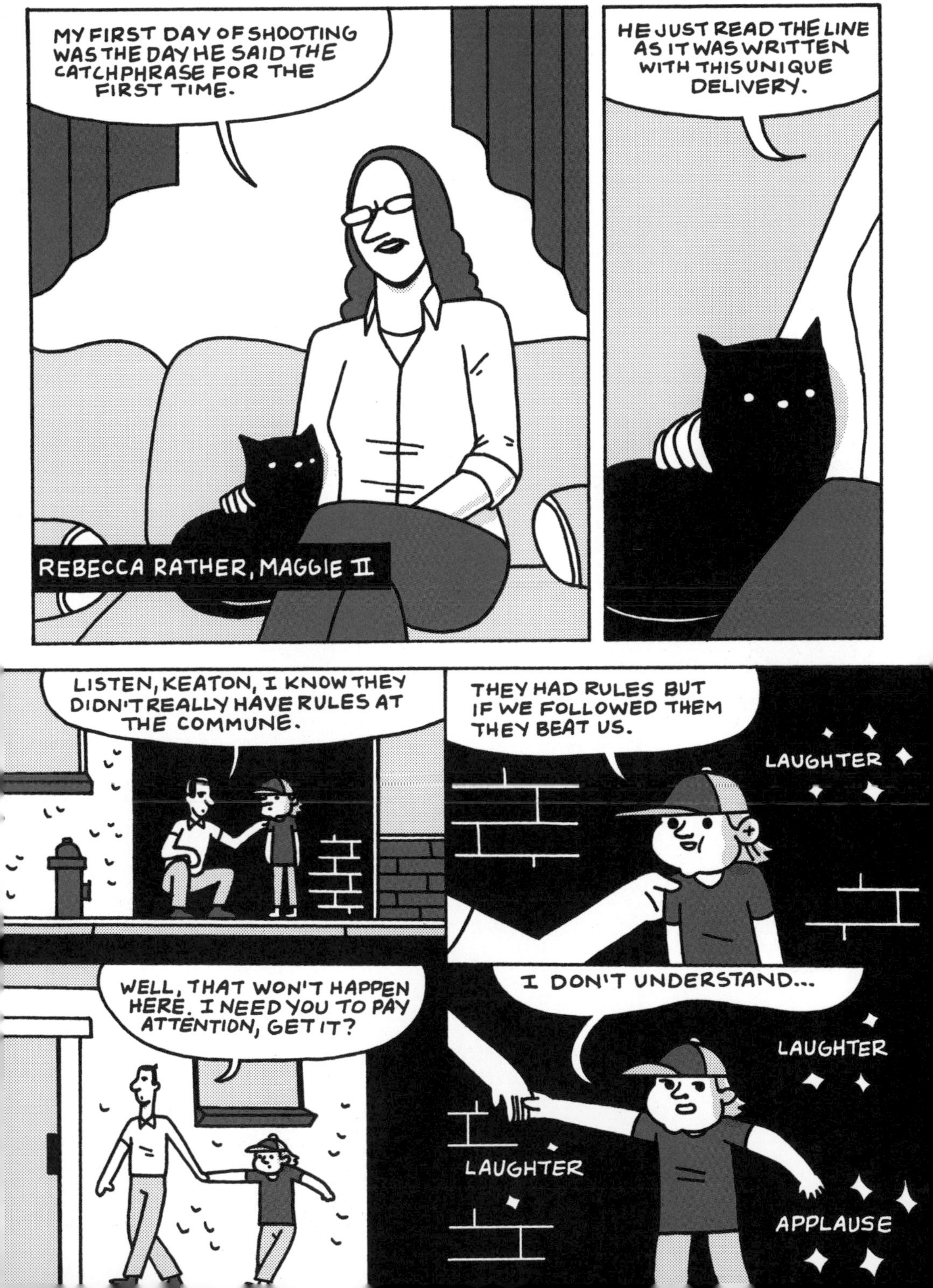

MY FIRST DAY OF SHOOTING WAS THE DAY HE SAID THE CATCHPHRASE FOR THE FIRST TIME.
REBECCA RATHER, MAGGIE II
HE JUST READ THE LINE AS IT WAS WRITTEN WITH THIS UNIQUE DELIVERY.
LISTEN, KEATON, I KNOW THEY DIDN'T REALLY HAVE RULES AT THE COMMUNE.
THEY HAD RULES BUT IF WE FOLLOWED THEM THEY BEAT US.
LAUGHTER
WELL, THAT WON'T HAPPEN HERE. I NEED YOU TO PAY ATTENTION, GET IT?
I DON'T UNDERSTAND...
LAUGHTER
LAUGHTER
APPLAUSE

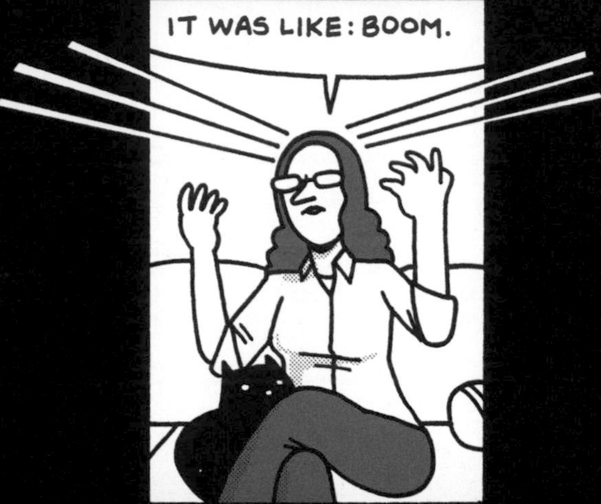
IT WAS LIKE: BOOM.

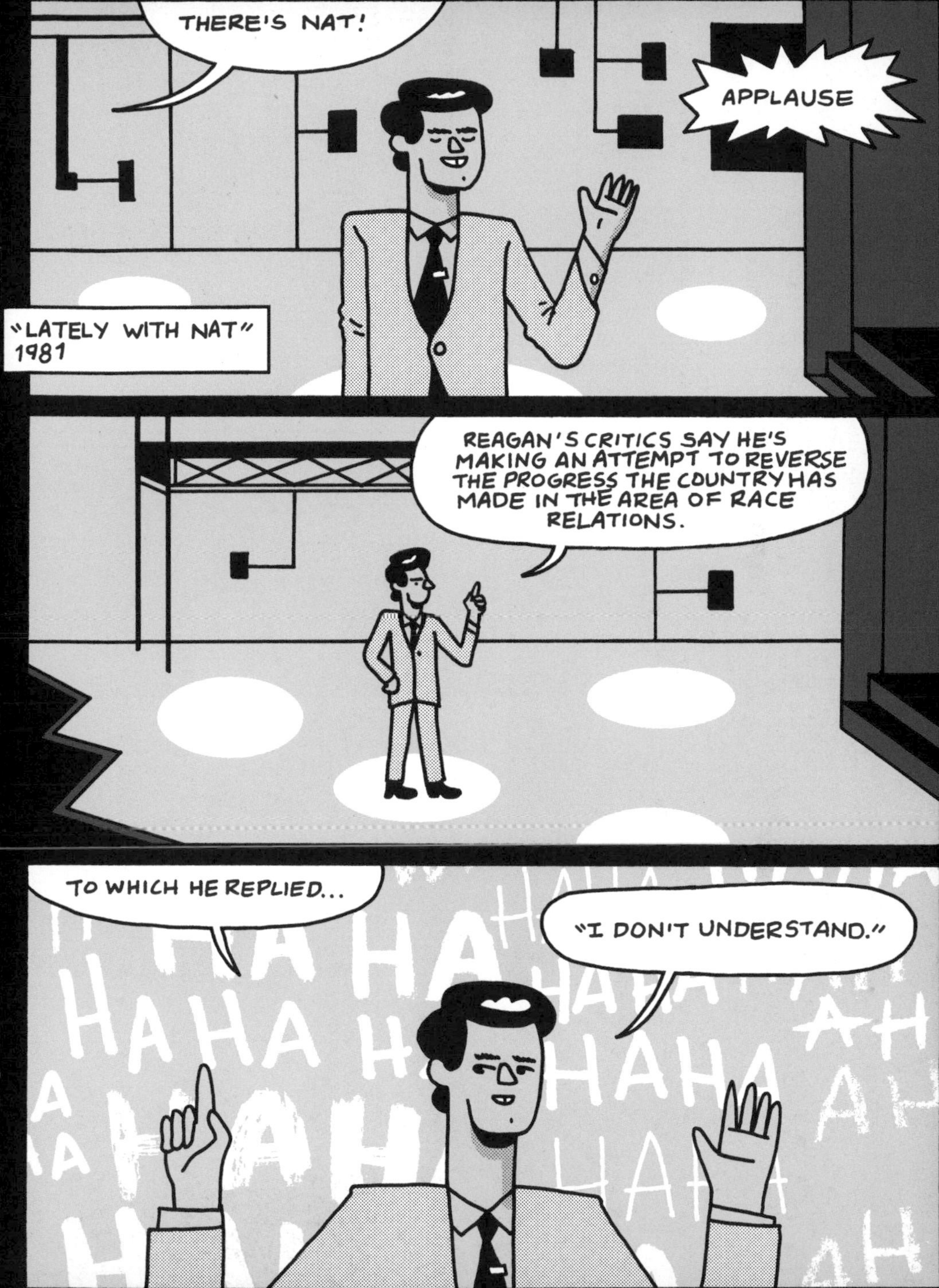
THERE'S NAT!
APPLAUSE
"LATELY WITH NAT" 1981
REAGAN'S CRITICS SAY HE'S MAKING AN ATTEMPT TO REVERSE THE PROGRESS THE COUNTRY HAS MADE IN THE AREA OF RACE RELATIONS.
TO WHICH HE REPLIED...
"I DON'T UNDERSTAND."
HA HA HA HA HA HA HA HA

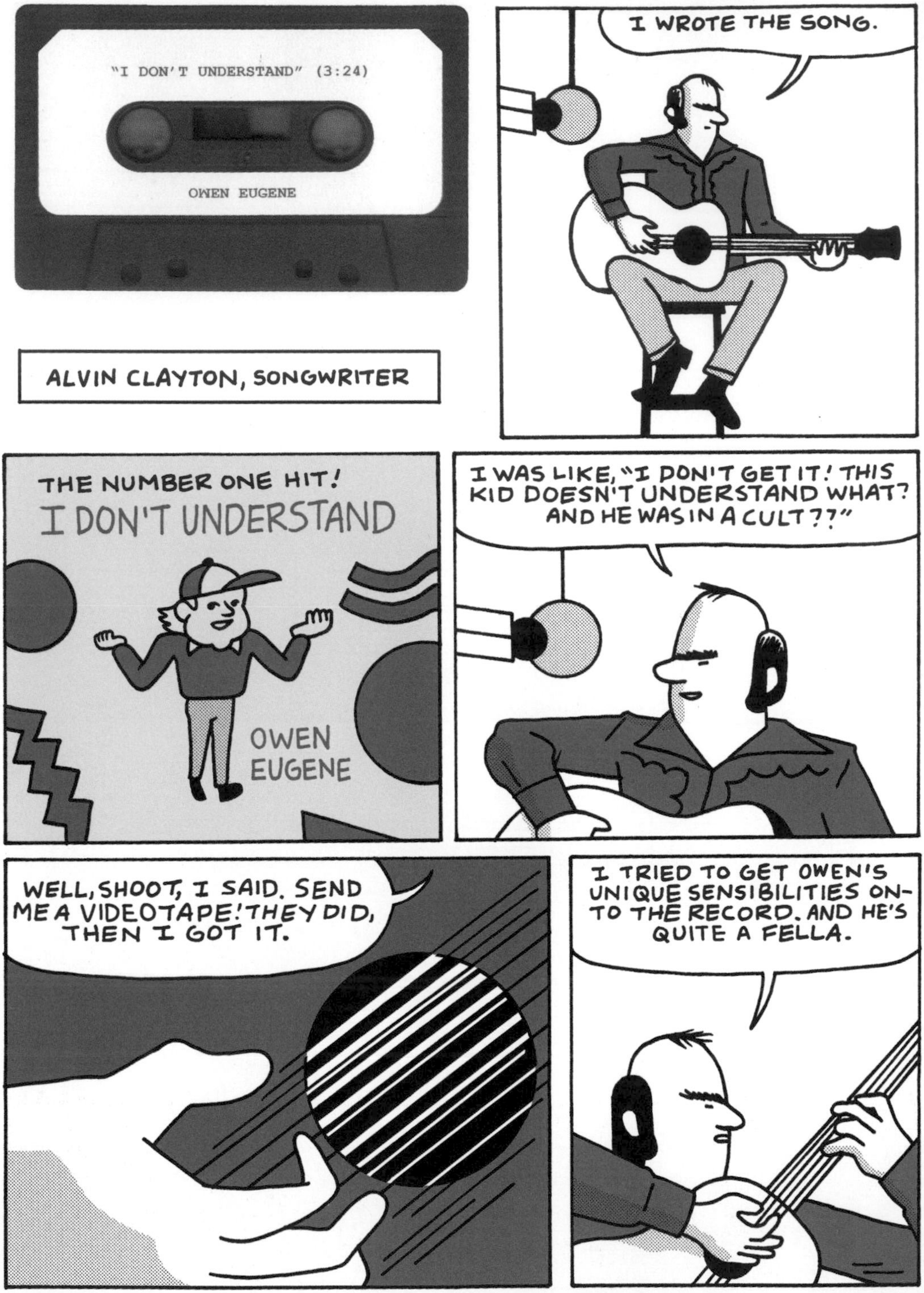
"I DON'T UNDERSTAND" (3:24)
OWEN EUGENE
ALVIN CLAYTON, SONGWRITER
I WROTE THE SONG.
THE NUMBER ONE HIT!
I DON'T UNDERSTAND
OWEN EUGENE
I WAS LIKE, "I DON'T GET IT! THIS KID DOESN'T UNDERSTAND WHAT? AND HE WAS IN A CULT??"
WELL, SHOOT, I SAID. SEND ME A VIDEOTAPE! THEY DID, THEN I GOT IT.
I TRIED TO GET OWEN'S UNIQUE SENSIBILITIES ON-TO THE RECORD. AND HE'S QUITE A FELLA.

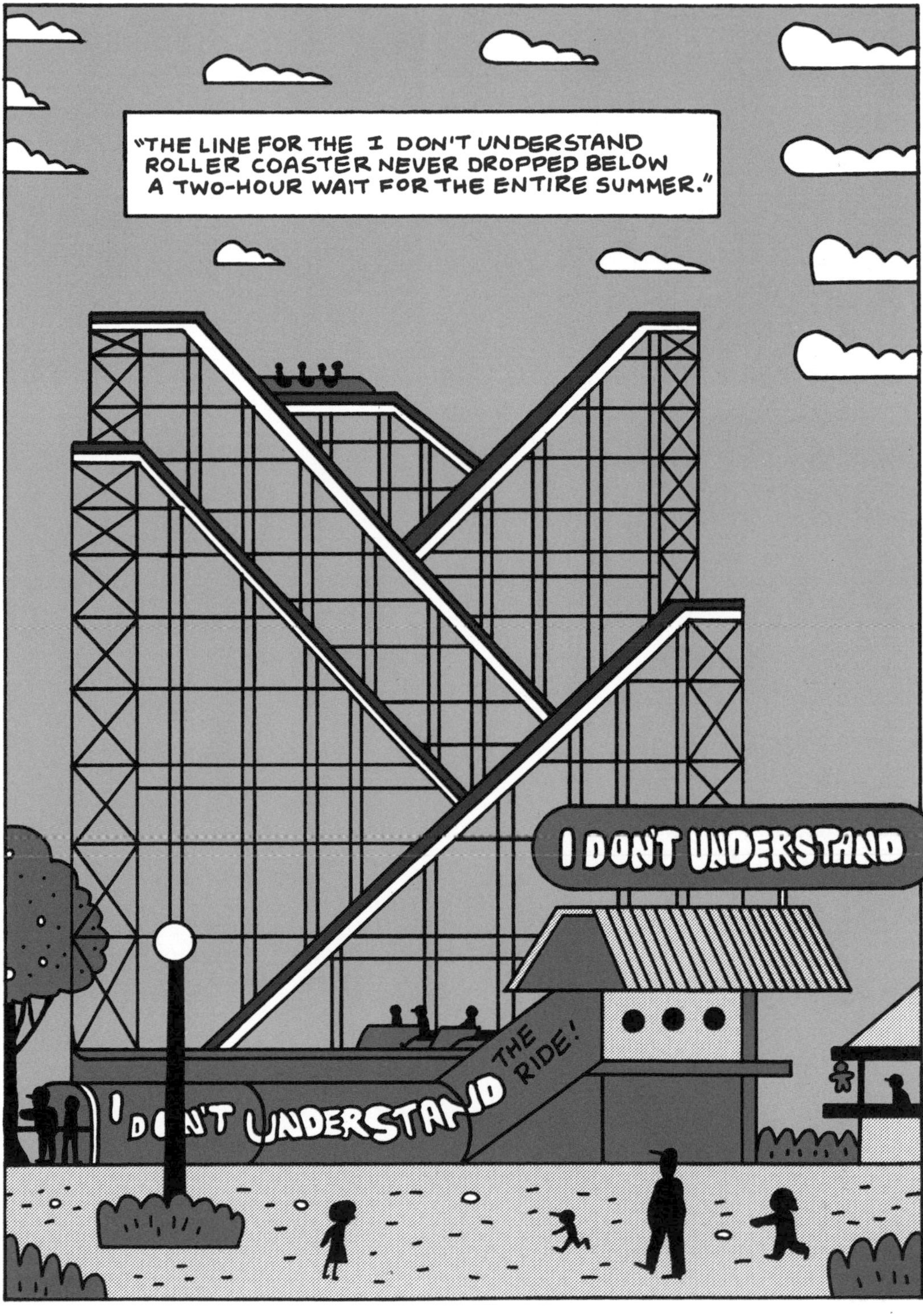
"THE LINE FOR THE I DON'T UNDERSTAND ROLLER COASTER NEVER DROPPED BELOW A TWO-HOUR WAIT FOR THE ENTIRE SUMMER."
I DON'T UNDERSTAND
I DON'T UNDERSTAND
THE RIDE!

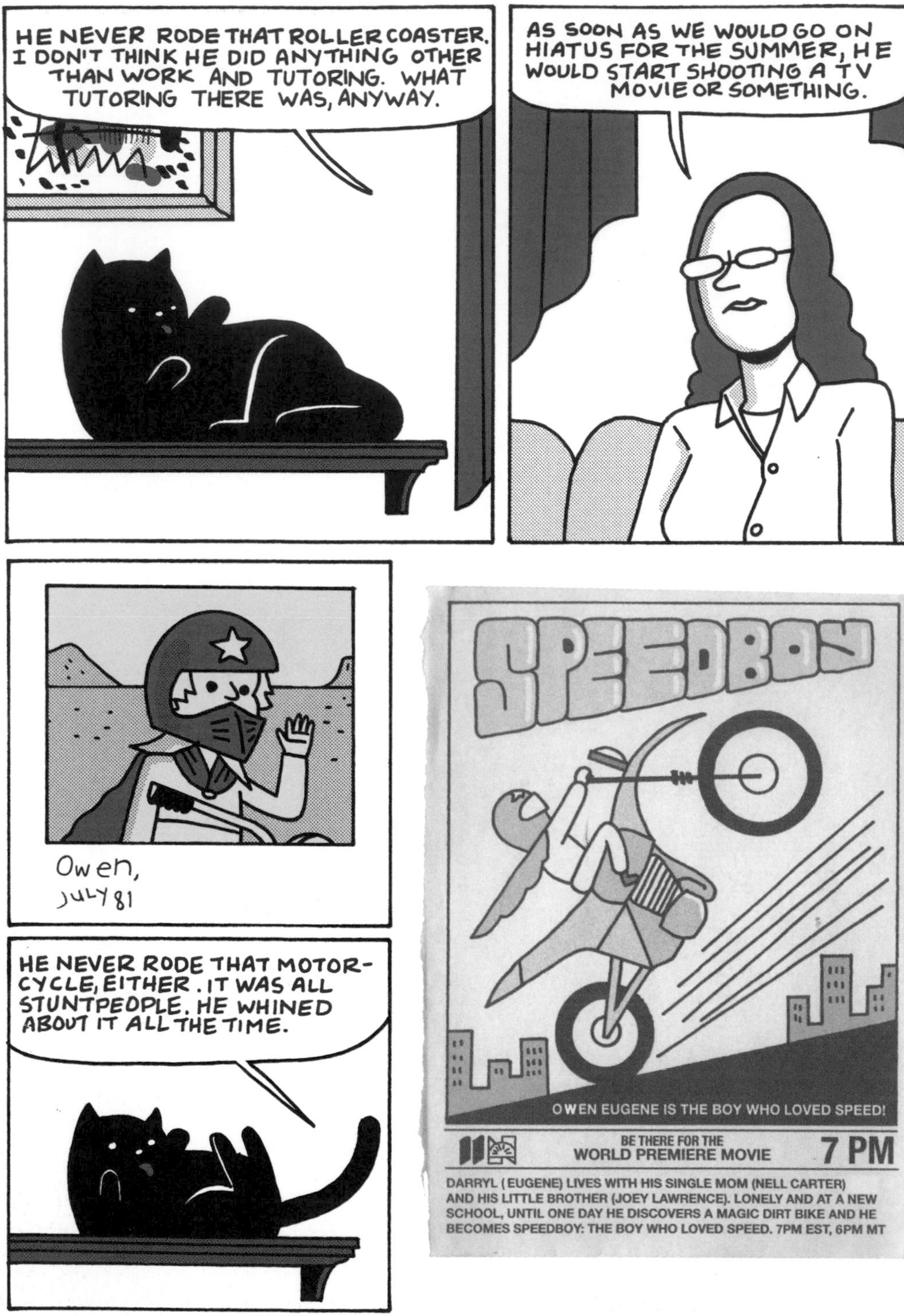
HE NEVER RODE THAT ROLLER COASTER. I DON'T THINK HE DID ANYTHING OTHER THAN WORK AND TUTORING. WHAT TUTORING THERE WAS, ANYWAY.
AS SOON AS WE WOULD GO ON HIATUS FOR THE SUMMER, HE WOULD START SHOOTING A TV MOVIE OR SOMETHING.
Owen,
JULY 81
SPEEDBOY
OWEN EUGENE IS THE BOY WHO LOVED SPEED!
BE THERE FOR THE
WORLD PREMIERE MOVIE
7 PM
DARRYL (EUGENE) LIVES WITH HIS SINGLE MOM (NELL CARTER) AND HIS LITTLE BROTHER (JOEY LAWRENCE). LONELY AND AT A NEW SCHOOL, UNTIL ONE DAY HE DISCOVERS A MAGIC DIRT BIKE AND HE BECOMES SPEEDBOY: THE BOY WHO LOVED SPEED. 7PM EST, 6PM MT
HE NEVER RODE THAT MOTORCYCLE, EITHER. IT WAS ALL STUNTPEOPLE. HE WHINED ABOUT IT ALL THE TIME.

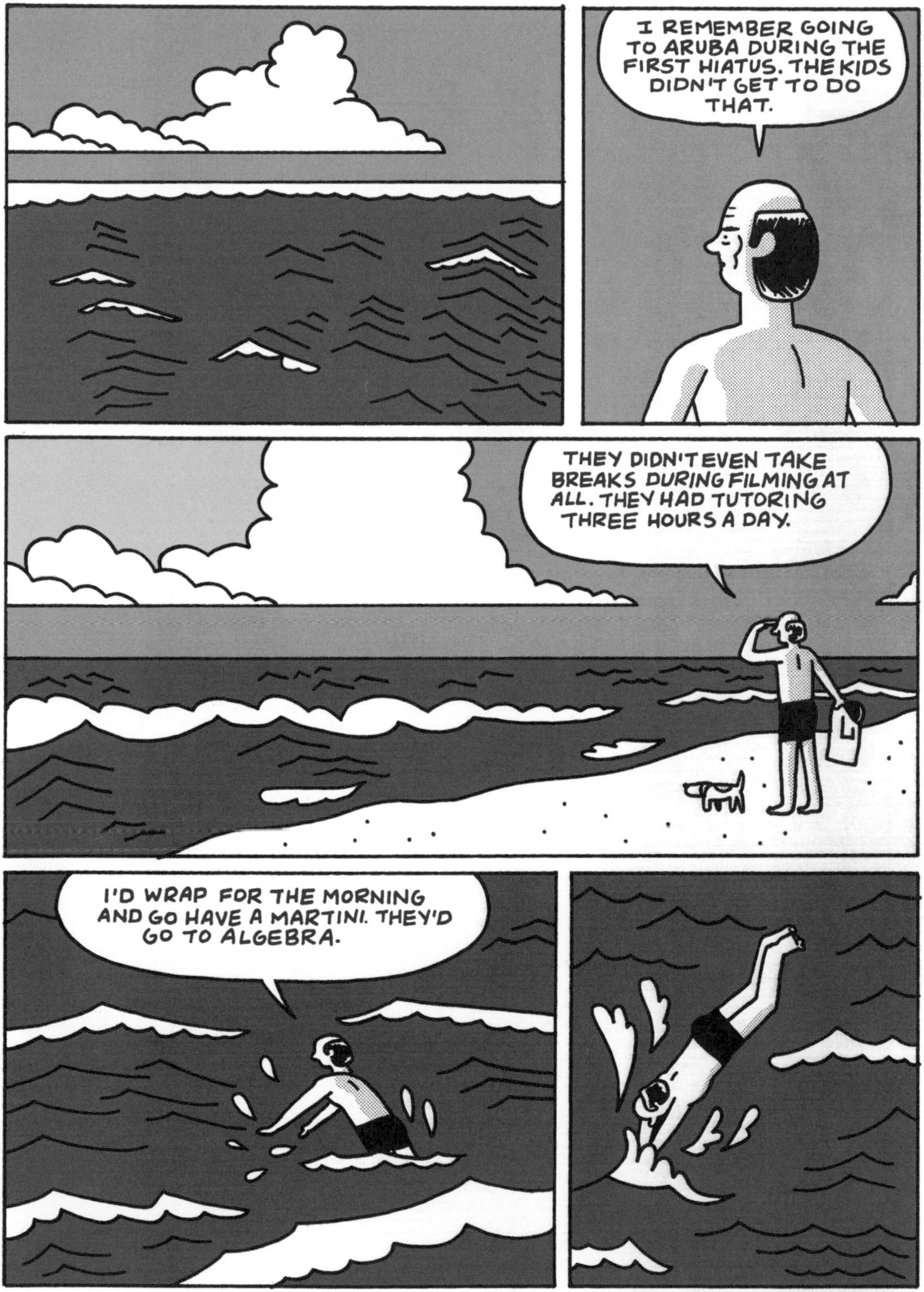
I REMEMBER GOING TO ARUBA DURING THE FIRST HIATUS. THE KIDS DIDN'T GET TO DO THAT.
THEY DIDN'T EVEN TAKE BREAKS DURING FILMING AT ALL. THEY HAD TUTORING THREE HOURS A DAY.
I'D WRAP FOR THE MORNING AND GO HAVE A MARTINI. THEY'D GO TO ALGEBRA.

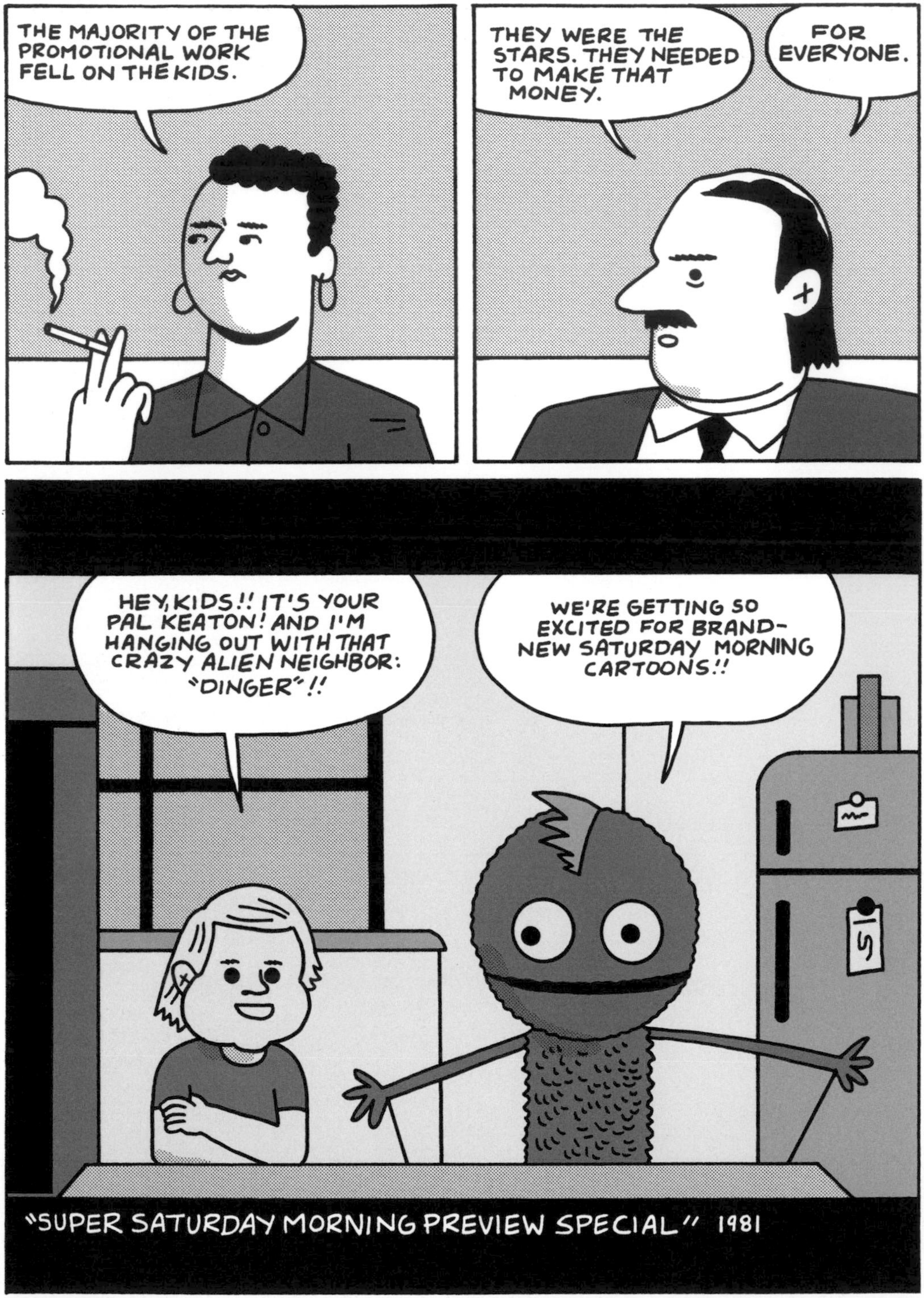
THE MAJORITY OF THE PROMOTIONAL WORK FELL ON THE KIDS.
THEY WERE THE STARS. THEY NEEDED TO MAKE THAT MONEY.
FOR EVERYONE.
HEY, KIDS!! IT'S YOUR PAL KEATON! AND I'M HANGING OUT WITH THAT CRAZY ALIEN NEIGHBOR: "DINGER"!!
WE'RE GETTING SO EXCITED FOR BRAND-NEW SATURDAY MORNING CARTOONS!!
"SUPER SATURDAY MORNING PREVIEW SPECIAL" 1981

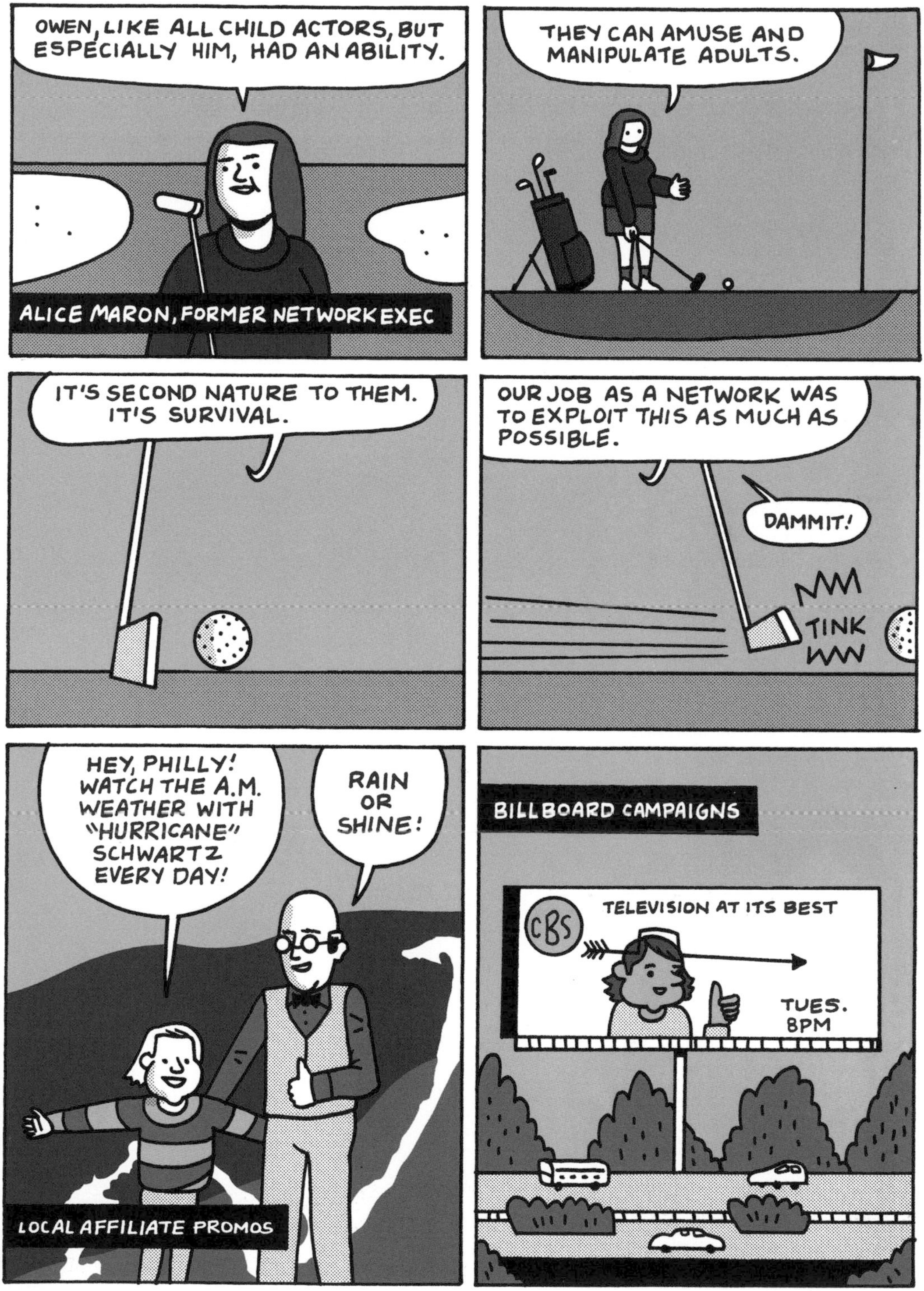
OWEN, LIKE ALL CHILD ACTORS, BUT ESPECIALLY HIM, HAD AN ABILITY.
ALICE MARON, FORMER NETWORK EXEC
THEY CAN AMUSE AND MANIPULATE ADULTS.
IT'S SECOND NATURE TO THEM. IT'S SURVIVAL.
OUR JOB AS A NETWORK WAS TO EXPLOIT THIS AS MUCH AS POSSIBLE.
DAMMIT!
TINK
HEY, PHILLY! WATCH THE A.M. WEATHER WITH "HURRICANE" SCHWARTZ EVERY DAY!
RAIN OR SHINE!
LOCAL AFFILIATE PROMOS
BILLBOARD CAMPAIGNS
CBS
TELEVISION AT ITS BEST
TUES. 8PM

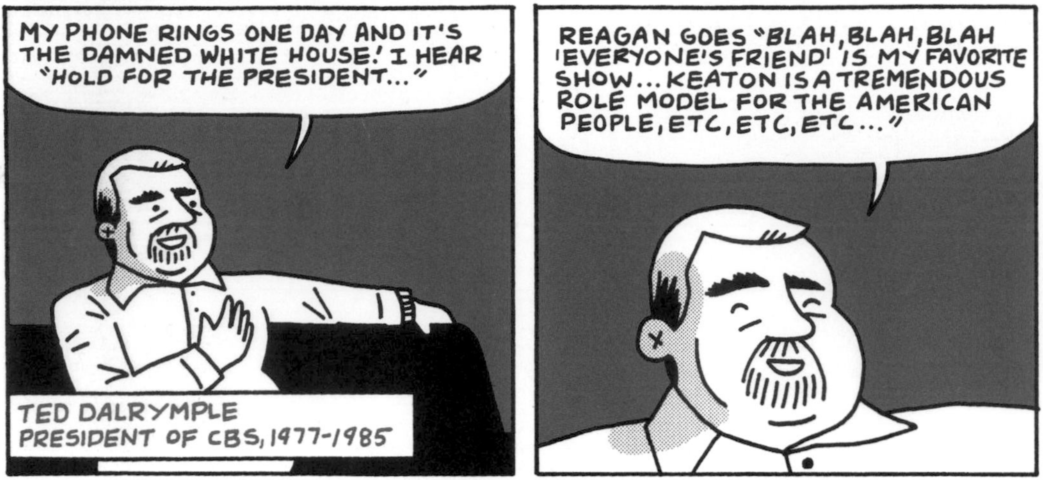
MY PHONE RINGS ONE DAY AND IT'S THE DAMNED WHITE HOUSE! I HEAR "HOLD FOR THE PRESIDENT..."
TED DALRYMPLE
PRESIDENT OF CBS, 1977-1985
REAGAN GOES "BLAH, BLAH, BLAH 'EVERYONE'S FRIEND' IS MY FAVORITE SHOW... KEATON IS A TREMENDOUS ROLE MODEL FOR THE AMERICAN PEOPLE, ETC, ETC, ETC..."

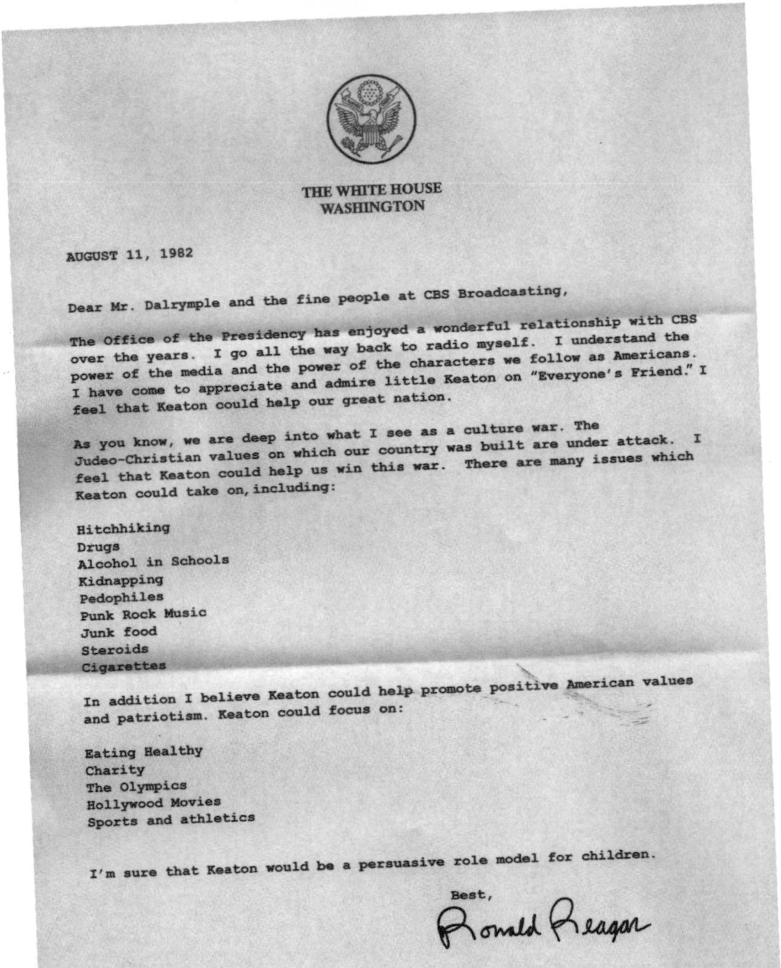

THE WHITE HOUSE
WASHINGTON

AUGUST 11, 1982

Dear Mr. Dalrymple and the fine people at CBS Broadcasting,

The Office of the Presidency has enjoyed a wonderful relationship with CBS over the years. I go all the way back to radio myself. I understand the power of the media and the power of the characters we follow as Americans. I have come to appreciate and admire little Keaton on "Everyone's Friend." I feel that Keaton could help our great nation.

As you know, we are deep into what I see as a culture war. The Judeo-Christian values on which our country was built are under attack. I feel that Keaton could help us win this war. There are many issues which Keaton could take on, including:

Hitchhiking
Drugs
Alcohol in Schools
Kidnapping
Pedophiles
Punk Rock Music
Junk food
Steroids
Cigarettes

In addition I believe Keaton could help promote positive American values and patriotism. Keaton could focus on:

Eating Healthy
Charity
The Olympics
Hollywood Movies
Sports and athletics

I'm sure that Keaton would be a persuasive role model for children.

Best,

Ronald Reagan

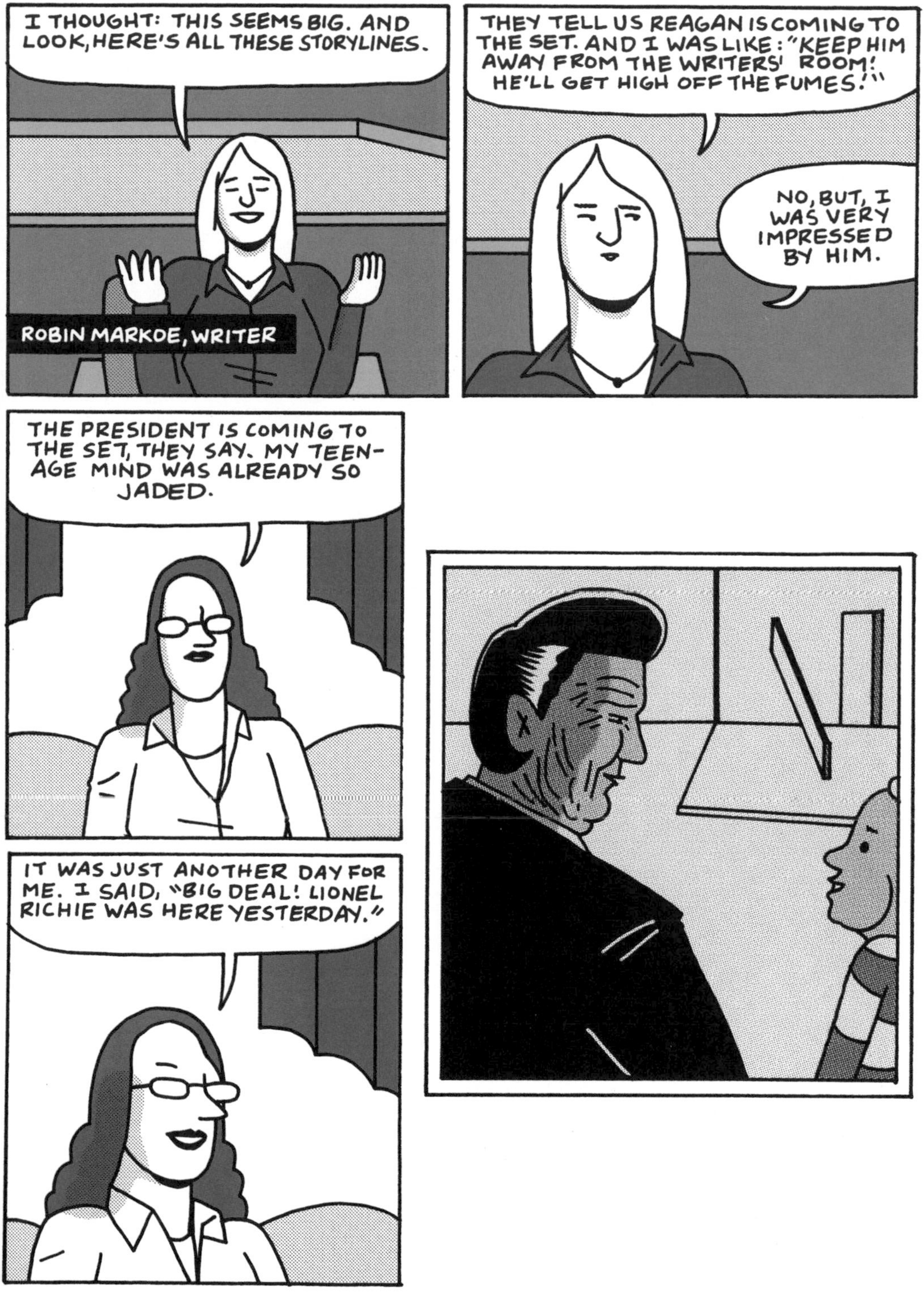
I THOUGHT: THIS SEEMS BIG. AND LOOK, HERE'S ALL THESE STORYLINES.
ROBIN MARKOE, WRITER
THEY TELL US REAGAN IS COMING TO THE SET. AND I WAS LIKE: "KEEP HIM AWAY FROM THE WRITERS' ROOM! HE'LL GET HIGH OFF THE FUMES!"
NO, BUT, I WAS VERY IMPRESSED BY HIM.
THE PRESIDENT IS COMING TO THE SET, THEY SAY. MY TEEN-AGE MIND WAS ALREADY SO JADED.
IT WAS JUST ANOTHER DAY FOR ME. I SAID, "BIG DEAL! LIONEL RICHIE WAS HERE YESTERDAY."

THE HITCHHIKERS SEASON TWO EPISODE ONE

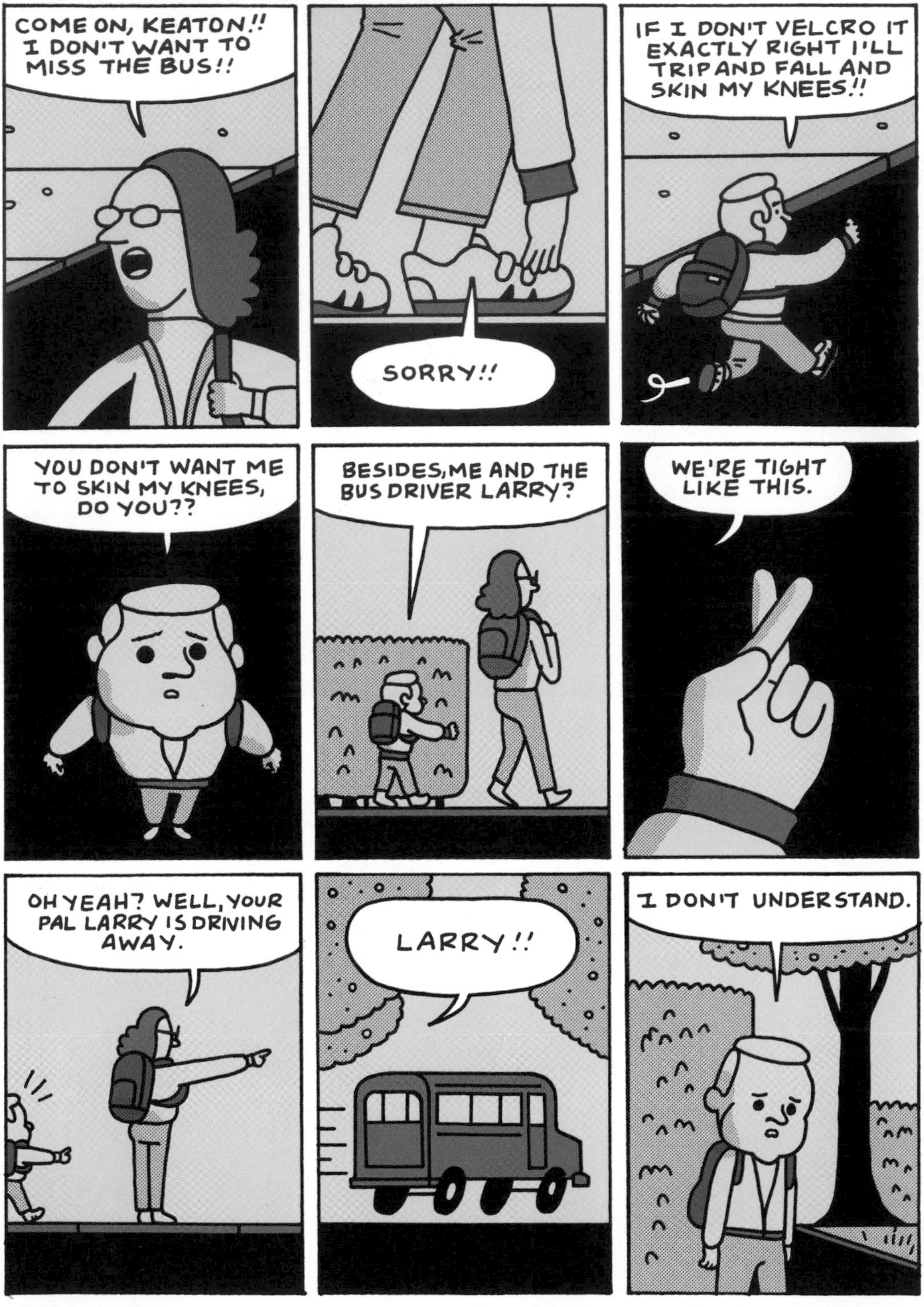
COME ON, KEATON!! I DON'T WANT TO MISS THE BUS!!
SORRY!!
IF I DON'T VELCRO IT EXACTLY RIGHT I'LL TRIP AND FALL AND SKIN MY KNEES!!
YOU DON'T WANT ME TO SKIN MY KNEES, DO YOU??
BESIDES, ME AND THE BUS DRIVER LARRY?
WE'RE TIGHT LIKE THIS.
OH YEAH? WELL, YOUR PAL LARRY IS DRIVING AWAY.
LARRY!!
I DON'T UNDERSTAND.

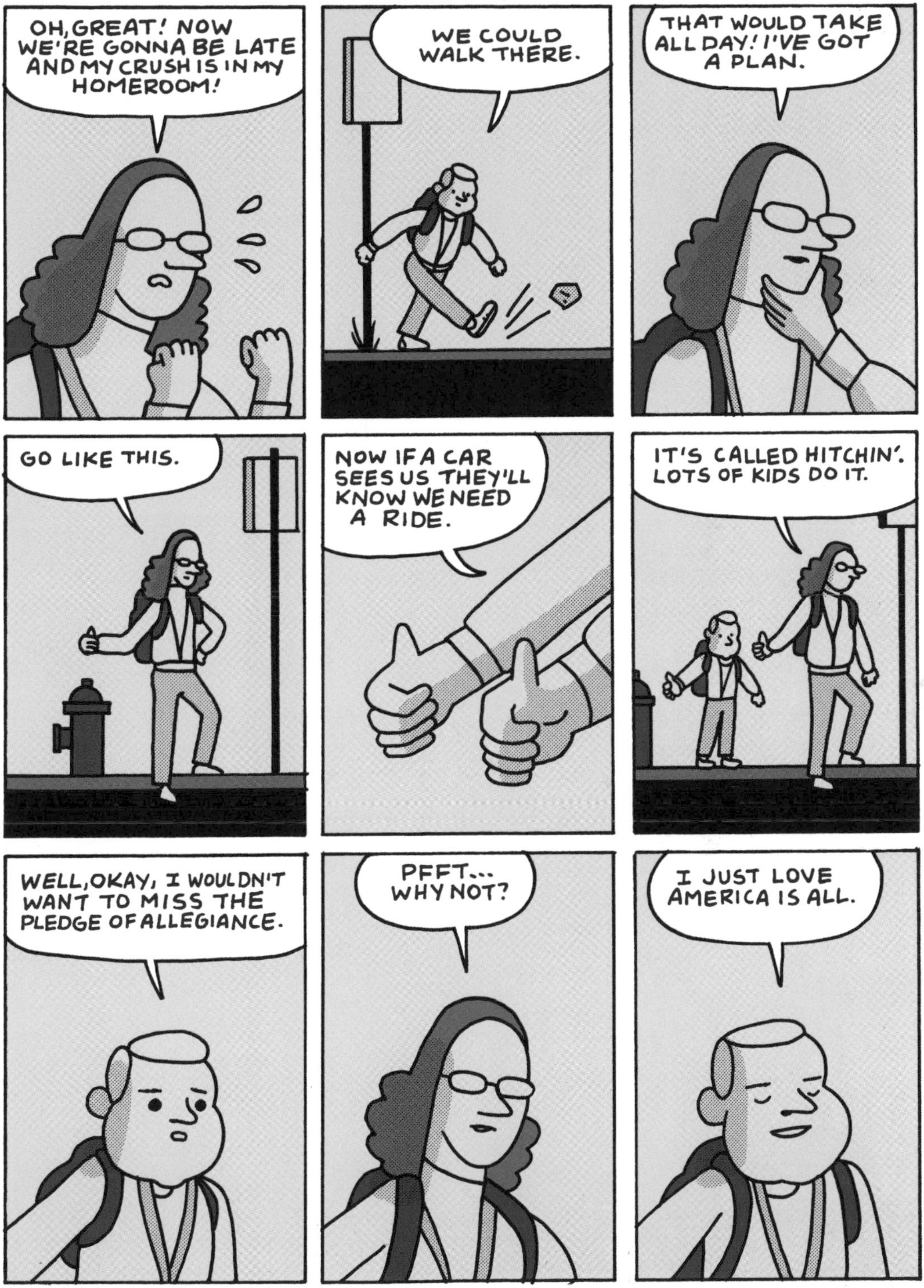
OH, GREAT! NOW WE'RE GONNA BE LATE AND MY CRUSH IS IN MY HOMEROOM!
WE COULD WALK THERE.
THAT WOULD TAKE ALL DAY! I'VE GOT A PLAN.
GO LIKE THIS.
NOW IF A CAR SEES US THEY'LL KNOW WE NEED A RIDE.
IT'S CALLED HITCHIN'. LOTS OF KIDS DO IT.
WELL, OKAY, I WOULDN'T WANT TO MISS THE PLEDGE OF ALLEGIANCE.
PFFT... WHY NOT?
I JUST LOVE AMERICA IS ALL.

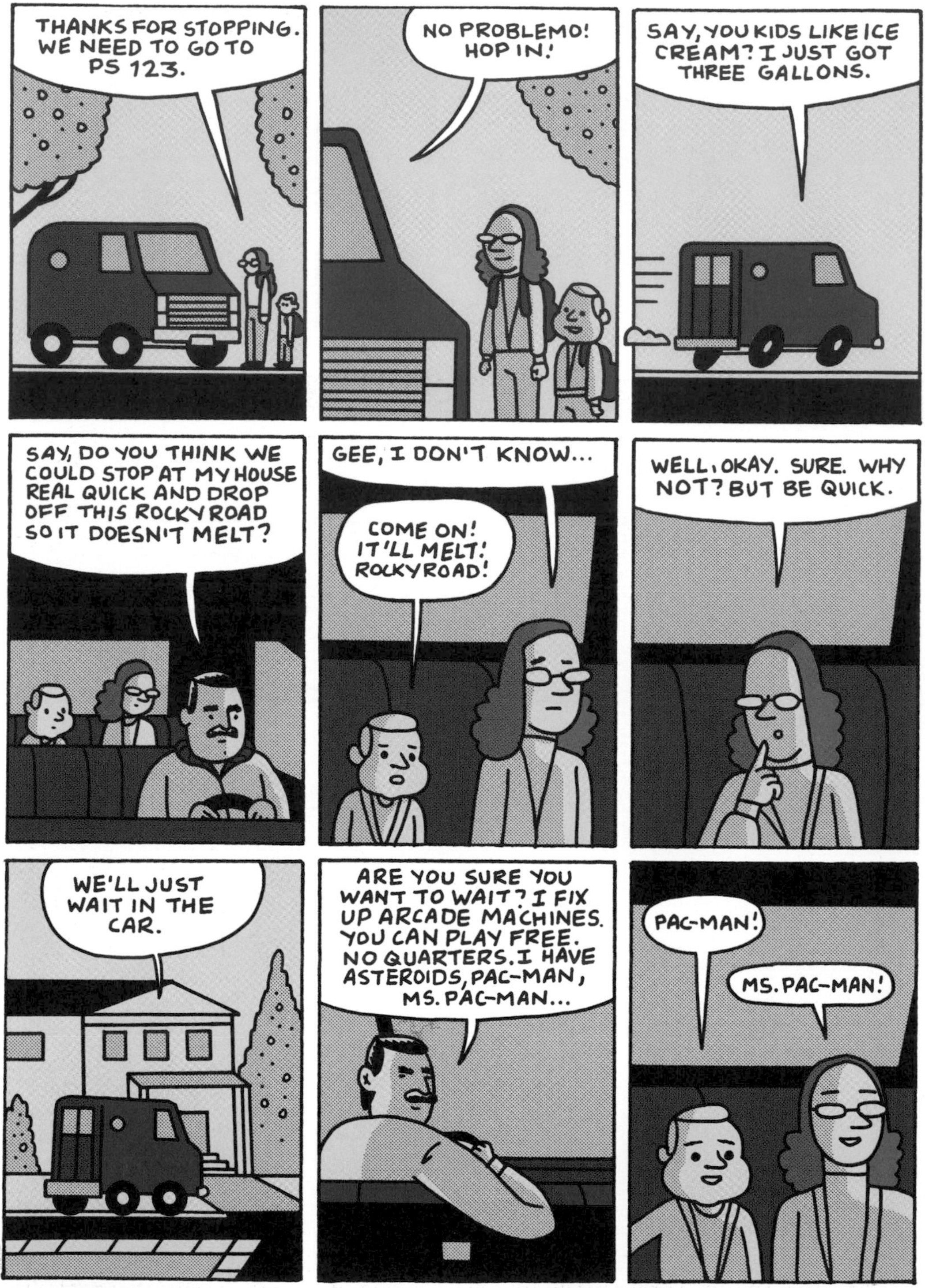
THANKS FOR STOPPING. WE NEED TO GO TO PS 123.
NO PROBLEMO! HOP IN!
SAY, YOU KIDS LIKE ICE CREAM? I JUST GOT THREE GALLONS.
SAY, DO YOU THINK WE COULD STOP AT MY HOUSE REAL QUICK AND DROP OFF THIS ROCKY ROAD SO IT DOESN'T MELT?
GEE, I DON'T KNOW...
COME ON! IT'LL MELT! ROCKY ROAD!
WELL, OKAY. SURE. WHY NOT? BUT BE QUICK.
WE'LL JUST WAIT IN THE CAR.
ARE YOU SURE YOU WANT TO WAIT? I FIX UP ARCADE MACHINES. YOU CAN PLAY FREE. NO QUARTERS. I HAVE ASTEROIDS, PAC-MAN, MS. PAC-MAN...
PAC-MAN!
MS. PAC-MAN!

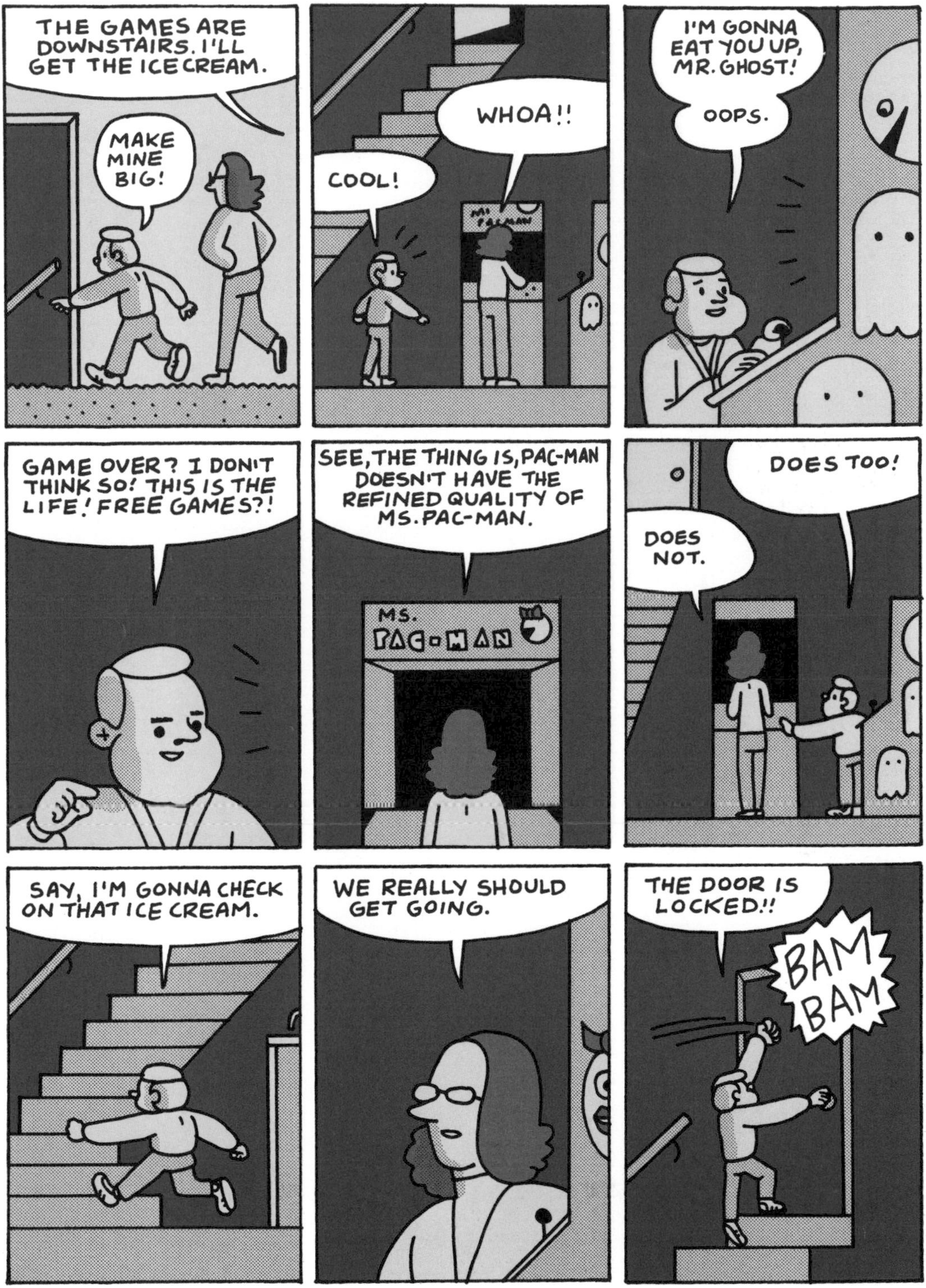
THE GAMES ARE DOWNSTAIRS. I'LL GET THE ICE CREAM.
MAKE MINE BIG!
WHOA!!
COOL!
MS PAC-MAN
I'M GONNA EAT YOU UP, MR. GHOST!
OOPS.
GAME OVER? I DON'T THINK SO! THIS IS THE LIFE! FREE GAMES?!
SEE, THE THING IS, PAC-MAN DOESN'T HAVE THE REFINED QUALITY OF MS. PAC-MAN.
MS. PAC-MAN
DOES TOO!
DOES NOT.
SAY, I'M GONNA CHECK ON THAT ICE CREAM.
WE REALLY SHOULD GET GOING.
THE DOOR IS LOCKED!!
BAM BAM

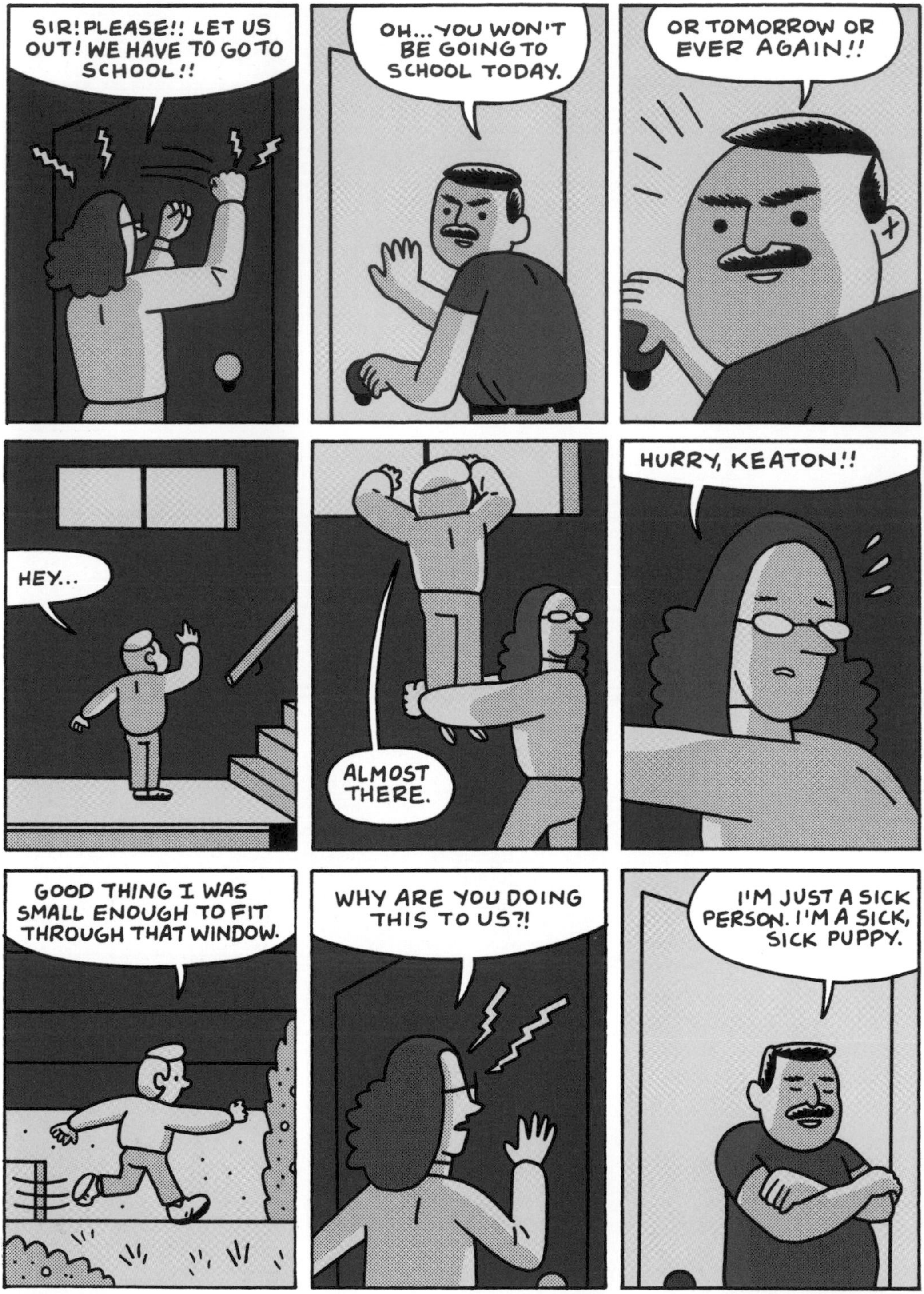
SIR! PLEASE!! LET US OUT! WE HAVE TO GO TO SCHOOL!!
OH... YOU WON'T BE GOING TO SCHOOL TODAY.
OR TOMORROW OR EVER AGAIN!!
HEY...
ALMOST THERE.
HURRY, KEATON!!
GOOD THING I WAS SMALL ENOUGH TO FIT THROUGH THAT WINDOW.
WHY ARE YOU DOING THIS TO US?!
I'M JUST A SICK PERSON. I'M A SICK, SICK PUPPY.

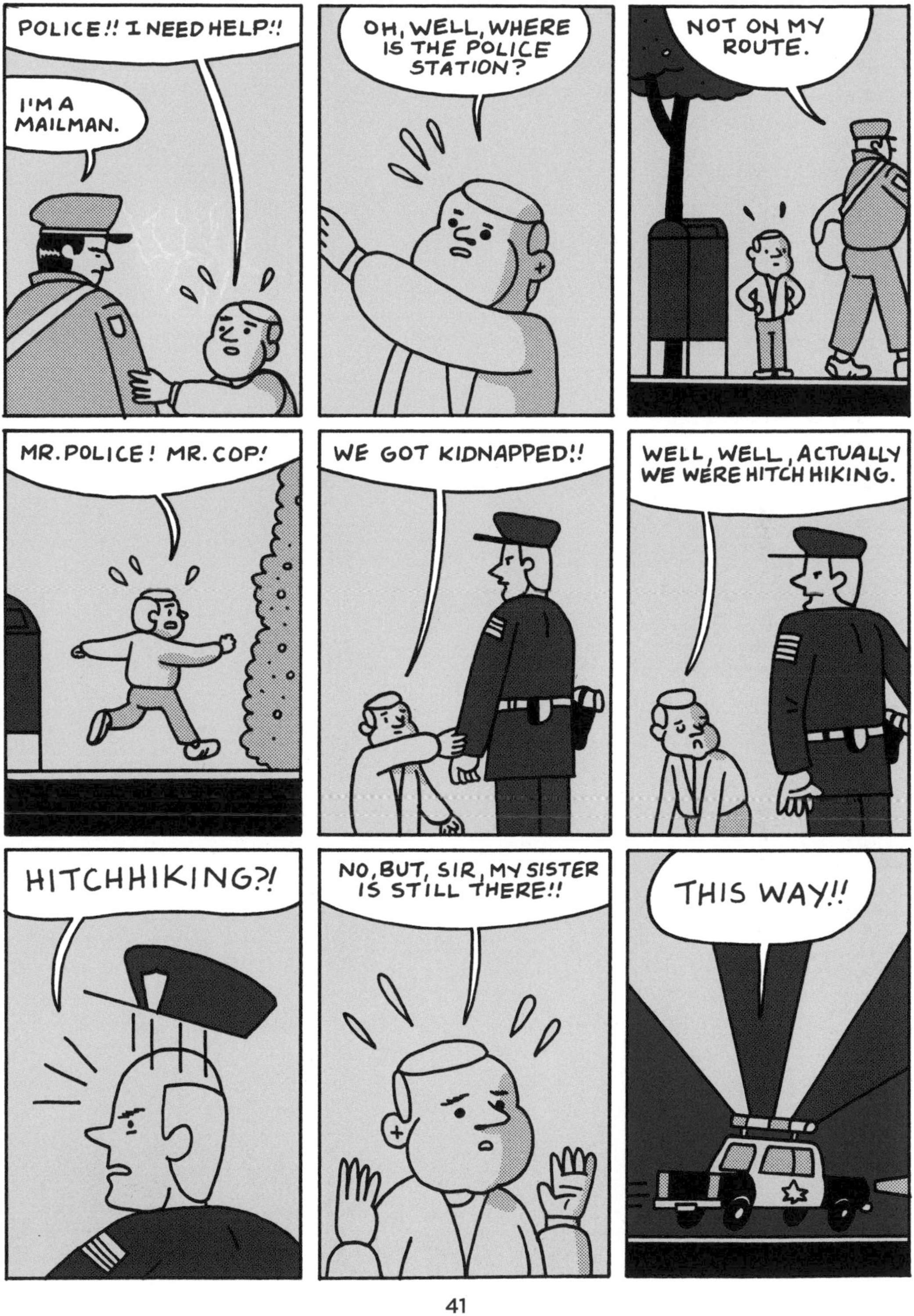
POLICE!! I NEED HELP!!
I'M A MAILMAN.
OH, WELL, WHERE IS THE POLICE STATION?
NOT ON MY ROUTE.
MR. POLICE! MR. COP!
WE GOT KIDNAPPED!!
WELL, WELL, ACTUALLY WE WERE HITCH HIKING.
HITCHHIKING?!
NO, BUT, SIR, MY SISTER IS STILL THERE!!
THIS WAY!!

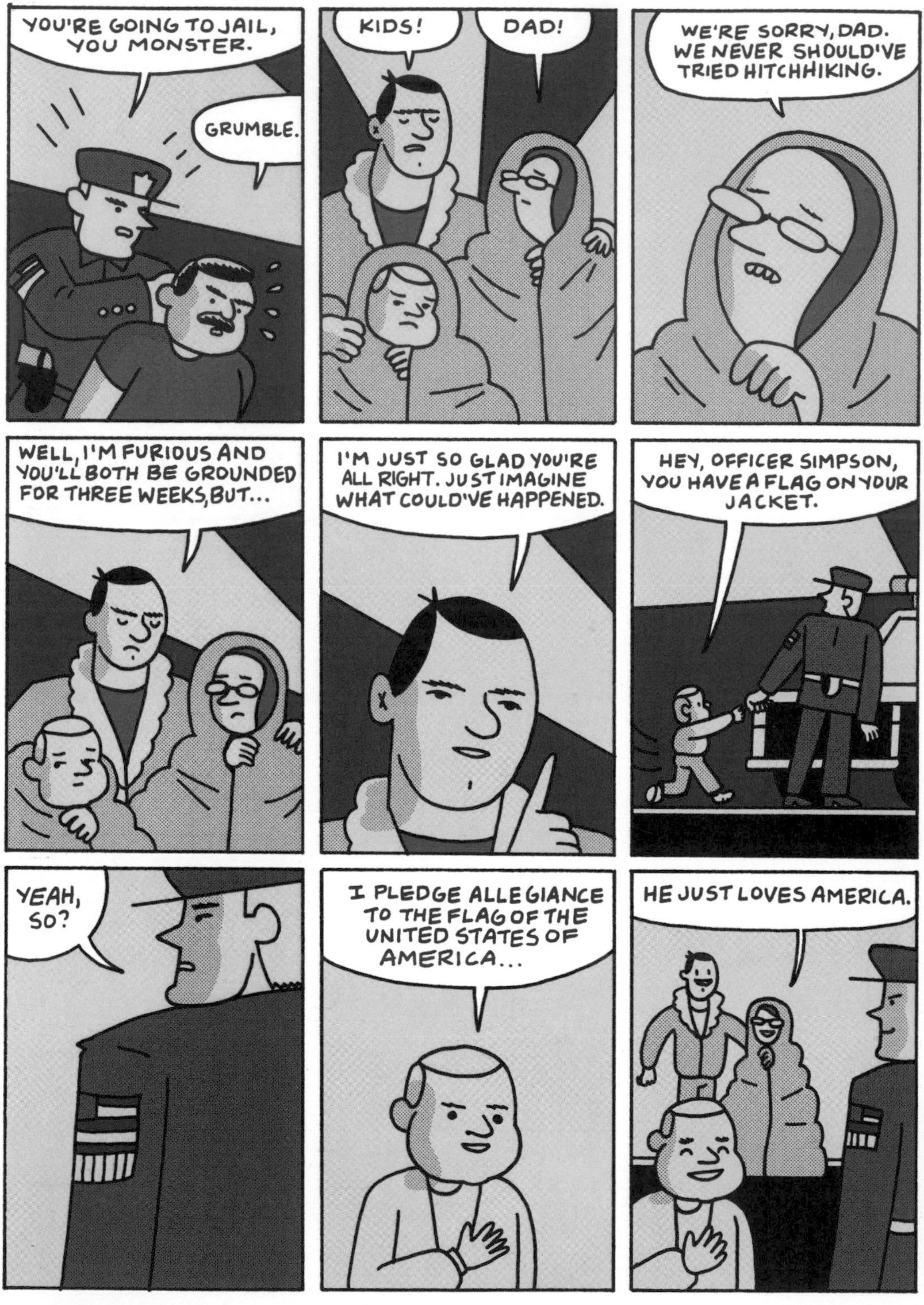
YOU'RE GOING TO JAIL, YOU MONSTER.
GRUMBLE.
KIDS!
DAD!
WE'RE SORRY, DAD. WE NEVER SHOULD'VE TRIED HITCHHIKING.
WELL, I'M FURIOUS AND YOU'LL BOTH BE GROUNDED FOR THREE WEEKS, BUT...
I'M JUST SO GLAD YOU'RE ALL RIGHT. JUST IMAGINE WHAT COULD'VE HAPPENED.
HEY, OFFICER SIMPSON, YOU HAVE A FLAG ON YOUR JACKET.
YEAH, SO?
I PLEDGE ALLEGIANCE TO THE FLAG OF THE UNITED STATES OF AMERICA...
HE JUST LOVES AMERICA.

I REMEMBER THEY HAD HIM GET A HAIRCUT HE DIDN'T LIKE VERY MUCH. I LIKED IT! MORE CLEAN CUT.

I REMEMBER BUYING US A MERCEDES THAT SUMMER AND ONE FOR HER IN THE FALL.

I WAS ONLY 16, BUT I WAS 100% ABSOLUTELY TREATED LIKE AN ADULT BY EVERY-ONE ON THE SET.

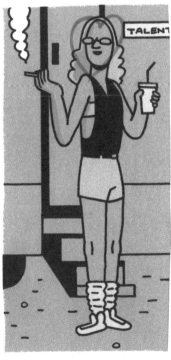

TALENT

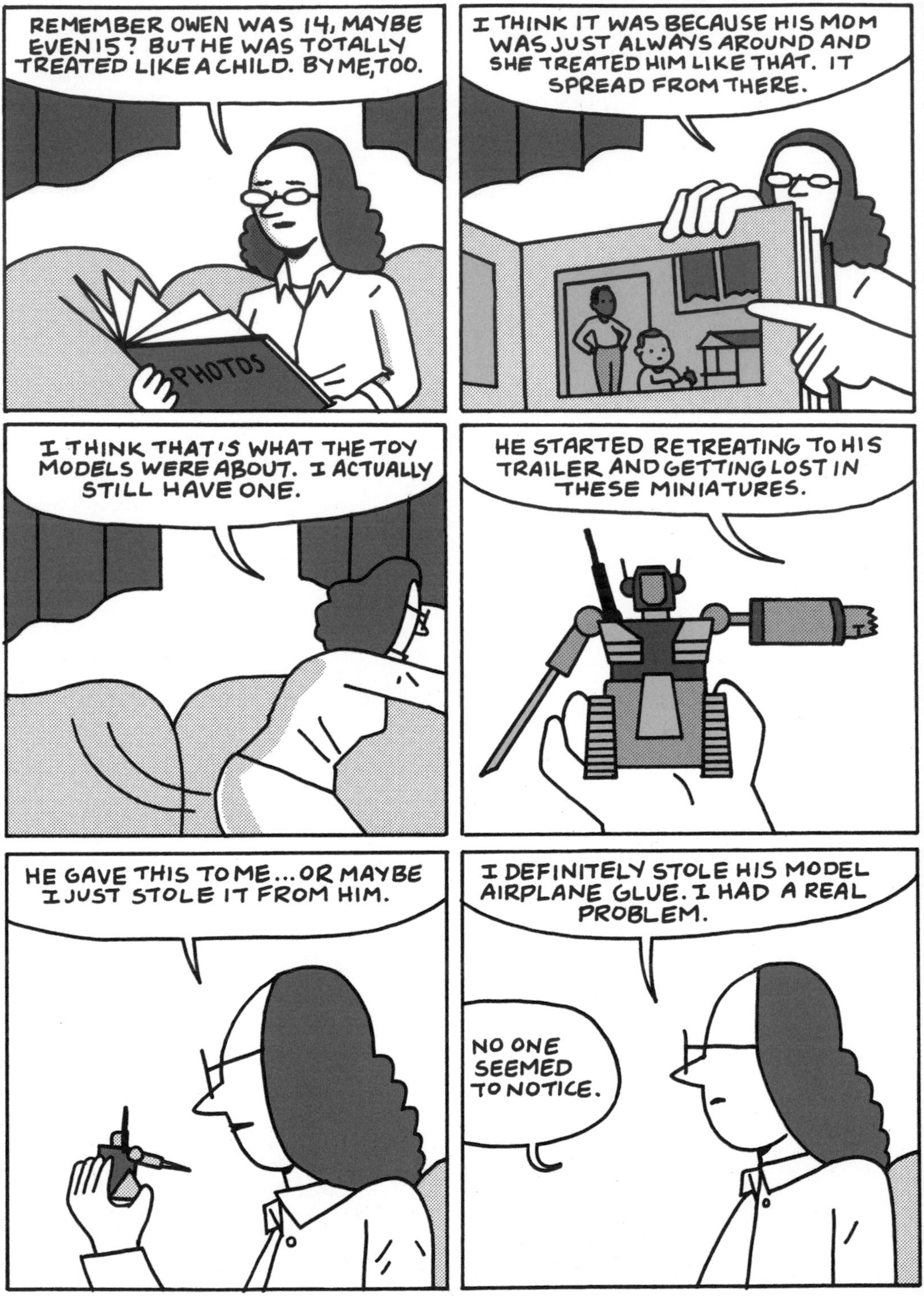
REMEMBER OWEN WAS 14, MAYBE EVEN 15? BUT HE WAS TOTALLY TREATED LIKE A CHILD. BY ME, TOO.
PHOTOS
I THINK IT WAS BECAUSE HIS MOM WAS JUST ALWAYS AROUND AND SHE TREATED HIM LIKE THAT. IT SPREAD FROM THERE.
I THINK THAT'S WHAT THE TOY MODELS WERE ABOUT. I ACTUALLY STILL HAVE ONE.
HE STARTED RETREATING TO HIS TRAILER AND GETTING LOST IN THESE MINIATURES.
HE GAVE THIS TO ME... OR MAYBE I JUST STOLE IT FROM HIM.
I DEFINITELY STOLE HIS MODEL AIRPLANE GLUE. I HAD A REAL PROBLEM.
NO ONE SEEMED TO NOTICE.

I HAVE TO ADMIT I WAS EMBARRASSED OF THE DOLLS AFTER A WHILE.

HERE WE ARE IN HOLLYWOOD, LIVING A GLAMOROUS LIFESTYLE AND MY SON IS HERE PLAYING WITH DOLLS...

I WAS HARD ON HIM.

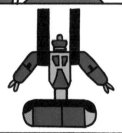

EVEN THOUGH HE WAS THIS BIG TV STAR HE STILL CRAVED ATTENTION AND ACTED OUT.

HE CRIED A LOT.

45

"THE EVERY NIGHT SHOW WITH SAMMY LARSON"

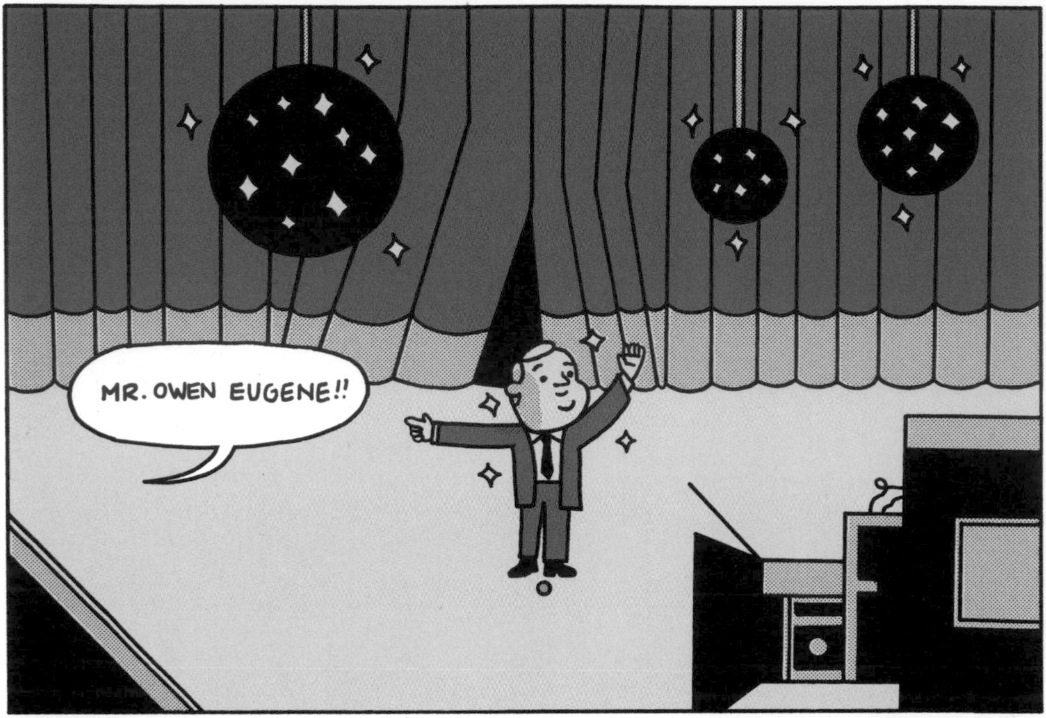
MR. OWEN EUGENE!!

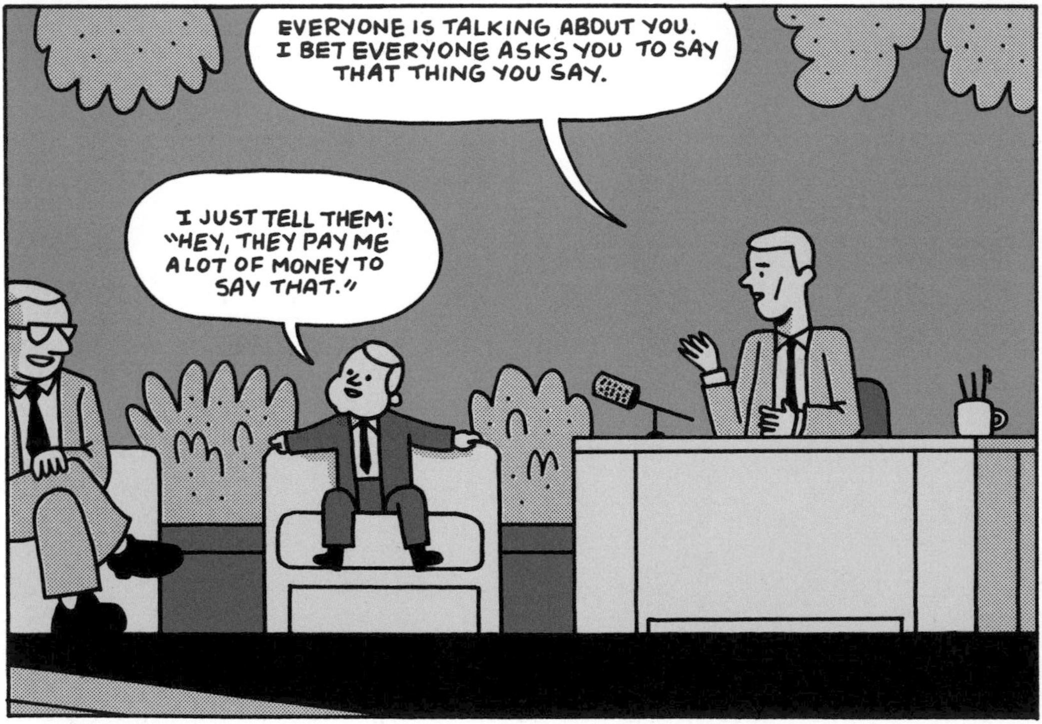
EVERYONE IS TALKING ABOUT YOU. I BET EVERYONE ASKS YOU TO SAY THAT THING YOU SAY.
I JUST TELL THEM: "HEY, THEY PAY ME A LOT OF MONEY TO SAY THAT."

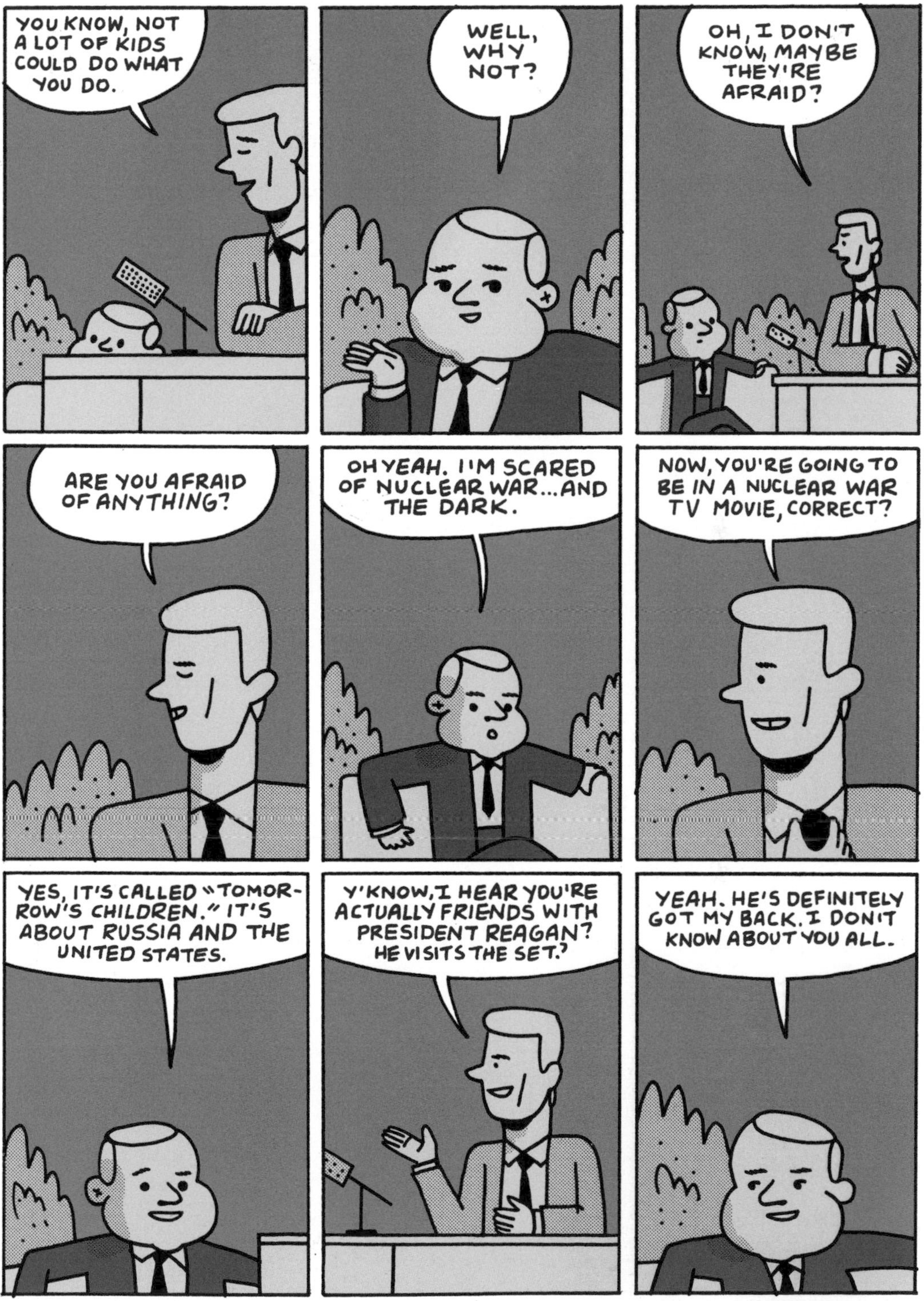
YOU KNOW, NOT A LOT OF KIDS COULD DO WHAT YOU DO.
WELL, WHY NOT?
OH, I DON'T KNOW, MAYBE THEY'RE AFRAID?
ARE YOU AFRAID OF ANYTHING?
OH YEAH. I'M SCARED OF NUCLEAR WAR...AND THE DARK.
NOW, YOU'RE GOING TO BE IN A NUCLEAR WAR TV MOVIE, CORRECT?
YES, IT'S CALLED "TOMORROW'S CHILDREN." IT'S ABOUT RUSSIA AND THE UNITED STATES.
Y'KNOW, I HEAR YOU'RE ACTUALLY FRIENDS WITH PRESIDENT REAGAN? HE VISITS THE SET?
YEAH. HE'S DEFINITELY GOT MY BACK. I DON'T KNOW ABOUT YOU ALL.

s include "Giving It
(60 min.)
D MAGAZINE—Bill

E NEWS
rer/Kamen
R—Discussion

etails. (60 min.)
cience Fiction
comes an antibody
energy-draining in-
nnihilated an en-
—and is about to
William Shatner.
noy. (60 min.)
ND SPECIAL

r is the host of a
d concert. Guests
olds, Louise Man-
Brothers, Brenda
2 hrs.)
om Jarriel
harles Osgood

Interior Secretary
Super Bowl MVP
90 min.)
BW
(1948) A married
rk Gable) develops
mance with his
er). Anne Baxter,
Collins. Mrs. Kir-
(2 hrs., 15 min.)
S—Reviews
Road to China"
e King of Comedy"
rry Lewis), "Tender
uvall), "My Tutor."

OCUS
CIAL—Music
st), Seals & Crofts,
the Family Stone.
Southern Nights,"
n.)
NT THIS WEEK

ennett, actors Ken
nson. (60 min.)
—Chris Clausen
AY NIGHT

CO
AIT OF A BIRD

tist Wendell Gilley.
who took up the
has created more

---

than 6000 carvings. He is seen at his
workshop.
11:55 **HBO MOVIE—Drama**
"Shoot the Moon." (1982) R: Strong
language, adult themes, violence.
Strong performances distinguish this
study of a marital break-up and its im-
pact on a family. Albert Finney, Diane
Keaton. (2 hrs.)
Mid. **72 ENTERTAINMENT THIS WEEK**
—Magazine
8 AL McGUIRE OnSPORTS
25 HEALTH FIELD
38 EXCHANGE—Alison McCann
12:10 **41 GLORY OF THE GARDEN**
—Documentary
See 4:50 P.M. for details. (60 min.)
12:30 **B SPORTSMAN'S FRIEND**
5 SATURDAY NIGHT
38 WALL STREET JOURNAL
REPORT
1 AM **4 SOLID GOLD—Music**
17 MORE—Newsmagazine
8 NEWS
38 FAITH FOR TODAY
41 GOLD FROM THE DEEP
—Documentary
ESN POOL
Luther Lassiter vs. U.J. Pluckett in the
Lengendary Pocket Billiards Stars,
taped at Atlantic City, N.J. (60 min.)
[Time approximate after basketball.]
1:30 **77 JACK ANDERSON**
CONFIDENTIAL
1:45 **5 SUNDAY OPEN HOUSE**
2 AM **72 13 CBS NEWS**
ESN SPORTSCENTER
HBO MOVIE—Drama
"Quest for Fire." (Canadian-French;
1982) R: Nudity, violence. Anthony
Burgess confected the primitive lan-
guages for this anthropological approach to prehistoric tribal life. Naoh:
Everett McGill. Amoukar: Ron Perl-
man. (1 hr., 40 min.)
3 AM **ESN NBA BASKETBALL**
Philadelphia at Detroit, taped earlier
tonight. (2 hrs., 30 min.)
3:35 **5 MOVIE—Comedy BW**
"No Minor Vices." (1948) An artist (Louis Jourdan) causes turmoil
when he claims his sketches of a
couple (Dana Andrews, Lilli Palm-
er) reveal their "real" selves.
Jane Wyatt. (1 hr., 50 min.)
3:45 **HBO MOVIE—Comedy**
"La Cage aux Folles II." (French-Ital-
ian; 1980) R: Adult themes. Disap-
pointing sequel about aging gays
caught up in espionage. Ugo Tognaz-
zi, Michel Serrault. (1 hr., 40 min.)

Perhaps the Most
Important Film Ever
Made

Can we protect them?

TOMORROW'S CHILDREN

A CBS TELEVISION MOTION PICTURE
Ted Glutenberger, Rebecca Klein
Sunday 8/7c

"TOMORROW'S CHILDREN" 3/14/83

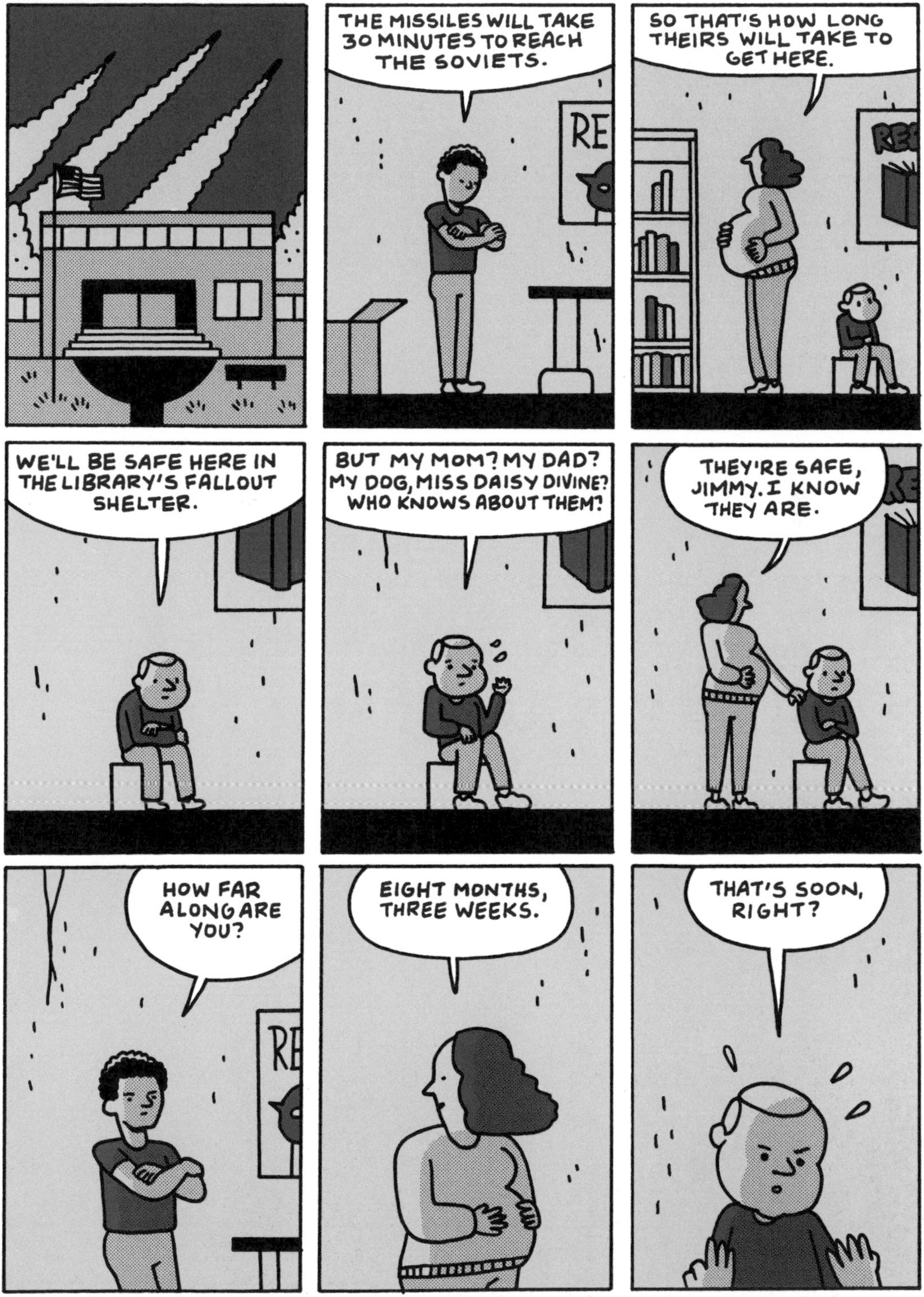
THE MISSILES WILL TAKE 30 MINUTES TO REACH THE SOVIETS.
SO THAT'S HOW LONG THEIRS WILL TAKE TO GET HERE.
WE'LL BE SAFE HERE IN THE LIBRARY'S FALLOUT SHELTER.
BUT MY MOM? MY DAD? MY DOG, MISS DAISY DIVINE? WHO KNOWS ABOUT THEM?
THEY'RE SAFE, JIMMY. I KNOW THEY ARE.
HOW FAR ALONG ARE YOU?
EIGHT MONTHS, THREE WEEKS.
THAT'S SOON, RIGHT?

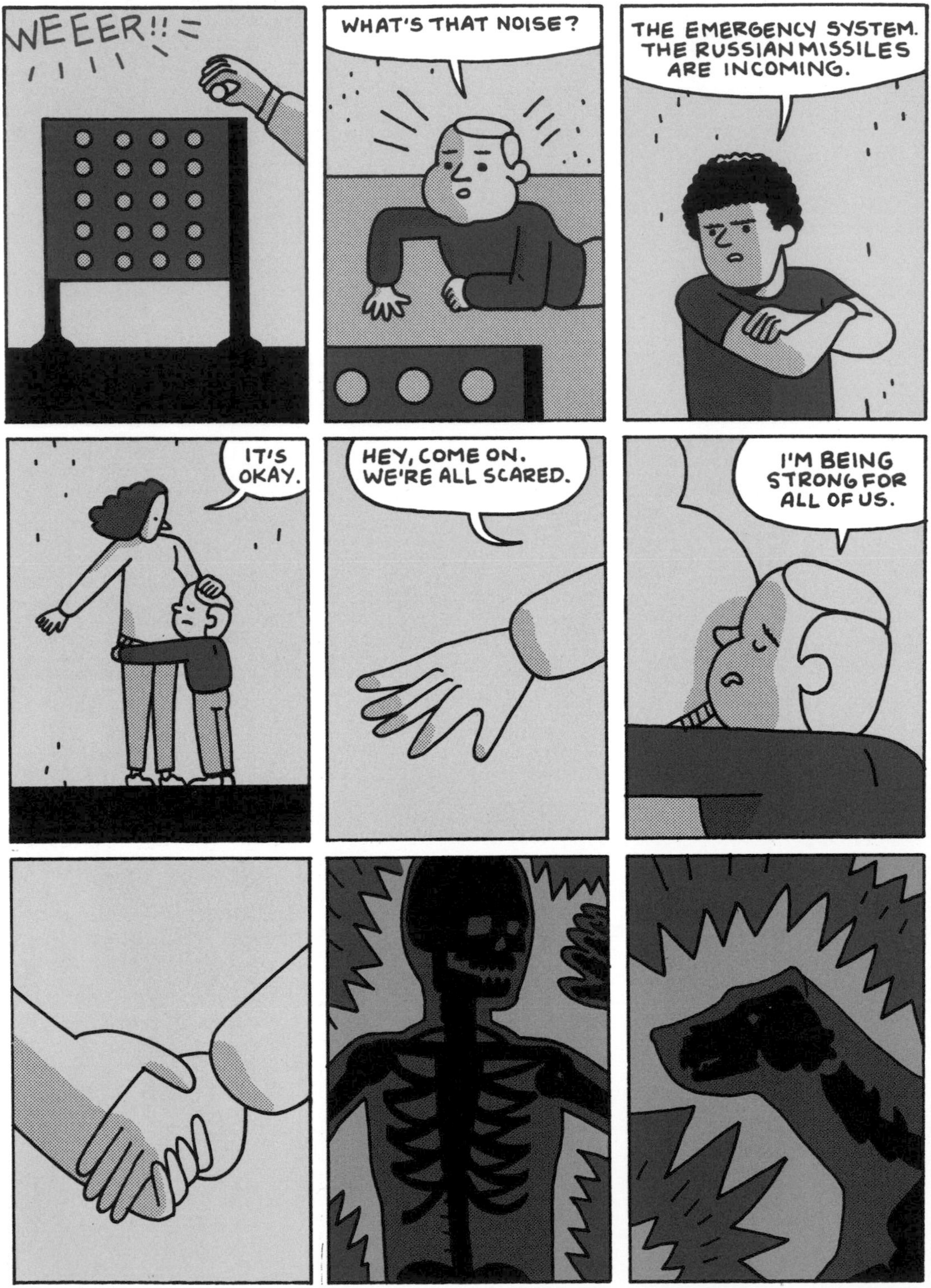
WEEER!!
WHAT'S THAT NOISE?
THE EMERGENCY SYSTEM. THE RUSSIAN MISSILES ARE INCOMING.
IT'S OKAY.
HEY, COME ON. WE'RE ALL SCARED.
I'M BEING STRONG FOR ALL OF US.

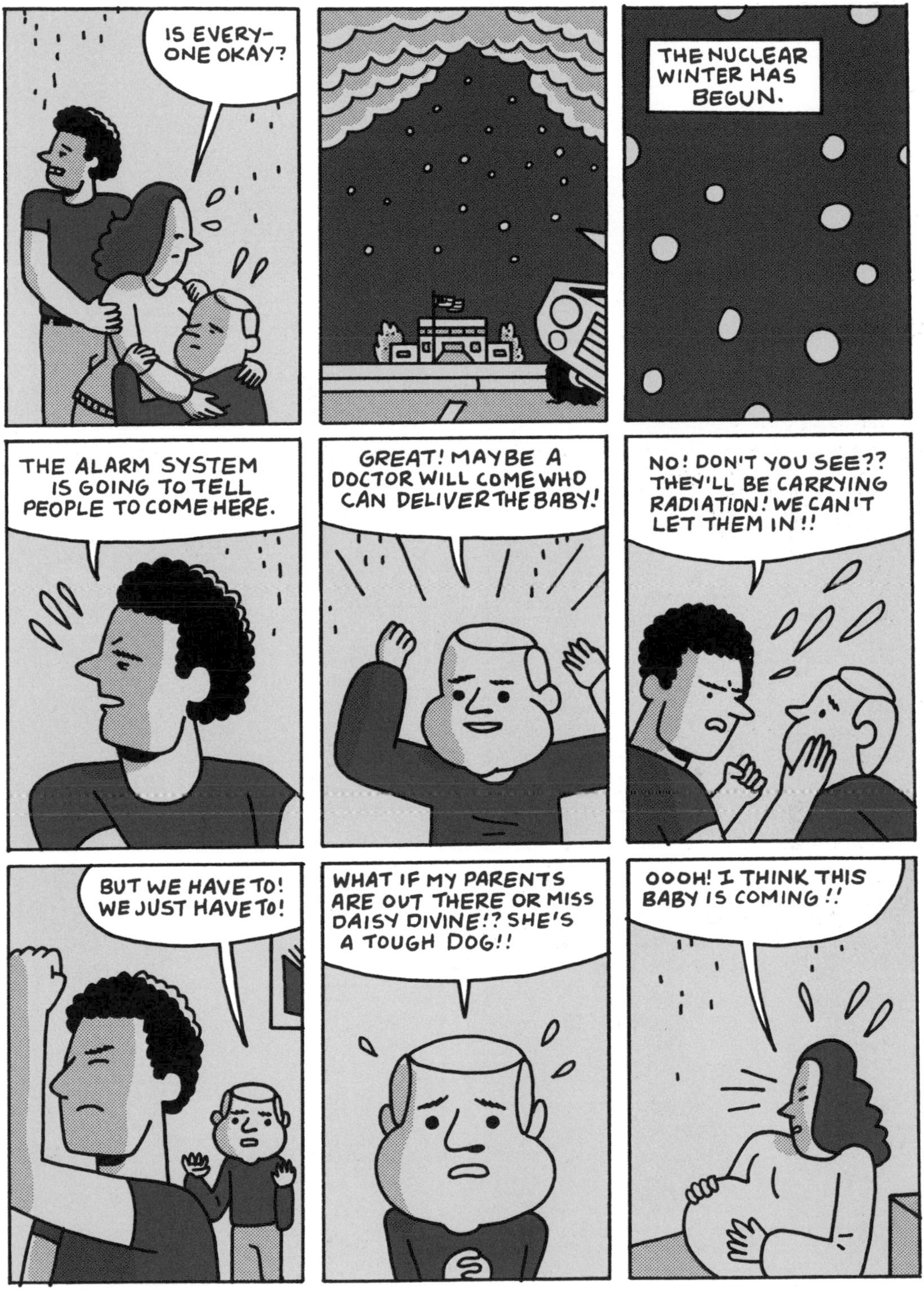
IS EVERY-ONE OKAY?
THE NUCLEAR WINTER HAS BEGUN.
THE ALARM SYSTEM IS GOING TO TELL PEOPLE TO COME HERE.
GREAT! MAYBE A DOCTOR WILL COME WHO CAN DELIVER THE BABY!
NO! DON'T YOU SEE?? THEY'LL BE CARRYING RADIATION! WE CAN'T LET THEM IN!!
BUT WE HAVE TO! WE JUST HAVE TO!
WHAT IF MY PARENTS ARE OUT THERE OR MISS DAISY DIVINE!? SHE'S A TOUGH DOG!!
OOOH! I THINK THIS BABY IS COMING!!

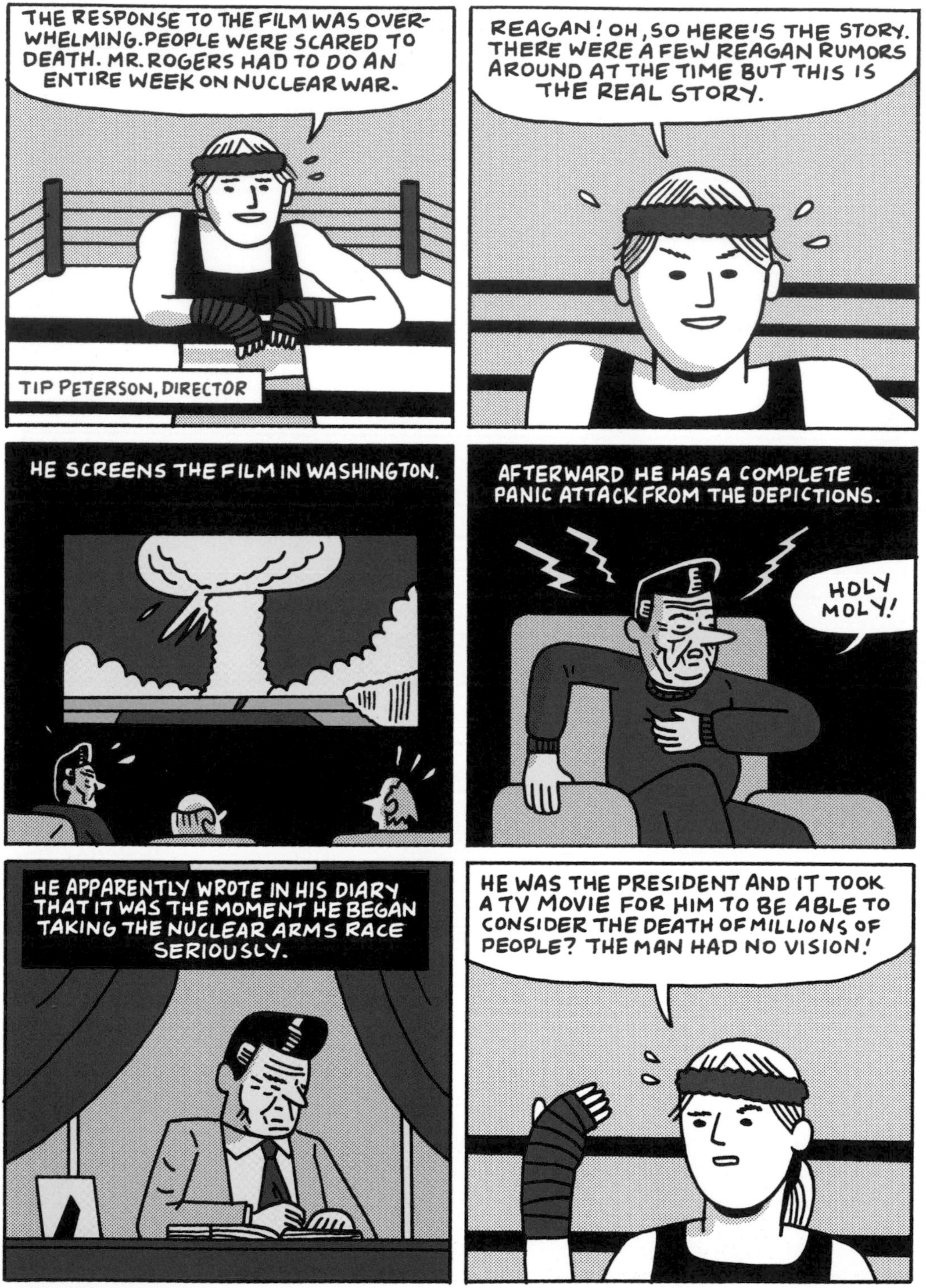
THE RESPONSE TO THE FILM WAS OVERWHELMING. PEOPLE WERE SCARED TO DEATH. MR. ROGERS HAD TO DO AN ENTIRE WEEK ON NUCLEAR WAR.
TIP PETERSON, DIRECTOR
REAGAN! OH, SO HERE'S THE STORY. THERE WERE A FEW REAGAN RUMORS AROUND AT THE TIME BUT THIS IS THE REAL STORY.
HE SCREENS THE FILM IN WASHINGTON.
AFTERWARD HE HAS A COMPLETE PANIC ATTACK FROM THE DEPICTIONS.
HOLY MOLY!
HE APPARENTLY WROTE IN HIS DIARY THAT IT WAS THE MOMENT HE BEGAN TAKING THE NUCLEAR ARMS RACE SERIOUSLY.
HE WAS THE PRESIDENT AND IT TOOK A TV MOVIE FOR HIM TO BE ABLE TO CONSIDER THE DEATH OF MILLIONS OF PEOPLE? THE MAN HAD NO VISION!

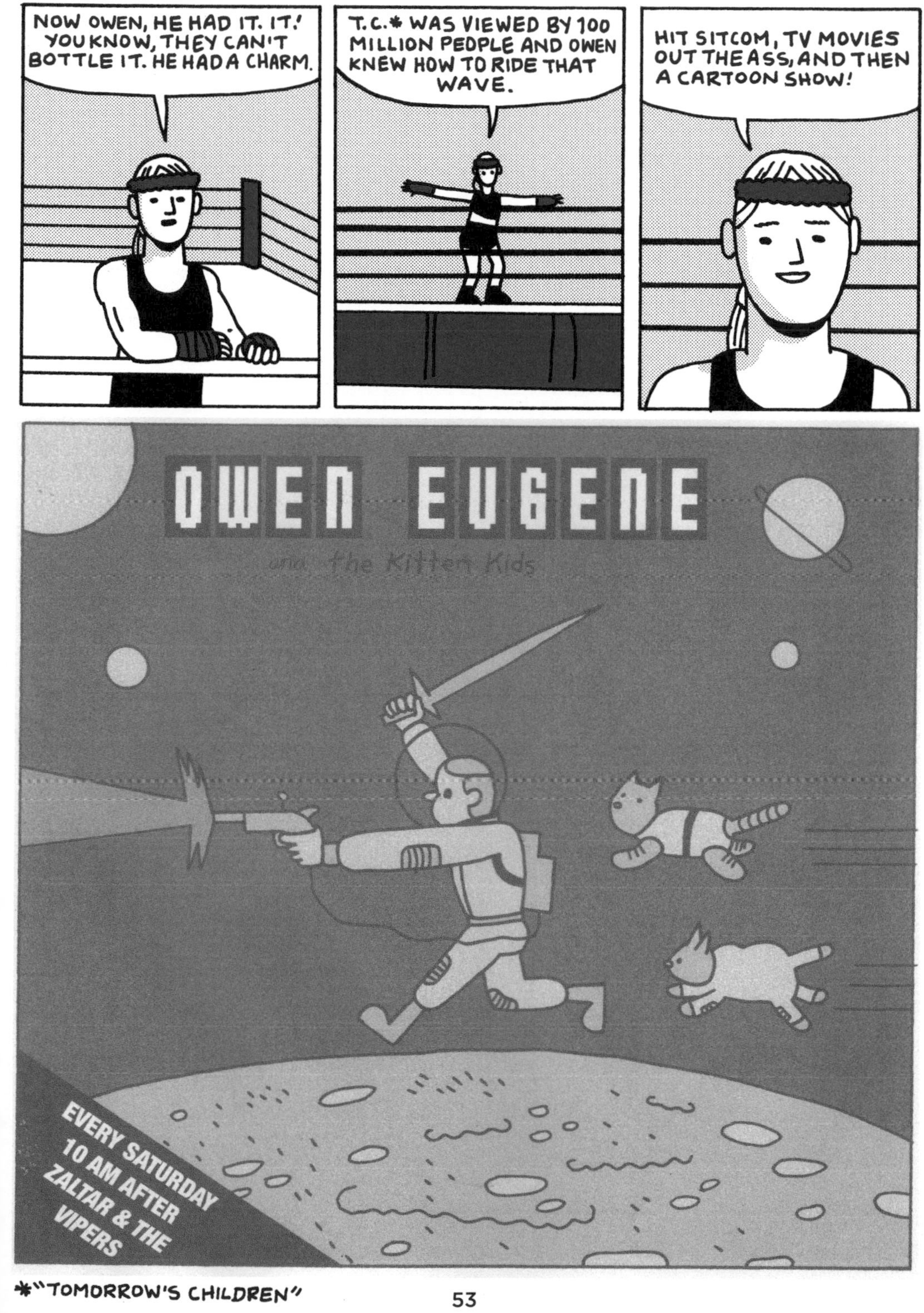
NOW OWEN, HE HAD IT. IT! YOU KNOW, THEY CAN'T BOTTLE IT. HE HAD A CHARM.
T.C.* WAS VIEWED BY 100 MILLION PEOPLE AND OWEN KNEW HOW TO RIDE THAT WAVE.
HIT SITCOM, TV MOVIES OUT THE ASS, AND THEN A CARTOON SHOW!
OWEN EUGENE
and the Kitten Kids
EVERY SATURDAY 10 AM AFTER ZALTAR & THE VIPERS

*"TOMORROW'S CHILDREN"

SO, THE BASIC PLOT WAS THAT THE KITTEN KIDS, WALDO AND GERALDO, HAVE TO SAVE THEIR PLANET FROM DISASTER. THEY SCOOP UP OWEN AND TAKE HIM ON THIS ADVENTURE TO DEFEAT LEMONSTRO, AN EVIL BIRD.

POD TRODSKIN, CREATOR OF OWEN EUGENE AND THE KITTEN KIDS

THERE WAS A LOT OF OPPORTUNITY FOR MERCHANDISING.

  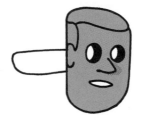 

OWEN RECORDED HIS OWN VOICE. IMAGINE ENDLESS SESSIONS OF HIM SAYING: "KITTEN KIDS, AMASS!!"

WHICH MADE THE KITTEN KIDS FORM SUPER KITTEN KING, NATURALLY.

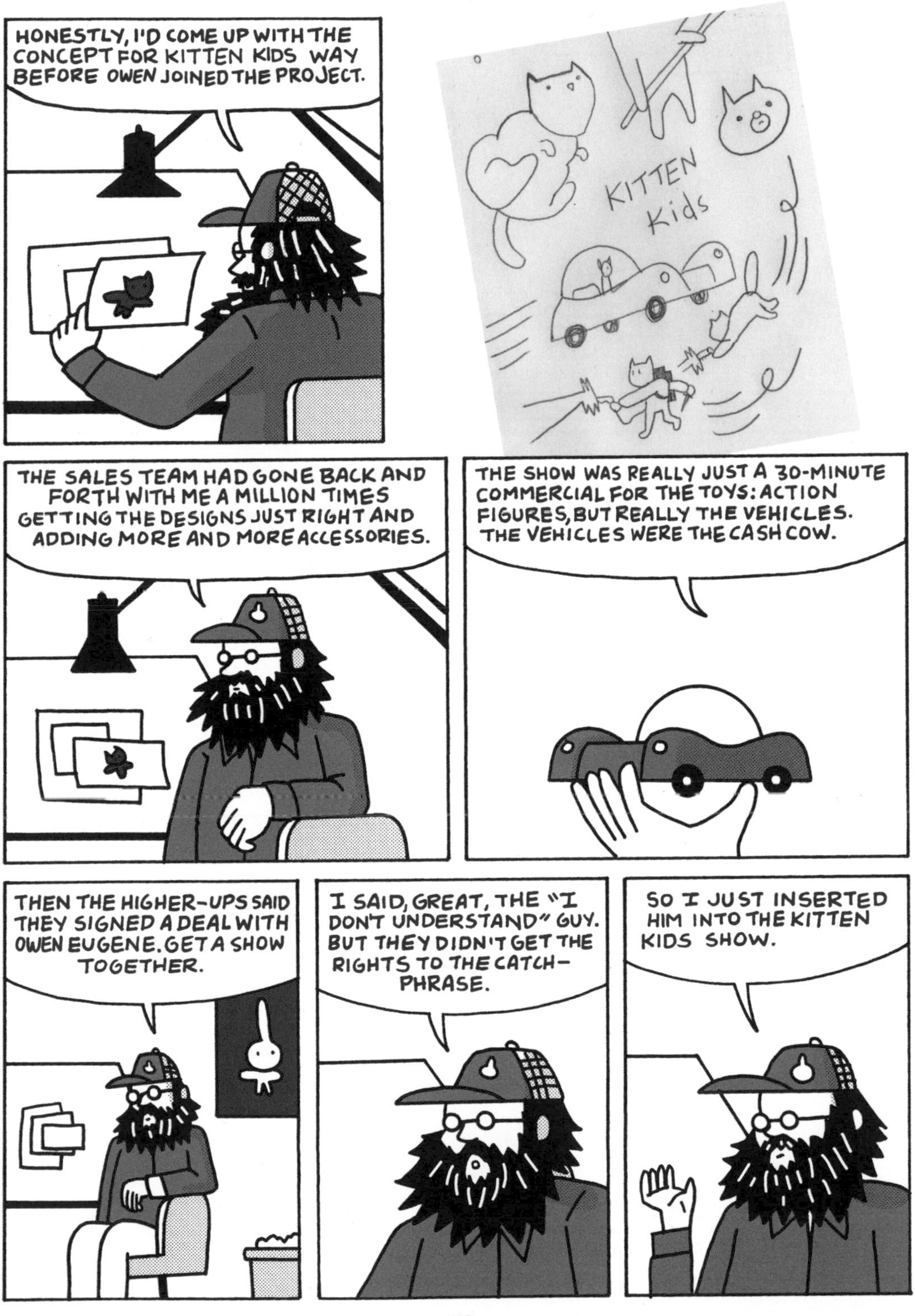
HONESTLY, I'D COME UP WITH THE CONCEPT FOR KITTEN KIDS WAY BEFORE OWEN JOINED THE PROJECT.
KITTEN Kids
THE SALES TEAM HAD GONE BACK AND FORTH WITH ME A MILLION TIMES GETTING THE DESIGNS JUST RIGHT AND ADDING MORE AND MORE ACCESSORIES.
THE SHOW WAS REALLY JUST A 30-MINUTE COMMERCIAL FOR THE TOYS: ACTION FIGURES, BUT REALLY THE VEHICLES. THE VEHICLES WERE THE CASH COW.
THEN THE HIGHER-UPS SAID THEY SIGNED A DEAL WITH OWEN EUGENE. GET A SHOW TOGETHER.
I SAID, GREAT, THE "I DON'T UNDERSTAND" GUY. BUT THEY DIDN'T GET THE RIGHTS TO THE CATCH-PHRASE.
SO I JUST INSERTED HIM INTO THE KITTEN KIDS SHOW.

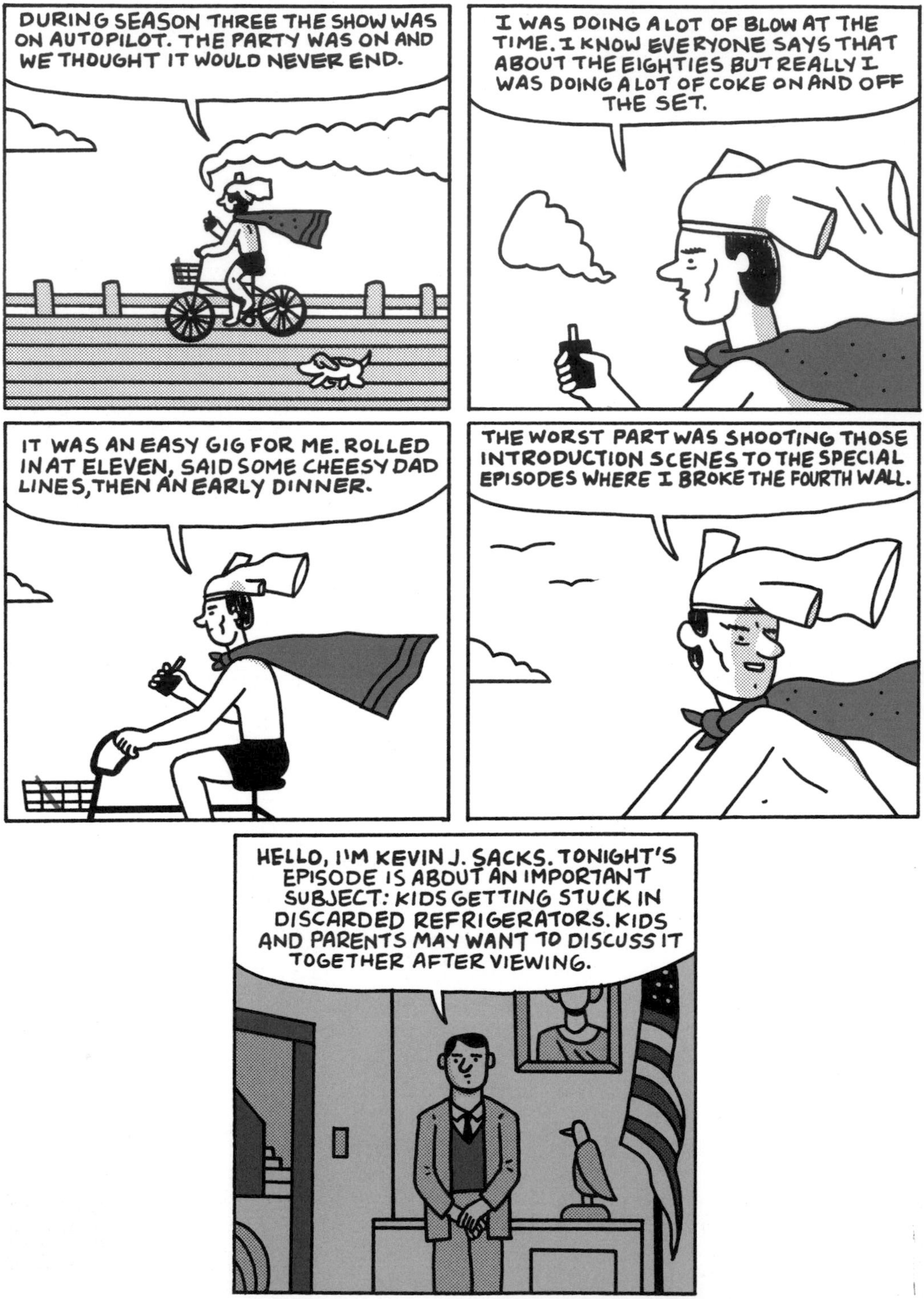
DURING SEASON THREE THE SHOW WAS ON AUTOPILOT. THE PARTY WAS ON AND WE THOUGHT IT WOULD NEVER END.
I WAS DOING A LOT OF BLOW AT THE TIME. I KNOW EVERYONE SAYS THAT ABOUT THE EIGHTIES BUT REALLY I WAS DOING A LOT OF COKE ON AND OFF THE SET.
IT WAS AN EASY GIG FOR ME. ROLLED IN AT ELEVEN, SAID SOME CHEESY DAD LINES, THEN AN EARLY DINNER.
THE WORST PART WAS SHOOTING THOSE INTRODUCTION SCENES TO THE SPECIAL EPISODES WHERE I BROKE THE FOURTH WALL.
HELLO, I'M KEVIN J. SACKS. TONIGHT'S EPISODE IS ABOUT AN IMPORTANT SUBJECT: KIDS GETTING STUCK IN DISCARDED REFRIGERATORS. KIDS AND PARENTS MAY WANT TO DISCUSS IT TOGETHER AFTER VIEWING.

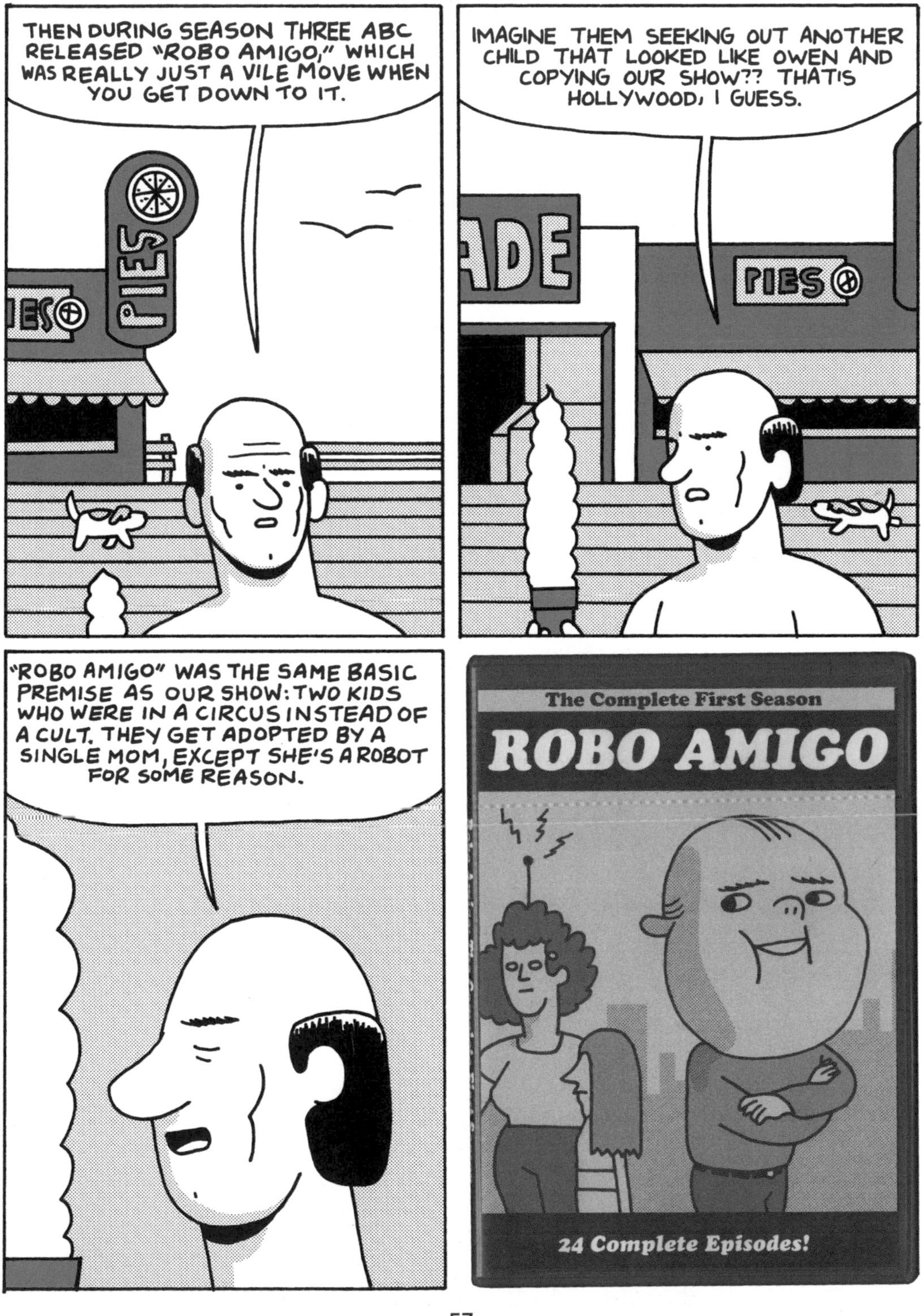
THEN DURING SEASON THREE ABC RELEASED "ROBO AMIGO," WHICH WAS REALLY JUST A VILE MOVE WHEN YOU GET DOWN TO IT.
PIES
IMAGINE THEM SEEKING OUT ANOTHER CHILD THAT LOOKED LIKE OWEN AND COPYING OUR SHOW?? THAT'S HOLLYWOOD, I GUESS.
ADE
PIES
"ROBO AMIGO" WAS THE SAME BASIC PREMISE AS OUR SHOW: TWO KIDS WHO WERE IN A CIRCUS INSTEAD OF A CULT. THEY GET ADOPTED BY A SINGLE MOM, EXCEPT SHE'S A ROBOT FOR SOME REASON.
The Complete First Season
ROBO AMIGO
24 Complete Episodes!

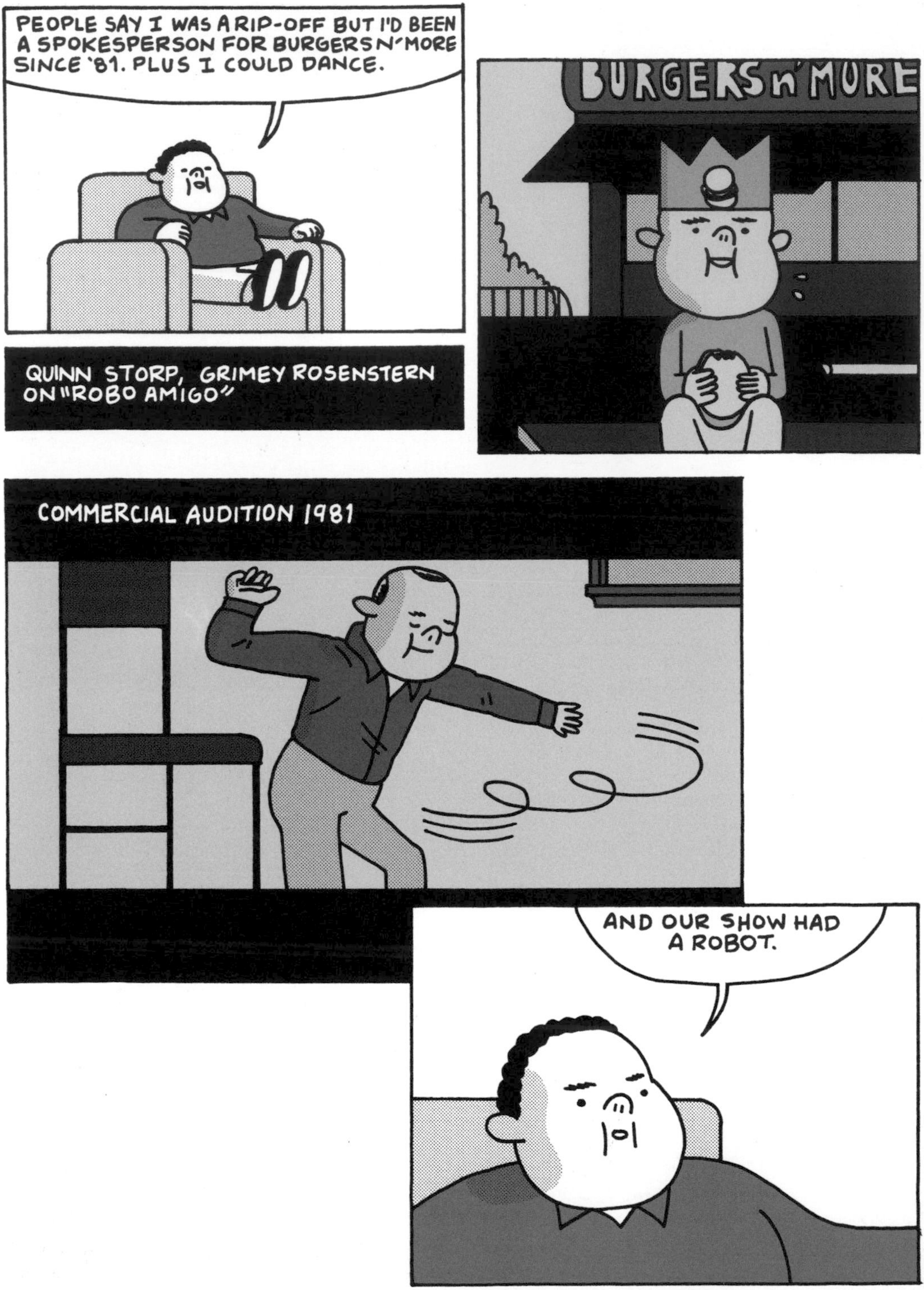
PEOPLE SAY I WAS A RIP-OFF BUT I'D BEEN A SPOKESPERSON FOR BURGERS N' MORE SINCE '81. PLUS I COULD DANCE.
QUINN STORP, GRIMEY ROSENSTERN ON "ROBO AMIGO"
BURGERS n' MORE
COMMERCIAL AUDITION 1981
AND OUR SHOW HAD A ROBOT.

"ROBO AMIGO" EPISODE 11

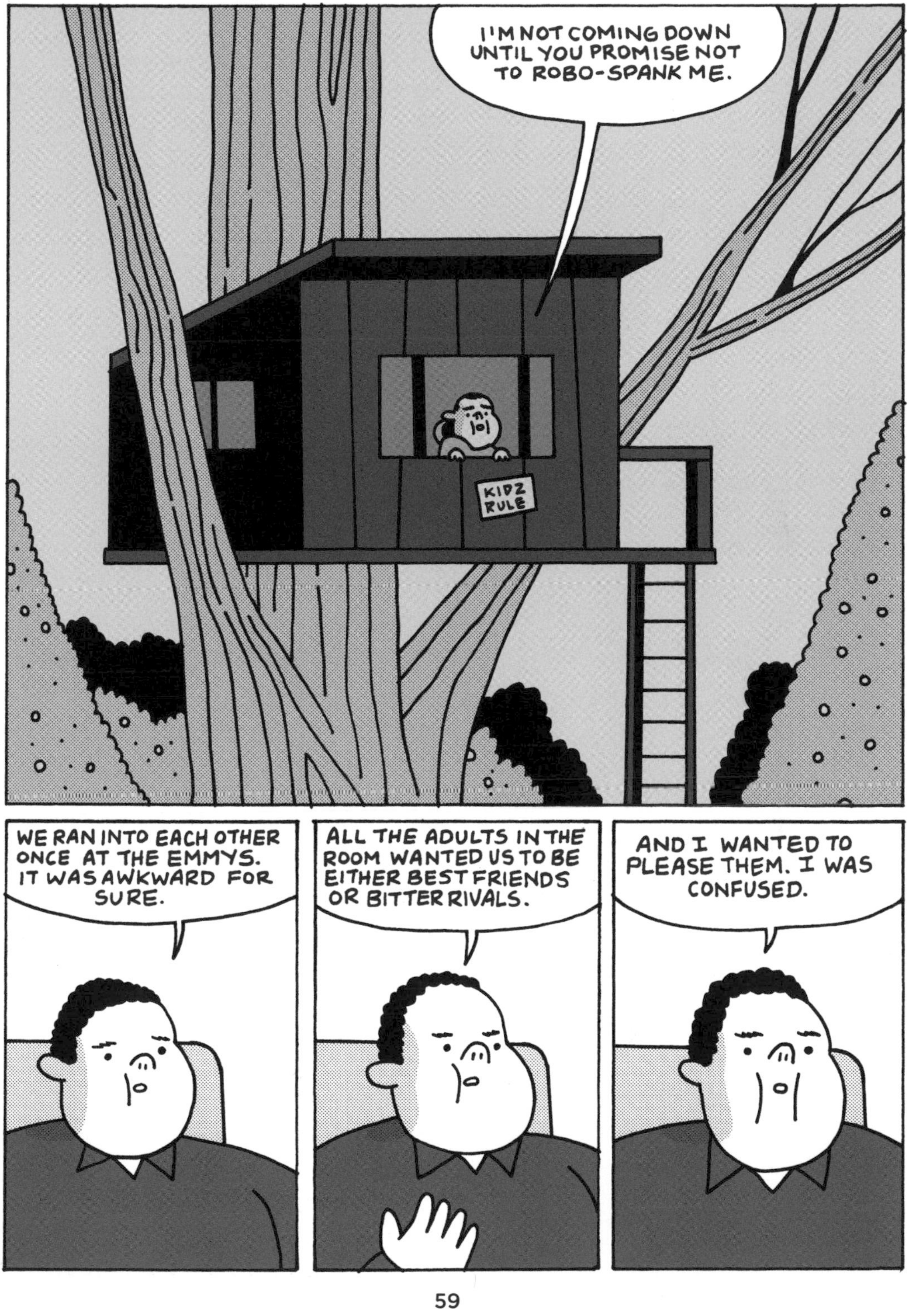

I'M NOT COMING DOWN UNTIL YOU PROMISE NOT TO ROBO-SPANK ME.
KIDZ RULE
WE RAN INTO EACH OTHER ONCE AT THE EMMYS. IT WAS AWKWARD FOR SURE.
ALL THE ADULTS IN THE ROOM WANTED US TO BE EITHER BEST FRIENDS OR BITTER RIVALS.
AND I WANTED TO PLEASE THEM. I WAS CONFUSED.

IN RETROSPECT I WISH I'D REACHED OUT. WE SHOULD'VE BEEN FRIENDS.

WE HAD SO MUCH IN COMMON, Y'KNOW? THE PHYSICAL CONDITION, THE INTENSE FAME THAT EVENTUALLY...

WELL, YOU KNOW HOW IT WENT WITH HIM.

BUT THESE ARE ALL THINGS I'VE LEARNED IN THERAPY AND BY WORKING ON MYSELF. YOGA HAS DONE WONDERS FOR ME PHYSICALLY, TOO.

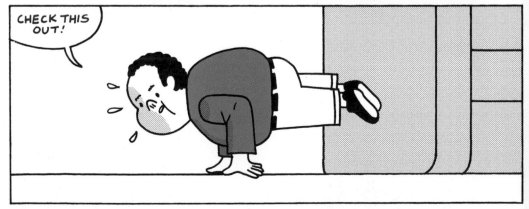

CHECK THIS OUT!

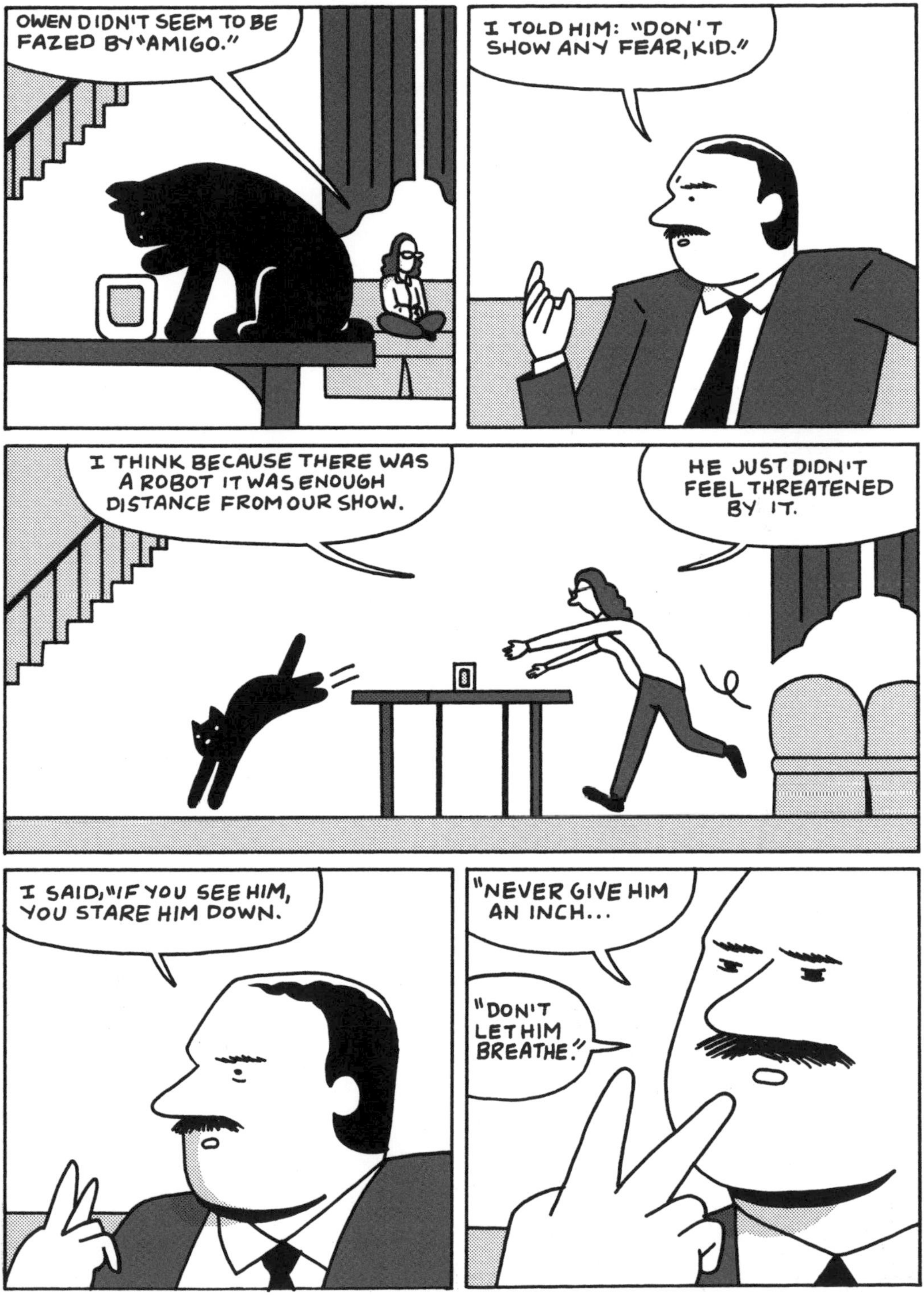
OWEN DIDN'T SEEM TO BE FAZED BY "AMIGO."
I TOLD HIM: "DON'T SHOW ANY FEAR, KID."
I THINK BECAUSE THERE WAS A ROBOT IT WAS ENOUGH DISTANCE FROM OUR SHOW.
HE JUST DIDN'T FEEL THREATENED BY IT.
I SAID, "IF YOU SEE HIM, YOU STARE HIM DOWN.
"NEVER GIVE HIM AN INCH...
"DON'T LET HIM BREATHE."

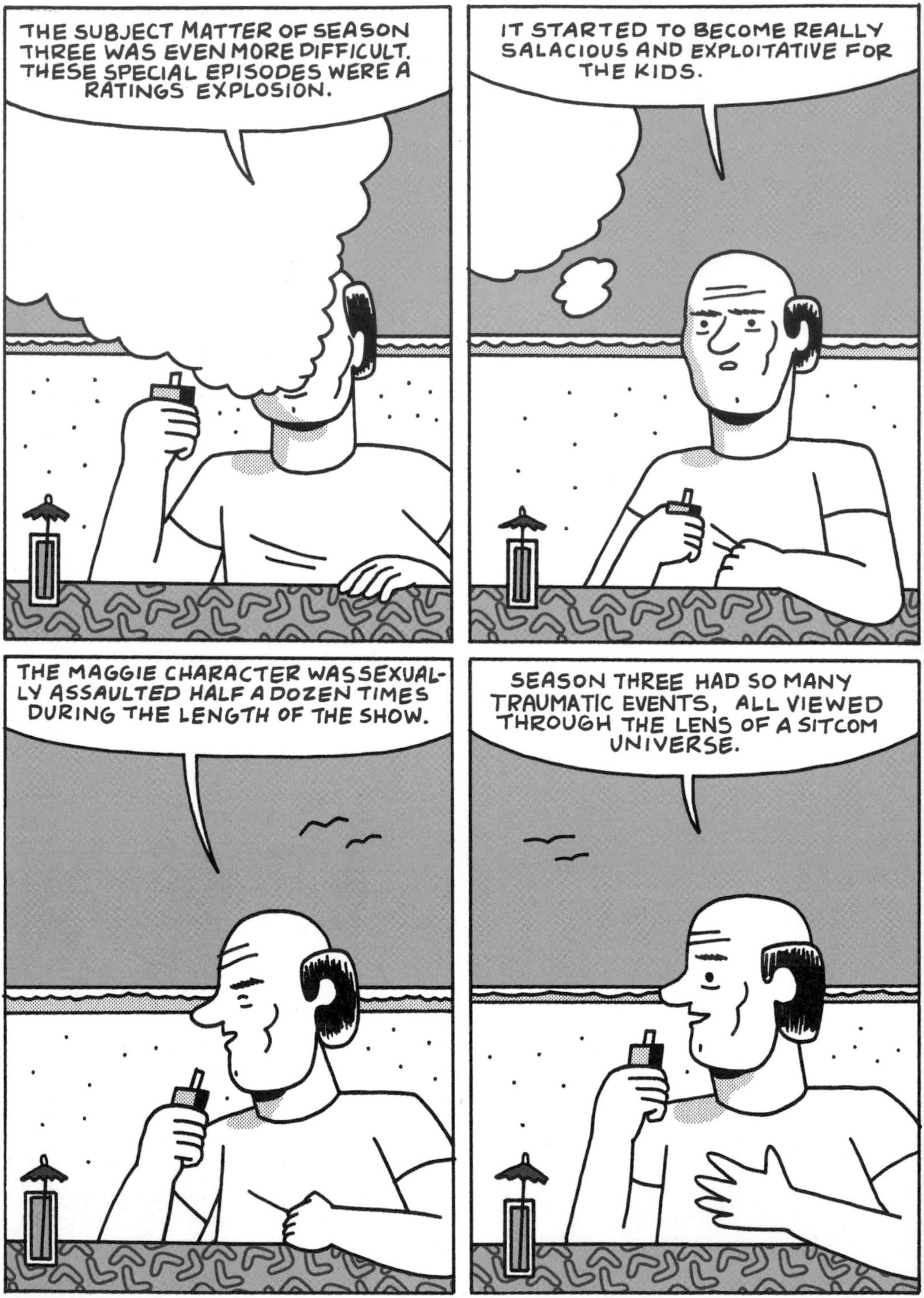
THE SUBJECT MATTER OF SEASON THREE WAS EVEN MORE DIFFICULT. THESE SPECIAL EPISODES WERE A RATINGS EXPLOSION.
IT STARTED TO BECOME REALLY SALACIOUS AND EXPLOITATIVE FOR THE KIDS.
THE MAGGIE CHARACTER WAS SEXUALLY ASSAULTED HALF A DOZEN TIMES DURING THE LENGTH OF THE SHOW.
SEASON THREE HAD SO MANY TRAUMATIC EVENTS, ALL VIEWED THROUGH THE LENS OF A SITCOM UNIVERSE.

"EVERYONE'S FRIEND" SEASON 3 EPISODE 6 11/24/83

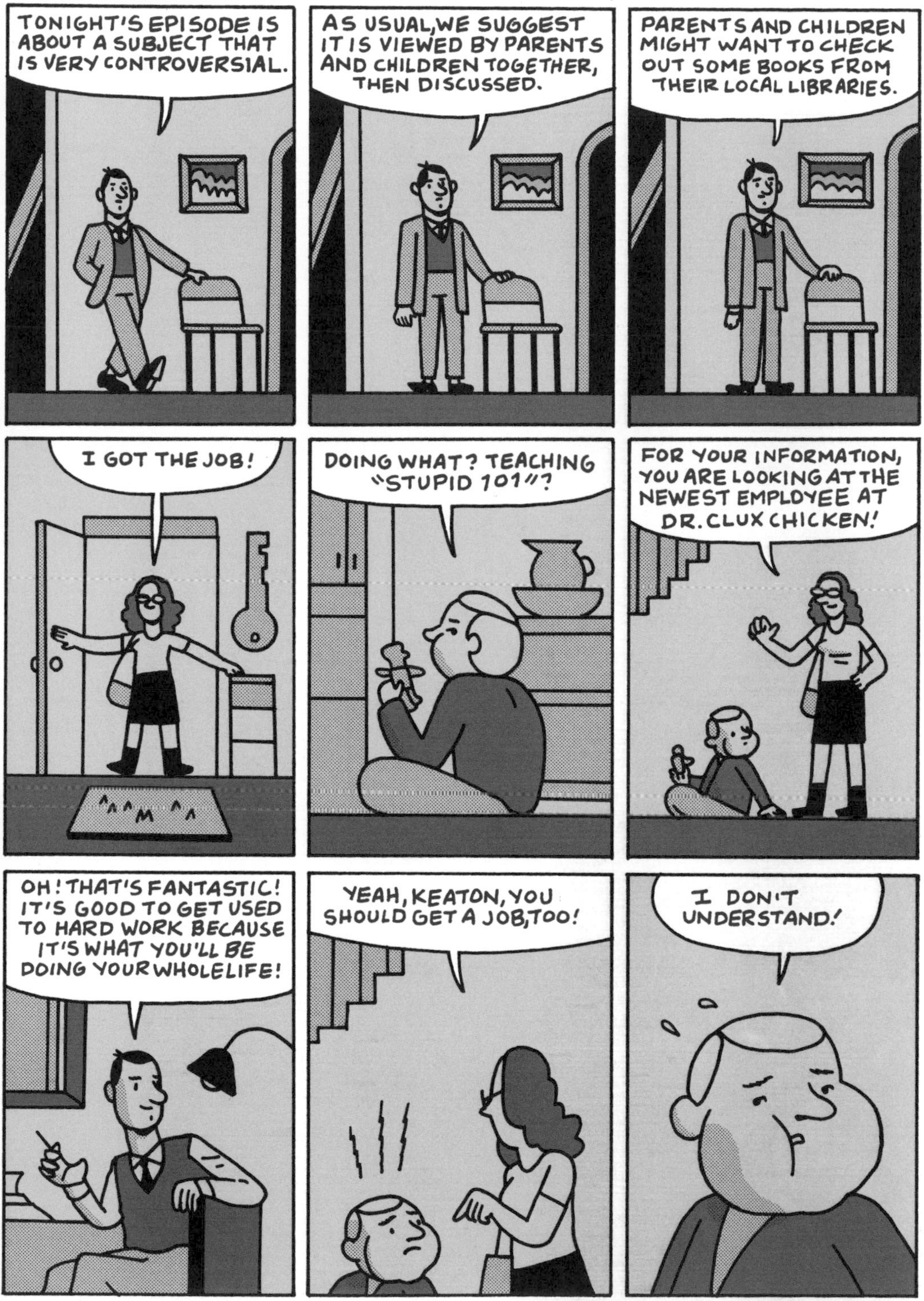
TONIGHT'S EPISODE IS ABOUT A SUBJECT THAT IS VERY CONTROVERSIAL.
AS USUAL, WE SUGGEST IT IS VIEWED BY PARENTS AND CHILDREN TOGETHER, THEN DISCUSSED.
PARENTS AND CHILDREN MIGHT WANT TO CHECK OUT SOME BOOKS FROM THEIR LOCAL LIBRARIES.
I GOT THE JOB!
DOING WHAT? TEACHING "STUPID 101"?
FOR YOUR INFORMATION, YOU ARE LOOKING AT THE NEWEST EMPLOYEE AT DR. CLUX CHICKEN!
OH! THAT'S FANTASTIC! IT'S GOOD TO GET USED TO HARD WORK BECAUSE IT'S WHAT YOU'LL BE DOING YOUR WHOLE LIFE!
YEAH, KEATON, YOU SHOULD GET A JOB, TOO!
I DON'T UNDERSTAND!

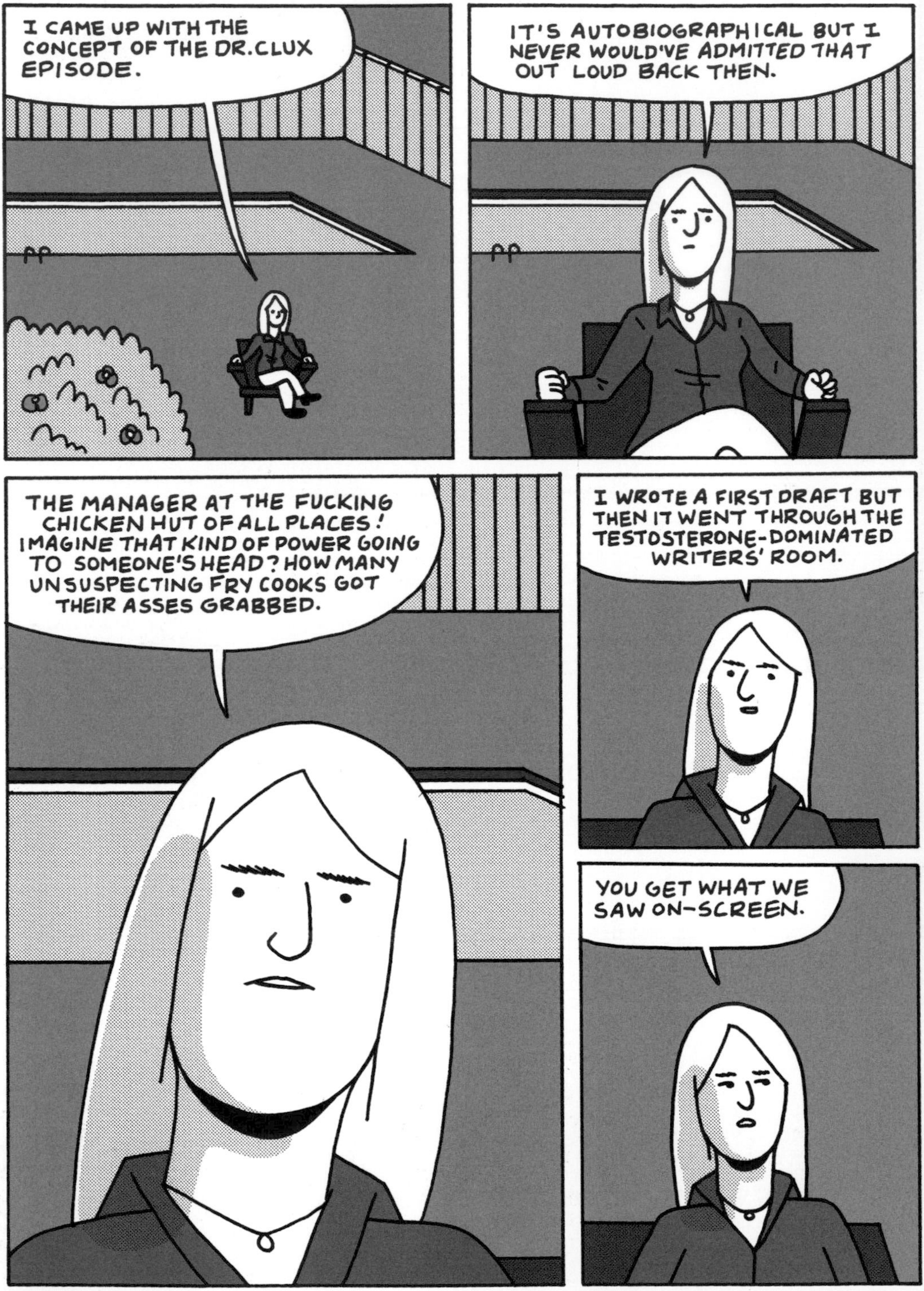
I CAME UP WITH THE CONCEPT OF THE DR. CLUX EPISODE.
IT'S AUTOBIOGRAPHICAL BUT I NEVER WOULD'VE ADMITTED THAT OUT LOUD BACK THEN.
THE MANAGER AT THE FUCKING CHICKEN HUT OF ALL PLACES! IMAGINE THAT KIND OF POWER GOING TO SOMEONE'S HEAD? HOW MANY UNSUSPECTING FRY COOKS GOT THEIR ASSES GRABBED.
I WROTE A FIRST DRAFT BUT THEN IT WENT THROUGH THE TESTOSTERONE-DOMINATED WRITERS' ROOM.
YOU GET WHAT WE SAW ON-SCREEN.

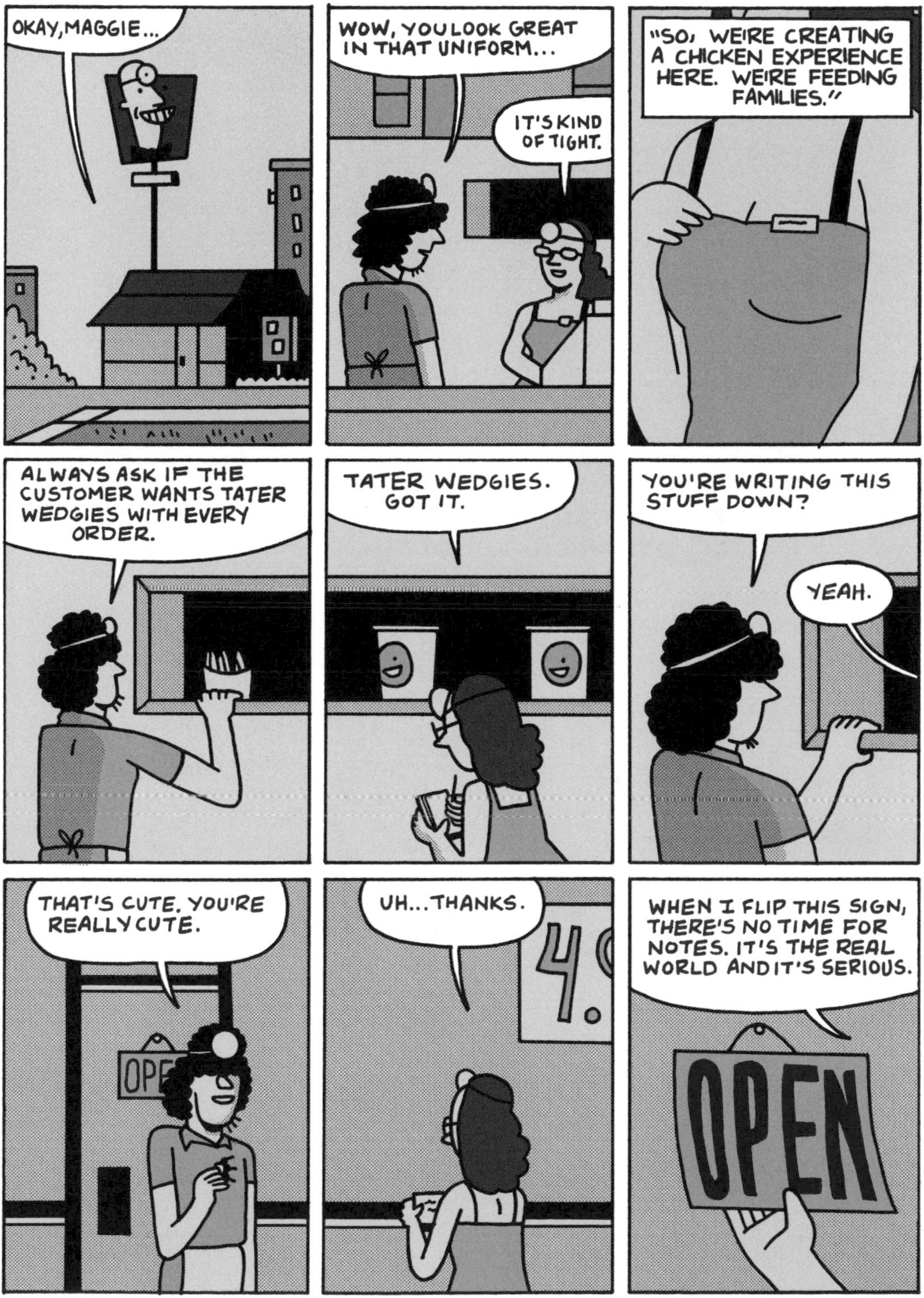
OKAY, MAGGIE...
WOW, YOU LOOK GREAT IN THAT UNIFORM...
IT'S KIND OF TIGHT.
"SO, WE'RE CREATING A CHICKEN EXPERIENCE HERE. WE'RE FEEDING FAMILIES."
ALWAYS ASK IF THE CUSTOMER WANTS TATER WEDGIES WITH EVERY ORDER.
TATER WEDGIES. GOT IT.
YOU'RE WRITING THIS STUFF DOWN?
YEAH.
THAT'S CUTE. YOU'RE REALLY CUTE.
UH... THANKS.
WHEN I FLIP THIS SIGN, THERE'S NO TIME FOR NOTES. IT'S THE REAL WORLD AND IT'S SERIOUS.
OPEN

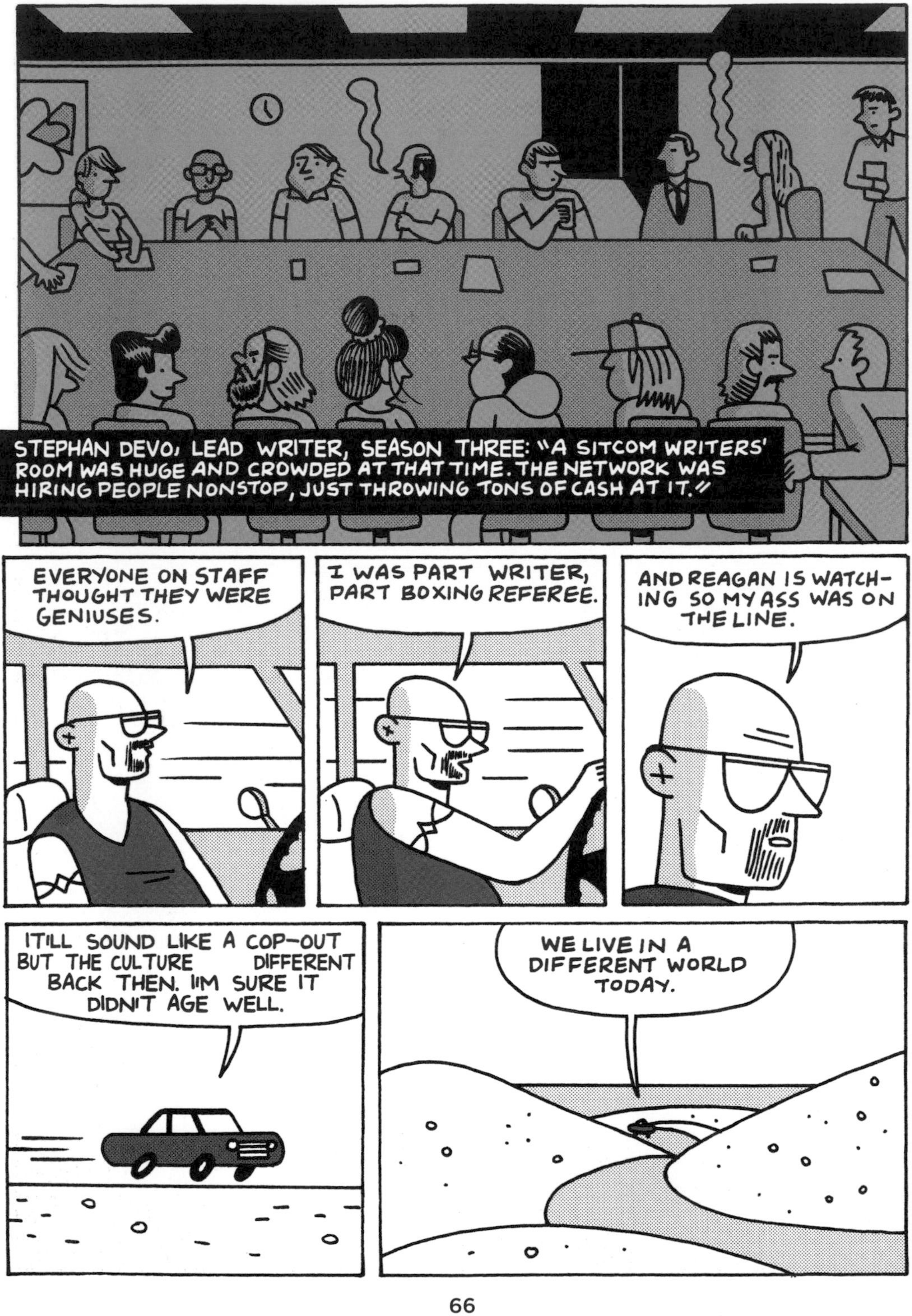

STEPHAN DEVO, LEAD WRITER, SEASON THREE: "A SITCOM WRITERS' ROOM WAS HUGE AND CROWDED AT THAT TIME. THE NETWORK WAS HIRING PEOPLE NONSTOP, JUST THROWING TONS OF CASH AT IT."
EVERYONE ON STAFF THOUGHT THEY WERE GENIUSES.
I WAS PART WRITER, PART BOXING REFEREE.
AND REAGAN IS WATCHING SO MY ASS WAS ON THE LINE.
IT'LL SOUND LIKE A COP-OUT BUT THE CULTURE DIFFERENT BACK THEN. I'M SURE IT DIDN'T AGE WELL.
WE LIVE IN A DIFFERENT WORLD TODAY.

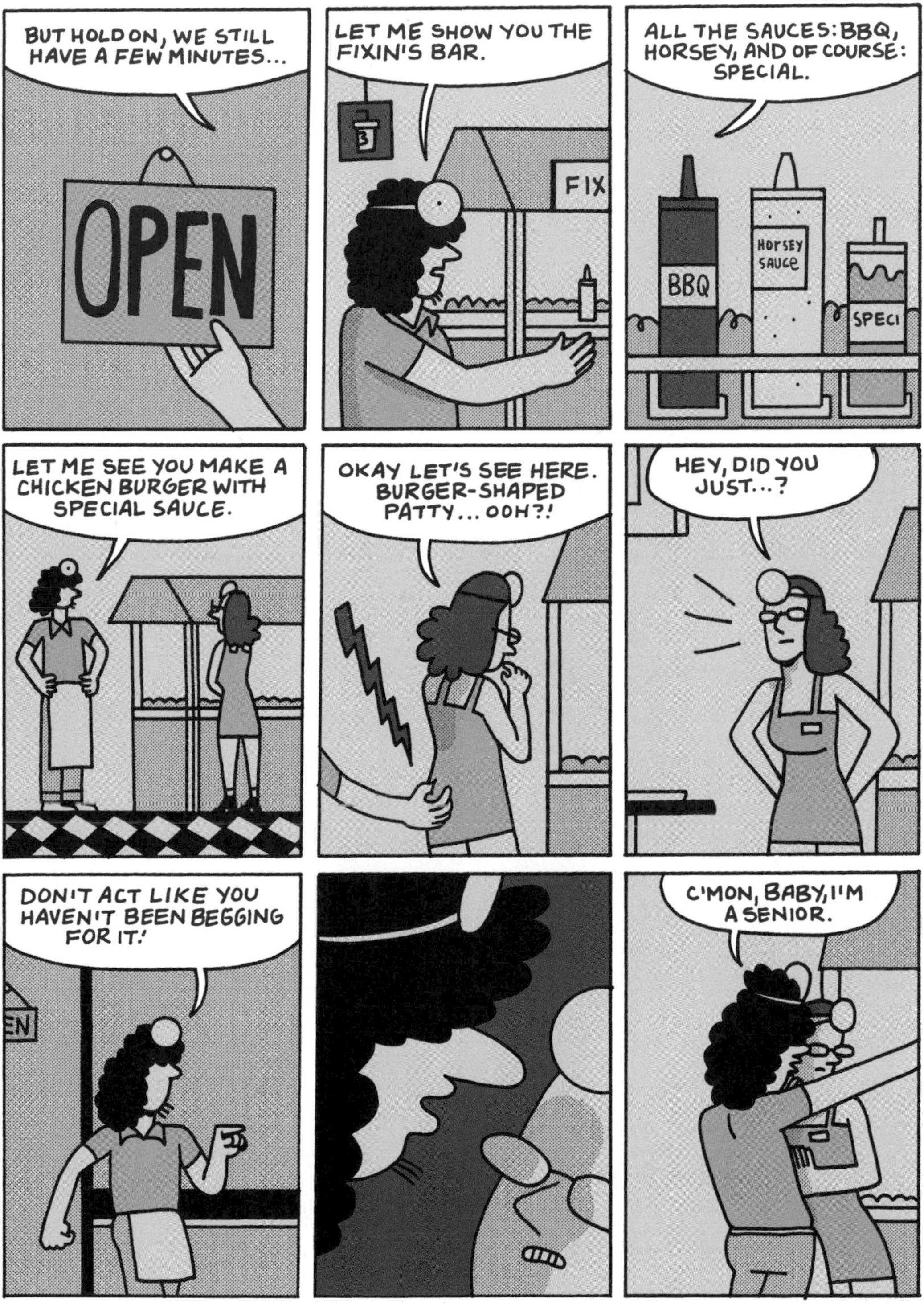
BUT HOLD ON, WE STILL HAVE A FEW MINUTES...
OPEN
LET ME SHOW YOU THE FIXIN'S BAR.
FIX
ALL THE SAUCES: BBQ, HORSEY, AND OF COURSE: SPECIAL.
BBQ
HORSEY SAUCE
SPECI
LET ME SEE YOU MAKE A CHICKEN BURGER WITH SPECIAL SAUCE.
OKAY LET'S SEE HERE. BURGER-SHAPED PATTY... OOH?!
HEY, DID YOU JUST...?
DON'T ACT LIKE YOU HAVEN'T BEEN BEGGING FOR IT.
EN
C'MON, BABY, I'M A SENIOR.

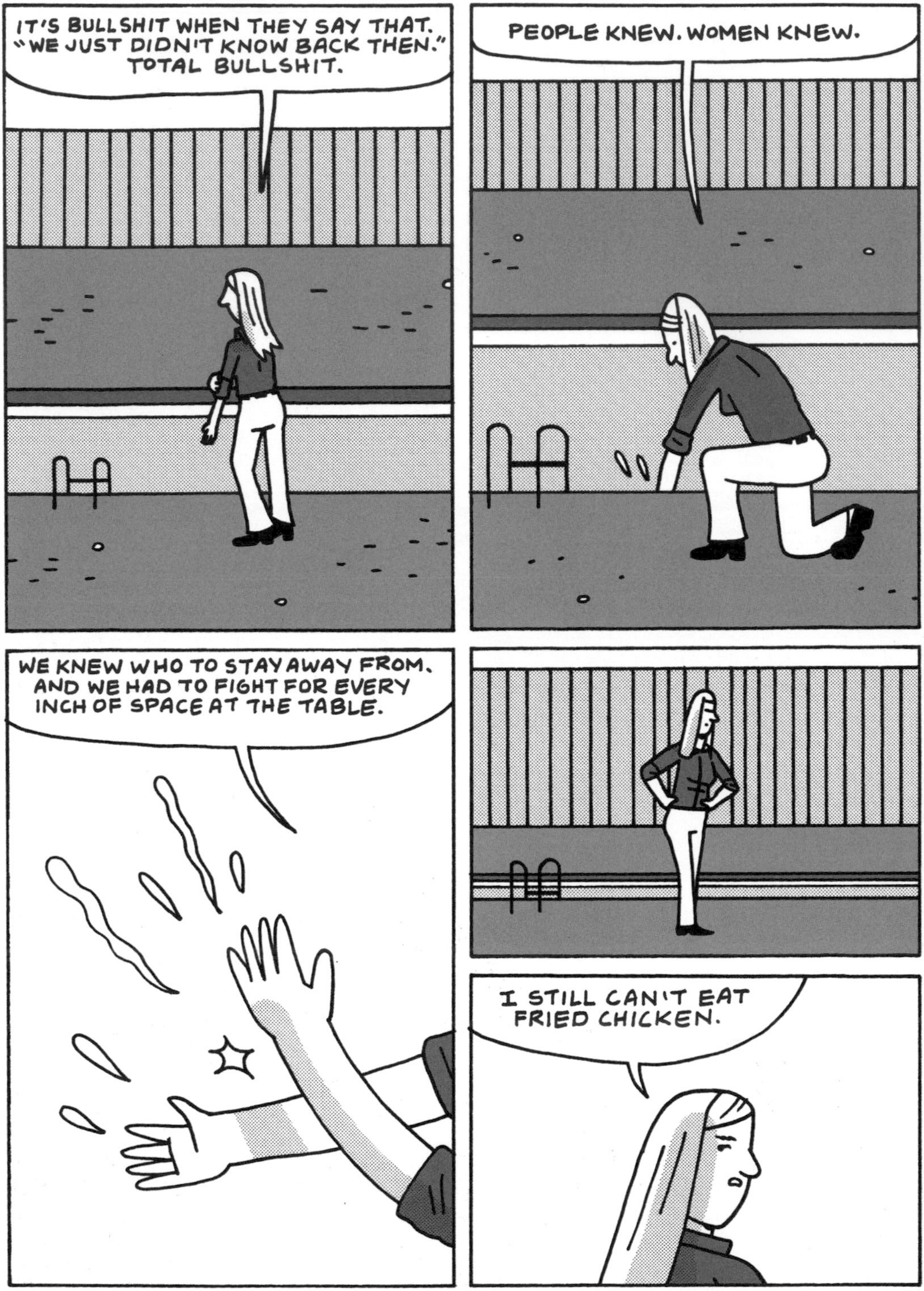
IT'S BULLSHIT WHEN THEY SAY THAT. "WE JUST DIDN'T KNOW BACK THEN." TOTAL BULLSHIT.
PEOPLE KNEW. WOMEN KNEW.
WE KNEW WHO TO STAY AWAY FROM. AND WE HAD TO FIGHT FOR EVERY INCH OF SPACE AT THE TABLE.
I STILL CAN'T EAT FRIED CHICKEN.

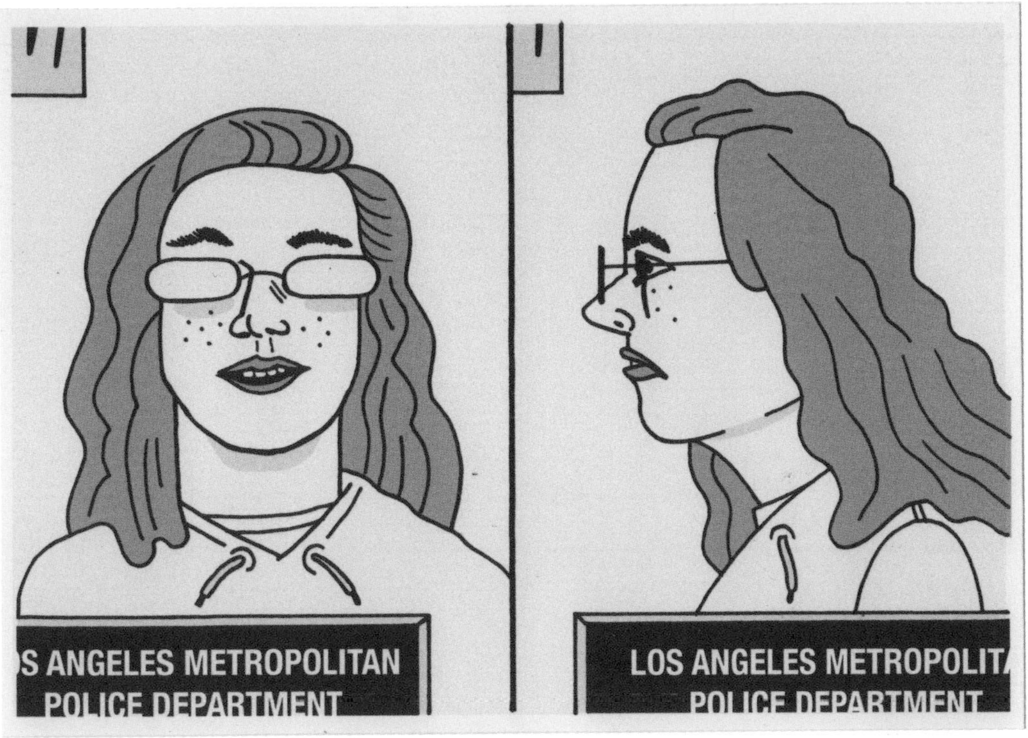
S ANGELES METROPOLITAN
POLICE DEPARTMENT
LOS ANGELES METROPOLIT
POLICE DEPARTMENT

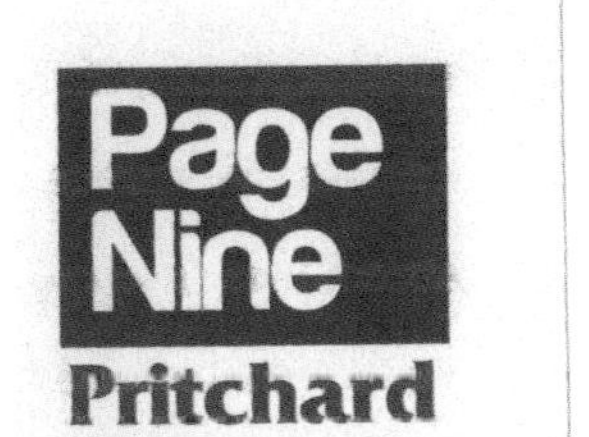

Page Nine

Pritchard Bronson

Sightings

A network TV star was seen stumbling and mumbling on the side of the freeway on Thursday evening. The police said they were slurring their words and swerving their fancy new car. The actor was issued a citation for allegedly driving under the influence after a hot party at Club Ricky Ronny....
Slip Lawrence of the daytime drama The Brilliantly Bold had lunch with two female friends at the Smoke A Joke Cafe in Santa Monica...
Elizabeth Whiz was seen thowing a hissy fit over a parking spot in Downtown Los Angeles. Allegedly her car needed to be towed but she refused to leave the car. She was also holding several baguettes from Brown's Downtown Bread Pound which has been the site of several recent celebrity car towings...
Serf Boyd sent his meal back to the

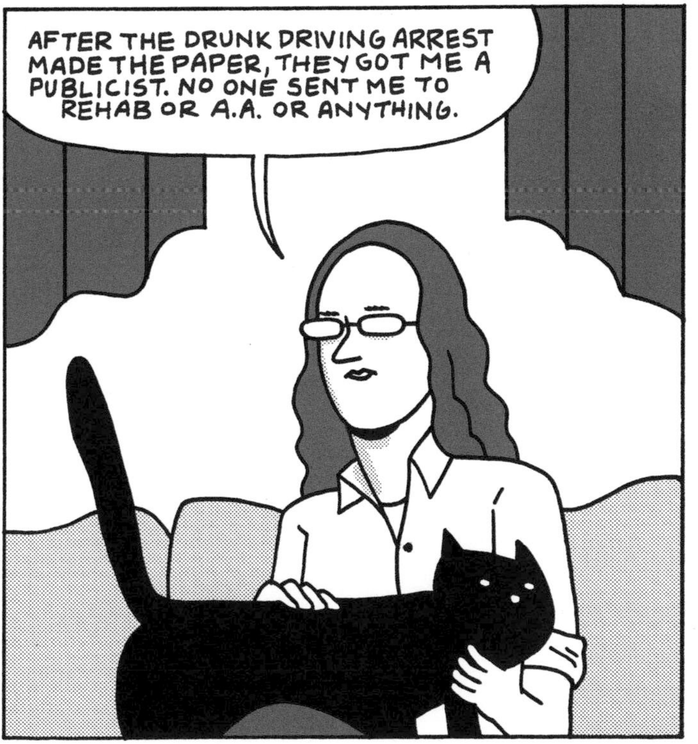
AFTER THE DRUNK DRIVING ARREST MADE THE PAPER, THEY GOT ME A PUBLICIST. NO ONE SENT ME TO REHAB OR A.A. OR ANYTHING.

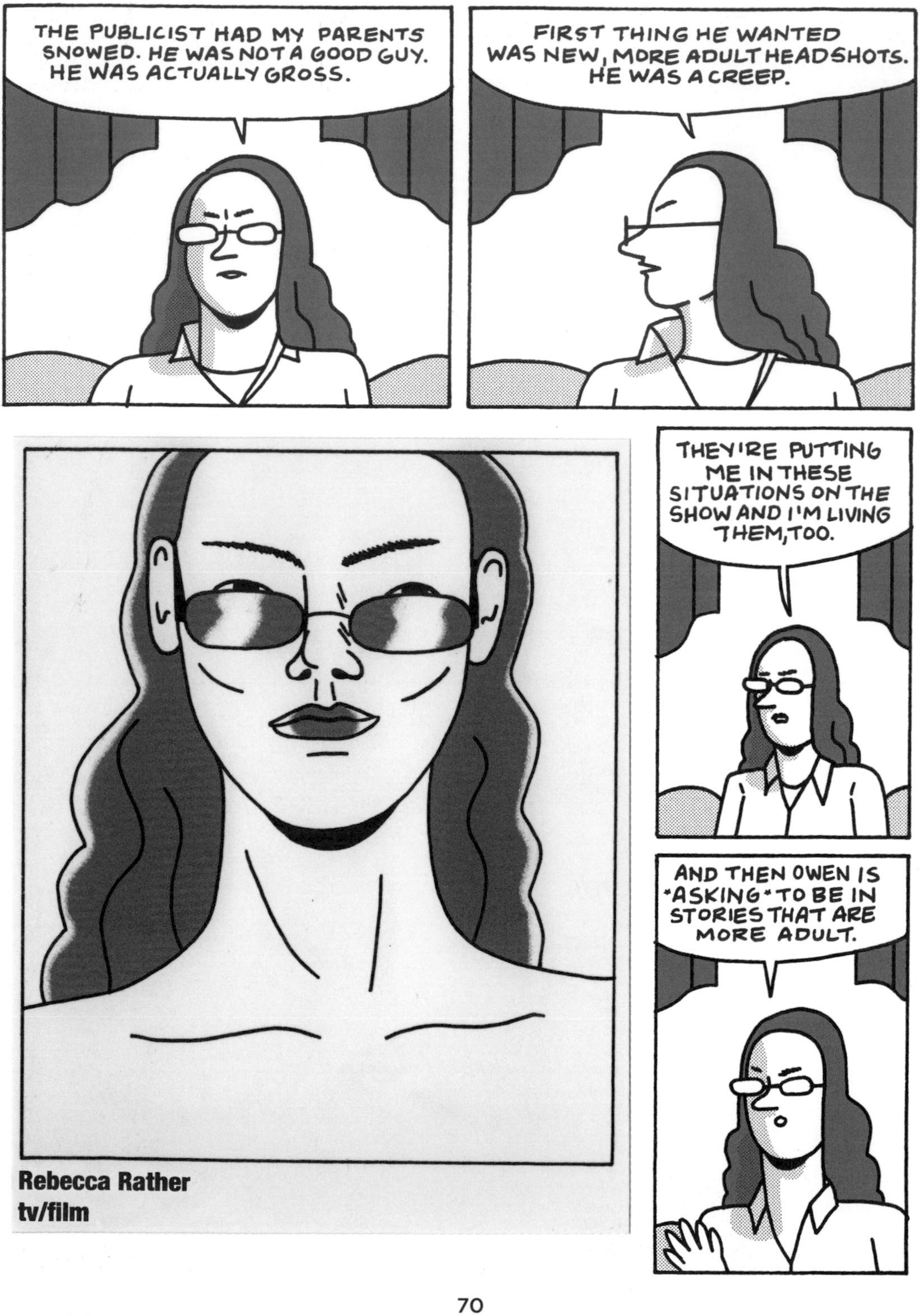
THE PUBLICIST HAD MY PARENTS SNOWED. HE WAS NOT A GOOD GUY. HE WAS ACTUALLY GROSS.
FIRST THING HE WANTED WAS NEW, MORE ADULT HEADSHOTS. HE WAS A CREEP.
Rebecca Rather
tv/film
THEY'RE PUTTING ME IN THESE SITUATIONS ON THE SHOW AND I'M LIVING THEM, TOO.
AND THEN OWEN IS *ASKING* TO BE IN STORIES THAT ARE MORE ADULT.

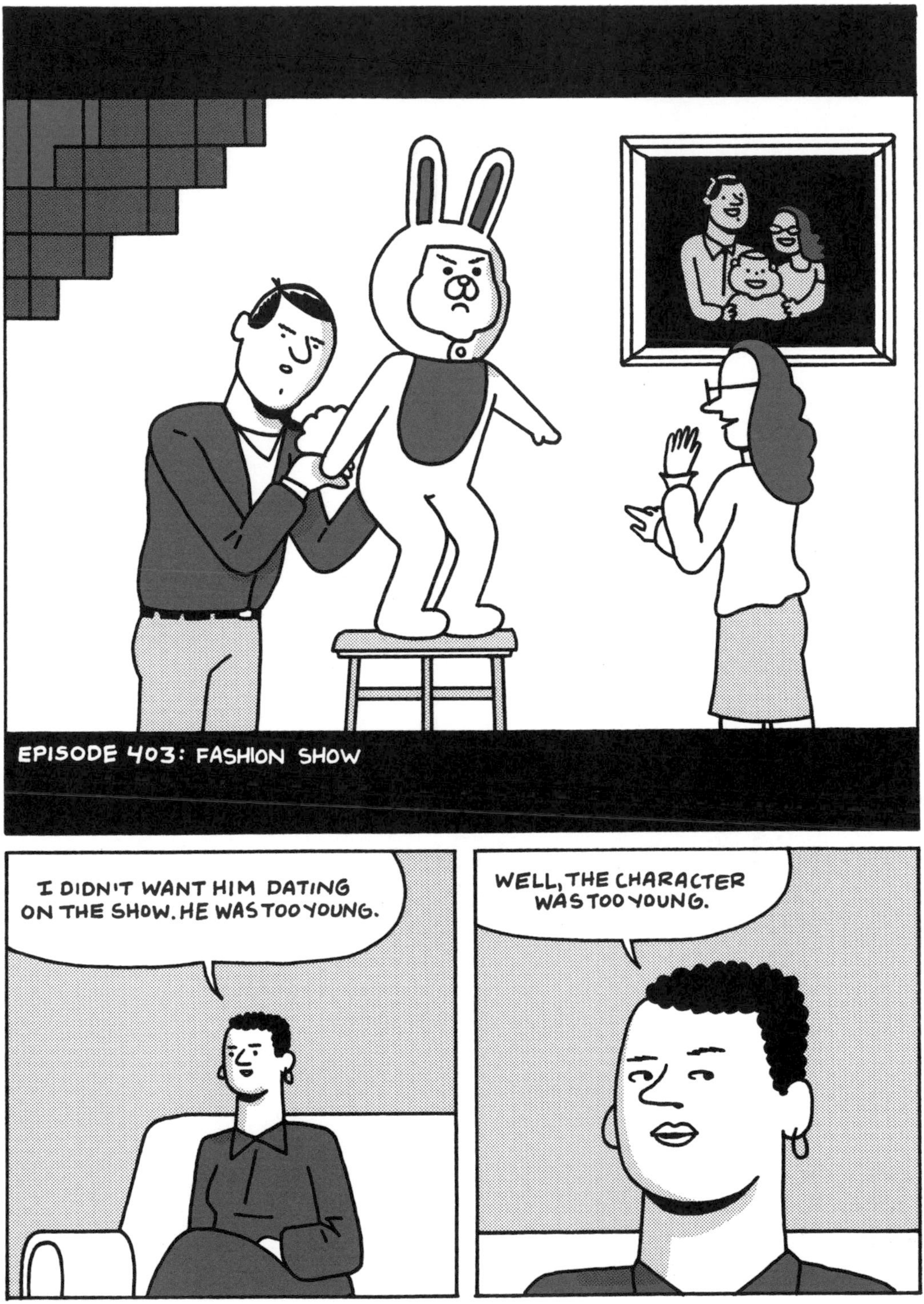
EPISODE 403: FASHION SHOW
I DIDN'T WANT HIM DATING ON THE SHOW. HE WAS TOO YOUNG.
WELL, THE CHARACTER WAS TOO YOUNG.

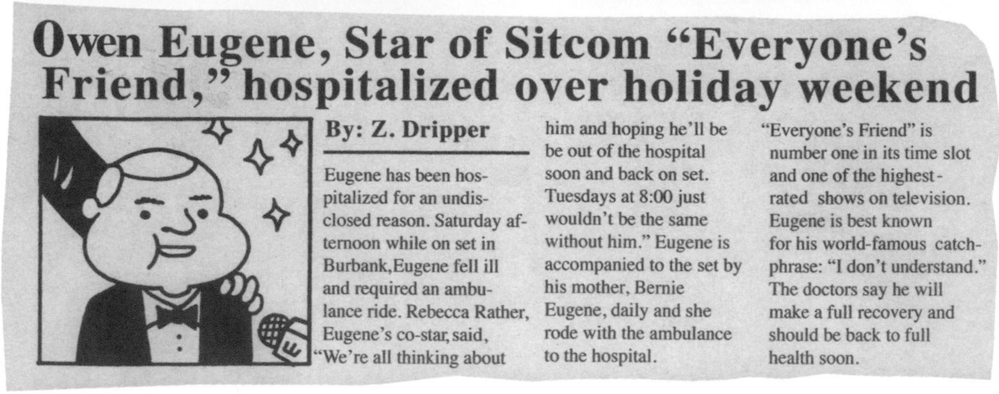

Owen Eugene, Star of Sitcom "Everyone's Friend," hospitalized over holiday weekend

By: Z. Dripper

Eugene has been hospitalized for an undisclosed reason. Saturday afternoon while on set in Burbank,Eugene fell ill and required an ambulance ride. Rebecca Rather, Eugene's co-star, said, "We're all thinking about him and hoping he'll be be out of the hospital soon and back on set. Tuesdays at 8:00 just wouldn't be the same without him." Eugene is accompanied to the set by his mother, Bernie Eugene, daily and she rode with the ambulance to the hospital.

"Everyone's Friend" is number one in its time slot and one of the highest-rated shows on television. Eugene is best known for his world-famous catchphrase: "I don't understand." The doctors say he will make a full recovery and should be back to full health soon.

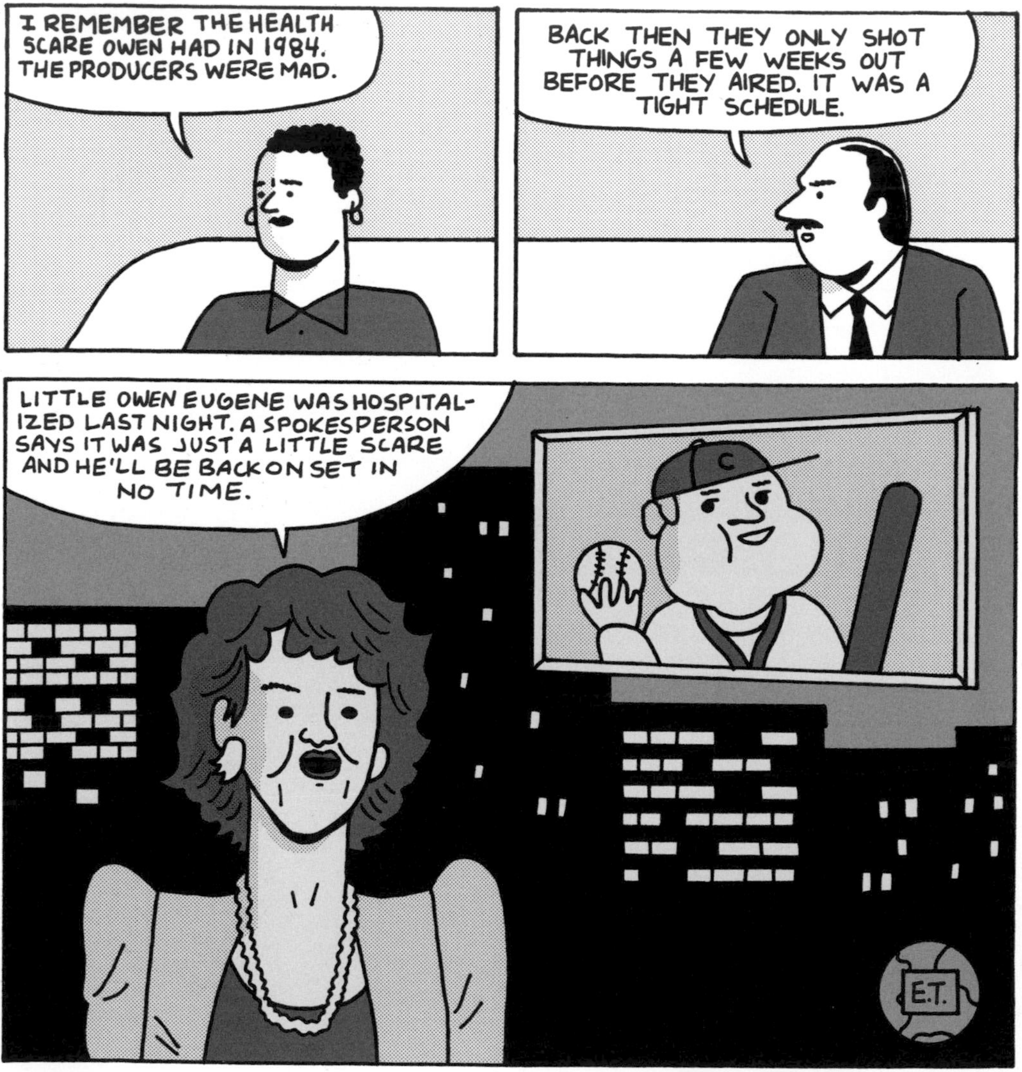

I REMEMBER THE HEALTH SCARE OWEN HAD IN 1984. THE PRODUCERS WERE MAD.
BACK THEN THEY ONLY SHOT THINGS A FEW WEEKS OUT BEFORE THEY AIRED. IT WAS A TIGHT SCHEDULE.
LITTLE OWEN EUGENE WAS HOSPITALIZED LAST NIGHT. A SPOKESPERSON SAYS IT WAS JUST A LITTLE SCARE AND HE'LL BE BACK ON SET IN NO TIME.
C
E.T.

THIS "LITTLE HEALTH SCARE," AS IT WAS REPORTED IN THE NEWS, WAS ACTUALLY VERY SEVERE.

HE HAD UNTREATED TYPE 1 DIABETES. HIS BLOOD SUGAR WAS SPIKING. FIVE TIMES NORMAL LEVELS, MAYBE MORE.

WHEN HE CAME INTO THE HOSPITAL HE'D BEEN VOMITING AND UNRESPONSIVE.

THEN BY SOME MIRACLE THEY STABILIZED HIM AND THEN HIS ENTIRE LIFE BECAME FINGER PRICKS AND INSULIN INJECTIONS. IT REQUIRES CONSTANT MAINTENANCE.

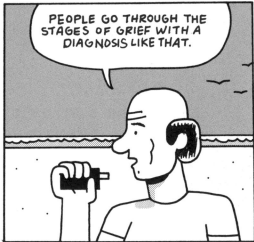

PEOPLE GO THROUGH THE STAGES OF GRIEF WITH A DIAGNOSIS LIKE THAT.

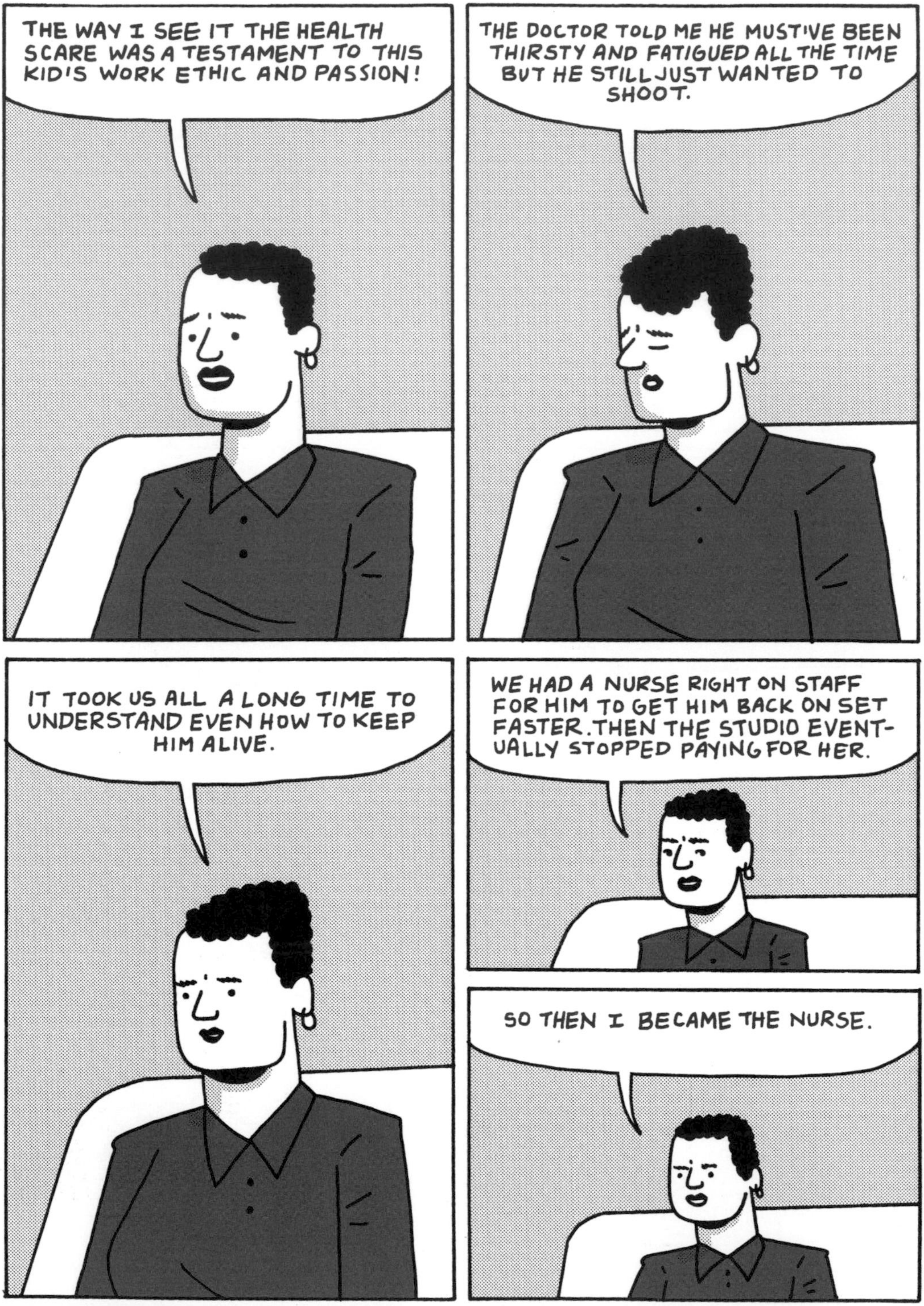
THE WAY I SEE IT THE HEALTH SCARE WAS A TESTAMENT TO THIS KID'S WORK ETHIC AND PASSION!
THE DOCTOR TOLD ME HE MUST'VE BEEN THIRSTY AND FATIGUED ALL THE TIME BUT HE STILL JUST WANTED TO SHOOT.
IT TOOK US ALL A LONG TIME TO UNDERSTAND EVEN HOW TO KEEP HIM ALIVE.
WE HAD A NURSE RIGHT ON STAFF FOR HIM TO GET HIM BACK ON SET FASTER. THEN THE STUDIO EVENT-UALLY STOPPED PAYING FOR HER.
SO THEN I BECAME THE NURSE.

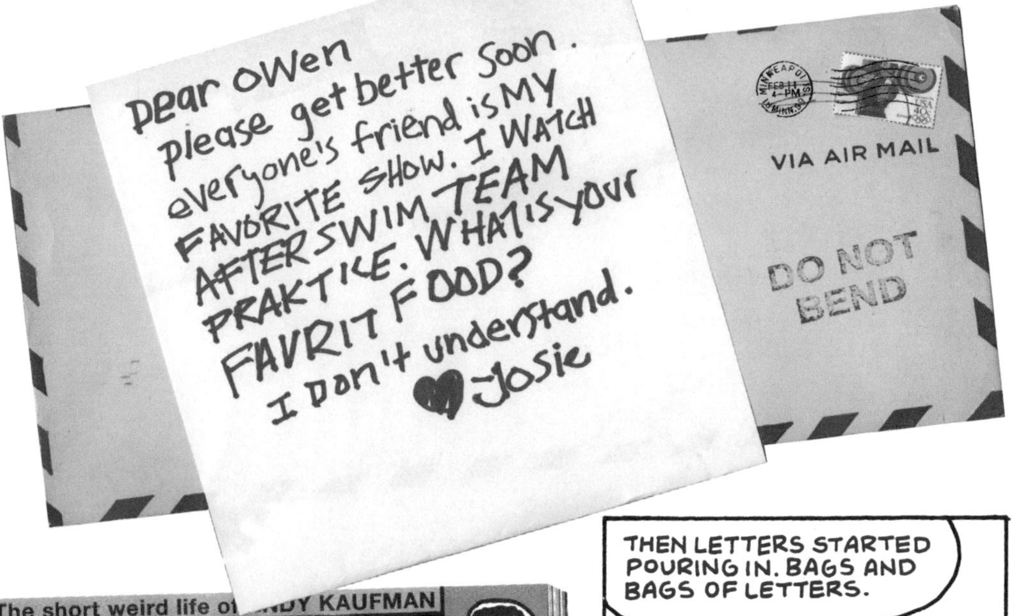
Dear OWen
please get better soon.
everyone's friend is MY
FAVORITE SHOW. I WATCH
AFTER SWIM TEAM
PRAKTICE. WHAT IS your
FAVRIT FOOD?
I Don't understand.
-Josie
VIA AIR MAIL
DO NOT
BEND

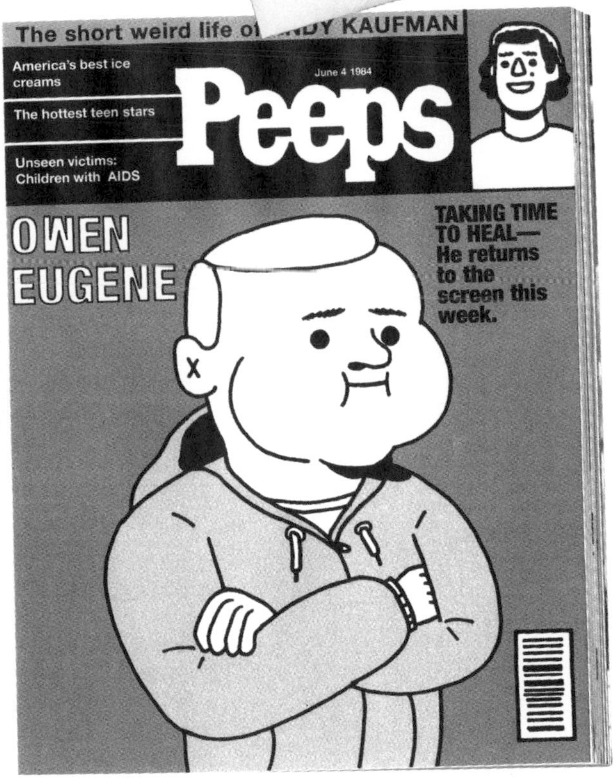
The short weird life o
NDY KAUFMAN
America's best ice creams
June 4 1984
Peeps
The hottest teen stars
Unseen victims: Children with AIDS
OWEN EUGENE
TAKING TIME TO HEAL— He returns to the screen this week.

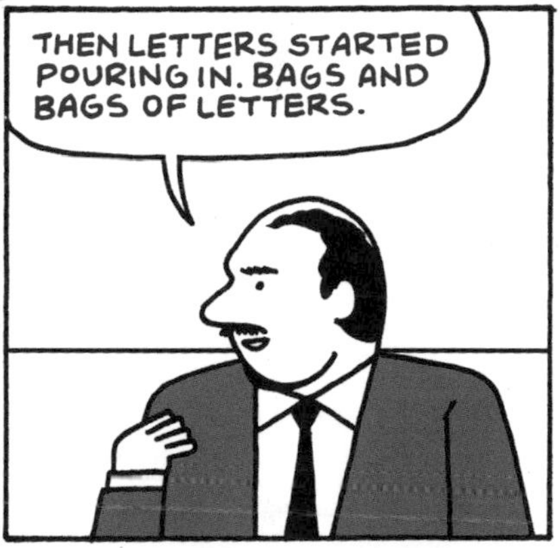
THEN LETTERS STARTED POURING IN. BAGS AND BAGS OF LETTERS.

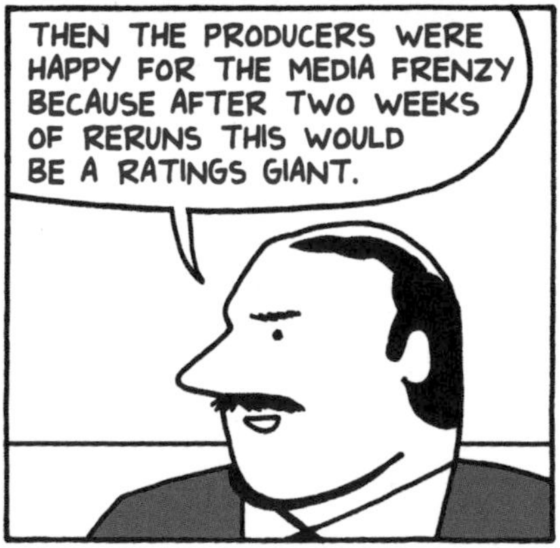
THEN THE PRODUCERS WERE HAPPY FOR THE MEDIA FRENZY BECAUSE AFTER TWO WEEKS OF RERUNS THIS WOULD BE A RATINGS GIANT.

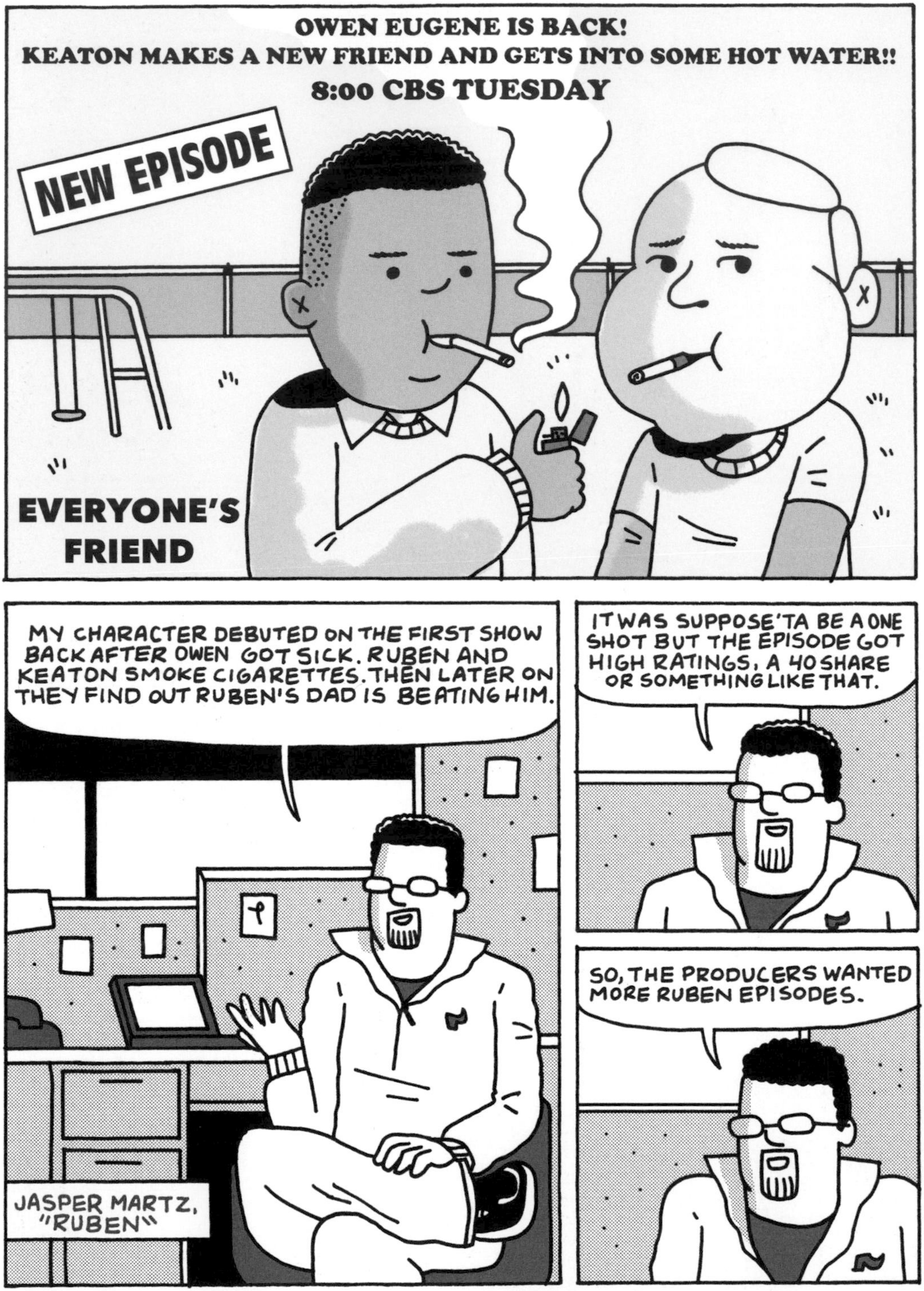
OWEN EUGENE IS BACK!
KEATON MAKES A NEW FRIEND AND GETS INTO SOME HOT WATER!!
8:00 CBS TUESDAY
NEW EPISODE
EVERYONE'S FRIEND
MY CHARACTER DEBUTED ON THE FIRST SHOW BACK AFTER OWEN GOT SICK. RUBEN AND KEATON SMOKE CIGARETTES. THEN LATER ON THEY FIND OUT RUBEN'S DAD IS BEATING HIM.
JASPER MARTZ, "RUBEN"
IT WAS SUPPOSE'TA BE A ONE SHOT BUT THE EPISODE GOT HIGH RATINGS, A 40 SHARE OR SOMETHING LIKE THAT.
SO, THE PRODUCERS WANTED MORE RUBEN EPISODES.

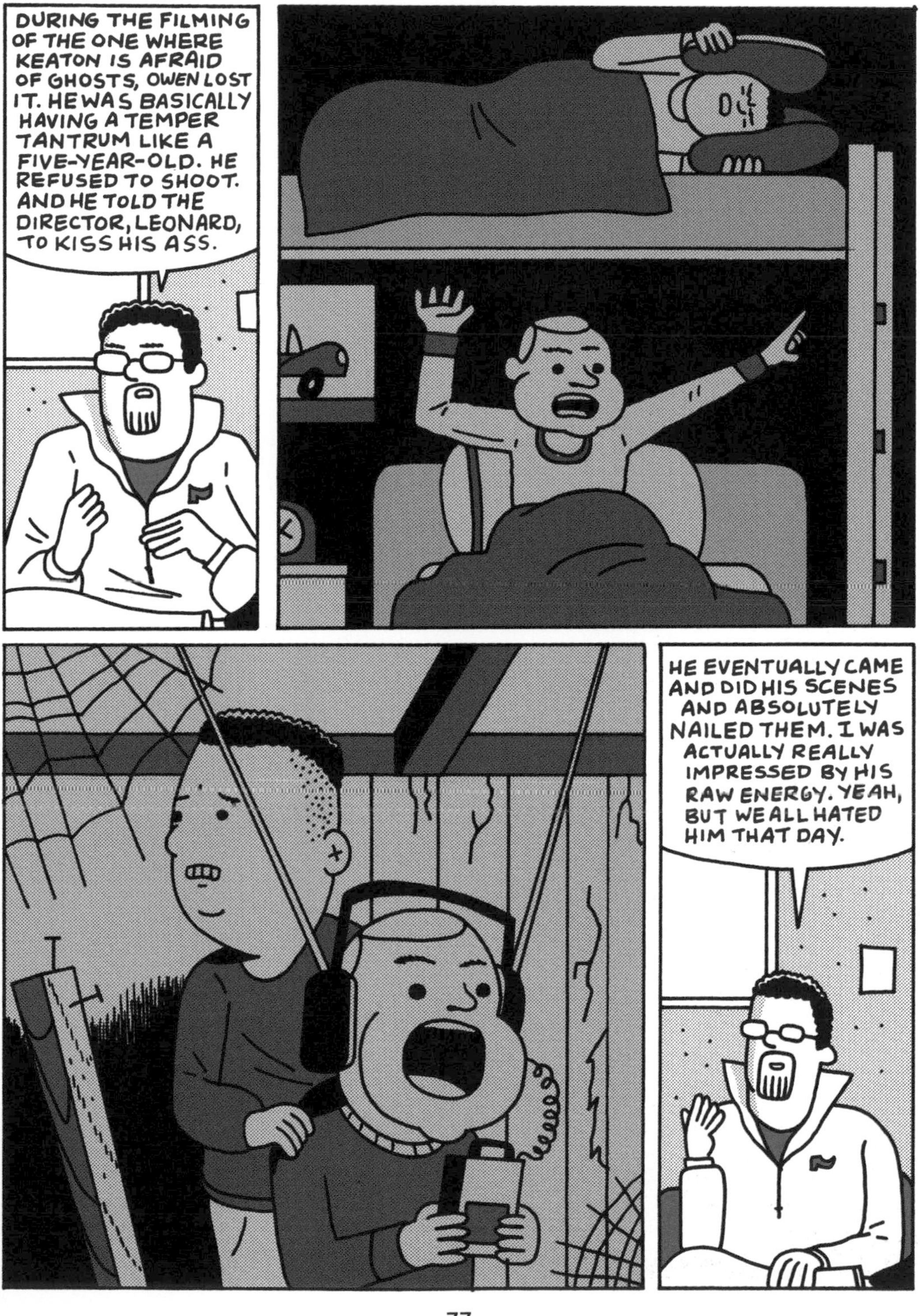
DURING THE FILMING OF THE ONE WHERE KEATON IS AFRAID OF GHOSTS, OWEN LOST IT. HE WAS BASICALLY HAVING A TEMPER TANTRUM LIKE A FIVE-YEAR-OLD. HE REFUSED TO SHOOT. AND HE TOLD THE DIRECTOR, LEONARD, TO KISS HIS ASS.
HE EVENTUALLY CAME AND DID HIS SCENES AND ABSOLUTELY NAILED THEM. I WAS ACTUALLY REALLY IMPRESSED BY HIS RAW ENERGY. YEAH, BUT WE ALL HATED HIM THAT DAY.

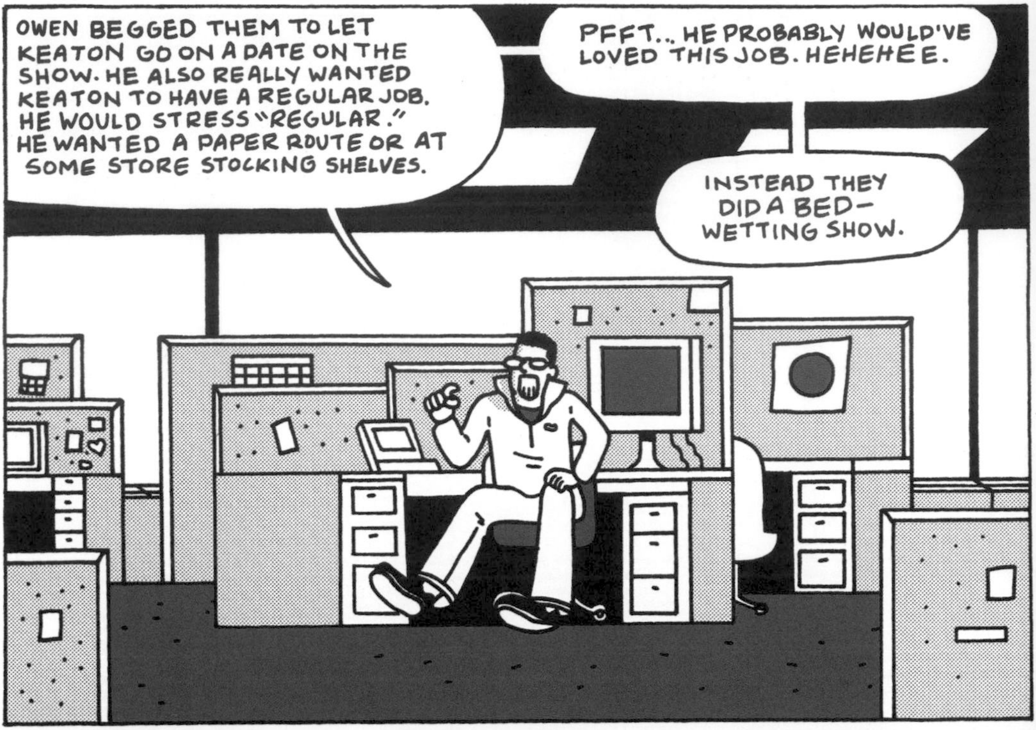
OWEN BEGGED THEM TO LET KEATON GO ON A DATE ON THE SHOW. HE ALSO REALLY WANTED KEATON TO HAVE A REGULAR JOB. HE WOULD STRESS "REGULAR." HE WANTED A PAPER ROUTE OR AT SOME STORE STOCKING SHELVES.
PFFT... HE PROBABLY WOULD'VE LOVED THIS JOB. HEHEHEE.
INSTEAD THEY DID A BED-WETTING SHOW.

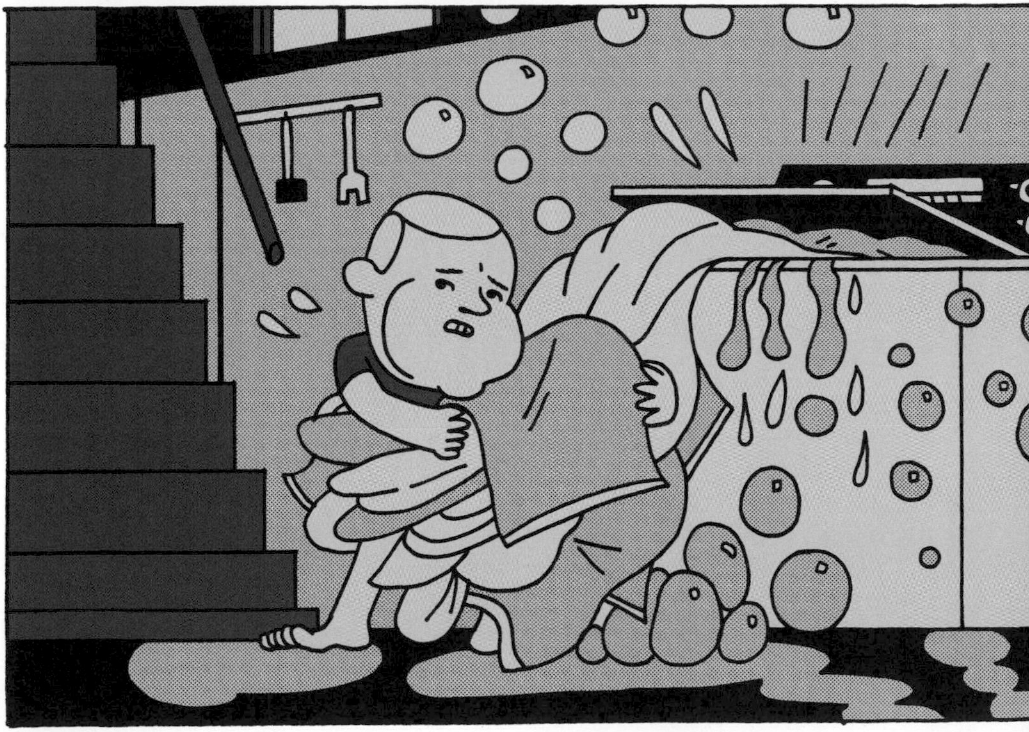

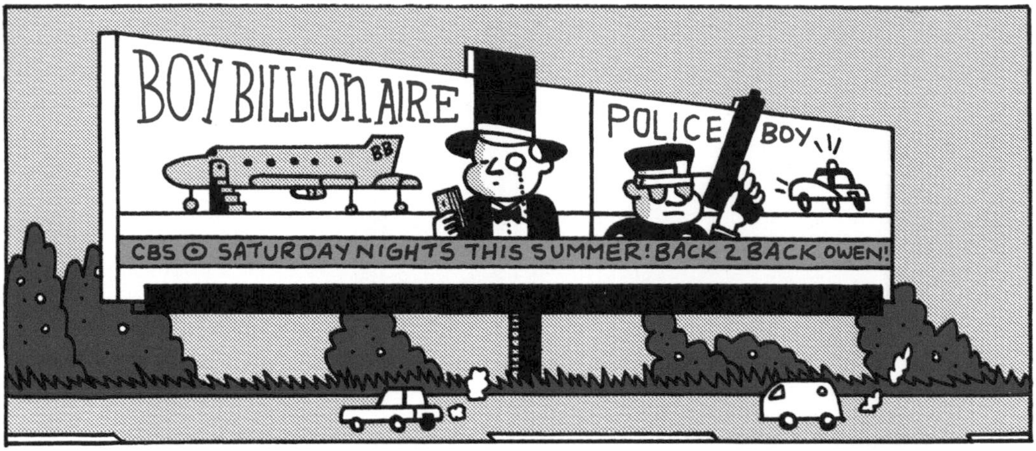
BOY BILLIONAIRE
BB
POLICE BOY
CBS SATURDAY NIGHTS THIS SUMMER! BACK 2 BACK OWEN!

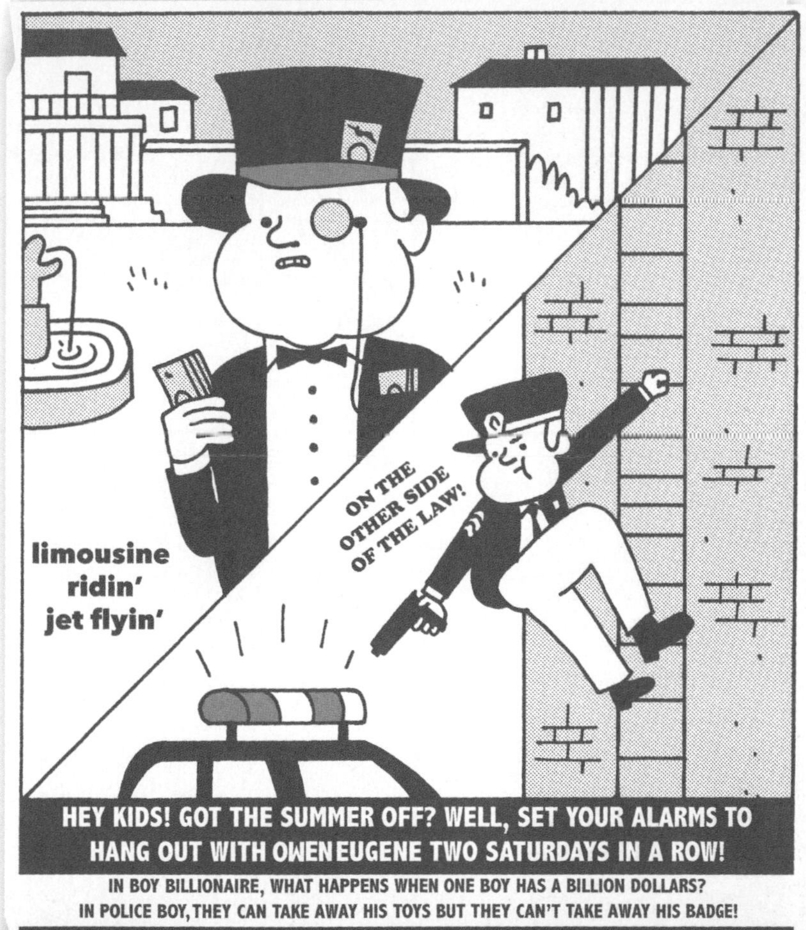
limousine ridin' jet flyin'
ON THE OTHER SIDE OF THE LAW!
HEY KIDS! GOT THE SUMMER OFF? WELL, SET YOUR ALARMS TO HANG OUT WITH OWEN EUGENE TWO SATURDAYS IN A ROW!
IN BOY BILLIONAIRE, WHAT HAPPENS WHEN ONE BOY HAS A BILLION DOLLARS?
IN POLICE BOY, THEY CAN TAKE AWAY HIS TOYS BUT THEY CAN'T TAKE AWAY HIS BADGE!
BACK 2 BACK SATURDAYS! JULY 6 & JULY 13 ONLY ON CBS

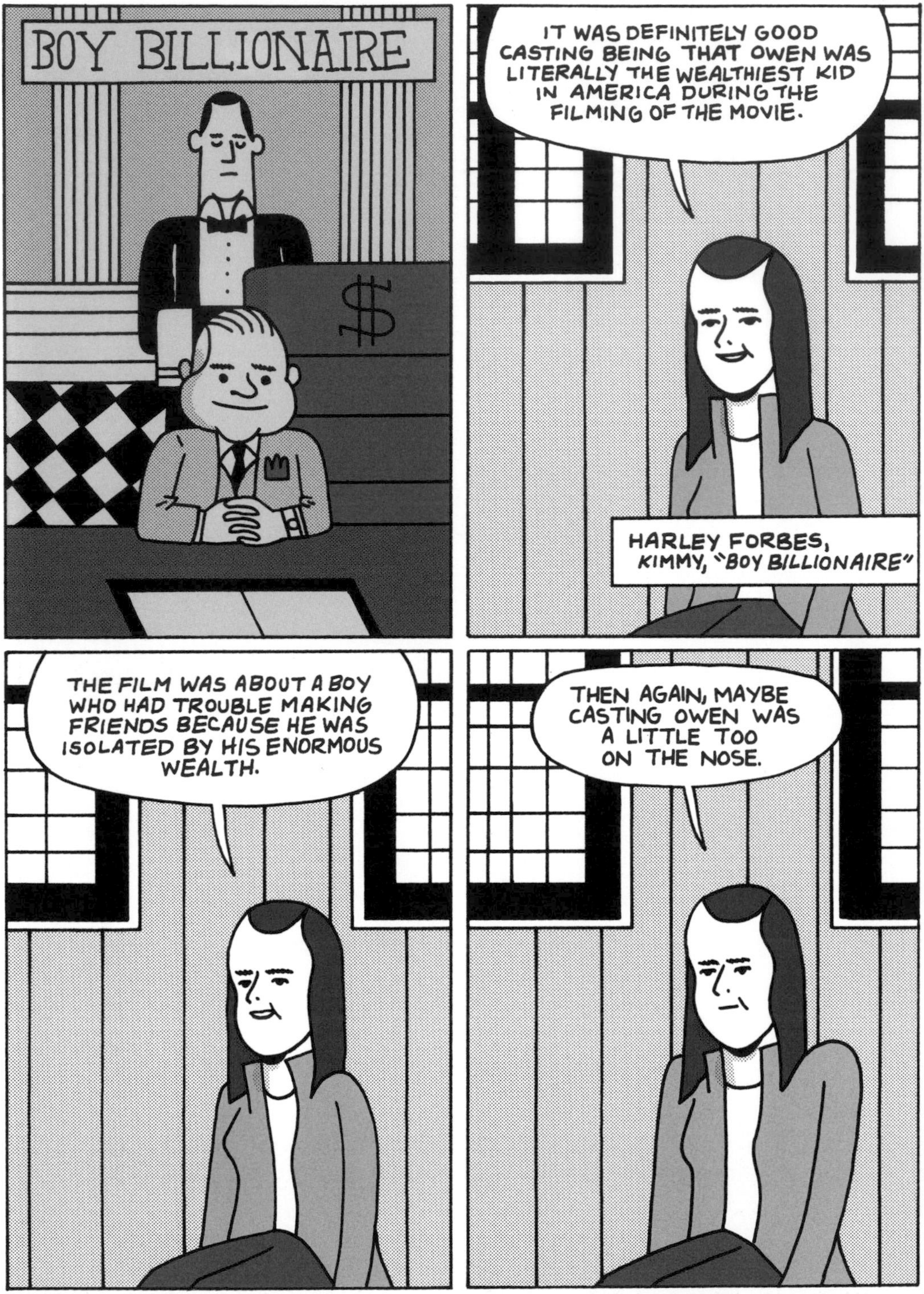
BOY BILLIONAIRE
$
IT WAS DEFINITELY GOOD CASTING BEING THAT OWEN WAS LITERALLY THE WEALTHIEST KID IN AMERICA DURING THE FILMING OF THE MOVIE.
HARLEY FORBES, KIMMY, "BOY BILLIONAIRE"
THE FILM WAS ABOUT A BOY WHO HAD TROUBLE MAKING FRIENDS BECAUSE HE WAS ISOLATED BY HIS ENORMOUS WEALTH.
THEN AGAIN, MAYBE CASTING OWEN WAS A LITTLE TOO ON THE NOSE.

"BOY BILLIONAIRE" 7/6/85

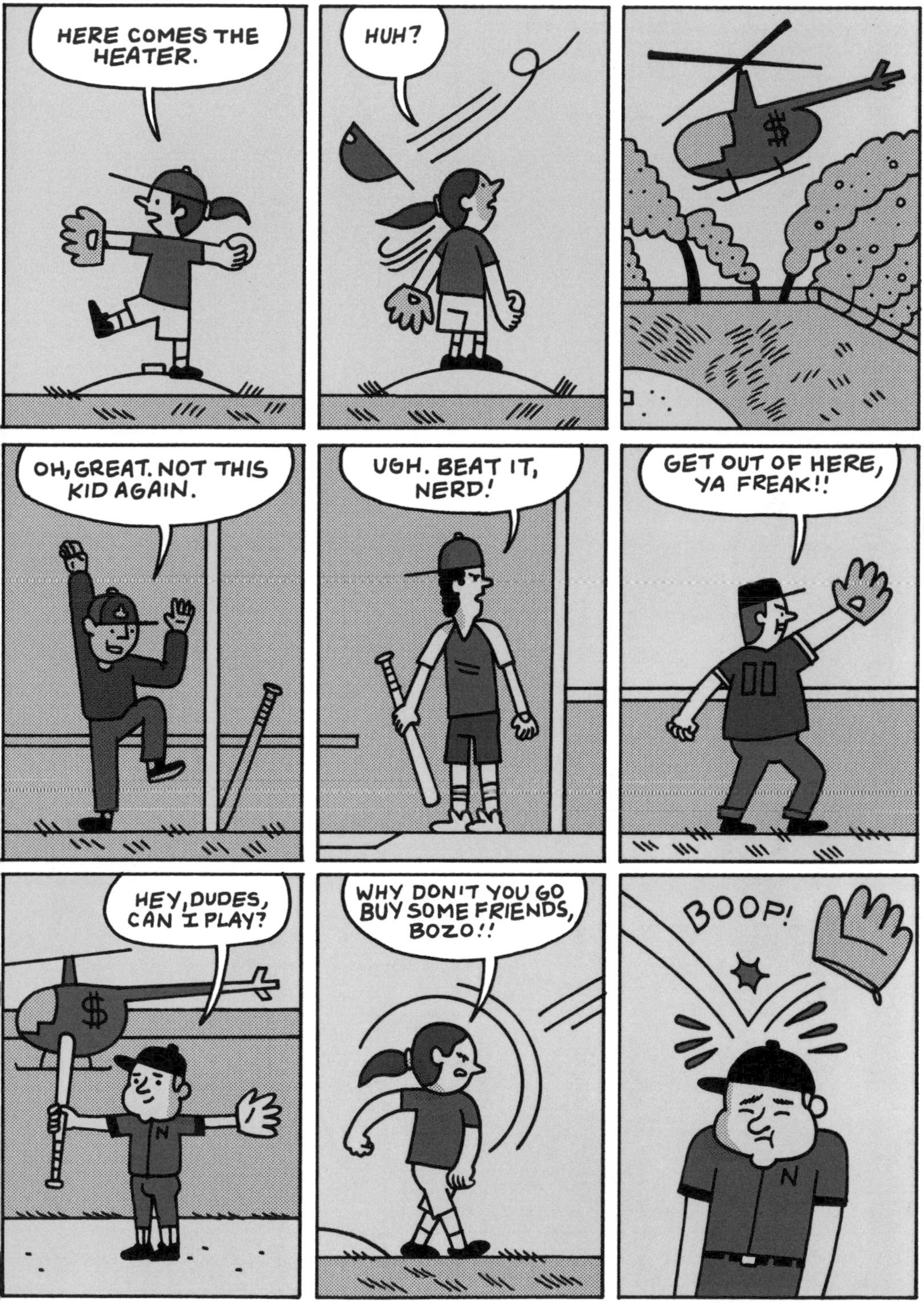
HERE COMES THE HEATER.
HUH?
OH, GREAT. NOT THIS KID AGAIN.
UGH. BEAT IT, NERD!
GET OUT OF HERE, YA FREAK!!
HEY, DUDES, CAN I PLAY?
WHY DON'T YOU GO BUY SOME FRIENDS, BOZO!!
BOOP!

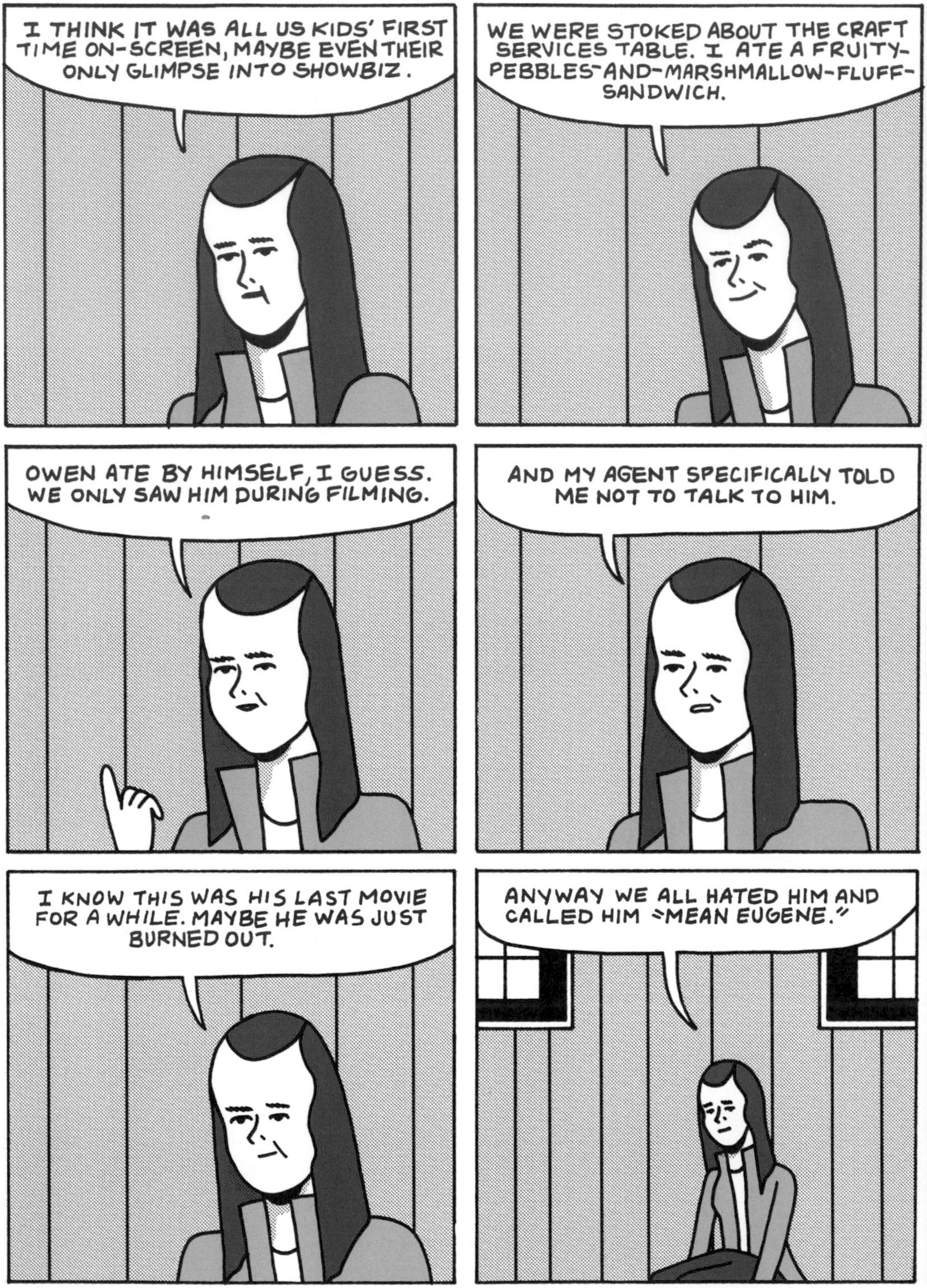
I THINK IT WAS ALL US KIDS' FIRST TIME ON-SCREEN, MAYBE EVEN THEIR ONLY GLIMPSE INTO SHOWBIZ.
WE WERE STOKED ABOUT THE CRAFT SERVICES TABLE. I ATE A FRUITY-PEBBLES-AND-MARSHMALLOW-FLUFF-SANDWICH.
OWEN ATE BY HIMSELF, I GUESS. WE ONLY SAW HIM DURING FILMING.
AND MY AGENT SPECIFICALLY TOLD ME NOT TO TALK TO HIM.
I KNOW THIS WAS HIS LAST MOVIE FOR A WHILE. MAYBE HE WAS JUST BURNED OUT.
ANYWAY WE ALL HATED HIM AND CALLED HIM "MEAN EUGENE."

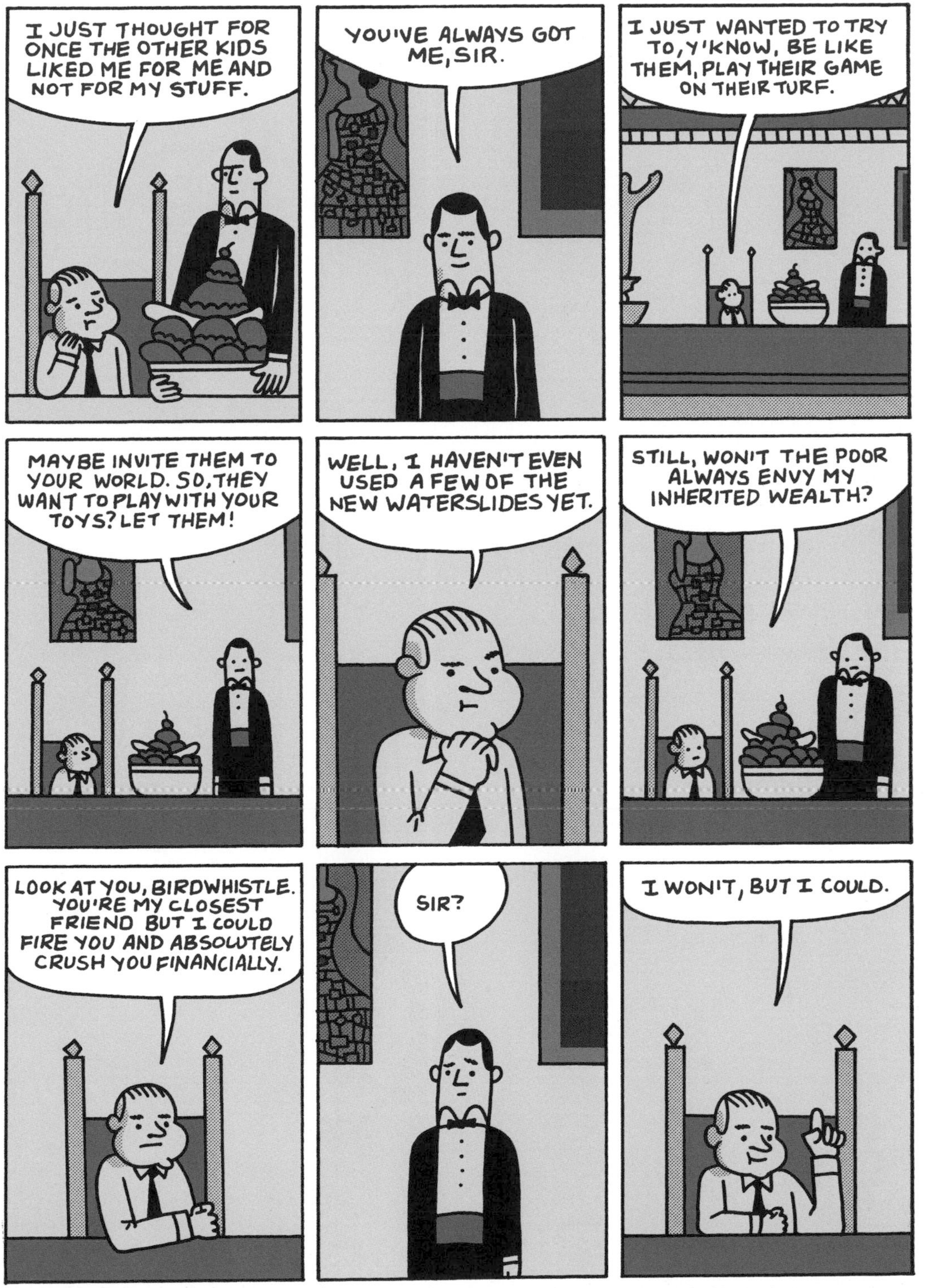
I JUST THOUGHT FOR ONCE THE OTHER KIDS LIKED ME FOR ME AND NOT FOR MY STUFF.
YOU'VE ALWAYS GOT ME, SIR.
I JUST WANTED TO TRY TO, Y'KNOW, BE LIKE THEM, PLAY THEIR GAME ON THEIR TURF.
MAYBE INVITE THEM TO YOUR WORLD. SO, THEY WANT TO PLAY WITH YOUR TOYS? LET THEM!
WELL, I HAVEN'T EVEN USED A FEW OF THE NEW WATERSLIDES YET.
STILL, WON'T THE POOR ALWAYS ENVY MY INHERITED WEALTH?
LOOK AT YOU, BIRDWHISTLE. YOU'RE MY CLOSEST FRIEND BUT I COULD FIRE YOU AND ABSOLUTELY CRUSH YOU FINANCIALLY.
SIR?
I WON'T, BUT I COULD.

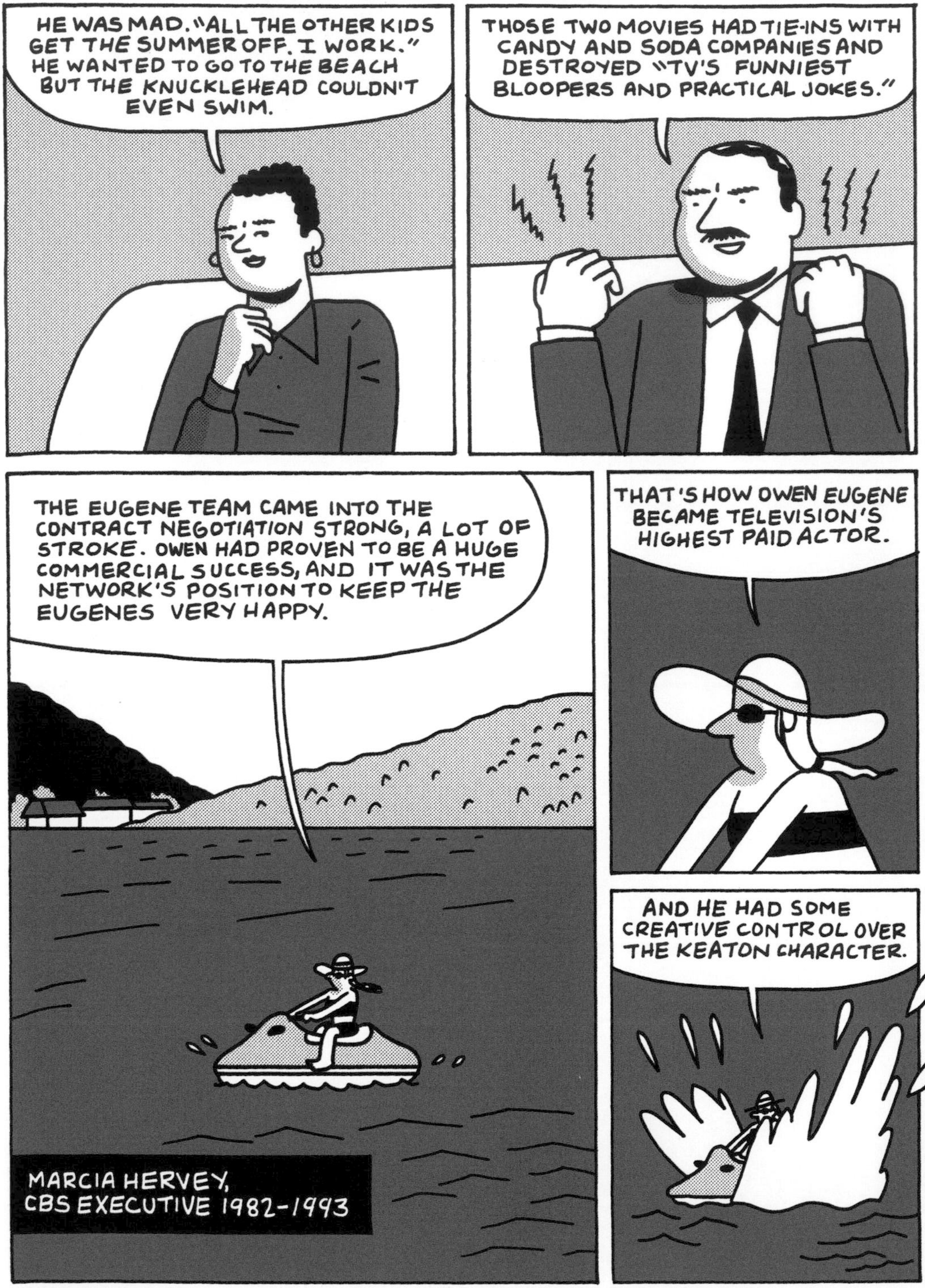
HE WAS MAD. "ALL THE OTHER KIDS GET THE SUMMER OFF. I WORK." HE WANTED TO GO TO THE BEACH BUT THE KNUCKLEHEAD COULDN'T EVEN SWIM.
THOSE TWO MOVIES HAD TIE-INS WITH CANDY AND SODA COMPANIES AND DESTROYED "TV'S FUNNIEST BLOOPERS AND PRACTICAL JOKES."
THE EUGENE TEAM CAME INTO THE CONTRACT NEGOTIATION STRONG, A LOT OF STROKE. OWEN HAD PROVEN TO BE A HUGE COMMERCIAL SUCCESS, AND IT WAS THE NETWORK'S POSITION TO KEEP THE EUGENES VERY HAPPY.
MARCIA HERVEY, CBS EXECUTIVE 1982-1993
THAT'S HOW OWEN EUGENE BECAME TELEVISION'S HIGHEST PAID ACTOR.
AND HE HAD SOME CREATIVE CONTROL OVER THE KEATON CHARACTER.

FILM | STAGE | TV

VARIETY

THE PAPER APRIL Nº 4

NEWS OF THE WEEK APRIL 16-22, 1985

REAL BILLION-DOLLAR BOY

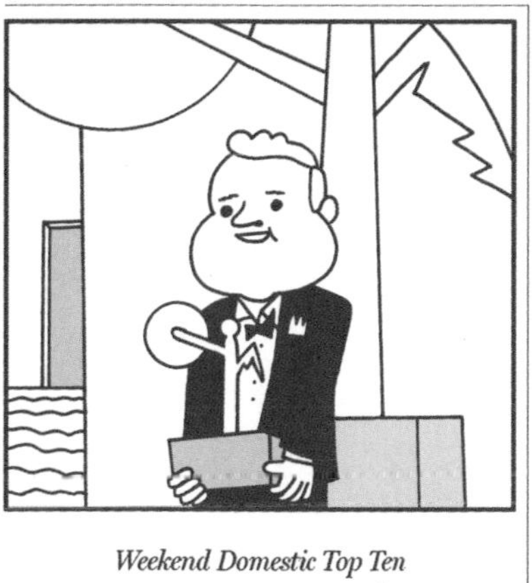

Weekend Domestic Top Ten

Title (weeks in release)	3-day gross*	Engmts.	$ per engagement	Cume*	% chg.
1. Police Academy 3: Back 2 Work	37.1	3,783	9,795	37.1	–
2. Money Is the Pits	17.7	3,250	5,454	53.8	-36
3. Autoworkers Are Different in Japan	9.2	3435	2,689	154.6	-30
4. Purple But Not the Color	6.2	3,402	1,808	22.8	-57
5. Pretty Girl Goes to the Prom	5.8	3,175	1,8[illegible]5	111.2	-47
6. The Mice Patrol Goes Cheesy	4.9	1,542	3,189	11.6	+26
7. Nightmare Killer 4: Wake Up Sleepy	4.5	2,638	1,699	88.8	-38
8. Government Robot	4.1	2,823	1,457	48.5	-57
8. Motorcycle Guy	4.1	2,330	1,740	38.5	-54
10. Space Is a Place	3.0	2,045	1,469	223.7	-39

Overseas Top Five

Title (weeks in release)	3-day gross*	Territories	Screens	Int'l cume*	Global cume*	% chg.
1. Police Academy 3: Back 2 Work	40.2	61	12,628	212.0	323.2	+187
2. Money Is the Pits	32.8	60	7744	111.2	148.3	-46
3. Motorcycle Guy	17.9	67	9,714	268.9	423.5	-30
4. Government Robot	3.2	29	931	64.5	136.1	+129
5. Space Is a Place	2.2	32	1,250	15.3	63.8	-24

*IN MILLIONS OF $

SOURCE: STUDIOS

HIGHEST PAID ACTOR ON TV

By ANDRE WART

Owen Eugene, star of CBS TV's ***Everyone's Friend***, is now the highest paid actor on television. It is said the 17-year-old actor will make $100,000 per episode, placing him at the absolute top of the list of big money earners in Hollywood. His new contract is said to include more TV movies and more episodes per season.

Eugene surpasses Tom Selleck of *Magnum P.I.* as the highest paid actor on network televison. His catchphrase, "I don't understand," is on the lips of kids and parents all over the country, as well as on the T-shirts of pretty much everyone under the age of 30.

Everyone's Friend dominates the ratings every Thursday night, often getting the lion's share of the ad money. This year it'll be followed by ***Pumps***, a show about two women who have struck out on their own to open a shoe store, a vehicle for new star Solaris Platertater.

There will also be a number of new Keaton products. The show has teamed up with Hasbro, Hefty Garbage Bags, Frosted Flakes, Nike, Snickers, Coca-Cola, Budweiser as well as a number of other brands to co-promote on the show. CBS executive Harpo Drummond calls the deal "Super duper."

Season five starts in September and will again be the flagship program for the network. The list of celebrity guest stars balloons this year to include: The Harlem Globetrotters, pro wrestling's Sgt. Slaughter, Ralph Macchio, Eddie Van Halen and even the First Lady of the United States, Nancy Reagan.

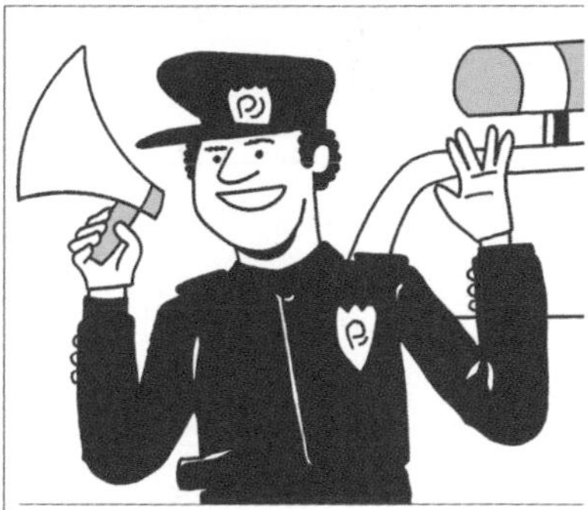

POLICE ACADEMY TO LIVE ON IN AT LEAST ONE MORE FILM

The producers of the Police Academy films have committed to at least one more film. Series producer Hammond Deggs says, "I think we've got the creative energy and the gas for one more film but can't see the series going beyond that. We've just really run out of ways to make this funny. I honestly didn't think we could've made the third film, but now it's done really well at the box office and we'll have to do a fourth film." When asked about the possibility of a fifth film the producer shrugged and answered, "I'd do it if they paid me more money."

MICE PATROL, TOO CHEESY FOR PARAMOUNT

The animated film seriers Mice Patrol could have developed into a legitimate franchise, Saturday morning cartoon, toys, etc. But Paramount says no. They've passed on ***Mice Patrol 3: Cheddar Weather***.

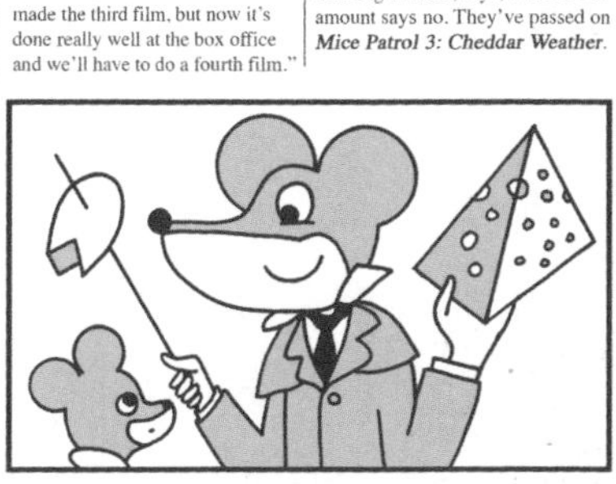

SEASON FIVE PREMIERE

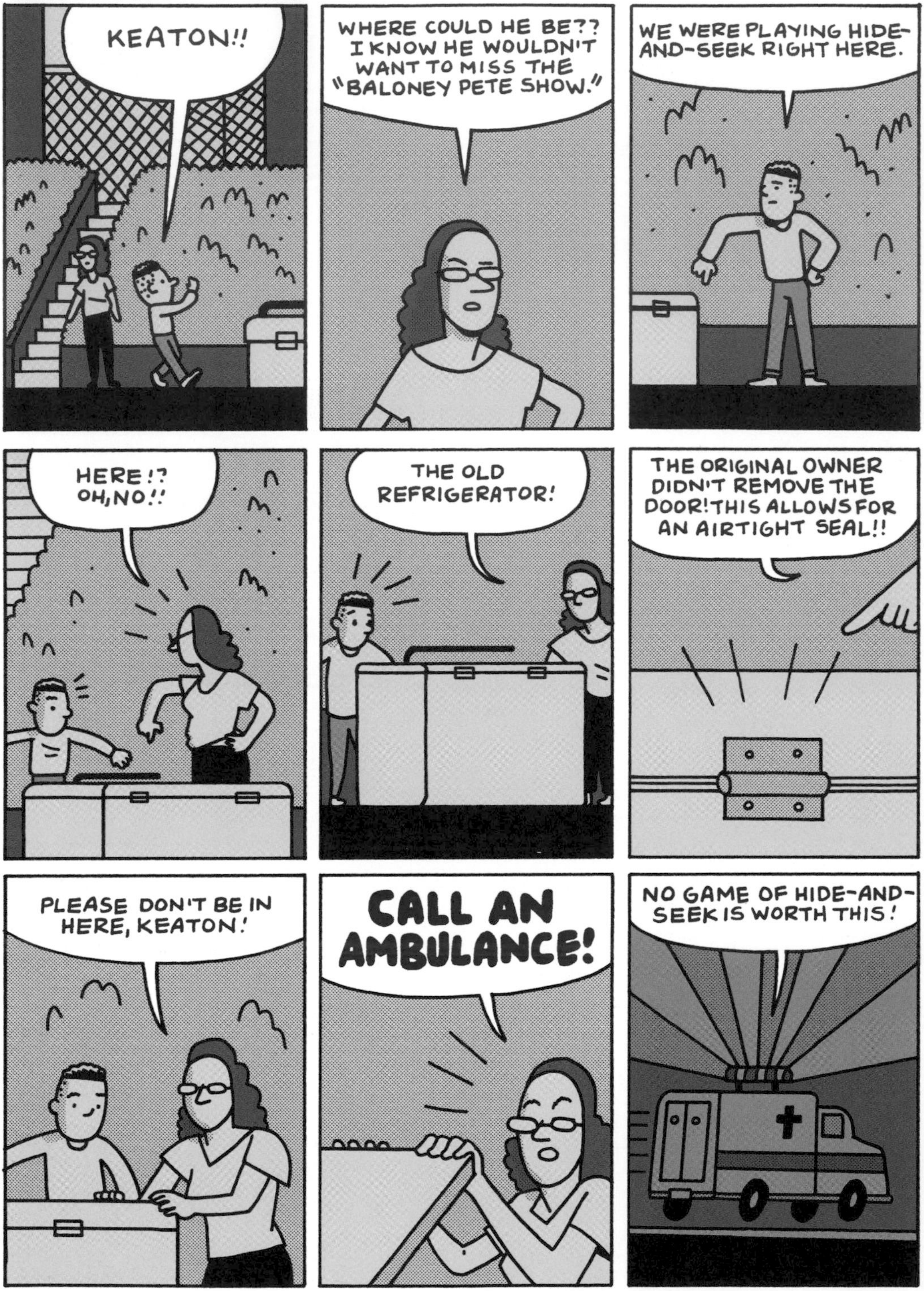
KEATON!!
WHERE COULD HE BE?? I KNOW HE WOULDN'T WANT TO MISS THE "BALONEY PETE SHOW."
WE WERE PLAYING HIDE-AND-SEEK RIGHT HERE.
HERE!? OH, NO!!
THE OLD REFRIGERATOR!
THE ORIGINAL OWNER DIDN'T REMOVE THE DOOR! THIS ALLOWS FOR AN AIRTIGHT SEAL!!
PLEASE DON'T BE IN HERE, KEATON!
CALL AN AMBULANCE!
NO GAME OF HIDE-AND-SEEK IS WORTH THIS!

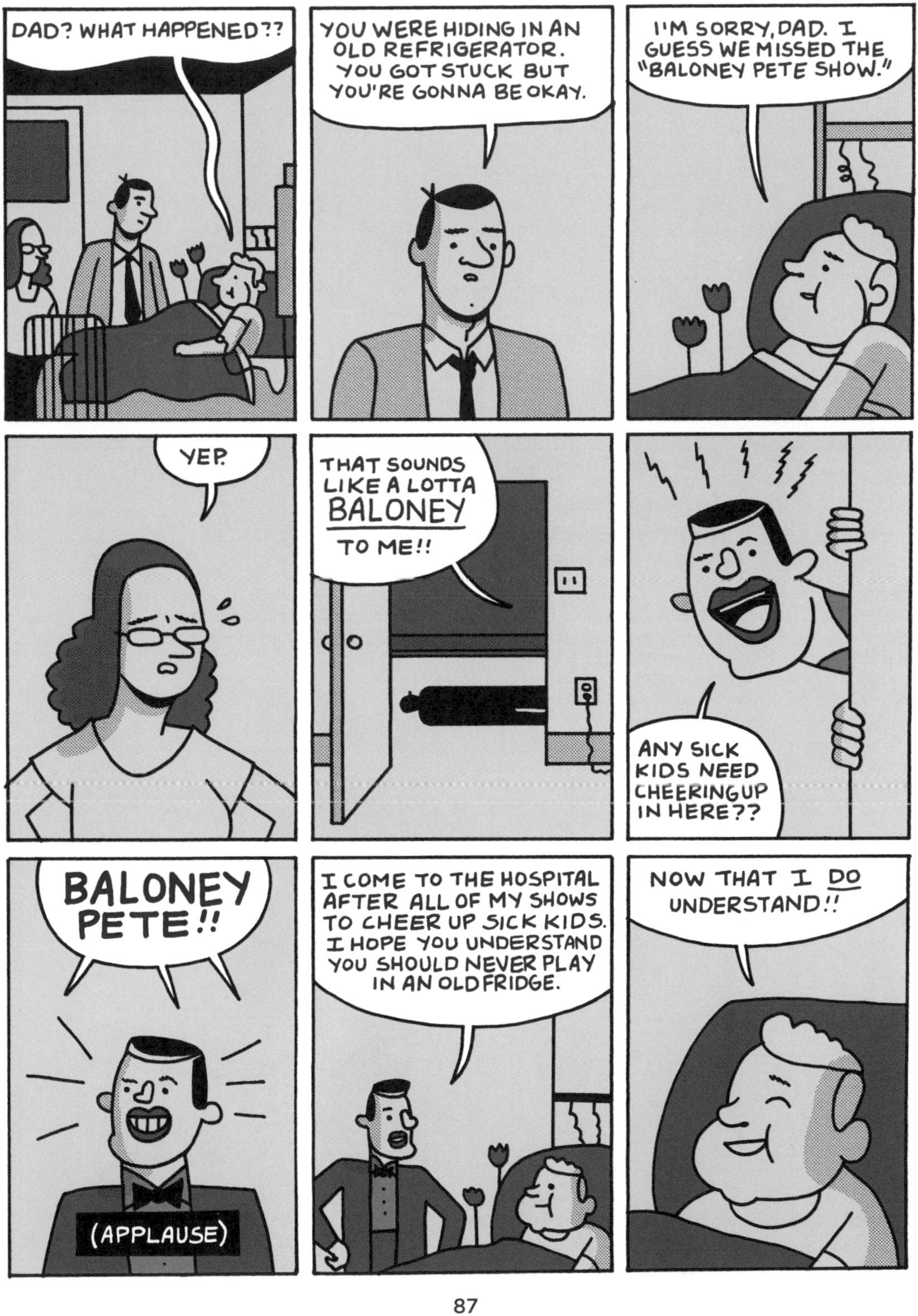
DAD? WHAT HAPPENED??
YOU WERE HIDING IN AN OLD REFRIGERATOR. YOU GOT STUCK BUT YOU'RE GONNA BE OKAY.
I'M SORRY, DAD. I GUESS WE MISSED THE "BALONEY PETE SHOW."
YEP.
THAT SOUNDS LIKE A LOTTA BALONEY TO ME!!
ANY SICK KIDS NEED CHEERING UP IN HERE??
BALONEY PETE!!
(APPLAUSE)
I COME TO THE HOSPITAL AFTER ALL OF MY SHOWS TO CHEER UP SICK KIDS. I HOPE YOU UNDERSTAND YOU SHOULD NEVER PLAY IN AN OLD FRIDGE.
NOW THAT I DO UNDERSTAND!!

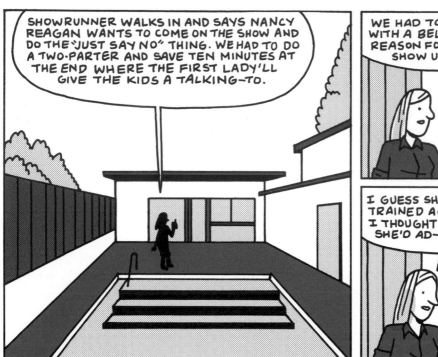

SHOWRUNNER WALKS IN AND SAYS NANCY REAGAN WANTS TO COME ON THE SHOW AND DO THE "JUST SAY NO" THING. WE HAD TO DO A TWO-PARTER AND SAVE TEN MINUTES AT THE END WHERE THE FIRST LADY'LL GIVE THE KIDS A TALKING-TO.

WE HAD TO COME UP WITH A BELIEVABLE REASON FOR HER TO SHOW UP.

I GUESS SHE WAS A TRAINED ACTRESS. I THOUGHT MAYBE SHE'D AD-LIB?

KEATON WAS ONLY SUPPOSED TO BE IN THE FIFTH GRADE BUT WE DECIDED TO MAKE ONE OF THE KIDS A DRUG DEALER. HE WAS ONLY NINE. SO CUTE.

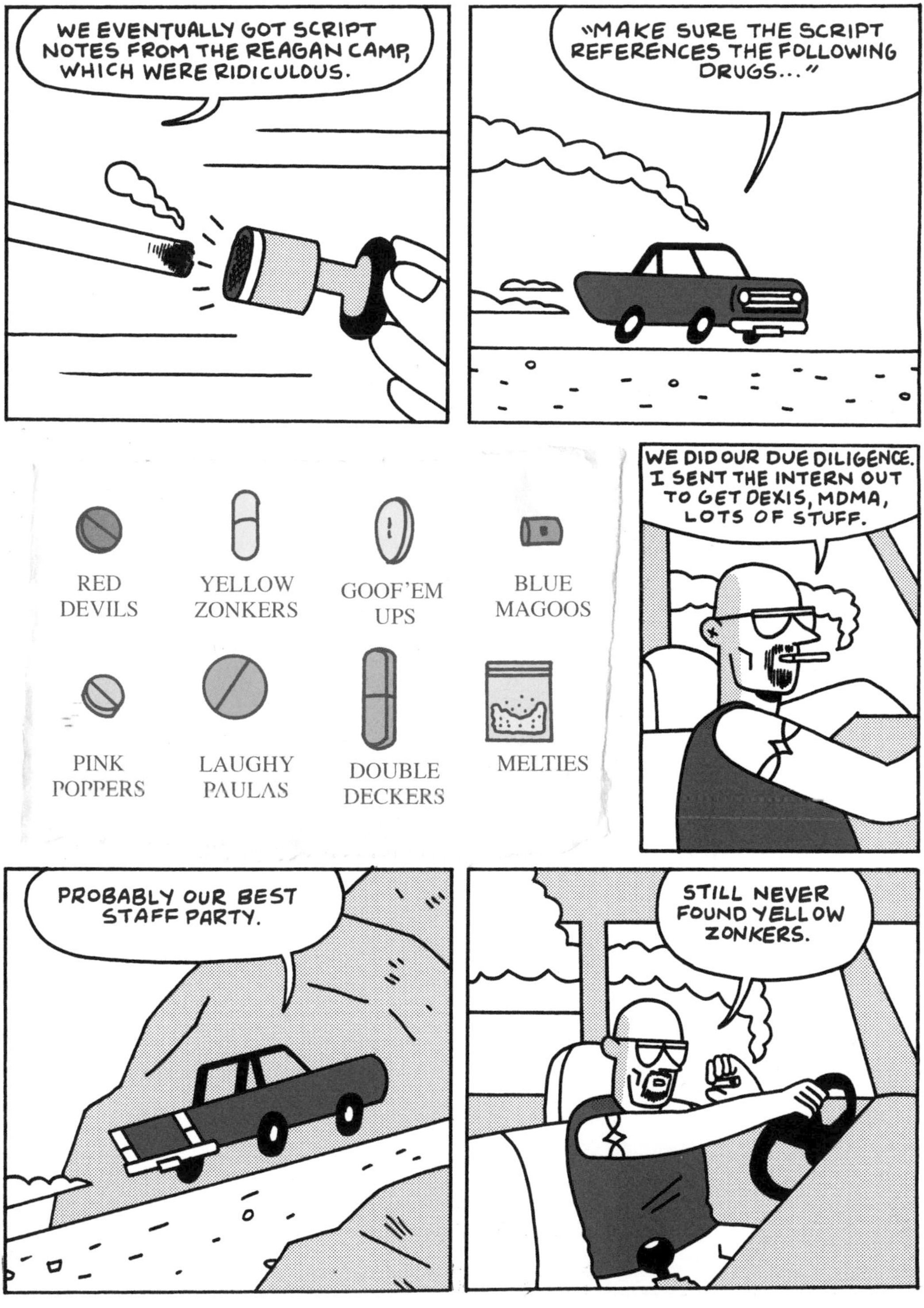
WE EVENTUALLY GOT SCRIPT NOTES FROM THE REAGAN CAMP, WHICH WERE RIDICULOUS.
"MAKE SURE THE SCRIPT REFERENCES THE FOLLOWING DRUGS..."
RED DEVILS
YELLOW ZONKERS
GOOF'EM UPS
BLUE MAGOOS
PINK POPPERS
LAUGHY PAULAS
DOUBLE DECKERS
MELTIES
WE DID OUR DUE DILIGENCE. I SENT THE INTERN OUT TO GET DEXIS, MDMA, LOTS OF STUFF.
PROBABLY OUR BEST STAFF PARTY.
STILL NEVER FOUND YELLOW ZONKERS.

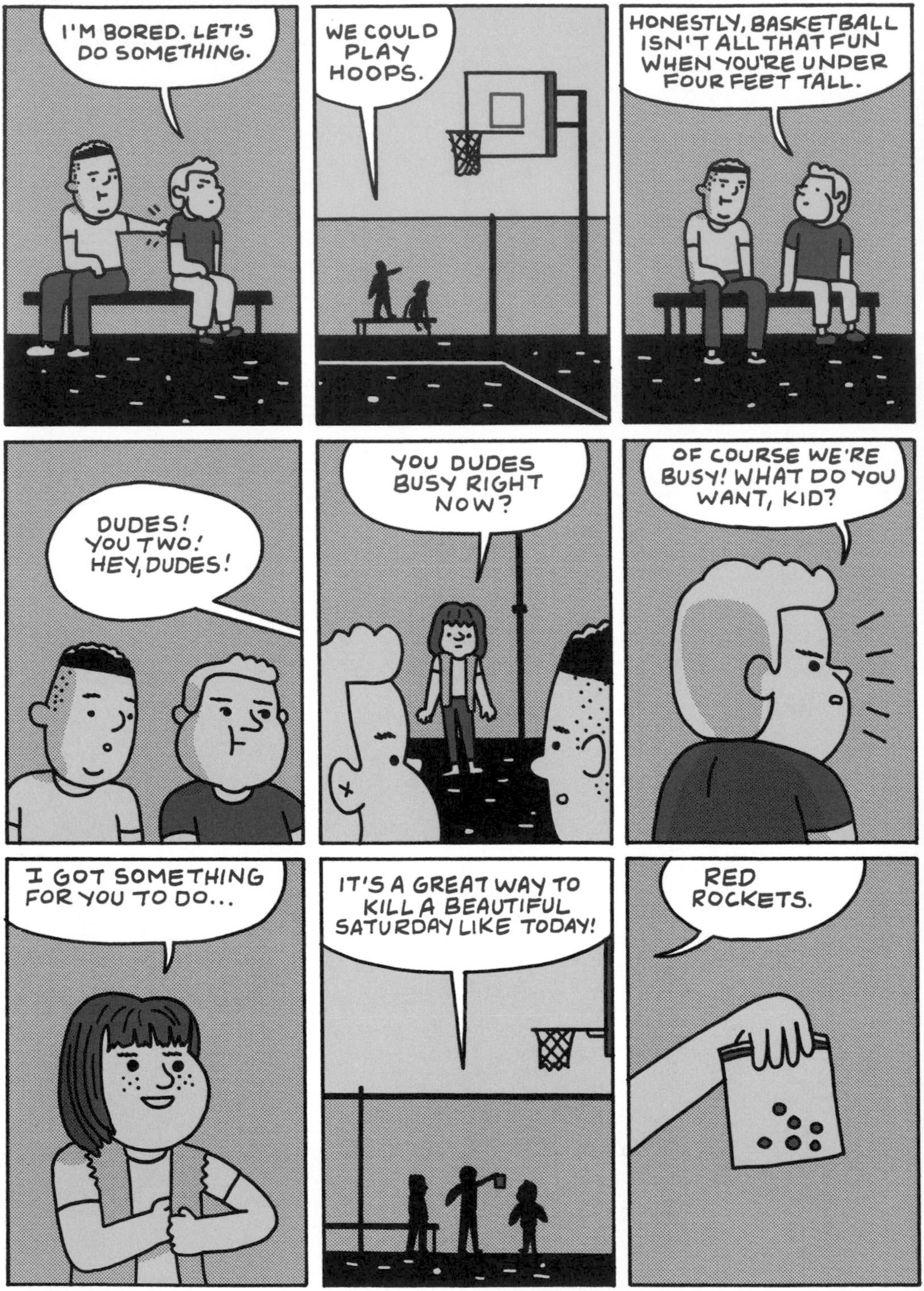
I'M BORED. LET'S DO SOMETHING.
WE COULD PLAY HOOPS.
HONESTLY, BASKETBALL ISN'T ALL THAT FUN WHEN YOU'RE UNDER FOUR FEET TALL.
DUDES! YOU TWO! HEY, DUDES!
YOU DUDES BUSY RIGHT NOW?
OF COURSE WE'RE BUSY! WHAT DO YOU WANT, KID?
I GOT SOMETHING FOR YOU TO DO...
IT'S A GREAT WAY TO KILL A BEAUTIFUL SATURDAY LIKE TODAY!
RED ROCKETS.

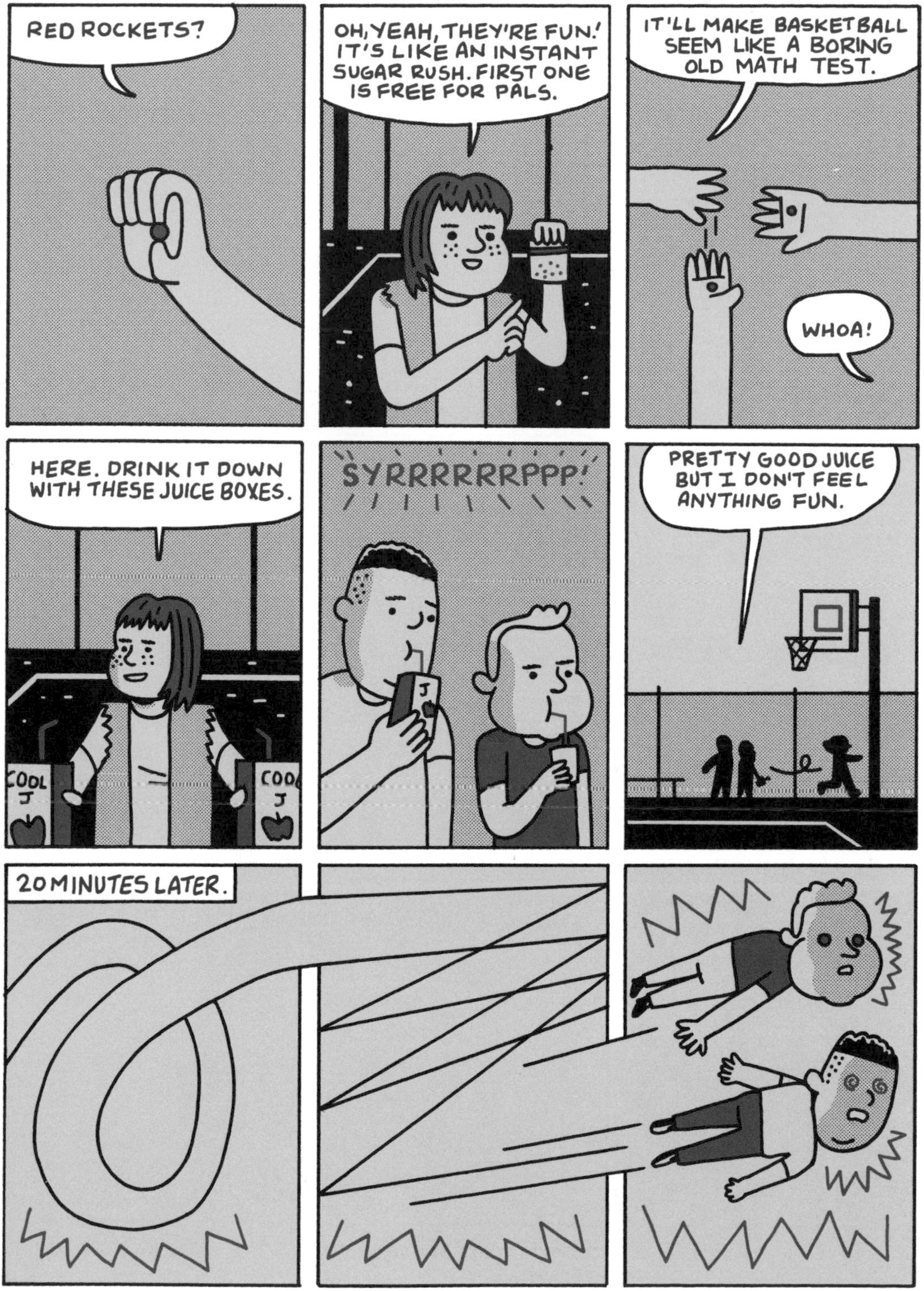
RED ROCKETS?
OH, YEAH, THEY'RE FUN! IT'S LIKE AN INSTANT SUGAR RUSH. FIRST ONE IS FREE FOR PALS.
IT'LL MAKE BASKETBALL SEEM LIKE A BORING OLD MATH TEST.
WHOA!
HERE. DRINK IT DOWN WITH THESE JUICE BOXES.
COOL J
COOL J
SYRRRRRRPPP!
J
PRETTY GOOD JUICE BUT I DON'T FEEL ANYTHING FUN.
20 MINUTES LATER.

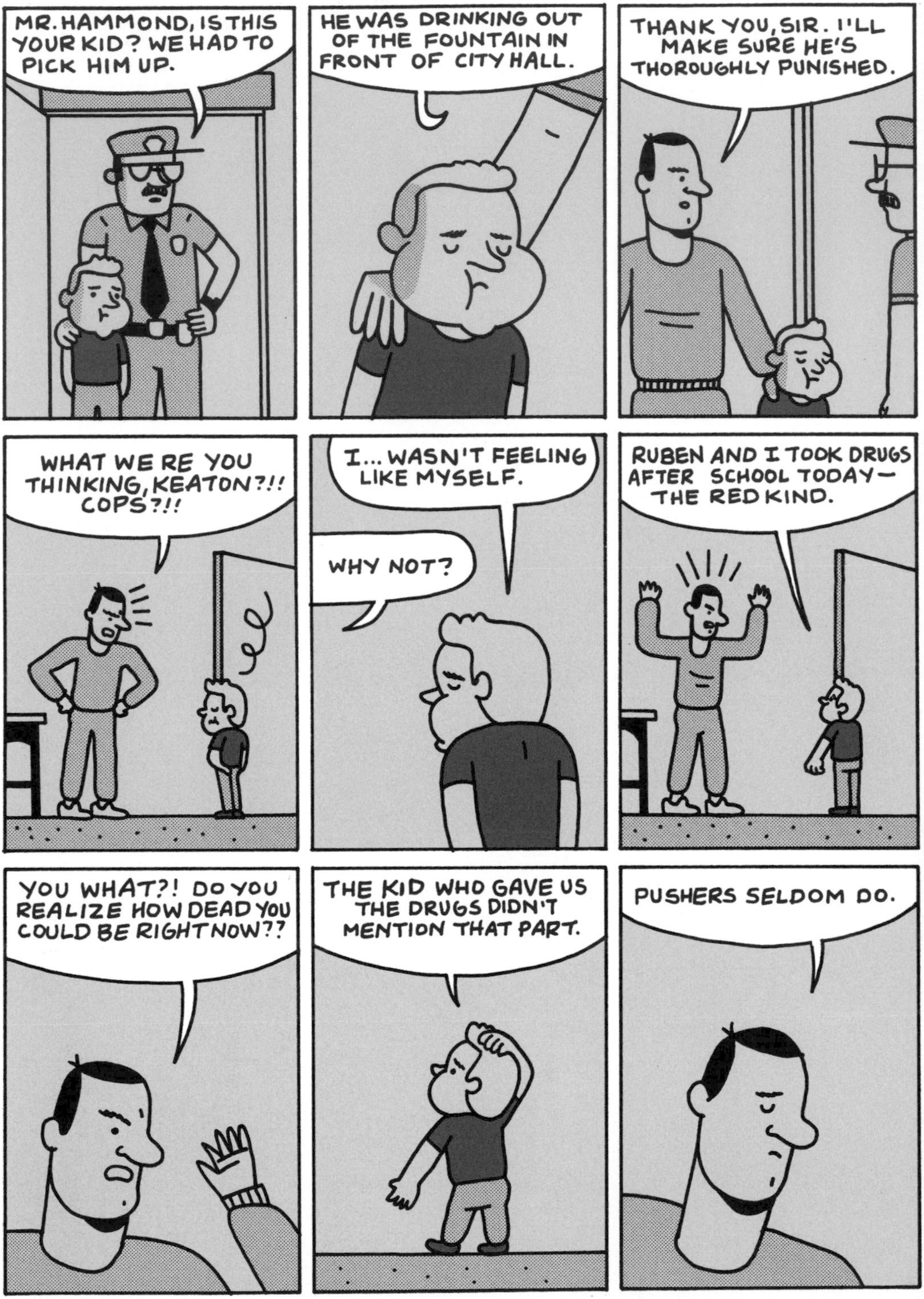
MR. HAMMOND, IS THIS YOUR KID? WE HAD TO PICK HIM UP.
HE WAS DRINKING OUT OF THE FOUNTAIN IN FRONT OF CITY HALL.
THANK YOU, SIR. I'LL MAKE SURE HE'S THOROUGHLY PUNISHED.
WHAT WERE YOU THINKING, KEATON?!! COPS?!!
I... WASN'T FEELING LIKE MYSELF.
WHY NOT?
RUBEN AND I TOOK DRUGS AFTER SCHOOL TODAY— THE RED KIND.
YOU WHAT?! DO YOU REALIZE HOW DEAD YOU COULD BE RIGHT NOW??
THE KID WHO GAVE US THE DRUGS DIDN'T MENTION THAT PART.
PUSHERS SELDOM DO.

YES, MR. TERRA, I'M FURIOUS, TOO. YES, I WILL BE PUNISHING KEATON HEAVILY.

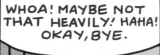

WHOA! MAYBE NOT THAT HEAVILY! HAHA! OKAY, BYE.

YOU'RE LUCKY I'M NOT RUBEN'S FATHER.

DAD, DO I HAVE TO GO TO SCHOOL TOMORROW? I DON'T FEEL WELL.

OH, YOU'RE GOING!! I DON'T CARE IF YOU LOSE YOUR LUNCH!

I HOPE I DON'T. IT'S CHICKEN NUGGETS TOMORROW!!

GO TO YOUR ROOM! YOU NEED TO THINK ABOUT WHAT YOU'VE DONE.

I'M NEVER HANGING OUT AT THE PARK AGAIN. I'M TOO CUTE TO DIE!!

HELLO, PETE? I'M CALLING IN MY FAVOR.

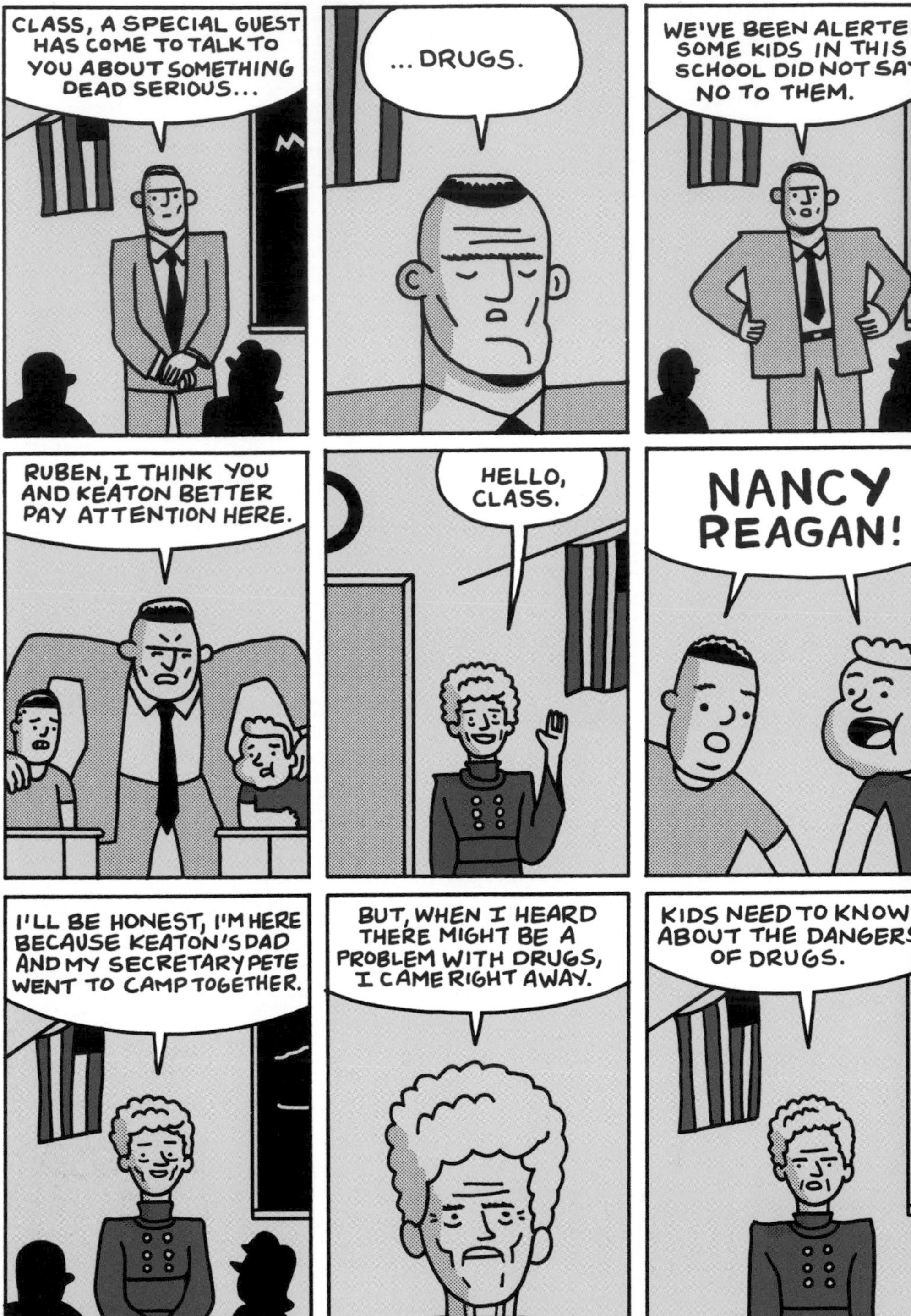
CLASS, A SPECIAL GUEST HAS COME TO TALK TO YOU ABOUT SOMETHING DEAD SERIOUS...
... DRUGS.
WE'VE BEEN ALERTED SOME KIDS IN THIS SCHOOL DID NOT SAY NO TO THEM.
RUBEN, I THINK YOU AND KEATON BETTER PAY ATTENTION HERE.
HELLO, CLASS.
NANCY REAGAN!
I'LL BE HONEST, I'M HERE BECAUSE KEATON'S DAD AND MY SECRETARY PETE WENT TO CAMP TOGETHER.
BUT, WHEN I HEARD THERE MIGHT BE A PROBLEM WITH DRUGS, I CAME RIGHT AWAY.
KIDS NEED TO KNOW ABOUT THE DANGERS OF DRUGS.

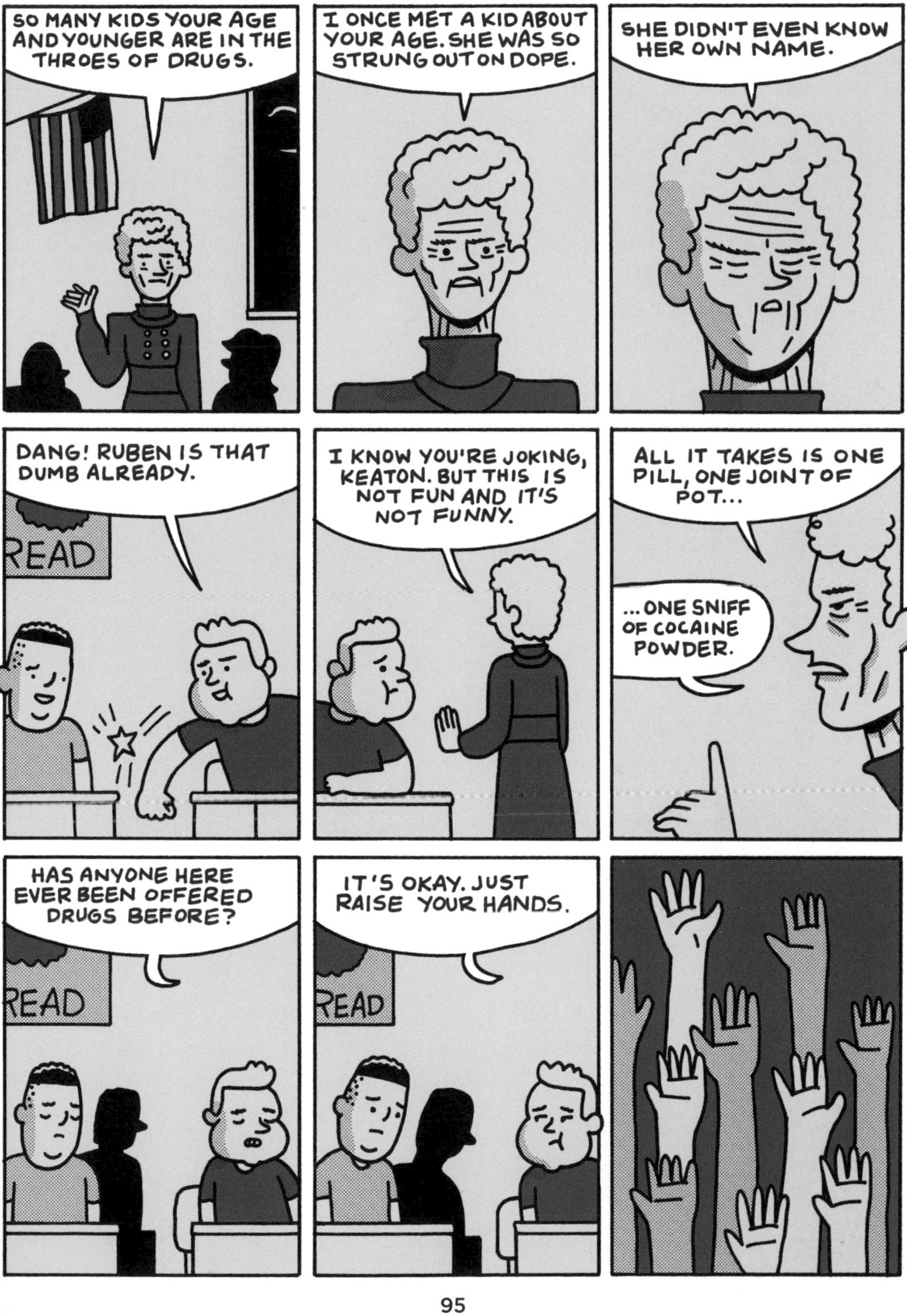
SO MANY KIDS YOUR AGE AND YOUNGER ARE IN THE THROES OF DRUGS.
I ONCE MET A KID ABOUT YOUR AGE. SHE WAS SO STRUNG OUT ON DOPE.
SHE DIDN'T EVEN KNOW HER OWN NAME.
DANG! RUBEN IS THAT DUMB ALREADY.
READ
I KNOW YOU'RE JOKING, KEATON. BUT THIS IS NOT FUN AND IT'S NOT FUNNY.
ALL IT TAKES IS ONE PILL, ONE JOINT OF POT...
...ONE SNIFF OF COCAINE POWDER.
HAS ANYONE HERE EVER BEEN OFFERED DRUGS BEFORE?
READ
IT'S OKAY. JUST RAISE YOUR HANDS.
READ

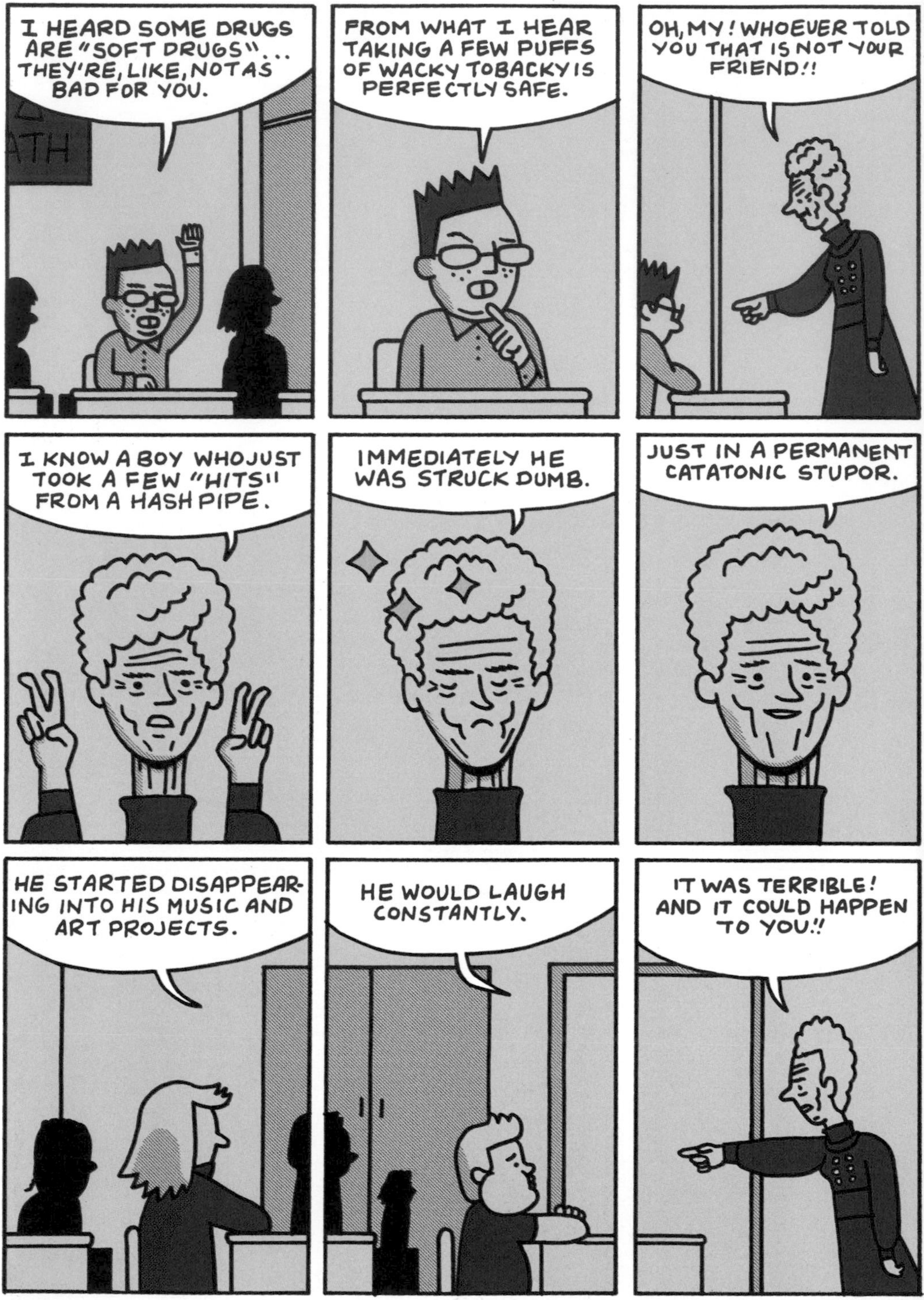
I HEARD SOME DRUGS ARE "SOFT DRUGS"... THEY'RE, LIKE, NOT AS BAD FOR YOU.
ATH
FROM WHAT I HEAR TAKING A FEW PUFFS OF WACKY TOBACKY IS PERFECTLY SAFE.
OH, MY! WHOEVER TOLD YOU THAT IS NOT YOUR FRIEND!!
I KNOW A BOY WHO JUST TOOK A FEW "HITS" FROM A HASH PIPE.
IMMEDIATELY HE WAS STRUCK DUMB.
JUST IN A PERMANENT CATATONIC STUPOR.
HE STARTED DISAPPEARING INTO HIS MUSIC AND ART PROJECTS.
HE WOULD LAUGH CONSTANTLY.
IT WAS TERRIBLE! AND IT COULD HAPPEN TO YOU!!

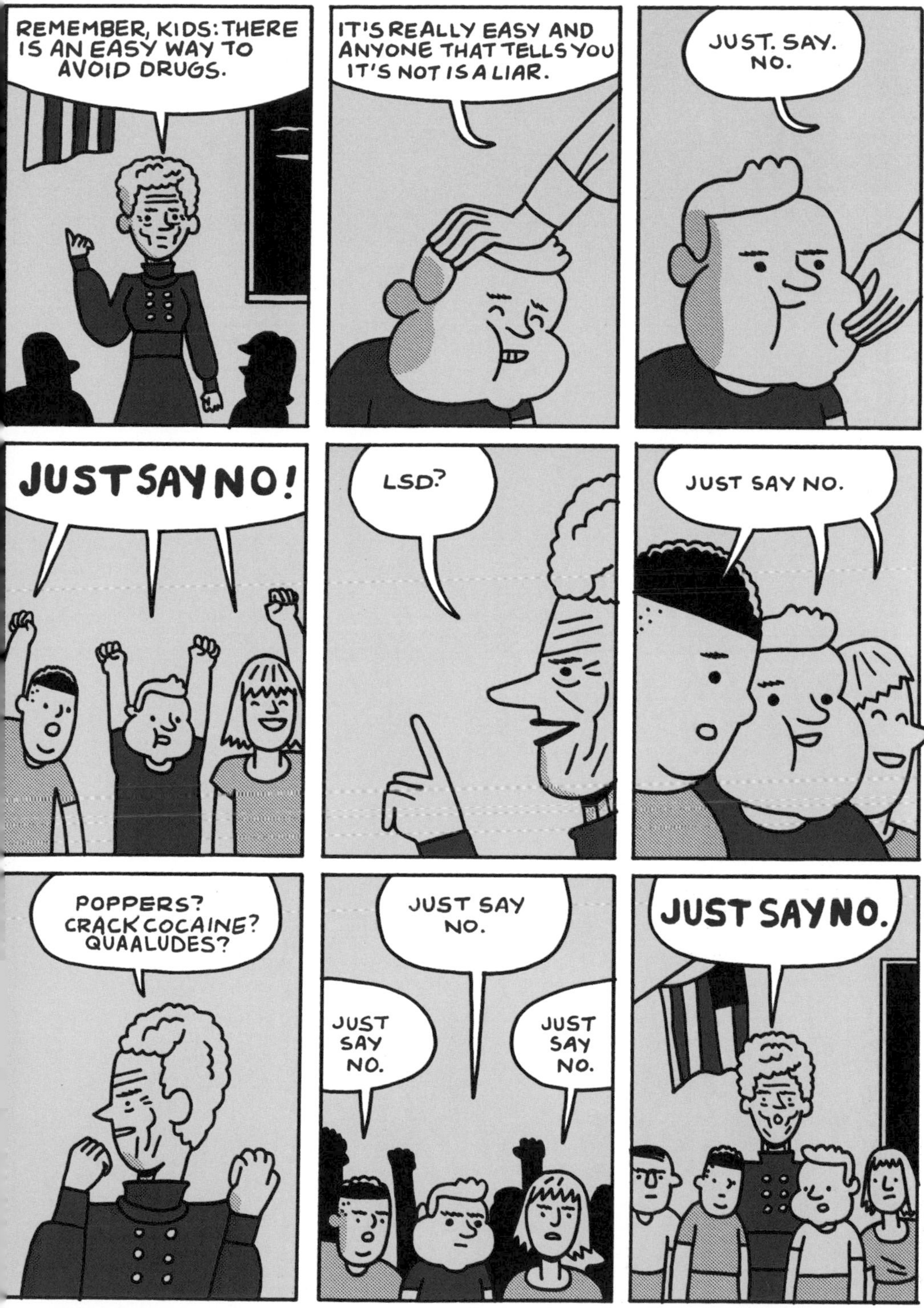
REMEMBER, KIDS: THERE IS AN EASY WAY TO AVOID DRUGS.
IT'S REALLY EASY AND ANYONE THAT TELLS YOU IT'S NOT IS A LIAR.
JUST. SAY. NO.
JUST SAY NO!
LSD?
JUST SAY NO.
POPPERS? CRACK COCAINE? QUAALUDES?
JUST SAY NO.
JUST SAY NO.
JUST SAY NO.
JUST SAY NO.

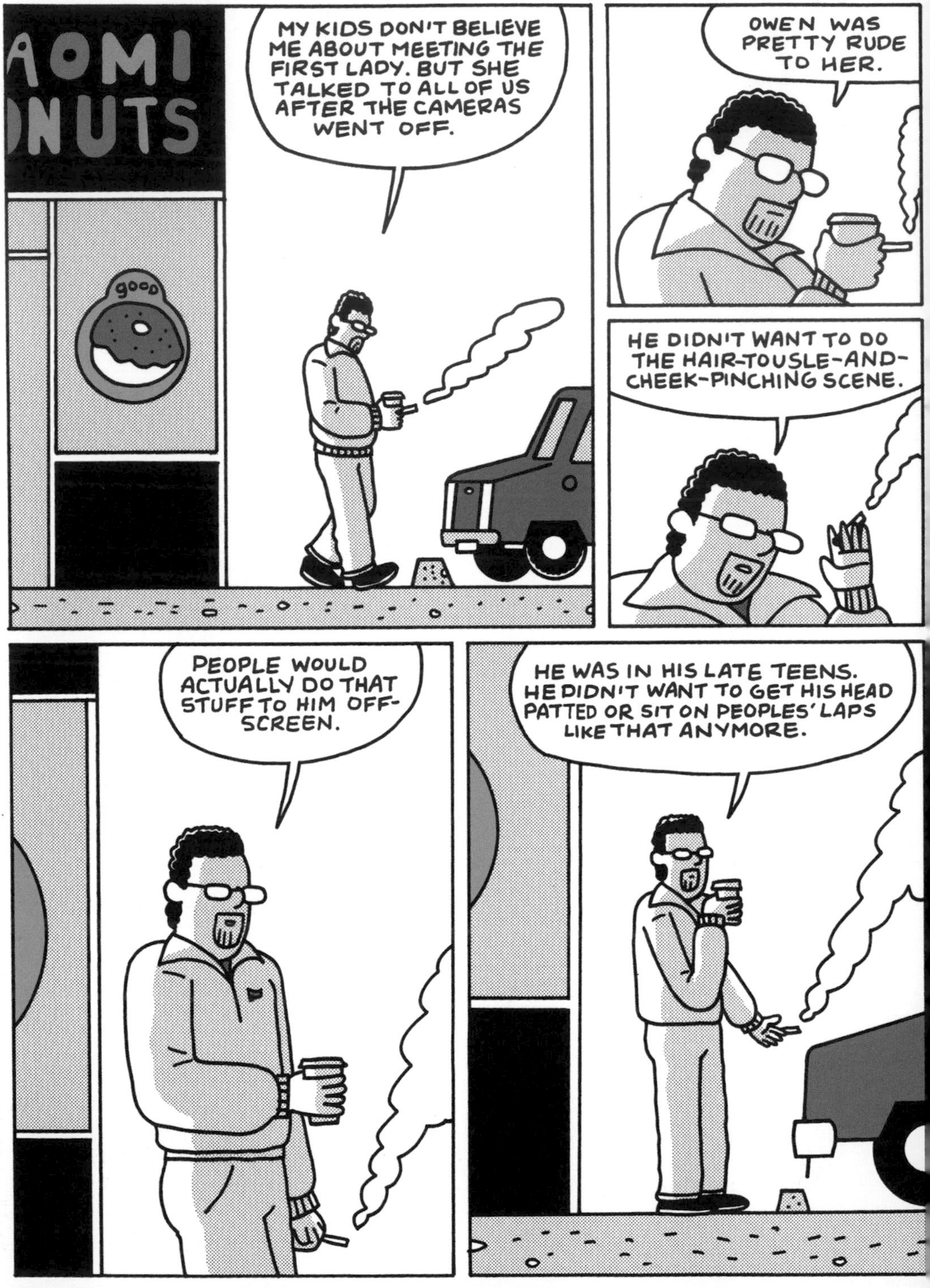
AOMI
NUTS
GOOD
MY KIDS DON'T BELIEVE ME ABOUT MEETING THE FIRST LADY. BUT SHE TALKED TO ALL OF US AFTER THE CAMERAS WENT OFF.
OWEN WAS PRETTY RUDE TO HER.
HE DIDN'T WANT TO DO THE HAIR-TOUSLE-AND-CHEEK-PINCHING SCENE.
PEOPLE WOULD ACTUALLY DO THAT STUFF TO HIM OFF-SCREEN.
HE WAS IN HIS LATE TEENS. HE DIDN'T WANT TO GET HIS HEAD PATTED OR SIT ON PEOPLES' LAPS LIKE THAT ANYMORE.

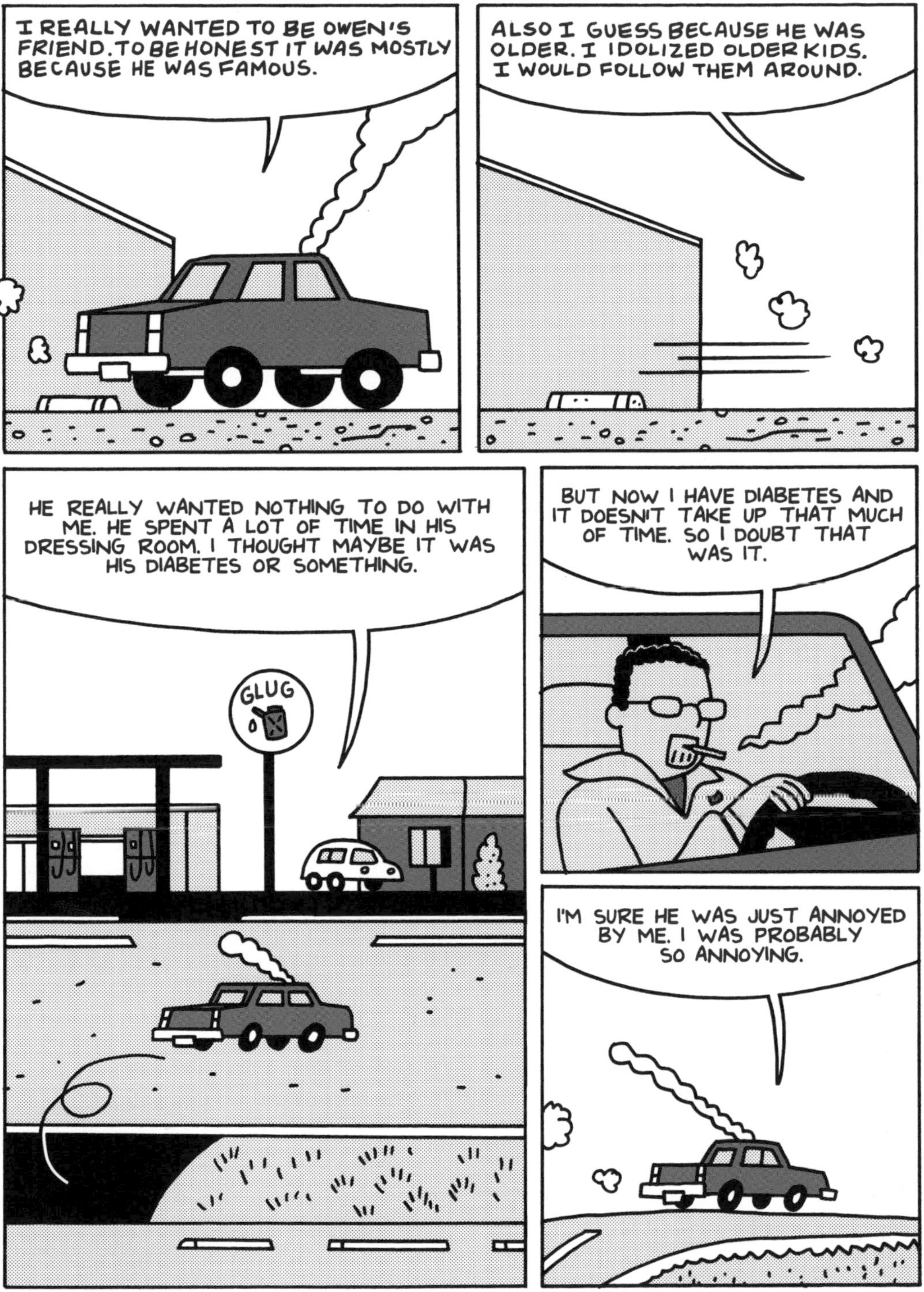
I REALLY WANTED TO BE OWEN'S FRIEND. TO BE HONEST IT WAS MOSTLY BECAUSE HE WAS FAMOUS.
ALSO I GUESS BECAUSE HE WAS OLDER. I IDOLIZED OLDER KIDS. I WOULD FOLLOW THEM AROUND.
HE REALLY WANTED NOTHING TO DO WITH ME. HE SPENT A LOT OF TIME IN HIS DRESSING ROOM. I THOUGHT MAYBE IT WAS HIS DIABETES OR SOMETHING.
GLUG
BUT NOW I HAVE DIABETES AND IT DOESN'T TAKE UP THAT MUCH OF TIME. SO I DOUBT THAT WAS IT.
I'M SURE HE WAS JUST ANNOYED BY ME. I WAS PROBABLY SO ANNOYING.

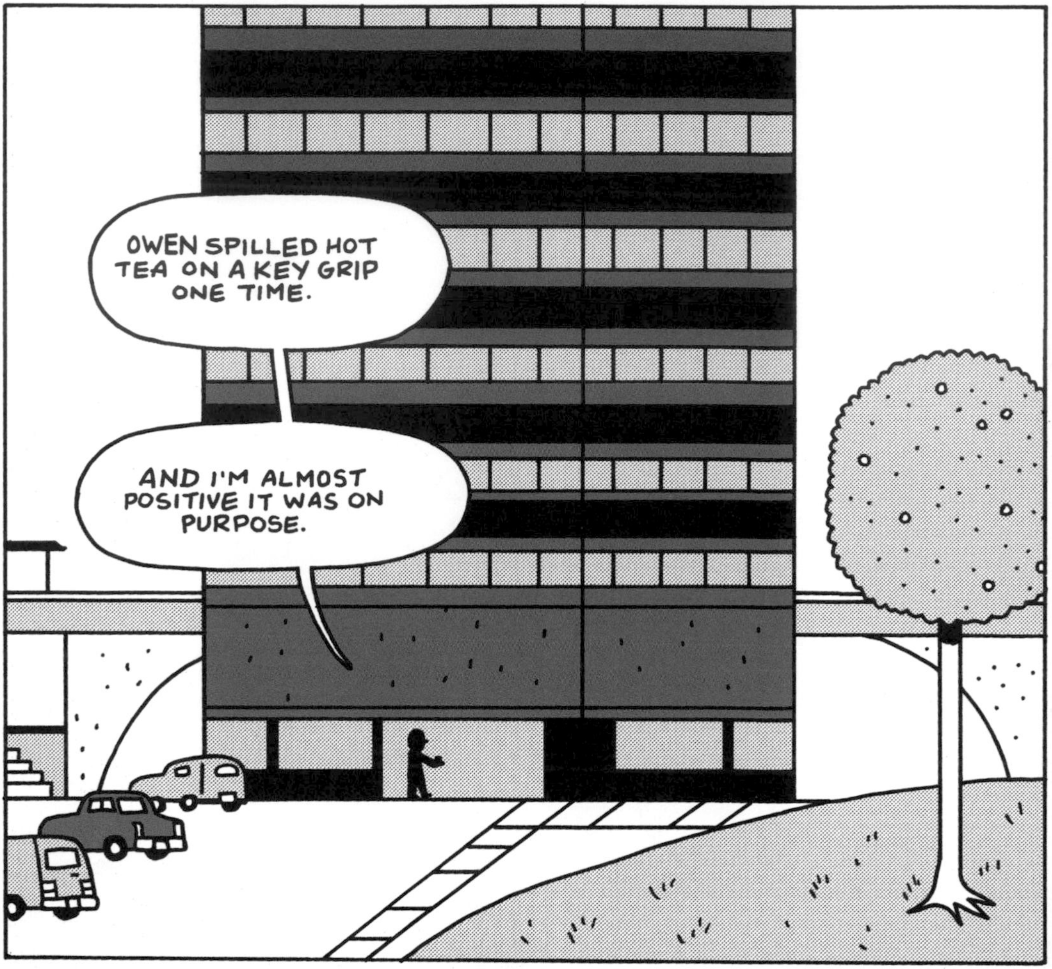
OWEN SPILLED HOT TEA ON A KEY GRIP ONE TIME.
AND I'M ALMOST POSITIVE IT WAS ON PURPOSE.

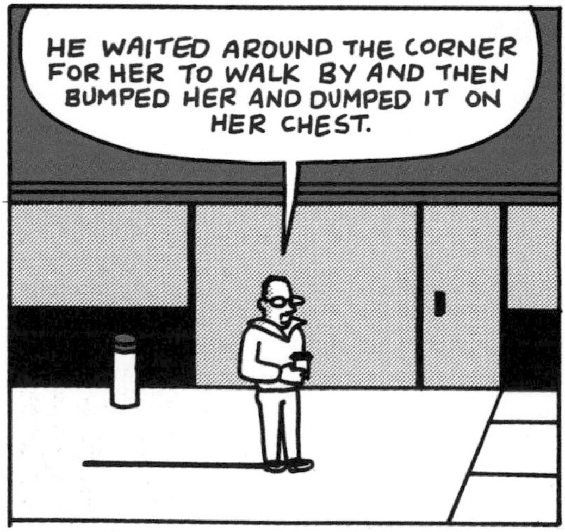
HE WAITED AROUND THE CORNER FOR HER TO WALK BY AND THEN BUMPED HER AND DUMPED IT ON HER CHEST.

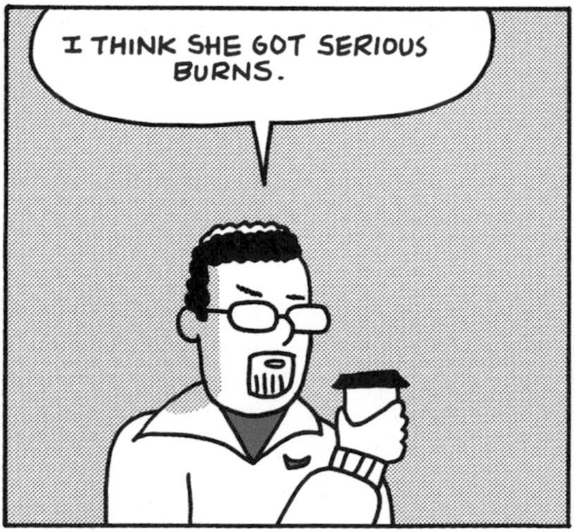
I THINK SHE GOT SERIOUS BURNS.

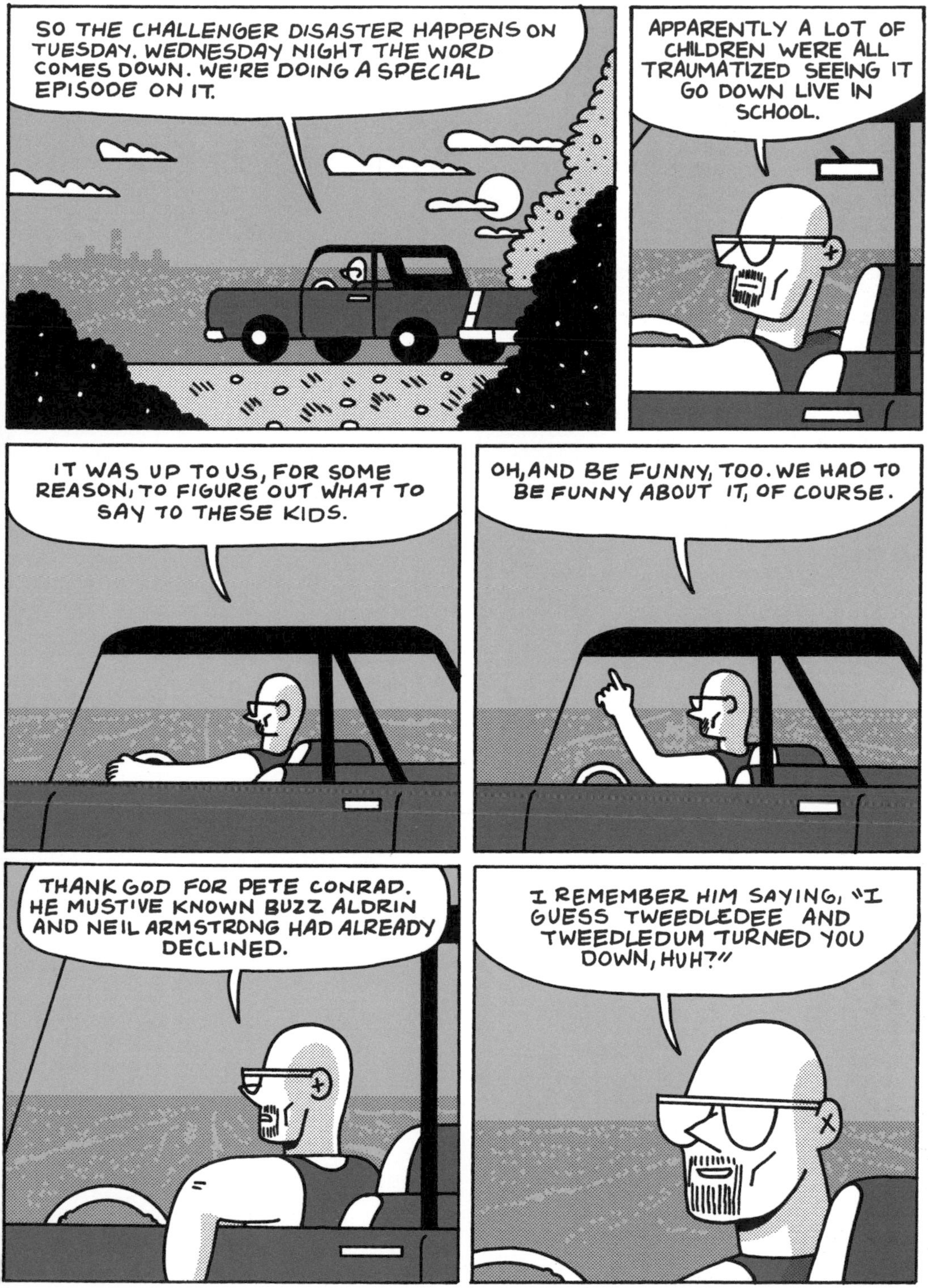
SO THE CHALLENGER DISASTER HAPPENS ON TUESDAY. WEDNESDAY NIGHT THE WORD COMES DOWN. WE'RE DOING A SPECIAL EPISODE ON IT.
APPARENTLY A LOT OF CHILDREN WERE ALL TRAUMATIZED SEEING IT GO DOWN LIVE IN SCHOOL.
IT WAS UP TO US, FOR SOME REASON, TO FIGURE OUT WHAT TO SAY TO THESE KIDS.
OH, AND BE FUNNY, TOO. WE HAD TO BE FUNNY ABOUT IT, OF COURSE.
THANK GOD FOR PETE CONRAD. HE MUST'VE KNOWN BUZZ ALDRIN AND NEIL ARMSTRONG HAD ALREADY DECLINED.
I REMEMBER HIM SAYING, "I GUESS TWEEDLEDEE AND TWEEDLEDUM TURNED YOU DOWN, HUH?"

THIS WAS ONE OF THOSE OCCASIONS WHERE I THANK FUCKIN' GOD WE HAD OWEN. HE WAS SO LIKABLE AND TELEGENIC.

HE REALLY MADE US ALL LOOK GOOD. AFTER "EVERYONE'S FRIEND" I WORKED ON A BUNCH OF SHORT-LIVED FAMILY SITCOMS.

I GOT PAID A LOT MORE BECAUSE OF MY EXPERIENCE BUT THEY NEVER WENT MORE THAN A SEASON. THOSE KIDS COULD NOT SELL THE MATERIAL.

OWEN EUGENE WAS A UNIQUE TALENT. I WAS LUCKY TO EVEN GET A PIECE OF HIS GREATNESS.

REEER

IN 1986, RIGHT AFTER WRITING THE CHALLENGER EPISODE, I DROVE HOME IN MY MASERATI, STRIPPED BUTT-NAKED AND JUMPED INTO MY POOL IN THE SHAPE OF A GUITAR.

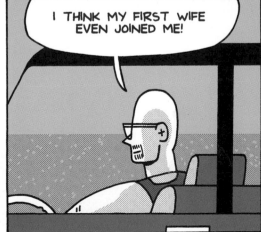

I THINK MY FIRST WIFE EVEN JOINED ME!

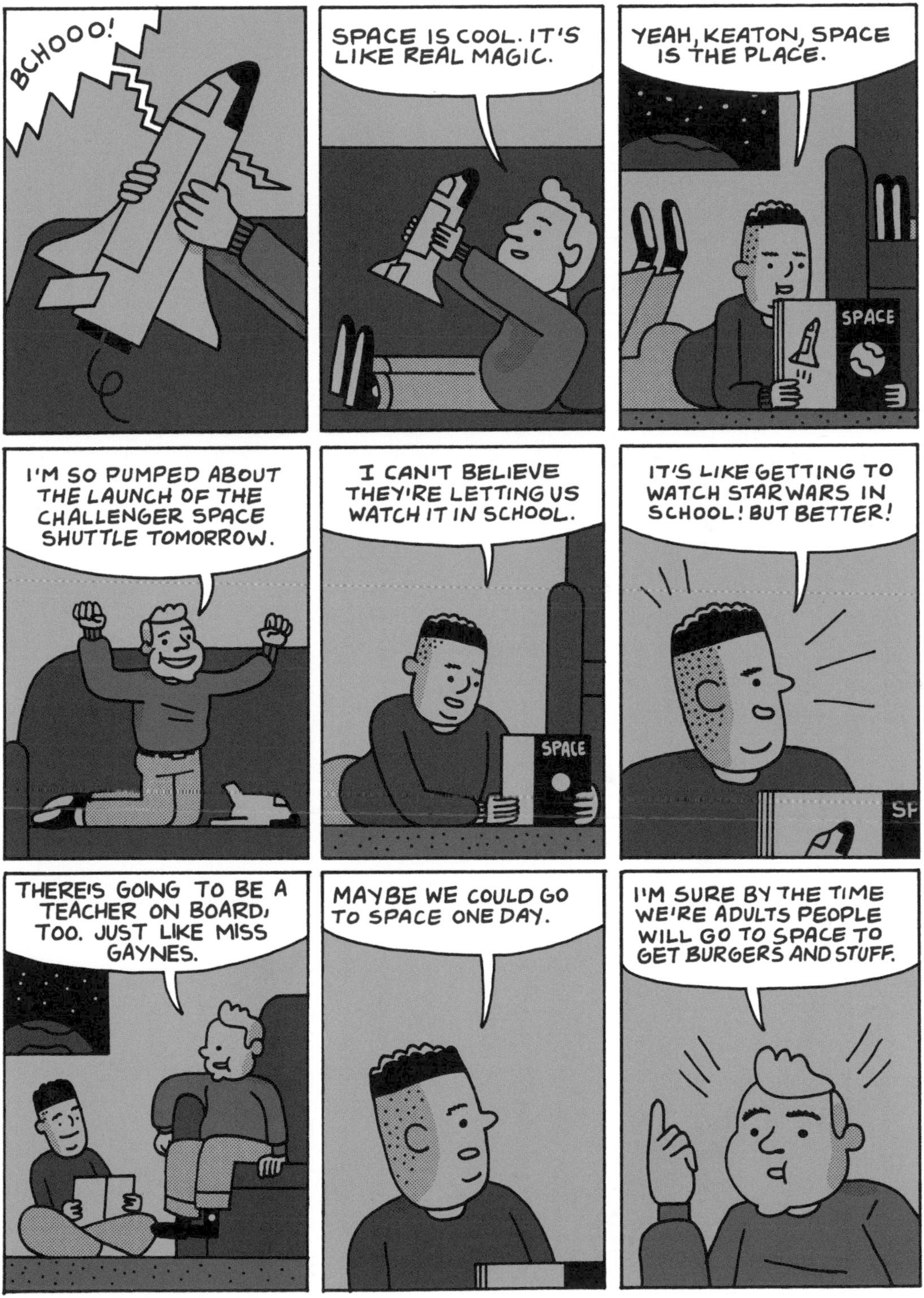
BCHOOO!
SPACE IS COOL. IT'S LIKE REAL MAGIC.
YEAH, KEATON, SPACE IS THE PLACE.
SPACE
I'M SO PUMPED ABOUT THE LAUNCH OF THE CHALLENGER SPACE SHUTTLE TOMORROW.
I CAN'T BELIEVE THEY'RE LETTING US WATCH IT IN SCHOOL.
SPACE
IT'S LIKE GETTING TO WATCH STAR WARS IN SCHOOL! BUT BETTER!
THERE'S GOING TO BE A TEACHER ON BOARD, TOO. JUST LIKE MISS GAYNES.
MAYBE WE COULD GO TO SPACE ONE DAY.
I'M SURE BY THE TIME WE'RE ADULTS PEOPLE WILL GO TO SPACE TO GET BURGERS AND STUFF.

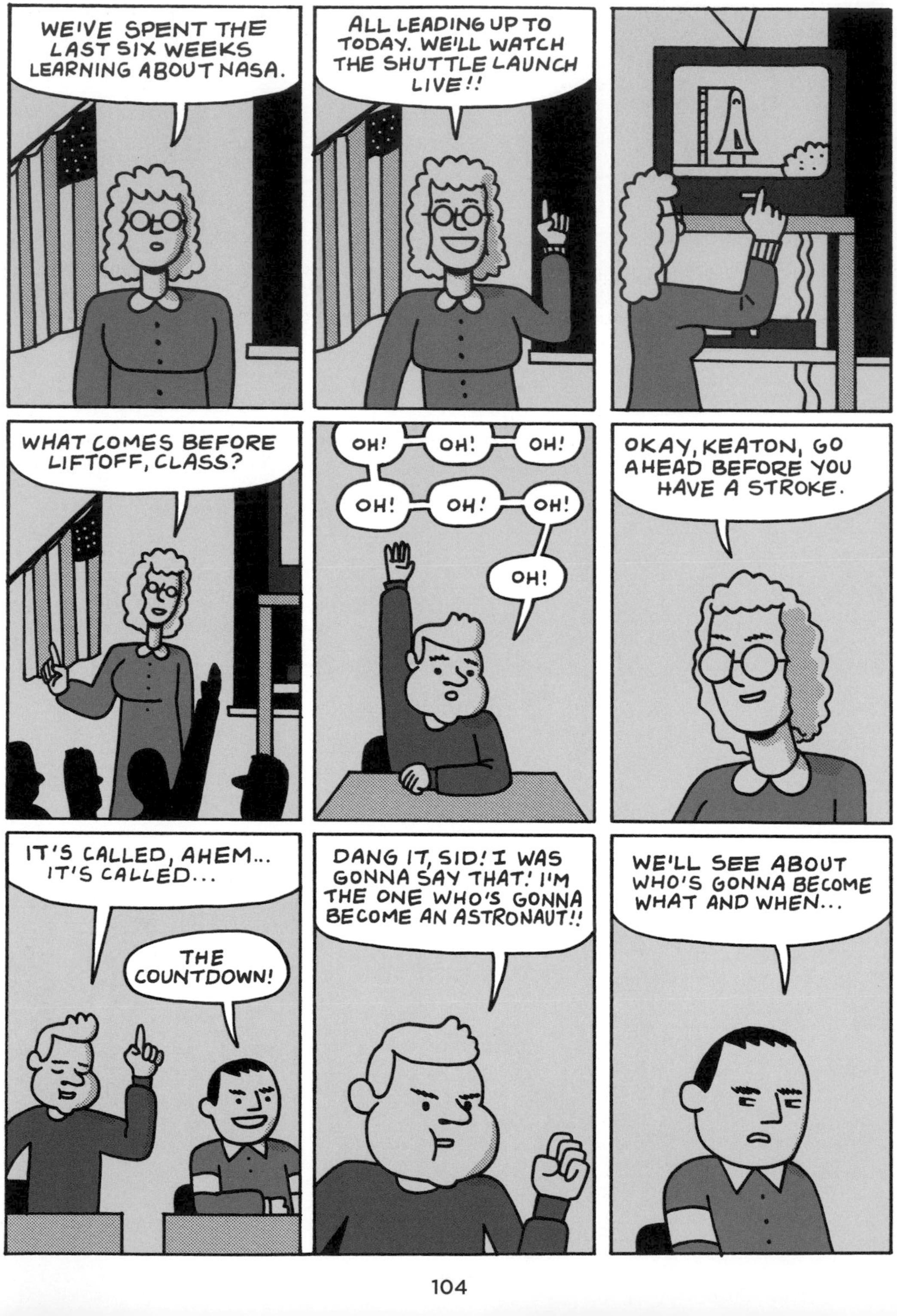
WE'VE SPENT THE LAST SIX WEEKS LEARNING ABOUT NASA.
ALL LEADING UP TO TODAY. WE'LL WATCH THE SHUTTLE LAUNCH LIVE!!
WHAT COMES BEFORE LIFTOFF, CLASS?
OH! OH! OH! OH! OH! OH! OH!
OKAY, KEATON, GO AHEAD BEFORE YOU HAVE A STROKE.
IT'S CALLED, AHEM... IT'S CALLED...
THE COUNTDOWN!
DANG IT, SID! I WAS GONNA SAY THAT! I'M THE ONE WHO'S GONNA BECOME AN ASTRONAUT!!
WE'LL SEE ABOUT WHO'S GONNA BECOME WHAT AND WHEN...

T-MINUS 22 SECONDS...

REMEMBER CHRISTA MCAULIFFE IS THE FIRST TEACHER IN SPACE!!

ESCAPE
READ

DOES THAT MEAN MISS GAYNES IS GOING TO SPACE?

NO, CAROL, BUT MAYBE YOU KIDS WILL.

THAT'S GONNA BE ME ONE DAY.

SHH... IT'S STARTING!

AND WE HAVE LIFTOFF!

WOW.

WHOA!

OH, NO!

NO, NO!

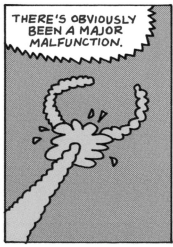

THERE'S OBVIOUSLY BEEN A MAJOR MALFUNCTION.

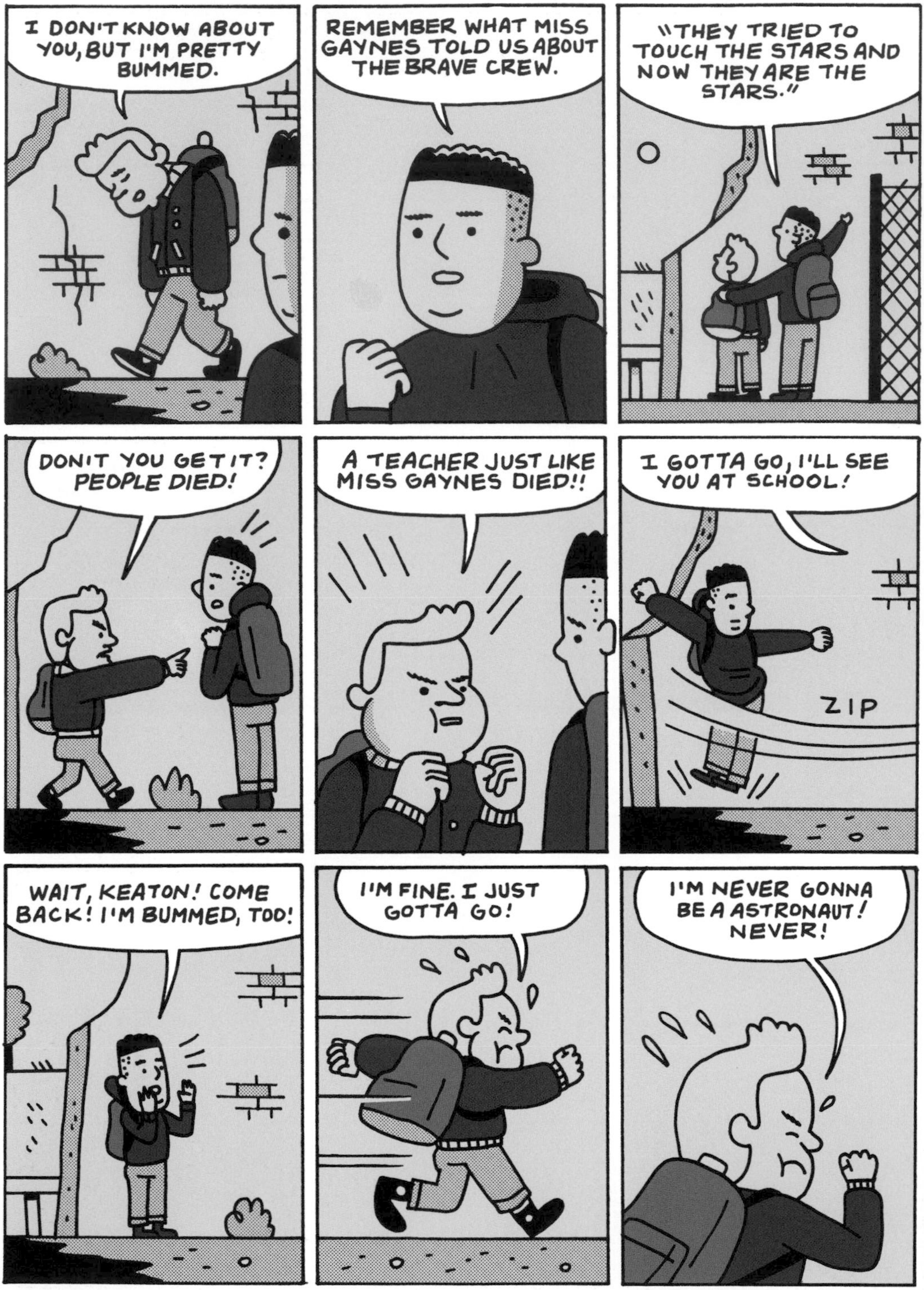
I DON'T KNOW ABOUT YOU, BUT I'M PRETTY BUMMED.
REMEMBER WHAT MISS GAYNES TOLD US ABOUT THE BRAVE CREW.
"THEY TRIED TO TOUCH THE STARS AND NOW THEY ARE THE STARS."
DON'T YOU GET IT? PEOPLE DIED!
A TEACHER JUST LIKE MISS GAYNES DIED!!
I GOTTA GO, I'LL SEE YOU AT SCHOOL!
ZIP
WAIT, KEATON! COME BACK! I'M BUMMED, TOO!
I'M FINE. I JUST GOTTA GO!
I'M NEVER GONNA BE A ASTRONAUT! NEVER!

SO I GUESS YOU'RE PRETTY UPSET ABOUT TODAY, HUH?

YEAH. REAL UPSET.

WHY'D THAT HAPPEN, DAD? WHY'D THE SHIP BLOW UP?

WELL, THEY SAID IT WAS THE O-RINGS OR SOMETHING.

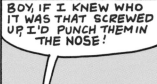

BOY, IF I KNEW WHO IT WAS THAT SCREWED UP, I'D PUNCH THEM IN THE NOSE!

IT'S JUST A FREAK ACCIDENT. NO ONE MEANT FOR THIS TO HAPPEN.

DAD, I THOUGHT SPACE WAS COOL AND FUN, BUT IT'S SCARY.

IT'S OKAY TO BE SCARED, KEATON. I'M SCARED, TOO.

BUT WE PUT ON OUR BRAVE FACES, RIGHT?

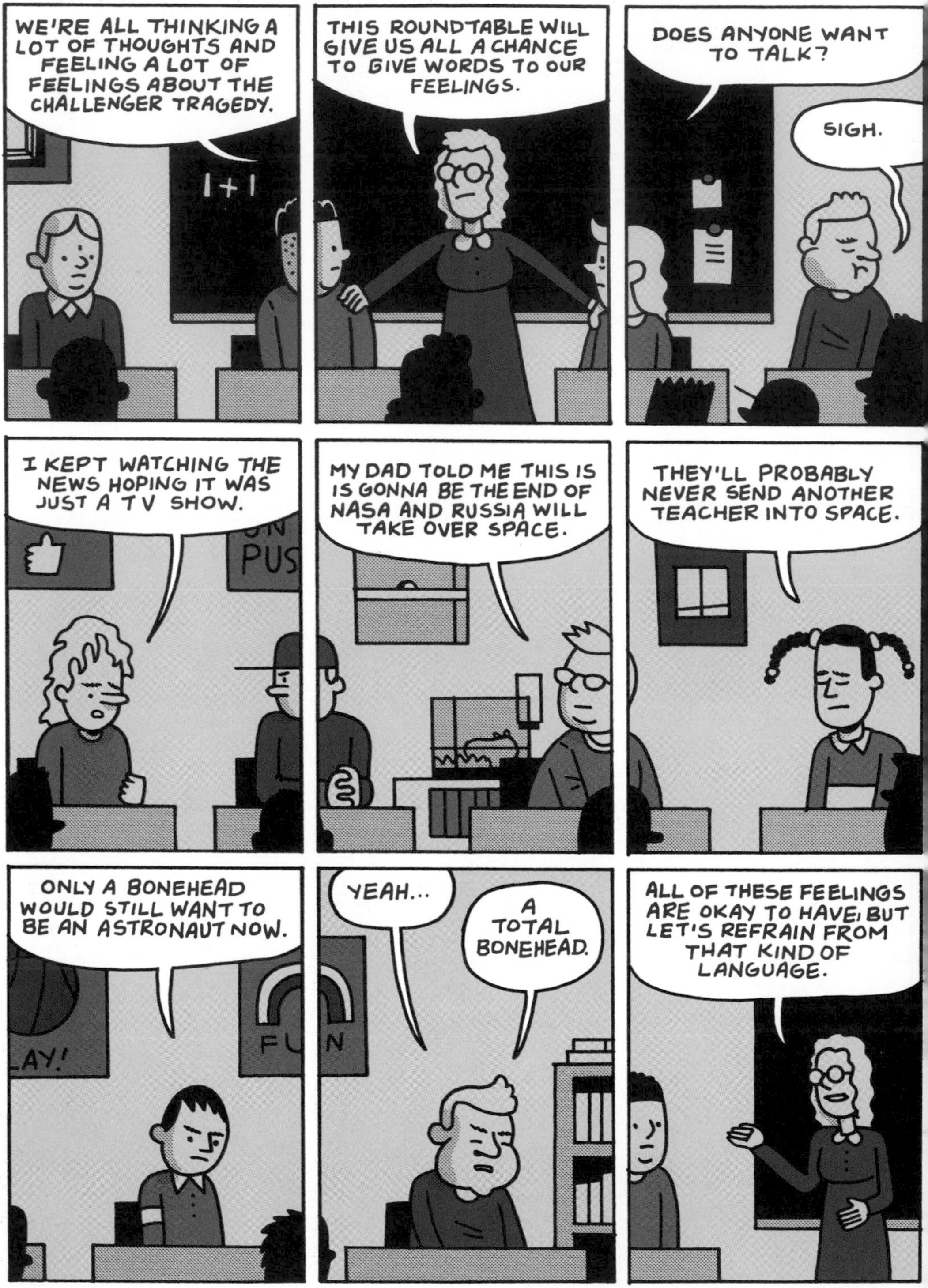
WE'RE ALL THINKING A LOT OF THOUGHTS AND FEELING A LOT OF FEELINGS ABOUT THE CHALLENGER TRAGEDY.
1+1
THIS ROUNDTABLE WILL GIVE US ALL A CHANCE TO GIVE WORDS TO OUR FEELINGS.
DOES ANYONE WANT TO TALK?
SIGH.
I KEPT WATCHING THE NEWS HOPING IT WAS JUST A TV SHOW.
PUS
MY DAD TOLD ME THIS IS IS GONNA BE THE END OF NASA AND RUSSIA WILL TAKE OVER SPACE.
THEY'LL PROBABLY NEVER SEND ANOTHER TEACHER INTO SPACE.
ONLY A BONEHEAD WOULD STILL WANT TO BE AN ASTRONAUT NOW.
AY!
FU N
YEAH...
A TOTAL BONEHEAD.
ALL OF THESE FEELINGS ARE OKAY TO HAVE; BUT LET'S REFRAIN FROM THAT KIND OF LANGUAGE.

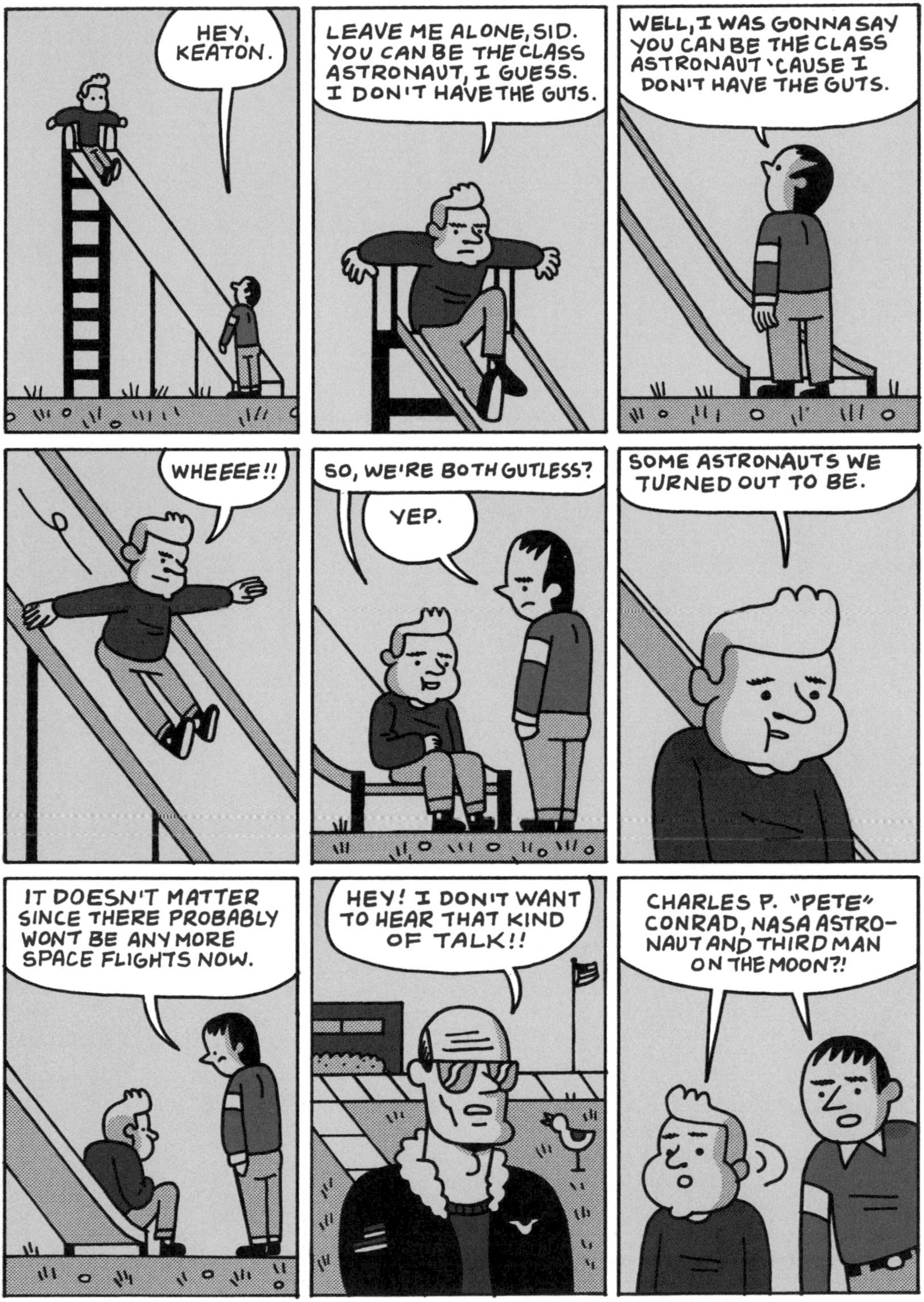
HEY, KEATON.
LEAVE ME ALONE, SID. YOU CAN BE THE CLASS ASTRONAUT, I GUESS. I DON'T HAVE THE GUTS.
WELL, I WAS GONNA SAY YOU CAN BE THE CLASS ASTRONAUT 'CAUSE I DON'T HAVE THE GUTS.
WHEEEE!!
SO, WE'RE BOTH GUTLESS?
YEP.
SOME ASTRONAUTS WE TURNED OUT TO BE.
IT DOESN'T MATTER SINCE THERE PROBABLY WON'T BE ANY MORE SPACE FLIGHTS NOW.
HEY! I DON'T WANT TO HEAR THAT KIND OF TALK!!
CHARLES P. "PETE" CONRAD, NASA ASTRONAUT AND THIRD MAN ON THE MOON?!

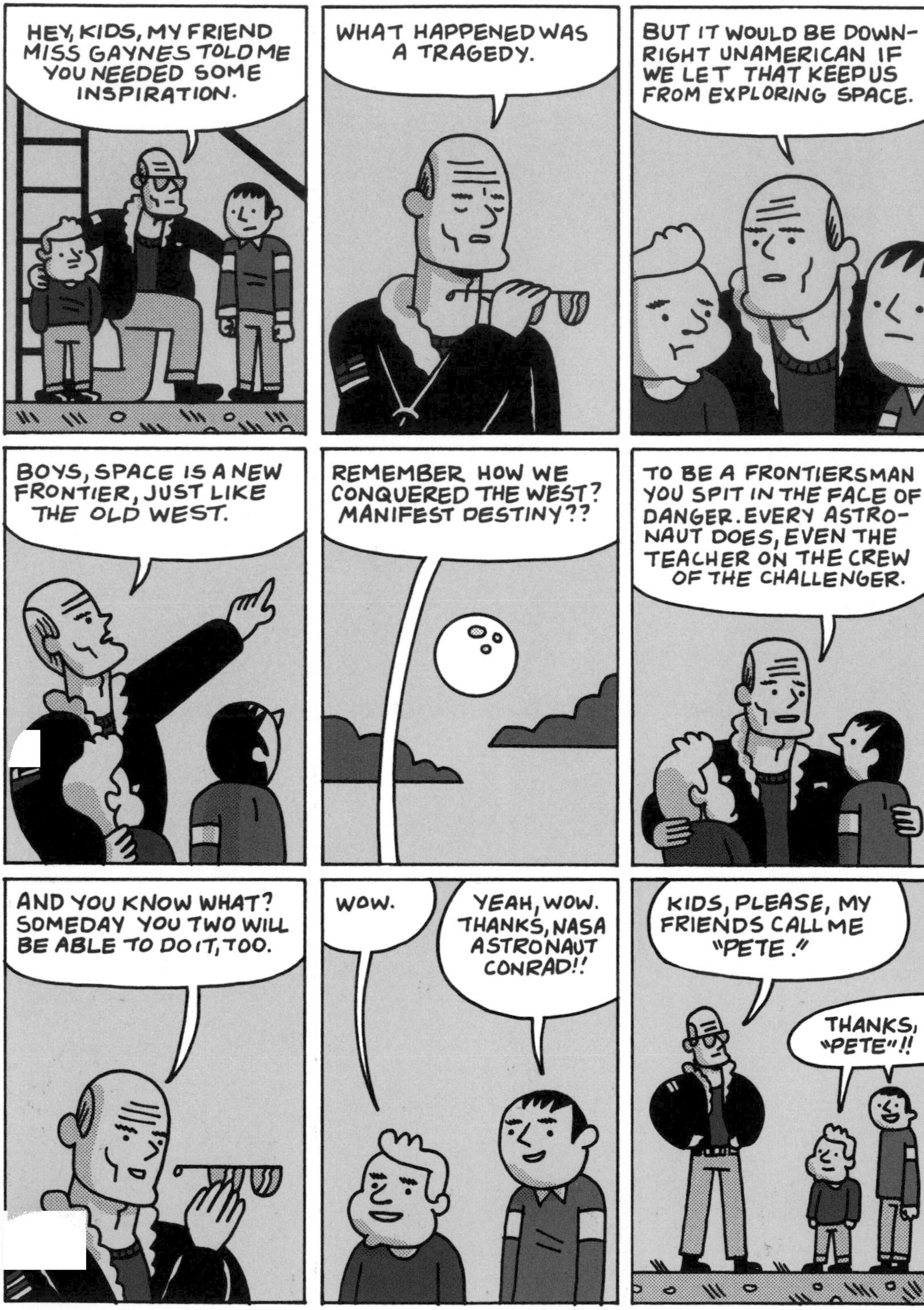
HEY, KIDS, MY FRIEND MISS GAYNES TOLD ME YOU NEEDED SOME INSPIRATION.
WHAT HAPPENED WAS A TRAGEDY.
BUT IT WOULD BE DOWN-RIGHT UNAMERICAN IF WE LET THAT KEEP US FROM EXPLORING SPACE.
BOYS, SPACE IS A NEW FRONTIER, JUST LIKE THE OLD WEST.
REMEMBER HOW WE CONQUERED THE WEST? MANIFEST DESTINY??
TO BE A FRONTIERSMAN YOU SPIT IN THE FACE OF DANGER. EVERY ASTRONAUT DOES, EVEN THE TEACHER ON THE CREW OF THE CHALLENGER.
AND YOU KNOW WHAT? SOMEDAY YOU TWO WILL BE ABLE TO DO IT, TOO.
WOW.
YEAH, WOW. THANKS, NASA ASTRONAUT CONRAD!!
KIDS, PLEASE, MY FRIENDS CALL ME "PETE."
THANKS, "PETE"!!

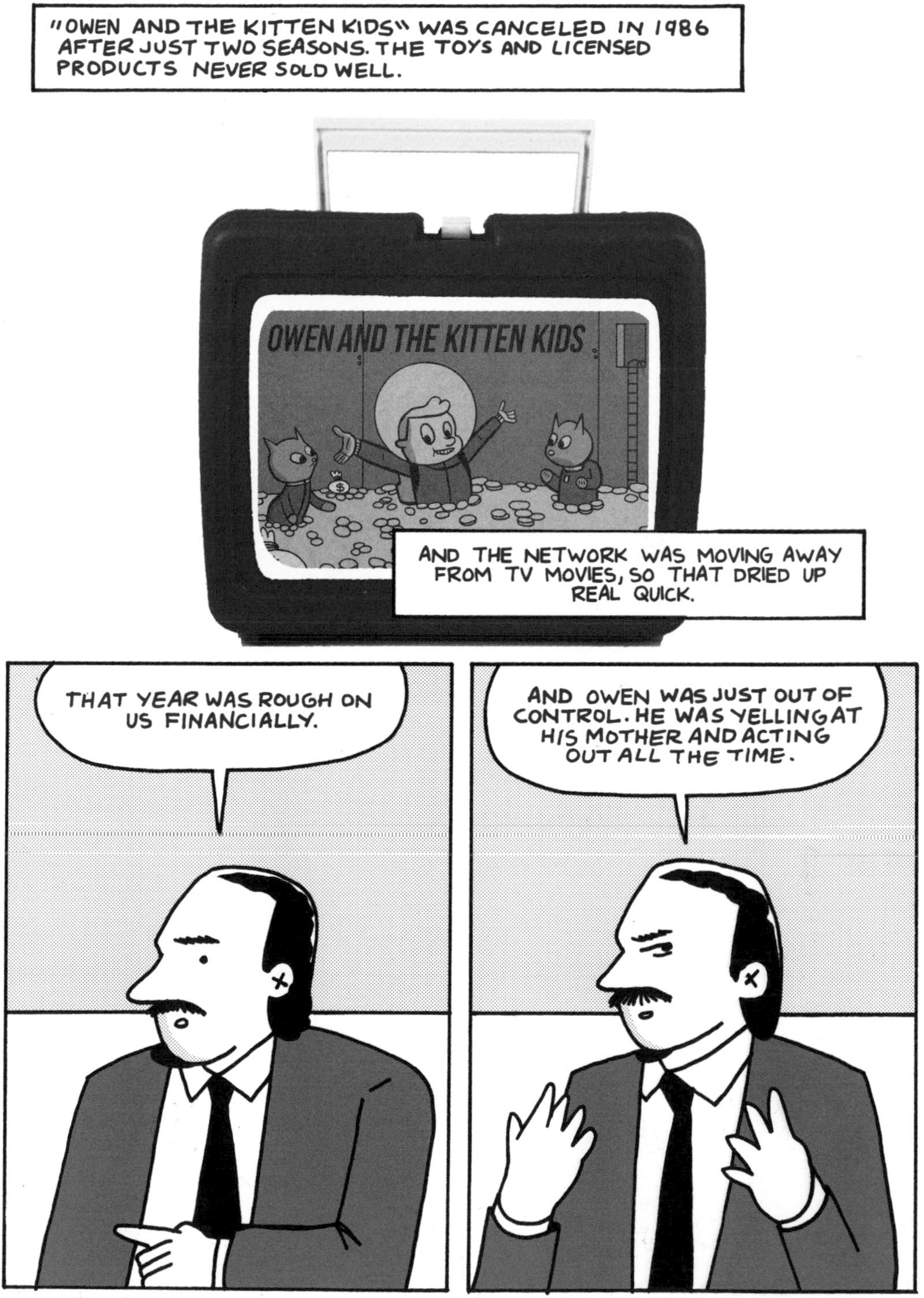
"OWEN AND THE KITTEN KIDS" WAS CANCELED IN 1986 AFTER JUST TWO SEASONS. THE TOYS AND LICENSED PRODUCTS NEVER SOLD WELL.
OWEN AND THE KITTEN KIDS
AND THE NETWORK WAS MOVING AWAY FROM TV MOVIES, SO THAT DRIED UP REAL QUICK.
THAT YEAR WAS ROUGH ON US FINANCIALLY.
AND OWEN WAS JUST OUT OF CONTROL. HE WAS YELLING AT HIS MOTHER AND ACTING OUT ALL THE TIME.

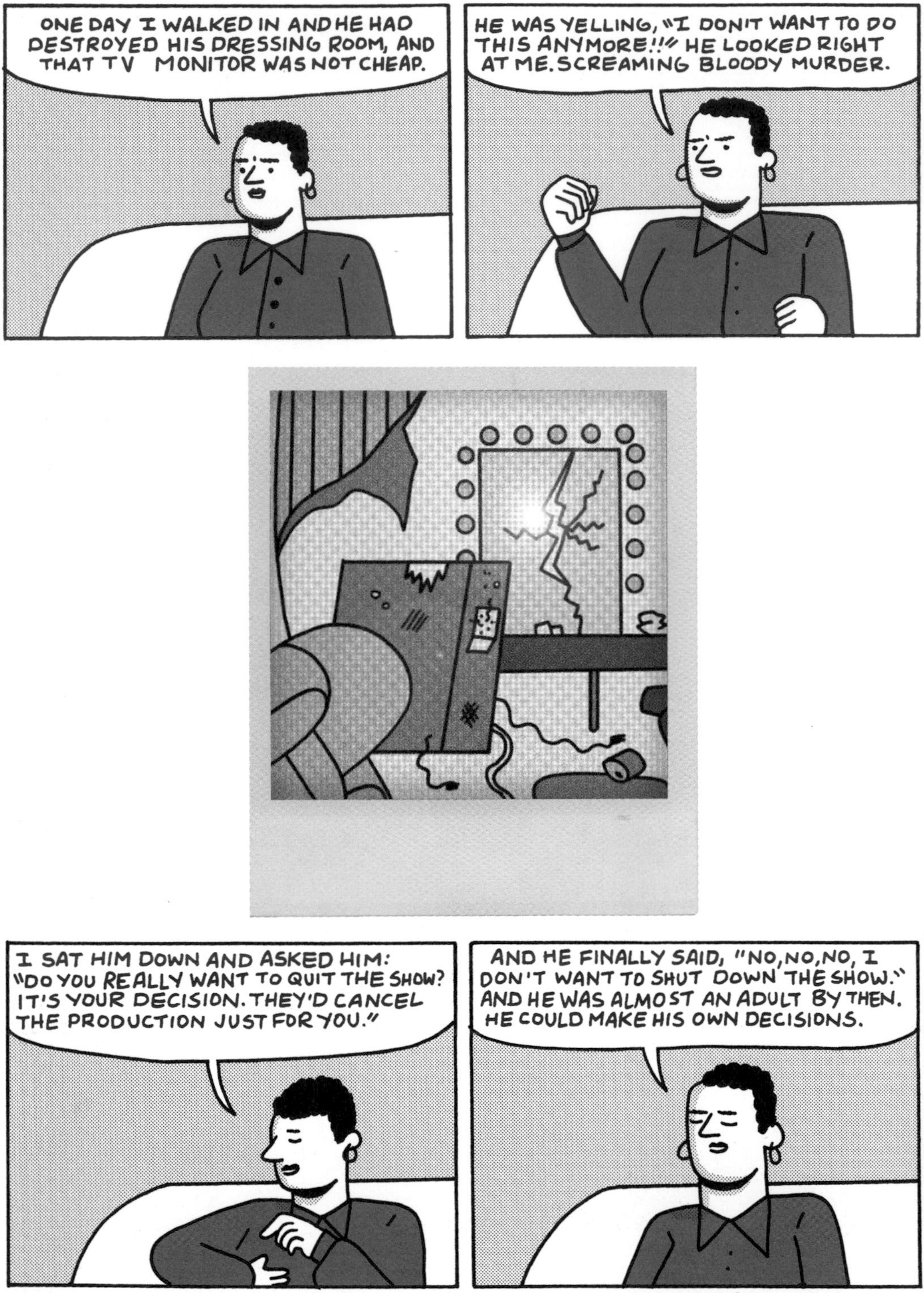
ONE DAY I WALKED IN AND HE HAD DESTROYED HIS DRESSING ROOM, AND THAT TV MONITOR WAS NOT CHEAP.
HE WAS YELLING, "I DON'T WANT TO DO THIS ANYMORE!!" HE LOOKED RIGHT AT ME. SCREAMING BLOODY MURDER.
I SAT HIM DOWN AND ASKED HIM: "DO YOU REALLY WANT TO QUIT THE SHOW? IT'S YOUR DECISION. THEY'D CANCEL THE PRODUCTION JUST FOR YOU."
AND HE FINALLY SAID, "NO, NO, NO, I DON'T WANT TO SHUT DOWN THE SHOW." AND HE WAS ALMOST AN ADULT BY THEN. HE COULD MAKE HIS OWN DECISIONS.

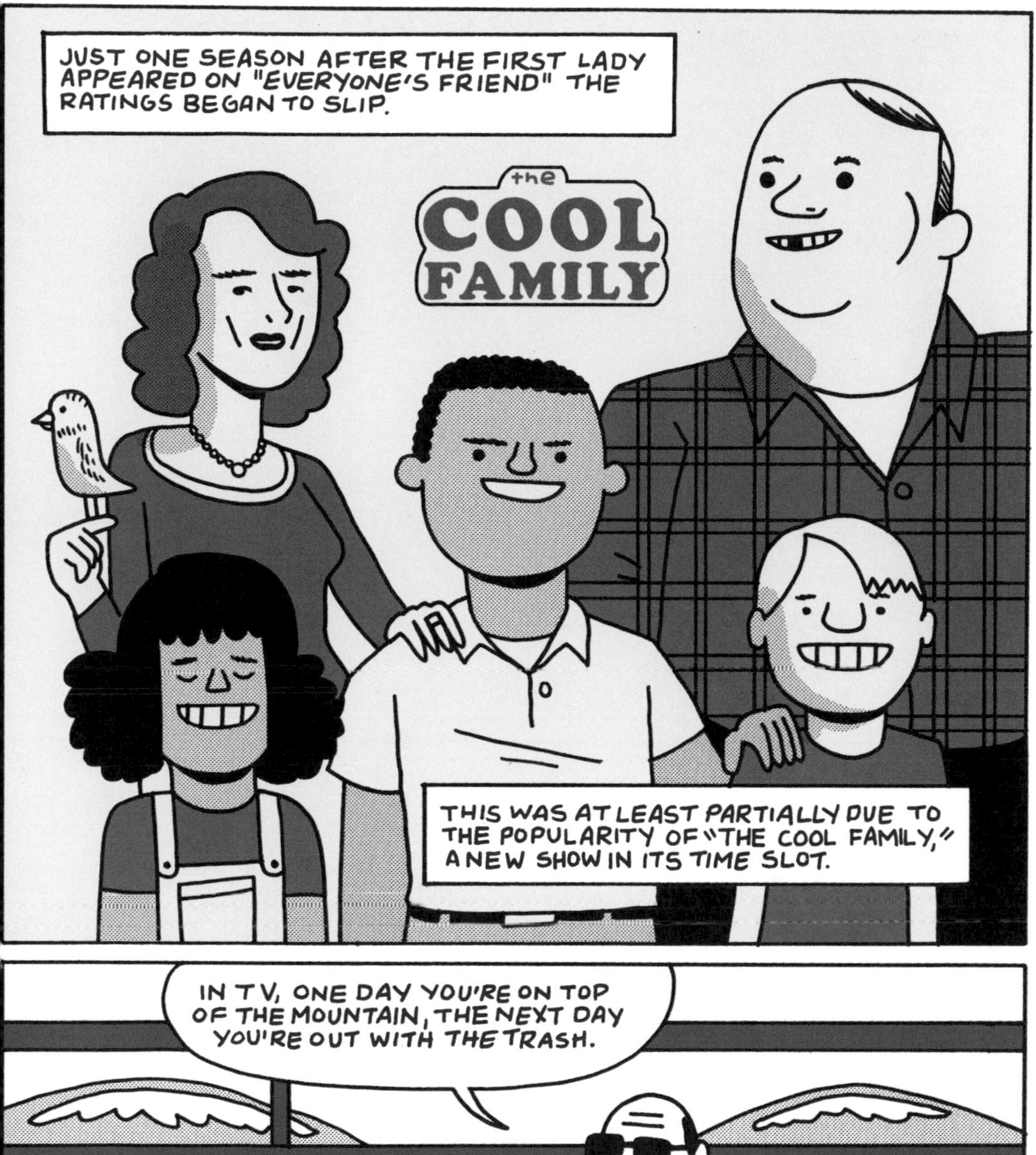
JUST ONE SEASON AFTER THE FIRST LADY APPEARED ON "EVERYONE'S FRIEND" THE RATINGS BEGAN TO SLIP.
the COOL FAMILY
THIS WAS AT LEAST PARTIALLY DUE TO THE POPULARITY OF "THE COOL FAMILY," A NEW SHOW IN ITS TIME SLOT.

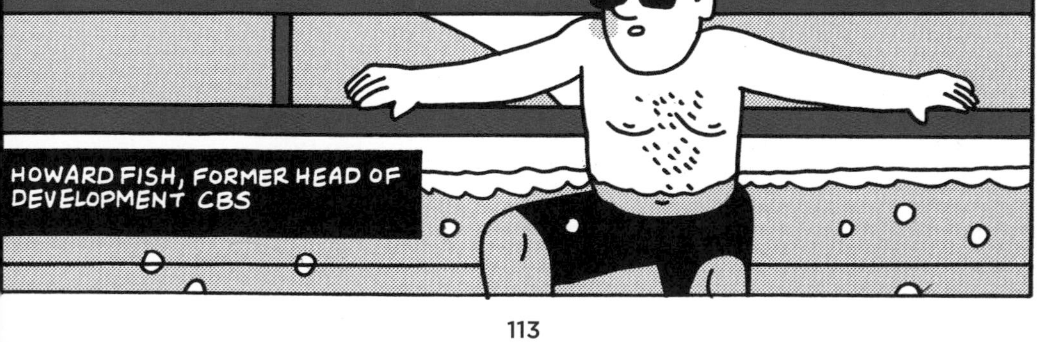
IN TV, ONE DAY YOU'RE ON TOP OF THE MOUNTAIN, THE NEXT DAY YOU'RE OUT WITH THE TRASH.
HOWARD FISH, FORMER HEAD OF DEVELOPMENT CBS

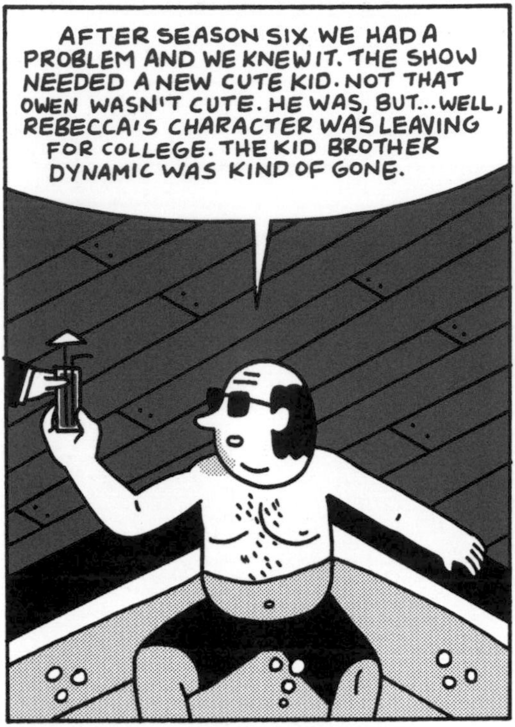
AFTER SEASON SIX WE HAD A PROBLEM AND WE KNEW IT. THE SHOW NEEDED A NEW CUTE KID. NOT THAT OWEN WASN'T CUTE. HE WAS, BUT... WELL, REBECCA'S CHARACTER WAS LEAVING FOR COLLEGE. THE KID BROTHER DYNAMIC WAS KIND OF GONE.

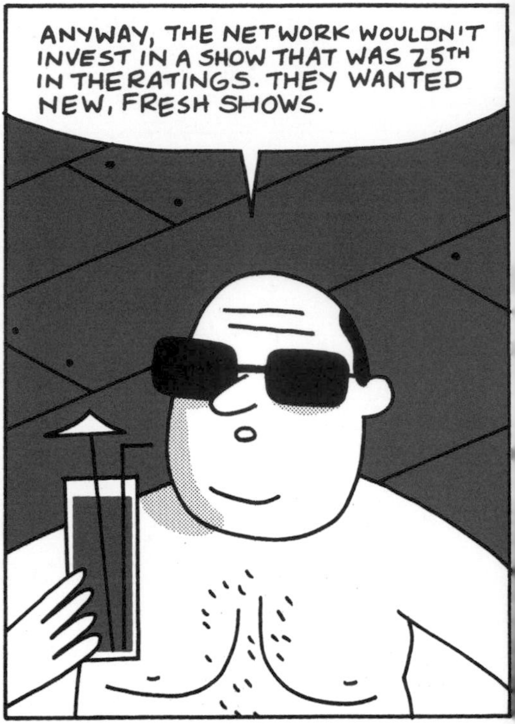
ANYWAY, THE NETWORK WOULDN'T INVEST IN A SHOW THAT WAS 25TH IN THE RATINGS. THEY WANTED NEW, FRESH SHOWS.

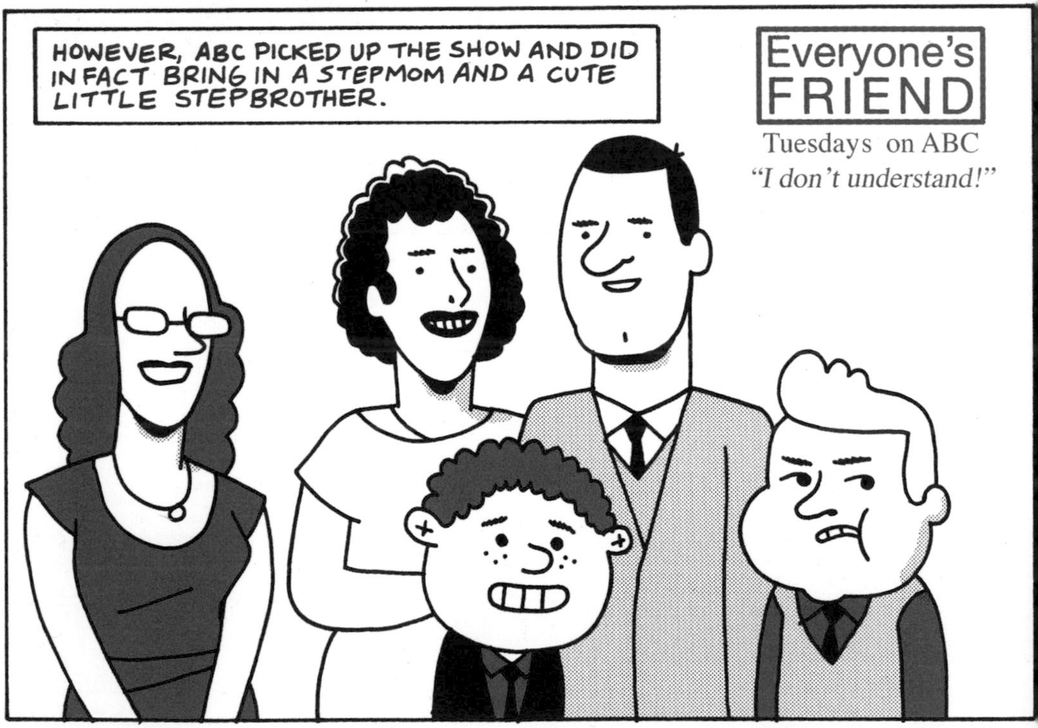
HOWEVER, ABC PICKED UP THE SHOW AND DID IN FACT BRING IN A STEPMOM AND A CUTE LITTLE STEPBROTHER.
Everyone's FRIEND
Tuesdays on ABC
"I don't understand!"

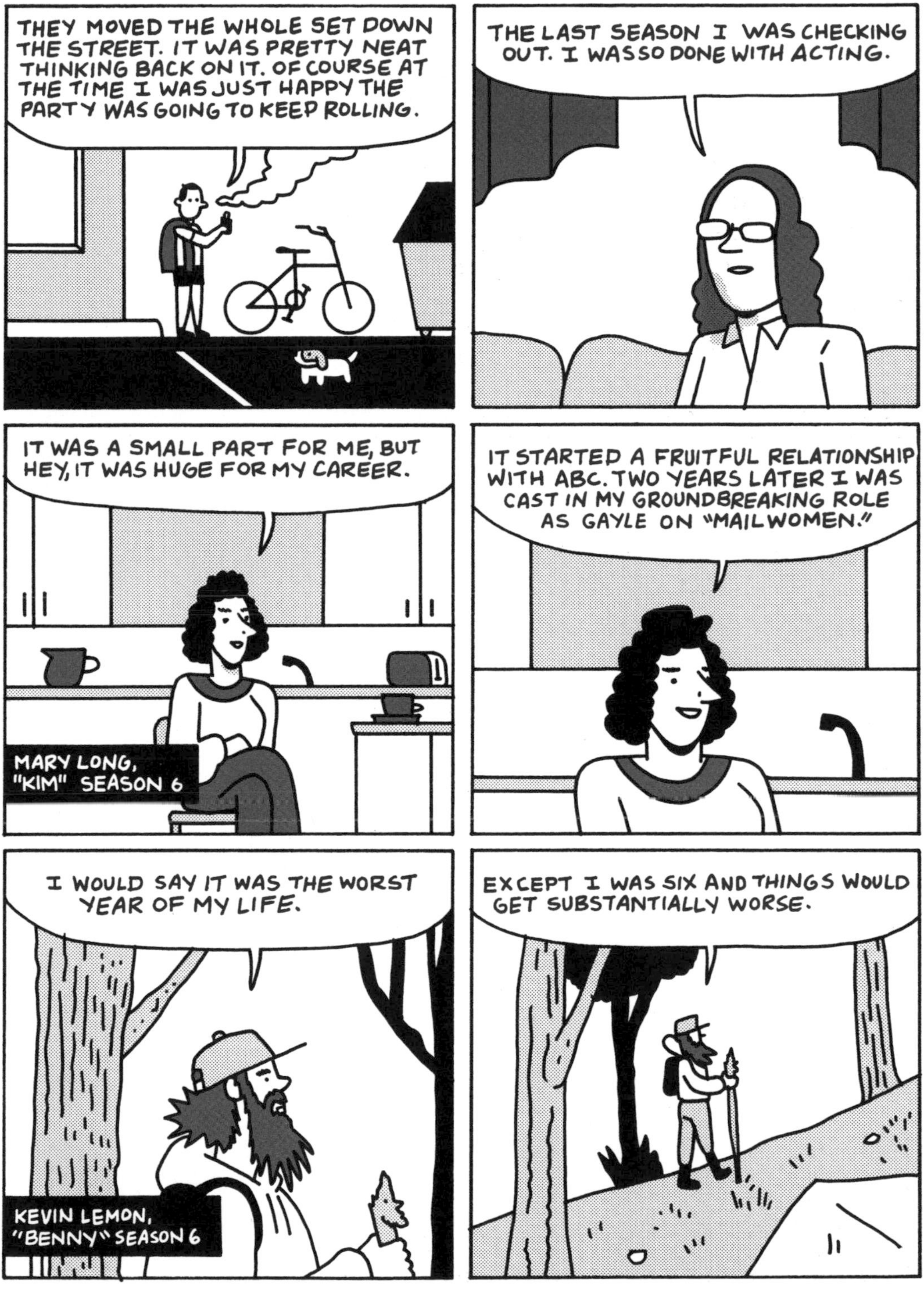
THEY MOVED THE WHOLE SET DOWN THE STREET. IT WAS PRETTY NEAT THINKING BACK ON IT. OF COURSE AT THE TIME I WAS JUST HAPPY THE PARTY WAS GOING TO KEEP ROLLING.
THE LAST SEASON I WAS CHECKING OUT. I WAS SO DONE WITH ACTING.
IT WAS A SMALL PART FOR ME, BUT HEY, IT WAS HUGE FOR MY CAREER.
MARY LONG, "KIM" SEASON 6
IT STARTED A FRUITFUL RELATIONSHIP WITH ABC. TWO YEARS LATER I WAS CAST IN MY GROUNDBREAKING ROLE AS GAYLE ON "MAILWOMEN."
I WOULD SAY IT WAS THE WORST YEAR OF MY LIFE.
KEVIN LEMON, "BENNY" SEASON 6
EXCEPT I WAS SIX AND THINGS WOULD GET SUBSTANTIALLY WORSE.

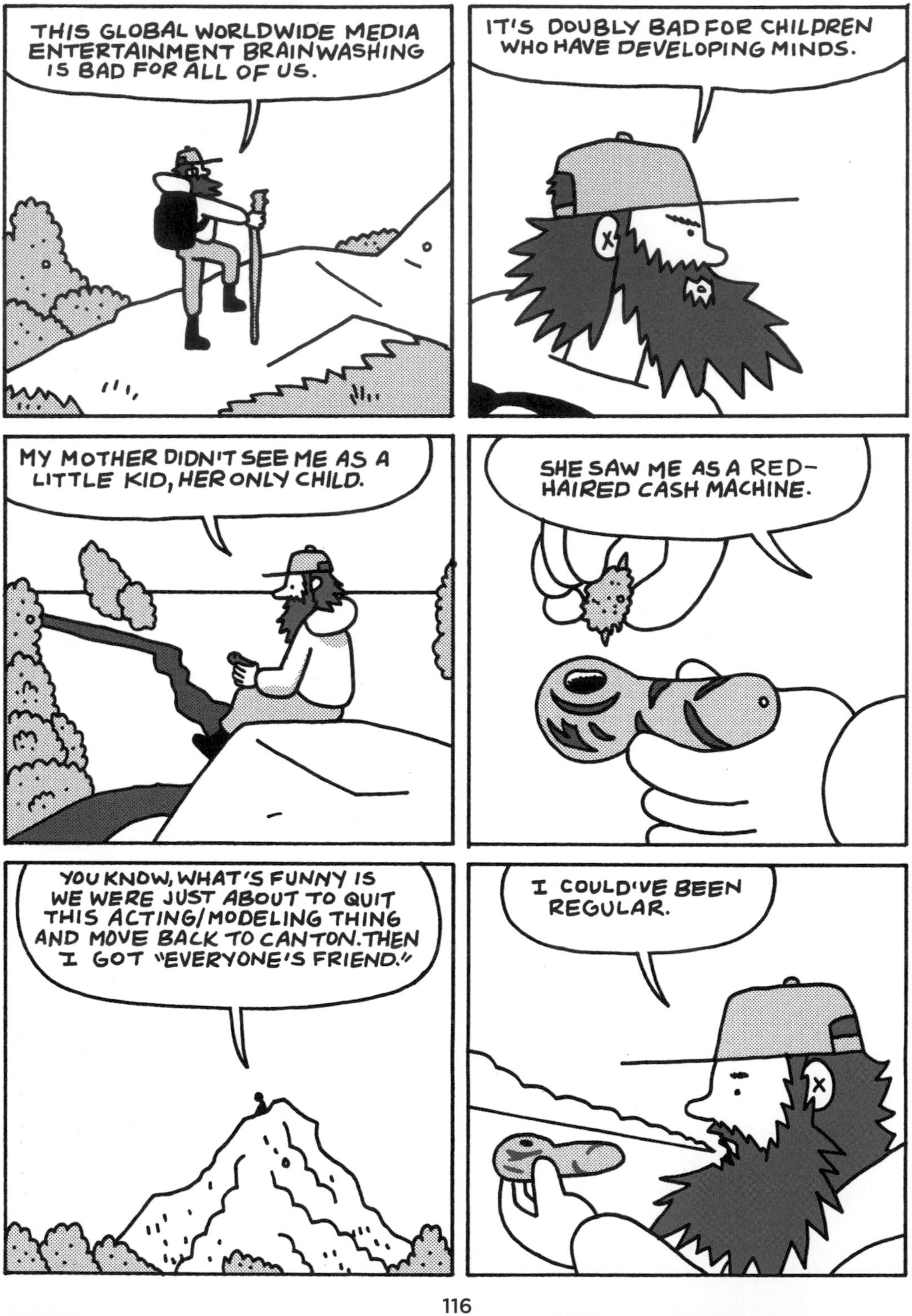
THIS GLOBAL WORLDWIDE MEDIA ENTERTAINMENT BRAINWASHING IS BAD FOR ALL OF US.
IT'S DOUBLY BAD FOR CHILDREN WHO HAVE DEVELOPING MINDS.
MY MOTHER DIDN'T SEE ME AS A LITTLE KID, HER ONLY CHILD.
SHE SAW ME AS A RED-HAIRED CASH MACHINE.
YOU KNOW, WHAT'S FUNNY IS WE WERE JUST ABOUT TO QUIT THIS ACTING/MODELING THING AND MOVE BACK TO CANTON. THEN I GOT "EVERYONE'S FRIEND."
I COULD'VE BEEN REGULAR.

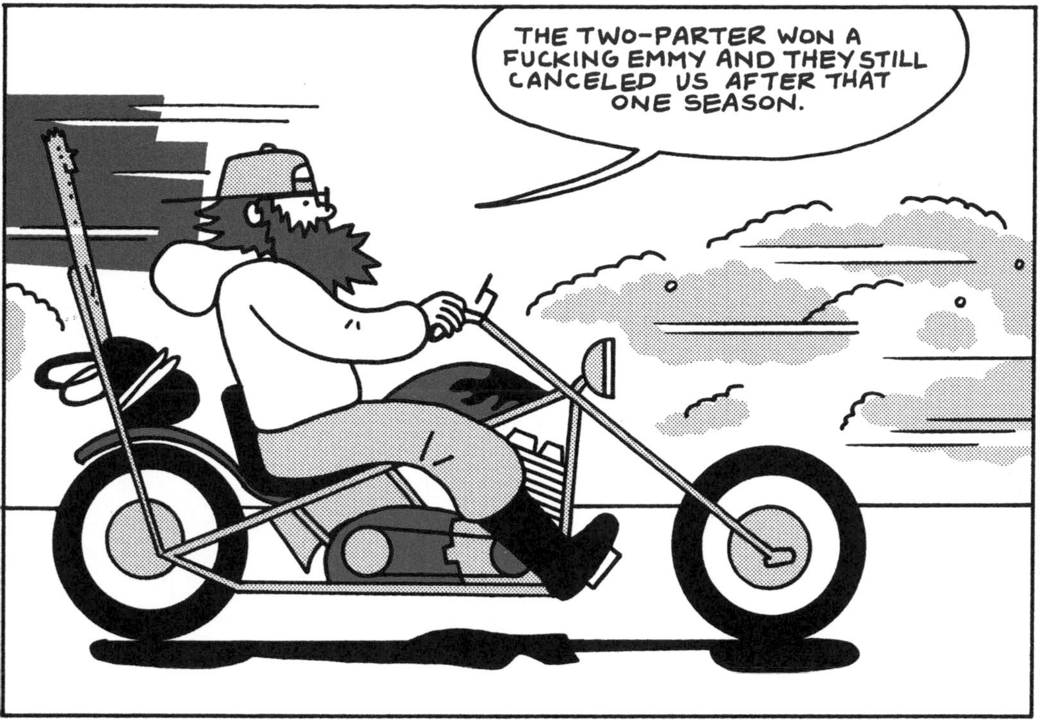
THE TWO-PARTER WON A FUCKING EMMY AND THEY STILL CANCELED US AFTER THAT ONE SEASON.

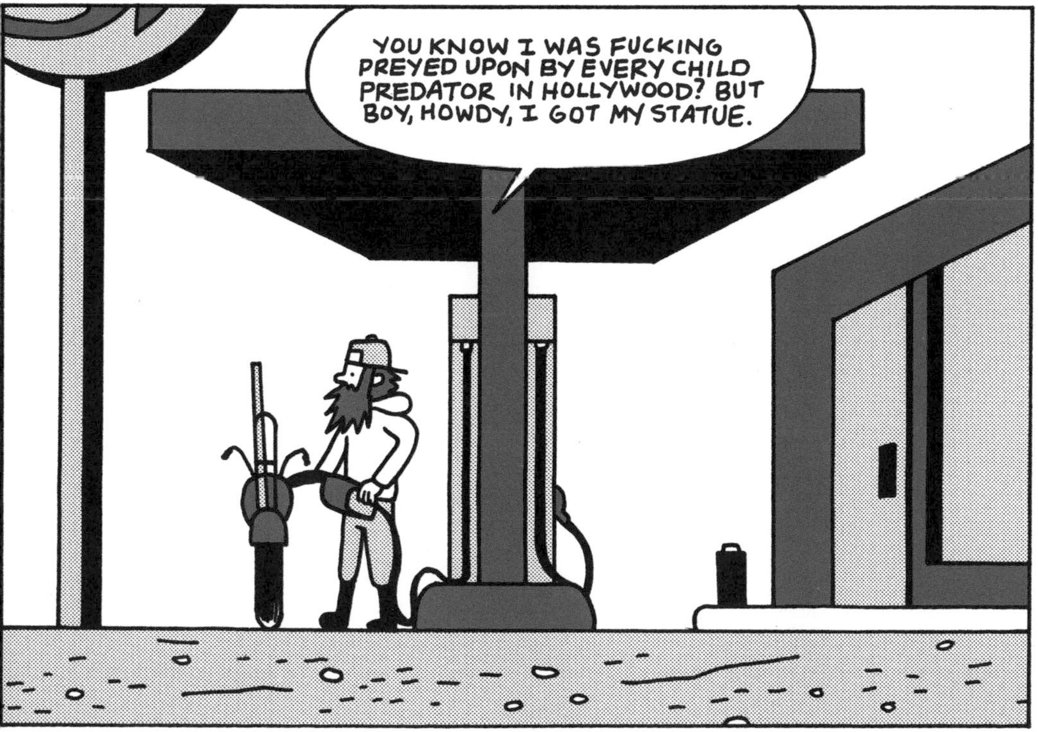
YOU KNOW I WAS FUCKING PREYED UPON BY EVERY CHILD PREDATOR IN HOLLYWOOD? BUT BOY, HOWDY, I GOT MY STATUE.

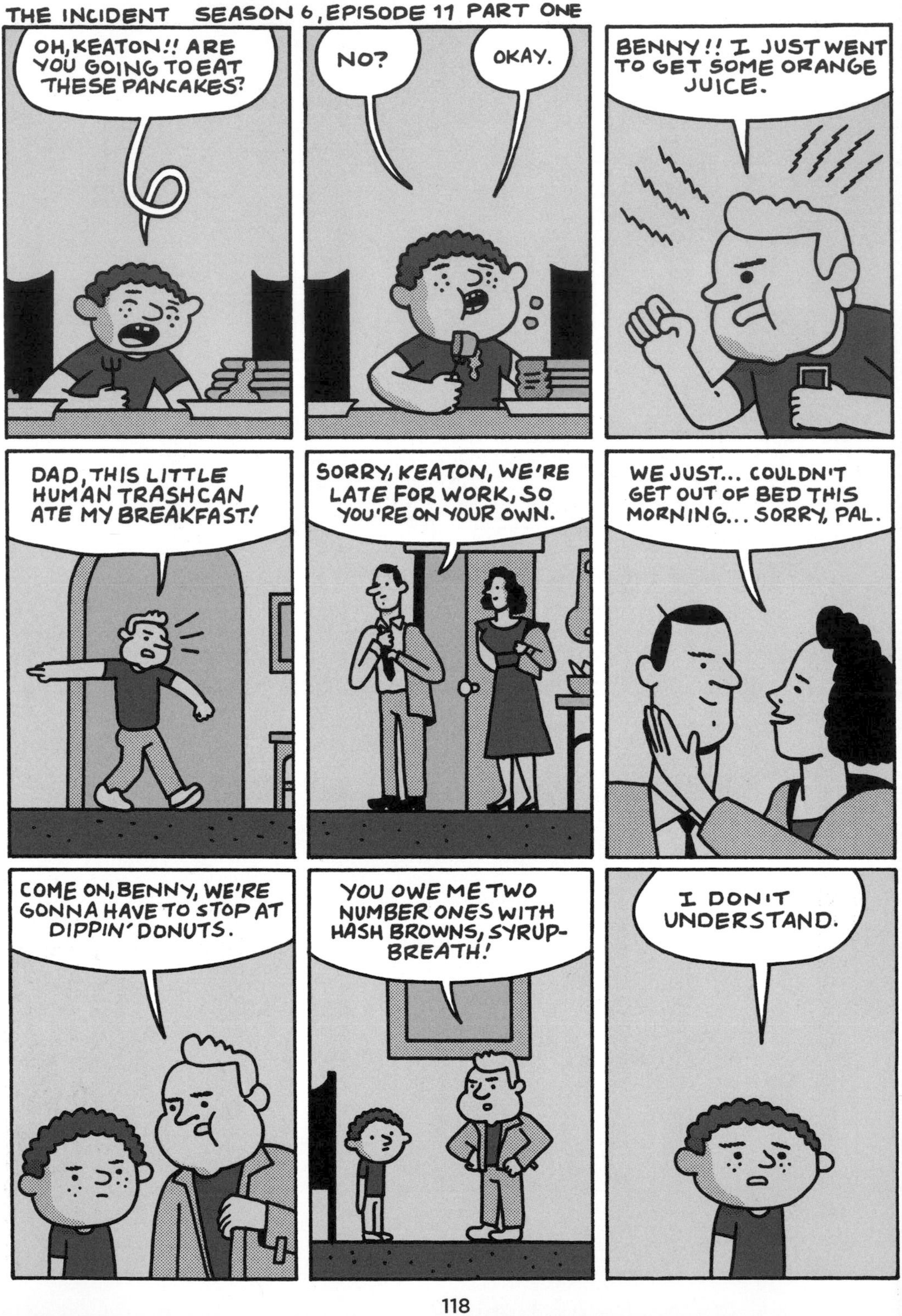
THE INCIDENT SEASON 6, EPISODE 11 PART ONE
OH, KEATON!! ARE YOU GOING TO EAT THESE PANCAKES?
NO?
OKAY.
BENNY!! I JUST WENT TO GET SOME ORANGE JUICE.
DAD, THIS LITTLE HUMAN TRASHCAN ATE MY BREAKFAST!
SORRY, KEATON, WE'RE LATE FOR WORK, SO YOU'RE ON YOUR OWN.
WE JUST... COULDN'T GET OUT OF BED THIS MORNING... SORRY, PAL.
COME ON, BENNY, WE'RE GONNA HAVE TO STOP AT DIPPIN' DONUTS.
YOU OWE ME TWO NUMBER ONES WITH HASH BROWNS, SYRUP-BREATH!
I DON'T UNDERSTAND.

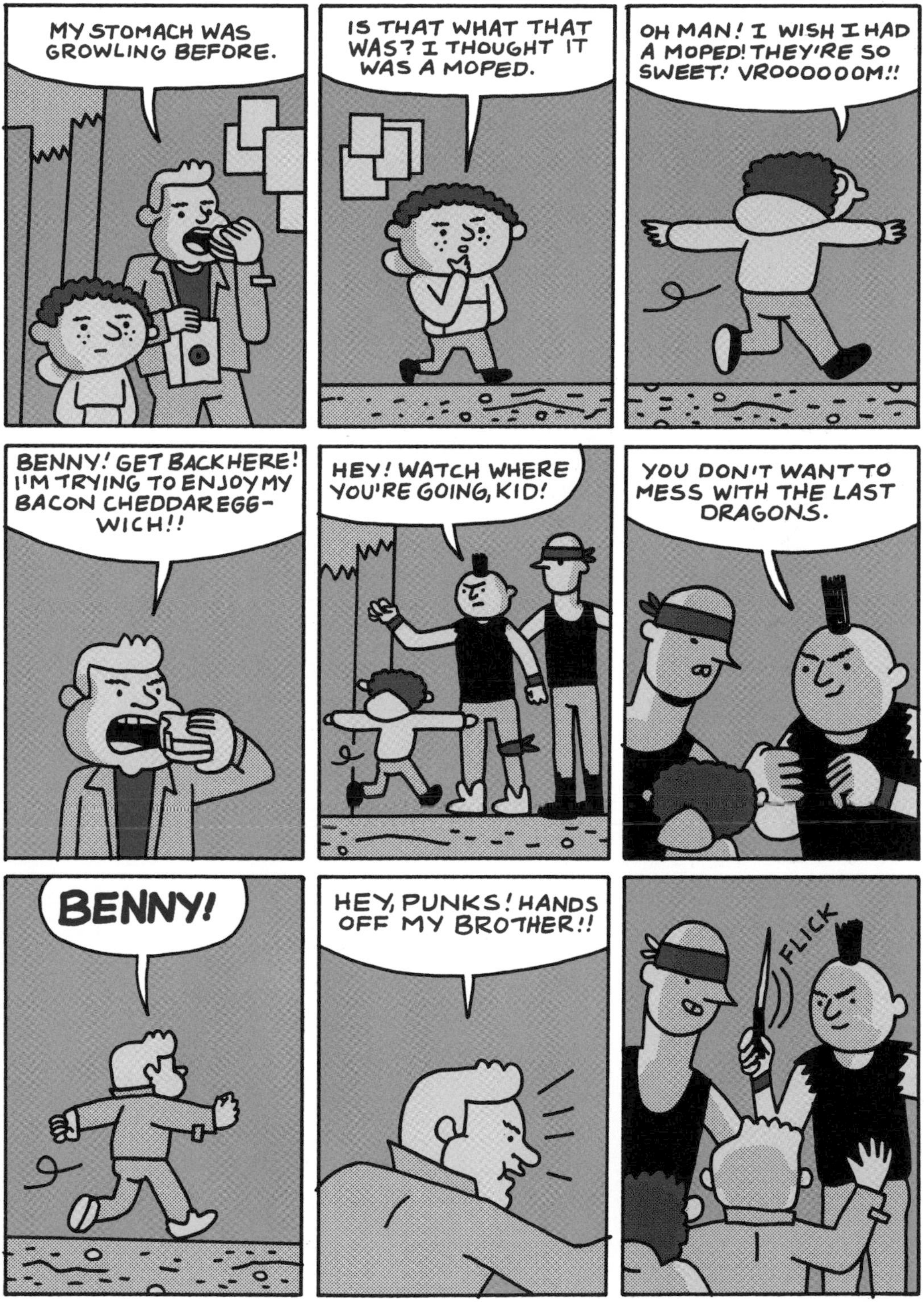
MY STOMACH WAS GROWLING BEFORE.
IS THAT WHAT THAT WAS? I THOUGHT IT WAS A MOPED.
OH MAN! I WISH I HAD A MOPED! THEY'RE SO SWEET! VROOOOOOM!!
BENNY! GET BACK HERE! I'M TRYING TO ENJOY MY BACON CHEDDAR EGG-WICH!!
HEY! WATCH WHERE YOU'RE GOING, KID!
YOU DON'T WANT TO MESS WITH THE LAST DRAGONS.
BENNY!
HEY, PUNKS! HANDS OFF MY BROTHER!!
FLICK

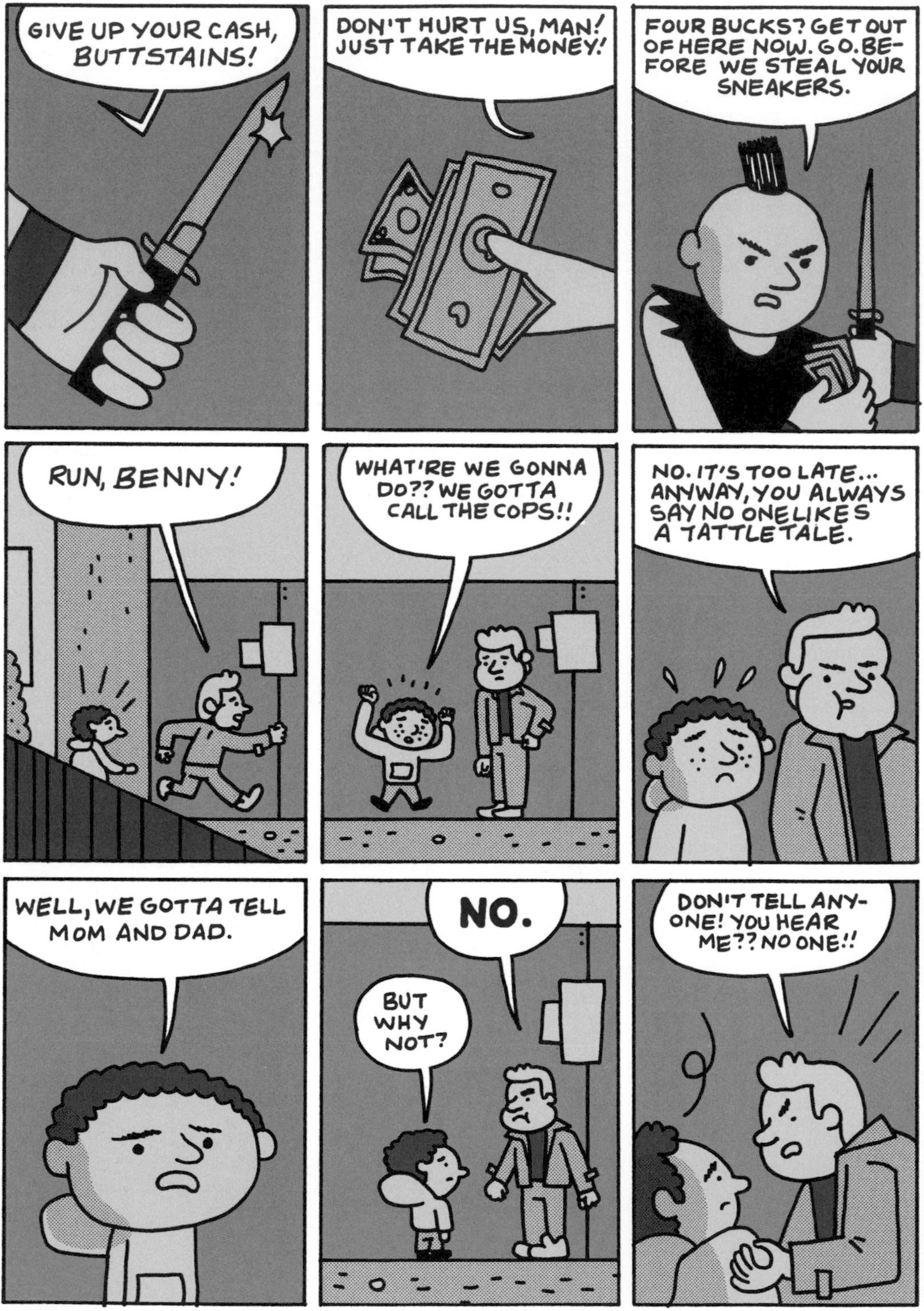
GIVE UP YOUR CASH, BUTTSTAINS!
DON'T HURT US, MAN! JUST TAKE THE MONEY!
FOUR BUCKS? GET OUT OF HERE NOW. GO. BEFORE WE STEAL YOUR SNEAKERS.
RUN, BENNY!
WHAT'RE WE GONNA DO?? WE GOTTA CALL THE COPS!!
NO. IT'S TOO LATE... ANYWAY, YOU ALWAYS SAY NO ONE LIKES A TATTLETALE.
WELL, WE GOTTA TELL MOM AND DAD.
NO.
BUT WHY NOT?
DON'T TELL ANYONE! YOU HEAR ME?? NO ONE!!

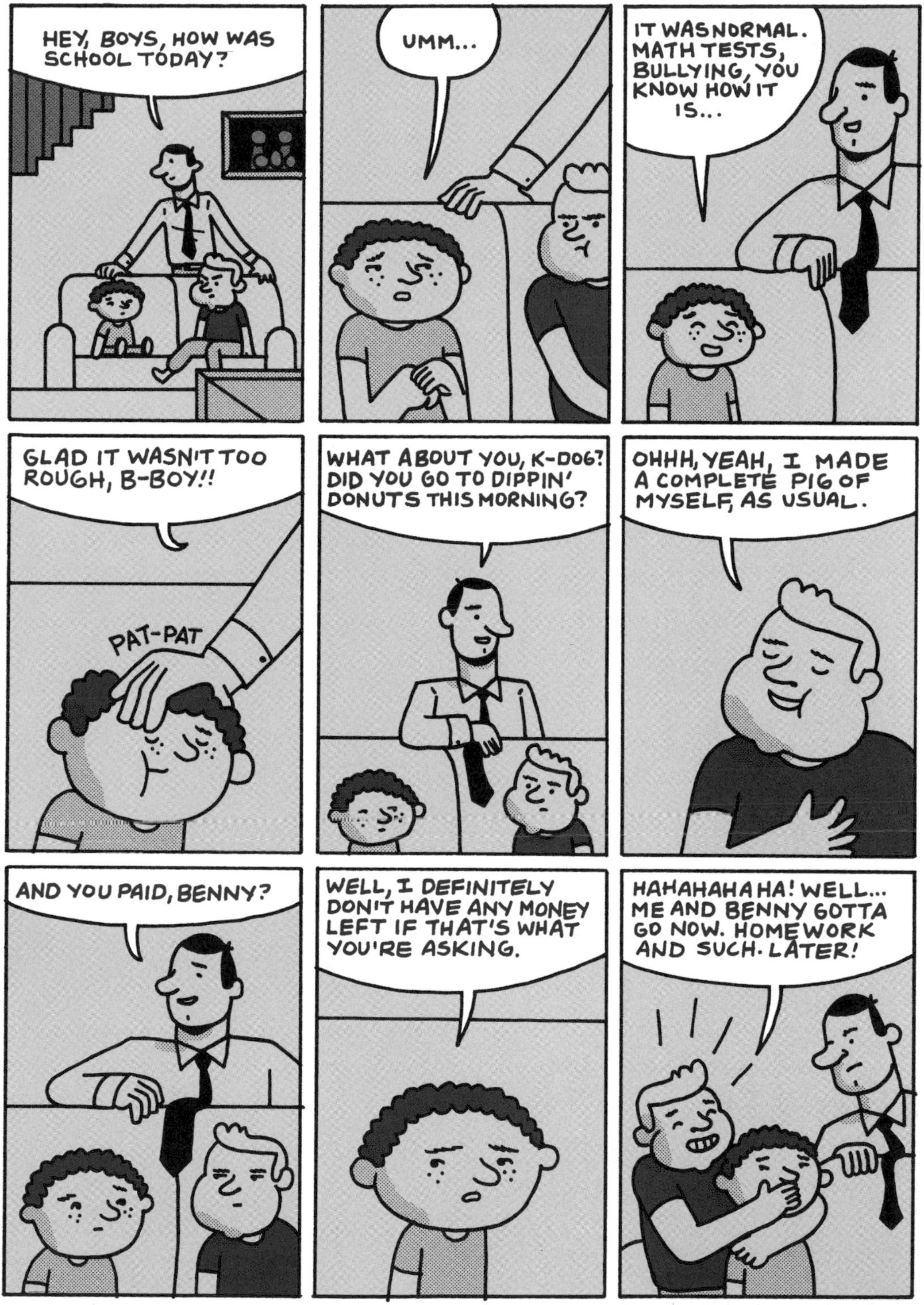
HEY, BOYS, HOW WAS SCHOOL TODAY?
UMM...
IT WAS NORMAL. MATH TESTS, BULLYING, YOU KNOW HOW IT IS...
GLAD IT WASN'T TOO ROUGH, B-BOY!!
PAT-PAT
WHAT ABOUT YOU, K-DOG? DID YOU GO TO DIPPIN' DONUTS THIS MORNING?
OHHH, YEAH, I MADE A COMPLETE PIG OF MYSELF, AS USUAL.
AND YOU PAID, BENNY?
WELL, I DEFINITELY DON'T HAVE ANY MONEY LEFT IF THAT'S WHAT YOU'RE ASKING.
HAHAHAHAHA! WELL... ME AND BENNY GOTTA GO NOW. HOMEWORK AND SUCH. LATER!

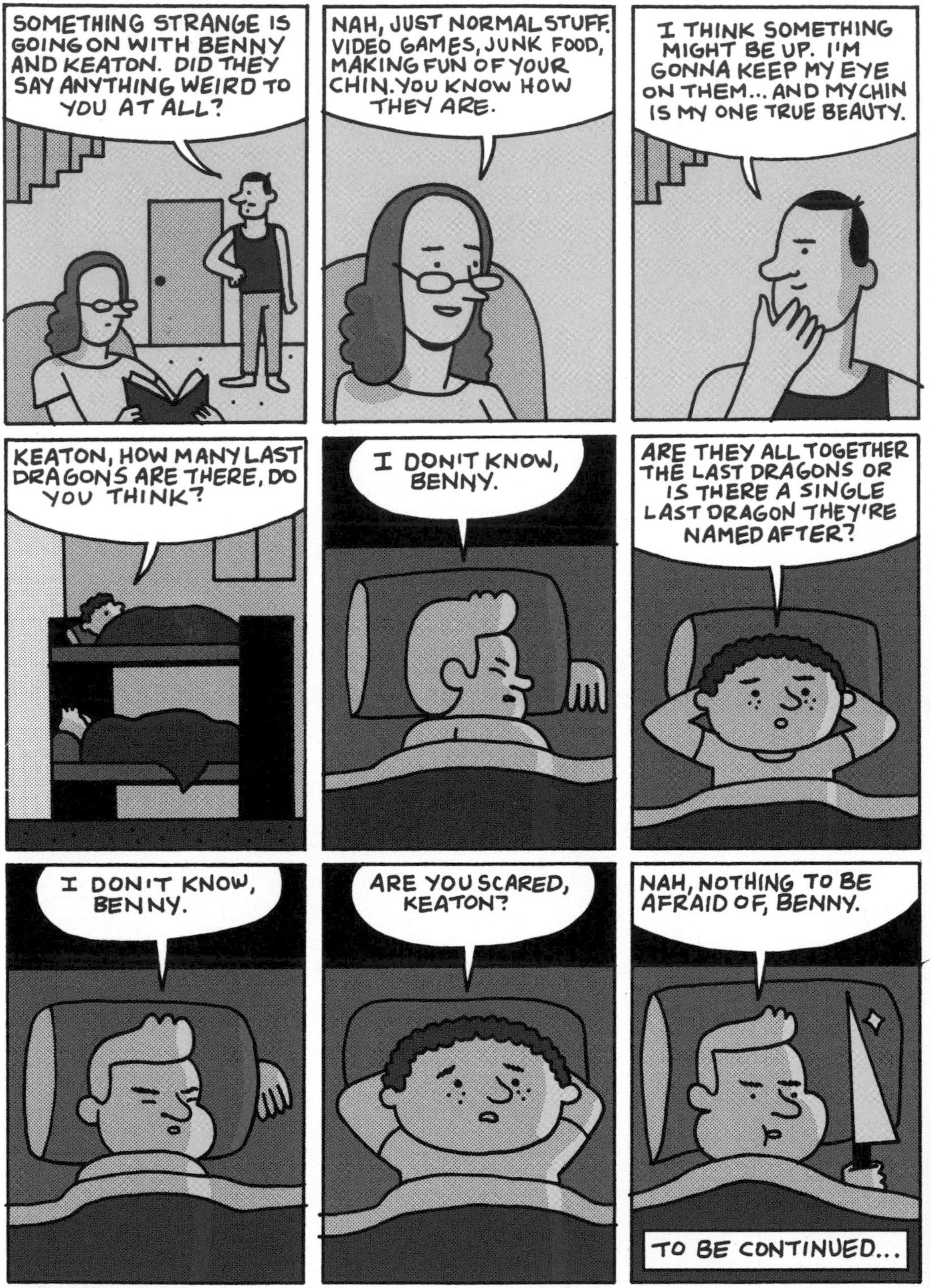
SOMETHING STRANGE IS GOING ON WITH BENNY AND KEATON. DID THEY SAY ANYTHING WEIRD TO YOU AT ALL?
NAH, JUST NORMAL STUFF. VIDEO GAMES, JUNK FOOD, MAKING FUN OF YOUR CHIN. YOU KNOW HOW THEY ARE.
I THINK SOMETHING MIGHT BE UP. I'M GONNA KEEP MY EYE ON THEM... AND MY CHIN IS MY ONE TRUE BEAUTY.
KEATON, HOW MANY LAST DRAGONS ARE THERE, DO YOU THINK?
I DON'T KNOW, BENNY.
ARE THEY ALL TOGETHER THE LAST DRAGONS OR IS THERE A SINGLE LAST DRAGON THEY'RE NAMED AFTER?
I DON'T KNOW, BENNY.
ARE YOU SCARED, KEATON?
NAH, NOTHING TO BE AFRAID OF, BENNY.
TO BE CONTINUED...

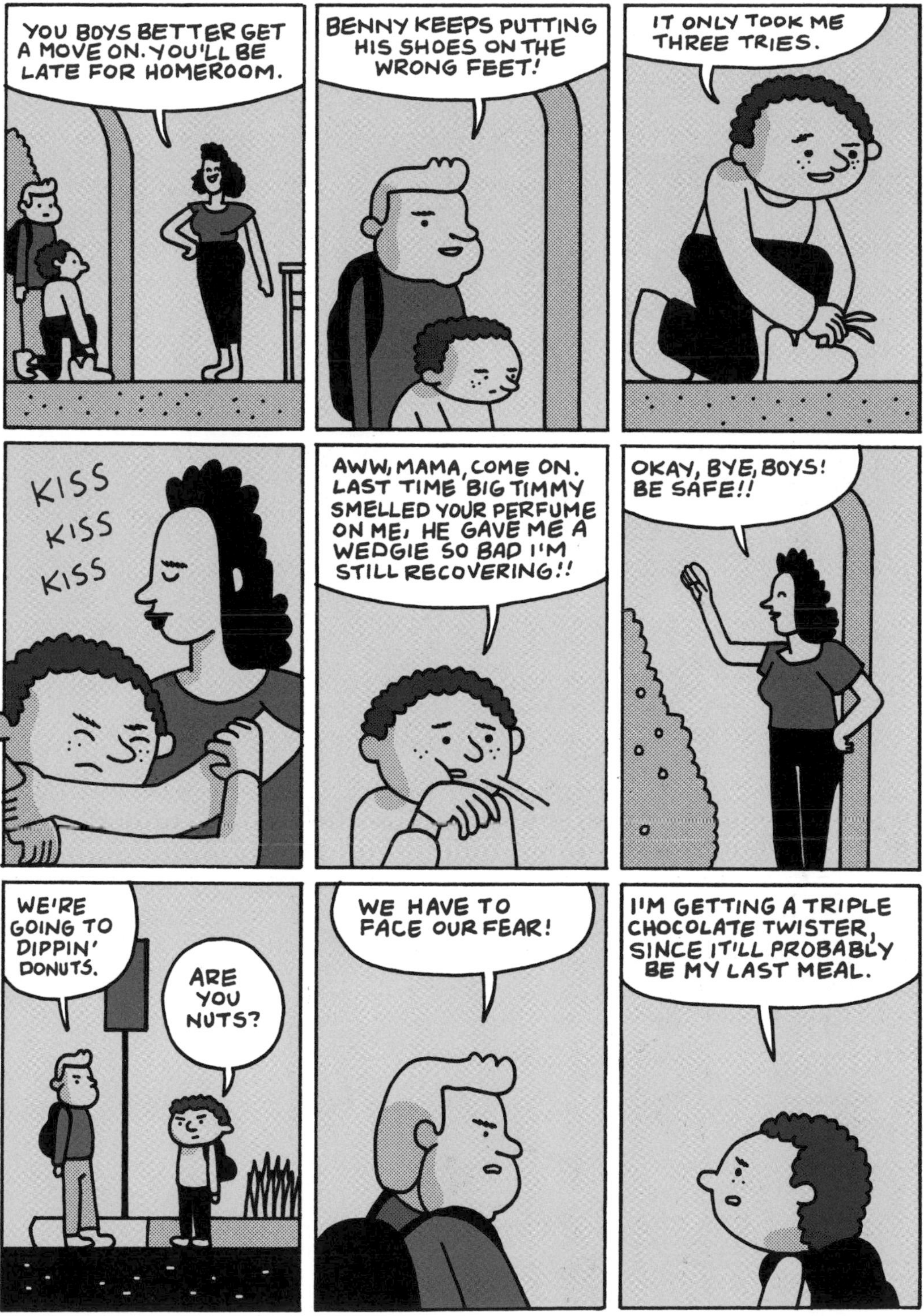
YOU BOYS BETTER GET A MOVE ON. YOU'LL BE LATE FOR HOMEROOM.
BENNY KEEPS PUTTING HIS SHOES ON THE WRONG FEET!
IT ONLY TOOK ME THREE TRIES.
KISS KISS KISS
AWW, MAMA, COME ON. LAST TIME BIG TIMMY SMELLED YOUR PERFUME ON ME, HE GAVE ME A WEDGIE SO BAD I'M STILL RECOVERING!!
OKAY, BYE, BOYS! BE SAFE!!
WE'RE GOING TO DIPPIN' DONUTS.
ARE YOU NUTS?
WE HAVE TO FACE OUR FEAR!
I'M GETTING A TRIPLE CHOCOLATE TWISTER, SINCE IT'LL PROBABLY BE MY LAST MEAL.

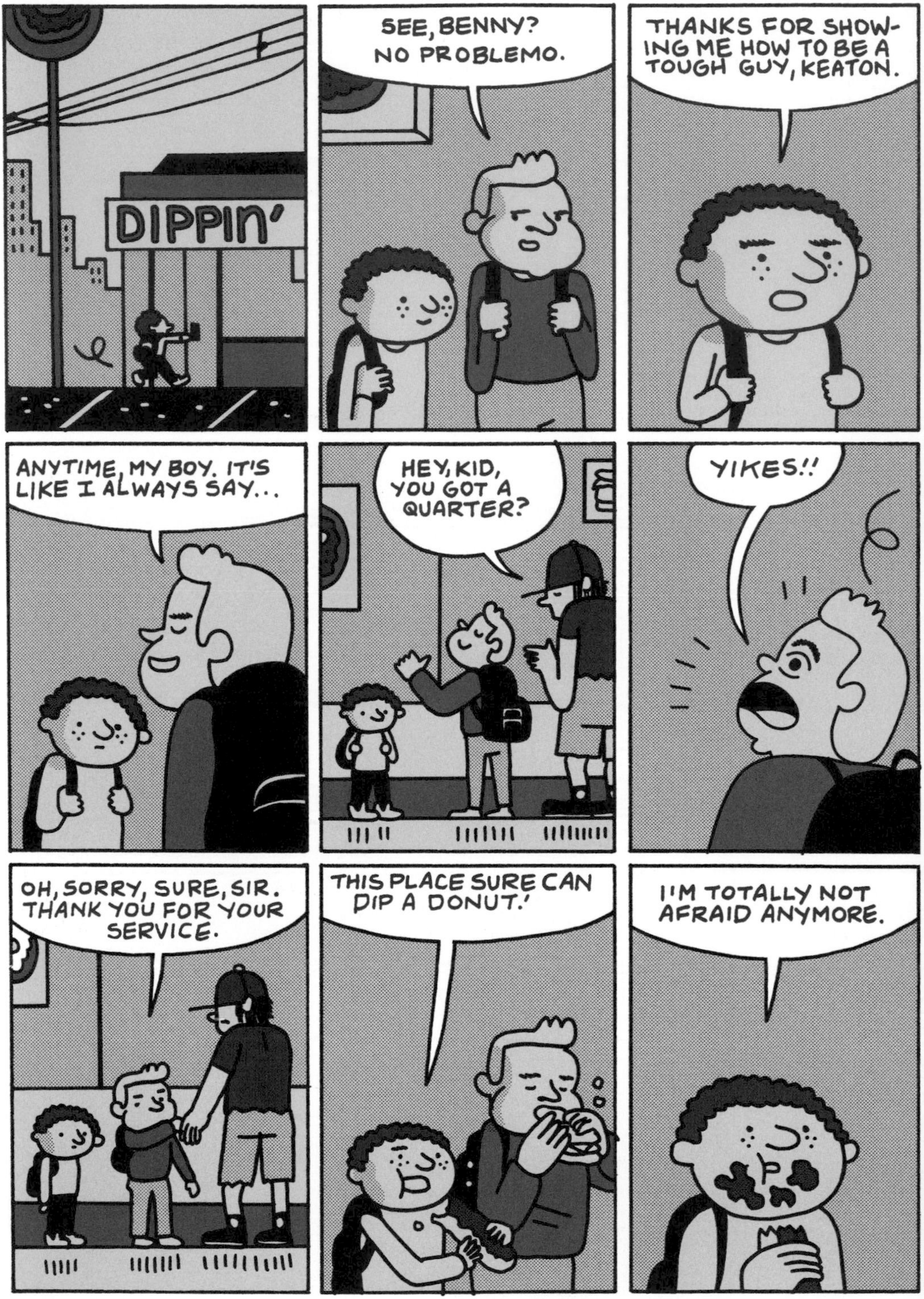
DIPPIN'
SEE, BENNY? NO PROBLEMO.
THANKS FOR SHOW-ING ME HOW TO BE A TOUGH GUY, KEATON.
ANYTIME, MY BOY. IT'S LIKE I ALWAYS SAY...
HEY, KID, YOU GOT A QUARTER?
YIKES!!
OH, SORRY, SURE, SIR. THANK YOU FOR YOUR SERVICE.
THIS PLACE SURE CAN DIP A DONUT!
I'M TOTALLY NOT AFRAID ANYMORE.

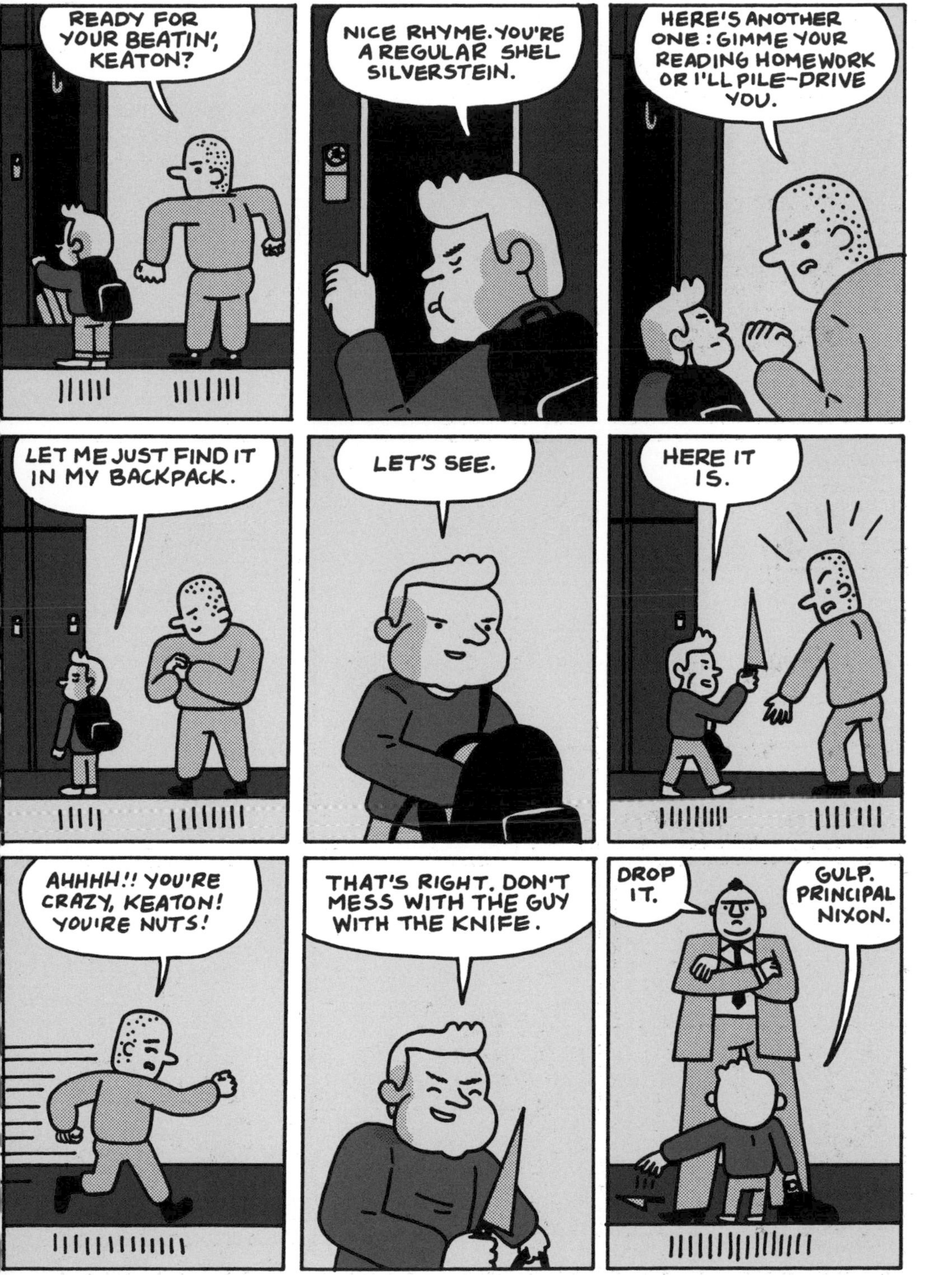
READY FOR YOUR BEATIN', KEATON?
NICE RHYME. YOU'RE A REGULAR SHEL SILVERSTEIN.
HERE'S ANOTHER ONE: GIMME YOUR READING HOMEWORK OR I'LL PILE-DRIVE YOU.
LET ME JUST FIND IT IN MY BACKPACK.
LET'S SEE.
HERE IT IS.
AHHHH!! YOU'RE CRAZY, KEATON! YOU'RE NUTS!
THAT'S RIGHT. DON'T MESS WITH THE GUY WITH THE KNIFE.
DROP IT.
GULP. PRINCIPAL NIXON.

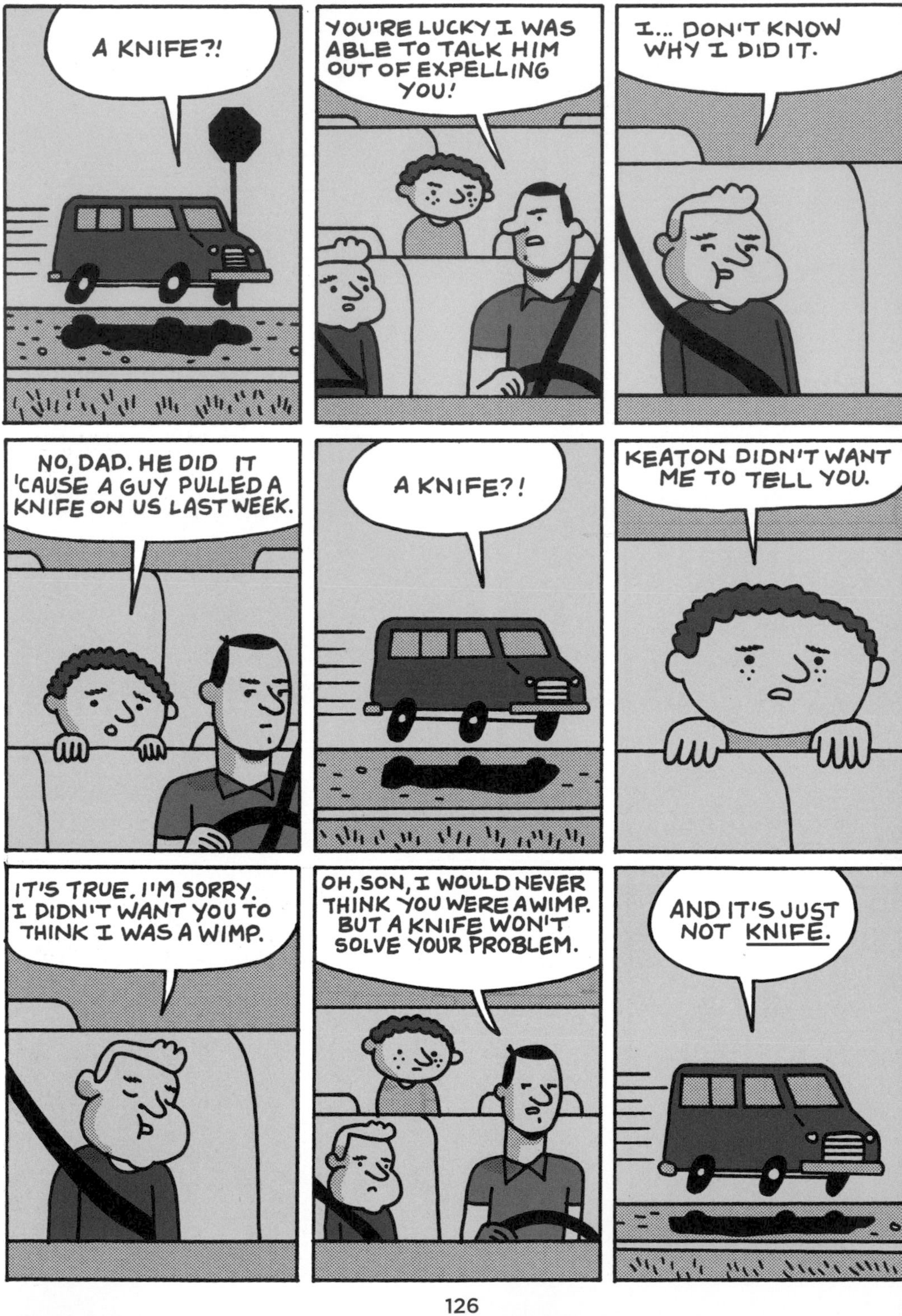
A KNIFE?!
YOU'RE LUCKY I WAS ABLE TO TALK HIM OUT OF EXPELLING YOU!
I... DON'T KNOW WHY I DID IT.
NO, DAD. HE DID IT 'CAUSE A GUY PULLED A KNIFE ON US LAST WEEK.
A KNIFE?!
KEATON DIDN'T WANT ME TO TELL YOU.
IT'S TRUE. I'M SORRY. I DIDN'T WANT YOU TO THINK I WAS A WIMP.
OH, SON, I WOULD NEVER THINK YOU WERE A WIMP. BUT A KNIFE WON'T SOLVE YOUR PROBLEM.
AND IT'S JUST NOT KNIFE.

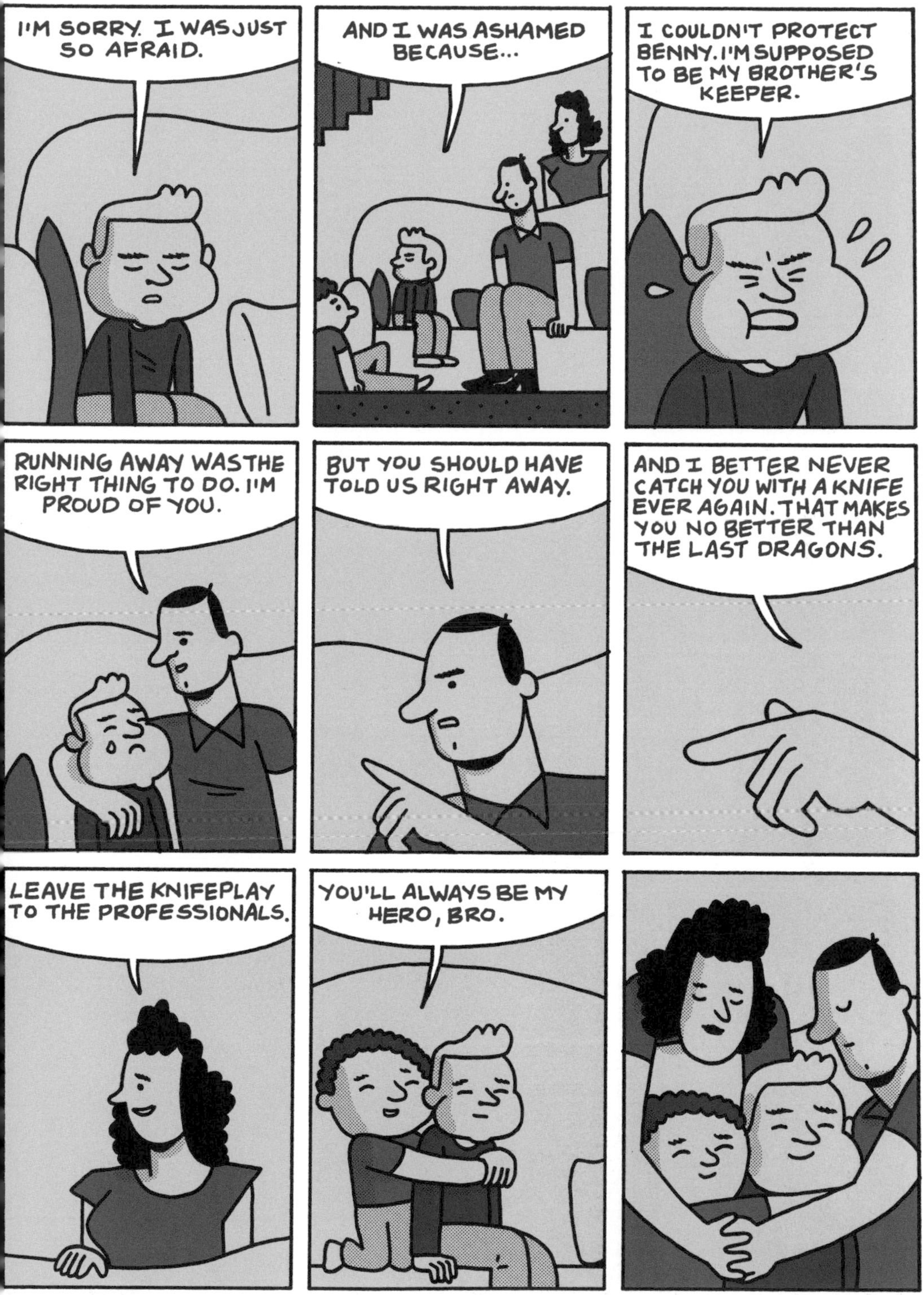
I'M SORRY. I WAS JUST SO AFRAID.
AND I WAS ASHAMED BECAUSE...
I COULDN'T PROTECT BENNY. I'M SUPPOSED TO BE MY BROTHER'S KEEPER.
RUNNING AWAY WAS THE RIGHT THING TO DO. I'M PROUD OF YOU.
BUT YOU SHOULD HAVE TOLD US RIGHT AWAY.
AND I BETTER NEVER CATCH YOU WITH A KNIFE EVER AGAIN. THAT MAKES YOU NO BETTER THAN THE LAST DRAGONS.
LEAVE THE KNIFEPLAY TO THE PROFESSIONALS.
YOU'LL ALWAYS BE MY HERO, BRO.

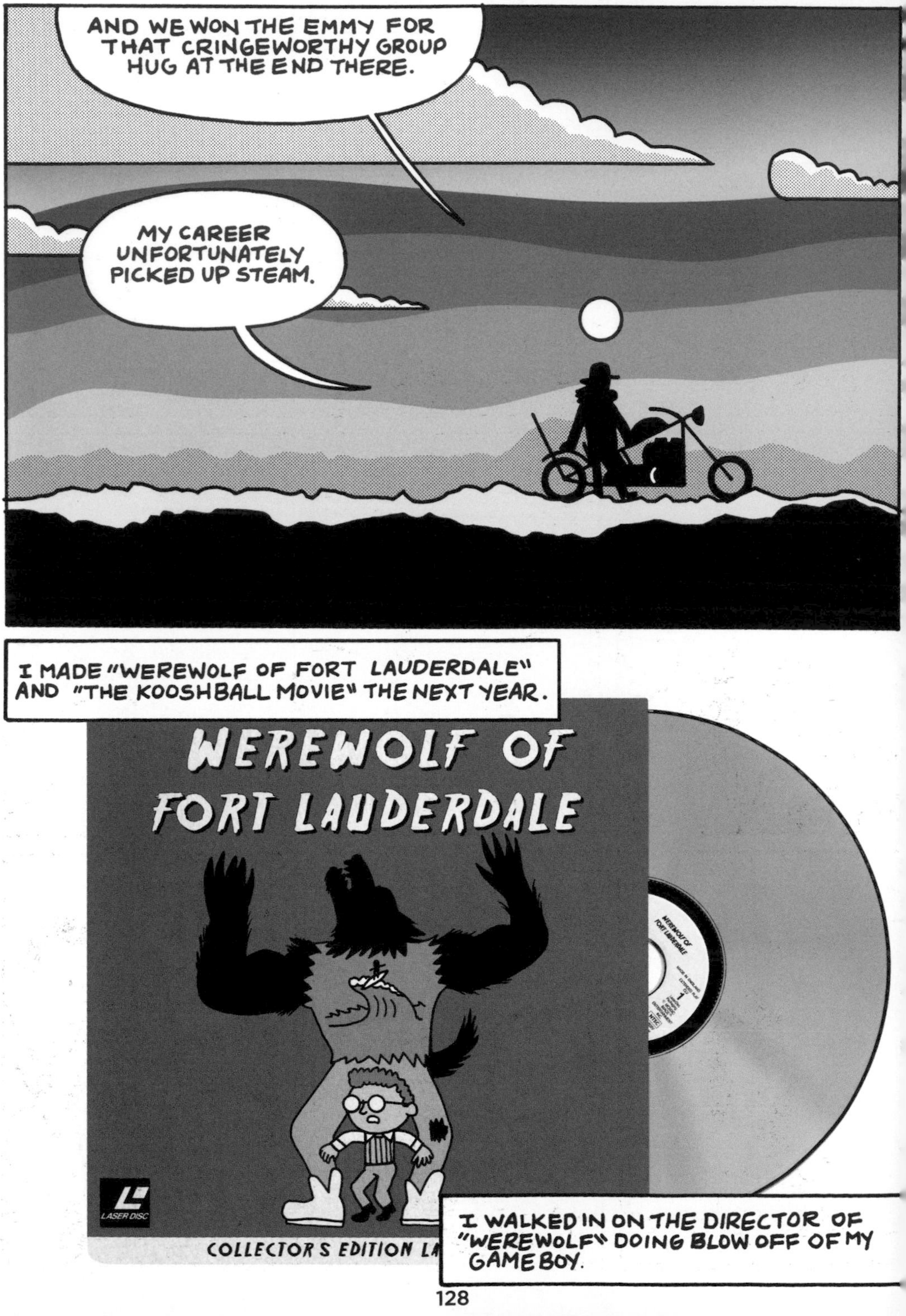
AND WE WON THE EMMY FOR THAT CRINGEWORTHY GROUP HUG AT THE END THERE.
MY CAREER UNFORTUNATELY PICKED UP STEAM.
I MADE "WEREWOLF OF FORT LAUDERDALE" AND "THE KOOSHBALL MOVIE" THE NEXT YEAR.
WEREWOLF OF FORT LAUDERDALE
LASER DISC
COLLECTOR S EDITION
I WALKED IN ON THE DIRECTOR OF "WEREWOLF" DOING BLOW OFF OF MY GAME BOY.

OWEN EUGENE'S EMMY ACCEPTANCE SPEECH 1987

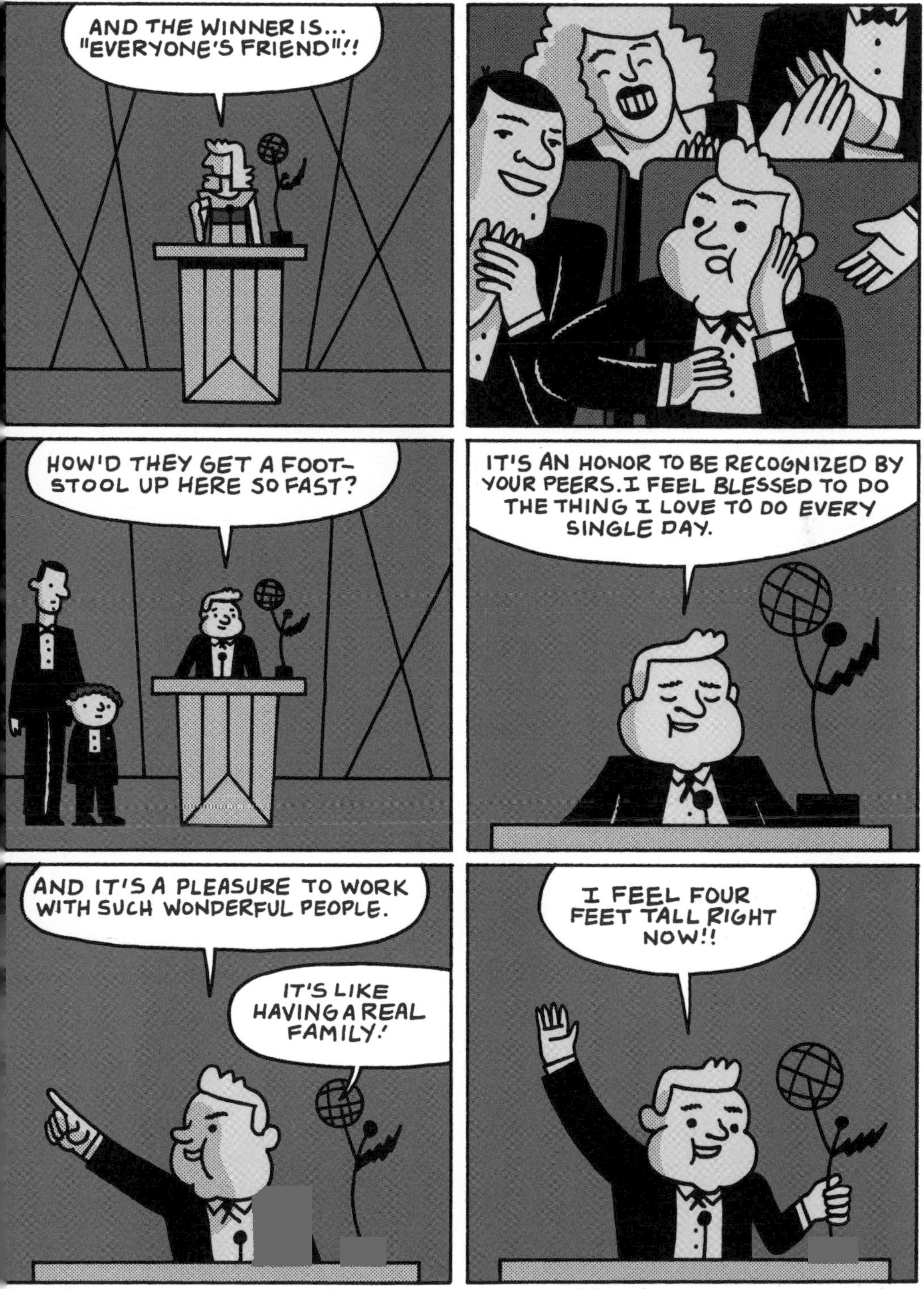
AND THE WINNER IS... "EVERYONE'S FRIEND"!!
HOW'D THEY GET A FOOT-STOOL UP HERE SO FAST?
IT'S AN HONOR TO BE RECOGNIZED BY YOUR PEERS. I FEEL BLESSED TO DO THE THING I LOVE TO DO EVERY SINGLE DAY.
AND IT'S A PLEASURE TO WORK WITH SUCH WONDERFUL PEOPLE.
IT'S LIKE HAVING A REAL FAMILY!
I FEEL FOUR FEET TALL RIGHT NOW!!

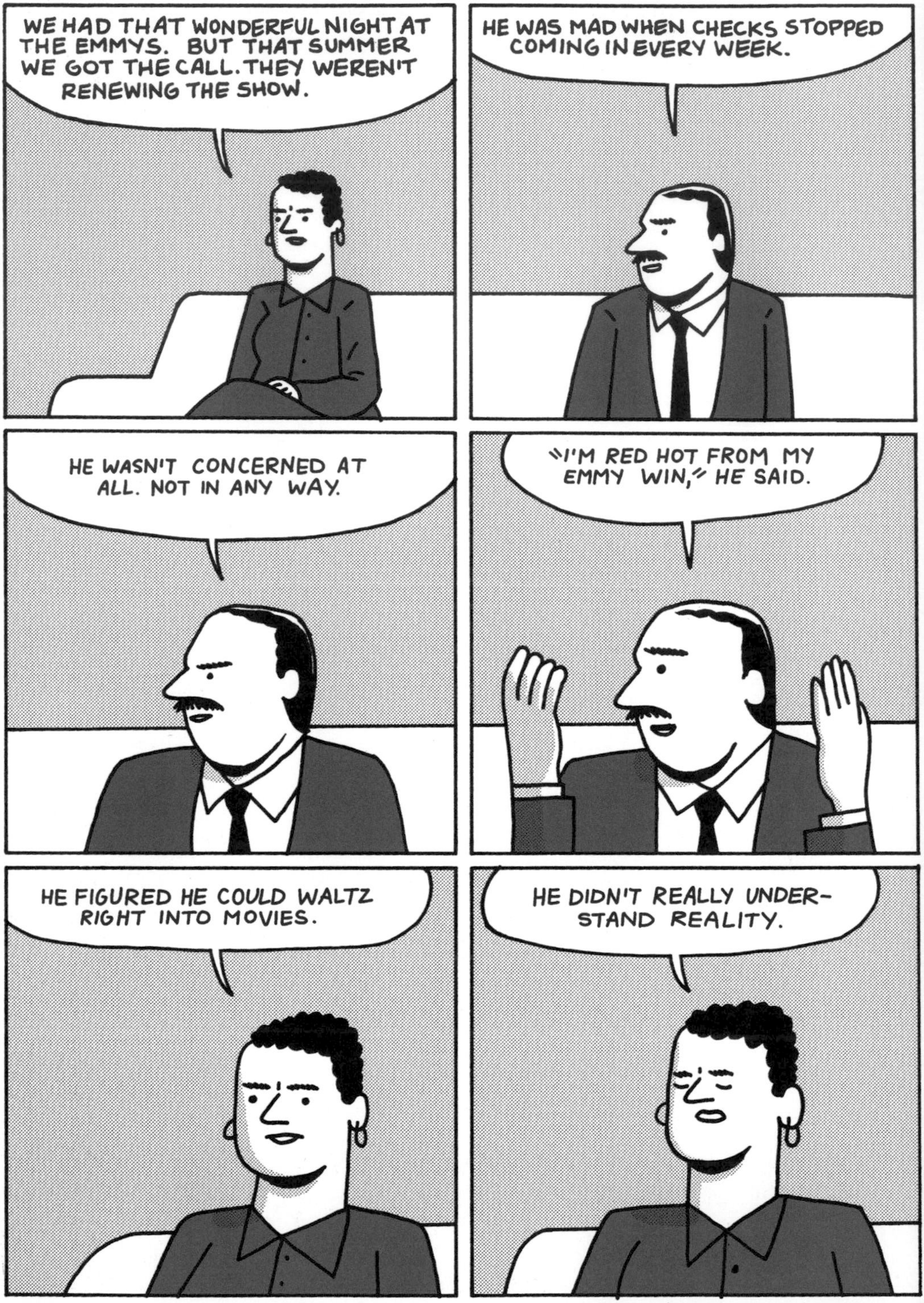
WE HAD THAT WONDERFUL NIGHT AT THE EMMYS. BUT THAT SUMMER WE GOT THE CALL. THEY WEREN'T RENEWING THE SHOW.
HE WAS MAD WHEN CHECKS STOPPED COMING IN EVERY WEEK.
HE WASN'T CONCERNED AT ALL. NOT IN ANY WAY.
"I'M RED HOT FROM MY EMMY WIN," HE SAID.
HE FIGURED HE COULD WALTZ RIGHT INTO MOVIES.
HE DIDN'T REALLY UNDER-STAND REALITY.

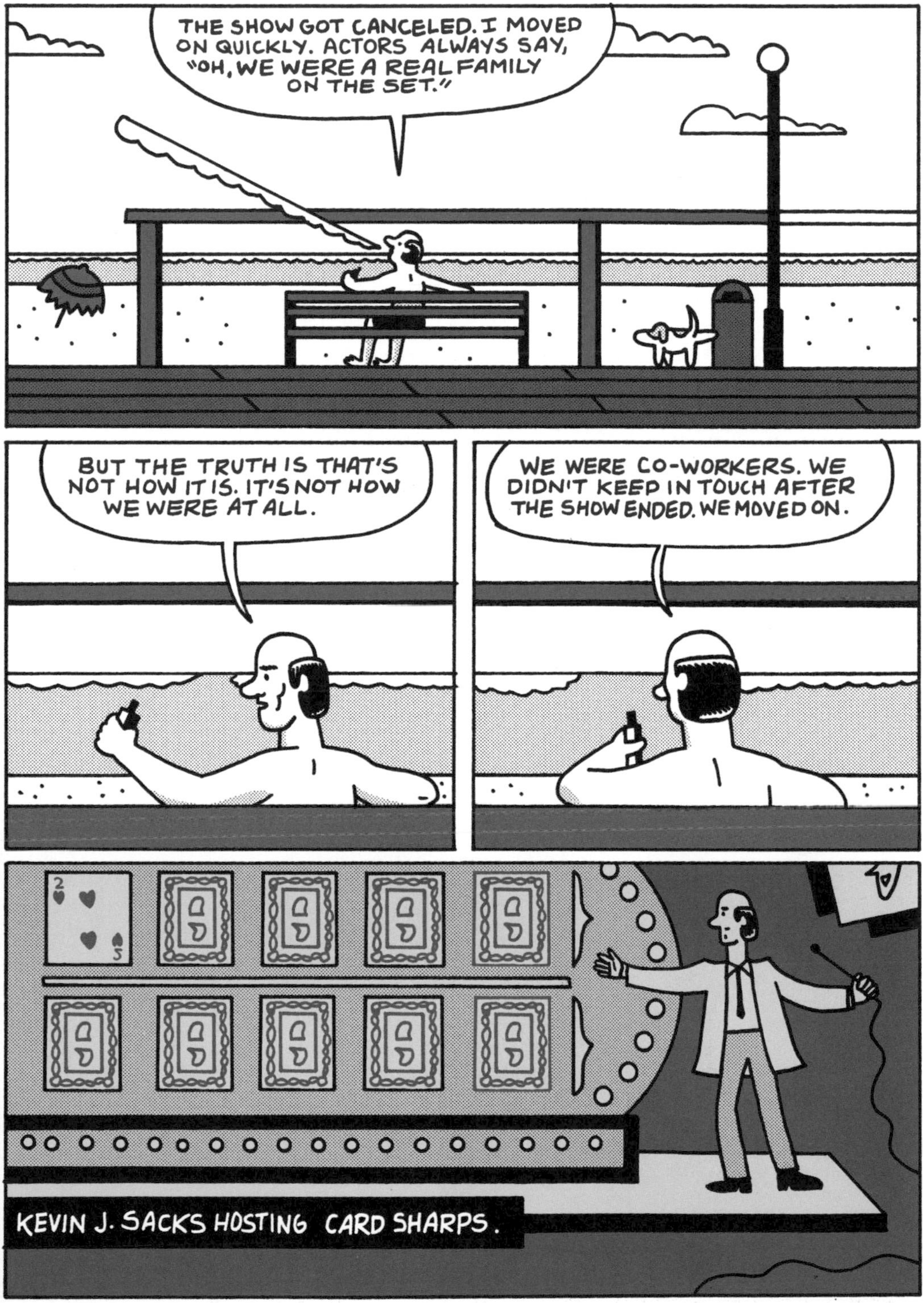
THE SHOW GOT CANCELED. I MOVED ON QUICKLY. ACTORS ALWAYS SAY, "OH, WE WERE A REAL FAMILY ON THE SET."
BUT THE TRUTH IS THAT'S NOT HOW IT IS. IT'S NOT HOW WE WERE AT ALL.
WE WERE CO-WORKERS. WE DIDN'T KEEP IN TOUCH AFTER THE SHOW ENDED. WE MOVED ON.
KEVIN J. SACKS HOSTING CARD SHARPS.

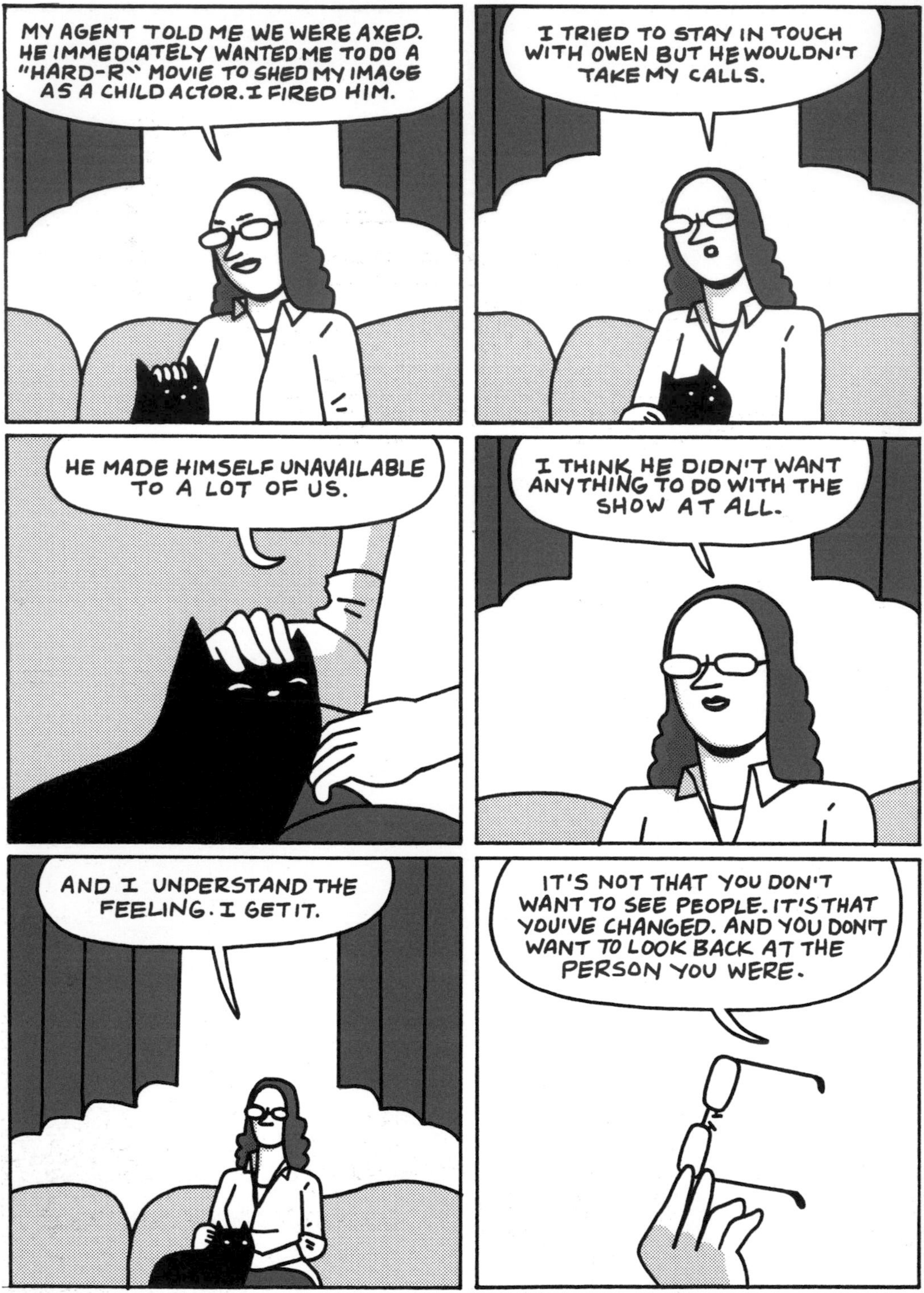
MY AGENT TOLD ME WE WERE AXED. HE IMMEDIATELY WANTED ME TO DO A "HARD-R" MOVIE TO SHED MY IMAGE AS A CHILD ACTOR. I FIRED HIM.
I TRIED TO STAY IN TOUCH WITH OWEN BUT HE WOULDN'T TAKE MY CALLS.
HE MADE HIMSELF UNAVAILABLE TO A LOT OF US.
I THINK HE DIDN'T WANT ANYTHING TO DO WITH THE SHOW AT ALL.
AND I UNDERSTAND THE FEELING. I GET IT.
IT'S NOT THAT YOU DON'T WANT TO SEE PEOPLE. IT'S THAT YOU'VE CHANGED. AND YOU DON'T WANT TO LOOK BACK AT THE PERSON YOU WERE.

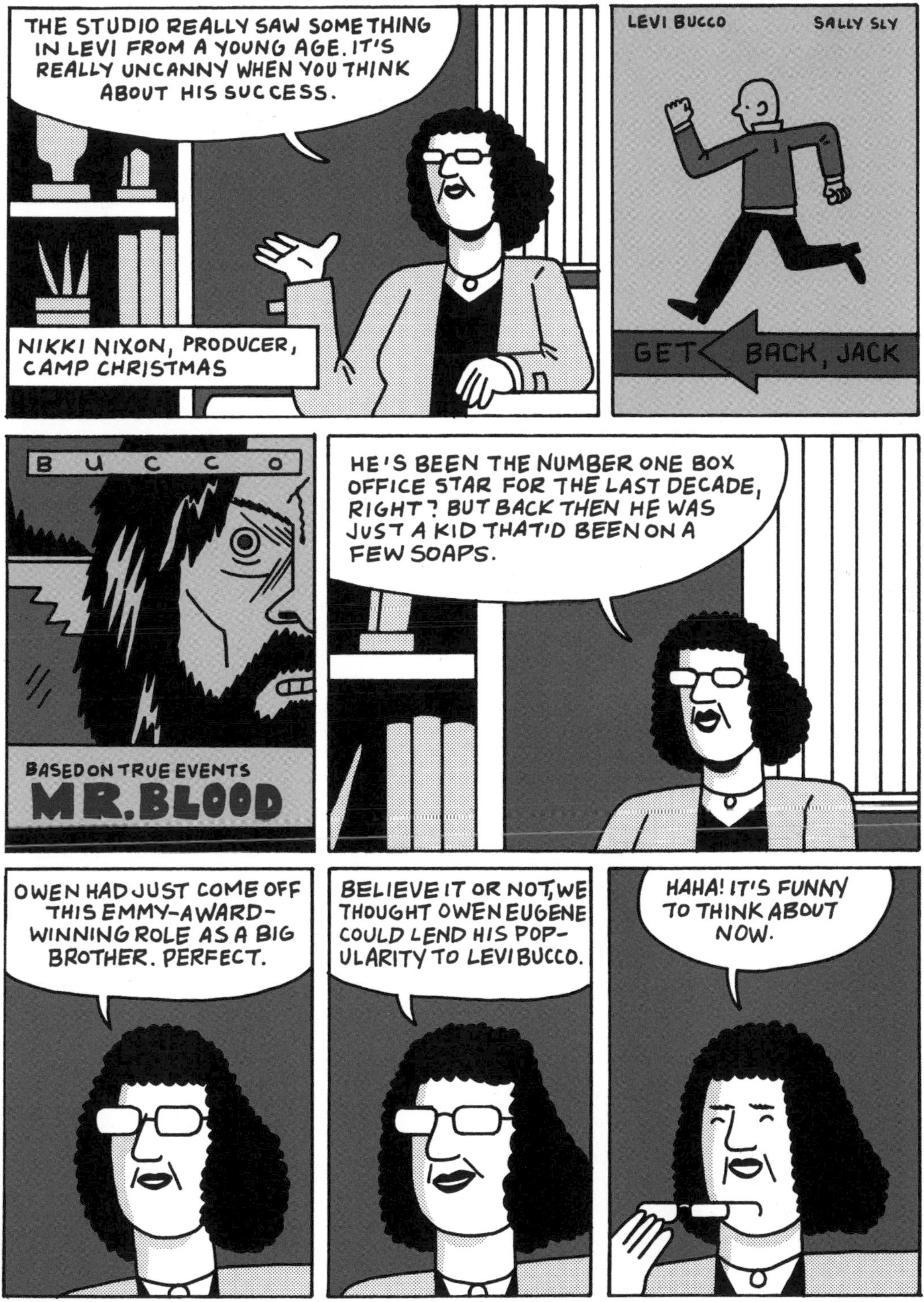
THE STUDIO REALLY SAW SOMETHING IN LEVI FROM A YOUNG AGE. IT'S REALLY UNCANNY WHEN YOU THINK ABOUT HIS SUCCESS.
NIKKI NIXON, PRODUCER, CAMP CHRISTMAS
LEVI BUCCO
SALLY SLY
GET BACK, JACK
BUCCO
BASED ON TRUE EVENTS
MR. BLOOD
HE'S BEEN THE NUMBER ONE BOX OFFICE STAR FOR THE LAST DECADE, RIGHT? BUT BACK THEN HE WAS JUST A KID THAT'D BEEN ON A FEW SOAPS.
OWEN HAD JUST COME OFF THIS EMMY-AWARD-WINNING ROLE AS A BIG BROTHER. PERFECT.
BELIEVE IT OR NOT, WE THOUGHT OWEN EUGENE COULD LEND HIS POPULARITY TO LEVI BUCCO.
HAHA! IT'S FUNNY TO THINK ABOUT NOW.

CAMP CHRISTMAS (1990)

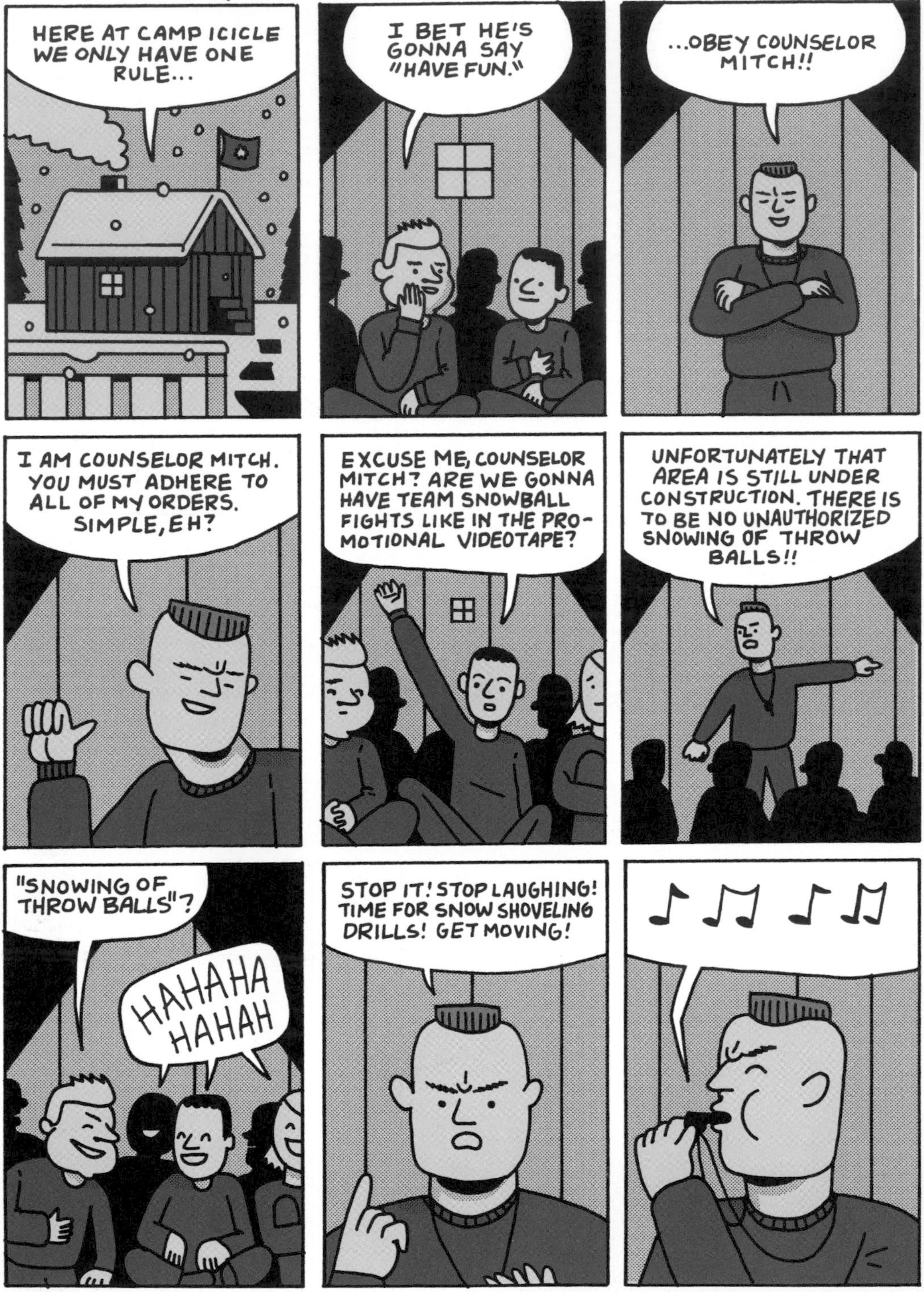
HERE AT CAMP ICICLE WE ONLY HAVE ONE RULE...
I BET HE'S GONNA SAY "HAVE FUN."
...OBEY COUNSELOR MITCH!!
I AM COUNSELOR MITCH. YOU MUST ADHERE TO ALL OF MY ORDERS. SIMPLE, EH?
EXCUSE ME, COUNSELOR MITCH? ARE WE GONNA HAVE TEAM SNOWBALL FIGHTS LIKE IN THE PROMOTIONAL VIDEOTAPE?
UNFORTUNATELY THAT AREA IS STILL UNDER CONSTRUCTION. THERE IS TO BE NO UNAUTHORIZED SNOWING OF THROW BALLS!!
"SNOWING OF THROW BALLS"?
HAHAHA HAHAH
STOP IT! STOP LAUGHING! TIME FOR SNOW SHOVELING DRILLS! GET MOVING!

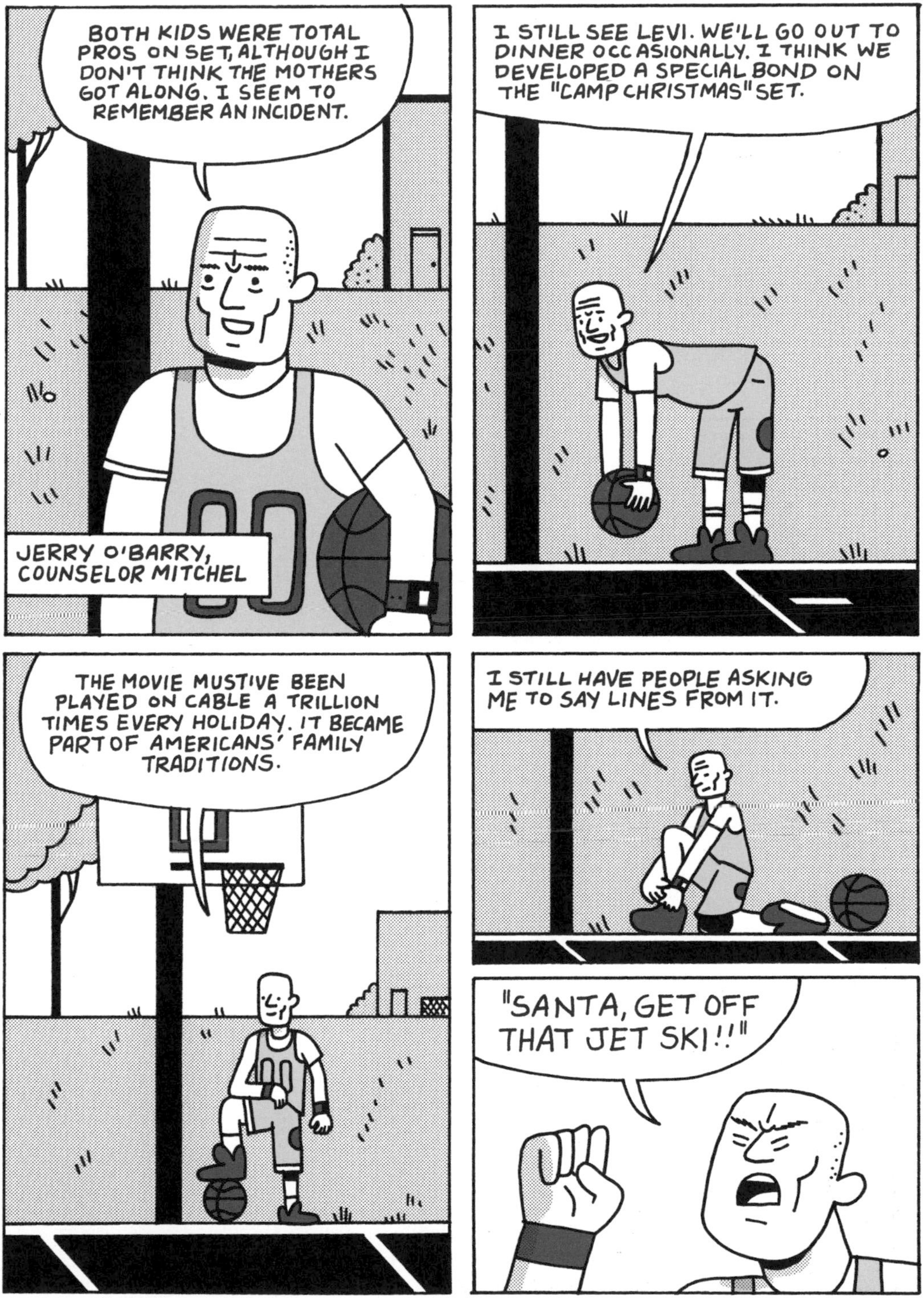

BOTH KIDS WERE TOTAL PROS ON SET, ALTHOUGH I DON'T THINK THE MOTHERS GOT ALONG. I SEEM TO REMEMBER AN INCIDENT.
JERRY O'BARRY, COUNSELOR MITCHEL
I STILL SEE LEVI. WE'LL GO OUT TO DINNER OCCASIONALLY. I THINK WE DEVELOPED A SPECIAL BOND ON THE "CAMP CHRISTMAS" SET.
THE MOVIE MUST'VE BEEN PLAYED ON CABLE A TRILLION TIMES EVERY HOLIDAY. IT BECAME PART OF AMERICANS' FAMILY TRADITIONS.
I STILL HAVE PEOPLE ASKING ME TO SAY LINES FROM IT.
"SANTA, GET OFF THAT JET SKI!!"

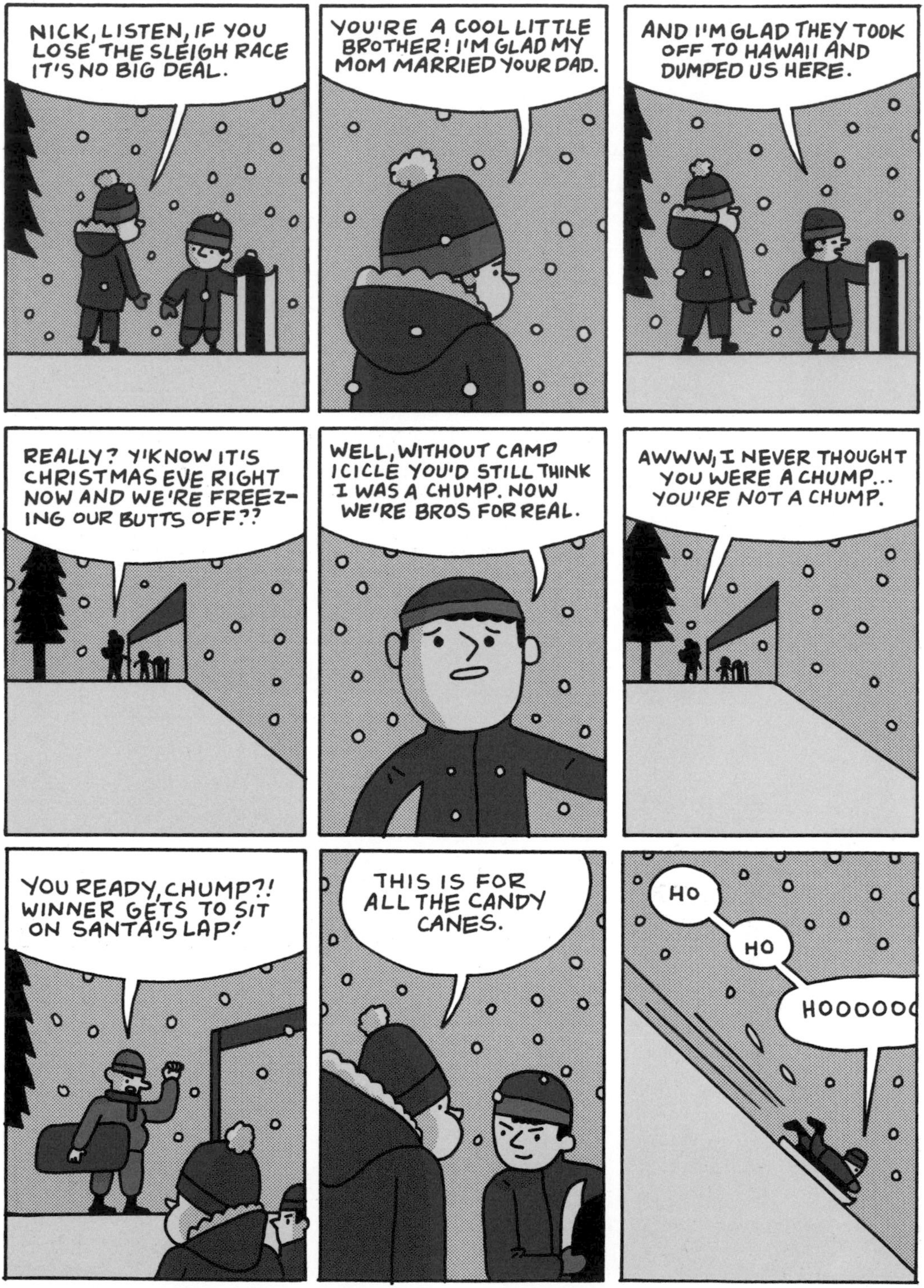
NICK, LISTEN, IF YOU LOSE THE SLEIGH RACE IT'S NO BIG DEAL.
YOU'RE A COOL LITTLE BROTHER! I'M GLAD MY MOM MARRIED YOUR DAD.
AND I'M GLAD THEY TOOK OFF TO HAWAII AND DUMPED US HERE.
REALLY? Y'KNOW IT'S CHRISTMAS EVE RIGHT NOW AND WE'RE FREEZ-ING OUR BUTTS OFF??
WELL, WITHOUT CAMP ICICLE YOU'D STILL THINK I WAS A CHUMP. NOW WE'RE BROS FOR REAL.
AWWW, I NEVER THOUGHT YOU WERE A CHUMP... YOU'RE NOT A CHUMP.
YOU READY, CHUMP?! WINNER GETS TO SIT ON SANTA'S LAP!
THIS IS FOR ALL THE CANDY CANES.
HO
HO
HOOOOOO

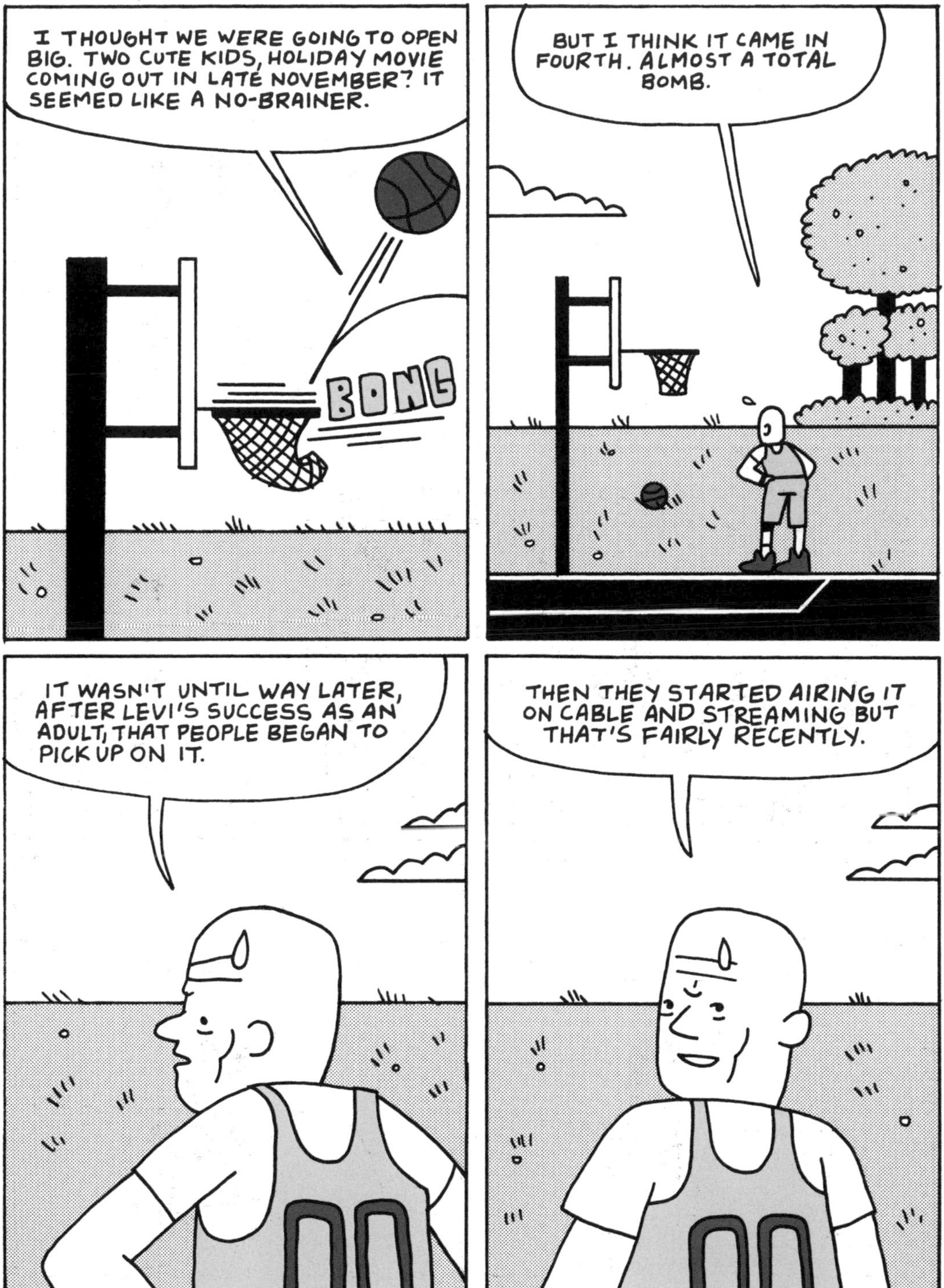
I THOUGHT WE WERE GOING TO OPEN BIG. TWO CUTE KIDS, HOLIDAY MOVIE COMING OUT IN LATE NOVEMBER? IT SEEMED LIKE A NO-BRAINER.
BONG
BUT I THINK IT CAME IN FOURTH. ALMOST A TOTAL BOMB.
IT WASN'T UNTIL WAY LATER, AFTER LEVI'S SUCCESS AS AN ADULT, THAT PEOPLE BEGAN TO PICK UP ON IT.
THEN THEY STARTED AIRING IT ON CABLE AND STREAMING BUT THAT'S FAIRLY RECENTLY.

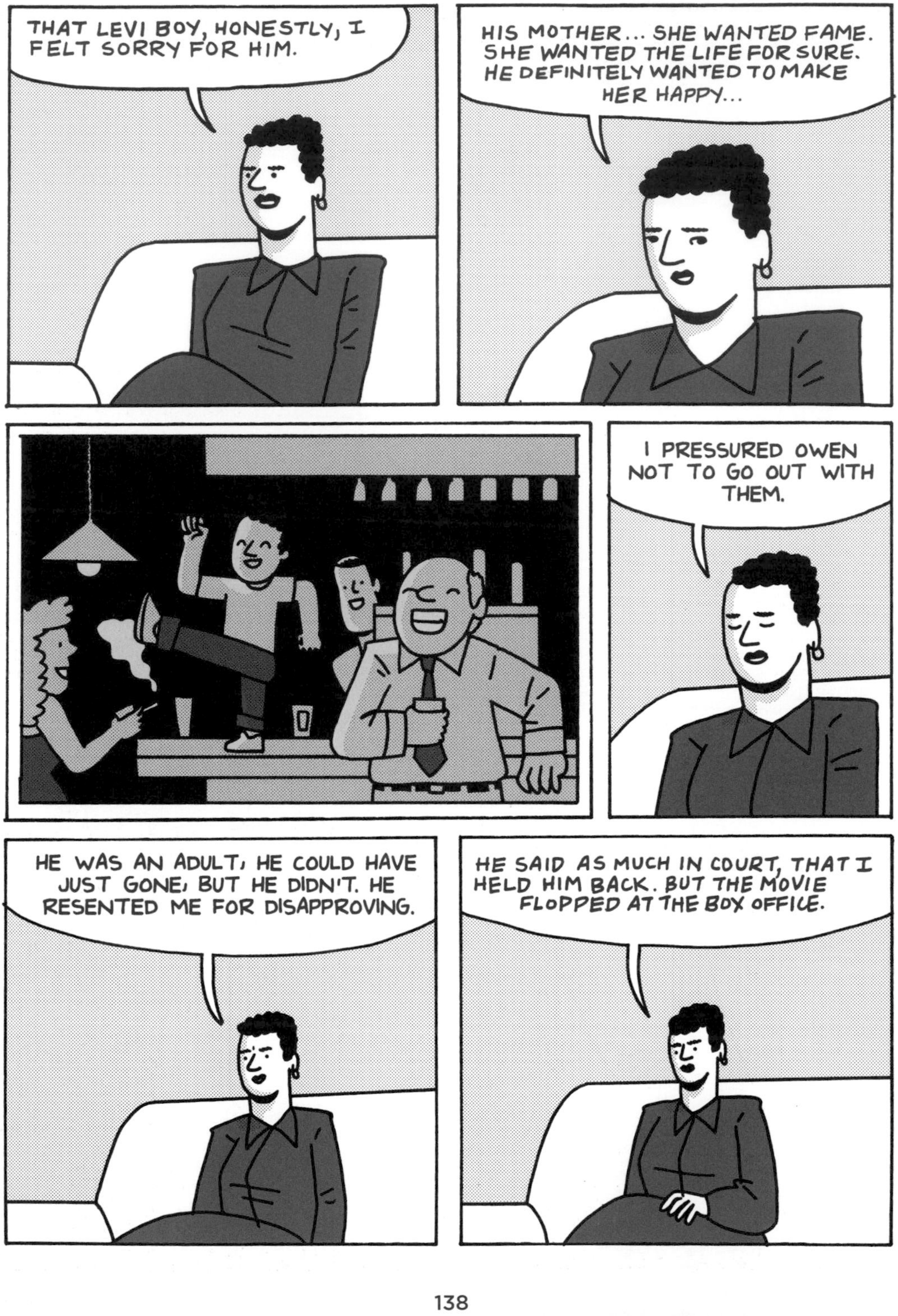
THAT LEVI BOY, HONESTLY, I FELT SORRY FOR HIM.
HIS MOTHER... SHE WANTED FAME. SHE WANTED THE LIFE FOR SURE. HE DEFINITELY WANTED TO MAKE HER HAPPY...
I PRESSURED OWEN NOT TO GO OUT WITH THEM.
HE WAS AN ADULT, HE COULD HAVE JUST GONE, BUT HE DIDN'T. HE RESENTED ME FOR DISAPPROVING.
HE SAID AS MUCH IN COURT, THAT I HELD HIM BACK. BUT THE MOVIE FLOPPED AT THE BOX OFFICE.

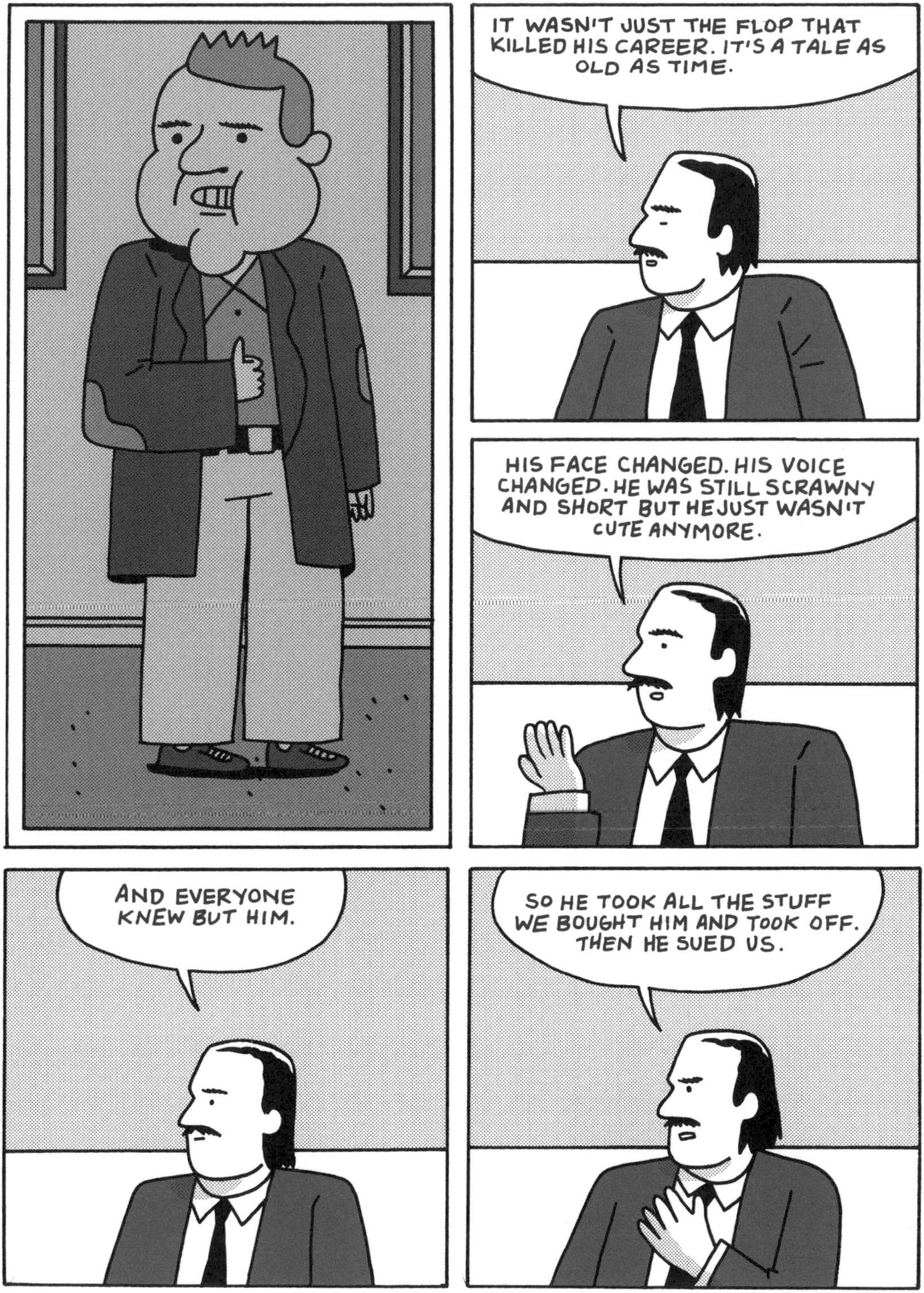
IT WASN'T JUST THE FLOP THAT KILLED HIS CAREER. IT'S A TALE AS OLD AS TIME.
HIS FACE CHANGED. HIS VOICE CHANGED. HE WAS STILL SCRAWNY AND SHORT BUT HE JUST WASN'T CUTE ANYMORE.
AND EVERYONE KNEW BUT HIM.
SO HE TOOK ALL THE STUFF WE BOUGHT HIM AND TOOK OFF. THEN HE SUED US.

PART TWO

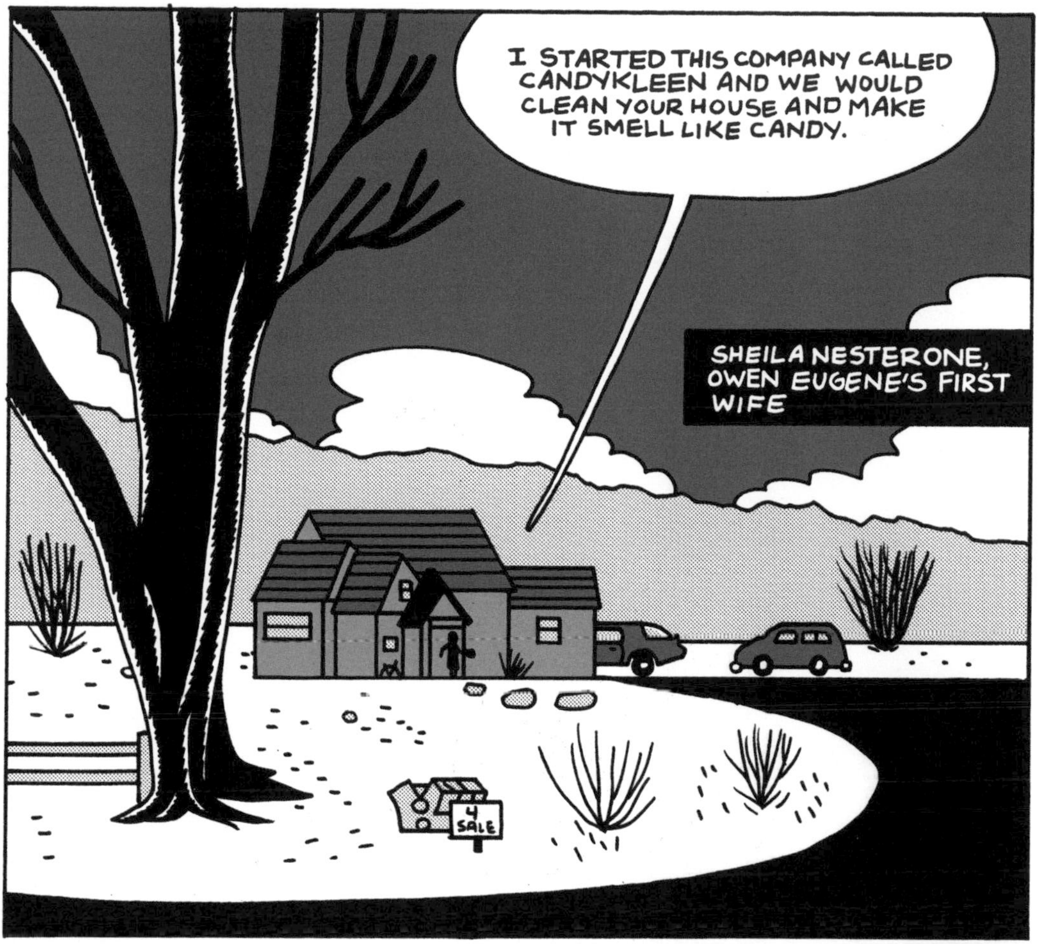
I STARTED THIS COMPANY CALLED CANDYKLEEN AND WE WOULD CLEAN YOUR HOUSE AND MAKE IT SMELL LIKE CANDY.
SHEILA NESTERONE, OWEN EUGENE'S FIRST WIFE
4 SALE

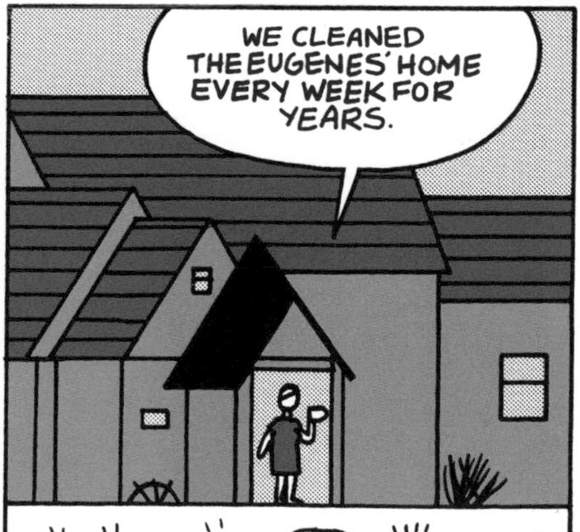
WE CLEANED THE EUGENES' HOME EVERY WEEK FOR YEARS.

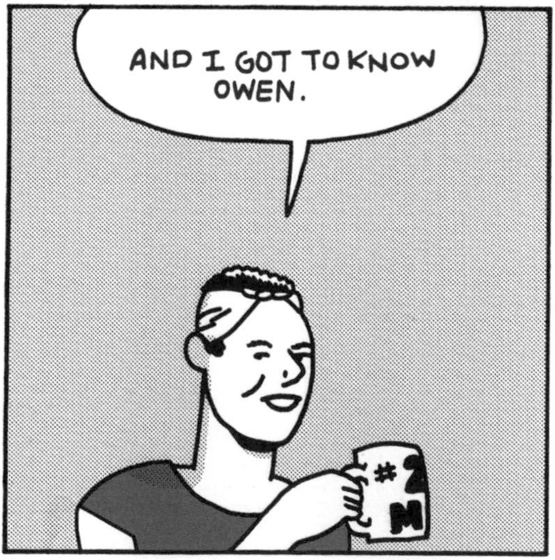
AND I GOT TO KNOW OWEN.

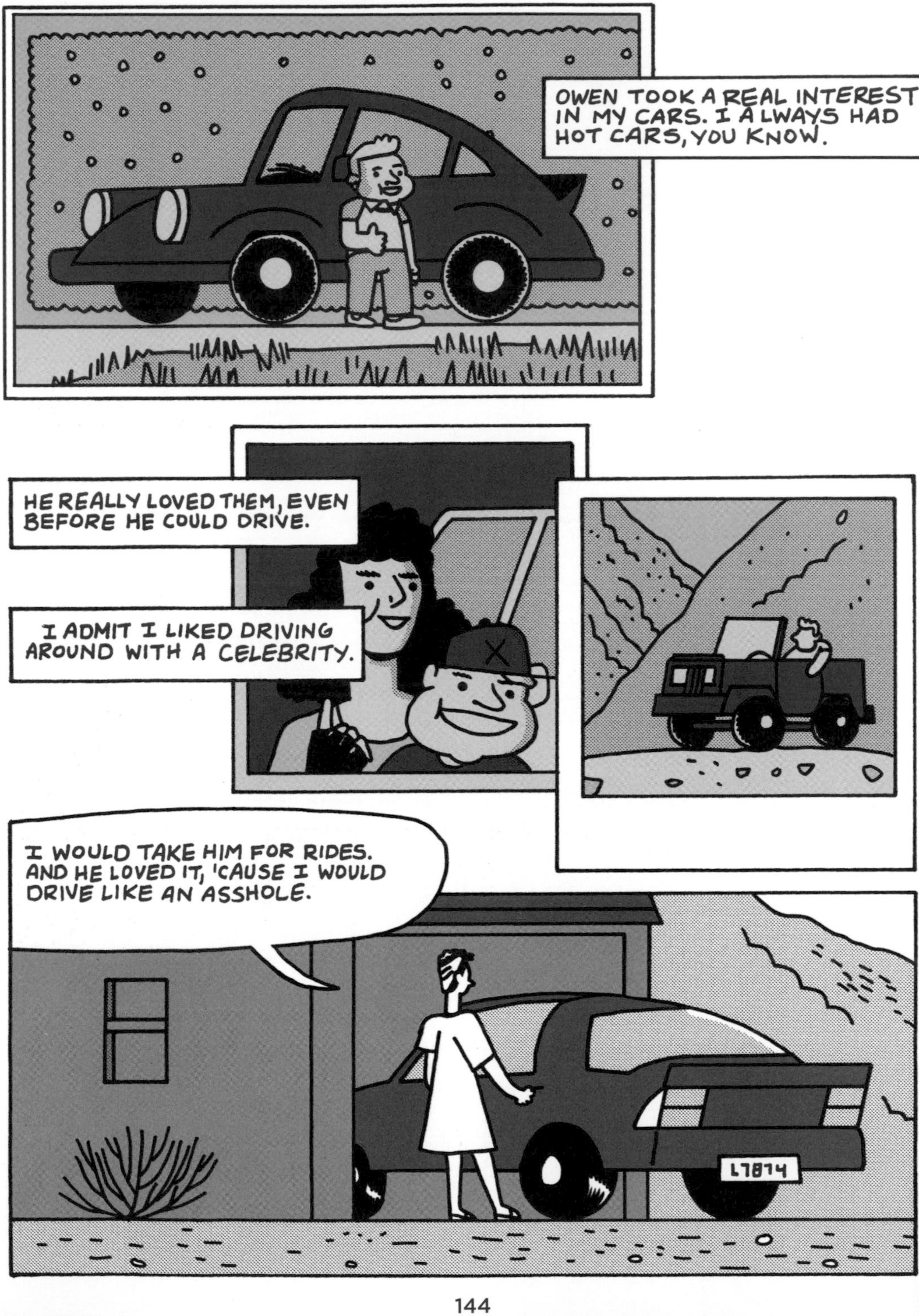
OWEN TOOK A REAL INTEREST IN MY CARS. I ALWAYS HAD HOT CARS, YOU KNOW.
HE REALLY LOVED THEM, EVEN BEFORE HE COULD DRIVE.
I ADMIT I LIKED DRIVING AROUND WITH A CELEBRITY.
I WOULD TAKE HIM FOR RIDES. AND HE LOVED IT, 'CAUSE I WOULD DRIVE LIKE AN ASSHOLE.
L7874

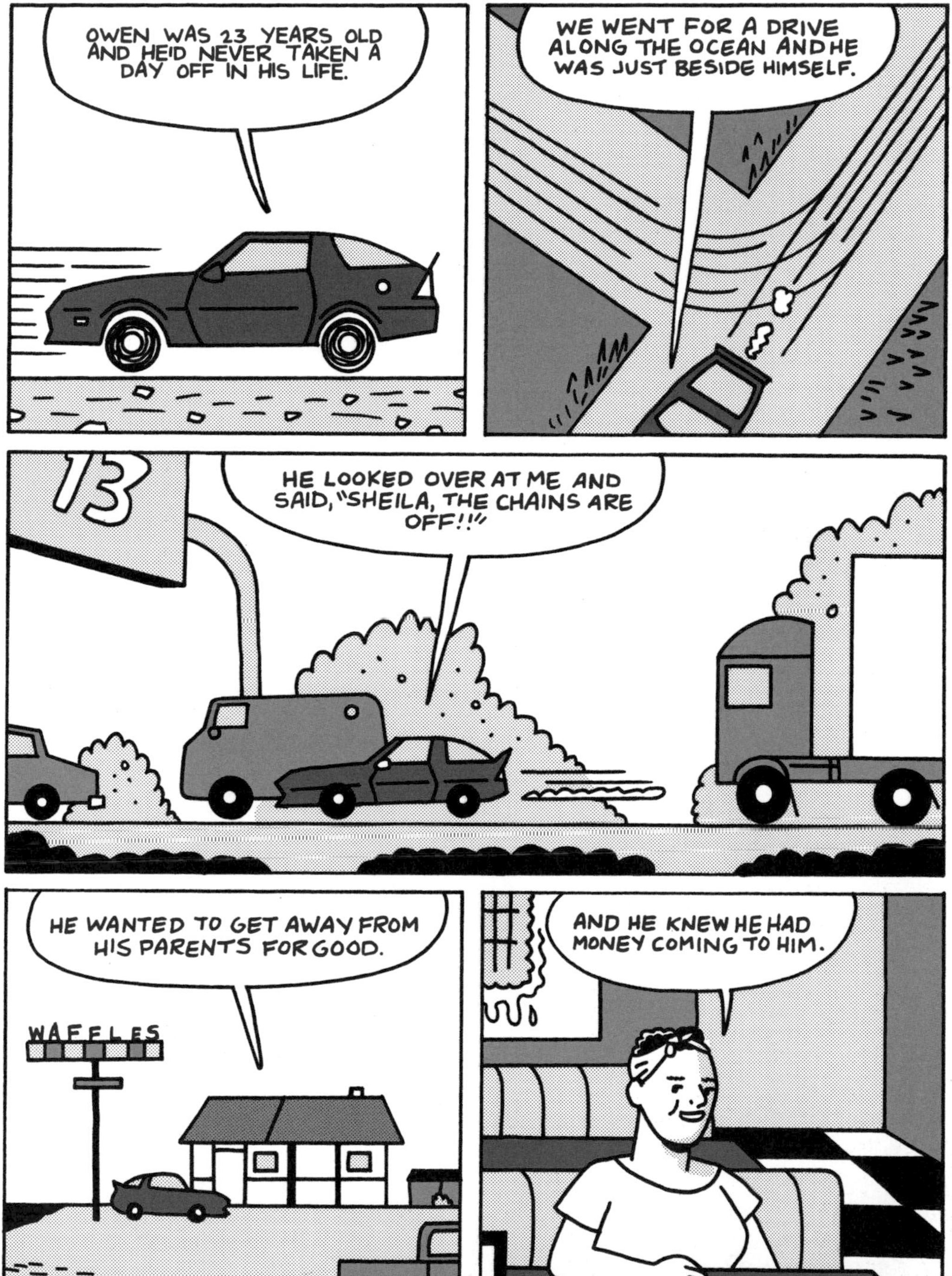
OWEN WAS 23 YEARS OLD AND HE'D NEVER TAKEN A DAY OFF IN HIS LIFE.
WE WENT FOR A DRIVE ALONG THE OCEAN AND HE WAS JUST BESIDE HIMSELF.
13
HE LOOKED OVER AT ME AND SAID, "SHEILA, THE CHAINS ARE OFF!!"
HE WANTED TO GET AWAY FROM HIS PARENTS FOR GOOD.
WAFFLES
AND HE KNEW HE HAD MONEY COMING TO HIM.

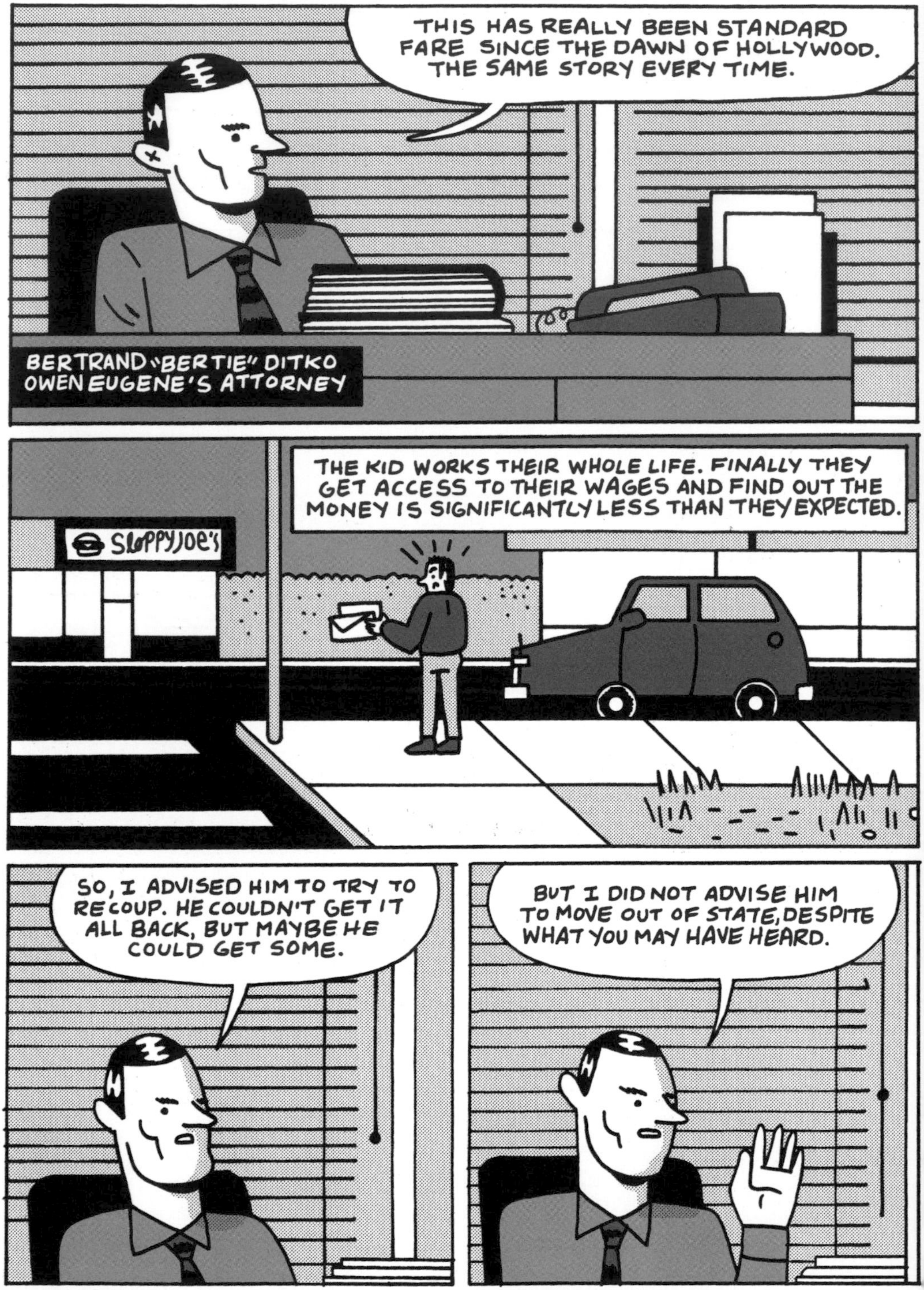
THIS HAS REALLY BEEN STANDARD FARE SINCE THE DAWN OF HOLLYWOOD. THE SAME STORY EVERY TIME.
BERTRAND "BERTIE" DITKO
OWEN EUGENE'S ATTORNEY
THE KID WORKS THEIR WHOLE LIFE. FINALLY THEY GET ACCESS TO THEIR WAGES AND FIND OUT THE MONEY IS SIGNIFICANTLY LESS THAN THEY EXPECTED.
SLOPPY JOE'S
SO, I ADVISED HIM TO TRY TO RECOUP. HE COULDN'T GET IT ALL BACK, BUT MAYBE HE COULD GET SOME.
BUT I DID NOT ADVISE HIM TO MOVE OUT OF STATE, DESPITE WHAT YOU MAY HAVE HEARD.

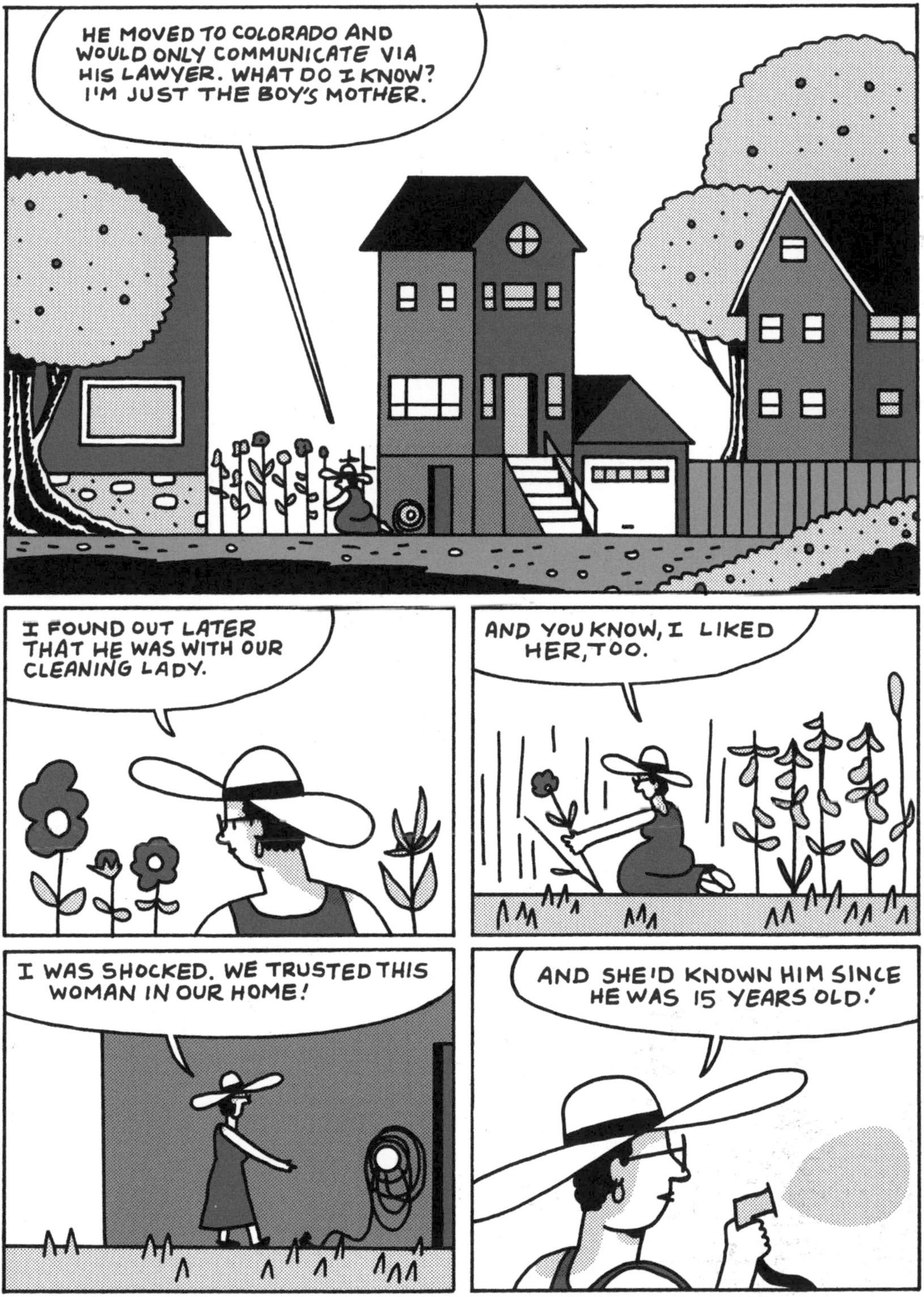
HE MOVED TO COLORADO AND WOULD ONLY COMMUNICATE VIA HIS LAWYER. WHAT DO I KNOW? I'M JUST THE BOY'S MOTHER.
I FOUND OUT LATER THAT HE WAS WITH OUR CLEANING LADY.
AND YOU KNOW, I LIKED HER, TOO.
I WAS SHOCKED. WE TRUSTED THIS WOMAN IN OUR HOME!
AND SHE'D KNOWN HIM SINCE HE WAS 15 YEARS OLD.'

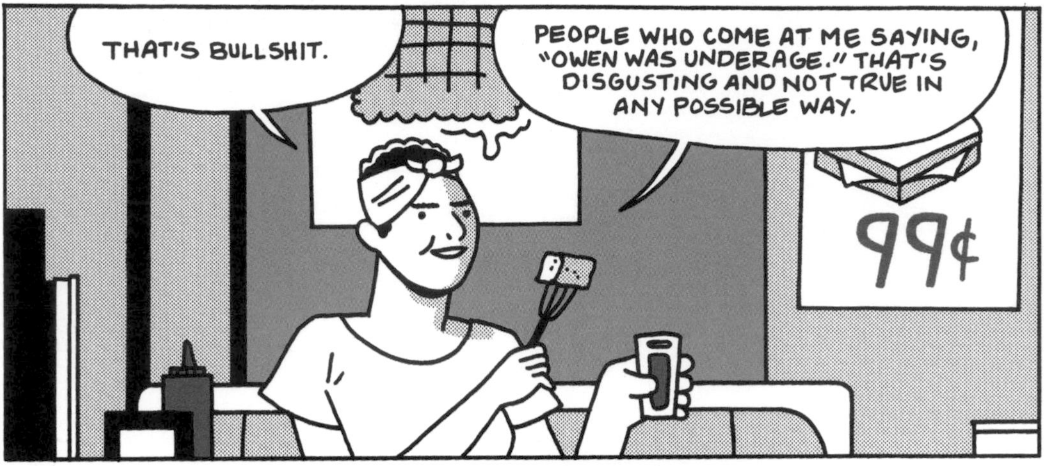
THAT'S BULLSHIT.
PEOPLE WHO COME AT ME SAYING, "OWEN WAS UNDERAGE." THAT'S DISGUSTING AND NOT TRUE IN ANY POSSIBLE WAY.
99¢

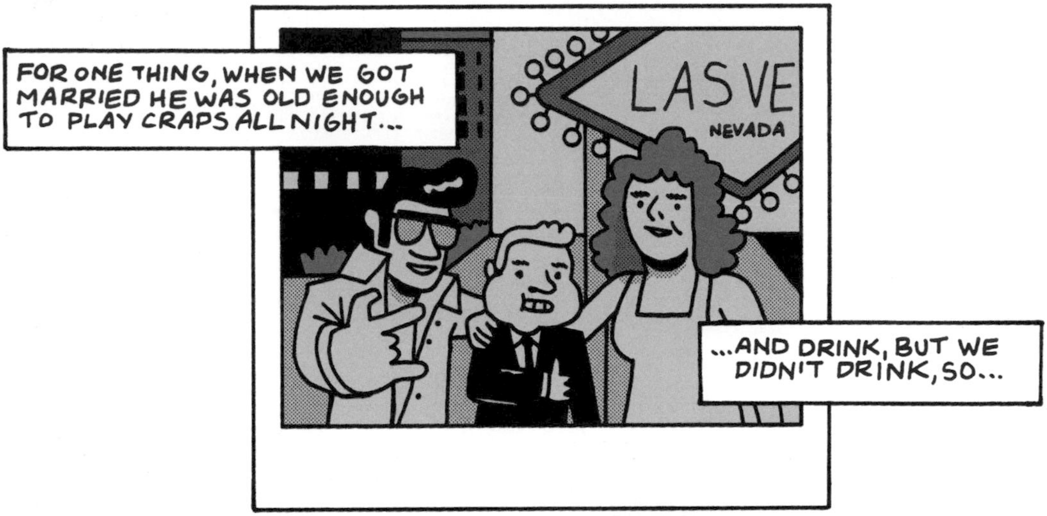
FOR ONE THING, WHEN WE GOT MARRIED HE WAS OLD ENOUGH TO PLAY CRAPS ALL NIGHT...
LAS VE
NEVADA
...AND DRINK, BUT WE DIDN'T DRINK, SO...

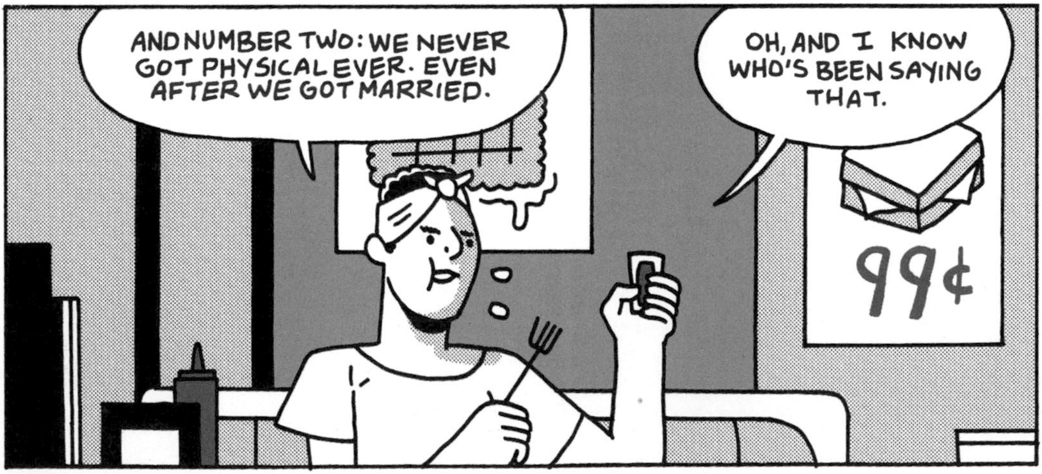
AND NUMBER TWO: WE NEVER GOT PHYSICAL EVER. EVEN AFTER WE GOT MARRIED.
OH, AND I KNOW WHO'S BEEN SAYING THAT.
99¢

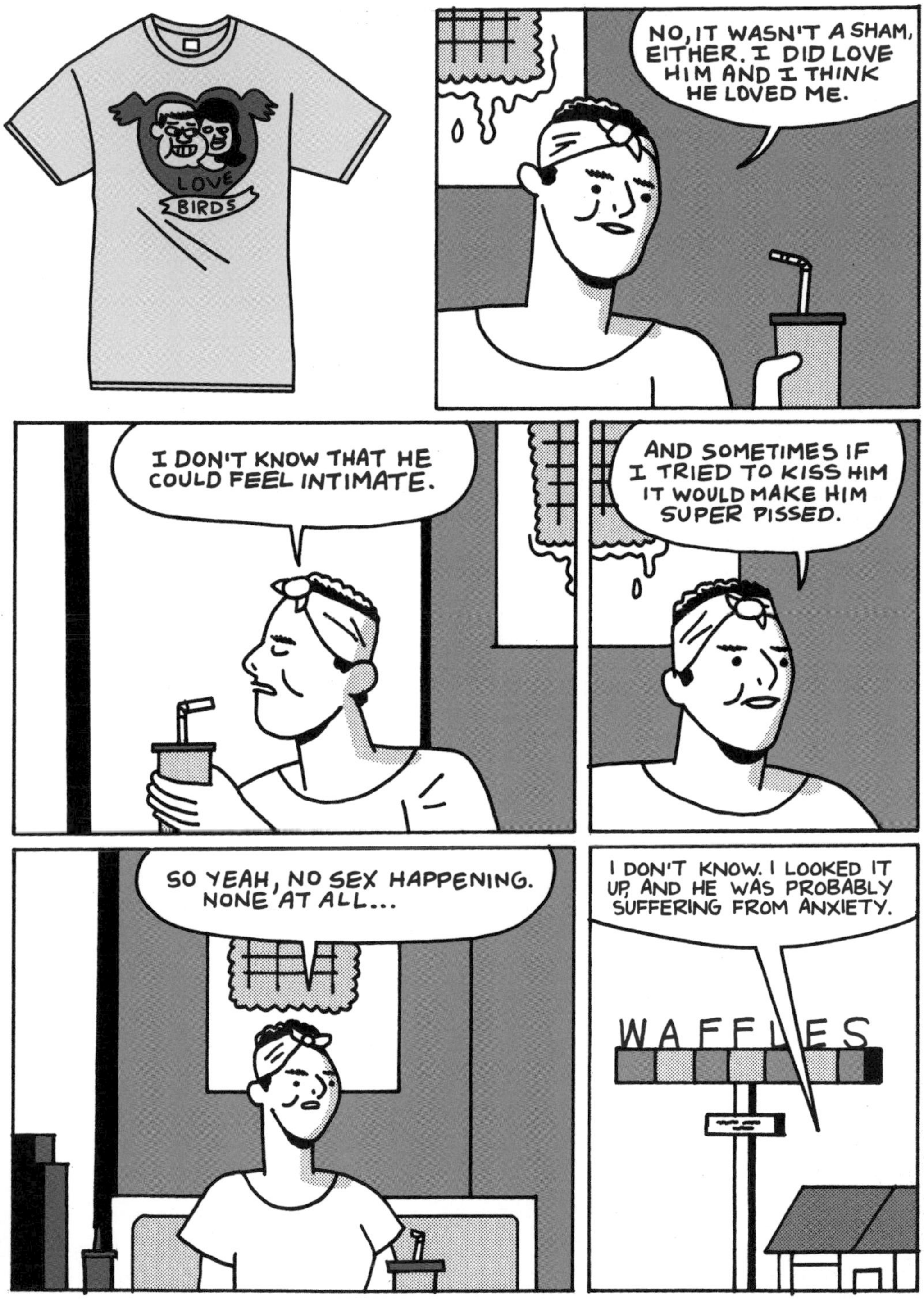
LOVE BIRDS
NO, IT WASN'T A SHAM, EITHER. I DID LOVE HIM AND I THINK HE LOVED ME.
I DON'T KNOW THAT HE COULD FEEL INTIMATE.
AND SOMETIMES IF I TRIED TO KISS HIM IT WOULD MAKE HIM SUPER PISSED.
SO YEAH, NO SEX HAPPENING. NONE AT ALL...
I DON'T KNOW. I LOOKED IT UP, AND HE WAS PROBABLY SUFFERING FROM ANXIETY.
WAFFLES

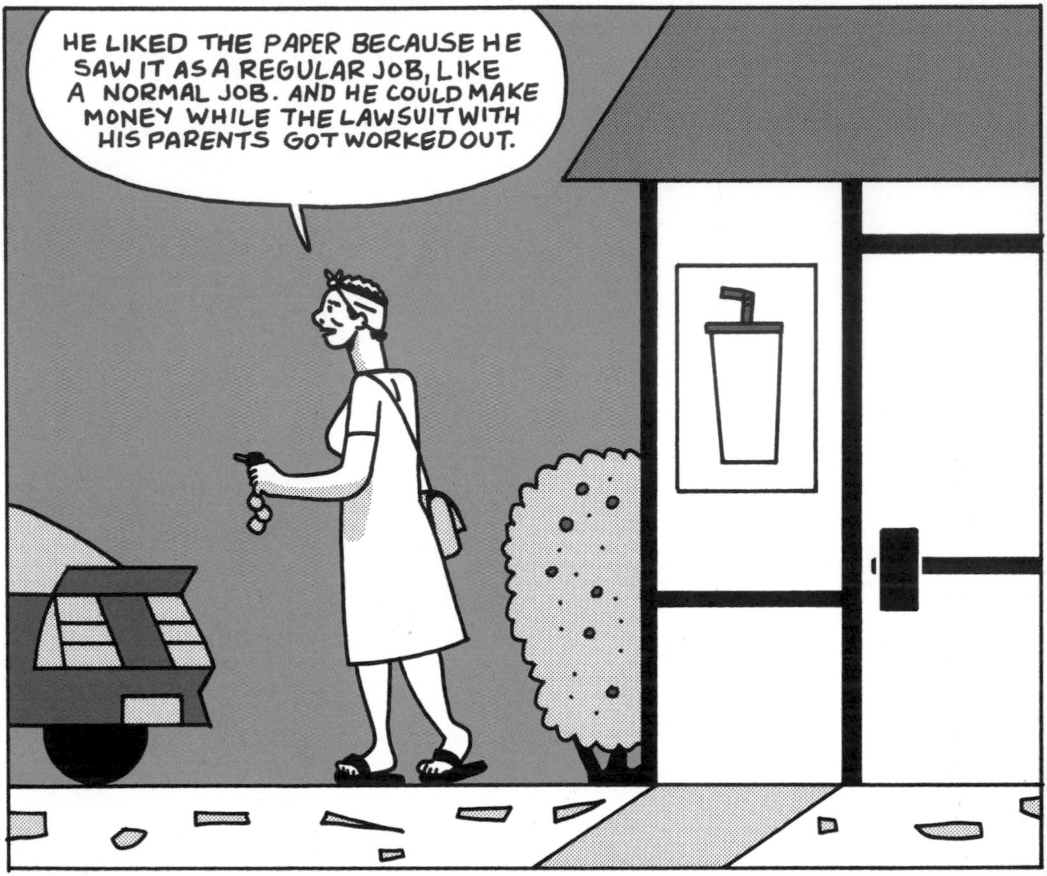
HE LIKED THE PAPER BECAUSE HE SAW IT AS A REGULAR JOB, LIKE A NORMAL JOB. AND HE COULD MAKE MONEY WHILE THE LAWSUIT WITH HIS PARENTS GOT WORKED OUT.

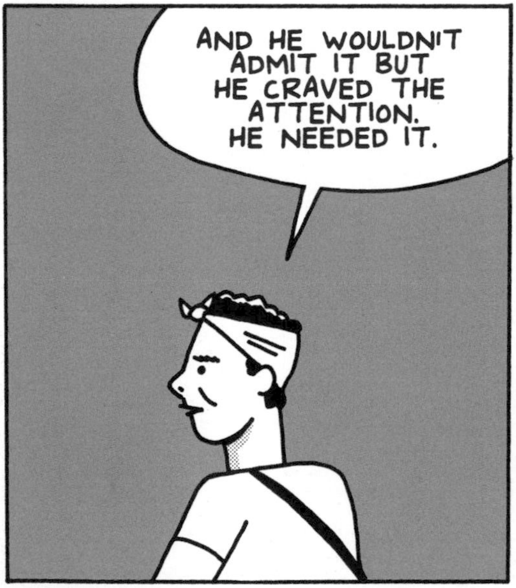
AND HE WOULDN'T ADMIT IT BUT HE CRAVED THE ATTENTION. HE NEEDED IT.

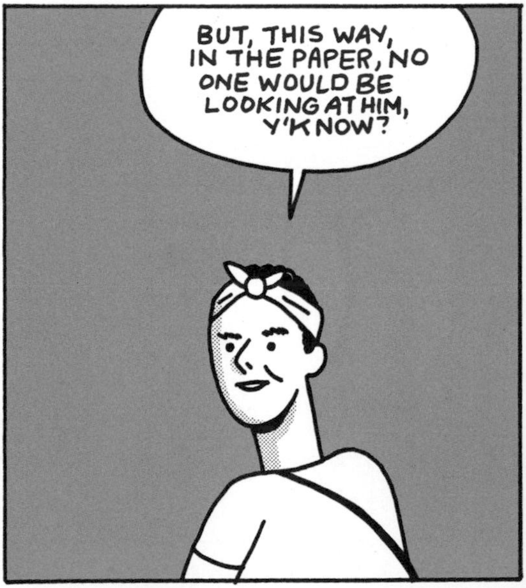
BUT, THIS WAY, IN THE PAPER, NO ONE WOULD BE LOOKING AT HIM, Y'KNOW?

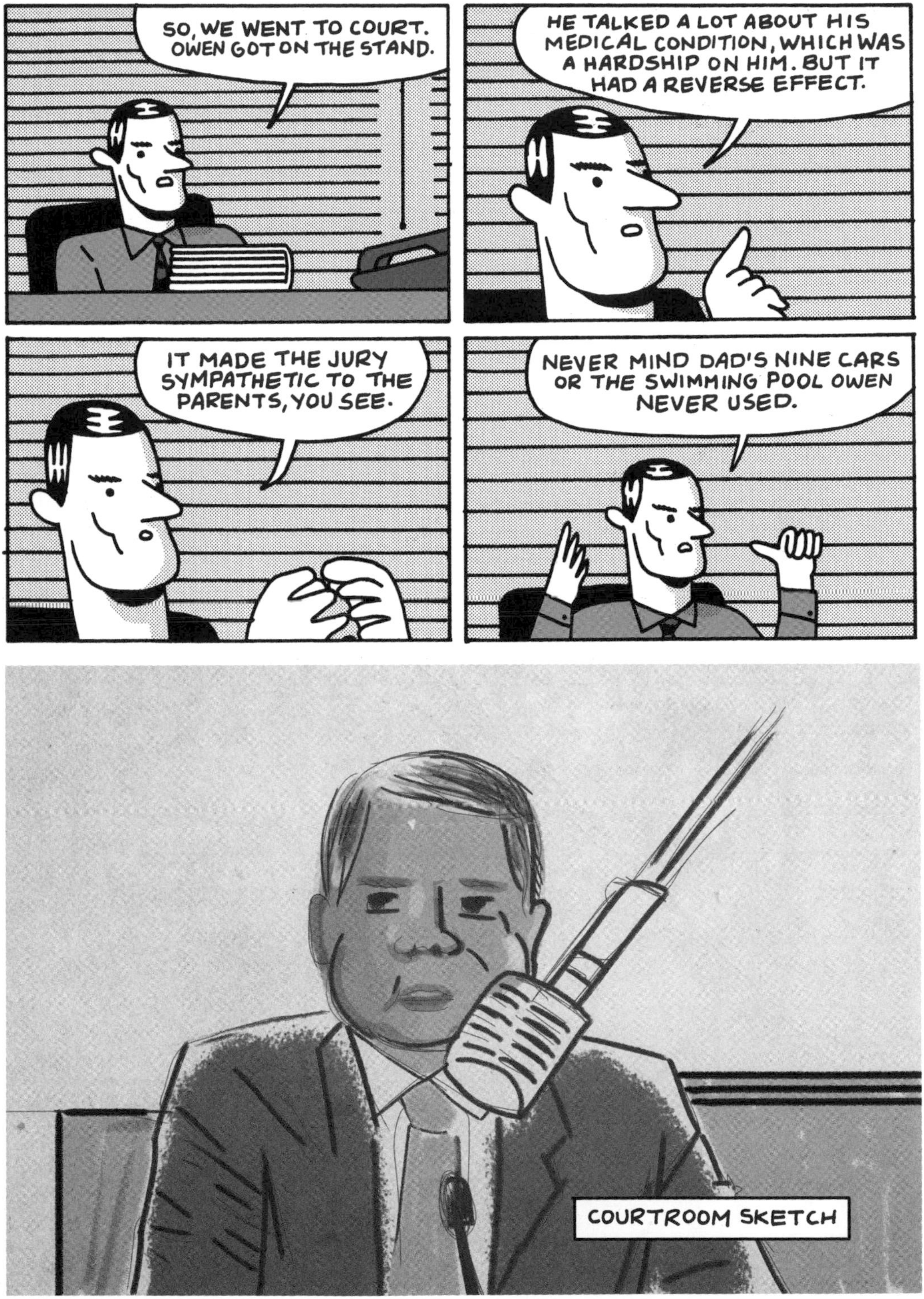
SO, WE WENT TO COURT. OWEN GOT ON THE STAND.
HE TALKED A LOT ABOUT HIS MEDICAL CONDITION, WHICH WAS A HARDSHIP ON HIM. BUT IT HAD A REVERSE EFFECT.
IT MADE THE JURY SYMPATHETIC TO THE PARENTS, YOU SEE.
NEVER MIND DAD'S NINE CARS OR THE SWIMMING POOL OWEN NEVER USED.
COURTROOM SKETCH

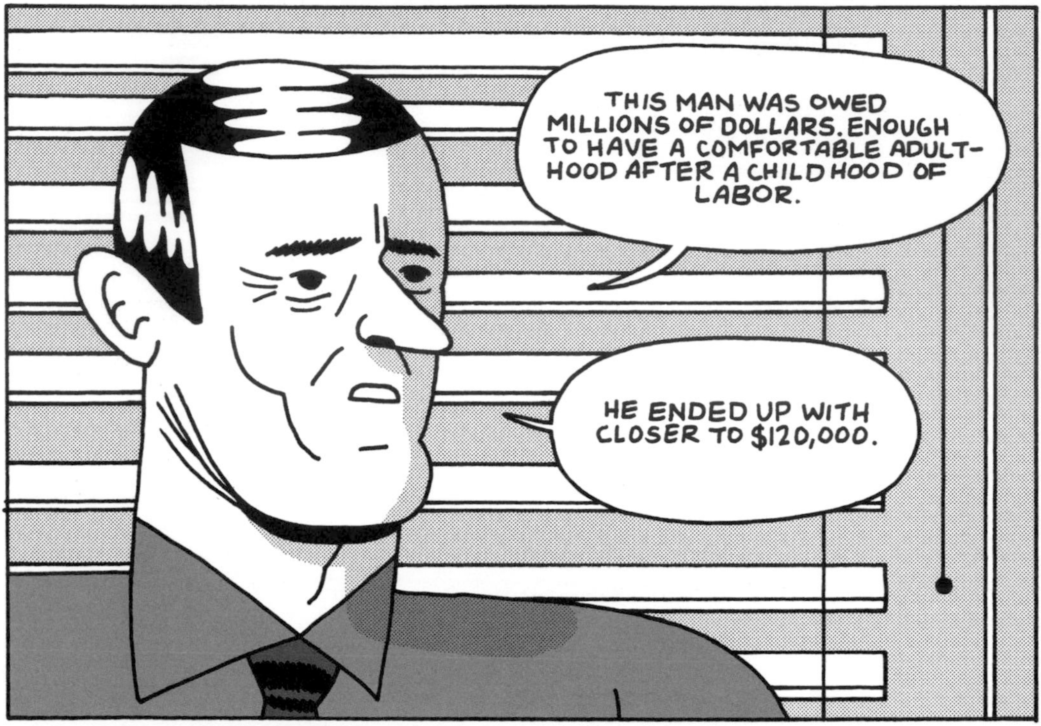
THIS MAN WAS OWED MILLIONS OF DOLLARS. ENOUGH TO HAVE A COMFORTABLE ADULT-HOOD AFTER A CHILDHOOD OF LABOR.
HE ENDED UP WITH CLOSER TO $120,000.

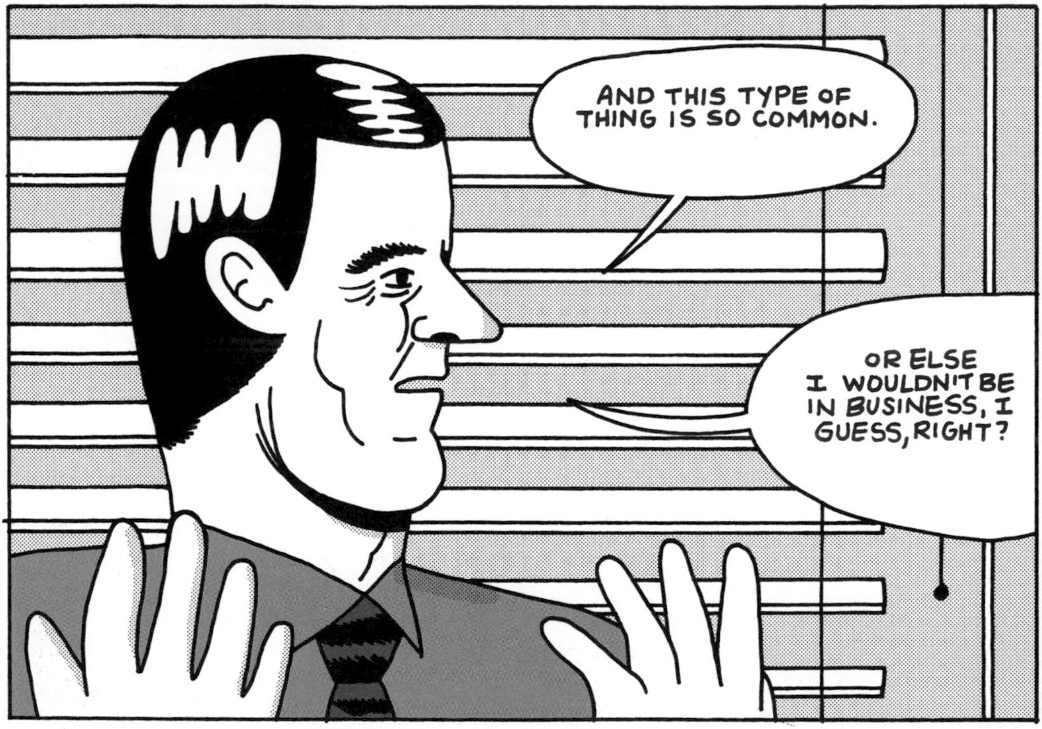
AND THIS TYPE OF THING IS SO COMMON.
OR ELSE I WOULDN'T BE IN BUSINESS, I GUESS, RIGHT?

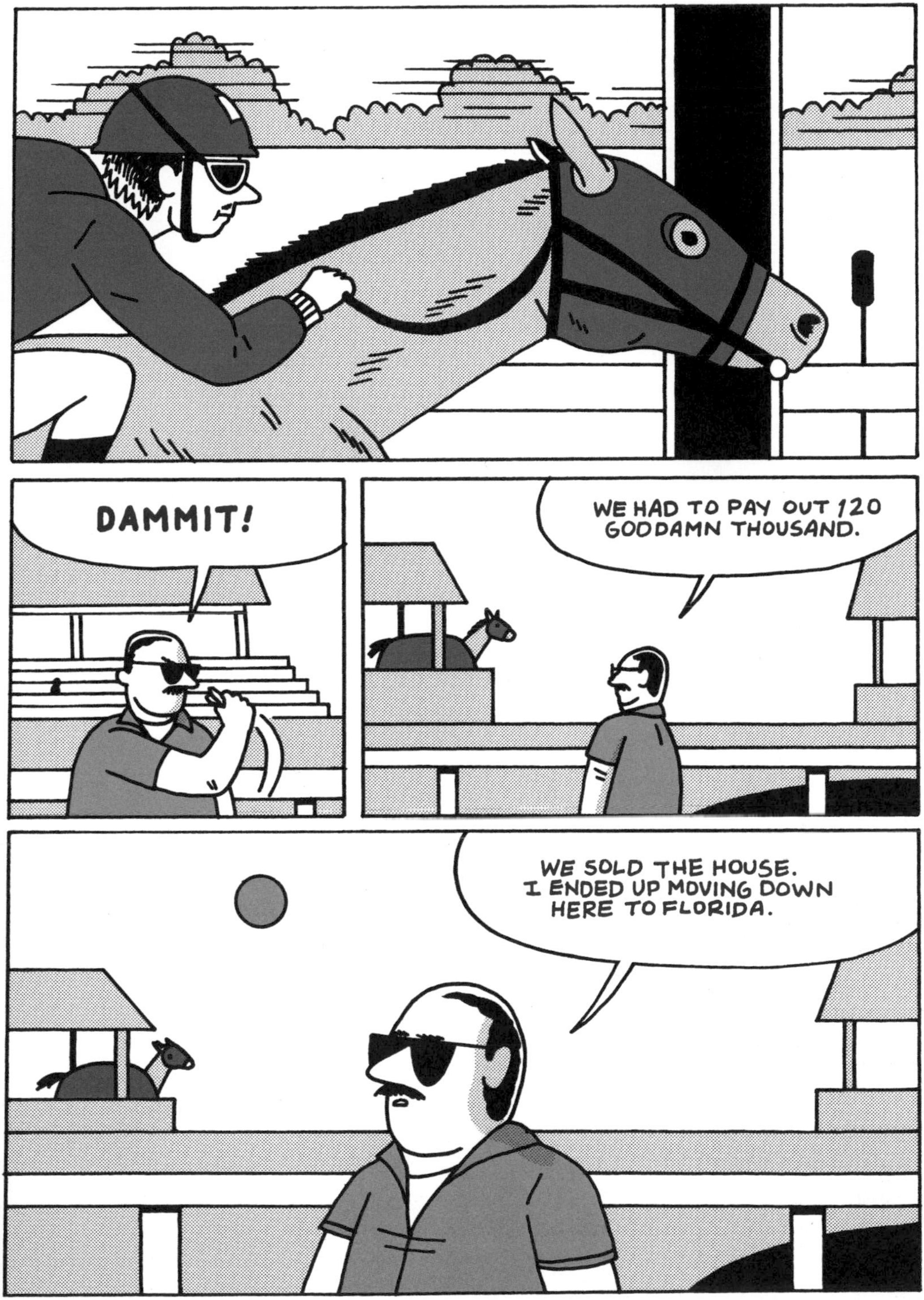
DAMMIT!
WE HAD TO PAY OUT 120 GODDAMN THOUSAND.
WE SOLD THE HOUSE. I ENDED UP MOVING DOWN HERE TO FLORIDA.

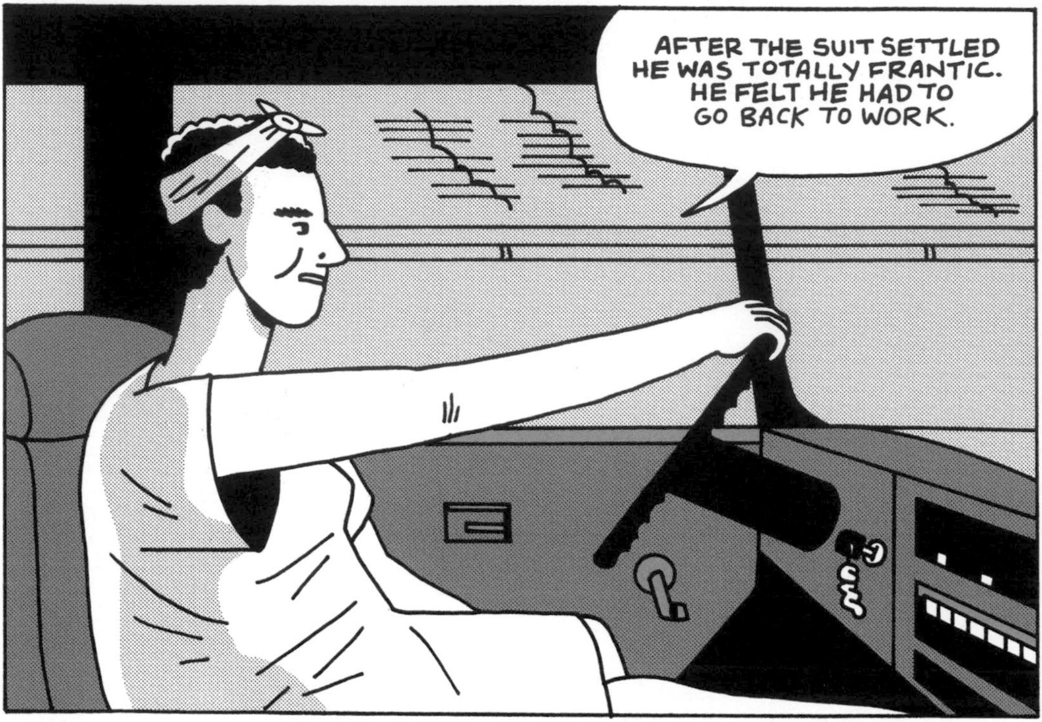
AFTER THE SUIT SETTLED HE WAS TOTALLY FRANTIC. HE FELT HE HAD TO GO BACK TO WORK.

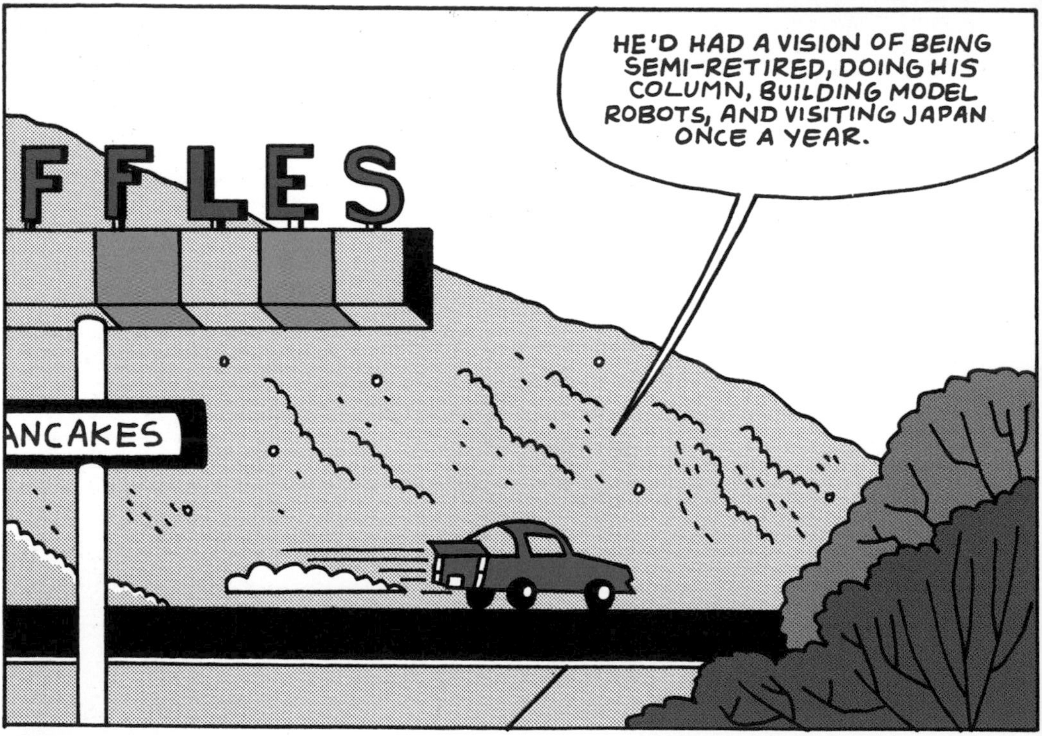
HE'D HAD A VISION OF BEING SEMI-RETIRED, DOING HIS COLUMN, BUILDING MODEL ROBOTS, AND VISITING JAPAN ONCE A YEAR.
FFLES
ANCAKES

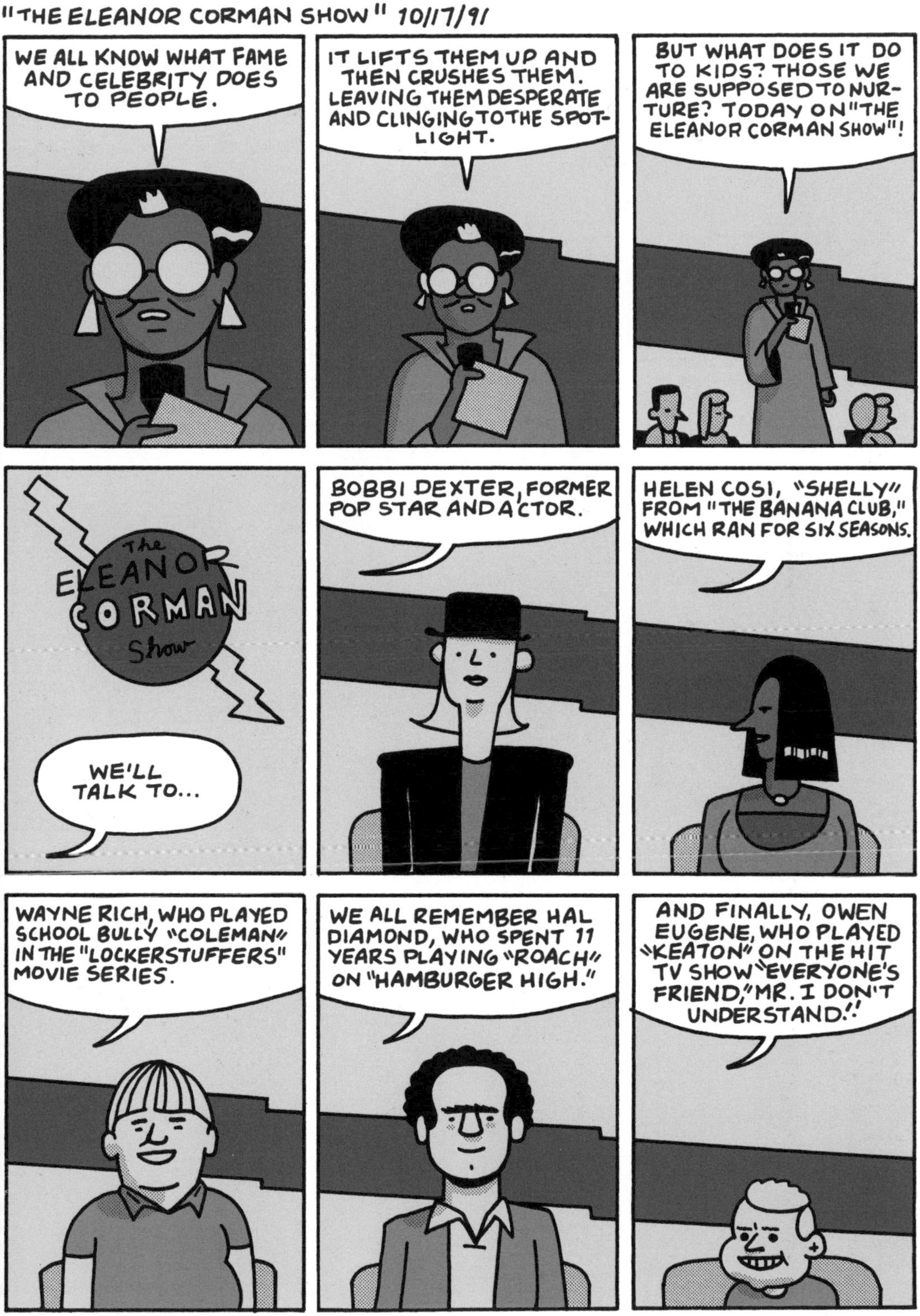
"THE ELEANOR CORMAN SHOW" 10/17/91
WE ALL KNOW WHAT FAME AND CELEBRITY DOES TO PEOPLE.
IT LIFTS THEM UP AND THEN CRUSHES THEM. LEAVING THEM DESPERATE AND CLINGING TO THE SPOTLIGHT.
BUT WHAT DOES IT DO TO KIDS? THOSE WE ARE SUPPOSED TO NURTURE? TODAY ON "THE ELEANOR CORMAN SHOW"!
The ELEANOR CORMAN Show
WE'LL TALK TO...
BOBBI DEXTER, FORMER POP STAR AND ACTOR.
HELEN COSI, "SHELLY" FROM "THE BANANA CLUB," WHICH RAN FOR SIX SEASONS.
WAYNE RICH, WHO PLAYED SCHOOL BULLY "COLEMAN" IN THE "LOCKERSTUFFERS" MOVIE SERIES.
WE ALL REMEMBER HAL DIAMOND, WHO SPENT 11 YEARS PLAYING "ROACH" ON "HAMBURGER HIGH."
AND FINALLY, OWEN EUGENE, WHO PLAYED "KEATON" ON THE HIT TV SHOW "EVERYONE'S FRIEND," MR. I DON'T UNDERSTAND!!

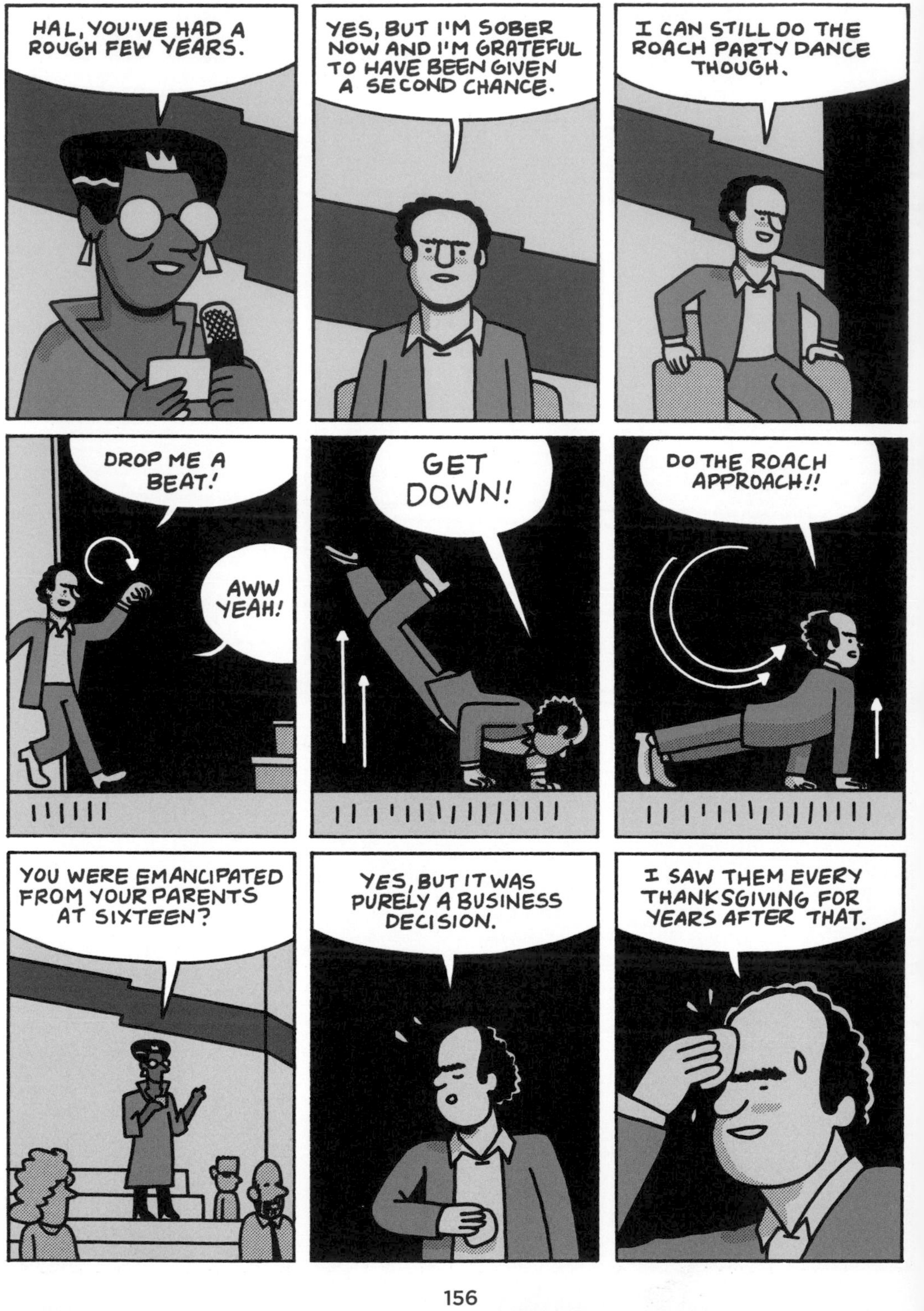
HAL, YOU'VE HAD A ROUGH FEW YEARS.
YES, BUT I'M SOBER NOW AND I'M GRATEFUL TO HAVE BEEN GIVEN A SECOND CHANCE.
I CAN STILL DO THE ROACH PARTY DANCE THOUGH.
DROP ME A BEAT!
AWW YEAH!
GET DOWN!
DO THE ROACH APPROACH!!
YOU WERE EMANCIPATED FROM YOUR PARENTS AT SIXTEEN?
YES, BUT IT WAS PURELY A BUSINESS DECISION.
I SAW THEM EVERY THANKSGIVING FOR YEARS AFTER THAT.

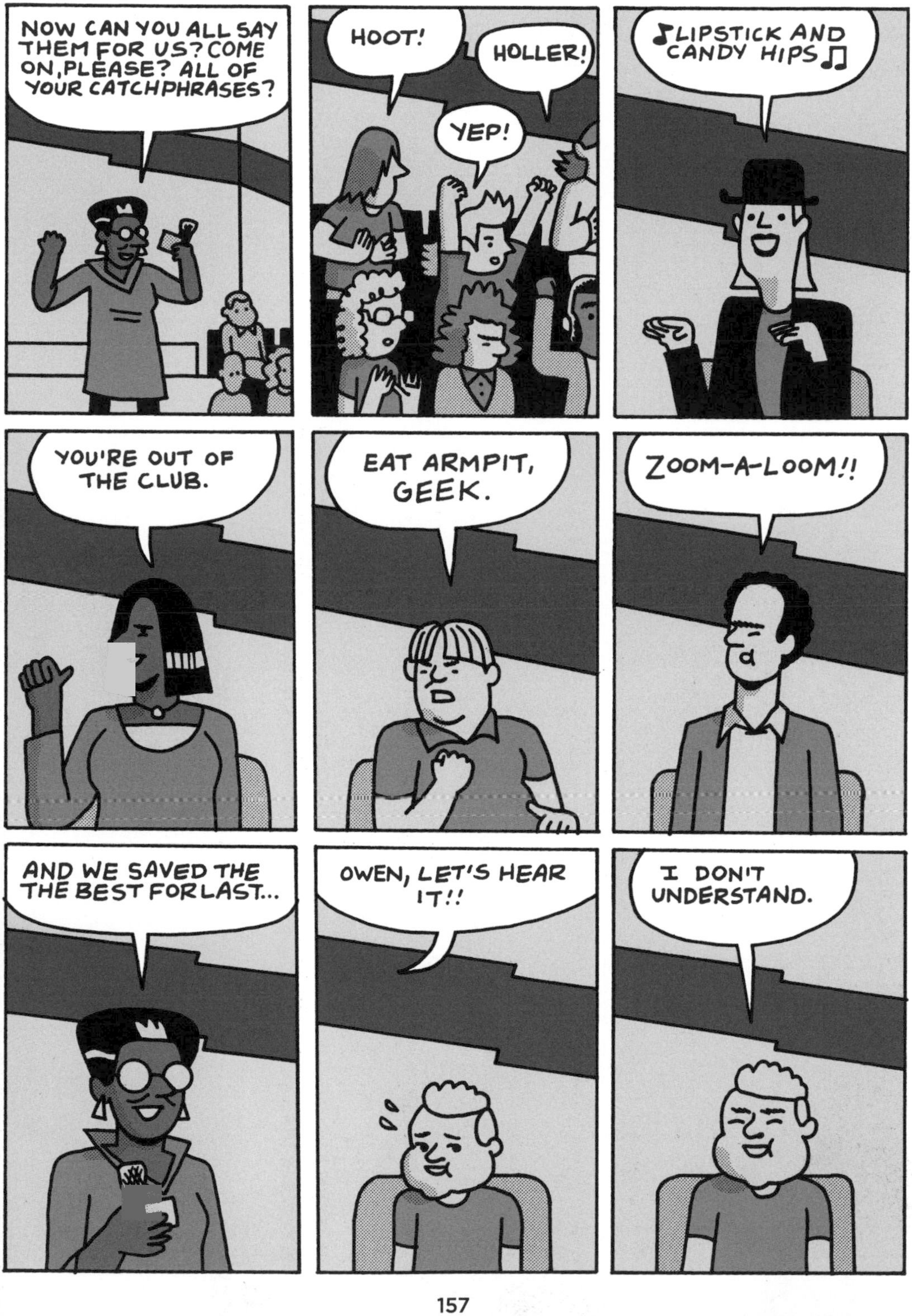
NOW CAN YOU ALL SAY THEM FOR US? COME ON, PLEASE? ALL OF YOUR CATCHPHRASES?
HOOT!
HOLLER!
YEP!
♪LIPSTICK AND CANDY HIPS♫
YOU'RE OUT OF THE CLUB.
EAT ARMPIT, GEEK.
ZOOM-A-LOOM!!
AND WE SAVED THE THE BEST FOR LAST...
OWEN, LET'S HEAR IT!!
I DON'T UNDERSTAND.

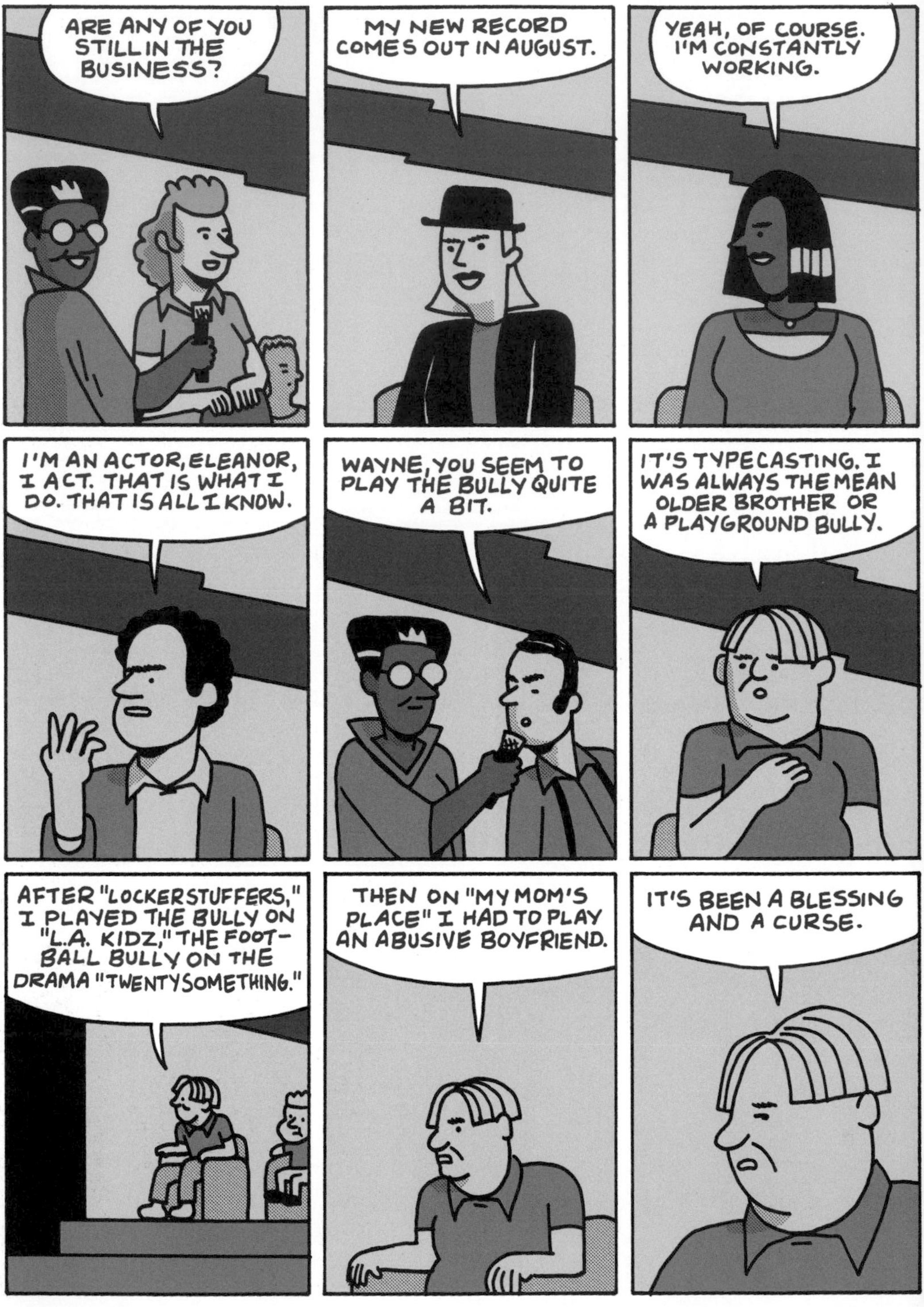
ARE ANY OF YOU STILL IN THE BUSINESS?
MY NEW RECORD COMES OUT IN AUGUST.
YEAH, OF COURSE. I'M CONSTANTLY WORKING.
I'M AN ACTOR, ELEANOR, I ACT. THAT IS WHAT I DO. THAT IS ALL I KNOW.
WAYNE, YOU SEEM TO PLAY THE BULLY QUITE A BIT.
IT'S TYPECASTING. I WAS ALWAYS THE MEAN OLDER BROTHER OR A PLAYGROUND BULLY.
AFTER "LOCKERSTUFFERS," I PLAYED THE BULLY ON "L.A. KIDZ," THE FOOT-BALL BULLY ON THE DRAMA "TWENTYSOMETHING."
THEN ON "MY MOM'S PLACE" I HAD TO PLAY AN ABUSIVE BOYFRIEND.
IT'S BEEN A BLESSING AND A CURSE.

OWEN EUGENE IS GOING TO PLAY US OUT WITH HIS NEW SOON-TO-BE-HIT SINGLE...

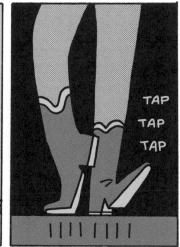

TAP

TAP

TAP

KICK IT, COWBOY...

I'M A COWBOY, HOSS. CALL ME THE BOSS.

ROCK MY BODY WITH A SHOOT-OUT, PISTOLS AT DAWN.

COWBOY DANCER ALL NIGHT!

COWBOY DANCER

HEYYYYYY!

159

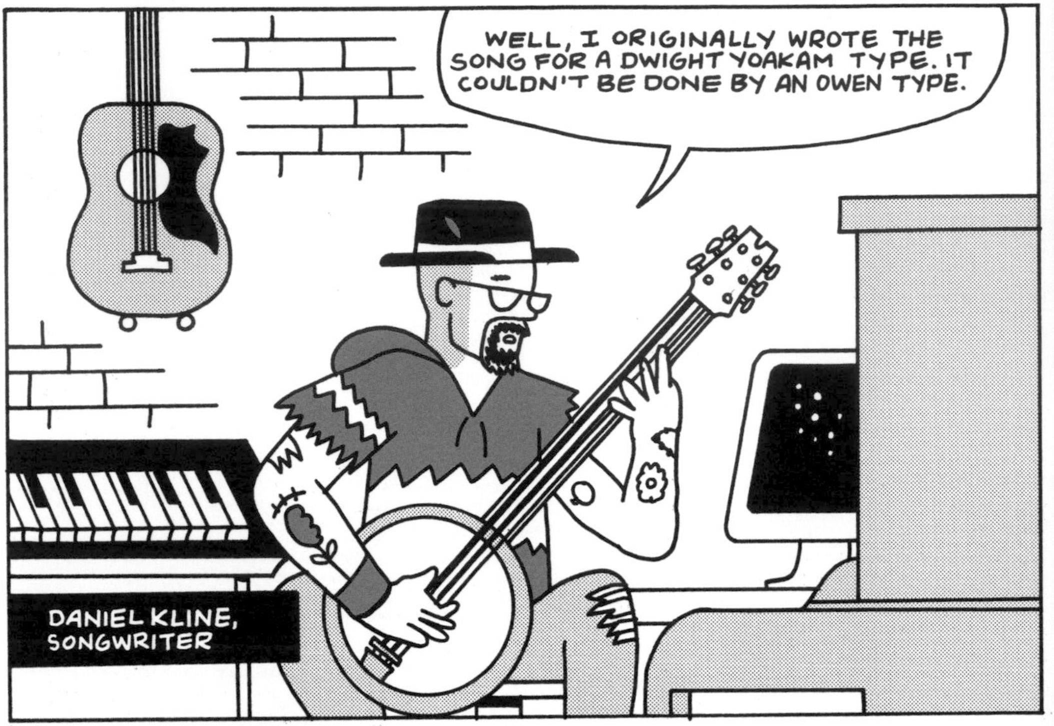
WELL, I ORIGINALLY WROTE THE SONG FOR A DWIGHT YOAKAM TYPE. IT COULDN'T BE DONE BY AN OWEN TYPE.
DANIEL KLINE, SONGWRITER

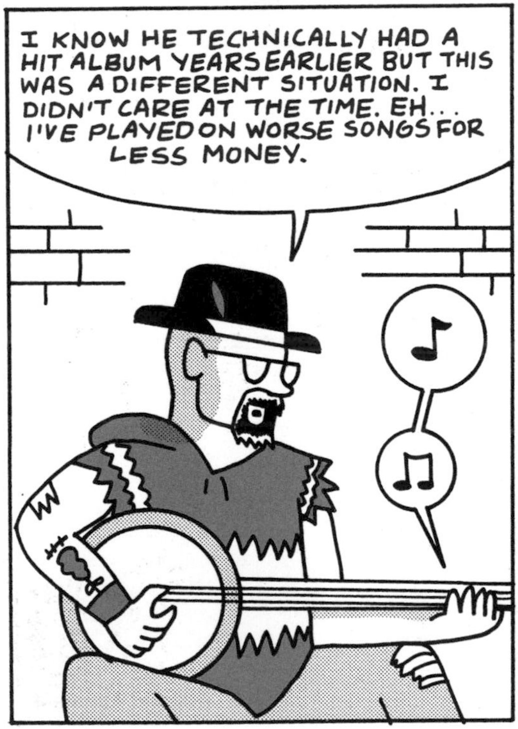
I KNOW HE TECHNICALLY HAD A HIT ALBUM YEARS EARLIER BUT THIS WAS A DIFFERENT SITUATION. I DIDN'T CARE AT THE TIME. EH... I'VE PLAYED ON WORSE SONGS FOR LESS MONEY.

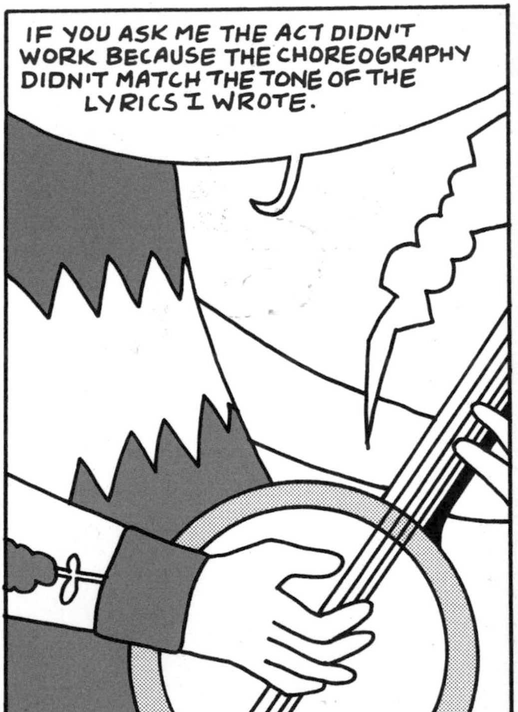
IF YOU ASK ME THE ACT DIDN'T WORK BECAUSE THE CHOREOGRAPHY DIDN'T MATCH THE TONE OF THE LYRICS I WROTE.

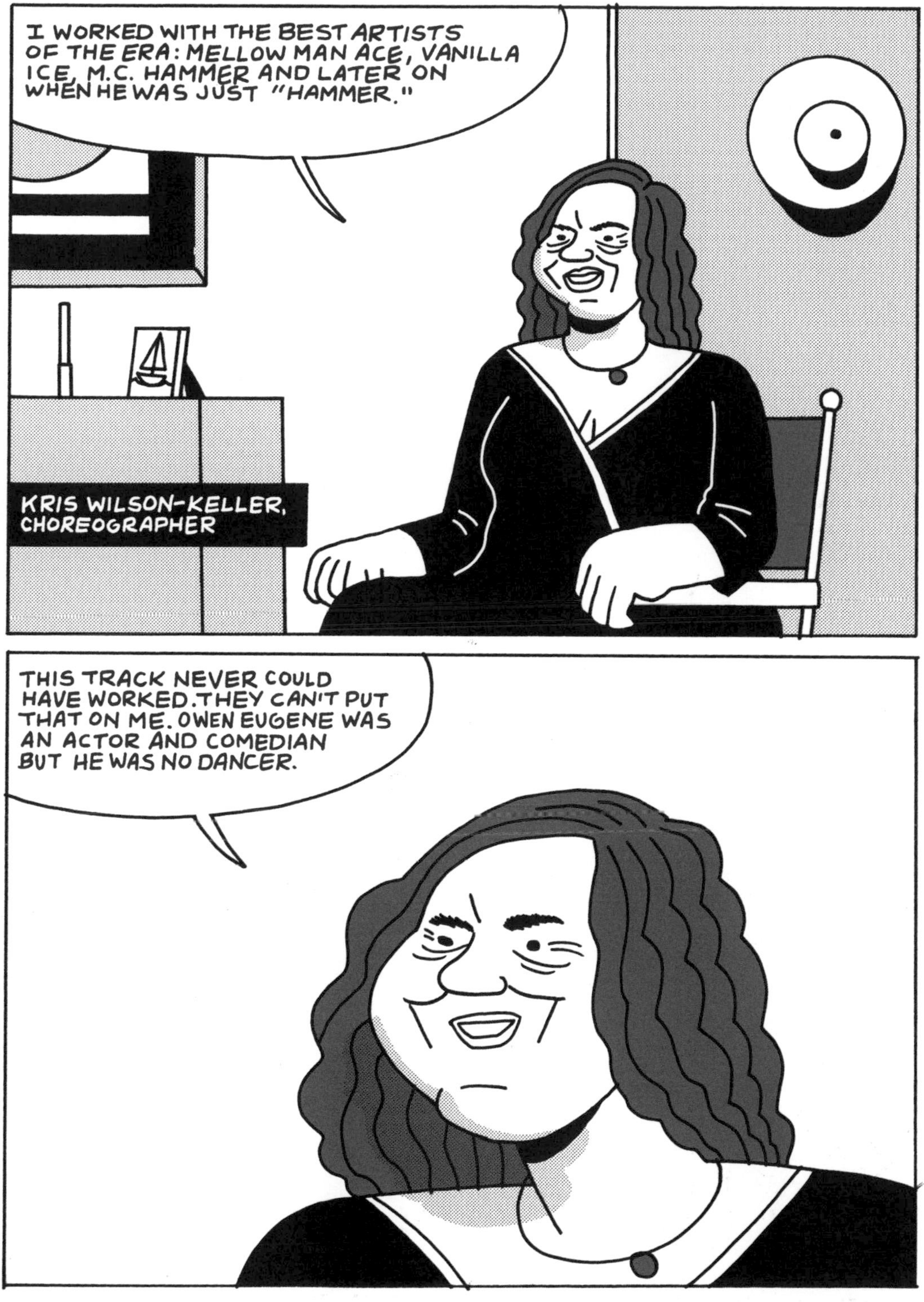
I WORKED WITH THE BEST ARTISTS OF THE ERA: MELLOW MAN ACE, VANILLA ICE, M.C. HAMMER AND LATER ON WHEN HE WAS JUST "HAMMER."
KRIS WILSON-KELLER, CHOREOGRAPHER
THIS TRACK NEVER COULD HAVE WORKED. THEY CAN'T PUT THAT ON ME. OWEN EUGENE WAS AN ACTOR AND COMEDIAN BUT HE WAS NO DANCER.

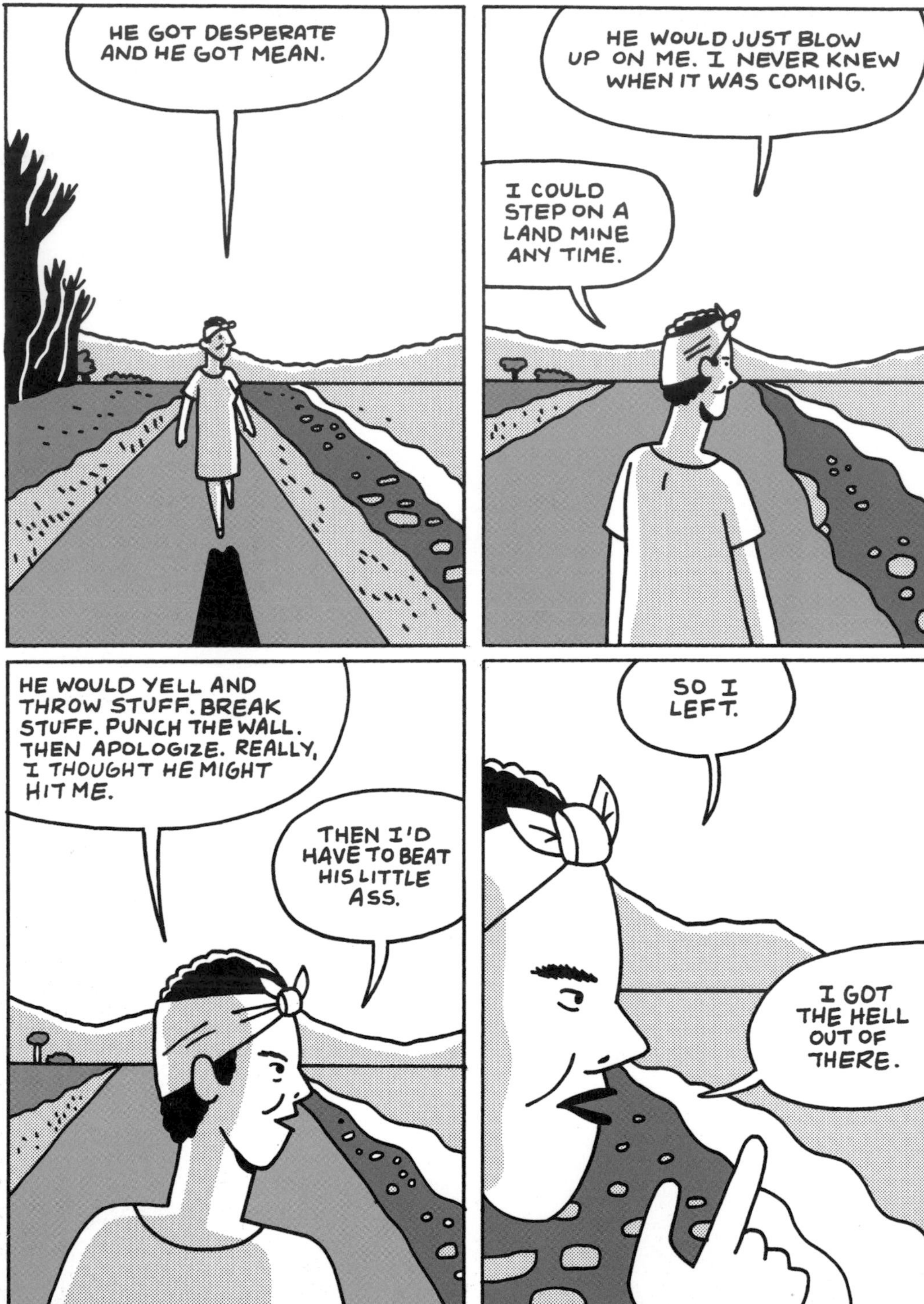
HE GOT DESPERATE AND HE GOT MEAN.
HE WOULD JUST BLOW UP ON ME. I NEVER KNEW WHEN IT WAS COMING.
I COULD STEP ON A LAND MINE ANY TIME.
HE WOULD YELL AND THROW STUFF. BREAK STUFF. PUNCH THE WALL. THEN APOLOGIZE. REALLY, I THOUGHT HE MIGHT HIT ME.
THEN I'D HAVE TO BEAT HIS LITTLE ASS.
SO I LEFT.
I GOT THE HELL OUT OF THERE.

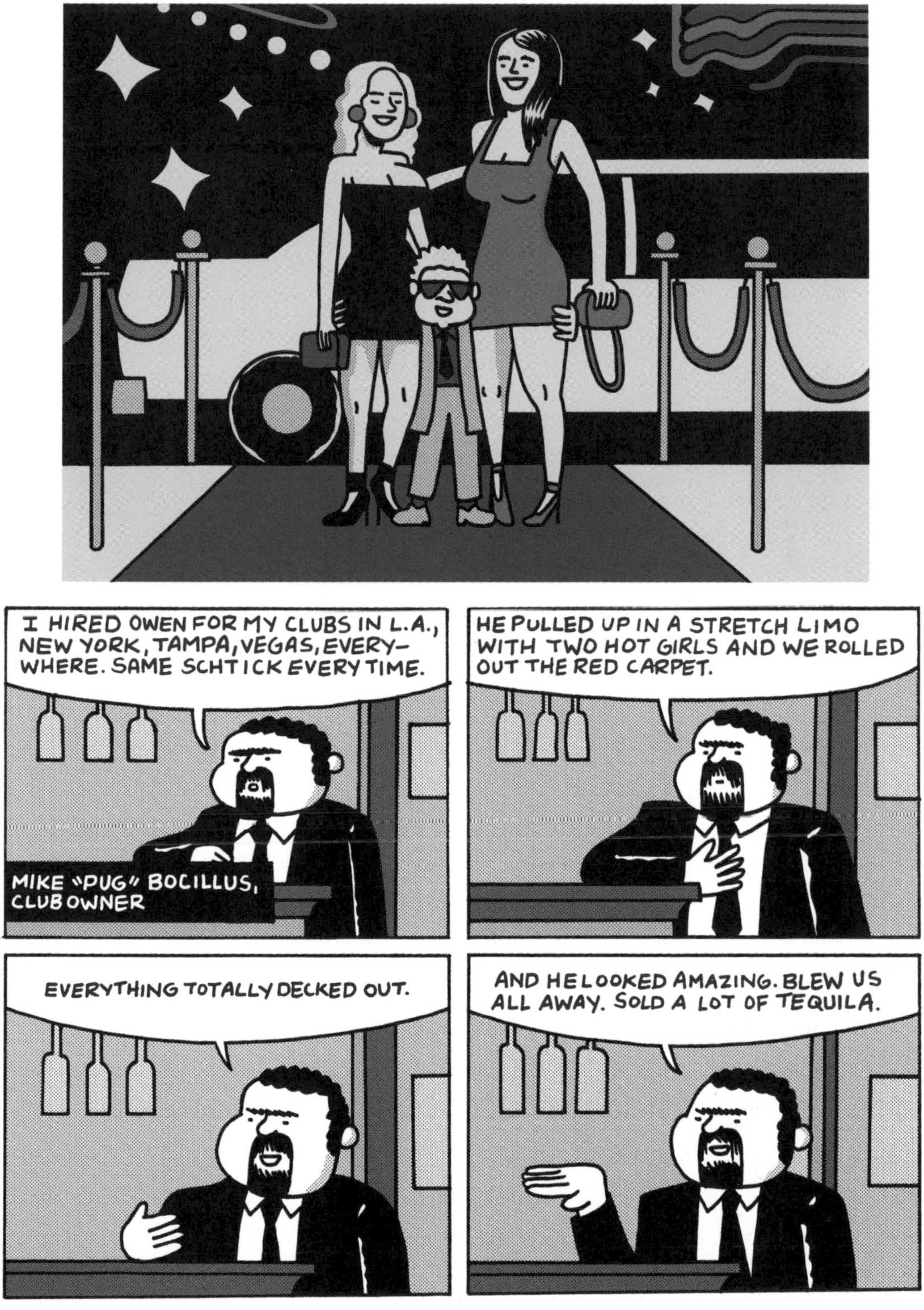
I HIRED OWEN FOR MY CLUBS IN L.A., NEW YORK, TAMPA, VEGAS, EVERYWHERE. SAME SCHTICK EVERY TIME.
MIKE "PUG" BOCILLUS, CLUB OWNER
HE PULLED UP IN A STRETCH LIMO WITH TWO HOT GIRLS AND WE ROLLED OUT THE RED CARPET.
EVERYTHING TOTALLY DECKED OUT.
AND HE LOOKED AMAZING. BLEW US ALL AWAY. SOLD A LOT OF TEQUILA.

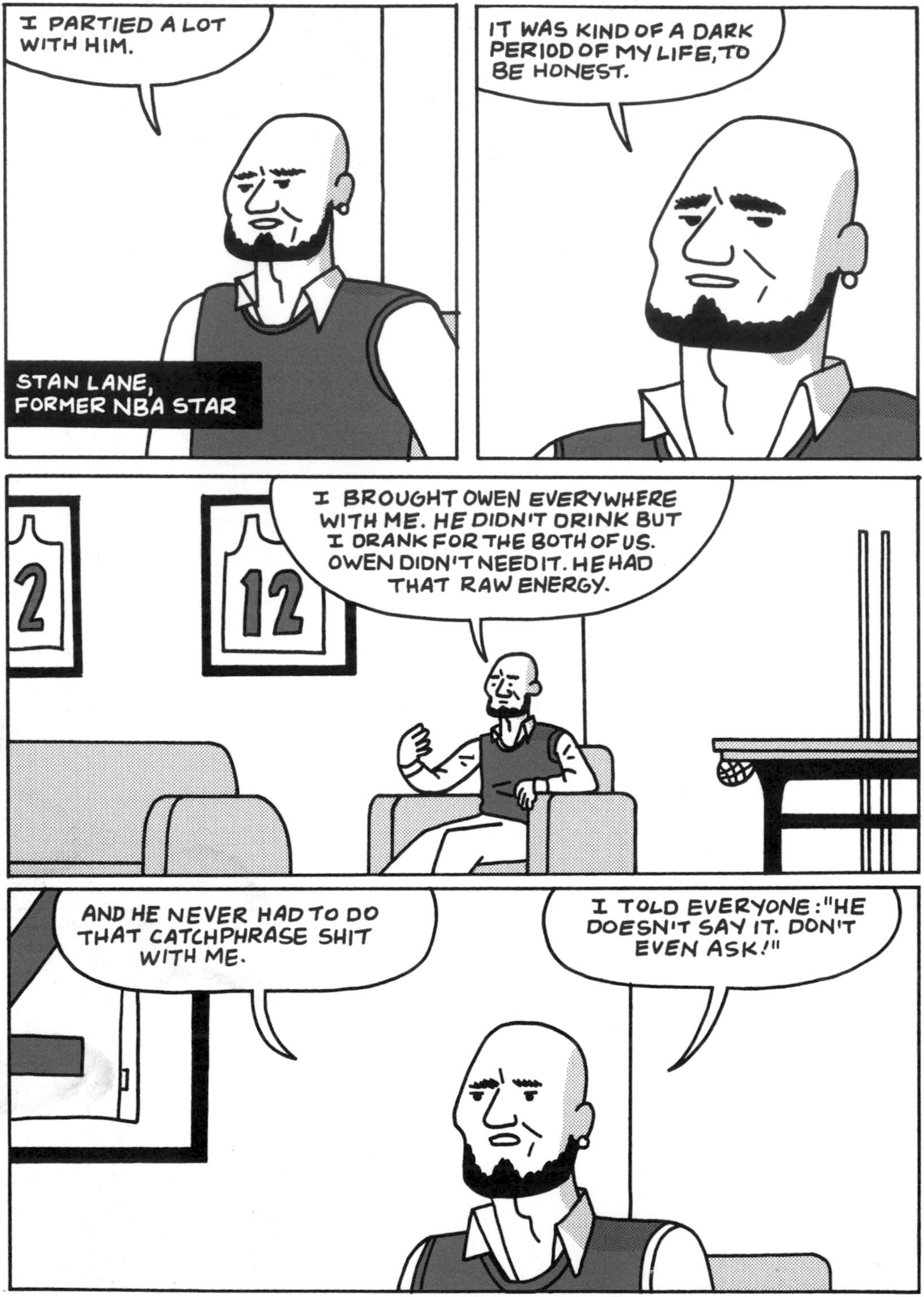
I PARTIED A LOT WITH HIM.
STAN LANE, FORMER NBA STAR
IT WAS KIND OF A DARK PERIOD OF MY LIFE, TO BE HONEST.
2
12
I BROUGHT OWEN EVERYWHERE WITH ME. HE DIDN'T DRINK BUT I DRANK FOR THE BOTH OF US. OWEN DIDN'T NEED IT. HE HAD THAT RAW ENERGY.
AND HE NEVER HAD TO DO THAT CATCHPHRASE SHIT WITH ME.
I TOLD EVERYONE: "HE DOESN'T SAY IT. DON'T EVEN ASK!"

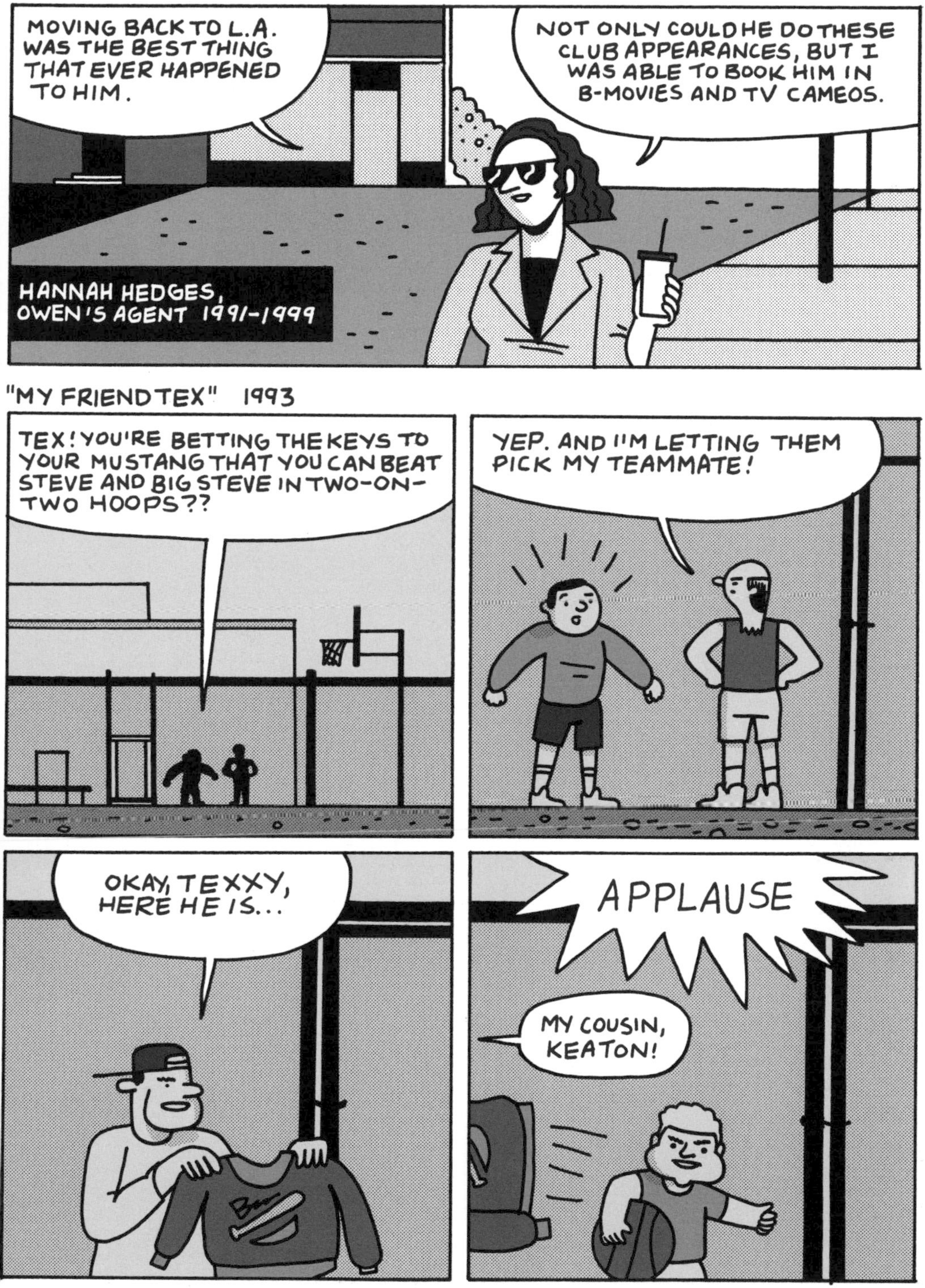
MOVING BACK TO L.A. WAS THE BEST THING THAT EVER HAPPENED TO HIM.
NOT ONLY COULD HE DO THESE CLUB APPEARANCES, BUT I WAS ABLE TO BOOK HIM IN B-MOVIES AND TV CAMEOS.
HANNAH HEDGES, OWEN'S AGENT 1991-1999
"MY FRIEND TEX" 1993
TEX! YOU'RE BETTING THE KEYS TO YOUR MUSTANG THAT YOU CAN BEAT STEVE AND BIG STEVE IN TWO-ON-TWO HOOPS??
YEP. AND I'M LETTING THEM PICK MY TEAMMATE!
OKAY, TEXXY, HERE HE IS...
APPLAUSE
MY COUSIN, KEATON!

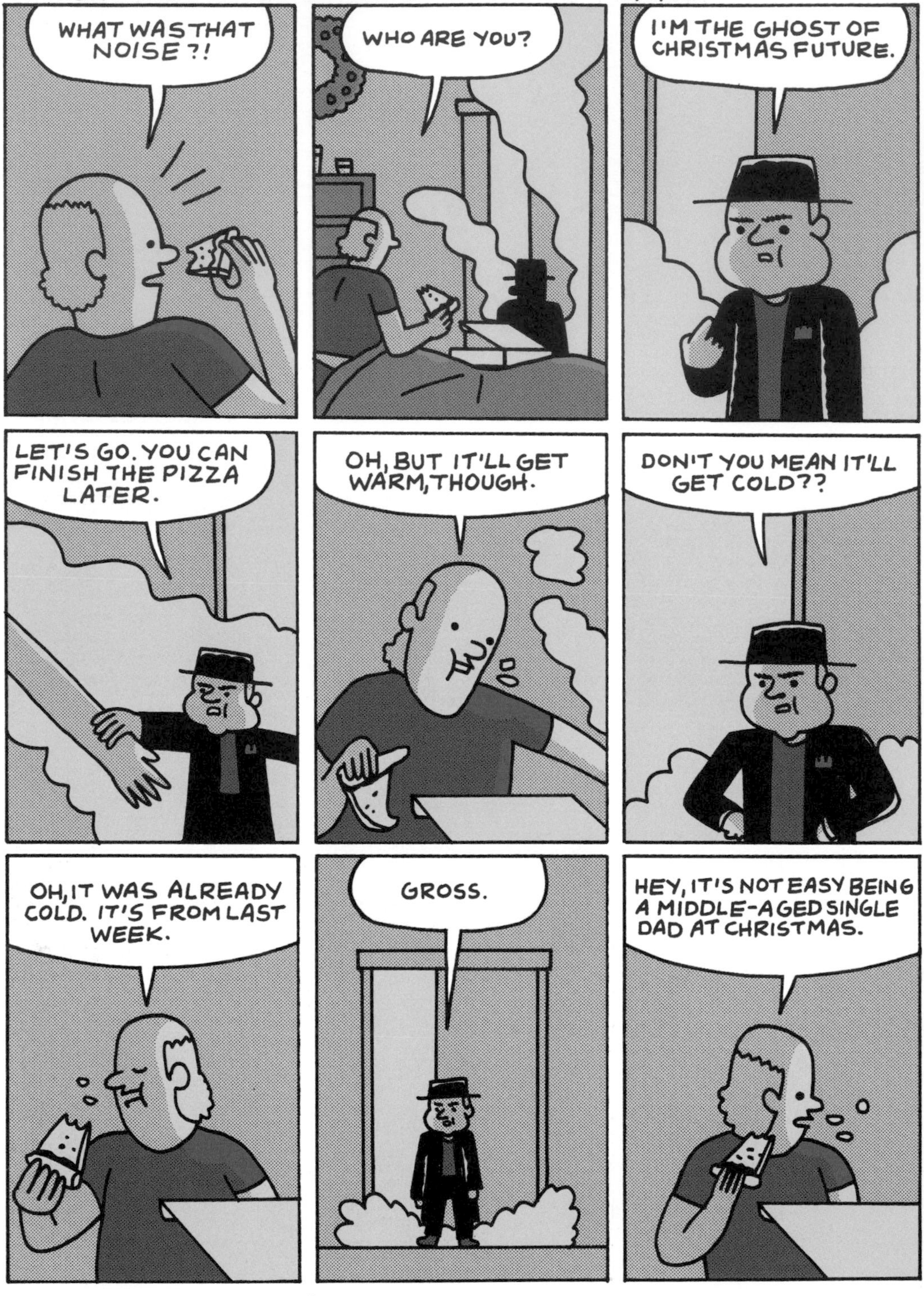
WHAT WAS THAT NOISE?!
WHO ARE YOU?
I'M THE GHOST OF CHRISTMAS FUTURE.
LET'S GO. YOU CAN FINISH THE PIZZA LATER.
OH, BUT IT'LL GET WARM, THOUGH.
DON'T YOU MEAN IT'LL GET COLD??
OH, IT WAS ALREADY COLD. IT'S FROM LAST WEEK.
GROSS.
HEY, IT'S NOT EASY BEING A MIDDLE-AGED SINGLE DAD AT CHRISTMAS.

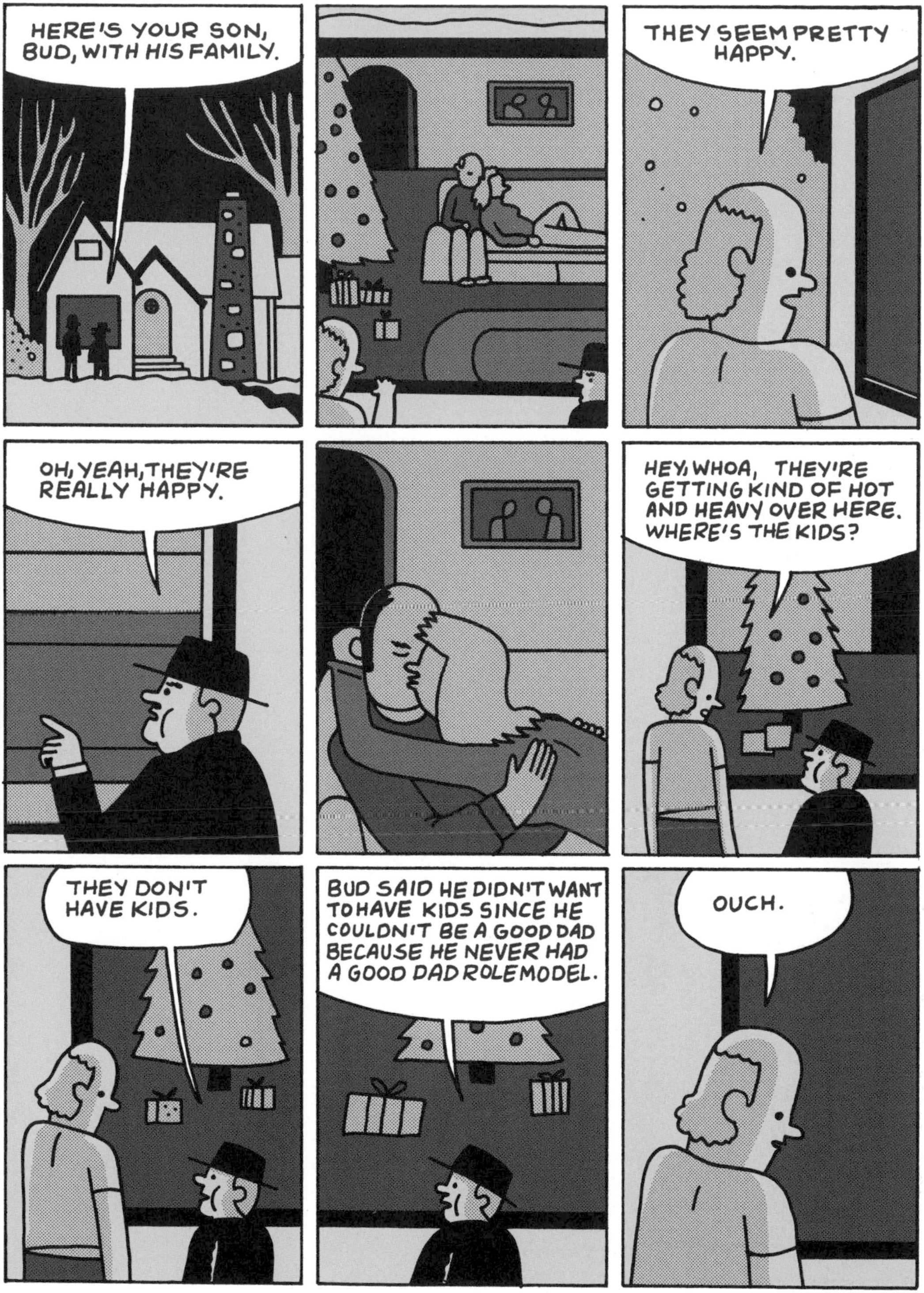
HERE'S YOUR SON, BUD, WITH HIS FAMILY.
THEY SEEM PRETTY HAPPY.
OH, YEAH, THEY'RE REALLY HAPPY.
HEY, WHOA, THEY'RE GETTING KIND OF HOT AND HEAVY OVER HERE. WHERE'S THE KIDS?
THEY DON'T HAVE KIDS.
BUD SAID HE DIDN'T WANT TO HAVE KIDS SINCE HE COULDN'T BE A GOOD DAD BECAUSE HE NEVER HAD A GOOD DAD ROLE MODEL.
OUCH.

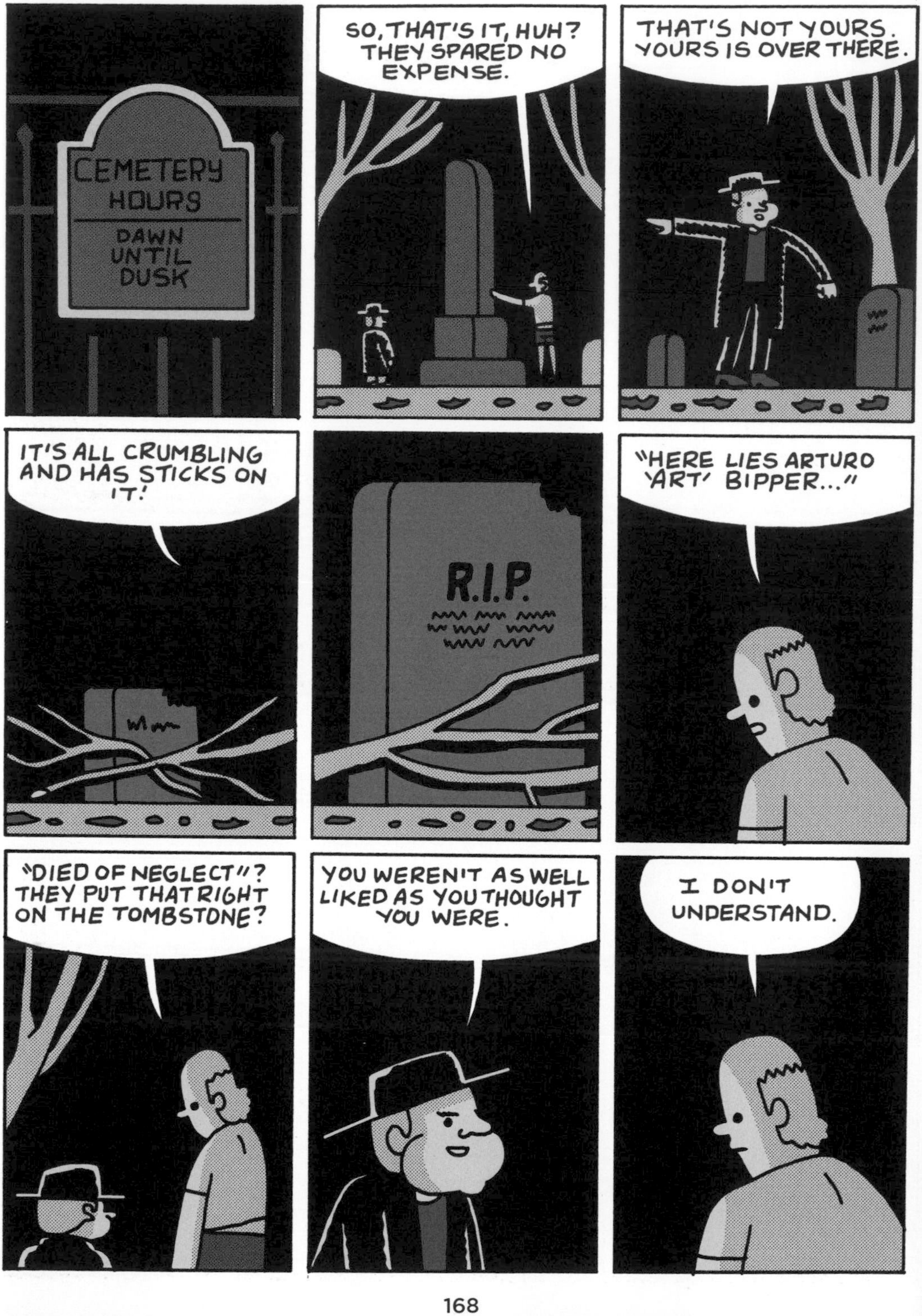
CEMETERY HOURS
DAWN UNTIL DUSK
SO, THAT'S IT, HUH? THEY SPARED NO EXPENSE.
THAT'S NOT YOURS. YOURS IS OVER THERE.
IT'S ALL CRUMBLING AND HAS STICKS ON IT!
R.I.P.
"HERE LIES ARTURO 'ART' BIPPER..."
"DIED OF NEGLECT"? THEY PUT THAT RIGHT ON THE TOMBSTONE?
YOU WEREN'T AS WELL LIKED AS YOU THOUGHT YOU WERE.
I DON'T UNDERSTAND.

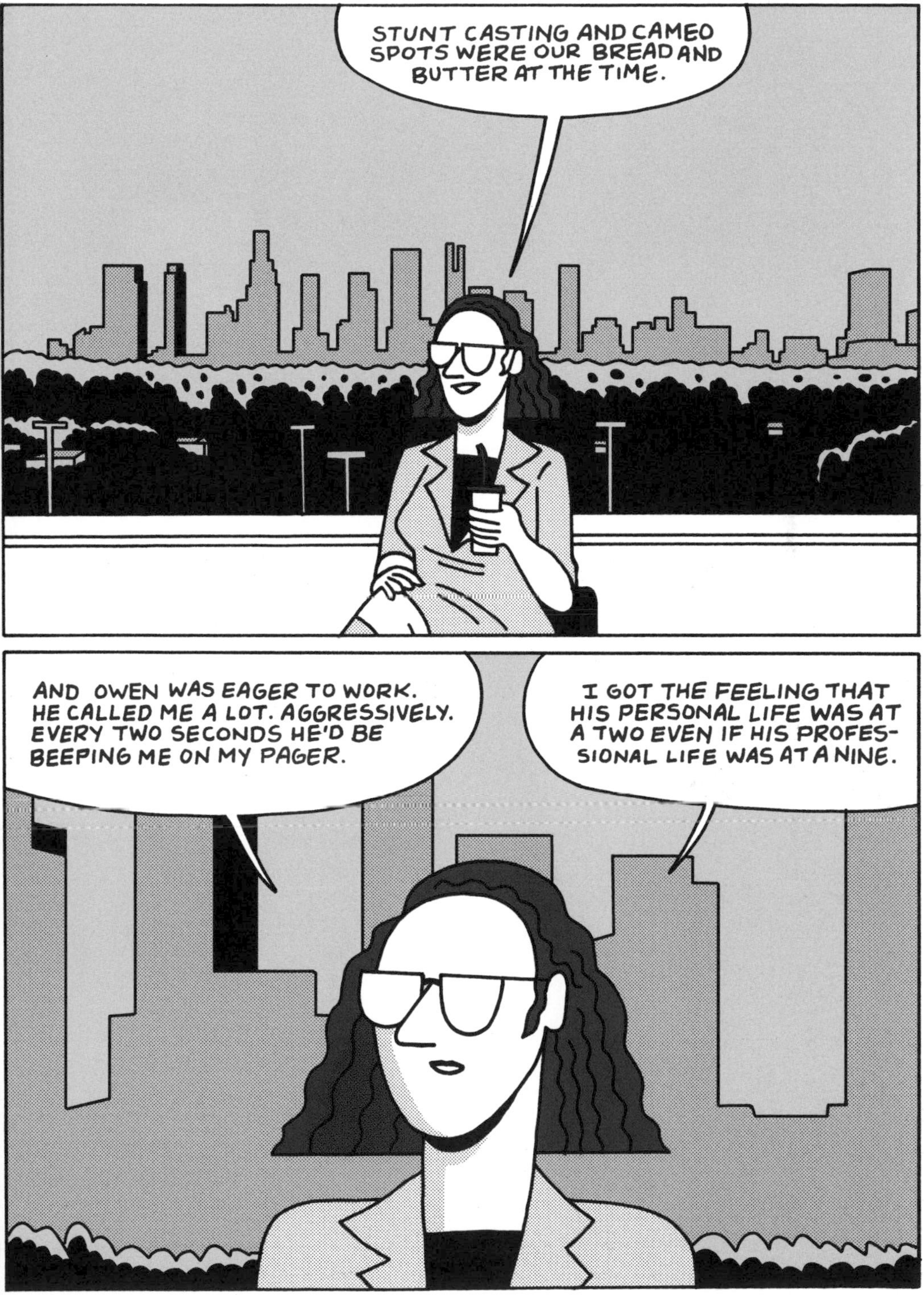
STUNT CASTING AND CAMEO SPOTS WERE OUR BREAD AND BUTTER AT THE TIME.
AND OWEN WAS EAGER TO WORK. HE CALLED ME A LOT. AGGRESSIVELY. EVERY TWO SECONDS HE'D BE BEEPING ME ON MY PAGER.
I GOT THE FEELING THAT HIS PERSONAL LIFE WAS AT A TWO EVEN IF HIS PROFES-SIONAL LIFE WAS AT A NINE.

"TAKING WHAT I'M GIVEN" JAILBIRD CHRIS 1994

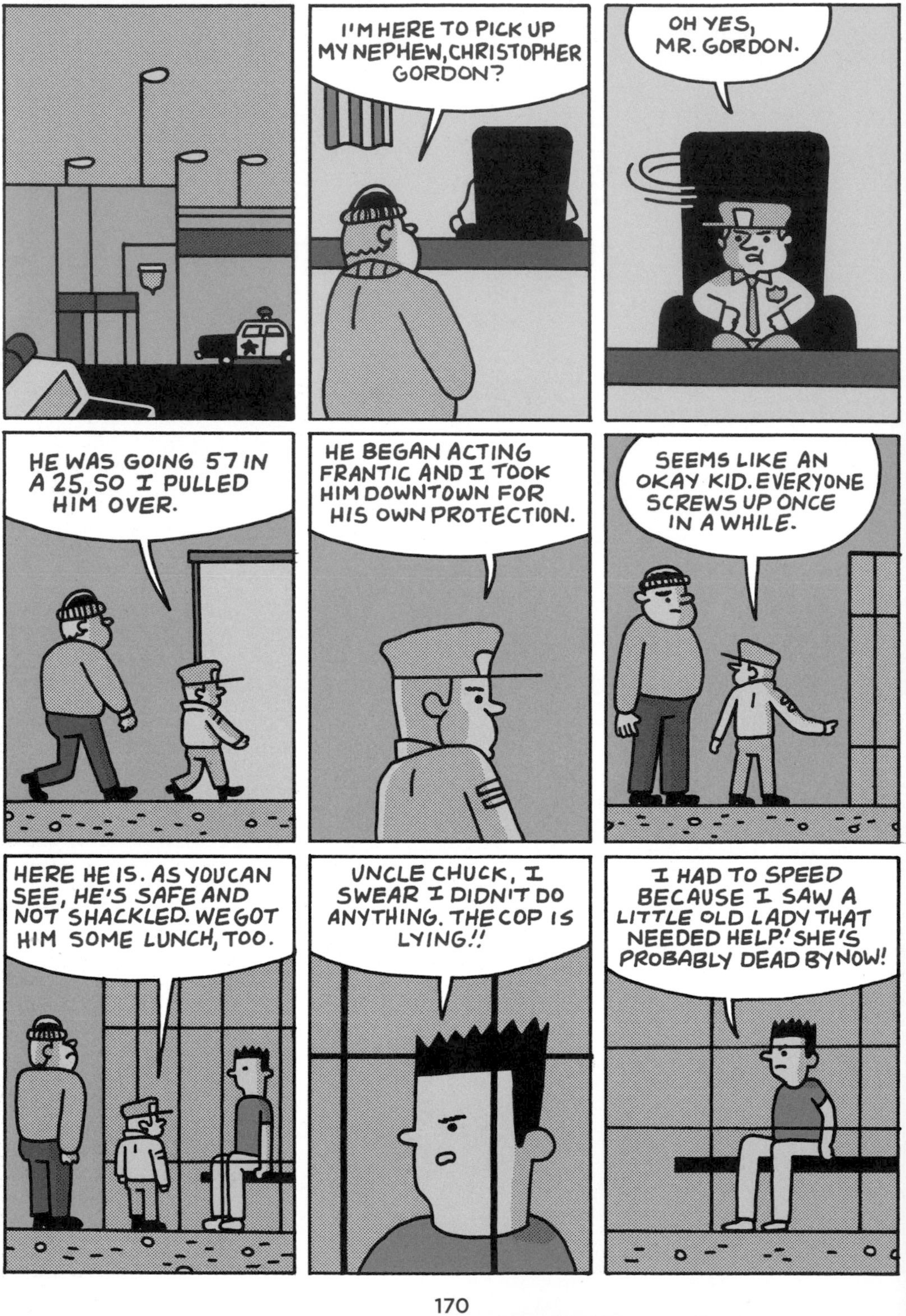
I'M HERE TO PICK UP MY NEPHEW, CHRISTOPHER GORDON?
OH YES, MR. GORDON.
HE WAS GOING 57 IN A 25, SO I PULLED HIM OVER.
HE BEGAN ACTING FRANTIC AND I TOOK HIM DOWNTOWN FOR HIS OWN PROTECTION.
SEEMS LIKE AN OKAY KID. EVERYONE SCREWS UP ONCE IN A WHILE.
HERE HE IS. AS YOU CAN SEE, HE'S SAFE AND NOT SHACKLED. WE GOT HIM SOME LUNCH, TOO.
UNCLE CHUCK, I SWEAR I DIDN'T DO ANYTHING. THE COP IS LYING!!
I HAD TO SPEED BECAUSE I SAW A LITTLE OLD LADY THAT NEEDED HELP! SHE'S PROBABLY DEAD BY NOW!

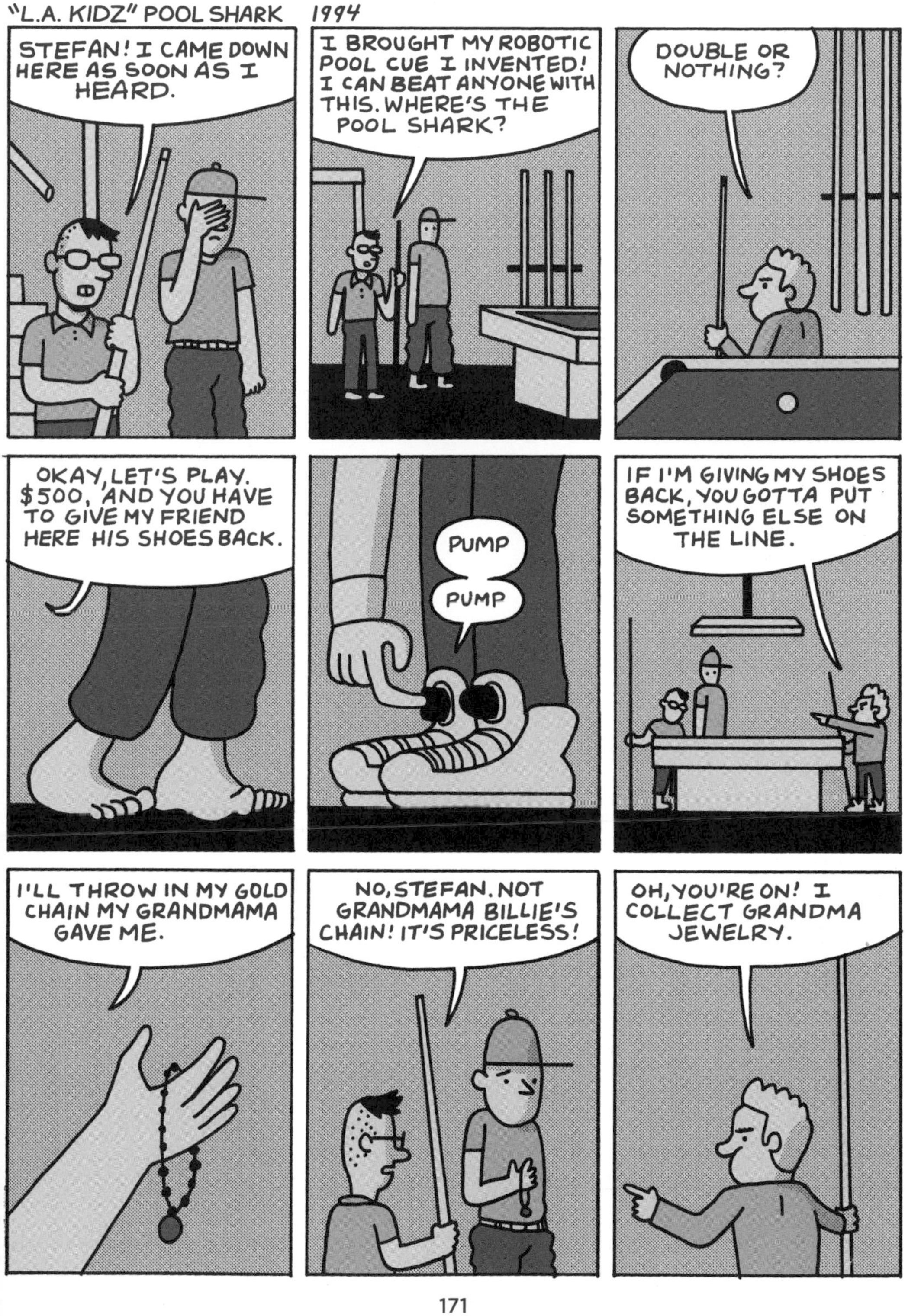
"L.A. KIDZ" POOL SHARK 1994
STEFAN! I CAME DOWN HERE AS SOON AS I HEARD.
I BROUGHT MY ROBOTIC POOL CUE I INVENTED! I CAN BEAT ANYONE WITH THIS. WHERE'S THE POOL SHARK?
DOUBLE OR NOTHING?
OKAY, LET'S PLAY. $500, AND YOU HAVE TO GIVE MY FRIEND HERE HIS SHOES BACK.
PUMP
PUMP
IF I'M GIVING MY SHOES BACK, YOU GOTTA PUT SOMETHING ELSE ON THE LINE.
I'LL THROW IN MY GOLD CHAIN MY GRANDMAMA GAVE ME.
NO, STEFAN. NOT GRANDMAMA BILLIE'S CHAIN! IT'S PRICELESS!
OH, YOU'RE ON! I COLLECT GRANDMA JEWELRY.

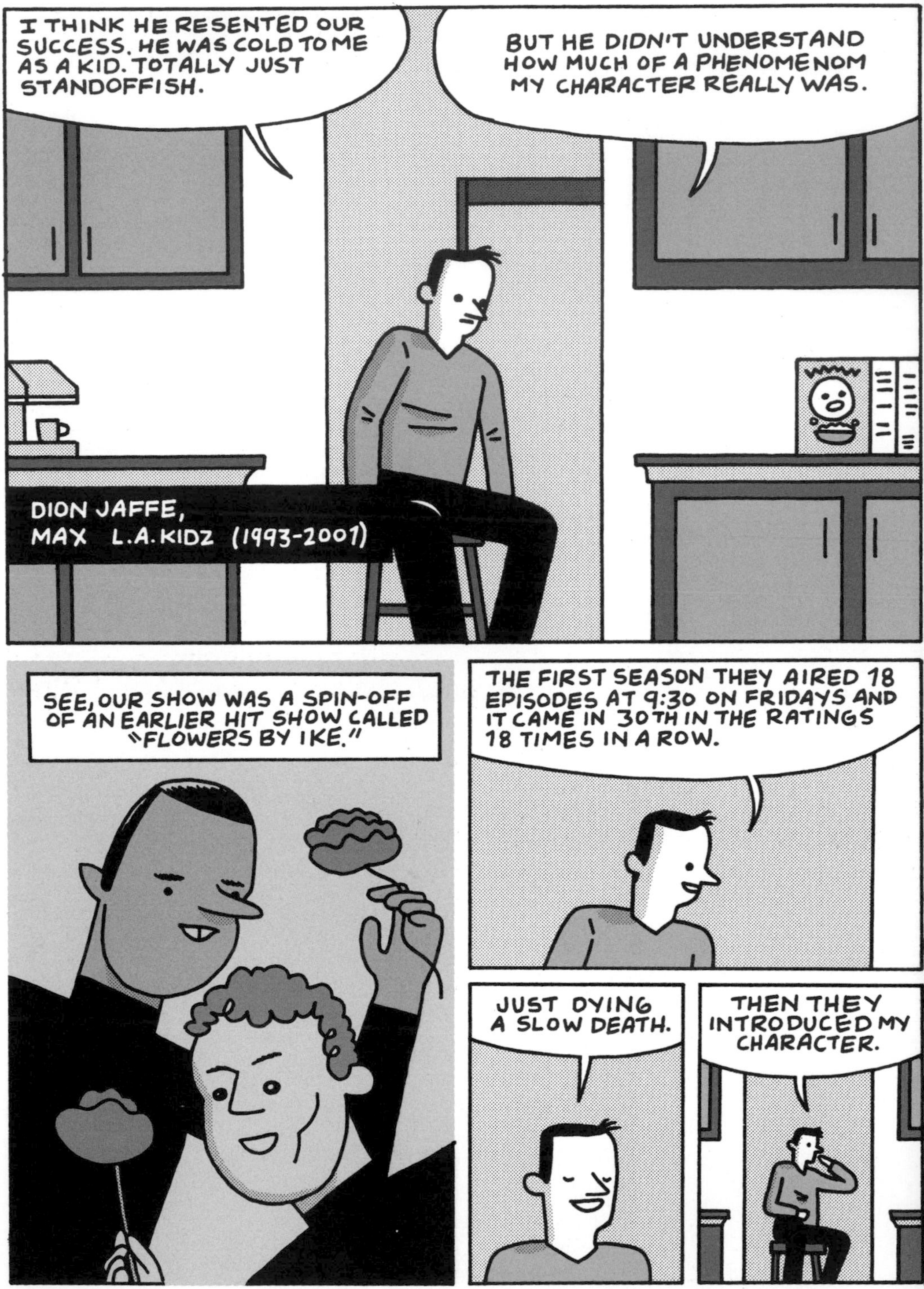
I THINK HE RESENTED OUR SUCCESS. HE WAS COLD TO ME AS A KID. TOTALLY JUST STANDOFFISH.
BUT HE DIDN'T UNDERSTAND HOW MUCH OF A PHENOMENOM MY CHARACTER REALLY WAS.
DION JAFFE, MAX L.A. KIDZ (1993-2001)
SEE, OUR SHOW WAS A SPIN-OFF OF AN EARLIER HIT SHOW CALLED "FLOWERS BY IKE."
THE FIRST SEASON THEY AIRED 18 EPISODES AT 9:30 ON FRIDAYS AND IT CAME IN 30TH IN THE RATINGS 18 TIMES IN A ROW.
JUST DYING A SLOW DEATH.
THEN THEY INTRODUCED MY CHARACTER.

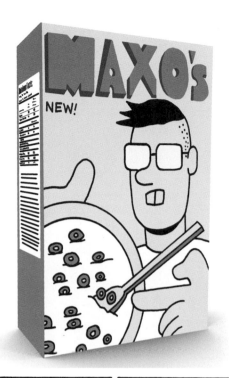

THE MAX CHARACTER WAS JUST SUPPOSED TO BE A ONE SHOT. ONE EPISODE. STEFAN NEEDED A NERDY OBNOXIOUS FRIEND.

BY THE END OF THE FILMING OF IT, THE LIVE AUDIENCE HAD STARTED CHANTING "MAX, MAX, MAX!"

LISTEN: I'D HAD ABOUT THREE MINUTES OF SCREEN TIME IN MY WHOLE LIFE.

I WAS JUST ABLE TO EMBODY THE CHARACTER. IT WAS THE POWER OF GOD IN ME.

BY THE END OF THE TAPING WE'D SIGNED A NEW CONTRACT.

THEY CHANGED THE WHOLE FOCUS OF THE SHOW.

I DID ALMOST ALL OF MY SCENES IN ONE TAKE, TOO.

MY PARENTS DIDN'T STEAL MY MONEY. I BOUGHT MY MOM A HOUSE.

I THINK MAYBE HE COULD JUST SENSE THAT ENERGY.

THAT WAS THE RESENTMENT I FELT FROM HIM.

"SEXY LIFEGUARDS ON THE BAY" WHAT IS LIFE? WHO AM I? 10/17/95

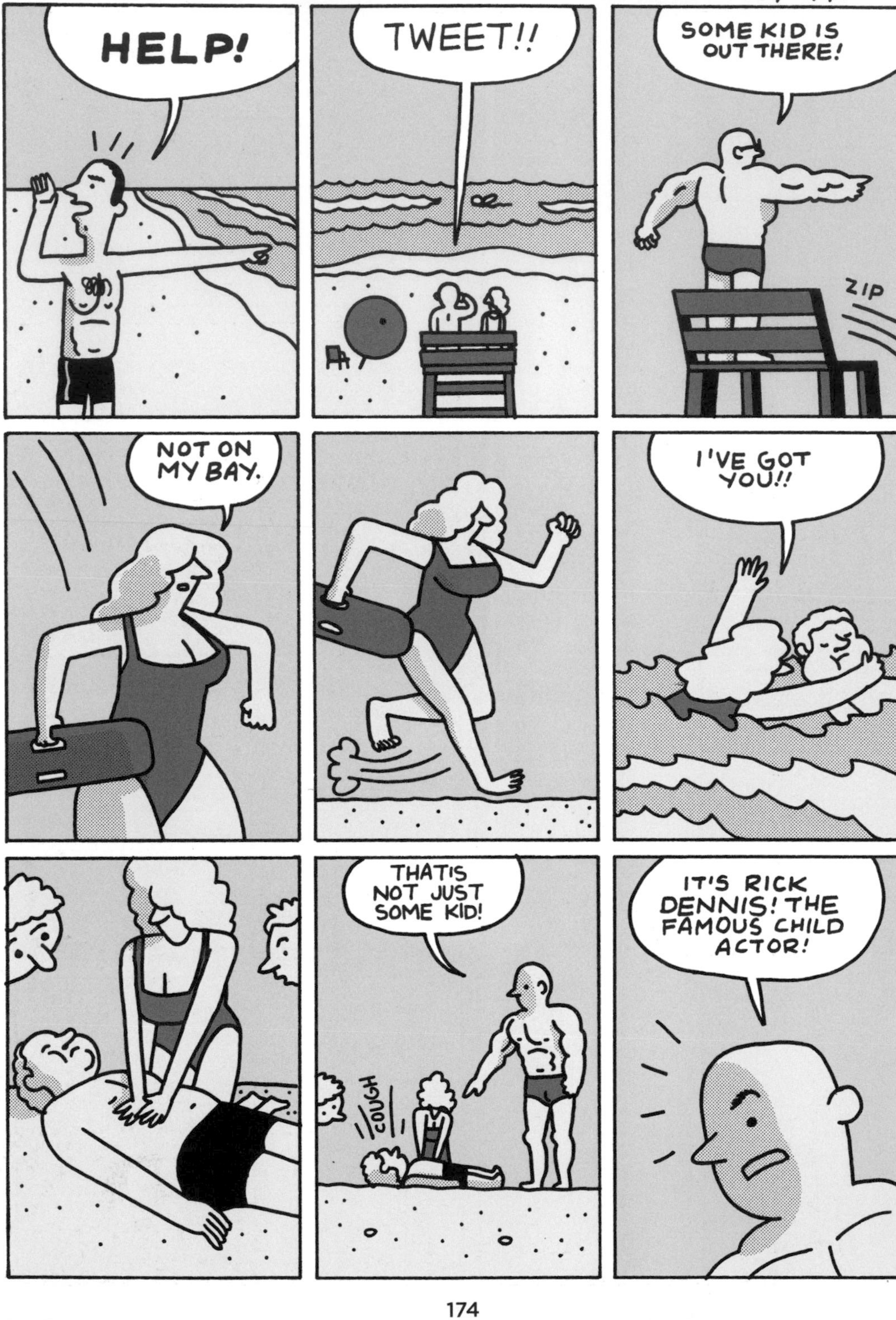
HELP!
TWEET!!
SOME KID IS OUT THERE!
ZIP
NOT ON MY BAY.
I'VE GOT YOU!!
COUGH
THAT'S NOT JUST SOME KID!
IT'S RICK DENNIS! THE FAMOUS CHILD ACTOR!

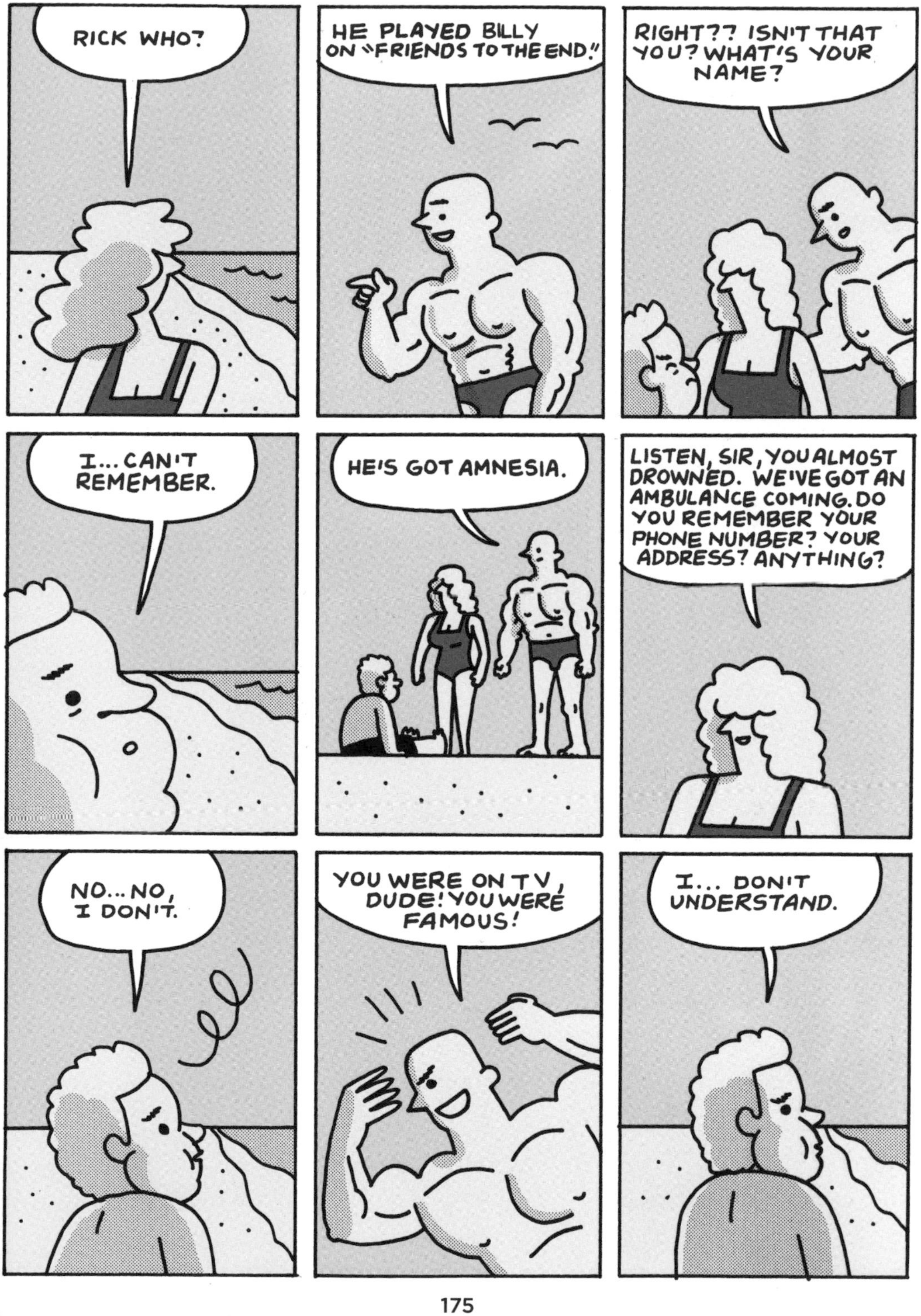
RICK WHO?
HE PLAYED BILLY ON "FRIENDS TO THE END."
RIGHT?? ISN'T THAT YOU? WHAT'S YOUR NAME?
I... CAN'T REMEMBER.
HE'S GOT AMNESIA.
LISTEN, SIR, YOU ALMOST DROWNED. WE'VE GOT AN AMBULANCE COMING. DO YOU REMEMBER YOUR PHONE NUMBER? YOUR ADDRESS? ANYTHING?
NO... NO, I DON'T.
YOU WERE ON TV, DUDE! YOU WERE FAMOUS!
I... DON'T UNDERSTAND.

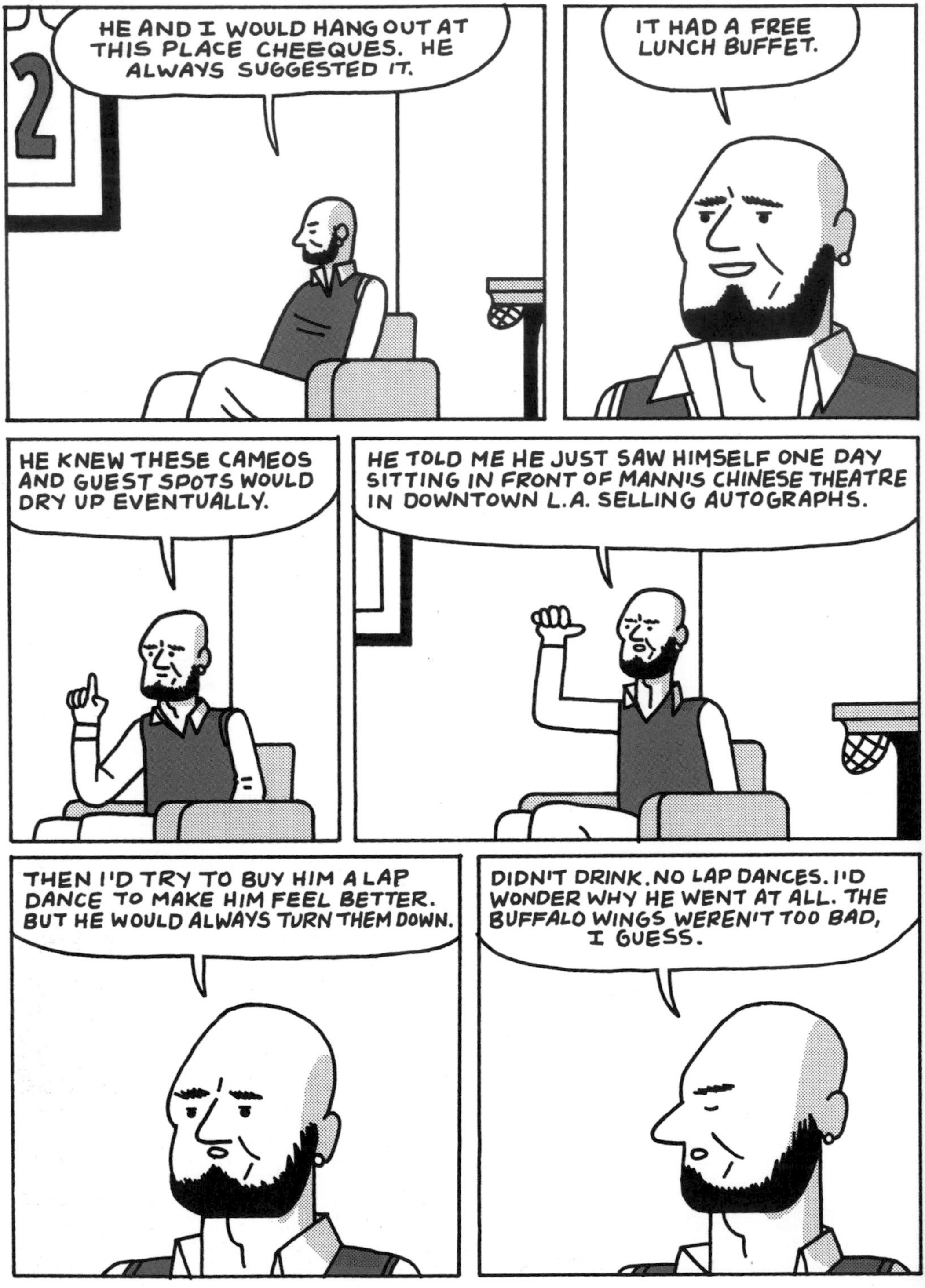
HE AND I WOULD HANG OUT AT THIS PLACE CHEEQUES. HE ALWAYS SUGGESTED IT.
IT HAD A FREE LUNCH BUFFET.
HE KNEW THESE CAMEOS AND GUEST SPOTS WOULD DRY UP EVENTUALLY.
HE TOLD ME HE JUST SAW HIMSELF ONE DAY SITTING IN FRONT OF MANN'S CHINESE THEATRE IN DOWNTOWN L.A. SELLING AUTOGRAPHS.
THEN I'D TRY TO BUY HIM A LAP DANCE TO MAKE HIM FEEL BETTER. BUT HE WOULD ALWAYS TURN THEM DOWN.
DIDN'T DRINK. NO LAP DANCES. I'D WONDER WHY HE WENT AT ALL. THE BUFFALO WINGS WEREN'T TOO BAD, I GUESS.

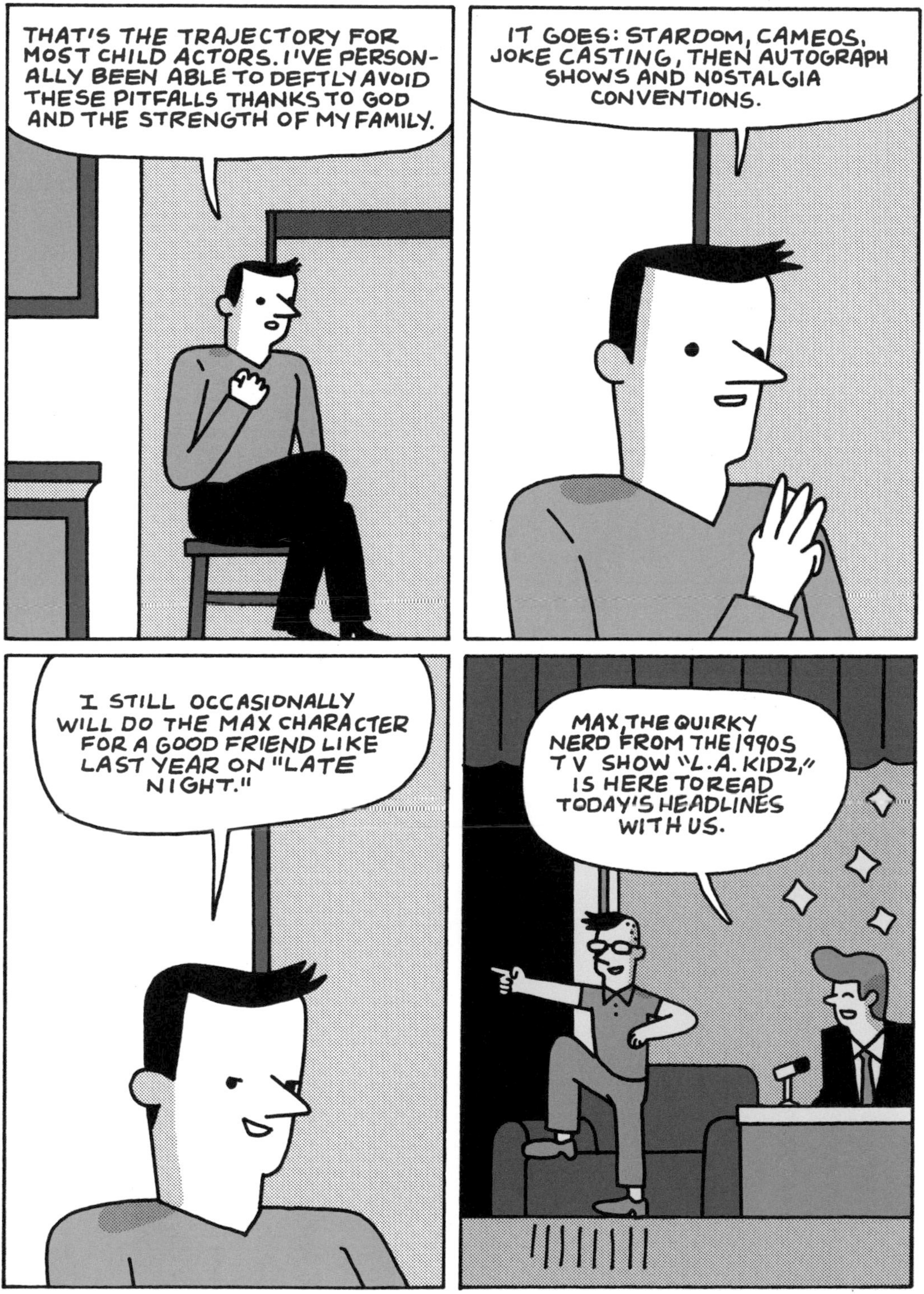
THAT'S THE TRAJECTORY FOR MOST CHILD ACTORS. I'VE PERSONALLY BEEN ABLE TO DEFTLY AVOID THESE PITFALLS THANKS TO GOD AND THE STRENGTH OF MY FAMILY.
IT GOES: STARDOM, CAMEOS, JOKE CASTING, THEN AUTOGRAPH SHOWS AND NOSTALGIA CONVENTIONS.
I STILL OCCASIONALLY WILL DO THE MAX CHARACTER FOR A GOOD FRIEND LIKE LAST YEAR ON "LATE NIGHT."
MAX, THE QUIRKY NERD FROM THE 1990S TV SHOW "L.A. KIDZ," IS HERE TO READ TODAY'S HEADLINES WITH US.

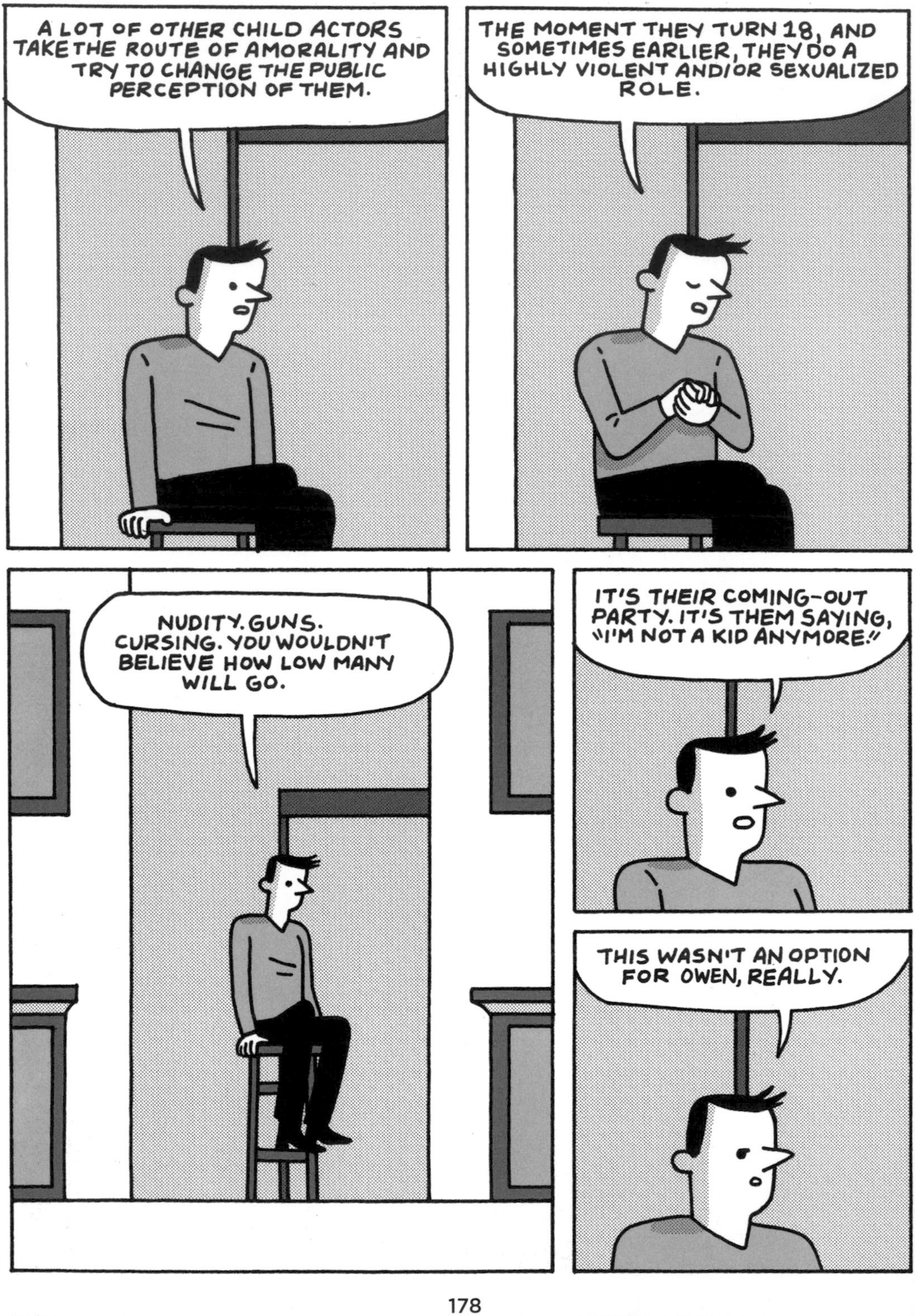
A LOT OF OTHER CHILD ACTORS TAKE THE ROUTE OF AMORALITY AND TRY TO CHANGE THE PUBLIC PERCEPTION OF THEM.
THE MOMENT THEY TURN 18, AND SOMETIMES EARLIER, THEY DO A HIGHLY VIOLENT AND/OR SEXUALIZED ROLE.
NUDITY. GUNS. CURSING. YOU WOULDN'T BELIEVE HOW LOW MANY WILL GO.
IT'S THEIR COMING-OUT PARTY. IT'S THEM SAYING, "I'M NOT A KID ANYMORE."
THIS WASN'T AN OPTION FOR OWEN, REALLY.

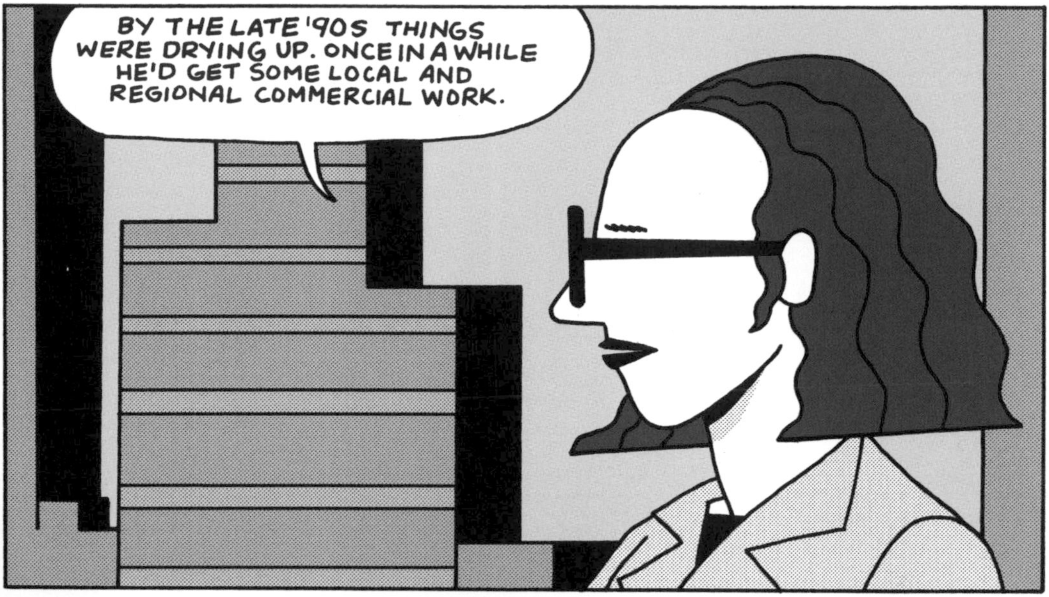
BY THE LATE '90S THINGS WERE DRYING UP. ONCE IN A WHILE HE'D GET SOME LOCAL AND REGIONAL COMMERCIAL WORK.

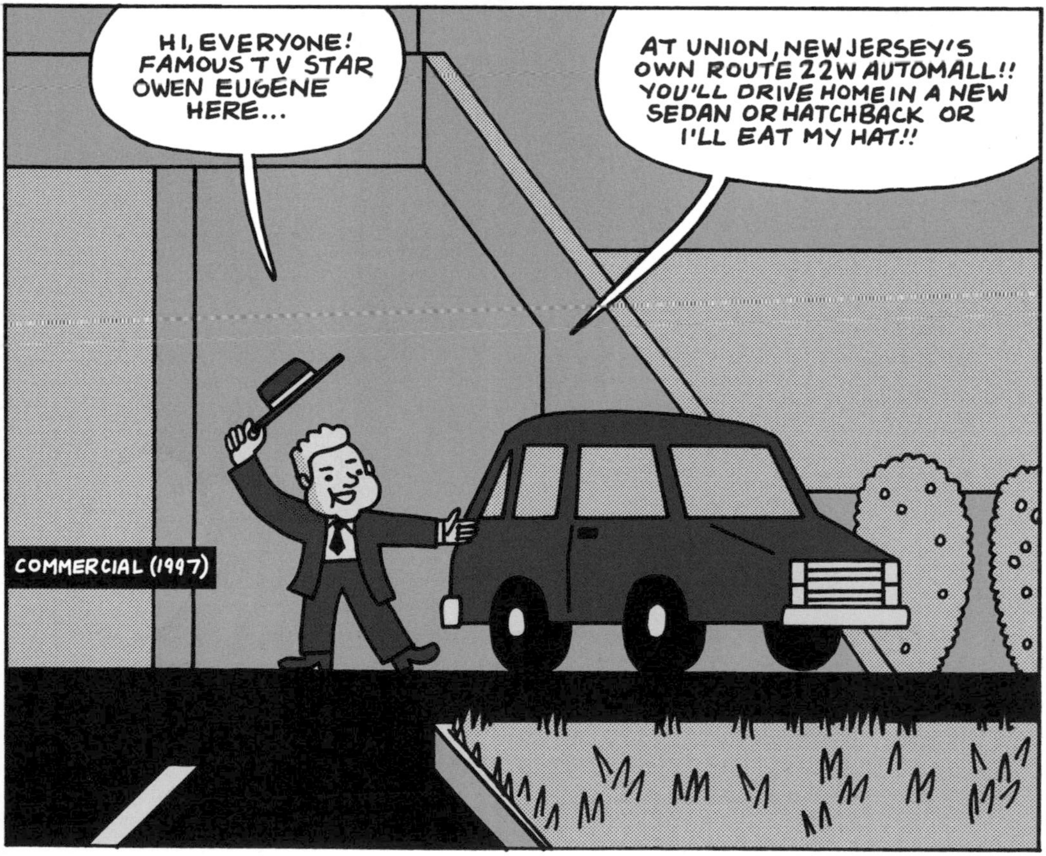
HI, EVERYONE! FAMOUS TV STAR OWEN EUGENE HERE...
AT UNION, NEW JERSEY'S OWN ROUTE 22W AUTOMALL!! YOU'LL DRIVE HOME IN A NEW SEDAN OR HATCHBACK OR I'LL EAT MY HAT!!
COMMERCIAL (1997)

THE PASTA PRO $39.99 INFOMERCIAL (1/97)

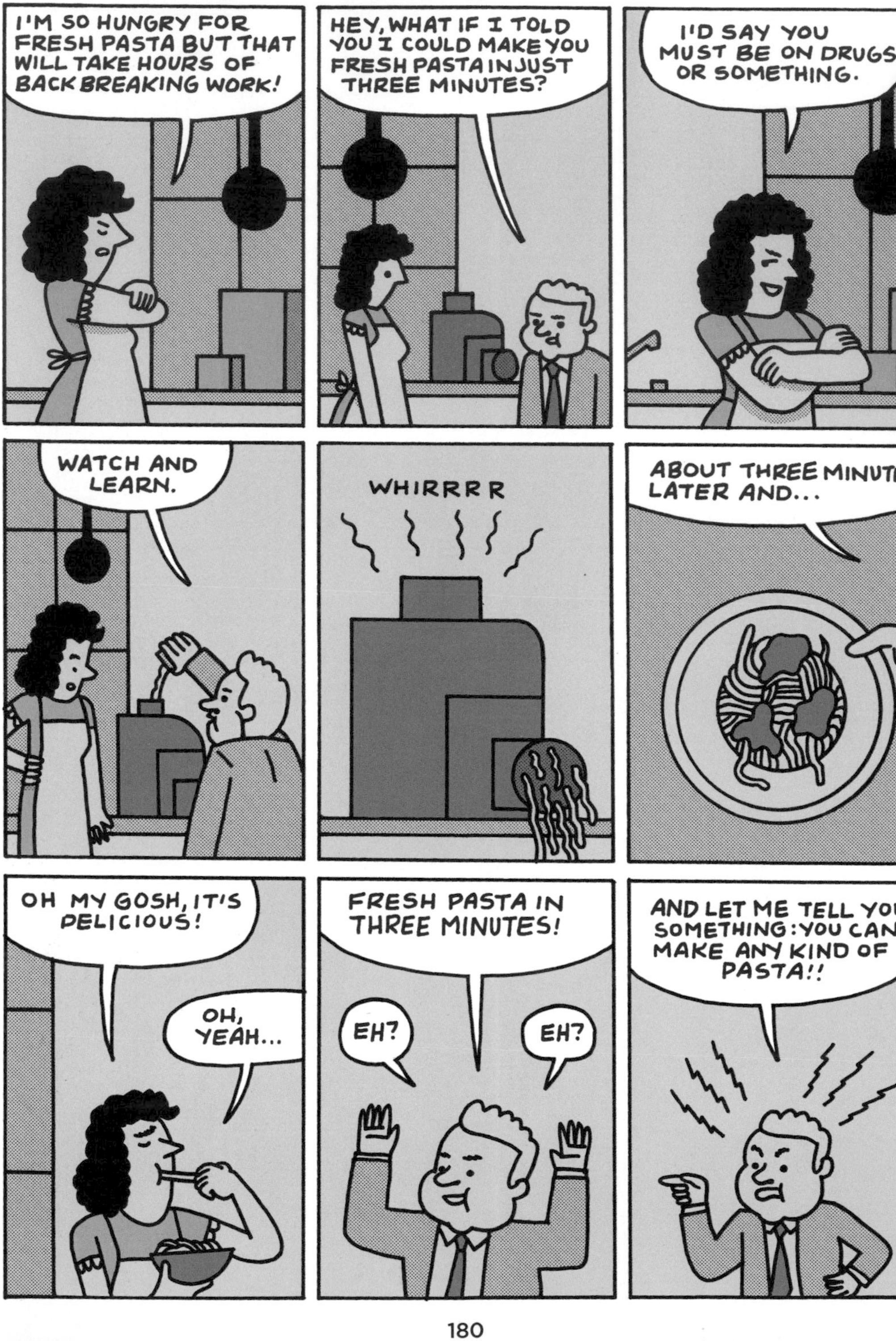
I'M SO HUNGRY FOR FRESH PASTA BUT THAT WILL TAKE HOURS OF BACK BREAKING WORK!
HEY, WHAT IF I TOLD YOU I COULD MAKE YOU FRESH PASTA IN JUST THREE MINUTES?
I'D SAY YOU MUST BE ON DRUGS OR SOMETHING.
WATCH AND LEARN.
WHIRRRR
ABOUT THREE MINUTES LATER AND...
OH MY GOSH, IT'S DELICIOUS!
OH, YEAH...
FRESH PASTA IN THREE MINUTES!
EH?
EH?
AND LET ME TELL YOU SOMETHING: YOU CAN MAKE ANY KIND OF PASTA!!

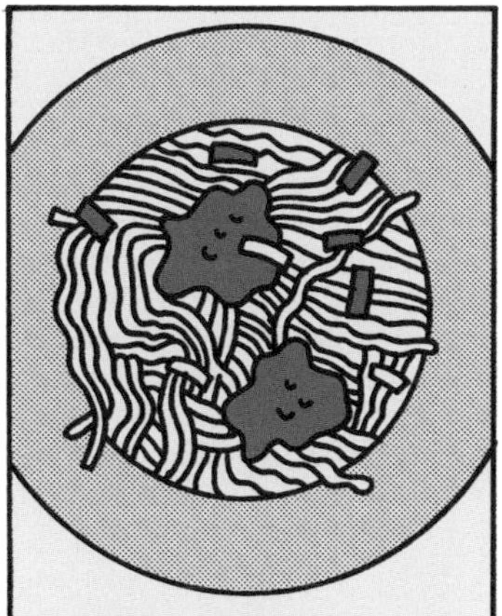

SOUTHWEST PASTA

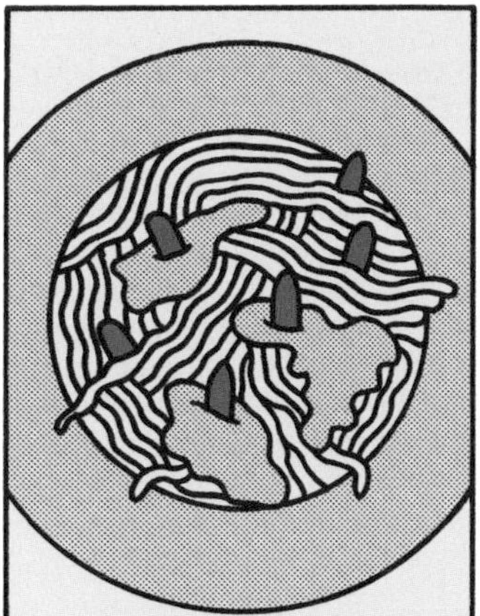

CHINESE PASTA

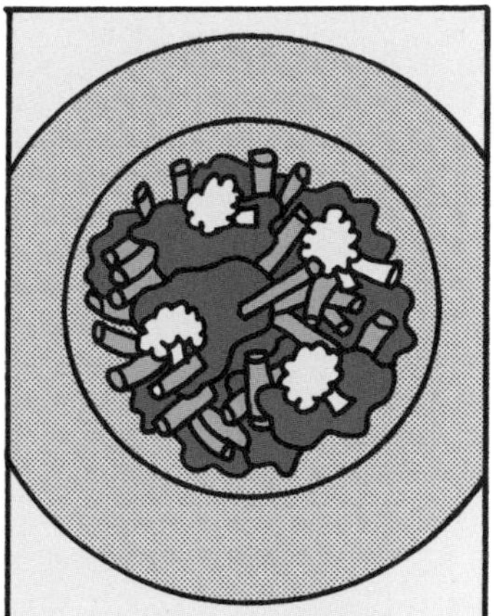

INDIAN PASTA

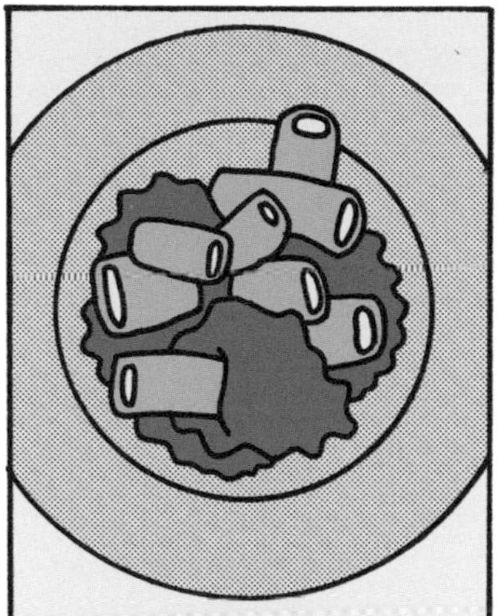

PASTA SALAD

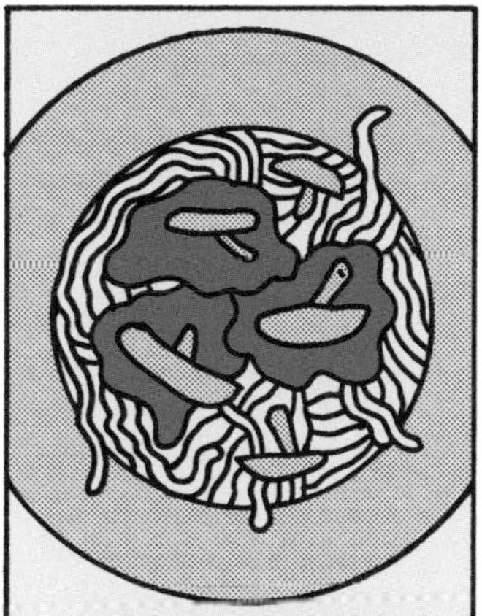

MUSHROOM PASTA

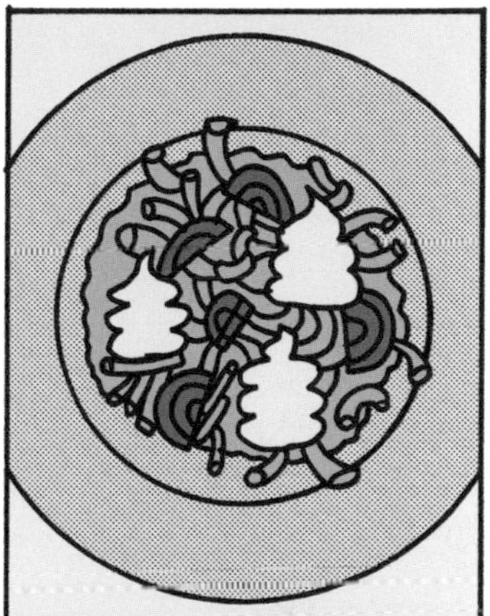

SOUR CREAM &ONION PASTA

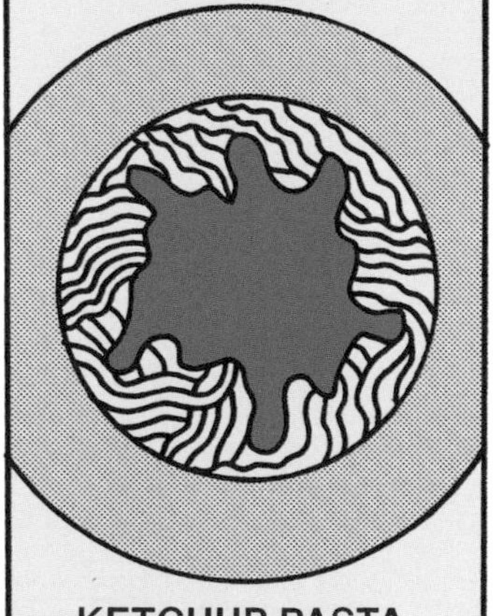

KETCHUP PASTA

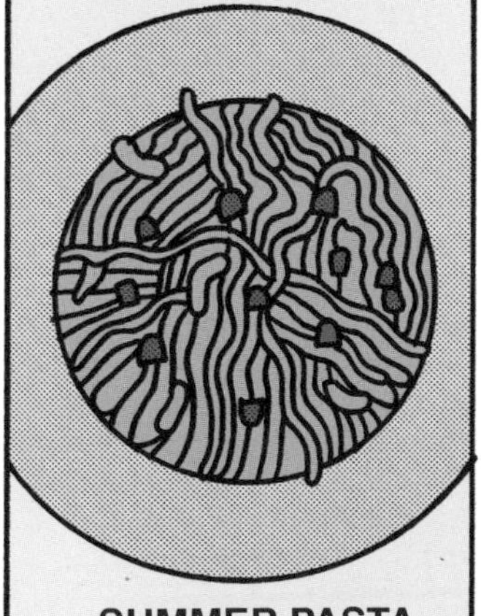

SUMMER PASTA

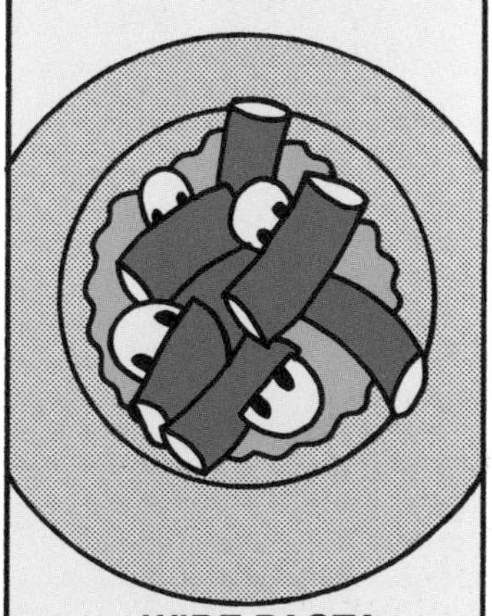

WIDE PASTA

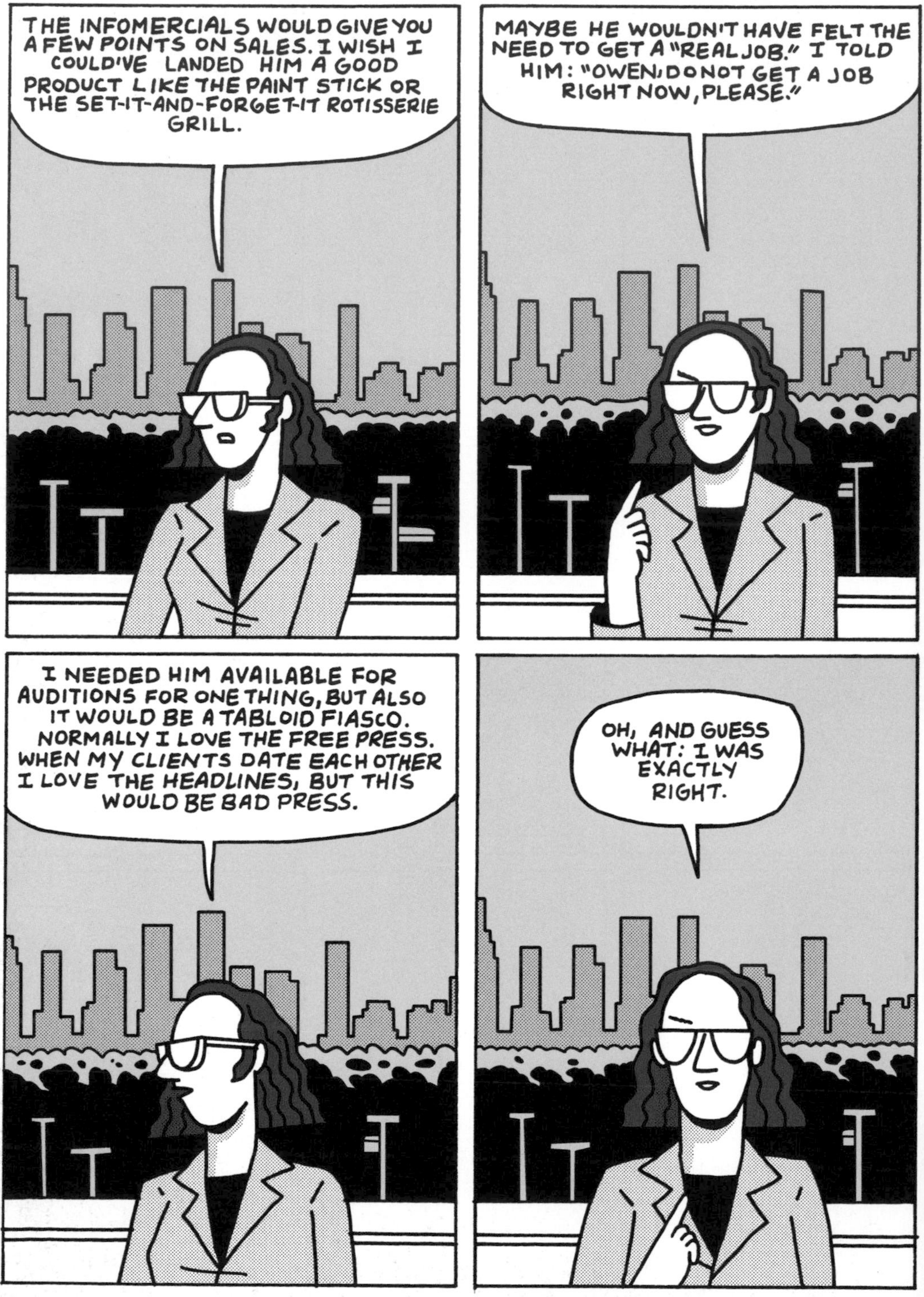
THE INFOMERCIALS WOULD GIVE YOU A FEW POINTS ON SALES. I WISH I COULD'VE LANDED HIM A GOOD PRODUCT LIKE THE PAINT STICK OR THE SET-IT-AND-FORGET-IT ROTISSERIE GRILL.
MAYBE HE WOULDN'T HAVE FELT THE NEED TO GET A "REAL JOB." I TOLD HIM: "OWEN, DO NOT GET A JOB RIGHT NOW, PLEASE."
I NEEDED HIM AVAILABLE FOR AUDITIONS FOR ONE THING, BUT ALSO IT WOULD BE A TABLOID FIASCO. NORMALLY I LOVE THE FREE PRESS. WHEN MY CLIENTS DATE EACH OTHER I LOVE THE HEADLINES, BUT THIS WOULD BE BAD PRESS.
OH, AND GUESS WHAT: I WAS EXACTLY RIGHT.

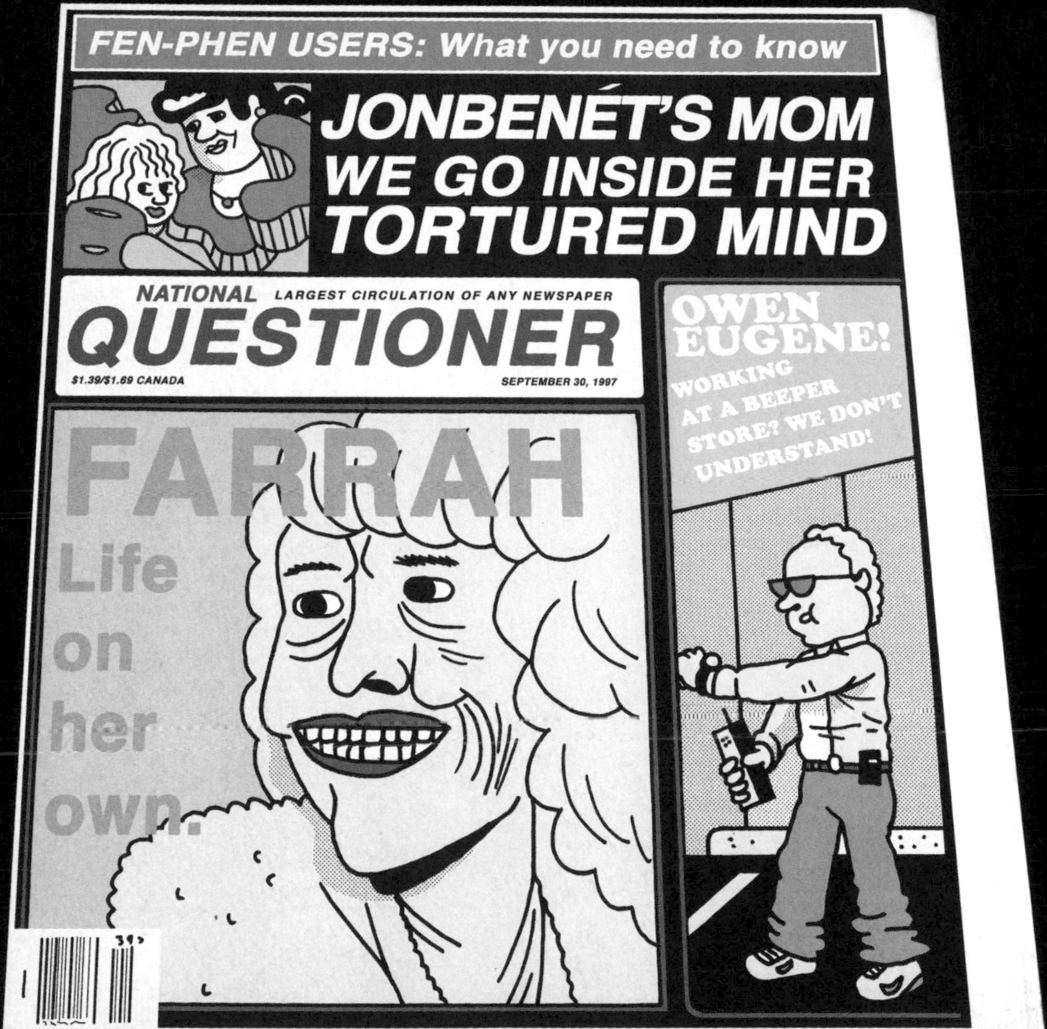
FEN-PHEN USERS: What you need to know
JONBENÉT'S MOM WE GO INSIDE HER TORTURED MIND
NATIONAL QUESTIONER
LARGEST CIRCULATION OF ANY NEWSPAPER
$1.39/$1.69 CANADA
SEPTEMBER 30, 1997
OWEN EUGENE!
WORKING AT A BEEPER STORE? WE DON'T UNDERSTAND!
FARRAH
Life on her own.

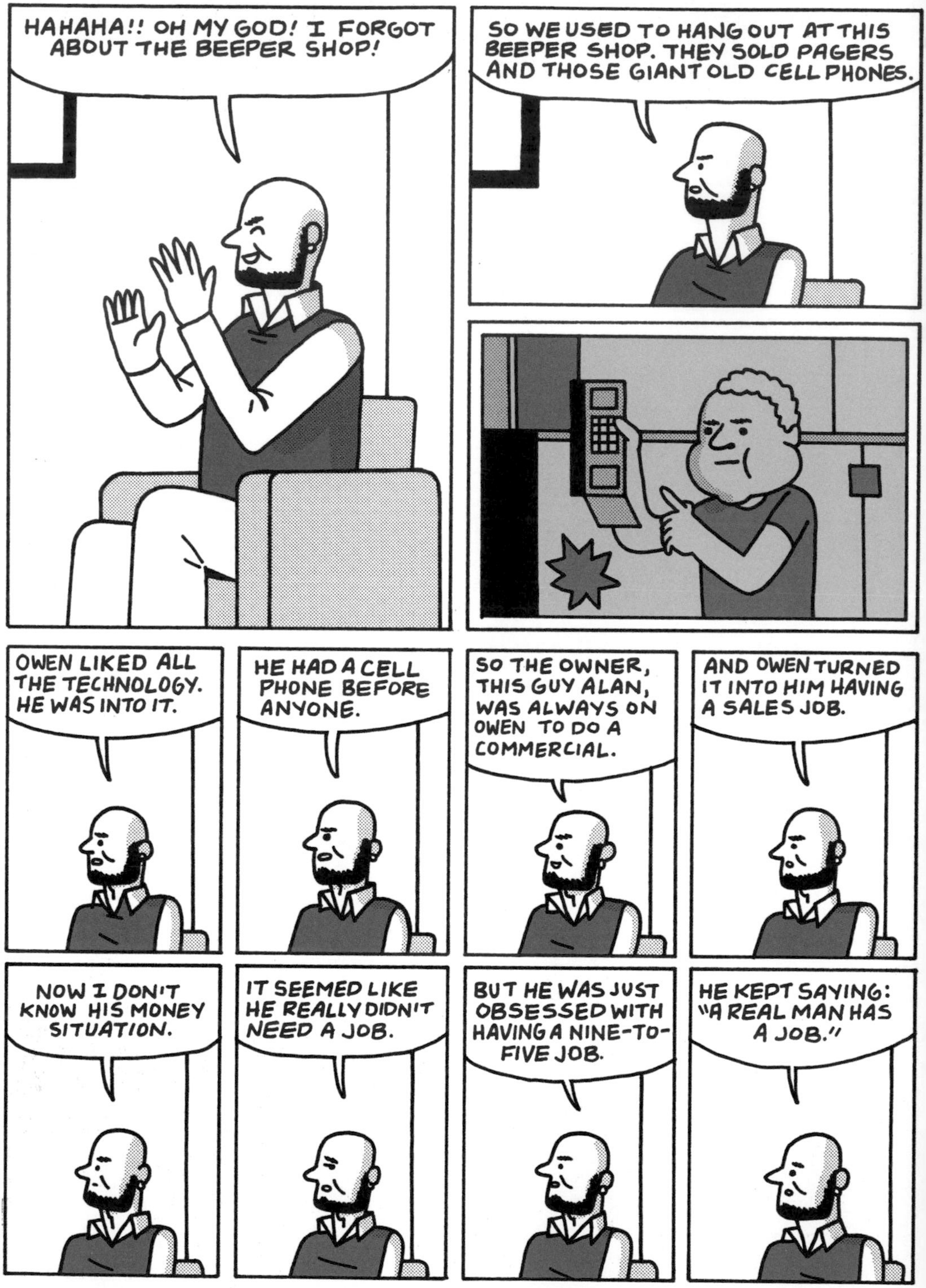
HAHAHA!! OH MY GOD! I FORGOT ABOUT THE BEEPER SHOP!
SO WE USED TO HANG OUT AT THIS BEEPER SHOP. THEY SOLD PAGERS AND THOSE GIANT OLD CELL PHONES.
OWEN LIKED ALL THE TECHNOLOGY. HE WAS INTO IT.
HE HAD A CELL PHONE BEFORE ANYONE.
SO THE OWNER, THIS GUY ALAN, WAS ALWAYS ON OWEN TO DO A COMMERCIAL.
AND OWEN TURNED IT INTO HIM HAVING A SALES JOB.
NOW I DON'T KNOW HIS MONEY SITUATION.
IT SEEMED LIKE HE REALLY DIDN'T NEED A JOB.
BUT HE WAS JUST OBSESSED WITH HAVING A NINE-TO-FIVE JOB.
HE KEPT SAYING: "A REAL MAN HAS A JOB."

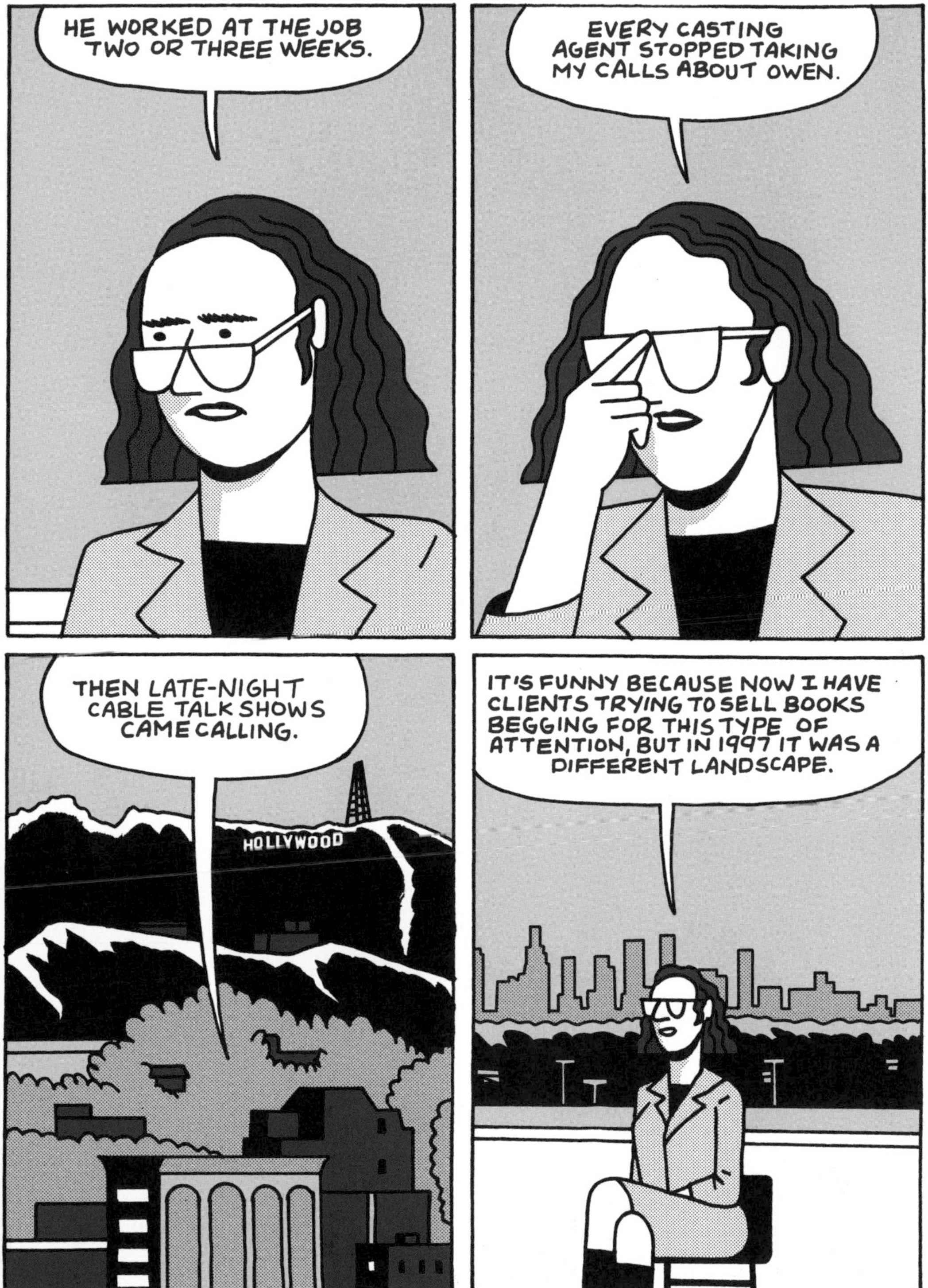
HE WORKED AT THE JOB TWO OR THREE WEEKS.
EVERY CASTING AGENT STOPPED TAKING MY CALLS ABOUT OWEN.
THEN LATE-NIGHT CABLE TALK SHOWS CAME CALLING.
HOLLYWOOD
IT'S FUNNY BECAUSE NOW I HAVE CLIENTS TRYING TO SELL BOOKS BEGGING FOR THIS TYPE OF ATTENTION, BUT IN 1997 IT WAS A DIFFERENT LANDSCAPE.

"THE LEE KING SHOW" 2/9/99

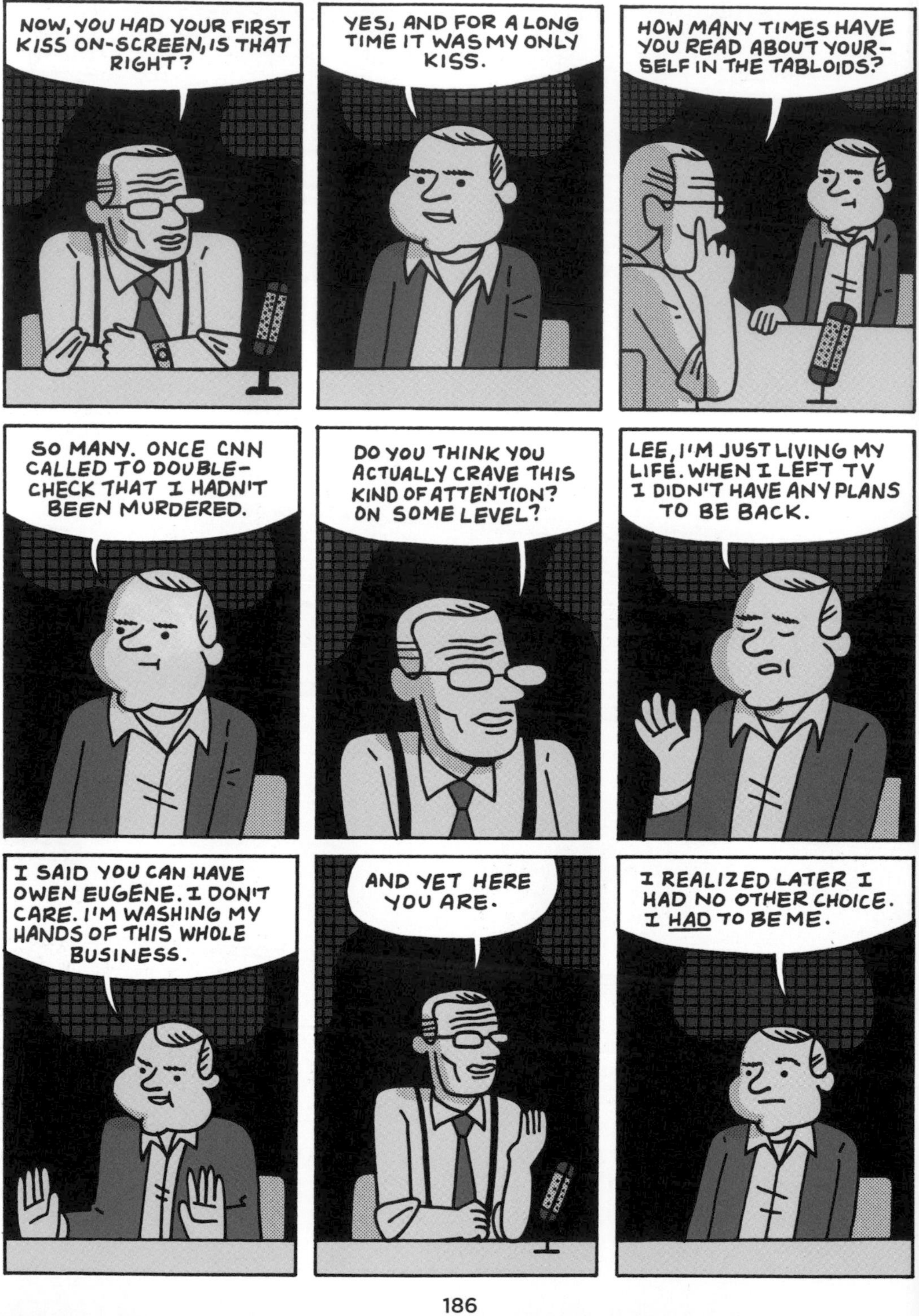
NOW, YOU HAD YOUR FIRST KISS ON-SCREEN, IS THAT RIGHT?
YES, AND FOR A LONG TIME IT WAS MY ONLY KISS.
HOW MANY TIMES HAVE YOU READ ABOUT YOURSELF IN THE TABLOIDS?
SO MANY. ONCE CNN CALLED TO DOUBLE-CHECK THAT I HADN'T BEEN MURDERED.
DO YOU THINK YOU ACTUALLY CRAVE THIS KIND OF ATTENTION? ON SOME LEVEL?
LEE, I'M JUST LIVING MY LIFE. WHEN I LEFT TV I DIDN'T HAVE ANY PLANS TO BE BACK.
I SAID YOU CAN HAVE OWEN EUGENE. I DON'T CARE. I'M WASHING MY HANDS OF THIS WHOLE BUSINESS.
AND YET HERE YOU ARE.
I REALIZED LATER I HAD NO OTHER CHOICE. I HAD TO BE ME.

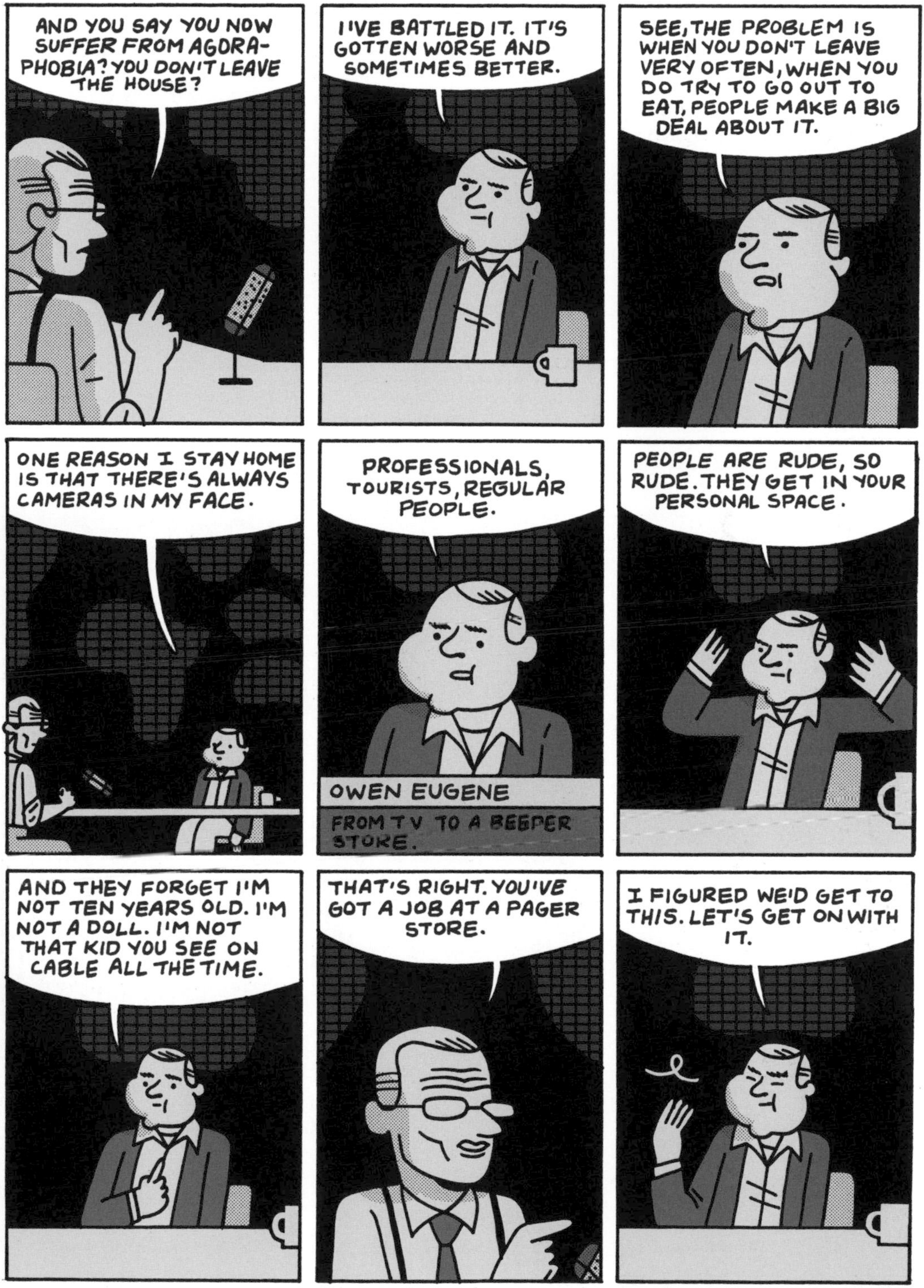
AND YOU SAY YOU NOW SUFFER FROM AGORAPHOBIA? YOU DON'T LEAVE THE HOUSE?
I'VE BATTLED IT. IT'S GOTTEN WORSE AND SOMETIMES BETTER.
SEE, THE PROBLEM IS WHEN YOU DON'T LEAVE VERY OFTEN, WHEN YOU DO TRY TO GO OUT TO EAT, PEOPLE MAKE A BIG DEAL ABOUT IT.
ONE REASON I STAY HOME IS THAT THERE'S ALWAYS CAMERAS IN MY FACE.
PROFESSIONALS, TOURISTS, REGULAR PEOPLE.
OWEN EUGENE
FROM TV TO A BEEPER STORE.
PEOPLE ARE RUDE, SO RUDE. THEY GET IN YOUR PERSONAL SPACE.
AND THEY FORGET I'M NOT TEN YEARS OLD. I'M NOT A DOLL. I'M NOT THAT KID YOU SEE ON CABLE ALL THE TIME.
THAT'S RIGHT. YOU'VE GOT A JOB AT A PAGER STORE.
I FIGURED WE'D GET TO THIS. LET'S GET ON WITH IT.

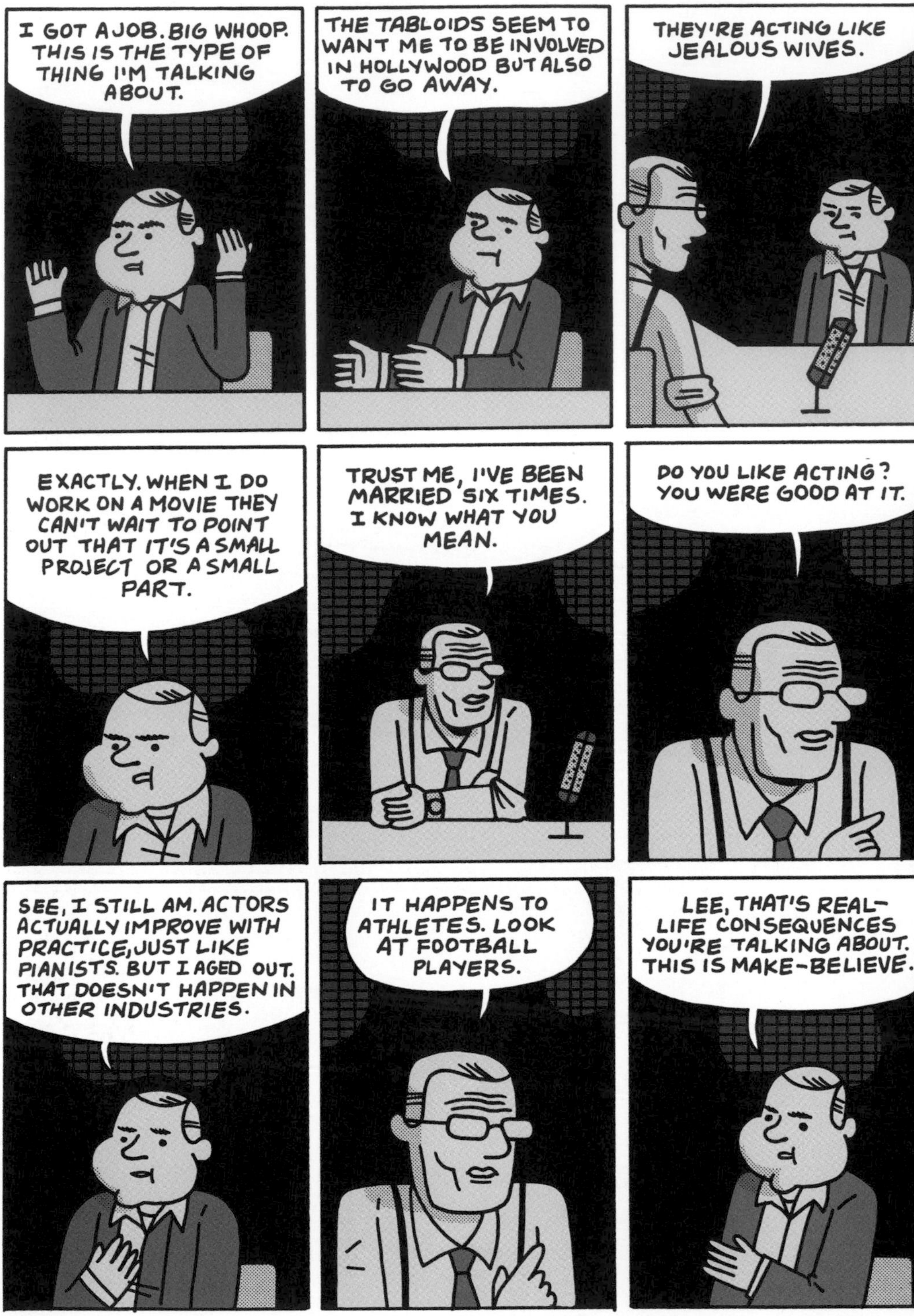
I GOT A JOB. BIG WHOOP. THIS IS THE TYPE OF THING I'M TALKING ABOUT.
THE TABLOIDS SEEM TO WANT ME TO BE INVOLVED IN HOLLYWOOD BUT ALSO TO GO AWAY.
THEY'RE ACTING LIKE JEALOUS WIVES.
EXACTLY. WHEN I DO WORK ON A MOVIE THEY CAN'T WAIT TO POINT OUT THAT IT'S A SMALL PROJECT OR A SMALL PART.
TRUST ME, I'VE BEEN MARRIED SIX TIMES. I KNOW WHAT YOU MEAN.
DO YOU LIKE ACTING? YOU WERE GOOD AT IT.
SEE, I STILL AM. ACTORS ACTUALLY IMPROVE WITH PRACTICE, JUST LIKE PIANISTS. BUT I AGED OUT. THAT DOESN'T HAPPEN IN OTHER INDUSTRIES.
IT HAPPENS TO ATHLETES. LOOK AT FOOTBALL PLAYERS.
LEE, THAT'S REAL-LIFE CONSEQUENCES YOU'RE TALKING ABOUT. THIS IS MAKE-BELIEVE.

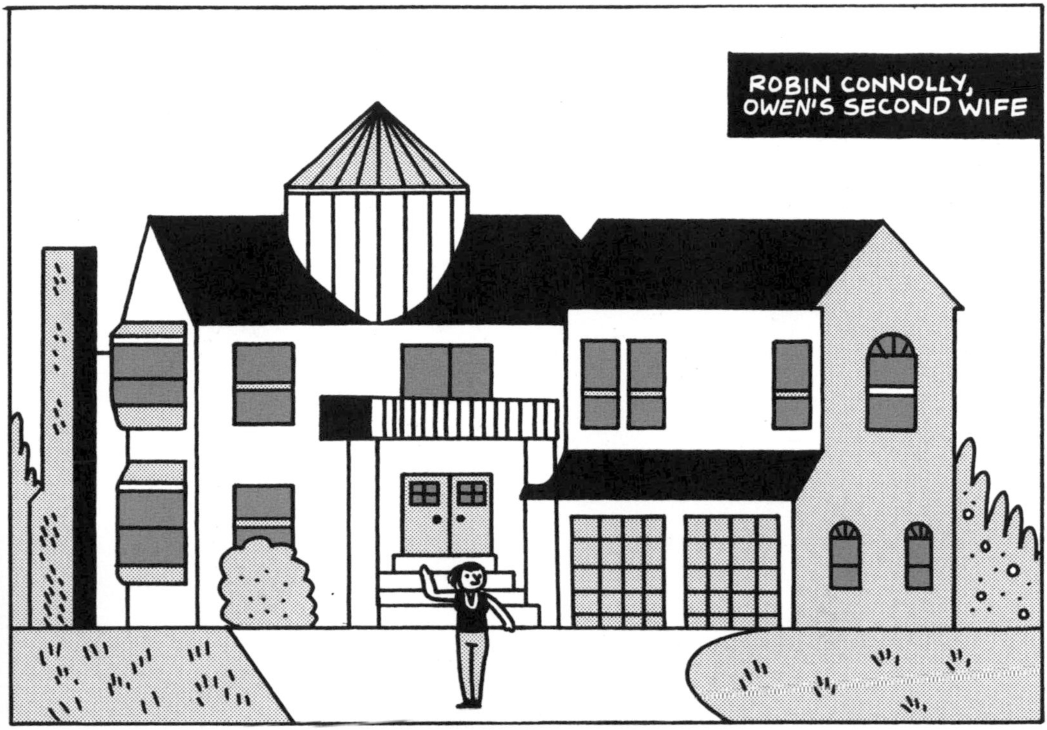
ROBIN CONNOLLY, OWEN'S SECOND WIFE

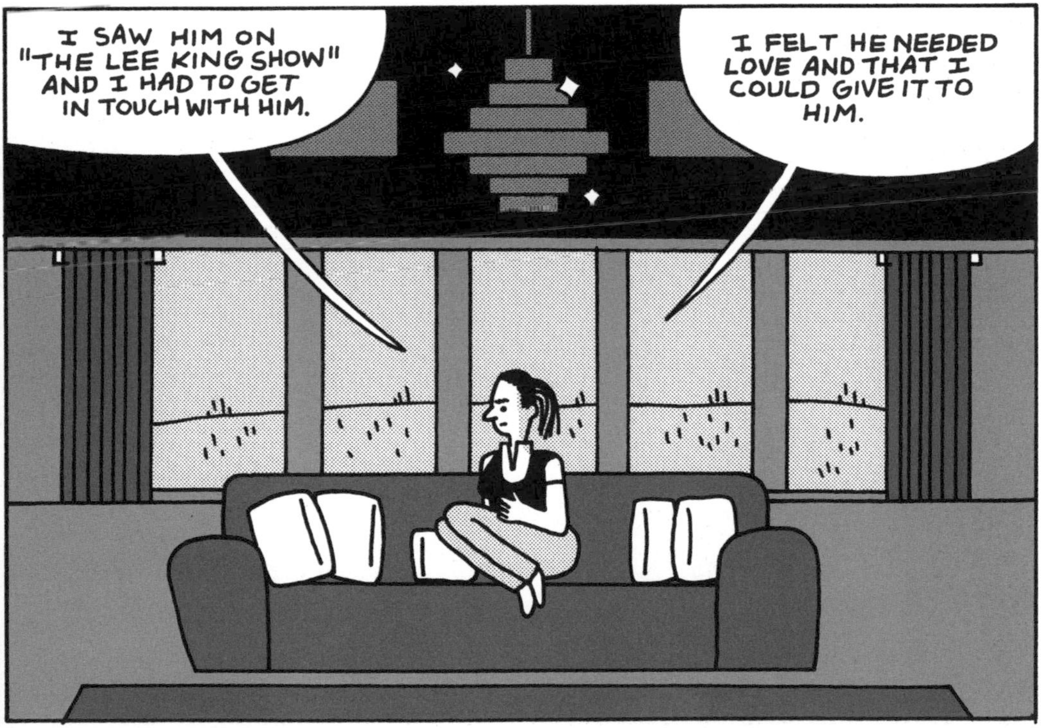
I SAW HIM ON "THE LEE KING SHOW" AND I HAD TO GET IN TOUCH WITH HIM.
I FELT HE NEEDED LOVE AND THAT I COULD GIVE IT TO HIM.

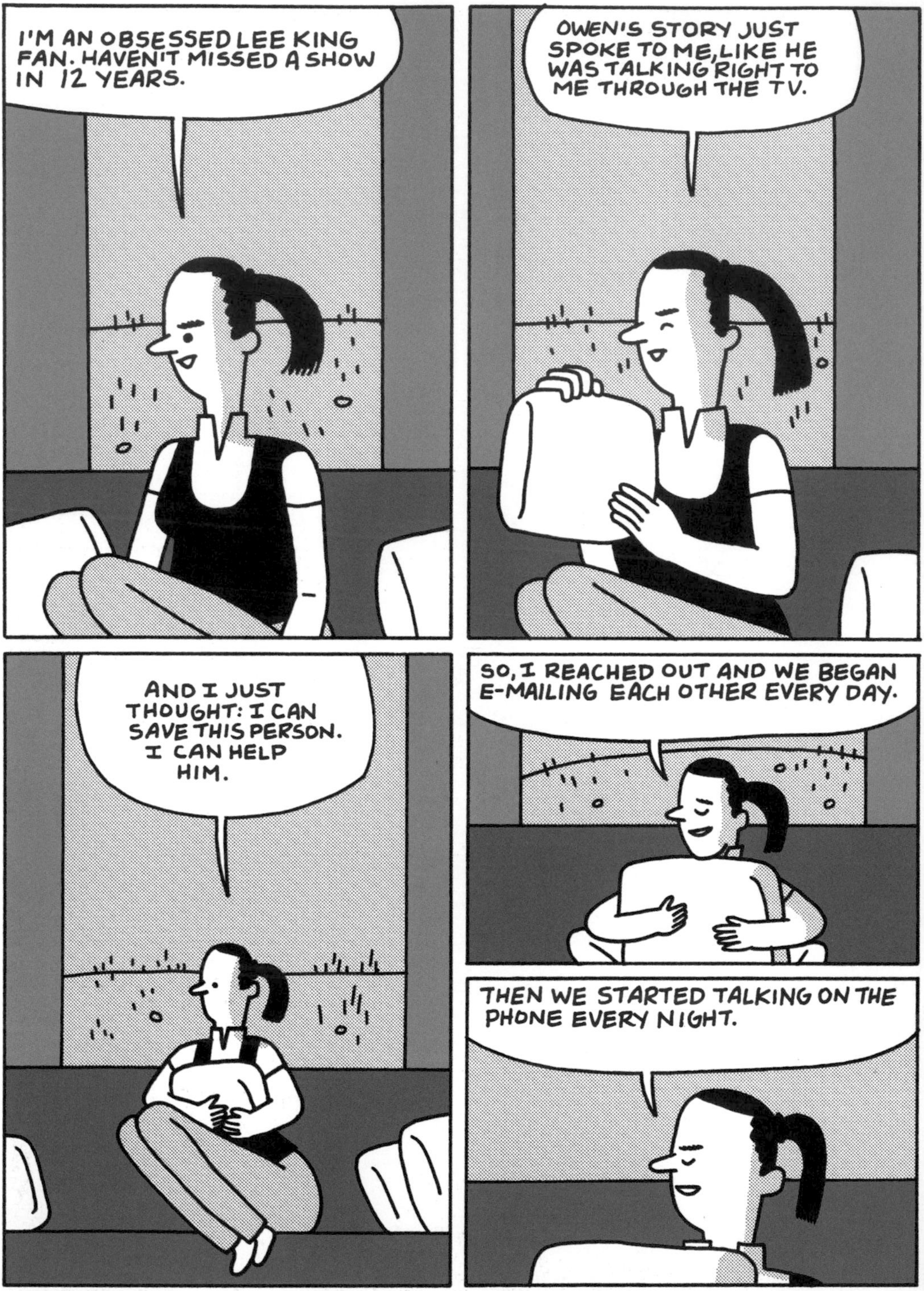
I'M AN OBSESSED LEE KING FAN. HAVEN'T MISSED A SHOW IN 12 YEARS.
OWEN'S STORY JUST SPOKE TO ME, LIKE HE WAS TALKING RIGHT TO ME THROUGH THE TV.
AND I JUST THOUGHT: I CAN SAVE THIS PERSON. I CAN HELP HIM.
SO, I REACHED OUT AND WE BEGAN E-MAILING EACH OTHER EVERY DAY.
THEN WE STARTED TALKING ON THE PHONE EVERY NIGHT.

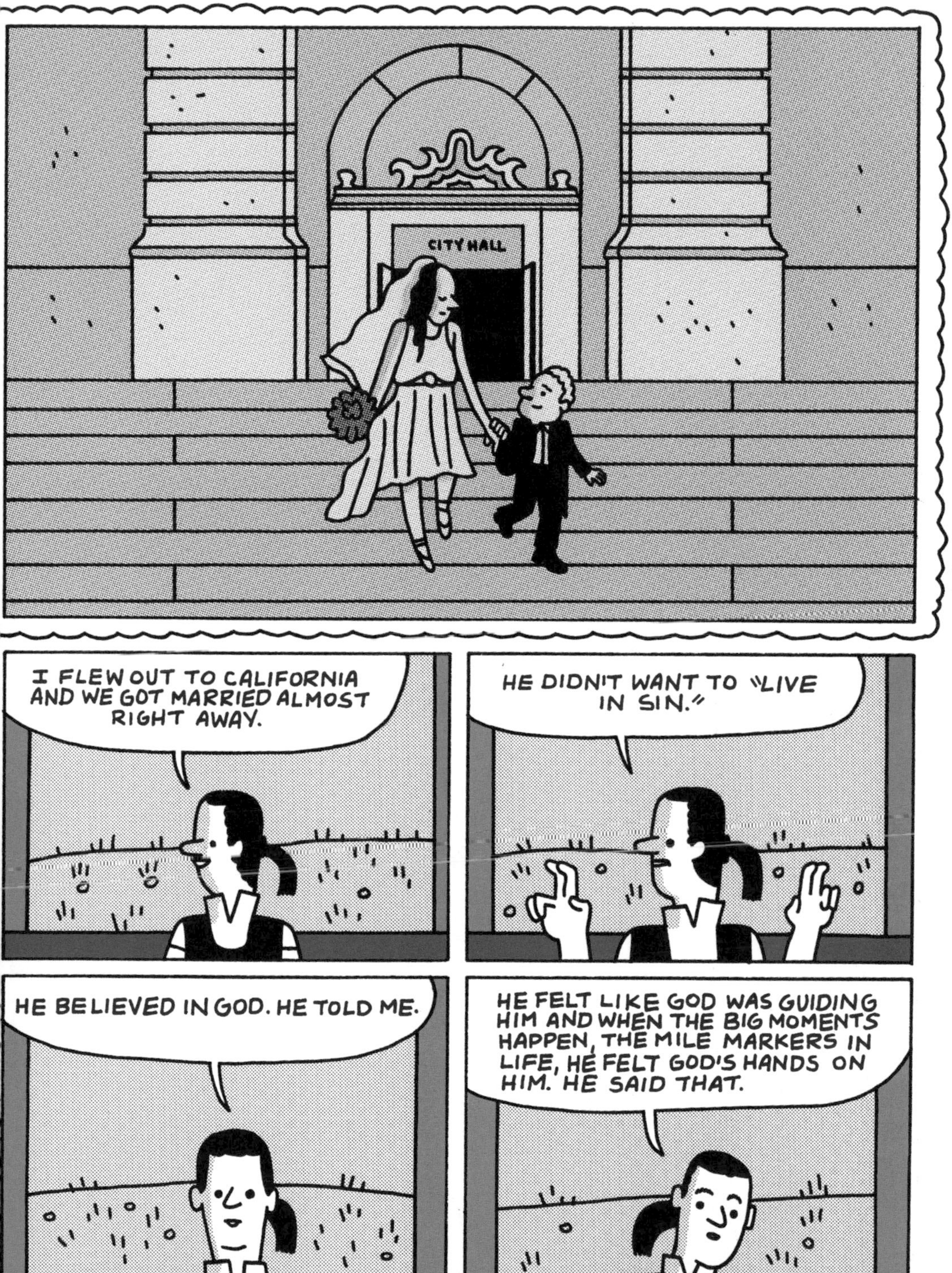
CITY HALL
I FLEW OUT TO CALIFORNIA AND WE GOT MARRIED ALMOST RIGHT AWAY.
HE DIDN'T WANT TO "LIVE IN SIN."
HE BELIEVED IN GOD. HE TOLD ME.
HE FELT LIKE GOD WAS GUIDING HIM AND WHEN THE BIG MOMENTS HAPPEN, THE MILE MARKERS IN LIFE, HE FELT GOD'S HANDS ON HIM. HE SAID THAT.

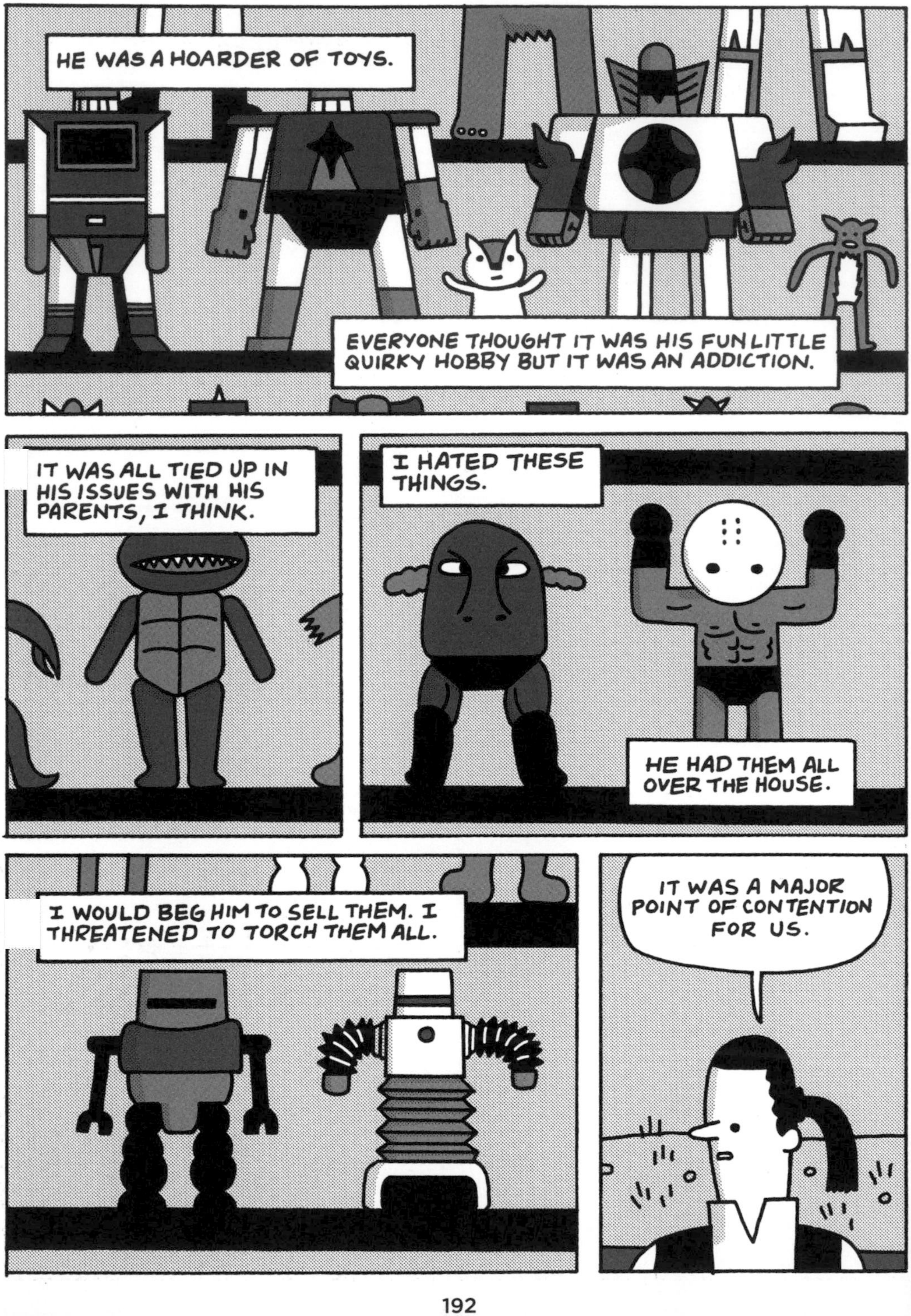
HE WAS A HOARDER OF TOYS.
EVERYONE THOUGHT IT WAS HIS FUN LITTLE QUIRKY HOBBY BUT IT WAS AN ADDICTION.
IT WAS ALL TIED UP IN HIS ISSUES WITH HIS PARENTS, I THINK.
I HATED THESE THINGS.
HE HAD THEM ALL OVER THE HOUSE.
I WOULD BEG HIM TO SELL THEM. I THREATENED TO TORCH THEM ALL.
IT WAS A MAJOR POINT OF CONTENTION FOR US.

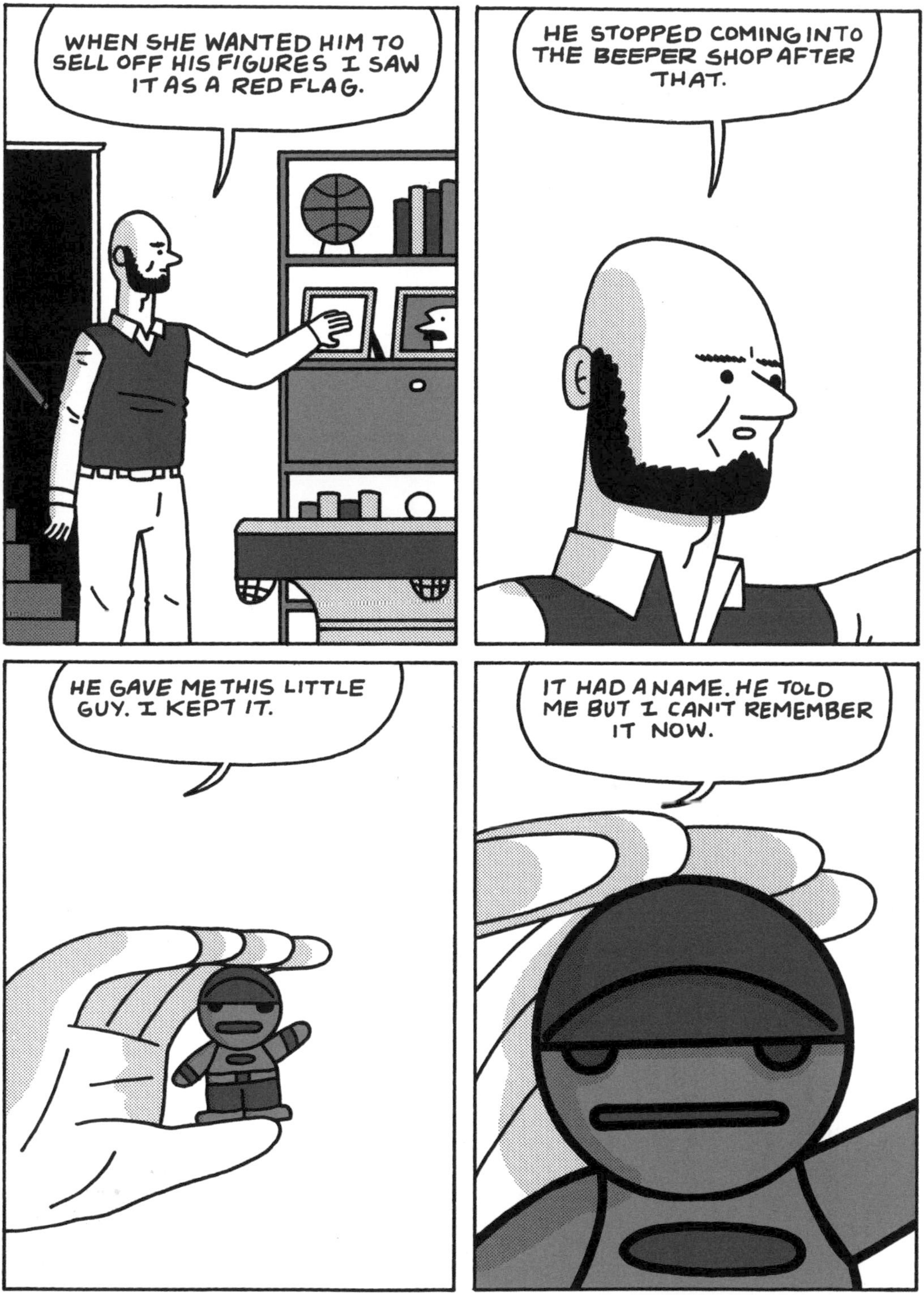
WHEN SHE WANTED HIM TO SELL OFF HIS FIGURES I SAW IT AS A RED FLAG.
HE STOPPED COMING INTO THE BEEPER SHOP AFTER THAT.
HE GAVE ME THIS LITTLE GUY. I KEPT IT.
IT HAD A NAME. HE TOLD ME BUT I CAN'T REMEMBER IT NOW.

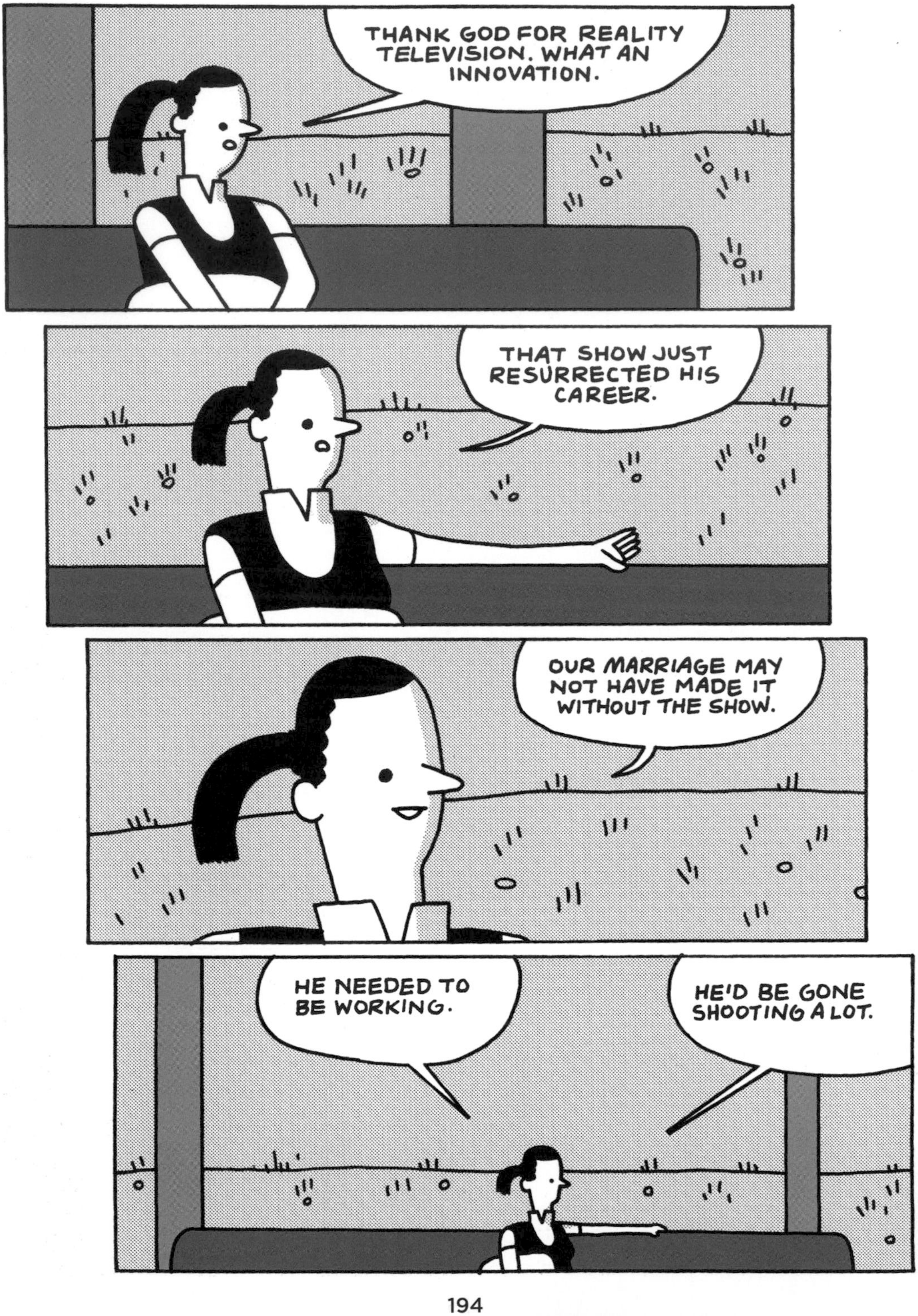
THANK GOD FOR REALITY TELEVISION. WHAT AN INNOVATION.
THAT SHOW JUST RESURRECTED HIS CAREER.
OUR MARRIAGE MAY NOT HAVE MADE IT WITHOUT THE SHOW.
HE NEEDED TO BE WORKING.
HE'D BE GONE SHOOTING A LOT.

"THIS IS THE LIFE" SEASON 1 EPISODE 3 MEETING THE ROOMMATES 1/12/03

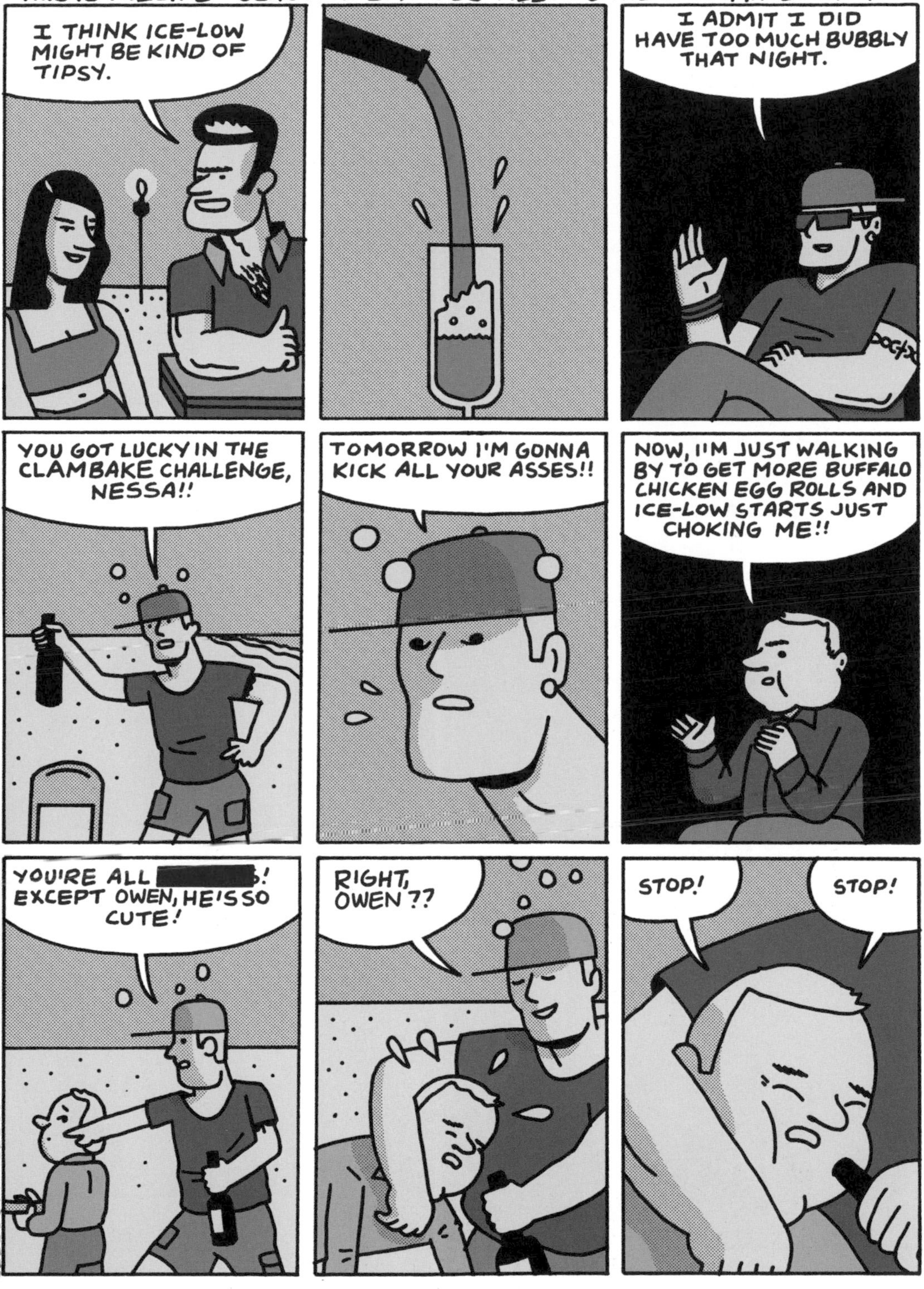
I THINK ICE-LOW MIGHT BE KIND OF TIPSY.
I ADMIT I DID HAVE TOO MUCH BUBBLY THAT NIGHT.
YOU GOT LUCKY IN THE CLAMBAKE CHALLENGE, NESSA!!
TOMORROW I'M GONNA KICK ALL YOUR ASSES!!
NOW, I'M JUST WALKING BY TO GET MORE BUFFALO CHICKEN EGG ROLLS AND ICE-LOW STARTS JUST CHOKING ME!!
YOU'RE ALL [redacted]! EXCEPT OWEN, HE'S SO CUTE!
RIGHT, OWEN??
STOP!
STOP!

PEOPLE SEE ME ON TV AND THEY THINK I'M LARGER THAN LIFE BUT I'M SMALL AND HOSPITAL BILLS ARE EXPENSIVE. PEOPLE FORGET.
HE LOVES IT!
HE LOVES IT!
LET HIM GO, ICE!!
AIGHT, AIGHT! CALM THE [redacted] DOWN!
I'M JUST SCREWING AROUND, NOT THINKING HE'D FLIP OUT LIKE THAT.
THAT'S ASSAULT! MY NECK! I COULDN'T BREATHE! CALL THE COPS! CALL THE COPS, MARK!
I'M NOT EVEN SURE IF I'M EVEN OFF PROBATION AT THIS POINT!
WHAT'S THE PROBLEM HERE??

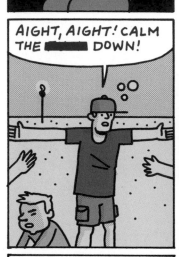

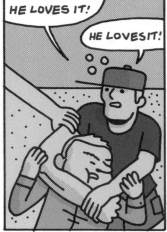

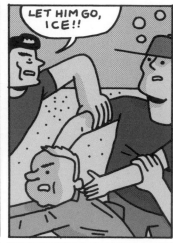

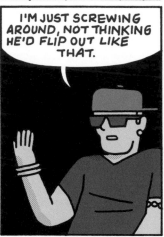

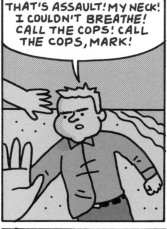

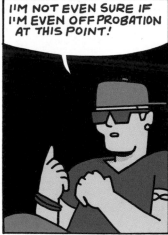

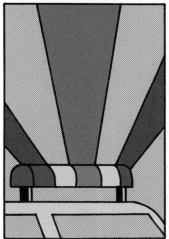

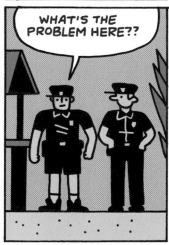

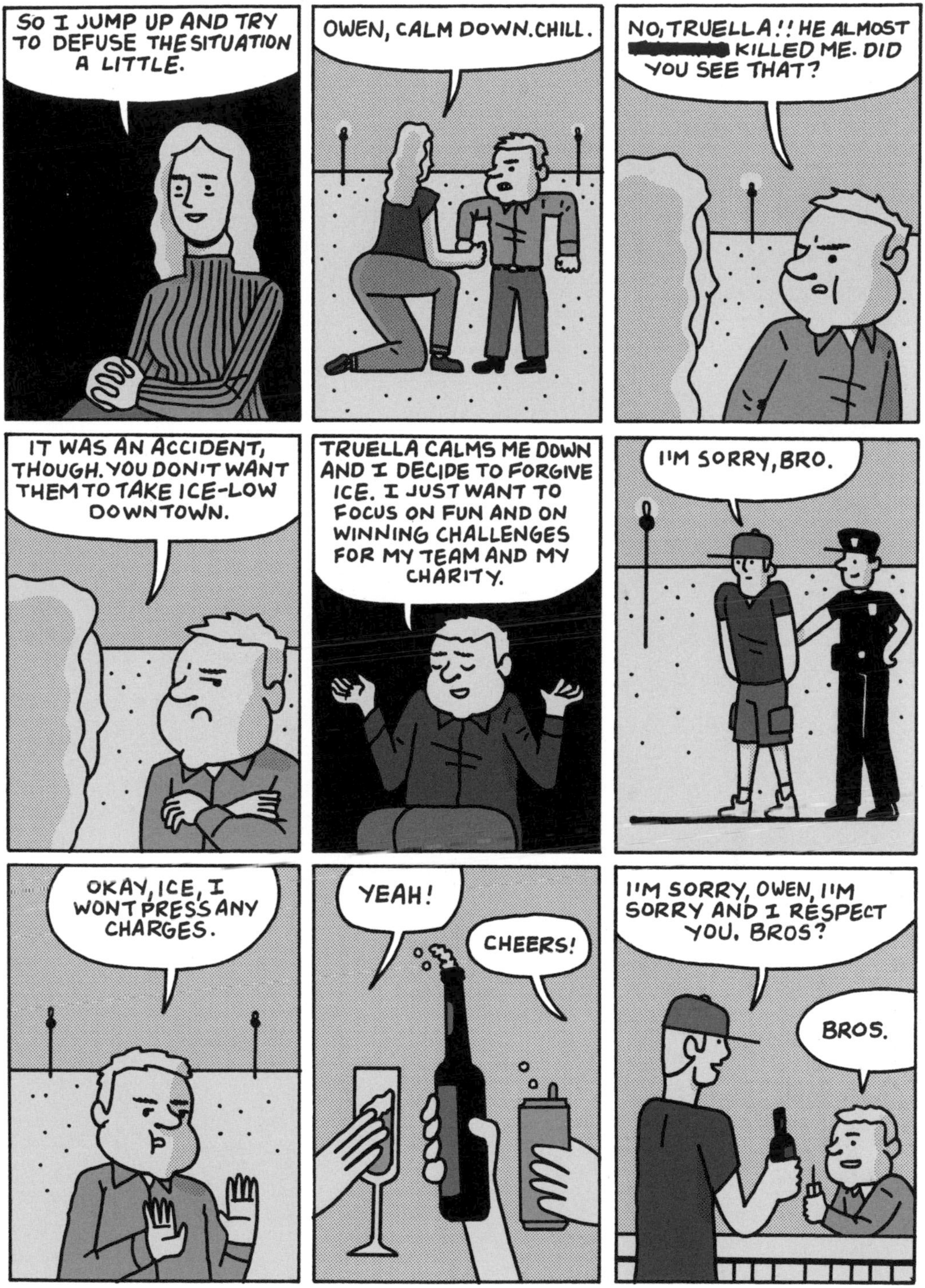
SO I JUMP UP AND TRY TO DEFUSE THE SITUATION A LITTLE.
OWEN, CALM DOWN. CHILL.
NO, TRUELLA!! HE ALMOST [redacted] KILLED ME. DID YOU SEE THAT?
IT WAS AN ACCIDENT, THOUGH. YOU DON'T WANT THEM TO TAKE ICE-LOW DOWNTOWN.
TRUELLA CALMS ME DOWN AND I DECIDE TO FORGIVE ICE. I JUST WANT TO FOCUS ON FUN AND ON WINNING CHALLENGES FOR MY TEAM AND MY CHARITY.
I'M SORRY, BRO.
OKAY, ICE, I WONT PRESS ANY CHARGES.
YEAH!
CHEERS!
I'M SORRY, OWEN, I'M SORRY AND I RESPECT YOU. BROS?
BROS.

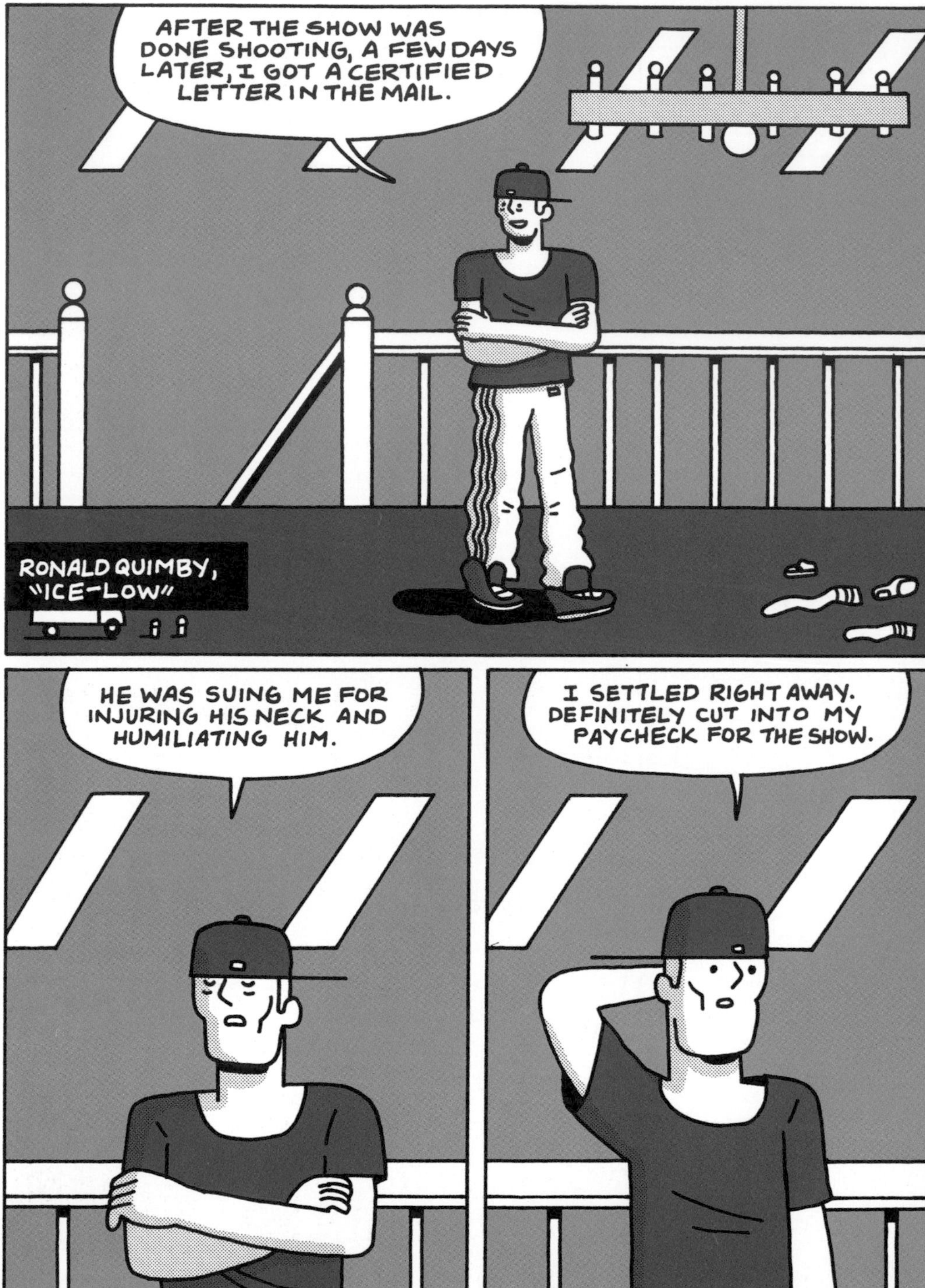
AFTER THE SHOW WAS DONE SHOOTING, A FEW DAYS LATER, I GOT A CERTIFIED LETTER IN THE MAIL.
RONALD QUIMBY, "ICE-LOW"
HE WAS SUING ME FOR INJURING HIS NECK AND HUMILIATING HIM.
I SETTLED RIGHT AWAY. DEFINITELY CUT INTO MY PAYCHECK FOR THE SHOW.

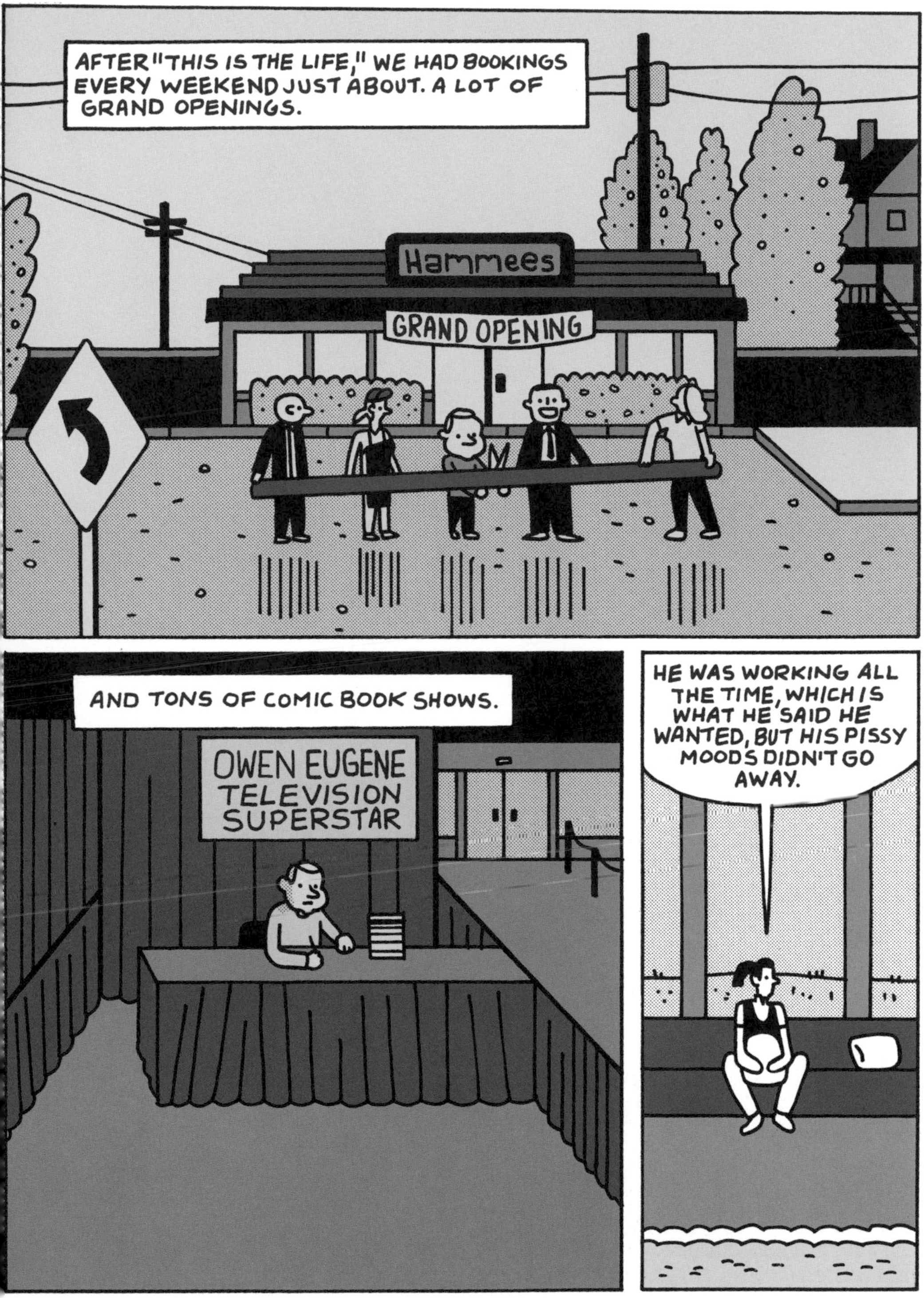
AFTER "THIS IS THE LIFE," WE HAD BOOKINGS EVERY WEEKEND JUST ABOUT. A LOT OF GRAND OPENINGS.
Hammees
GRAND OPENING
AND TONS OF COMIC BOOK SHOWS.
OWEN EUGENE TELEVISION SUPERSTAR
HE WAS WORKING ALL THE TIME, WHICH IS WHAT HE SAID HE WANTED, BUT HIS PISSY MOODS DIDN'T GO AWAY.

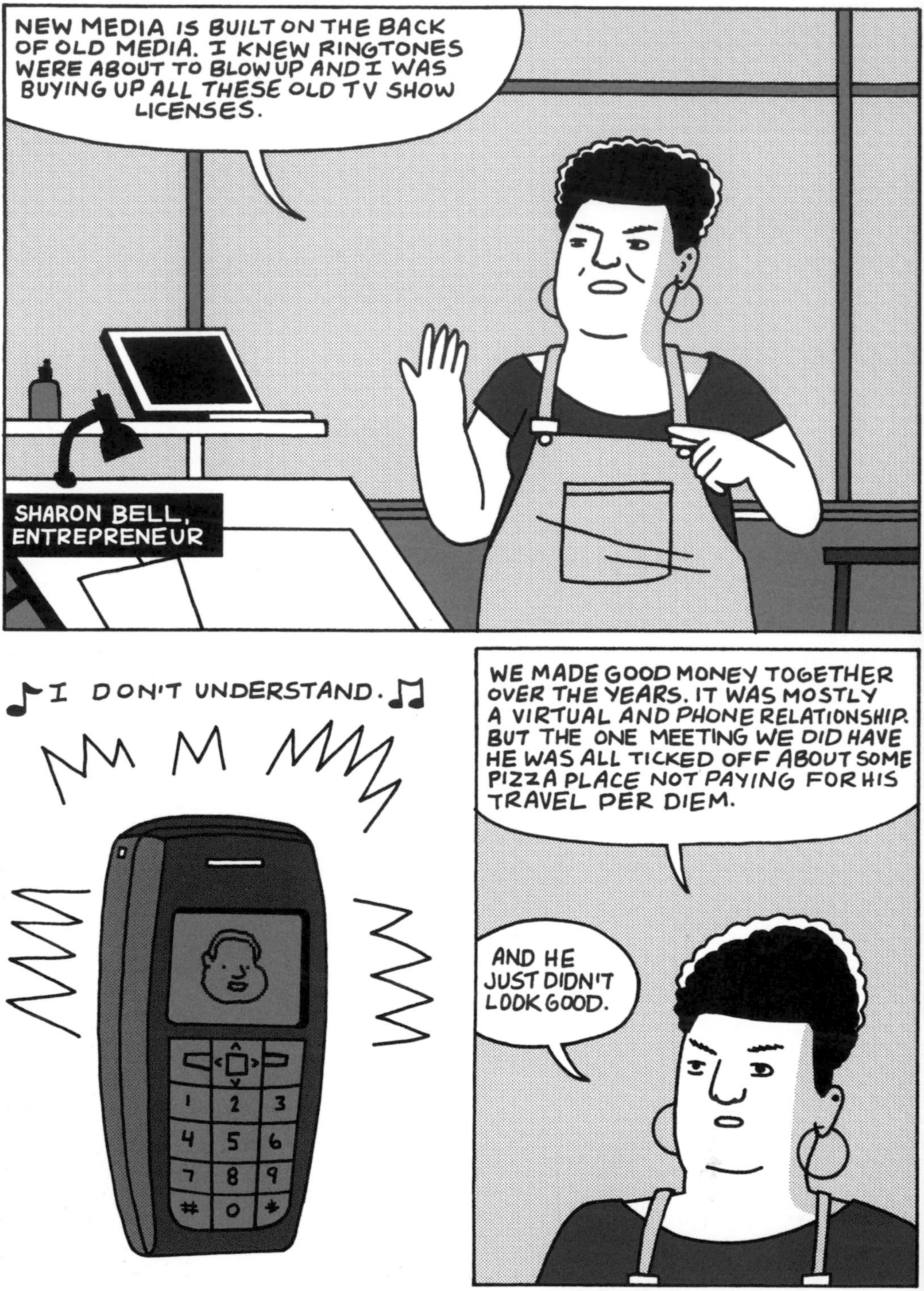
NEW MEDIA IS BUILT ON THE BACK OF OLD MEDIA. I KNEW RINGTONES WERE ABOUT TO BLOW UP AND I WAS BUYING UP ALL THESE OLD TV SHOW LICENSES.
SHARON BELL, ENTREPRENEUR
I DON'T UNDERSTAND.
WE MADE GOOD MONEY TOGETHER OVER THE YEARS. IT WAS MOSTLY A VIRTUAL AND PHONE RELATIONSHIP. BUT THE ONE MEETING WE DID HAVE HE WAS ALL TICKED OFF ABOUT SOME PIZZA PLACE NOT PAYING FOR HIS TRAVEL PER DIEM.
AND HE JUST DIDN'T LOOK GOOD.

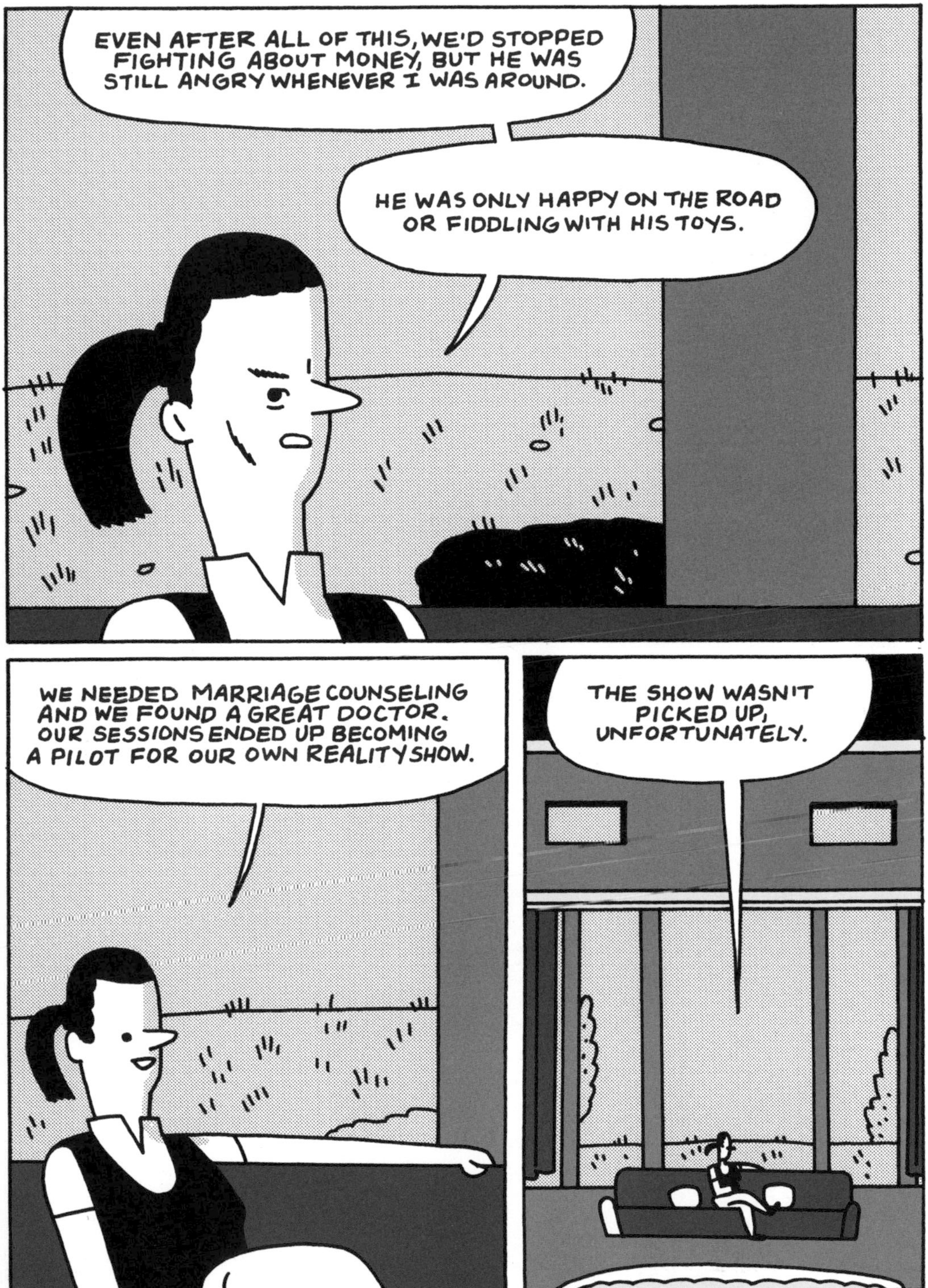
EVEN AFTER ALL OF THIS, WE'D STOPPED FIGHTING ABOUT MONEY, BUT HE WAS STILL ANGRY WHENEVER I WAS AROUND.
HE WAS ONLY HAPPY ON THE ROAD OR FIDDLING WITH HIS TOYS.
WE NEEDED MARRIAGE COUNSELING AND WE FOUND A GREAT DOCTOR. OUR SESSIONS ENDED UP BECOMING A PILOT FOR OUR OWN REALITY SHOW.
THE SHOW WASN'T PICKED UP, UNFORTUNATELY.

"OWEN AND ROBIN IRON IT OUT" PILOT 6/28/08

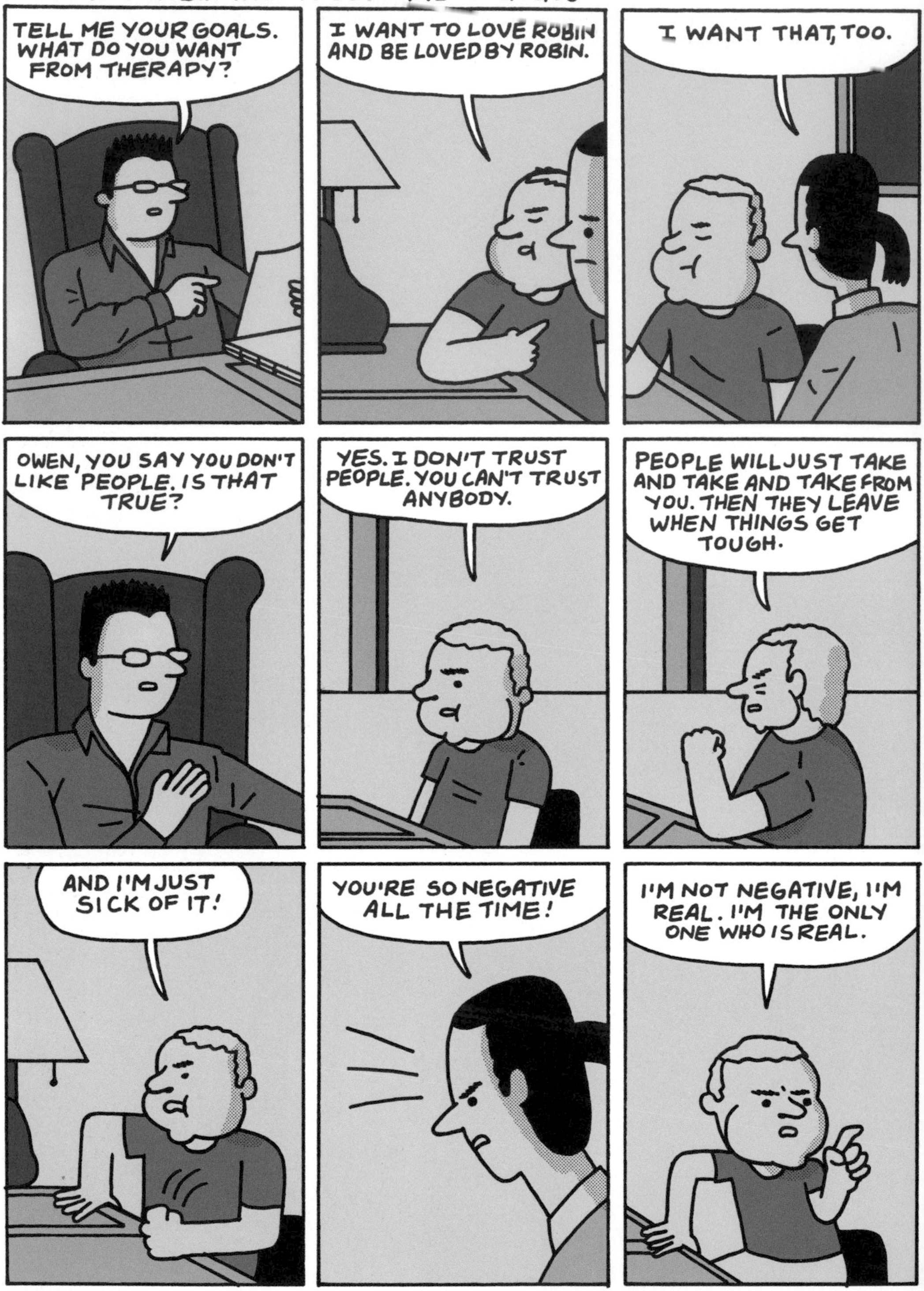
TELL ME YOUR GOALS. WHAT DO YOU WANT FROM THERAPY?
I WANT TO LOVE ROBIN AND BE LOVED BY ROBIN.
I WANT THAT, TOO.
OWEN, YOU SAY YOU DON'T LIKE PEOPLE. IS THAT TRUE?
YES. I DON'T TRUST PEOPLE. YOU CAN'T TRUST ANYBODY.
PEOPLE WILL JUST TAKE AND TAKE AND TAKE FROM YOU. THEN THEY LEAVE WHEN THINGS GET TOUGH.
AND I'M JUST SICK OF IT!
YOU'RE SO NEGATIVE ALL THE TIME!
I'M NOT NEGATIVE, I'M REAL. I'M THE ONLY ONE WHO IS REAL.

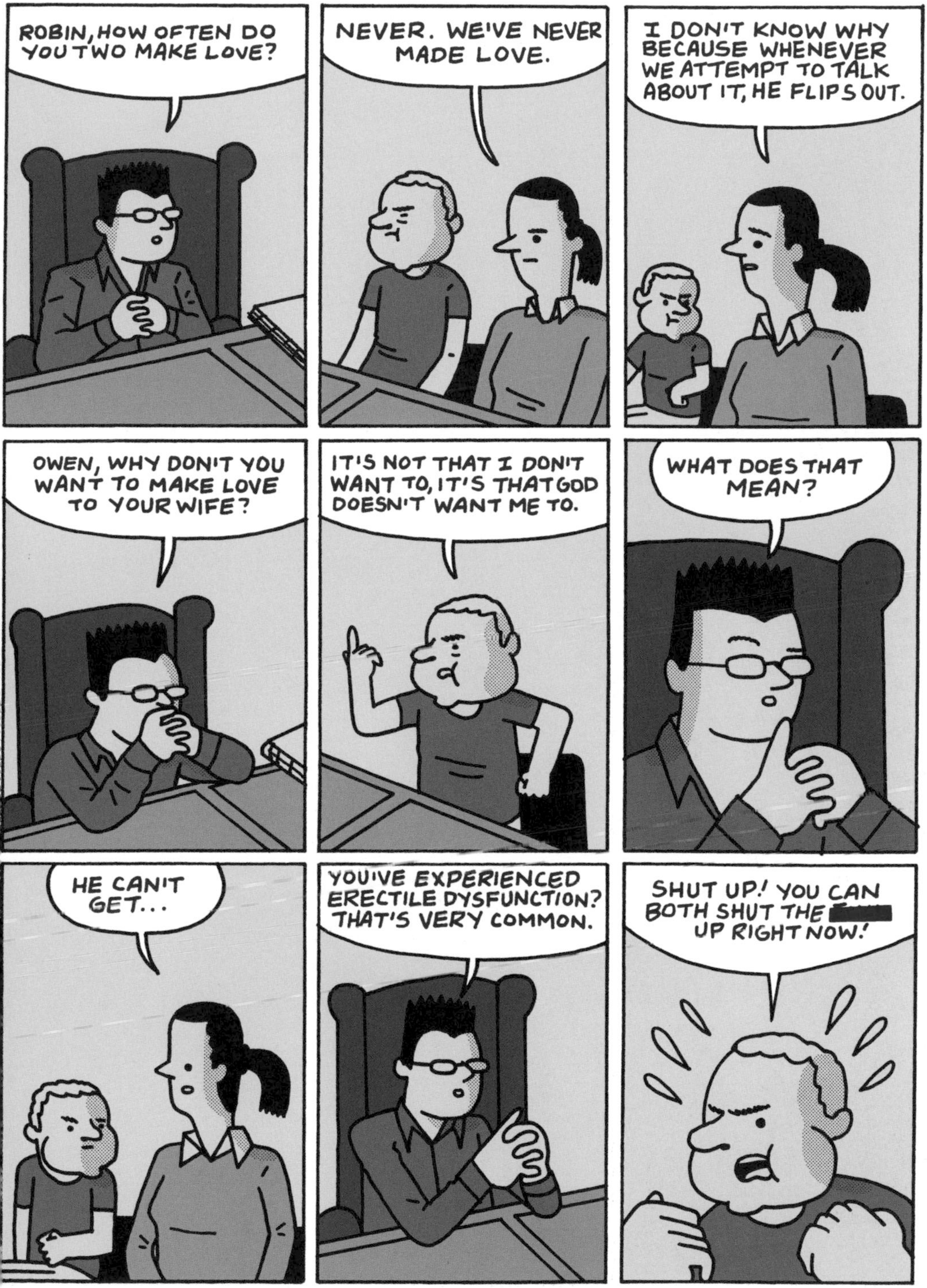
ROBIN, HOW OFTEN DO YOU TWO MAKE LOVE?
NEVER. WE'VE NEVER MADE LOVE.
I DON'T KNOW WHY BECAUSE WHENEVER WE ATTEMPT TO TALK ABOUT IT, HE FLIPS OUT.
OWEN, WHY DON'T YOU WANT TO MAKE LOVE TO YOUR WIFE?
IT'S NOT THAT I DON'T WANT TO, IT'S THAT GOD DOESN'T WANT ME TO.
WHAT DOES THAT MEAN?
HE CAN'T GET...
YOU'VE EXPERIENCED ERECTILE DYSFUNCTION? THAT'S VERY COMMON.
SHUT UP! YOU CAN BOTH SHUT THE [redacted] UP RIGHT NOW!

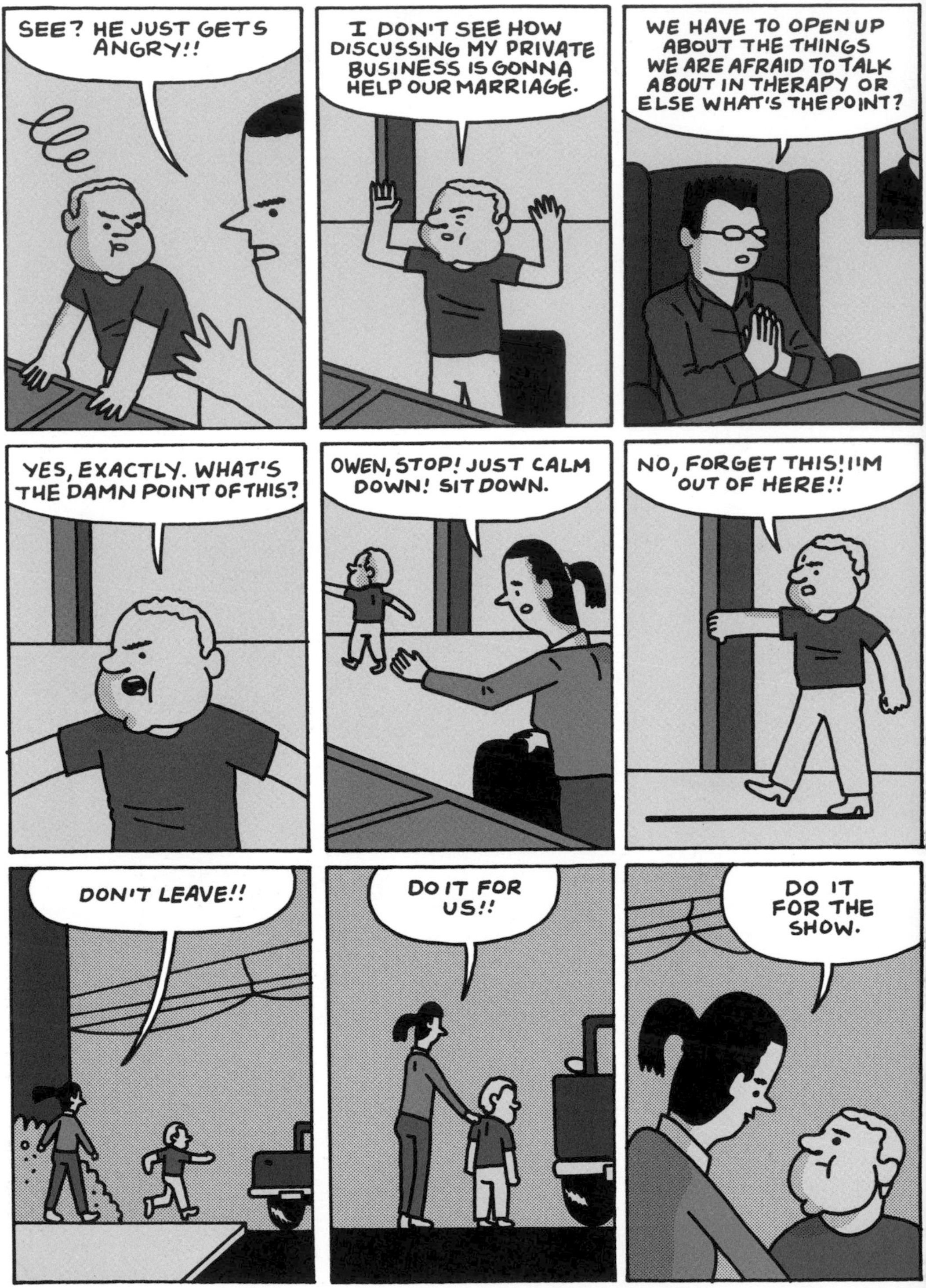
SEE? HE JUST GETS ANGRY!!
I DON'T SEE HOW DISCUSSING MY PRIVATE BUSINESS IS GONNA HELP OUR MARRIAGE.
WE HAVE TO OPEN UP ABOUT THE THINGS WE ARE AFRAID TO TALK ABOUT IN THERAPY OR ELSE WHAT'S THE POINT?
YES, EXACTLY. WHAT'S THE DAMN POINT OF THIS?
OWEN, STOP! JUST CALM DOWN! SIT DOWN.
NO, FORGET THIS! I'M OUT OF HERE!!
DON'T LEAVE!!
DO IT FOR US!!
DO IT FOR THE SHOW.

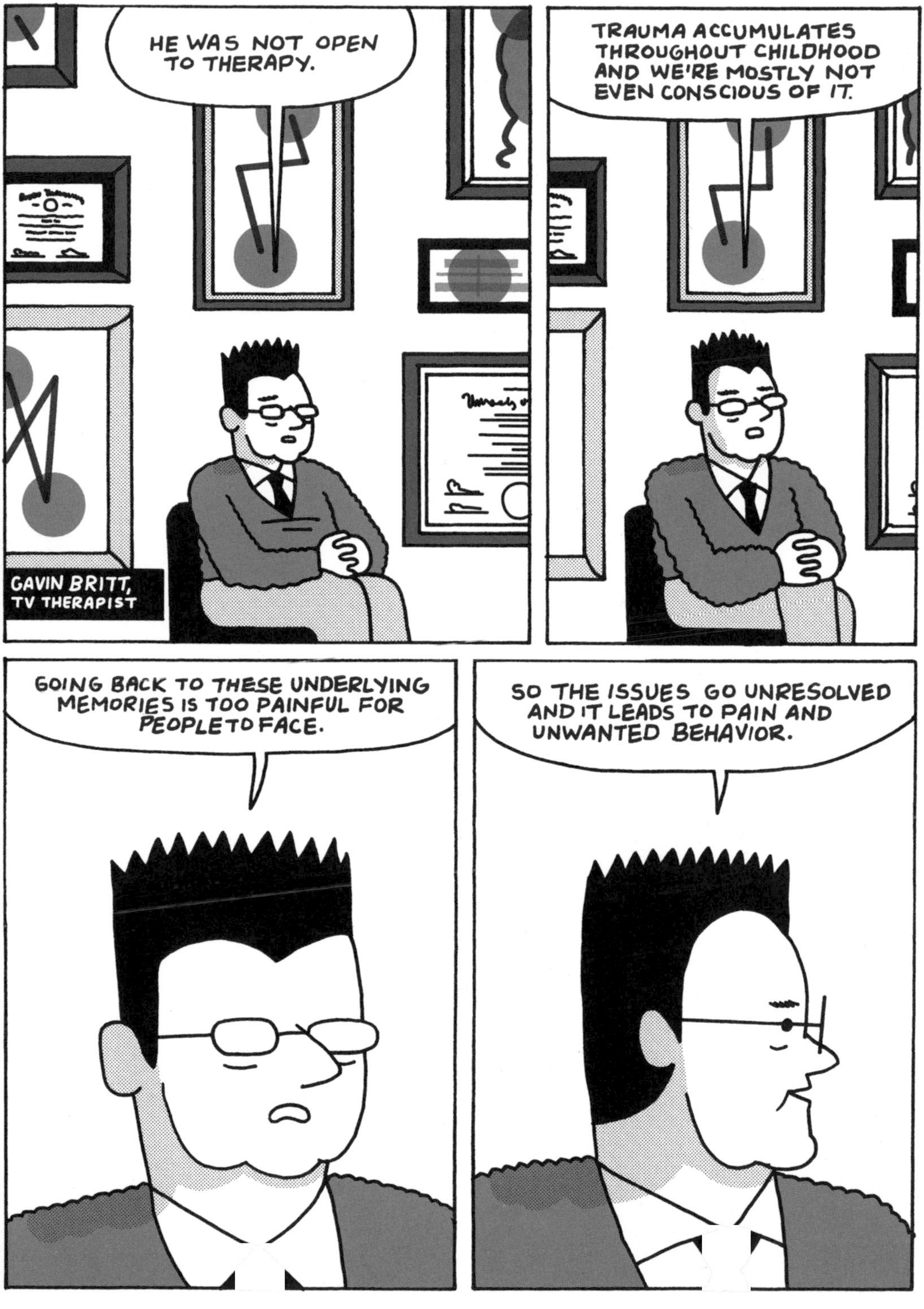
HE WAS NOT OPEN TO THERAPY.
GAVIN BRITT, TV THERAPIST
TRAUMA ACCUMULATES THROUGHOUT CHILDHOOD AND WE'RE MOSTLY NOT EVEN CONSCIOUS OF IT.
GOING BACK TO THESE UNDERLYING MEMORIES IS TOO PAINFUL FOR PEOPLE TO FACE.
SO THE ISSUES GO UNRESOLVED AND IT LEADS TO PAIN AND UNWANTED BEHAVIOR.

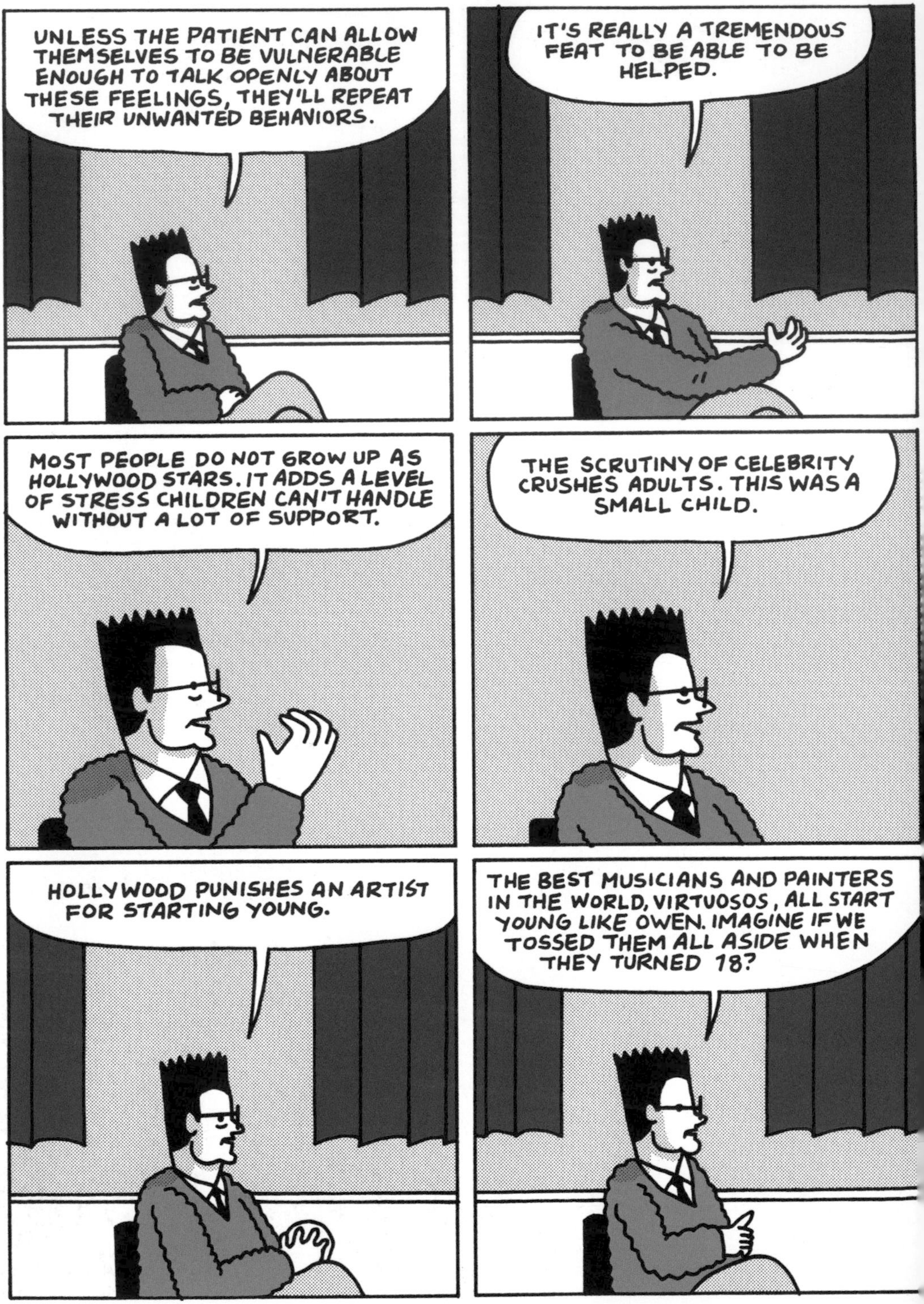
UNLESS THE PATIENT CAN ALLOW THEMSELVES TO BE VULNERABLE ENOUGH TO TALK OPENLY ABOUT THESE FEELINGS, THEY'LL REPEAT THEIR UNWANTED BEHAVIORS.
IT'S REALLY A TREMENDOUS FEAT TO BE ABLE TO BE HELPED.
MOST PEOPLE DO NOT GROW UP AS HOLLYWOOD STARS. IT ADDS A LEVEL OF STRESS CHILDREN CAN'T HANDLE WITHOUT A LOT OF SUPPORT.
THE SCRUTINY OF CELEBRITY CRUSHES ADULTS. THIS WAS A SMALL CHILD.
HOLLYWOOD PUNISHES AN ARTIST FOR STARTING YOUNG.
THE BEST MUSICIANS AND PAINTERS IN THE WORLD, VIRTUOSOS, ALL START YOUNG LIKE OWEN. IMAGINE IF WE TOSSED THEM ALL ASIDE WHEN THEY TURNED 18?

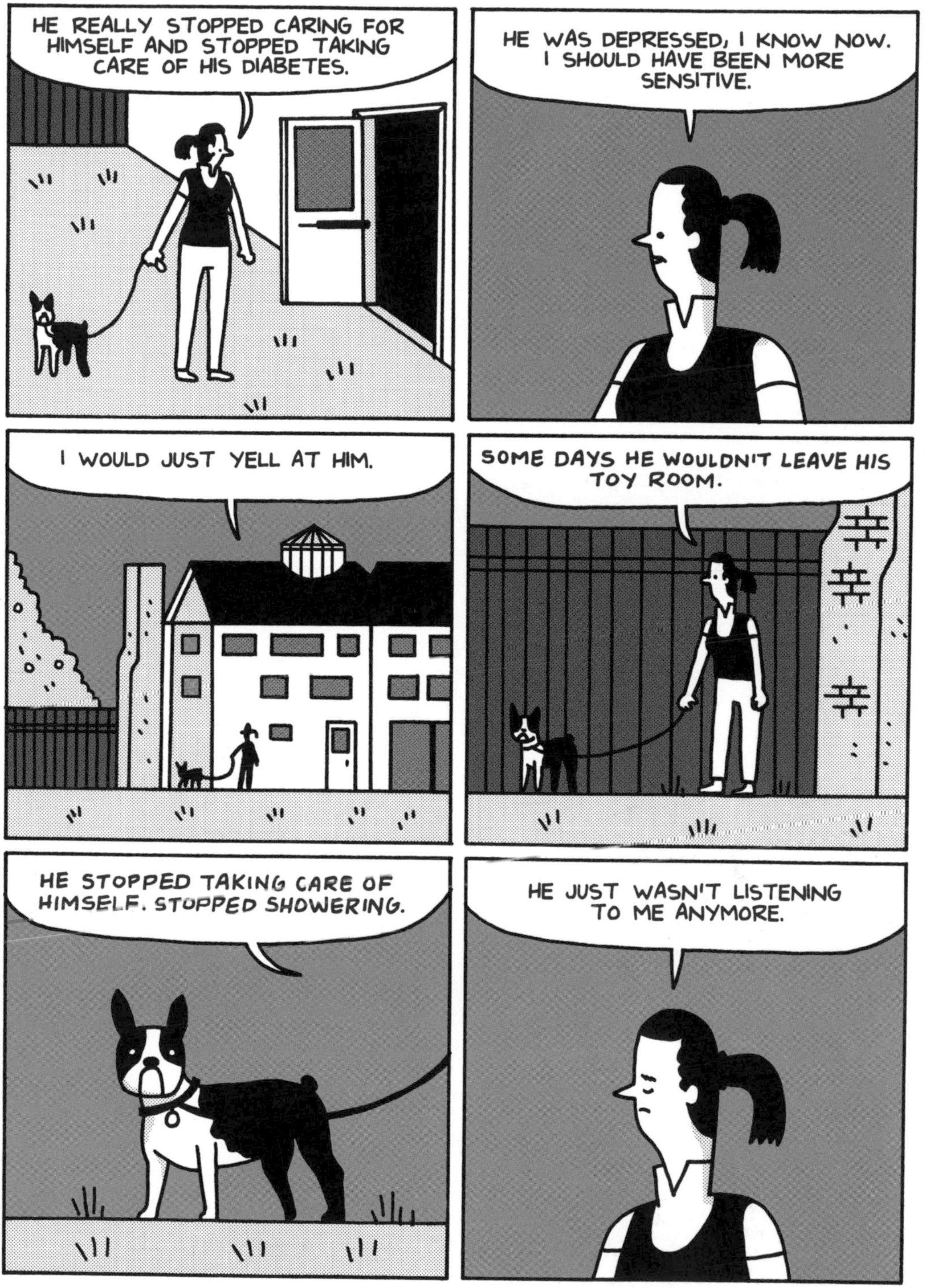
HE REALLY STOPPED CARING FOR HIMSELF AND STOPPED TAKING CARE OF HIS DIABETES.
HE WAS DEPRESSED, I KNOW NOW. I SHOULD HAVE BEEN MORE SENSITIVE.
I WOULD JUST YELL AT HIM.
SOME DAYS HE WOULDN'T LEAVE HIS TOY ROOM.
HE STOPPED TAKING CARE OF HIMSELF. STOPPED SHOWERING.
HE JUST WASN'T LISTENING TO ME ANYMORE.

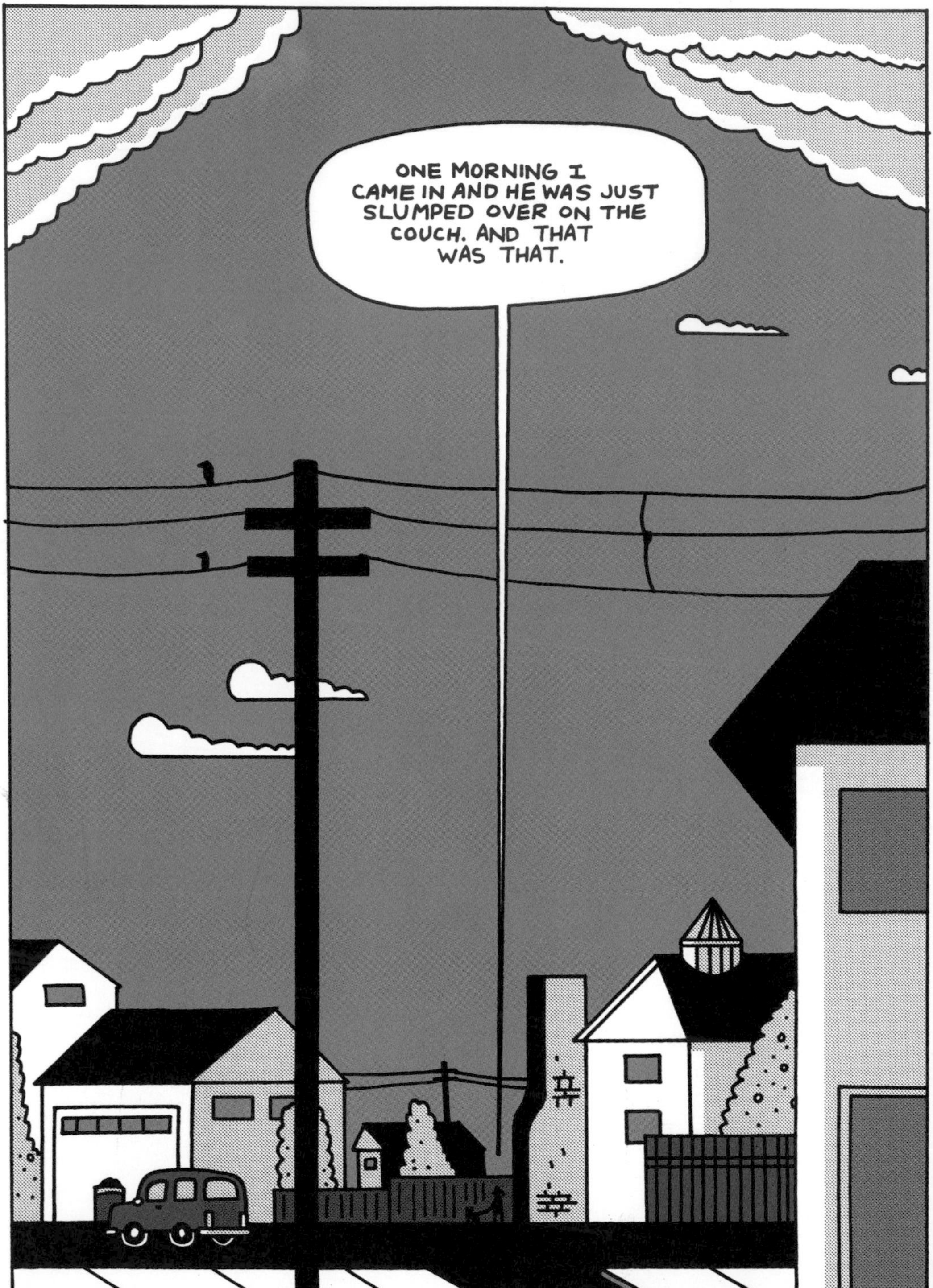
ONE MORNING I CAME IN AND HE WAS JUST SLUMPED OVER ON THE COUCH. AND THAT WAS THAT.

PART
THREE

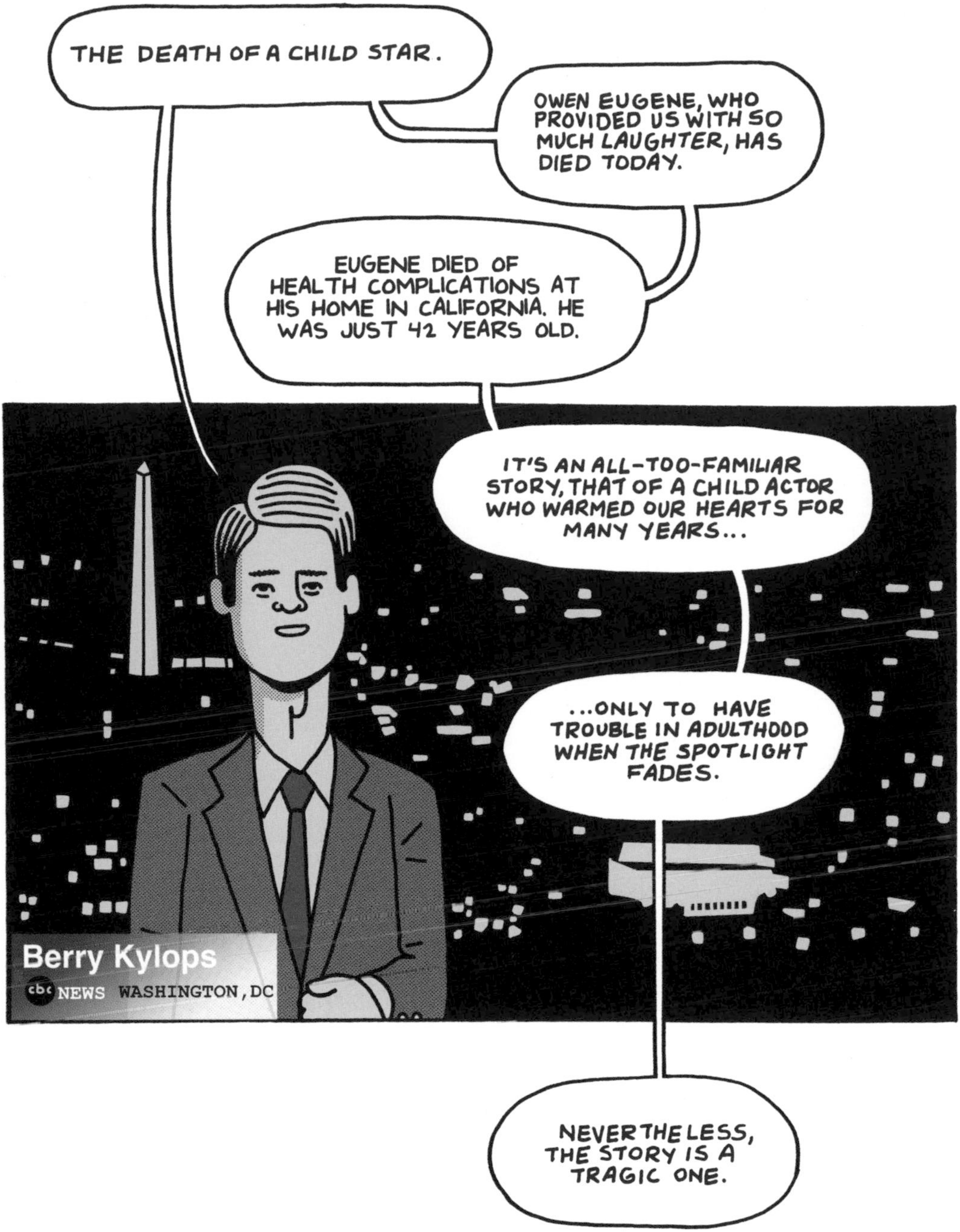
THE DEATH OF A CHILD STAR.
OWEN EUGENE, WHO PROVIDED US WITH SO MUCH LAUGHTER, HAS DIED TODAY.
EUGENE DIED OF HEALTH COMPLICATIONS AT HIS HOME IN CALIFORNIA. HE WAS JUST 42 YEARS OLD.
IT'S AN ALL-TOO-FAMILIAR STORY, THAT OF A CHILD ACTOR WHO WARMED OUR HEARTS FOR MANY YEARS...
...ONLY TO HAVE TROUBLE IN ADULTHOOD WHEN THE SPOTLIGHT FADES.
Berry Kylops
cbc NEWS WASHINGTON, DC
NEVERTHELESS, THE STORY IS A TRAGIC ONE.

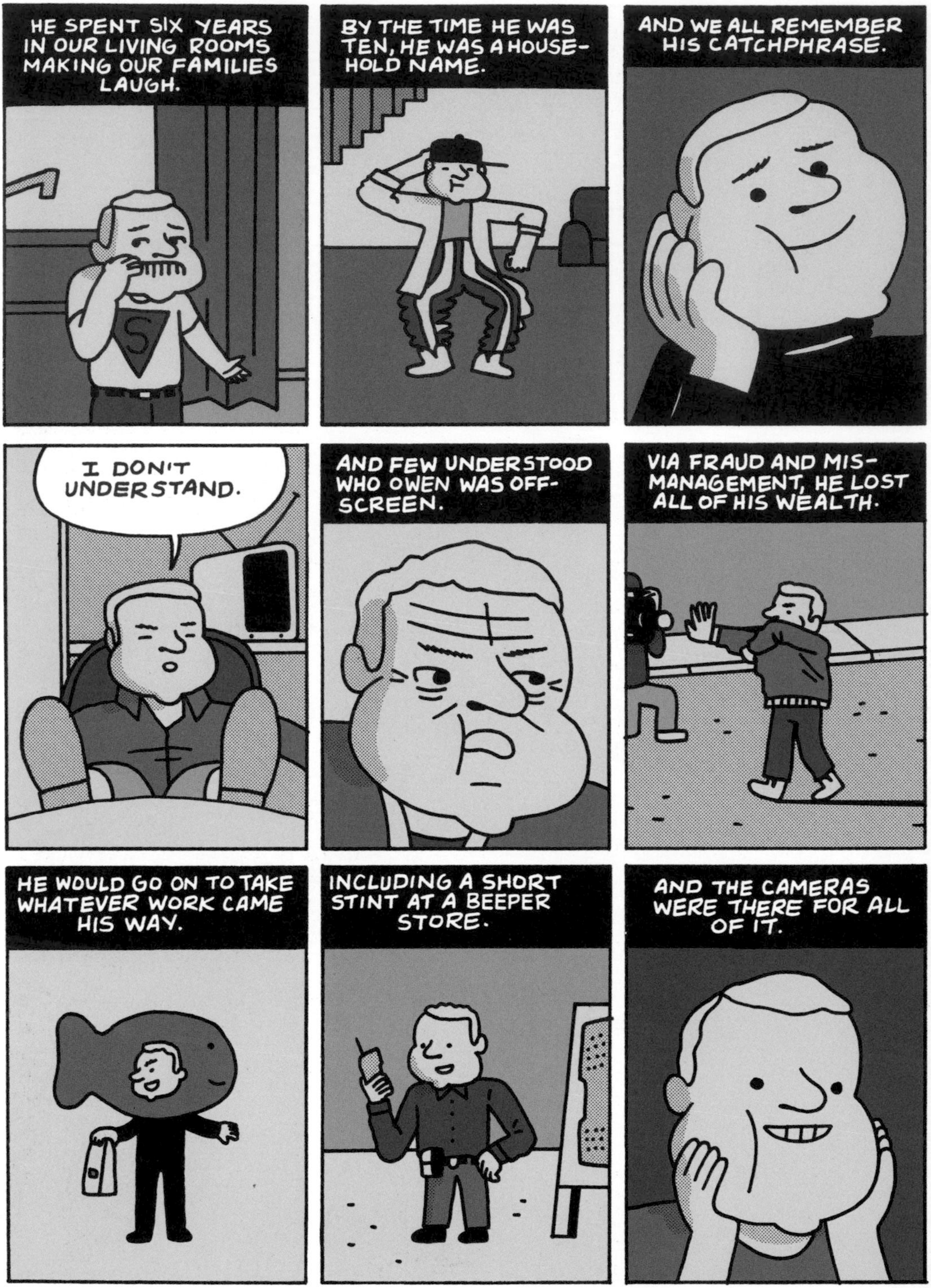
HE SPENT SIX YEARS IN OUR LIVING ROOMS MAKING OUR FAMILIES LAUGH.
BY THE TIME HE WAS TEN, HE WAS A HOUSE-HOLD NAME.
AND WE ALL REMEMBER HIS CATCHPHRASE.
I DON'T UNDERSTAND.
AND FEW UNDERSTOOD WHO OWEN WAS OFF-SCREEN.
VIA FRAUD AND MIS-MANAGEMENT, HE LOST ALL OF HIS WEALTH.
HE WOULD GO ON TO TAKE WHATEVER WORK CAME HIS WAY.
INCLUDING A SHORT STINT AT A BEEPER STORE.
AND THE CAMERAS WERE THERE FOR ALL OF IT.

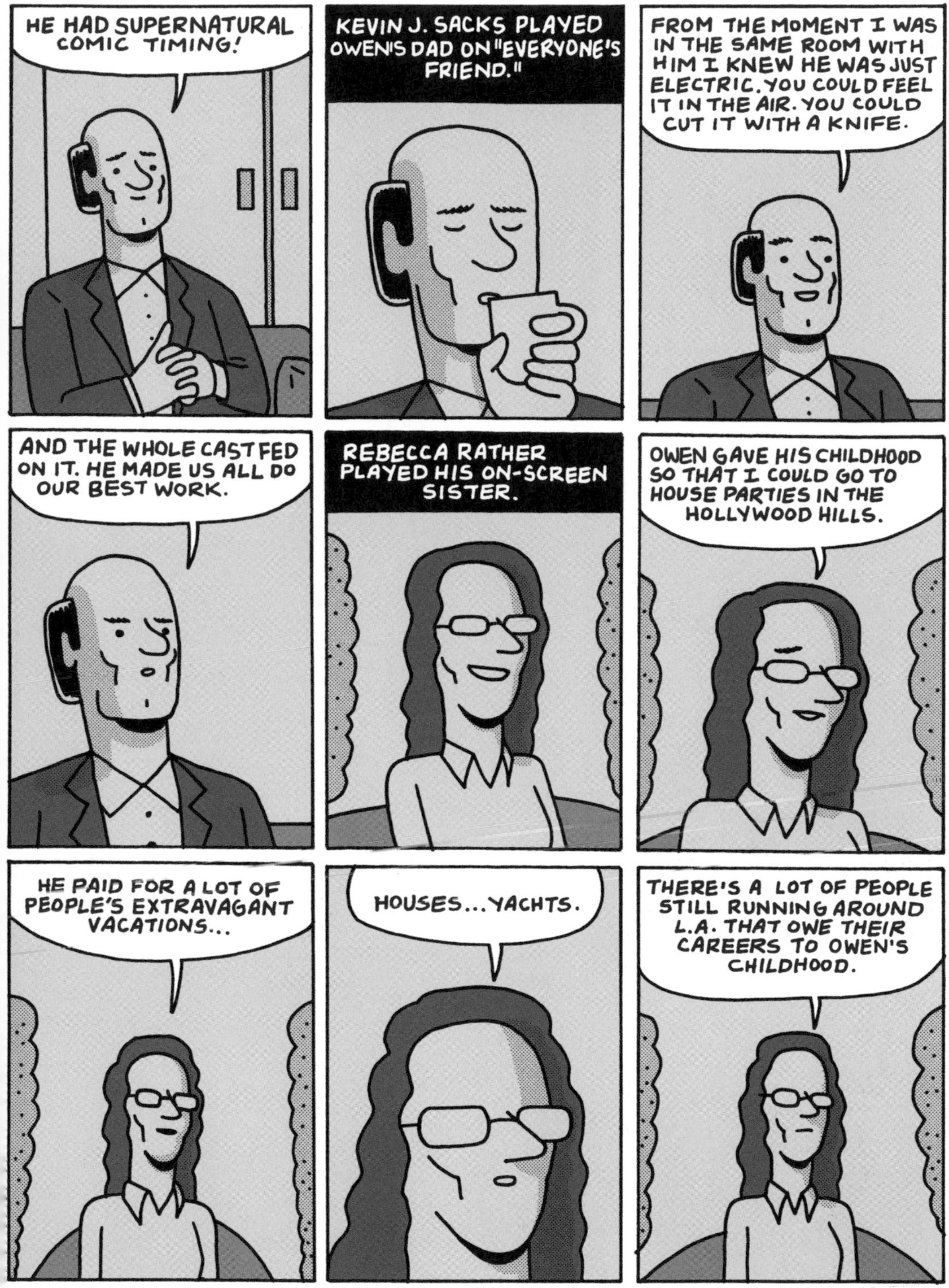
HE HAD SUPERNATURAL COMIC TIMING!
KEVIN J. SACKS PLAYED OWEN'S DAD ON "EVERYONE'S FRIEND."
FROM THE MOMENT I WAS IN THE SAME ROOM WITH HIM I KNEW HE WAS JUST ELECTRIC. YOU COULD FEEL IT IN THE AIR. YOU COULD CUT IT WITH A KNIFE.
AND THE WHOLE CAST FED ON IT. HE MADE US ALL DO OUR BEST WORK.
REBECCA RATHER PLAYED HIS ON-SCREEN SISTER.
OWEN GAVE HIS CHILDHOOD SO THAT I COULD GO TO HOUSE PARTIES IN THE HOLLYWOOD HILLS.
HE PAID FOR A LOT OF PEOPLE'S EXTRAVAGANT VACATIONS...
HOUSES... YACHTS.
THERE'S A LOT OF PEOPLE STILL RUNNING AROUND L.A. THAT OWE THEIR CAREERS TO OWEN'S CHILDHOOD.

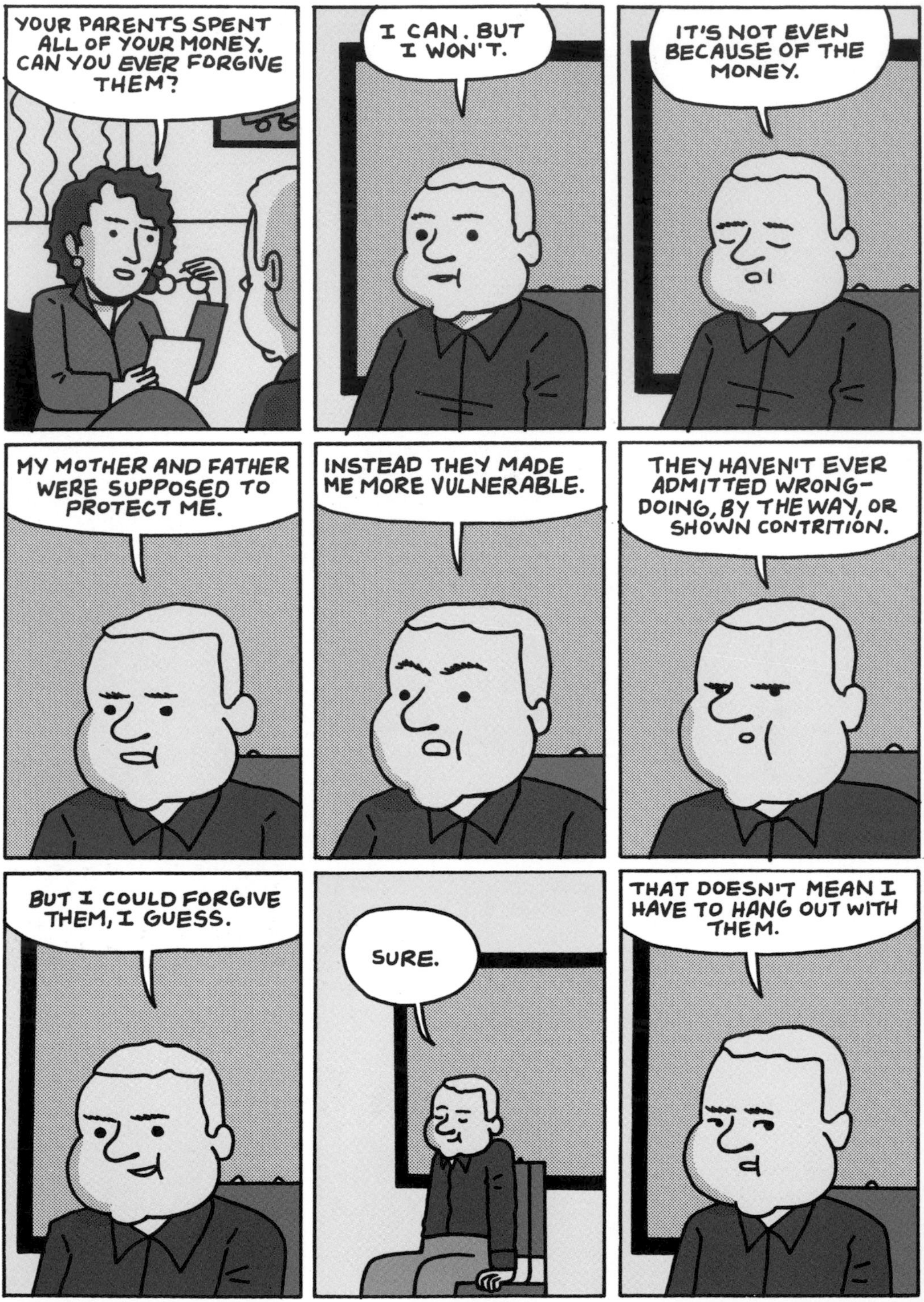
YOUR PARENTS SPENT ALL OF YOUR MONEY. CAN YOU *EVER* FORGIVE THEM?
I CAN. BUT I WON'T.
IT'S NOT EVEN BECAUSE OF THE MONEY.
MY MOTHER AND FATHER WERE SUPPOSED TO PROTECT ME.
INSTEAD THEY MADE ME MORE VULNERABLE.
THEY HAVEN'T EVER ADMITTED WRONG-DOING, BY THE WAY, OR SHOWN CONTRITION.
BUT I COULD FORGIVE THEM, I GUESS.
SURE.
THAT DOESN'T MEAN I HAVE TO HANG OUT WITH THEM.

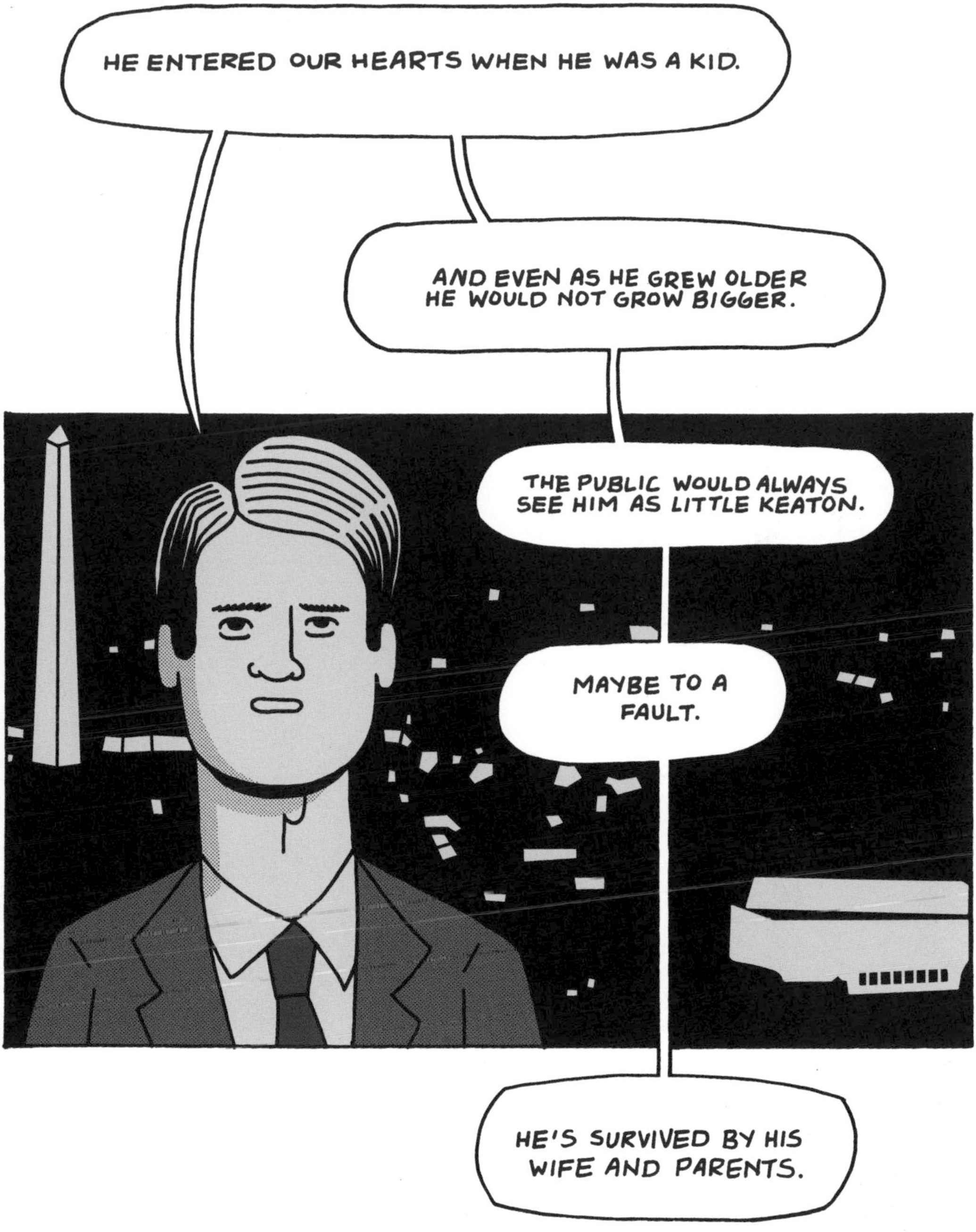
HE ENTERED OUR HEARTS WHEN HE WAS A KID.
AND EVEN AS HE GREW OLDER HE WOULD NOT GROW BIGGER.
THE PUBLIC WOULD ALWAYS SEE HIM AS LITTLE KEATON.
MAYBE TO A FAULT.
HE'S SURVIVED BY HIS WIFE AND PARENTS.

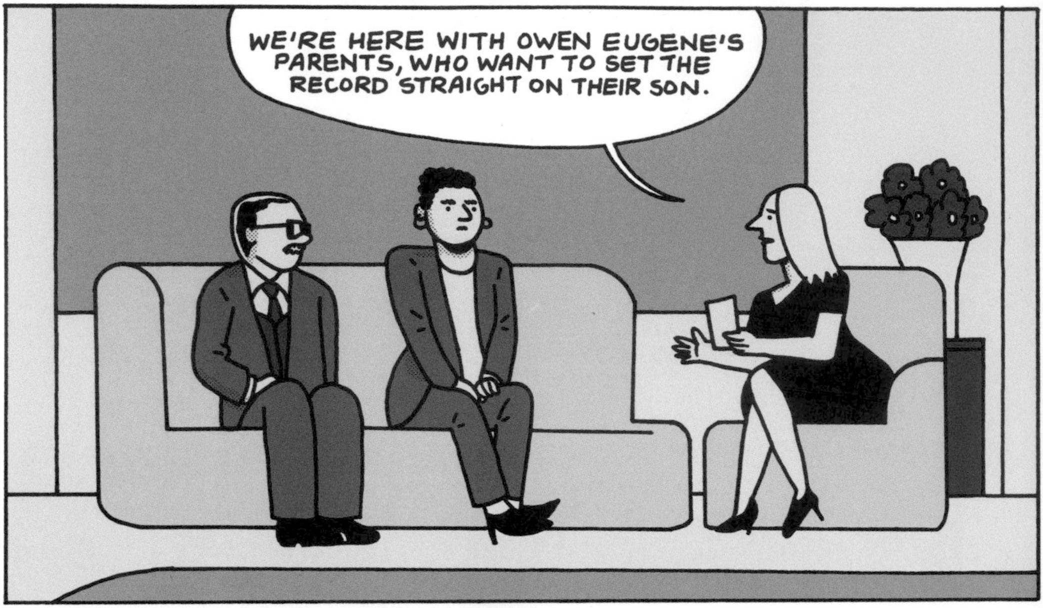
WE'RE HERE WITH OWEN EUGENE'S PARENTS, WHO WANT TO SET THE RECORD STRAIGHT ON THEIR SON.

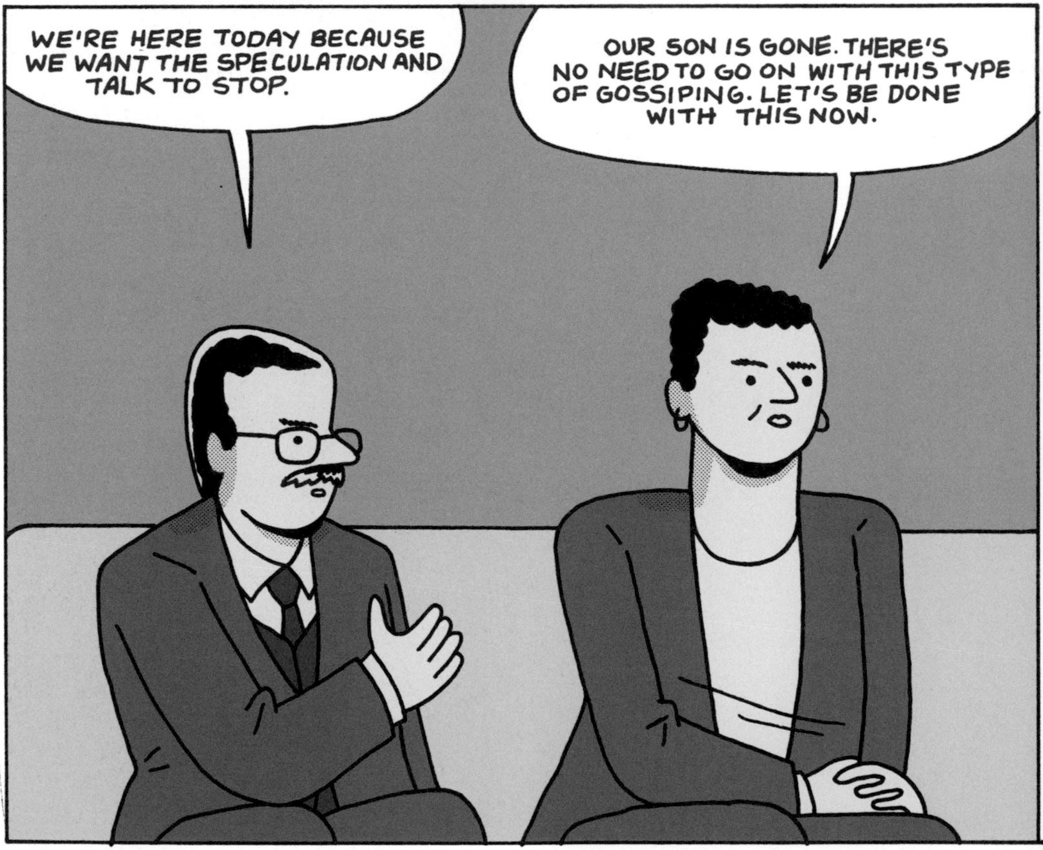
WE'RE HERE TODAY BECAUSE WE WANT THE SPECULATION AND TALK TO STOP.
OUR SON IS GONE. THERE'S NO NEED TO GO ON WITH THIS TYPE OF GOSSIPING. LET'S BE DONE WITH THIS NOW.

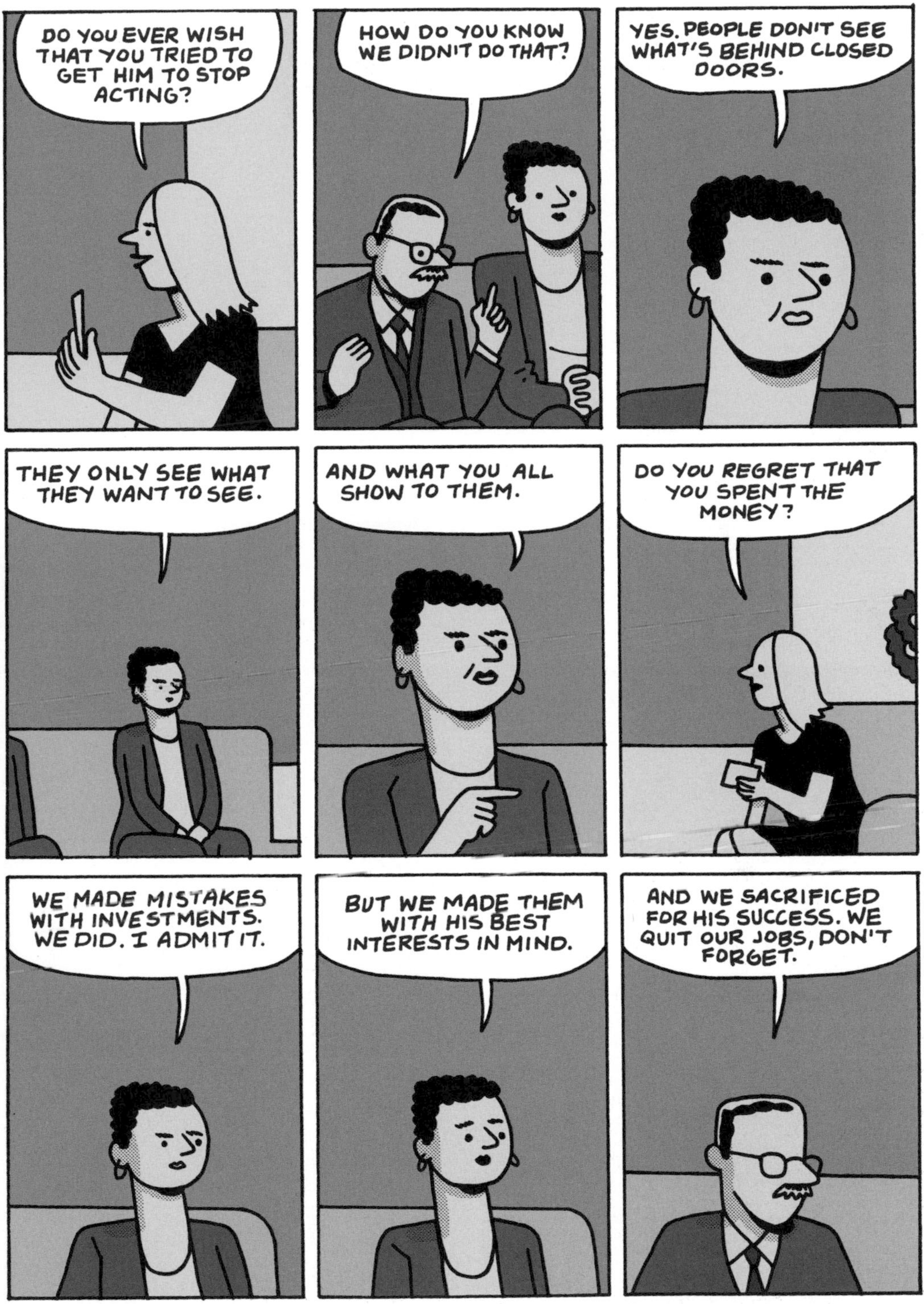
DO YOU EVER WISH THAT YOU TRIED TO GET HIM TO STOP ACTING?
HOW DO YOU KNOW WE DIDN'T DO THAT?
YES. PEOPLE DON'T SEE WHAT'S BEHIND CLOSED DOORS.
THEY ONLY SEE WHAT THEY WANT TO SEE.
AND WHAT YOU ALL SHOW TO THEM.
DO YOU REGRET THAT YOU SPENT THE MONEY?
WE MADE MISTAKES WITH INVESTMENTS. WE DID. I ADMIT IT.
BUT WE MADE THEM WITH HIS BEST INTERESTS IN MIND.
AND WE SACRIFICED FOR HIS SUCCESS. WE QUIT OUR JOBS, DON'T FORGET.

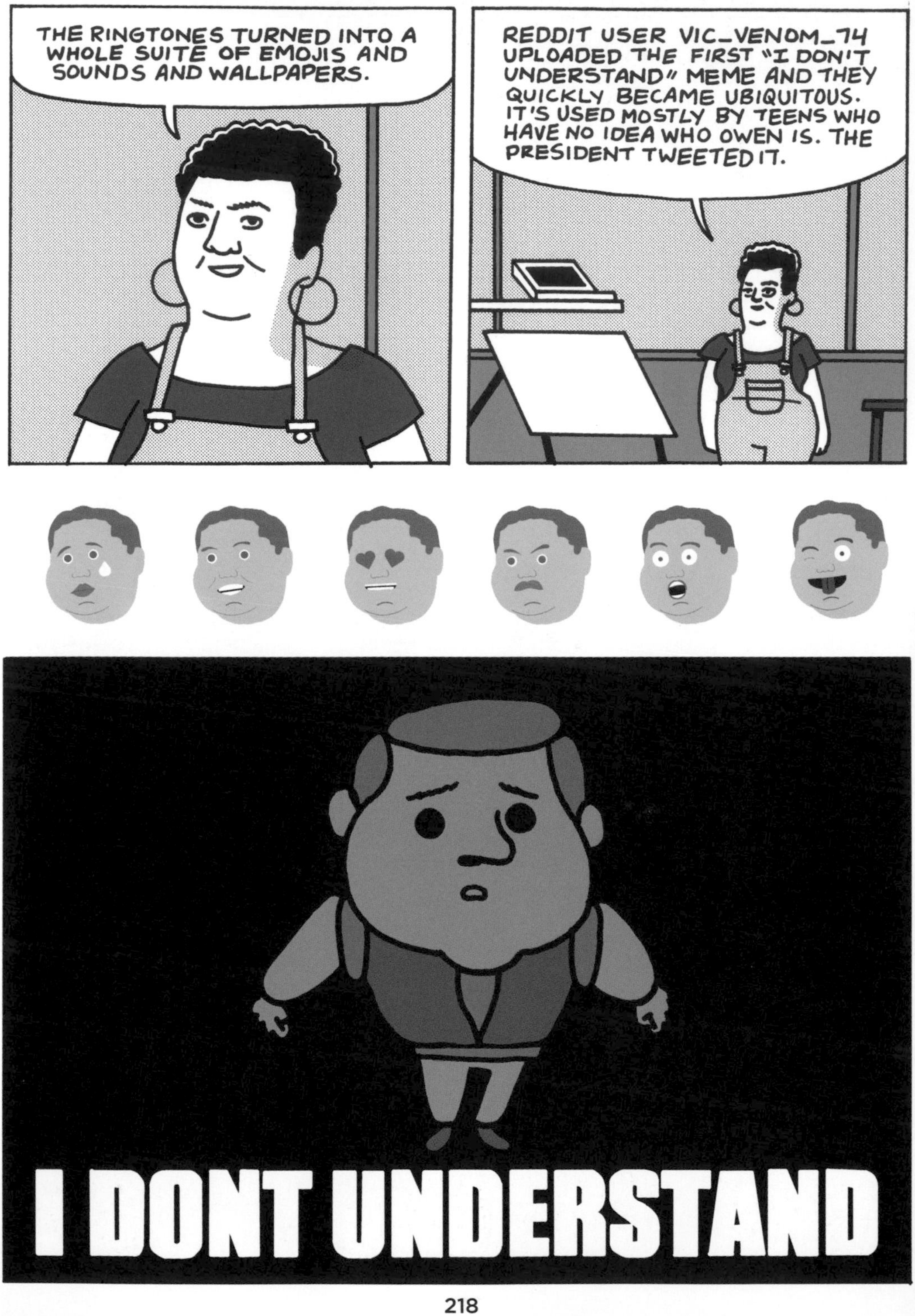
THE RINGTONES TURNED INTO A WHOLE SUITE OF EMOJIS AND SOUNDS AND WALLPAPERS.
REDDIT USER VIC_VENOM_74 UPLOADED THE FIRST "I DON'T UNDERSTAND" MEME AND THEY QUICKLY BECAME UBIQUITOUS. IT'S USED MOSTLY BY TEENS WHO HAVE NO IDEA WHO OWEN IS. THE PRESIDENT TWEETED IT.
I DONT UNDERSTAND

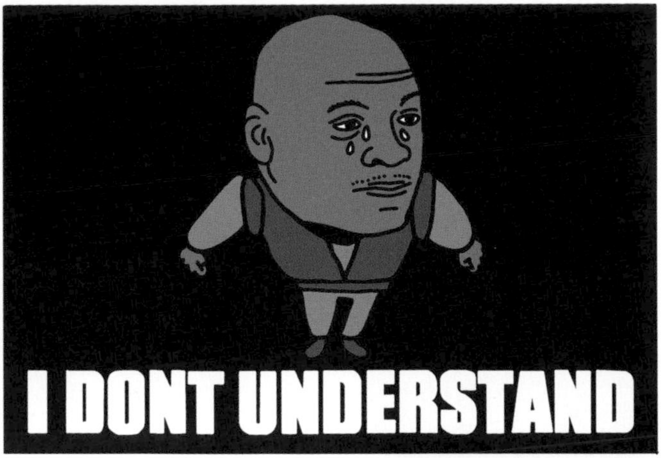
I DONT UNDERSTAND

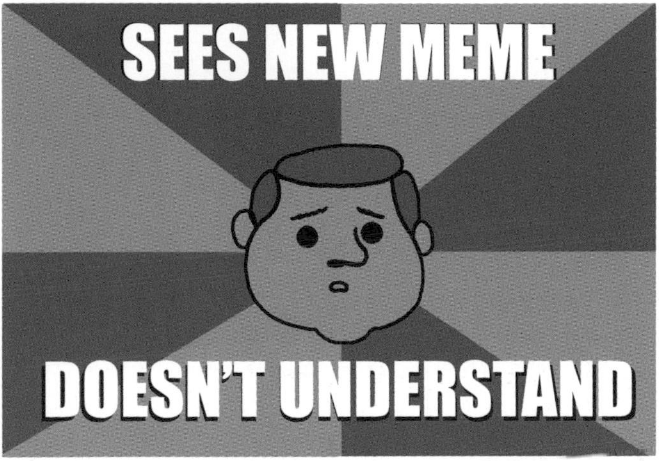
SEES NEW MEME
DOESN'T UNDERSTAND

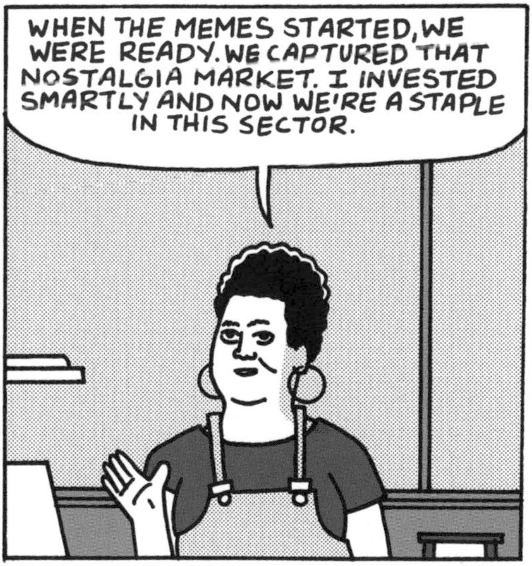
WHEN THE MEMES STARTED, WE WERE READY. WE CAPTURED THAT NOSTALGIA MARKET. I INVESTED SMARTLY AND NOW WE'RE A STAPLE IN THIS SECTOR.

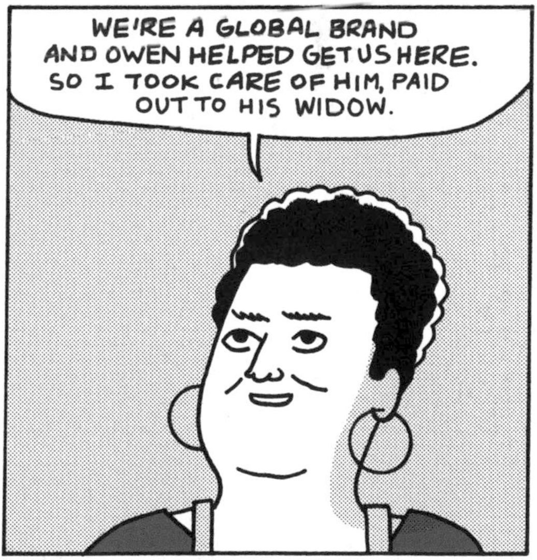
WE'RE A GLOBAL BRAND AND OWEN HELPED GET US HERE. SO I TOOK CARE OF HIM, PAID OUT TO HIS WIDOW.

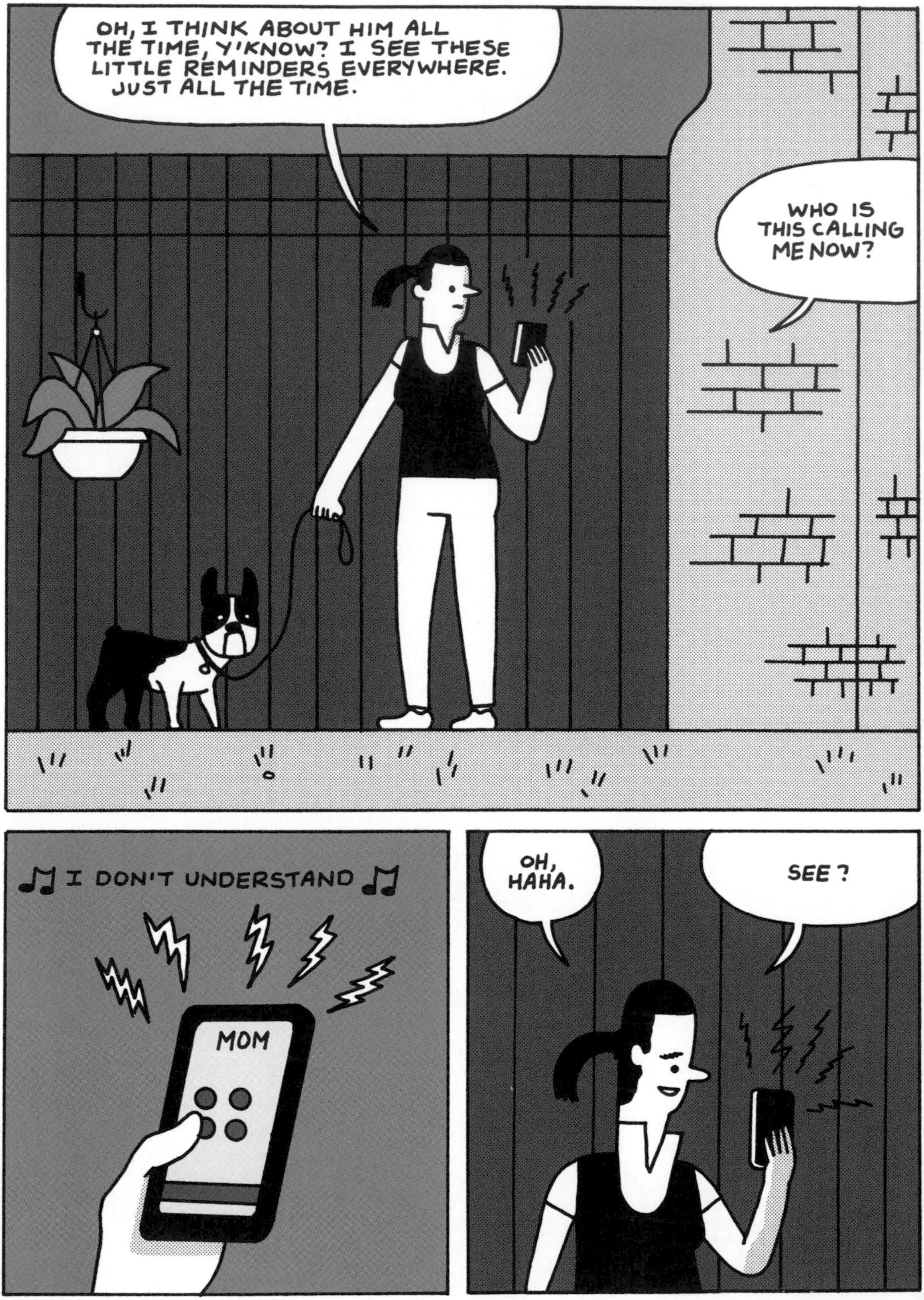
OH, I THINK ABOUT HIM ALL THE TIME, Y'KNOW? I SEE THESE LITTLE REMINDERS EVERYWHERE. JUST ALL THE TIME.
WHO IS THIS CALLING ME NOW?
I DON'T UNDERSTAND
MOM
OH, HAHA.
SEE?

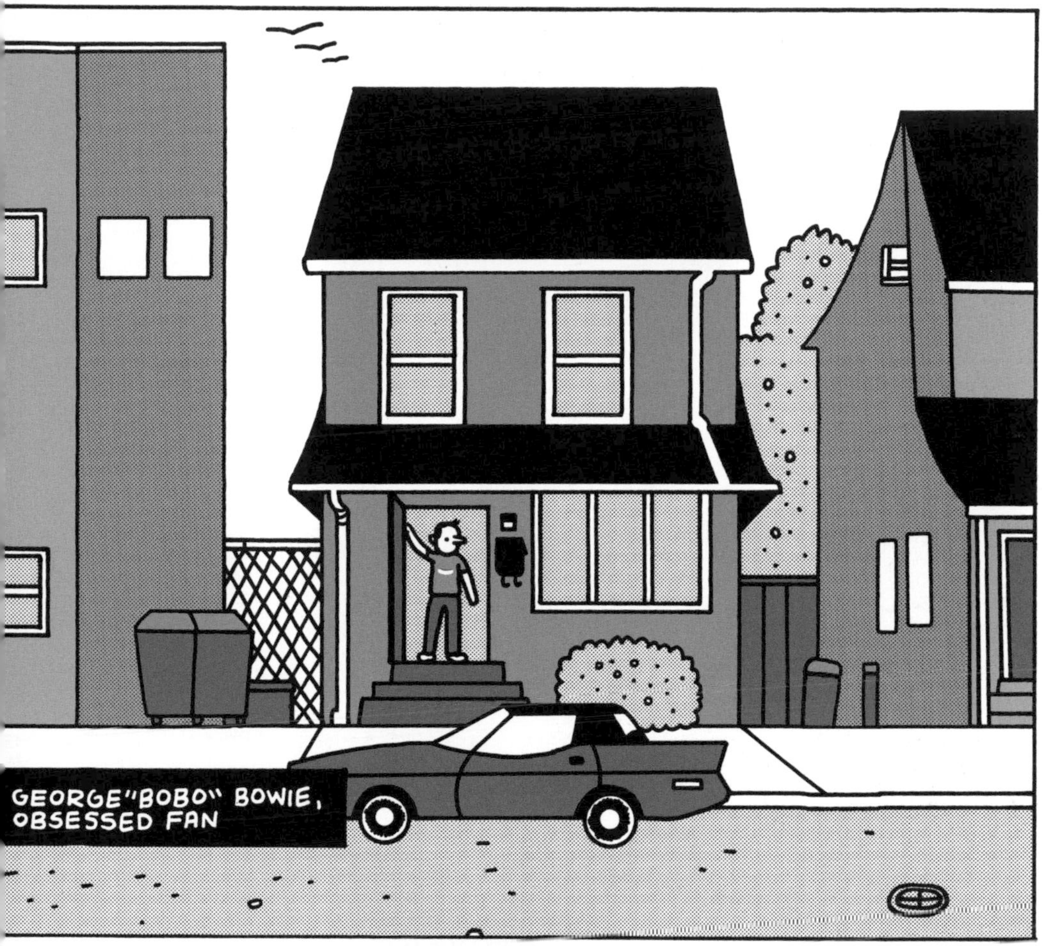
GEORGE "BOBO" BOWIE,
OBSESSED FAN

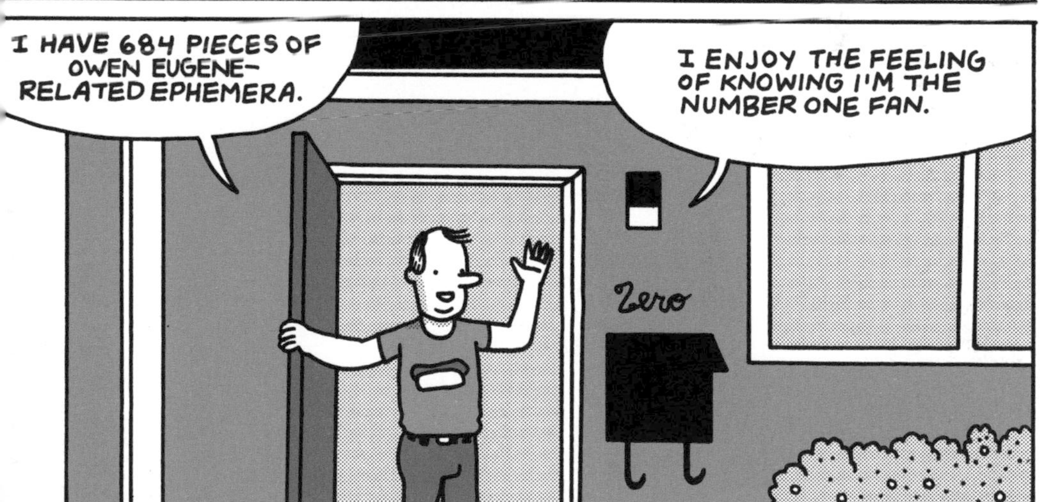
I HAVE 684 PIECES OF OWEN EUGENE-RELATED EPHEMERA.
I ENJOY THE FEELING OF KNOWING I'M THE NUMBER ONE FAN.
Zero

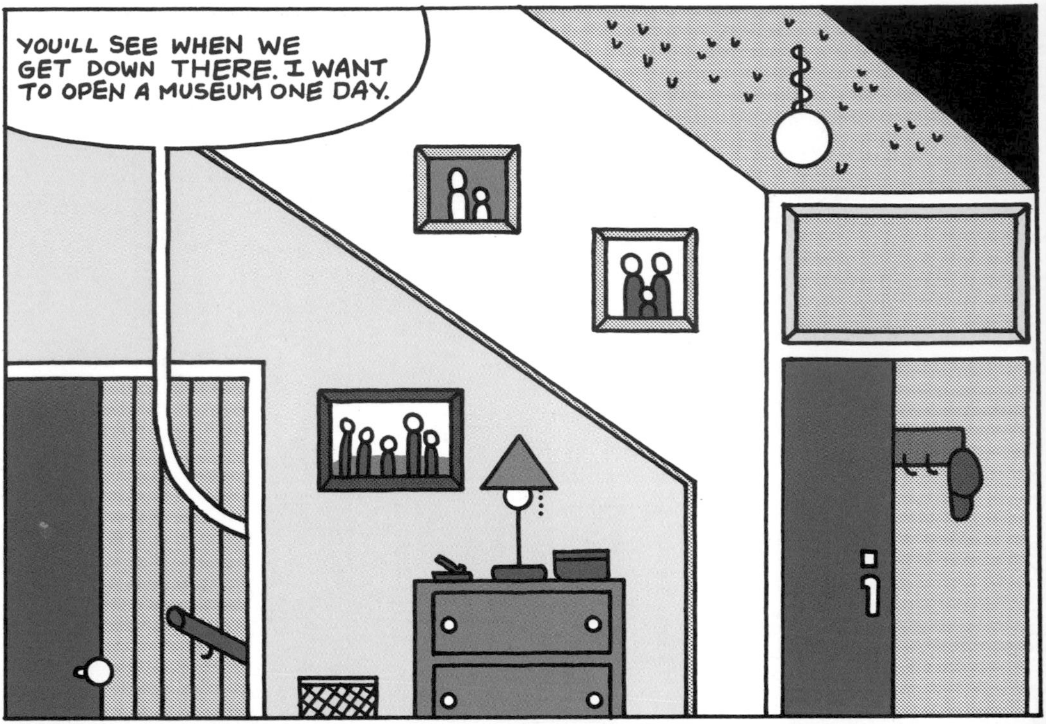
YOU'LL SEE WHEN WE GET DOWN THERE. I WANT TO OPEN A MUSEUM ONE DAY.

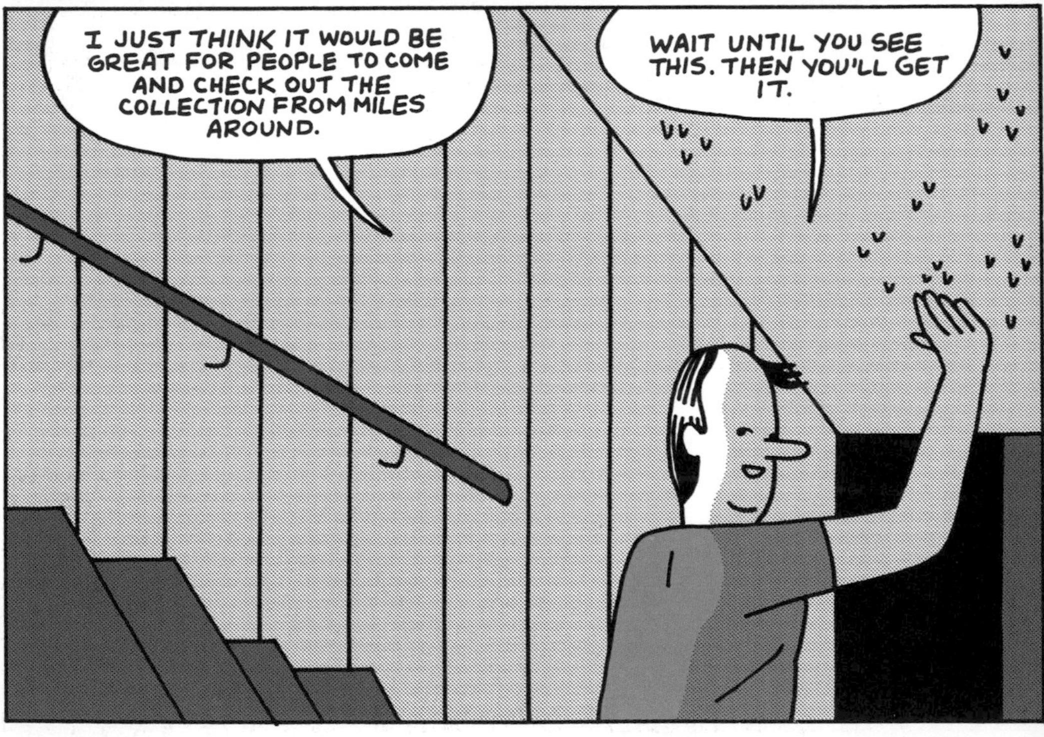
I JUST THINK IT WOULD BE GREAT FOR PEOPLE TO COME AND CHECK OUT THE COLLECTION FROM MILES AROUND.
WAIT UNTIL YOU SEE THIS. THEN YOU'LL GET IT.

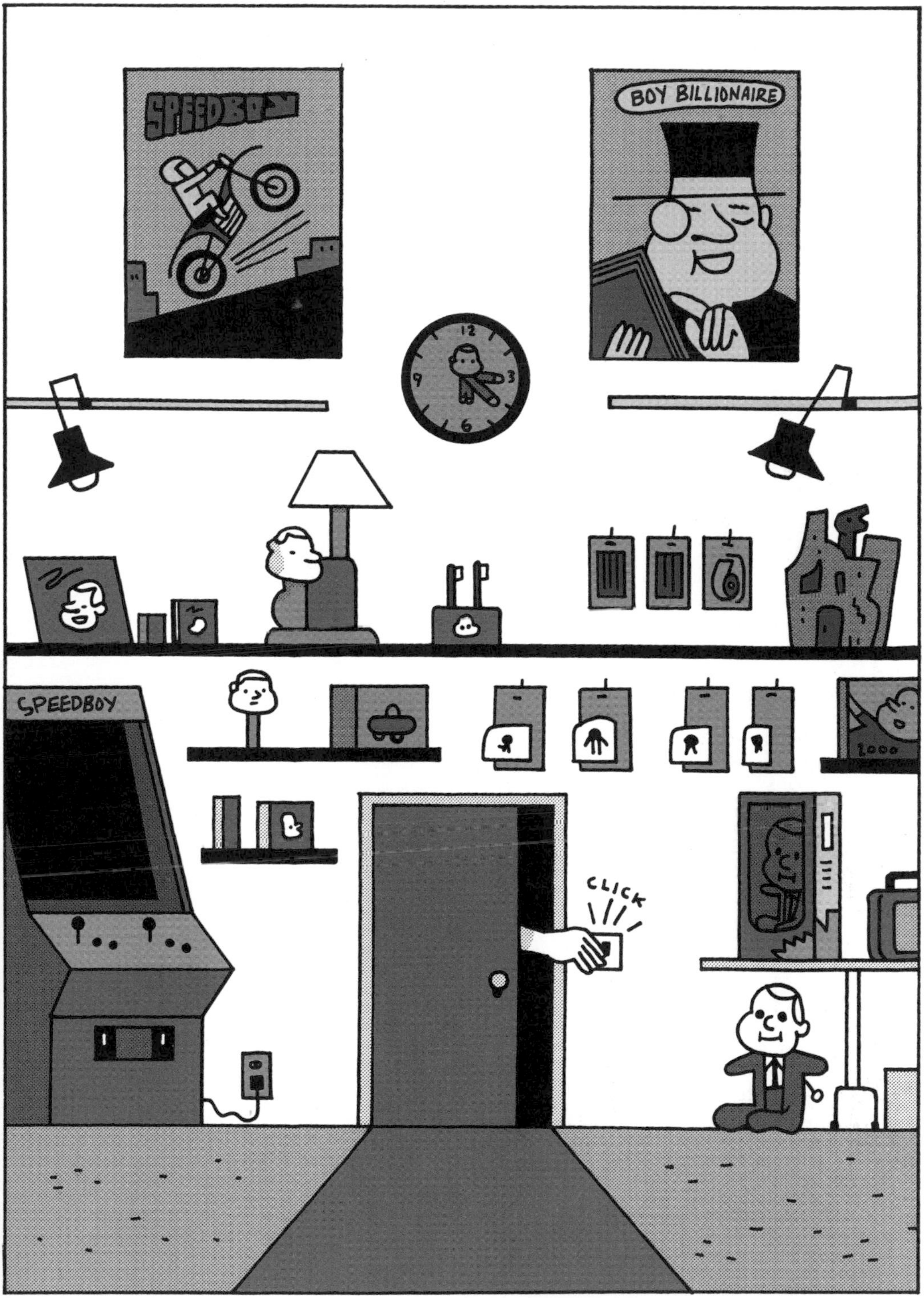
SPEEDBOY
BOY BILLIONAIRE
SPEEDBOY
2000
CLICK

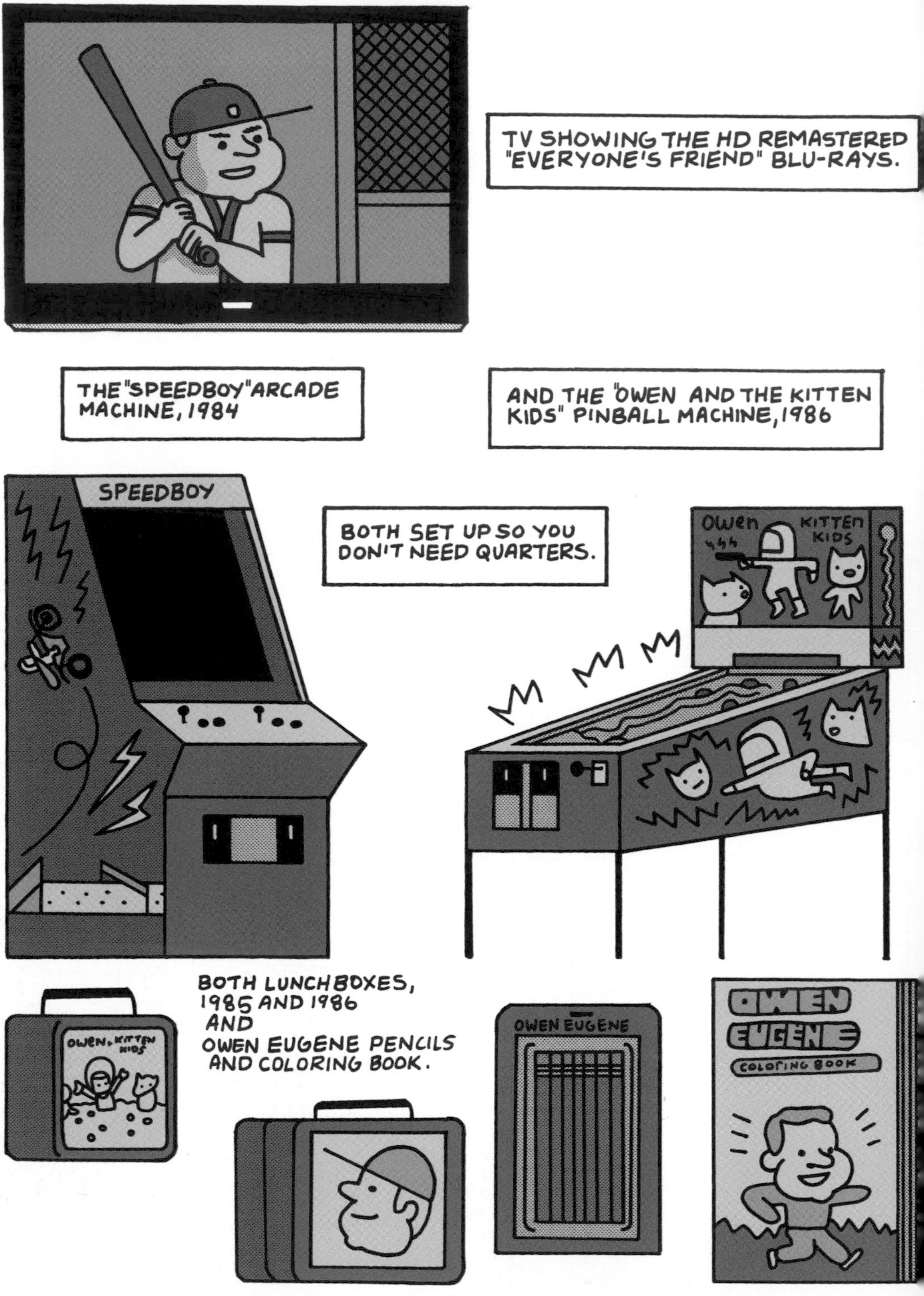
TV SHOWING THE HD REMASTERED "EVERYONE'S FRIEND" BLU-RAYS.
THE "SPEEDBOY" ARCADE MACHINE, 1984
AND THE "OWEN AND THE KITTEN KIDS" PINBALL MACHINE, 1986
SPEEDBOY
BOTH SET UP SO YOU DON'T NEED QUARTERS.
OWEN
KITTEN KIDS
BOTH LUNCHBOXES, 1985 AND 1986 AND OWEN EUGENE PENCILS AND COLORING BOOK.
OWEN, KITTEN KIDS
OWEN EUGENE
OWEN EUGENE
COLORING BOOK

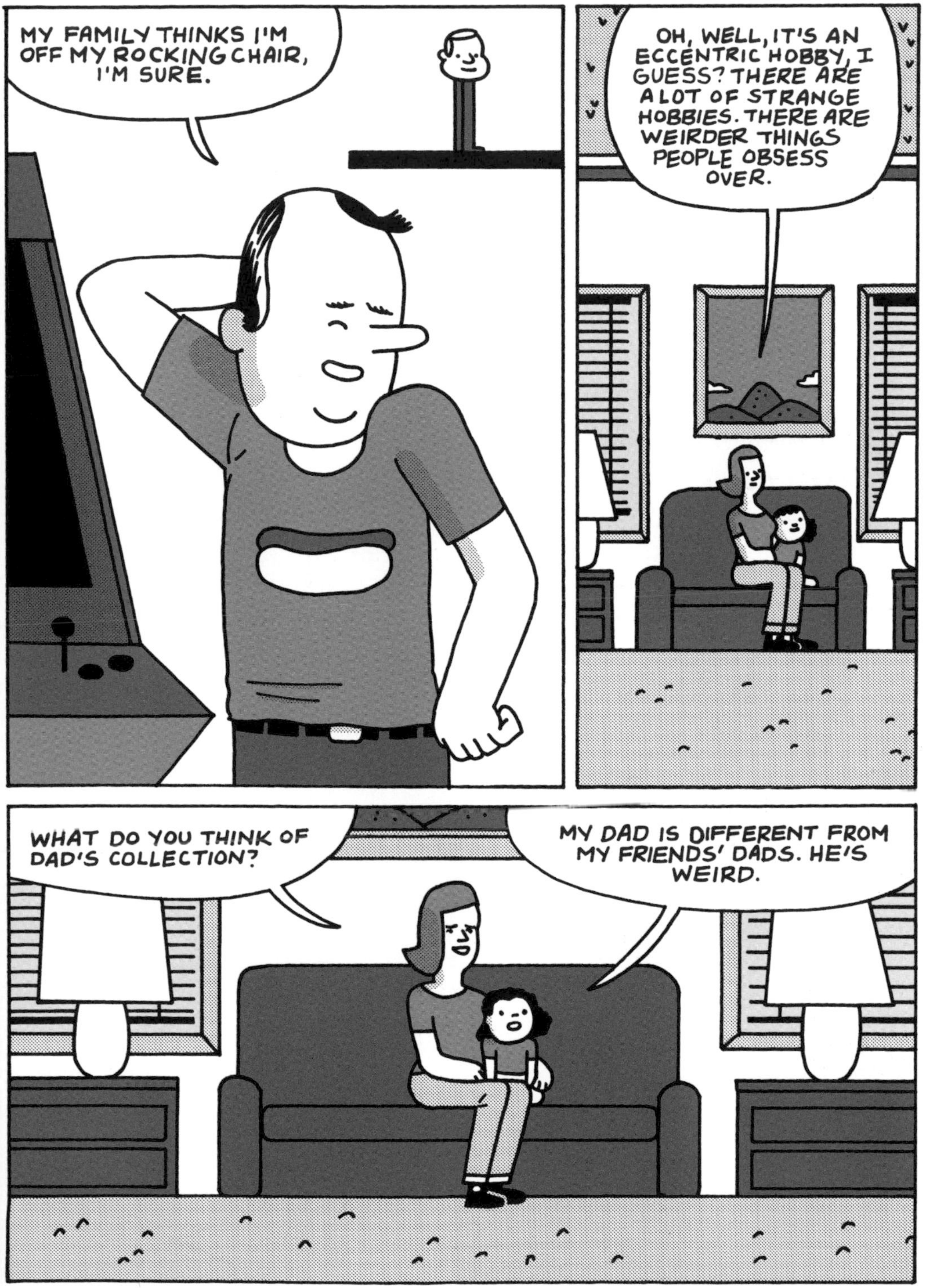
MY FAMILY THINKS I'M OFF MY ROCKING CHAIR, I'M SURE.
OH, WELL, IT'S AN ECCENTRIC HOBBY, I GUESS? THERE ARE A LOT OF STRANGE HOBBIES. THERE ARE WEIRDER THINGS PEOPLE OBSESS OVER.
WHAT DO YOU THINK OF DAD'S COLLECTION?
MY DAD IS DIFFERENT FROM MY FRIENDS' DADS. HE'S WEIRD.

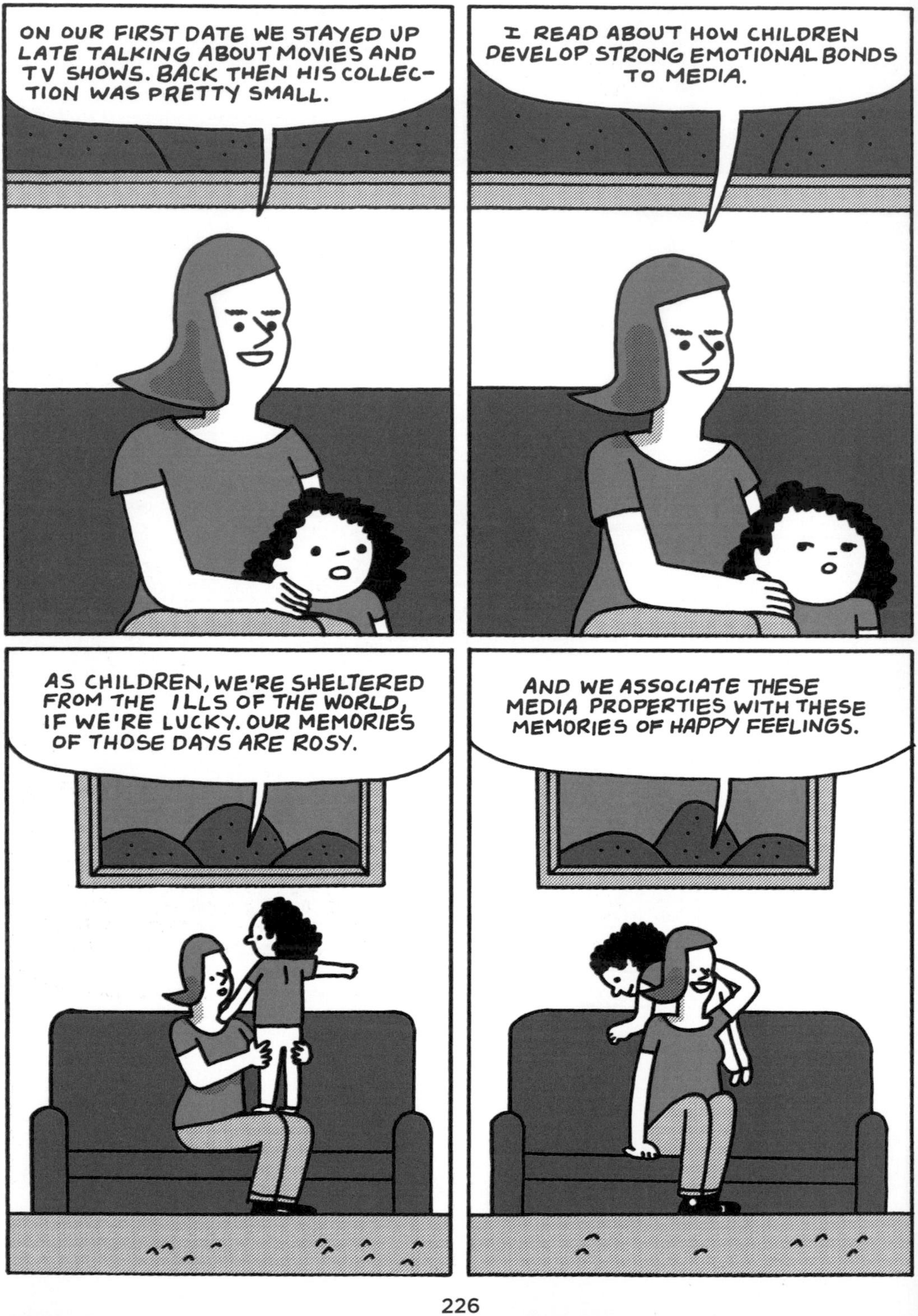
ON OUR FIRST DATE WE STAYED UP LATE TALKING ABOUT MOVIES AND TV SHOWS. BACK THEN HIS COLLECTION WAS PRETTY SMALL.
I READ ABOUT HOW CHILDREN DEVELOP STRONG EMOTIONAL BONDS TO MEDIA.
AS CHILDREN, WE'RE SHELTERED FROM THE ILLS OF THE WORLD, IF WE'RE LUCKY. OUR MEMORIES OF THOSE DAYS ARE ROSY.
AND WE ASSOCIATE THESE MEDIA PROPERTIES WITH THESE MEMORIES OF HAPPY FEELINGS.

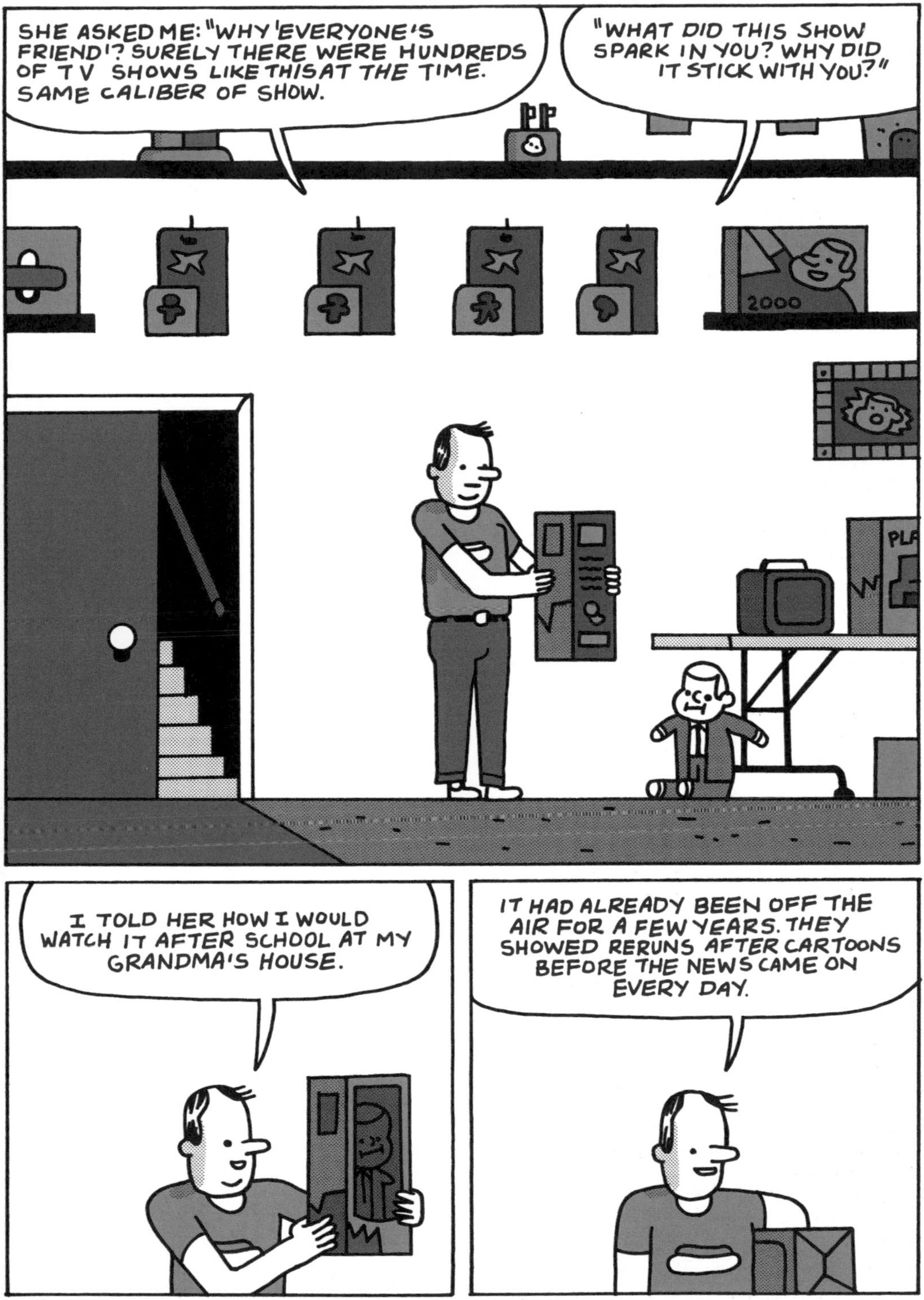
SHE ASKED ME: "WHY 'EVERYONE'S FRIEND'? SURELY THERE WERE HUNDREDS OF TV SHOWS LIKE THIS AT THE TIME. SAME CALIBER OF SHOW.
"WHAT DID THIS SHOW SPARK IN YOU? WHY DID IT STICK WITH YOU?"
2000
I TOLD HER HOW I WOULD WATCH IT AFTER SCHOOL AT MY GRANDMA'S HOUSE.
IT HAD ALREADY BEEN OFF THE AIR FOR A FEW YEARS. THEY SHOWED RERUNS AFTER CARTOONS BEFORE THE NEWS CAME ON EVERY DAY.

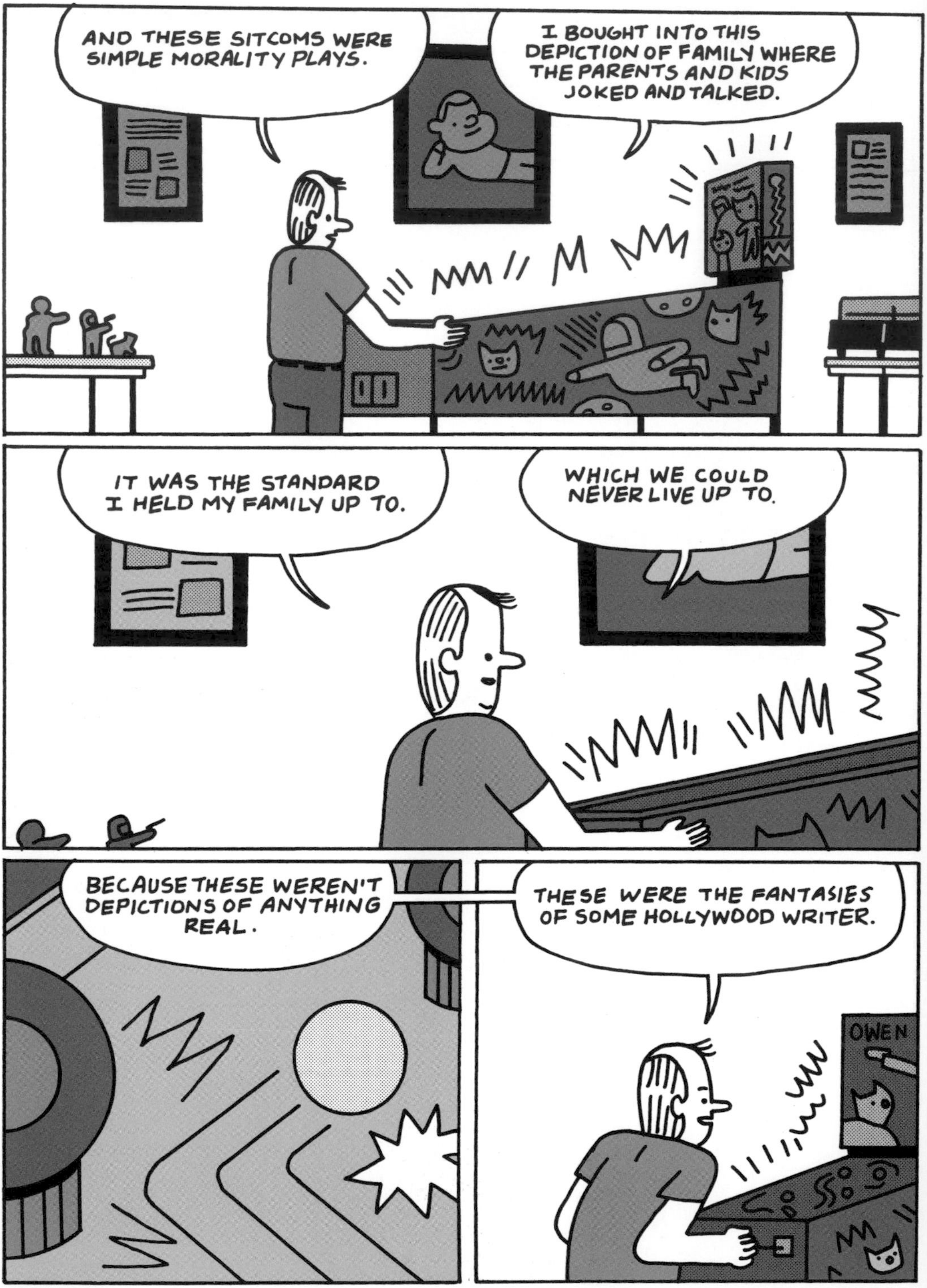
AND THESE SITCOMS WERE SIMPLE MORALITY PLAYS.
I BOUGHT INTO THIS DEPICTION OF FAMILY WHERE THE PARENTS AND KIDS JOKED AND TALKED.
IT WAS THE STANDARD I HELD MY FAMILY UP TO.
WHICH WE COULD NEVER LIVE UP TO.
BECAUSE THESE WEREN'T DEPICTIONS OF ANYTHING REAL.
THESE WERE THE FANTASIES OF SOME HOLLYWOOD WRITER.
OWEN

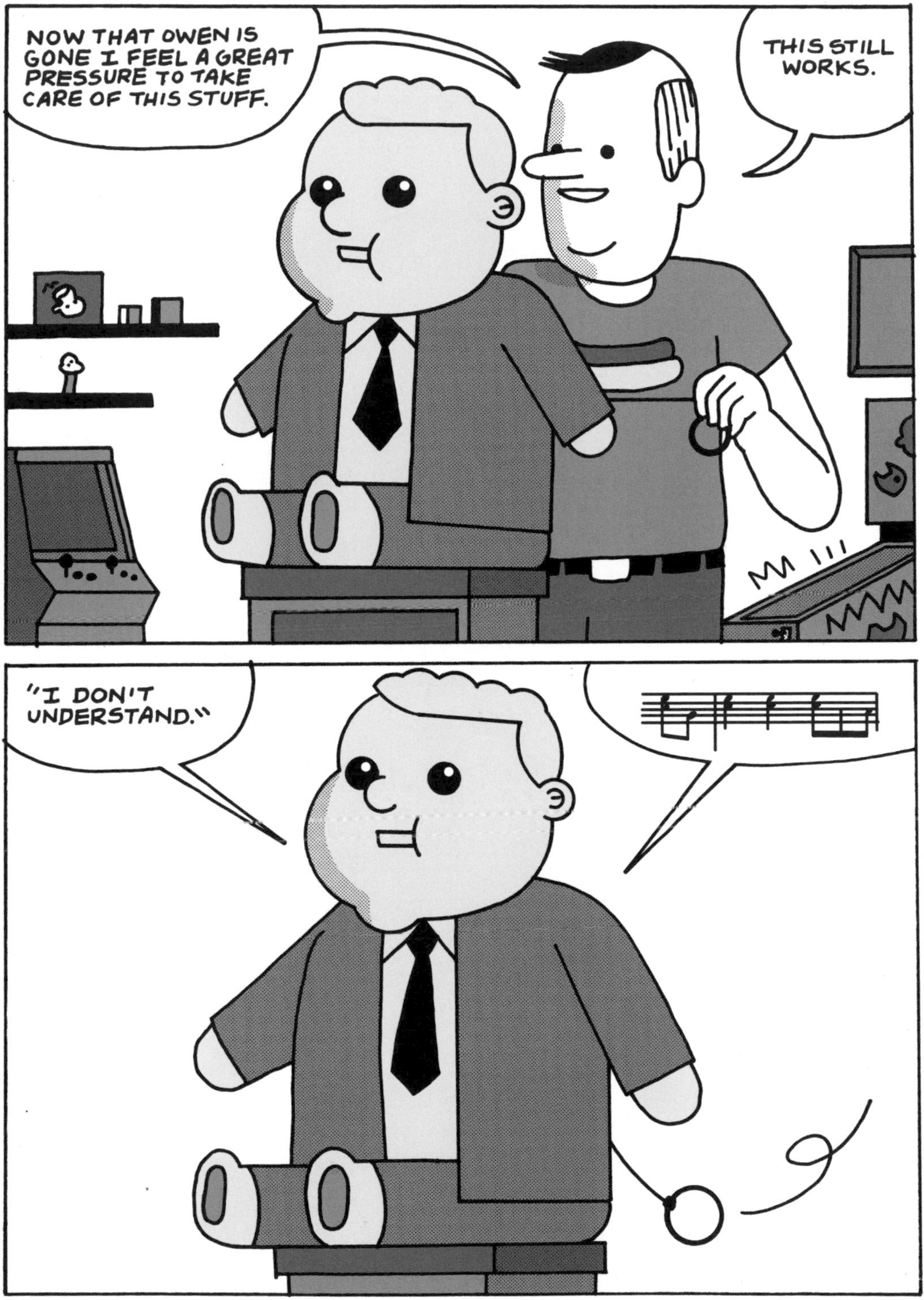
NOW THAT OWEN IS GONE I FEEL A GREAT PRESSURE TO TAKE CARE OF THIS STUFF.
THIS STILL WORKS.
"I DON'T UNDERSTAND."

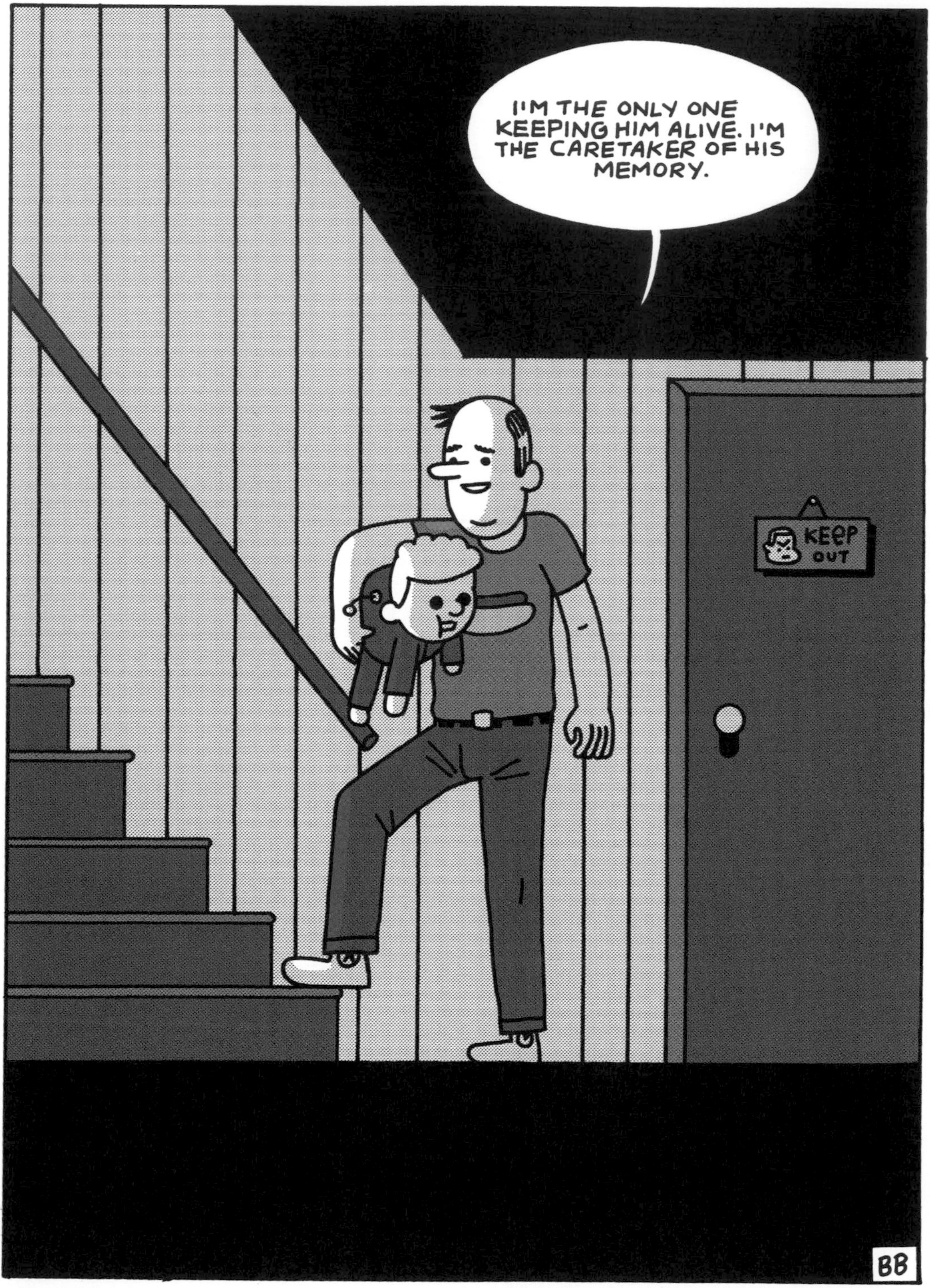
I'M THE ONLY ONE KEEPING HIM ALIVE. I'M THE CARETAKER OF HIS MEMORY.
KEEP OUT
BB

AUTHOR'S NOTE

I OFTEN REVISIT '80S TV SITCOMS BECAUSE THEY REMIND ME OF MY OWN CHILDHOOD. GROWING UP, I SPENT A LOT OF TIME AT MY GRANDMA'S HOUSE, SITTING ON HER COUCH, WATCHING TV. I REMEMBER FEELING SO BORED AT GRANDMA'S, WISHING I HAD MY NINTENDO, WHILE SHE COOKED INCREDIBLE DINNERS FOR THE FAMILY. I WOULD DRAW AND WATCH TV OR SNACK AND WATCH TV, KNOWING THAT AT 2 P.M. I WOULD HAVE TO FIND SOMETHING ELSE TO DO. (THAT WAS WHEN GRANDMA'S FAVORITE SOAP OPERA CAME ON.) BUT I SPENT THE REST OF MY TIME WATCHING SHOWS LIKE "DIFFRENT STROKES," "SMALL WONDER," "PUNKY BREWSTER," "WEBSTER," "WHAT'S HAPPENING!!," "MR. BELVEDERE," "ALF," "SILVER SPOONS," AND MORE, OUT OF BOREDOM. OF COURSE NOW, WHEN I THINK ABOUT THOSE SAME SHOWS AND THEIR FEATURED CHARACTERS, I FEEL HAPPY, WARM, AND LOVED. THEY MAKE ME FEEL LIKE THE WAY MY GRANDMA MADE ME FEEL.

I REMEMBER DOING THE THINGS THAT THE CHARACTERS ON TV DID. I WOULD SAY THE SAME THINGS THEY SAID. I TRIED TO RE-CREATE THE DRAMA THAT THE TV KIDS EXPERIENCED IN MY OWN LIFE. I WANTED TO BE THOSE KIDS.

EVEN THOUGH THESE SHOWS STILL SPARK A PARTICULAR TYPE OF NOSTALGIA IN ME, I KNOW THERE ARE REAL PEOPLE BEHIND THE CHARACTERS I LOVED. I THINK A LOT ABOUT HOW THE EVENTS OF OUR CHILDHOODS AFFECT OUR LIVES AS ADULTS. CHILDHOOD MEMORIES STAY WITH YOU AND SHAPE YOU. TODAY, I LOOK BACK AT OLD HOME MOVIES OF MYSELF AND CRINGE. BUT FOR FORMER CHILD ACTORS, THEY HAVE TO DEAL WITH EVERYONE WATCHING THEIR OLD HOME MOVIES ALL THE TIME.

LOOKING INTO THE BIOGRAPHIES OF MY CHILDHOOD TV FAVORITES, I FOUND THAT MANY OF THEIR LIFE STORIES HAVE A PARTICULAR TRAGEDY TO THEM. THE WORLD USES THEM UP AND THEN TOSSES THEM OUT. THE SAME INSECURITIES EVERYONE HAS GET MAGNIFIED IN EVERY POSSIBLE WAY. IT'S AN ISSUE THAT GOES BACK TO THE BIRTH OF MOVIES. EVEN SILENT FILMS HAD CHILD STARS WHO GOT CHEWED UP BY HOLLYWOOD.

OWEN EUGENE IS MY ATTEMPT TO DRAW FROM ALL OF THESE TRAGIC STORIES TO CREATE ONE CHARACTER. HONESTLY, IT'S QUITE A TASK TO CREATE A CHARACTER, AND THEN BASICALLY TORTURE THEM TO DEATH. AND IT'S ESPECIALLY TRUE WHEN THAT CHARACTER CAN ALSO BE SEEN AS A STAND-IN FOR YOUR OWN SON OR FOR YOURSELF. BUT I WANTED TO TELL OWEN'S STORY WITH THE UTMOST RESPECT FOR PEOPLE WHO WORKED UNDER SIMILAR CIRCUMSTANCES THROUGH THEIR OWN CHILDHOODS. THEY HOLD A SPECIAL PLACE IN MY HEART, A PLACE OF GREAT SYMPATHY.

THIS BOOK IS IN PRAISE OF THE CHILD ACTORS WHO ENDURED SO MUCH SO THAT KIDS LIKE ME COULD HAVE A FANTASY WORLD TO ESCAPE TO.

-BB

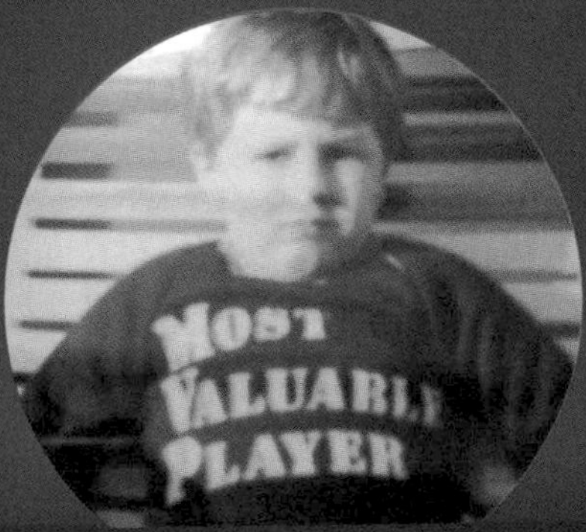
MOST
VALUABLE
PLAYER

SPECIAL THANKS TO KEN REID,

ROBYN, CALISTA, CHARLIE, AND MARI

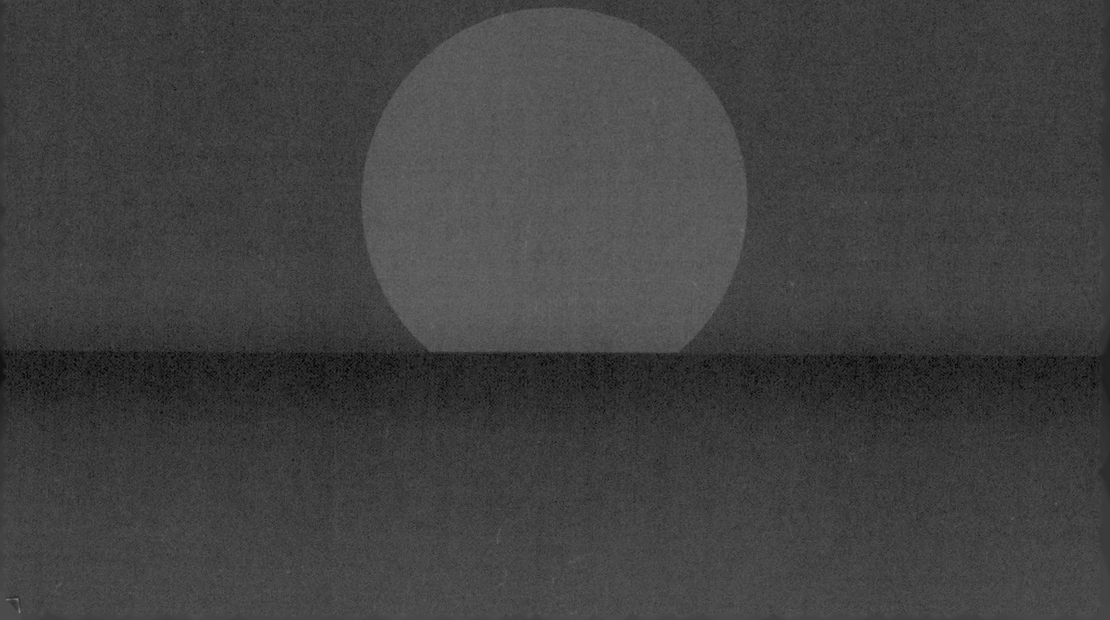

ALSO BY

BRIAN "BOX" BROWN

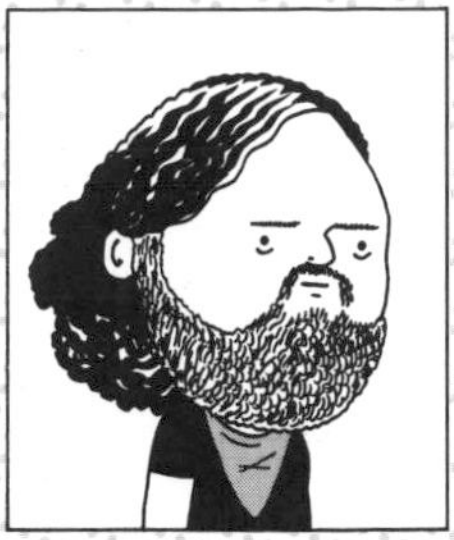

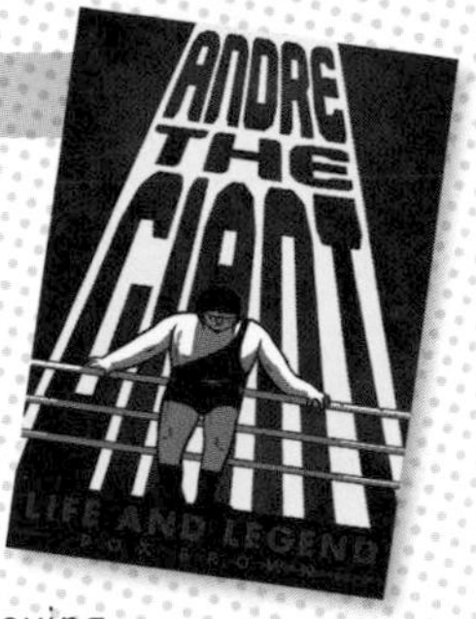
ANDRE THE GIANT
LIFE AND LEGEND

A ***USA Today*** Best Graphic Novel of the Year

★"A labor-of-love tribute, exquisitely rendered, to the larger-than-life wrestling giant."
***—Kirkus Reviews*, starred review**

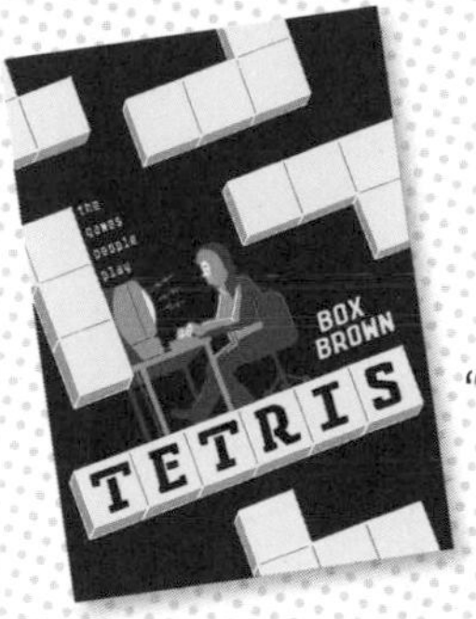
BOX BROWN
TETRIS

"The story never stops moving until its final pieces are in place."
—New York Times

"One of gaming's most intriguing tales . . . A book to watch."
—Nerdist

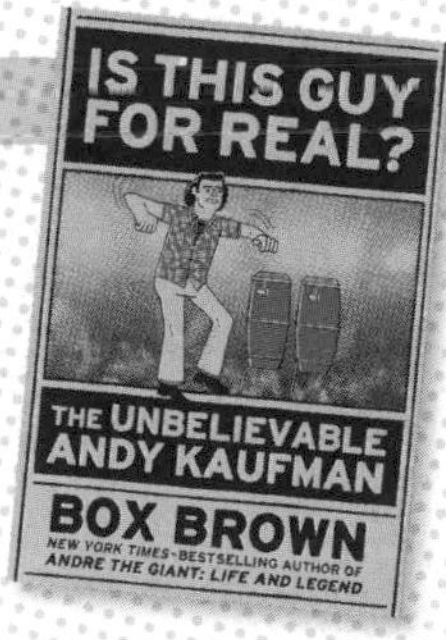
IS THIS GUY FOR REAL?
THE UNBELIEVABLE ANDY KAUFMAN
BOX BROWN
NEW YORK TIMES-BESTSELLING AUTHOR OF ANDRE THE GIANT: LIFE AND LEGEND

An **Eisner Award Winner** for Best Reality-Based Work

"[Kaufman's] fascinating, complicated persona is brought to gorgeous life in Brown's book, as are several fascinating tidbits."
—Entertainment Weekly

"A thorough character study that doesn't shy away from macro topics, giving readers a comprehensive look at Kaufman's rise to fame."
—AV Club

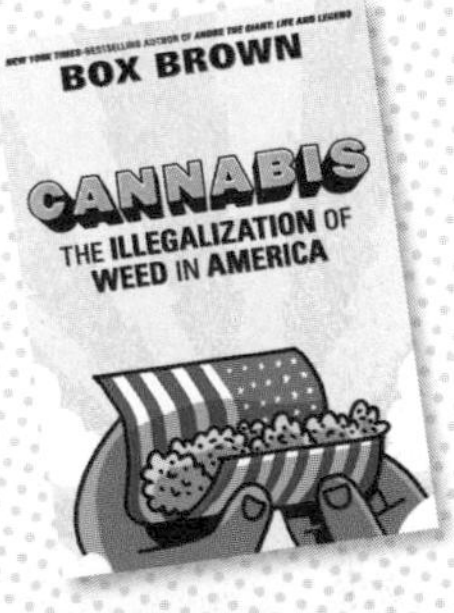
BOX BROWN
CANNABIS
THE ILLEGALIZATION OF WEED IN AMERICA

"Box Brown has a knack for using comics to illuminate tricky subjects . . . [His] pared-down drawings provide the perfect support for stories freighted with layers of misinformation and irony."
—NPR

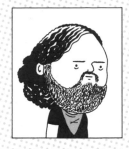

First Second

Published by First Second
First Second is an imprint of Roaring Brook Press,
a division of Holtzbrinck Publishing Holdings Limited Partnership
120 Broadway, New York, NY 10271

Don't miss your next favorite book from First Second!
For the latest updates go to firstsecondnewsletter.com and sign up for our enewsletter.

Library of Congress Control Number: 2019930655
ISBN: 978-1-250-15407-1

Our books may be purchased in bulk for promotional, educational, or business use. Please contact your local bookseller or the Macmillan Corporate and Premium Sales Department at (800) 221-7945 ext. 5442 or by email at MacmillanSpecialMarkets@macmillan.com.

FIRST EDITION

First edition, 2020
Edited by Calista Brill and Patrick Barb
Cover and interior book design by Kirk Benshoff
Printed in China

Penciled with Staedler Mars Lumigraph 3H and 5H pencils.
Inked with a Pentel Pocket Brush Pen and 08 Micron pen on Canson Recycled Bristol.
Cleaned up and toned with Photoshop CC and a Wacom tablet.

10 9 8 7 6 5 4 3 2 1

BY ART WE LIVE

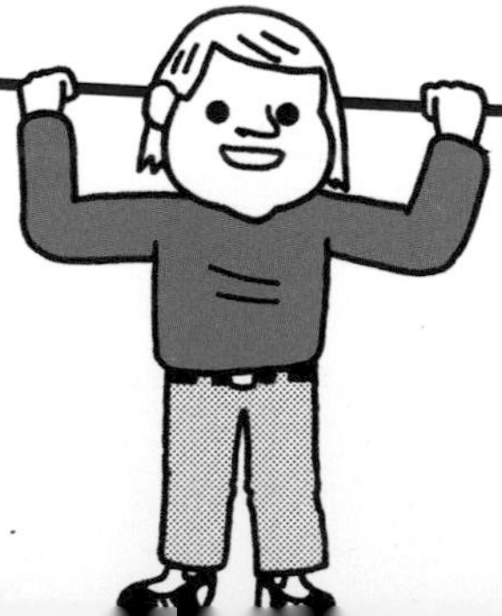